D1298796

Course	Legal and Ethical Environment of Business
Course Number	**FIN 3054**
	VIRGINIA TECH
	FINANCE

ISBN-10: 1308555997   ISBN-13: 9781308555997

Contents

Credits

An Introduction to Dynamic Business Law

LEARNING OBJECTIVES

After reading this chapter, you will be able to answer the following questions:

1 What is business law?

2 How does business law relate to business education?

3 What are the purposes of law?

4 What are alternative ways to classify the law?

5 What are the sources of the law?

6 What are the various schools of jurisprudence?

L01

What is business law?

This book is for future business managers, especially those who wish to be leaders. The preparation for that career requires, in part, an awareness of the legal issues arising in business. Businesses need to finance capital growth, purchase inputs, and hire and develop employees. They must sell to consumers, please owners, and comply with government rules. All these activities are full of potential legal conflicts. Appendix 1A explains the role of critical thinking in resolving these conflicts.

Business law consists of the enforceable rules of conduct that govern commercial relationships. For example, a firm is required by law to obey the antitrust laws when it considers merging with another firm. In other words, buyers and sellers interact in market exchanges within the rules that specify the boundaries of legal business behavior. Constitutions, legislatures, regulatory bodies, and courts spell out what market participants may and may not legally do. These rules and responsibilities provide the stability required in a thriving market economy.

L02

How does business law relate to business education?

Business activities must follow legal guidelines. All contracts, employment decisions, and payments to a supplier are constrained and protected by business law. Each of the six functional areas of business—management, production and transportation, marketing, research and development, accounting and finance, and human resource management—sits on a foundation of business law, as Exhibit 1-1 illustrates.

Law and Its Purposes

L03

What are the purposes of law?

As individuals, few of us can impose rules on others, but a majority of citizens in a democracy can agree to permit certain authorities to make and enforce rules of behavior in their community. These rules are the *law,* and they are enforceable in the courts the community maintains. Exhibit 1-2 lists just a few of the many purposes fulfilled by the law.

Each is important, but taken together they remind us why we are proud to say we are a society of laws. The respect we give the law as a source of authority is in part our recognition that in its absence, we would rely solely on the goodwill and dependability of one another. Most of us greatly prefer the law.

Classification of the Law

L04

What are alternative ways to classify the law?

There are many ways of dividing laws into different groups. Some include national versus international law, federal versus state law, and public versus private law. Private law regulates disputes between private individuals or groups. If a store owner is delinquent in paying rent to the landlord, the resulting dispute is governed by private law. Public law controls disputes between private individuals or groups and their government. If a store dumps waste behind its building in violation of local, state, or federal environmental regulations, public law will resolve the dispute.

Another distinction we make is between civil and criminal law. (See Exhibit 1-3.) Civil law delineates the rights and responsibilities implied in relationships between persons and between persons and their government. It also identifies the remedies available when someone's rights are violated. For example, in 1993 the restaurant chain Jack-In-the-Box was ordered to pay civil damages after a two-year-old child died of food poisoning and several other people became ill from eating meat tainted with *E. coli* bacteria.

Criminal law, in contrast, regulates incidents in which someone commits an act against the public as a whole, such as by conducting insider trading on the stock exchange. Insider trading occurs when an individual uses insider, or secret, company information to increase her or his own finances or those of family or friends. Several years ago an IBM secretary allegedly told her husband, who in turn told several other people, that the company was

Exhibit 1-1

Business Law and the Six Functional Areas of Business

FUNCTIONAL AREA OF BUSINESS	RELEVANT AREAS OF BUSINESS LAW
Corporate management	International and comparative law
	White-collar crime
	Contracts
	Corporate law
	Antitrust law
	Administrative law
	Agency law
	Insurance law
	Employment law
Production and transportation	Tort law
	Contracts
	Environmental law
	Consumer law
Marketing	Tort law
	Contracts
	Antitrust law
	Consumer law
	Intellectual property
Research and development	Product liability
	Intellectual property
	Property law
	Consumer law
Accounting and finance	Liability of accountants
	Contracts
	Negotiable instruments and banking
	Bankruptcy
	White-collar crime
Human resource management	Agency law
	Contracts
	Employment and labor law
	Employment discrimination

Exhibit 1-2

Purposes of the Law

- Providing order such that one can depend on a promise or an expectation of obligations
- Serving as an alternative to fighting
- Facilitating a sense that change is possible, but only after a rational consideration of options
- Encouraging social justice
- Guaranteeing personal freedoms
- Serving as a moral guide by indicating minimal expectations of citizens and organizations

Exhibit 1-3

Civil versus Criminal Law

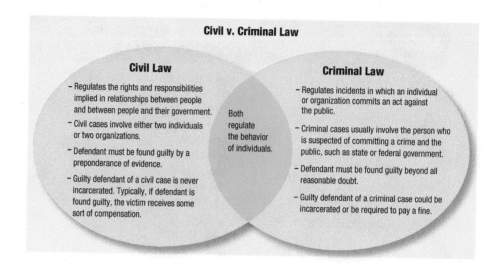

Civil v. Criminal Law

Civil Law

- Regulates the rights and responsibilities implied in relationships between people and between people and their government.
- Civil cases involve either two individuals or two organizations.
- Defendant must be found guilty by a preponderance of evidence.
- Guilty defendant of a civil case is never incarcerated. Typically, if defendant is found guilty, the victim receives some sort of compensation.

Both regulate the behavior of individuals.

Criminal Law

- Regulates incidents in which an individual or organization commits an act against the public.
- Criminal cases usually involve the person who is suspected of committing a crime and the public, such as state or federal government.
- Defendant must be found guilty beyond all reasonable doubt.
- Guilty defendant of a criminal case could be incarcerated or be required to pay a fine.

going to take over operations of Lotus Development. The leaked information spread among a number of individuals, 25 of whom bought stock that increased greatly in value following IBM's public announcement of the takeover. The Securities and Exchange Commission filed charges against them for creating an unfair trading environment for the public. Criminal law cases are prosecuted not by individuals but by the state, federal, or local government.

While some new laws have been adopted to regulate the kinds of activities businesses can now conduct online, cyberlaw is based primarily on existing laws. Laws governing contracts, for instance, are essentially the same in all situations, yet adaptations are necessary because contracts can now be made and signed online through retailers such as Amazon and eBay. Activities by companies such as Napster and YouTube have raised the question of whether and when the copying of certain intellectual property, such as music and video, constitutes theft.

I don't care if your enterprise exists only in cyberspace—you walk like a duck and quack like a duck, so you're a duck.

stus.com

Sources of Business Law

How is law created, and where do we look to find the laws? The sources of law are discussed below.

L05

What are the sources of the law?

CONSTITUTIONS

The United States Constitution and the constitution of each state establish the fundamental principles and rules by which the United States and the individual states are governed. The term constitutional law refers to the general limits and powers of these governments as stated in their written constitutions. The U.S. Constitution is the supreme law of the land, the foundation for all laws in the United States. It is the primary authority to study when trying to identify the relationship between business organizations and government.

STATUTES

The assortment of *statutes,* or rules and regulations put forth by legislatures, is what we call statutory law. These legislative acts are written into the United States Code when they are passed by Congress or into the appropriate state codes when they are enacted by state legislatures. The codes are a collection of all the laws in one convenient location.

Business managers must also be familiar with the local city and county ordinances that govern matters not covered by federal or state codes. These ordinances address important business considerations such as local taxes, environmental standards, zoning, and building codes. If you wish to open a Krispy Kreme franchise in Santa Fe, New Mexico, you must follow local guidelines regarding where you may build your store, the materials you may use, and the state minimum wage you must pay employees making donuts. The regulations will be different if you wish to open your franchise in Toledo, Ohio, or Seattle, Washington.

While they are not a source of law in the same sense as constitutions and statutory law, model or uniform laws serve as a basis for some statutory law at the state level. Business activity is made more difficult when laws vary from state to state. To prevent such problems, a group of legal scholars and lawyers formed the National Conference of Commissioners on Uniform State Laws (NCC). The NCC regularly urges states to enact model laws to provide greater uniformity. The response is entirely in the hands of the state legislatures. They can ignore a suggestion or adopt part or all of the proposed model law.

The proposals of the NCC, while not laws themselves, have been adopted on more than 200 occasions by state legislatures. The NCC is an especially important influence on business law. Paired with the publications of the American Law Institute, it became the source of the *Uniform Commercial Code (UCC).* The UCC is a body of law so significant for business activities that it will be the focus of intensive study in several chapters of this text. The UCC laws include sales laws and other regulations affecting commerce, such as bank deposits and collections, title documents, and warranties. For example, these laws govern the different types of warranties that companies such as Microsoft, Sony, and Honda provide with their products.

CASES

Constitutions, legislatures, and administrative agencies encourage certain behaviors and prevent others. But laws are seldom self-explanatory and often require interpretation. Case law, also called common law, is the collection of legal interpretations made by judges. These interpretations are law unless revoked later by new statutory law.

Case law is especially significant for businesses that operate in multiple legal jurisdictions. Courts in two different business locations may interpret similarly worded statutes differently.

Courts issue judicial decisions that often include interpretations of statutes and administrative regulations, as well as the reasoning they used to arrive at a decision. Such reasoning depends heavily on precedent, past decisions in similar cases that guide later decisions, thereby providing greater stability and predictability to the law.

Business managers must pay attention to changes in the law and cases in which new precedents are set and take them into account when making business decisions. After a woman was severely burned by very hot coffee, McDonald's was found negligent for failing to provide a warning label on its hot-beverage cups. Now many retailers provide warning labels on their beverage cups because of the precedent set by this case.

When courts rely on precedent, they are obeying the principle of stare decisis ("standing by their decision"), in which rulings made in higher courts become binding precedent for lower courts. When an issue is brought before a state court, the court will determine whether the state supreme court has made a decision on a similar issue, which creates a binding precedent or pattern of law the lower court must follow. If there is no binding decision, both state courts need to look for other rulings on similar cases.

They are not bound by each other's decisions and might decide differently on the same issue. Decisions in lower courts can be appealed to the state appeals court, however, and the appeals court's decision can be appealed to the state supreme court. If the state supreme court rules on the case, its decision is binding for the state in that and future cases but does not affect earlier decisions made by state courts.

Perhaps the most well-known case associated with stare decisis is *Roe v. Wade.*[1] This landmark case, decided in 1973, made a decision on the issue of abortion. The U.S. Supreme Court decided that until a fetus is "viable," a woman may terminate her pregnancy for any reason. The Court went on to define *viable* as the ability of the fetus "to live outside the mother's womb, albeit with artificial aid." The Court added that such a capability could occur around 24 weeks, although usually around 7 months. The decision in *Roe v. Wade* has been upheld in cases since. The precedent still stands today, despite attempts to overturn it. In 1992, *Planned Parenthood of Southeastern Pennsylvania v. Casey*[2] used the decision to determine that a woman has a constitutional right to have an abortion, although the standard for restricting abortions was lowered.

Another case that has been used in accordance with stare decisis as a binding precedent is *Brown v. Board of Education,*[3] which abolished discriminatory policies for individuals of different racial backgrounds. In *Regents of the University of California v. Bakke,*[4] the plaintiff, a white male, had applied to the University of California at Davis medical school two years in a row and been denied admittance. He alleged the admissions process was discriminatory because 16 of 100 slots were reserved for members of minority races. The U.S. Supreme Court found the school's admissions policy was not lawful, referencing *Brown* and stating that the basic principle behind it and similar cases was that individuals could not be excluded on the basis of race or ethnicity. The Court wrote, "Preferring members of any one group for no reason other than race or ethnic origin is discrimination for its own sake."

Another U.S. Supreme Court case that relied in part on *Brown v. Board of Education* was *Wygant v. Jackson Board of Education.*[5] The Board of Education and teachers' union

---

[1] 410 U.S. 113 (1973).
[2] 505 U.S. 833 (1992).
[3] 347 U.S. 483 (1954).
[4] 438 U.S. 265 (1978).
[5] 476 U.S. 267 (1986).

in Jackson, Michigan, had agreed that if teachers were laid off, those with more seniority would be retained and the minority teachers' percentage of the layoffs would not be higher than their percentage of all teachers employed by the school district at the time of the layoffs. When layoffs did occur, nonminority teachers were laid off and minority teachers with less seniority were retained. The nonminority teachers sued. When the case was brought before the Supreme Court, the Court ruled that the layoff policy was not lawful because "[c]arried to the logical extreme, the idea that black students are better off with black teachers could lead to the very system the Court rejected in *Brown v. Board of Education.*" Again in accordance with *Brown,* the Court ruled that singling people out on the basis of race was not lawful.

However, the case *Plessy v. Ferguson*[6] is an interesting circumstance in regard to stare decisis. In this case, the court decided that separate accommodations for blacks and whites were acceptable as long as such separation was "separate but equal." This case essentially made the legal acknowledgment of a difference between blacks and whites, and different treatment, acceptable. Interestingly, in 1954, *Brown v. Board of Education* did not follow the precedent established by *Plessy v. Ferguson.* In fact, the ruling established in *Plessy* was overturned. The Supreme Court determined that segregation of blacks and whites violated the equal protection clause of the Fourteenth Amendment of the Constitution. Thus, the court overturned the precedent and created a new one, one that has been used in decisions made by courts ever since.

Just as state statutes have been strongly influenced by the suggestions of the NCC, common law evolves with the assistance of a mechanism called Restatements of the Law. These are summaries of the common law rules in a particular area of the law that have been enacted by most states. The American Law Institute prepares these Restatements for contracts, agency, property, torts, and many other areas of law that affect business decisions. While the Restatements are not themselves a source of business law, judges frequently use them to guide their interpretations in a particular case.

In addition to the Restatements, many influences are at work in the minds of judges when they interpret constitutions, statutes, and regulations. Their own values and social backgrounds function as lights and shadows, moving the judges toward particular legal decisions.

Courts in one jurisdiction need not obey precedents in other jurisdictions, but they may be influenced by them. At least two current Supreme Court justices are using law in other countries as a basis for rethinking certain laws in the United States. The logic of this reliance on precedent is based on respect for those who have already wrestled with the issue and provided us guidance with their earlier decision.

ADMINISTRATIVE LAW

Constitutions and statutes never cover all the detailed rules that affect relationships between government and business. The federal, state, and local governments have dozens of administrative agencies whose task is to perform a particular government function. For example, the Environmental Protection Agency (EPA) has broad responsibilities to enforce federal statutes in the area of environmental protection. The Occupational Safety and Health Administration (OSHA) oversees health and workplace safety and makes sure working conditions are not hazardous. In 1994, OSHA settled a complaint that United Parcel Service (UPS) was not providing adequate safety measures and equipment for workers who handled hazardous waste by making sure UPS adapted its practices to follow federal safety guidelines.

[6] 163 U.S. 537 (1896).

Exhibit 1-4

Major Federal Administrative Agencies

INDEPENDENT AGENCIES	EXECUTIVE AGENCIES
• Commodity Futures Trading Commission (CFTC) http://www.cftc.gov/ • Consumer Product Safety Commission (CPSC) http://www.cpsc.gov/ • Equal Employment Opportunity Commission (EEOC) http://www.eeoc.gov/ • Federal Trade Commission (FTC) http://www.ftc.gov/ • Federal Communications Commission (FCC) http://www.fcc.gov/ • National Labor Relations Board (NLRB) http://www.nlrb.gov/ • National Transportation Safety Board (NTSB) http://www.ntsb.gov/ • Nuclear Regulatory Commission (NRC) http://www.nrc.gov/ • Securities and Exchange Commission (SEC) http://www.sec.gov/	• Federal Deposit Insurance Corporation (FDIC) http://www.fdic.gov/ • Occupational Safety and Health Administration (OSHA) http://www.osha.gov/ • General Services Administration (GSA) http://www.gsa.gov/ • National Aeronautics and Space Administration (NASA) http://www.nasa.gov/ • Small Business Administration (SBA) http://www.sba.gov • U.S. Agency for International Development (USAID) http://www.usaid.gov/ • National Science Foundation (NSF) http://www.nsf.gov/ • Veterans Administration (VA) http://www.va.gov/ • Office of Personnel Management (OPM) http://www.opm.gov/

Administrative law is the collection of rules and decisions made by all these agencies. Just glance at Exhibit 1-4 to get a sense of the scope of a few of the major federal administrative agencies.

TREATIES

A **treaty** is a binding agreement between two states or international organizations. It may be an international agreement, a covenant, an exchange of letters, a convention, or protocols. In the United States, a treaty is generally negotiated by the executive branch. To be binding, it must then be approved by two-thirds of the Senate.

A treaty is similar to a contract in two important ways. Both treaties and contracts are attempts by parties to determine rights and obligations among themselves, and when a party fails to obey a treaty or a contract, international law imposes liability on it.

EXECUTIVE ORDERS

The president and state governors can issue directives requiring that officials in the executive branch perform their functions in a particular manner. The Code of Federal Regulations (CFR) contains all the executive orders created by the president. (It is online at www.gpoaccess.gov/cfr/index.html.) Presidents claim the power to issue such orders on the basis of their Article II, Section 1, constitutional power to "take care that the laws be faithfully executed." President George W. Bush issued 284 executive orders during the eight years of his presidency.

An especially controversial executive order is Order 9066, issued by President Franklin Roosevelt during World War II, which sent Japanese-Americans on the West Coast, as well as thousands of Italian-American and German-American families, to internment camps for the duration of the war.

Exhibit 1-5 summarizes the various locations where you can find particular laws.

Exhibit 1-5   Where to Locate the Law

	Source by Level of Government		
TYPE OF LAW	**FEDERAL**	**STATE**	**LOCAL**
Statutes	United States Code (USC) United States Code Annotated (USCA) United States Statutes at Large	State code	Municipal ordinances
Administrative law	Code of Federal Regulations (CFR) *Federal Register*	State administrative code	Municipality administrative regulations
Common law	United States Reports (U.S.) United States Supreme Court Reporter (S. Ct.) Federal Reporter (F. F.2d) Federal Supplement (F.Supp.)	Regional reporters State reporters	Check the clerk's office at the local courthouse
Executive order	Title 3 of Code of Federal Regulations Codification of Presidential Proclamations and Executive Orders	See state government website	n/a
Treaty	See http://www.asil.org/treaty1.cfm	n/a	n/a

SCHOOLS OF JURISPRUDENCE

When legislators or courts make law, they do so guided by certain habits of mind and specific beliefs about human nature. Beliefs are deeply rooted within a person's emotions and habits, and thus they are sure to guide one's opinions and decisions. Such beliefs may be commonly held and thus create various larger schools of thought. Once one determines what schools of thought influence certain types of decisions and opinions, one is sure to better understand such decisions. This section briefly describes several of the more common guides to legal interpretation.

LO6

What are the various schools of jurisprudence?

Natural Law.   The term natural law describes certain ethical laws and principles believed to be morally right and "above" the laws devised by humans. Under natural law individuals have not only basic human rights but also the freedom to disobey a law enacted by people if their conscience goes against it and they believe it is wrong. Dow Chemical wants its suppliers to conform to U.S. environmental and labor laws, not just the local laws in the supplier's country, where regulations may not be as stringent. This policy reflects the beliefs that people have a right to be treated fairly in their jobs and a right as human beings to have a clean environment.

Legal Positivism.   The concept of legal positivism sees our proper role as obedience to duly authorized law. That law is quite distinct from morality, and moral questions about the law should not interfere with our inclination to obey it. A judge with leanings in the direction of legal positivism might write that she is deciding to enforce the law in question but that her decision does not necessarily mean she sees the law as the morally correct rule.

Identification with the Vulnerable.   Closely linked to pursuing legal change through natural law is pursuing change through identification with the vulnerable, on the grounds that some higher law or body of moral principles connects all of us in the human community. Some members of our society are able to take care of themselves in terms of most life situations. Others, especially the ill, children, the aged, the disabled, and the poor, require assistance to meet their fundamental needs of life, health, and education.

This guide to legal change is tied closely to the pursuit of fairness, a "level playing field," in our society. We might look at a particular employment contract and feel outrage that "it is just not fair." That outrage can be a stimulus for legal change. Minimum-wage laws reflect the belief that workers should receive a minimum hourly wage and that employers should not be allowed to pay them less.

Historical School: Tradition.   One of the guidelines most often used for shaping the law is tradition, or custom. Stare decisis is rooted in this *historical school*. When we follow tradition, instead of reinventing the wheel, we link our behavior to the behavior of those who faced similar problems in earlier periods. We assume past practice was the product of careful thought.

Legal Realism.   Legal realism is based on the idea that, when ruling on a case, judges need to consider more than just the law; they also weigh factors such as social and economic conditions, since legal guidelines were designed by humans and exist in an ever-changing environment. Judges who follow this school of thought are more likely to depart from past court decisions to account for the fact that our society is constantly shifting and evolving. They believe the law can never be enforced with complete consistency and argue that because judges are human, they will bring different methods of reasoning to very similar cases.

One law enacted to reflect social changes is the Family and Medical Leave Act. This act mandates that businesses employing more than 50 people provide their workers with up to 12 weeks' unpaid leave every year to take care of family-related affairs, including caring for oneself or ill parents and adopting or having a child. The law also protects pregnant women who take time off work, as their employers must provide them with the same pay and the same or an equivalent job when they return to work. More mothers are working outside the home, and more women are returning to work soon after they have a child. The act protects them against some types of discrimination that might occur after they return.

Cost-Benefit Analysis.   Suppose we could attach a monetary figure to the benefits of a particular law or legal decision. We would next need to examine all its costs and place a monetary value on it. If we possessed these figures, we could use cost-benefit analysis as a guide to legal change, choosing the alternatives that maximized benefits and minimized costs.

This approach is tied closely to the pursuit of efficiency. If the law to be applied yields more benefits than costs, then we have saved resources that we can, in turn, use to obtain more goods and services. Our economy is thus more efficient because it produces more with less.

Polluted land is an economic loss as it cannot be used for farming or recreation. Polluted water can be toxic for fish and cannot be used for drinking. Polluted air can cause health problems and result in higher health care costs. While complying with EPA pollution controls may cost companies more initially, the price of environmental cleanup and lost productivity in the economy as a whole may be even greater.

Global and Comparative Law

Advances in technology and transportation make trade with other countries far easier today than in the past. Boeing Co. can make hundreds of components for the same airliner all over the world and then assemble them in the United States. An antique store can operate in Poughkeepsie but sell to customers in Moscow or Taipei through a website.

This ease in trade means business managers must be familiar with laws that regulate business practices between nations. The United States has entered into trade agreements, such as the North American Free Trade Agreement (NAFTA) with Canada and Mexico and the General Agreement on Tariffs and Trade (GATT) with about 150 other countries, that help establish the conditions of global trade.

Future managers should also understand comparative law, which studies and compares the laws in different countries. The European Union (EU) regulates taxes on Internet sales and the amount of pollution firms can release differently than does the U.S. government. Companies doing business in the EU must take these standards into account. The Chinese government does not want its citizens to have access to certain information and websites. To do business in China, Google had to conform to Chinese standards by restricting the content of searches performed on Google.cn. Some felt that by thus restricting access to information, Google had violated its own mission statement to "do no evil."

Business law tells managers the basic rules of the business game. Play any game without having first studied the rules, and you will probably fail. But unlike an ordinary game, business has a rule book that is changing dynamically. So modern business managers must have an ongoing fascination with the law to function effectively.

KEY TERMS

administrative law 8
business law 2
case law 5
civil law 2
common law 5
constitutional law 5

cost-benefit analysis 10
criminal law 2
cyberlaw 4
identification with the
    vulnerable 9
legal positivism 9

legal realism 10
model (uniform)
    laws 5
natural law 9
precedent 6
private law 2

public law 2
Restatements of the
    Law 7
stare decisis 6
statutory law 5
treaty 8

APPENDIX 1A   CRITICAL THINKING AND BUSINESS LAW

Success in business requires the development of critical-thinking skills and attitudes—the ability and desire to understand the structure of what someone is saying and then apply a set of criteria to evaluate its worth. In other words, businesspeople need to be able to sort sense from nonsense by developing critical attitudes and abilities. There is no better context in which to develop these skills than the study of the laws that affect business.

Legal reasoning is like other kinds of reasoning in some ways. The stimulus that gets us thinking is an *issue,* stated as a question that requires us to *do* something, to think about answers.

We may be interested in such issues as the following:

- When are union organizers permitted under the National Labor Relations Act to trespass on an employer's property?
- Do tobacco manufacturers have liability for the deaths of smokers?
- Must a business fulfill a contract with an unlicensed contractor in a state requiring that all contractors be licensed?

These questions have several potential answers, but which best accomplishes a particular business objective? Which is consistent with the law? Here is where critical thinking is essential to business success. Some answers can get the decision maker into trouble; others will advance the intended purpose. Each answer is called a *conclusion.*

Business firms are both consumers of and contributors to legal conclusions. As they learn about and react to decisions or conclusions made by courts, businesspeople can respond in two ways:

1. Understand the conclusions in the case, and use this understanding as a guide for future business decisions.
2. Make judgments about the quality of the conclusions.

This book encourages you to do both. Critical thinking is active; it challenges each of us to form judgments about the quality of the link between a set of reasons and the conclusion derived from them. In particular, we will be focusing on the link between a court's reasons and its conclusions.

The following structure for critical thinking is a thoroughly tested method used by successful market decision makers. Every time you read a case, try to follow it.

1. Find the *facts.*

   Here we are looking for the most basic building blocks in a legal decision or argument. They provide the environment or context in which the legal issue is to be resolved. Certain events occurred; certain actions were or were not taken; particular persons behaved or failed to behave in specific ways. We always want to know, What happened in this case?

2. Look for the *issue.*

   The issue is the question that caused the lawyers and their clients to enter the legal system.

3. Identify the judge's *reasons and conclusion.*

   We want a world rich with opinions so that we can have a broad field of choice. But we should agree with only those legal opinions that have convincing reasons supporting the conclusion. Asking "Why?" is our respectful way of saying, "I want to believe you, but you have an obligation to help me by sharing the reasons for your conclusion."

4. Locate in the decision the *rules of law* that govern the judge's reasoning.

   Judges cannot offer just any reasoning that they please. They must always look back over their shoulders at the laws and previous court decisions that together provide an anchor for current and future decisions. What makes legal reasoning so complex is that statutes and legal findings are never crystal clear. They may seem very clear, but judges and businesspeople have room for interpretive flexibility in their reasoning.

5. Apply *critical thinking* to the reasoning.

   A judge's reasoning, once we have laid it out by following the steps discussed here, is a message we may either accept or reject. *Critical thinking in the legal context* consists of examining the legal opinion in search of potential problems in the reasoning.

One of the most exciting things about our legal system is its potential for change. Listed below is a small sample of some especially useful critical-thinking tools for business managers to use when thinking about business law. (See Exhibit 1-6.)

- Look for potential ambiguity in the reasoning. *Ambiguity* is a lack of clarity in a word or phrase. Many words have multiple meanings; until we know the intended one, we cannot tell whether we agree or disagree with the reasoning.

- Ask whether the analogies used in the decision are strong. When judges follow precedents, they are saying the facts in the precedent and those in the case at hand are so similar that it makes sense to apply the same rule of law in both. Are there key differences in the facts that raise questions about the quality of that analogy?

- Check the quality of the judge's reasoning. Is the judge's supporting evidence both abundant enough and reliable enough that we should agree with the reasoning?

Exhibit 1-6

Critical-Thinking Tools for Business Managers

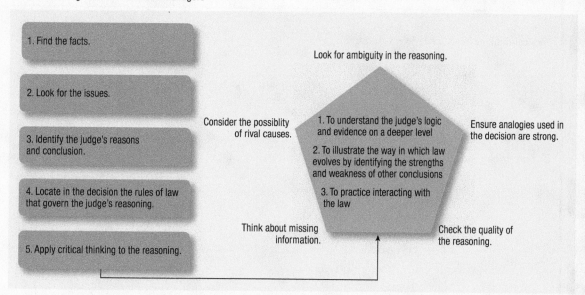

- Think about the extent to which missing information prevents you from being totally confident about the judge's reasoning. Is there information you would need to have before making up your mind?
- Consider the possibility of rival causes. When the judge claims one action caused another, think about whether some alternative cause may have been responsible.

Working through these steps accomplishes several things. First, walking through this process familiarizes you at a deeper level with what the judge is saying. You have to wrestle with the judge's logic and use of evidence to complete the critical-thinking activity. Second, the critical thinking provides a sense that the law evolves as we put together the strengths and weaknesses of previous thinking by judges and legal scholars. Most importantly, critical thinking enables us to practice interacting with the law, always with an eye to considering ways to improve our legal system.

This chapter has enabled you to understand several important things. First, you should now be acquainted with what business law is and how business law and business education are intertwined. Second, you should understand the purposes of law, be acquainted with different kinds of law, and have a basic understanding of how different courts and agencies cooperate with one another. You should also now know about the interplay between case law and stare decisis, or binding precedent. You should also be able to pinpoint where various kinds of laws come from.

More importantly, however, you should realize that all of our courts and legal documents are thought to be just and that justice is an idea based on other ideas. Different schools of thought arise from deep-rooted, commonly held beliefs, and these schools guide decisions about what is fair and just and why. Finally, you should be able to critically evaluate a judge's or court's opinion. Only by doing so can you sort through the logic of the decision and pinpoint all the factors that went into the decision, including not only precedent and case law but the perspective flowing from schools of legal thought, rooted in personal beliefs and opinions.

KEY TERM

critical-thinking skills 12

Business Ethics

LEARNING OBJECTIVES

After reading this chapter, you will be able to answer the following questions:

1 What are business ethics and the social responsibility of business?

2 How are business law and business ethics related?

3 How can we use the WPH framework for ethical business decisions?

CASE OPENER

Acne Medication and Gastrointestinal Injury

Since 1999, Kamie Kendall had experienced ongoing abdominal pain, and she was eventually diagnosed with ulcerative colitis and irritable bowel syndrome (IBD). Although Kendall had been taking an acne medication, Accutane, since 1997, the medication's warnings did not mention IBD or ulcerative colitis and, therefore, Kendall had never suspected that her ongoing illness was a result of the medication. Then, in April 2004, Kendall's grandmother informed her of a lawyer's television advertisement linking Accutane to ongoing IBD. On December 21, 2005, Kendall filed a lawsuit against Hoffman-LaRoche, the manufacturer of Accutane, alleging that the company was liable for her injuries because the medication's warnings failed to disclose the risk of developing IBD.

Kendall argued that, instead, the medication's warnings focused on pregnancy and suicide. Further, although the medication warned against "abdominal pain," there were no specific warnings, or mention on the consent form, of risk of IBD or colitis.

Hoffman-LaRoche moved to dismiss this lawsuit, arguing that the statute of limitations had expired and that Kendall's suit was untimely.

1. When is it usually considered untimely for plaintiffs to file failure-to-warn lawsuits?
2. If you were in charge of manufacturing acne medication, would you consider it your ethical obligation to list all potential illnesses that may result from your product?

The Wrap-Up at the end of the chapter will answer these questions.

What a business manager in the situation described in the opening scenario should do is not altogether clear. Ethical conversation is less about finding the one and only right thing to do than it is about finding the better thing to do. Whatever you choose to do, some stakeholders will be hurt and others will benefit. Business ethics requires a weighing of the benefits of a decision compared to their harm.

This chapter provides some assistance for thinking systematically about issues of right and wrong in business conduct. Initially, we need to sort through the meaning of key terms like *business ethics* and *social responsibility*. Then, because it is helpful to have a useful approach to ethical decision making, we provide a practical method by which future business managers can think more carefully about the ethical dilemmas they will face during their careers.

Business Ethics and Social Responsibility

L01

What are business ethics and the social responsibility of business?

Ethics is the study and practice of decisions about what is good, or right. Ethics guides us when we are wondering what we should be doing in a particular situation. Business ethics is the application of ethics to the special problems and opportunities experienced by businesspeople. For example, as a business manager, you might someday make a decision that you think is best for your company, as did the advertisers for Accutane, described in the Case Opener. Is a company doing the right thing when it attempts to reduce the costs of advertising by not listing all possible complications of the medicine for the consumer?

Such questions present businesses with ethical choices, each of which has advantages and disadvantages. An ethical dilemma is a problem about what a firm should do for which no clear, right decision is available.

For example, imagine yourself in the position of a business manager at Wells Fargo Bank. You know that providing bank accounts for customers has costs attached to it. You want to cover those costs by charging the customers the cost of their checking accounts. By doing so, you can preserve the bank's revenue for shareholders and employees of Wells Fargo. So far, the decision seems simple. But an ethical dilemma soon appears.

You learn from recent government reports that 12 million families cannot afford to have bank accounts when they are charged a fee to maintain one. You want to do the right thing in this situation. But what would that be? The study of business ethics can help you resolve this dilemma by suggesting approaches you can use that will show respect for others while maintaining a healthy business enterprise.

To see how ethics relates to accounting, please see the **Connecting to the Core** activity on the text website at www.mhhe.com/kubasek3e.

Making these decisions would be much easier if managers could focus only on the impact of decisions on the firm. If, for example, a firm had as its only objective the maximization of profits, the "right thing" to do would be the option that had the largest positive impact on the firm's profits.

But businesses operate in a community. Communities have expectations for behavior of individuals, groups, and businesses. Different communities have different expectations of businesses. Trying to identify what those expectations are and deciding whether to fulfill them complicate business ethics. The community often expects firms to do much more for it than just provide a useful good or service at a reasonable price. For example, a community may expect firms to resist paying bribes, even when the payment of such fees is an ordinary cost of doing business in certain global settings. The social responsibility of business consists of the expectations that the community imposes on firms doing business inside its borders. These expectations must be honored to a certain extent, even when a firm wishes to ignore them, because firms are always subject to the implicit threat that legislation will impose social obligations on them. So, if the community expects businesses to obey certain standards of fairness even when the standards interfere with profit maximization, firms that choose to ignore that expectation do so at their peril. See Exhibit 2-1 for a brief look at Pacific Gas and Electric's approach to social responsibility.

Consider also the financial meltdown of the largest insurance company in the United States, American International Group (AIG). In late October 2011, an investigation by the Government Accountability Office raised questions about the 2008 bailout of AIG by the Federal Reserve. In 2008, the company suddenly collapsed because of risky bets it made insuring mortgage-backed securities. AIG became the source of widespread public outrage after the media revealed that the company had paid $165 million in bonuses two days before its bailout; the public was especially distraught because these paid bonuses were even distributed to some members of the trading unit that had caused the company's collapse. The Federal Reserve spent $85 billion bailing out the company, but losses

---

Exhibit 2-1

Good Citizenship and Profits

Source: Code of Conduct from www.pgecorp.com/aboutus/ corp_gov/coce.shtml.

Given the number of corporate accounting scandals that have been revealed in the past few years, many corporations are making a point of assuring their investors that their corporate goals are not focused solely on profit. As investors lost millions of dollars during the collapse of companies such as WorldCom and Enron, some corporations have been placing increased emphasis on promoting themselves not only as profitable but as conscientious and ethical in their treatment of consumers, employees, and shareholders.

Whereas in years past companies may have focused solely on their profitability in an attempt to gain new investors, today many business managers realize that corporate honesty has become just as important to those who are seeking to buy stock. Tony Early, Chairman, CEO, and President of PG&E Corporation and Chris Johns, President of Pacific Gas and Electric Company, emphasize this in their message to employees in PG&E's Code of Conduct:

"... all of us at PG&E are working hard to ensure that our company is on a solid foundation for the future. Strong performance is critical to our success, but just as important is how we go about achieving results - with honesty and respect, without taking shortcuts, and by operating ethically and with integrity in all that we do.

[Our Employee Code of Conduct] supports our continuing commitment to honest and ethical conduct and compliance with both the letter and the spirit of all laws, rules, and regulations, and our company's policies, standards, and procedures."

continued to grow. Later, the government paid a total of $182 billion, setting the record as the largest federal bailout in U.S. history.

Business Law and Business Ethics

L02

How are business law and business ethics related?

Before business managers consider the social responsibilities of firms in their communities, they need to gather all relevant facts.

The legality of the decision in choosing a method of production, how to compete with competing firms, and the social responsibilities of the firm is the minimal standard that must be met for the firm to be an ethical business. But the existence of that minimum standard is essential for the development of business ethics. To make this point, let's take a look at the growing practice of bribery in the absence of such legal standards. In some countries businesses must pay bribes to receive legitimate supplies. Though the business-person may be morally opposed to paying the bribes, the supplies are necessary to stay in business and there may be no other means of obtaining them.

Thus, multinational companies face an ethical dilemma: They must decide whether to pay bribes or find alternative sources of supplies. For instance, when McDonald's opened its doors in Moscow, it made arrangements to receive its supplies from foreign providers. These arrangements ensured that the franchise did not have to engage in questionable business practices.

Regardless of the ethical and legal implications, there are still multinational corporations that choose to use bribes as a means of doing business in foreign markets. For example, in December 2008, multinational giant Siemens AG was ordered to pay the largest Foreign Corrupt Practices Act (FCPA) fine in history after admitting to acts of bribery worldwide. The company had been using off-the-book slush funds, middlemen posing as agents or company consultants, and even money-filled briefcases to bribe government officials and secure contracts overseas. An FBI agent involved in the Siemens investigation went so far as to say that executives for Siemens used bribery as "standard operating procedure" and "a business strategy." As a result, $1.6 billion later, Siemens AG is now forced to restructure itself to do business ethically and legally.

Future business professionals ought to consider not just the moral and monetary costs of engaging in unethical business practices but also the cost of lost business. A tarnished reputation could mean losing contracts, sales, and partnerships in the future.

Look at Case 2-1 as an exercise in comparing what is legal with what is ethical.

CASE 2-1 UNITED STATES OF AMERICA v. ALFRED CARONIA
U.S. DISTRICT COURT FOR THE EASTERN DISTRICT OF NEW YORK
576 F. SUPP. 2D 385 (2008)

The defendant, Alfred Caronia, was a sales representative for a pharmaceutical company named Orphan when he was charged for "off-label" promotion of a drug. The company, now called Jazz Pharmaceutical, had produced a drug named Xyrem, which was a depressant that induced sleep. The main active ingredient in the drug was gamma-hydroxybutyrate, also known as "GHB." At the time, the FDA reviewed the drug and stipulated that the drug was a safe way to treat only one condition: cataplexy, which is a narcoleptic condition. Several severe problems had been associated with Xyrem, including dependence and withdrawal symptoms. Other side effects included death, coma, or seizures. The FDA regulations regarding the drug stated that children under 16 should be kept from using the drug, as positive effects had not been observed. Additionally, elderly patients were advised not to use the drug, as limited observations linked positive effects with elderly patients. Caronia was discovered to be marketing Xyrem to physicians for an extra purpose: to combat excessive daytime sleepiness. This use had certainly not been approved by the FDA.

[continued]

The ethical ramifications of off-label promoting can be severe. In fact, promoting a drug for purposes not approved by the government has been a growing problem with both doctors and pharmaceutical sales representatives. These cases cast a light on the questionable financial partnerships between pharmaceutical companies and doctors who not only prescribe the drug but also advocate use of the drug. Having medicines prescribed for unapproved uses greatly increases the sales of the medicine and therefore the profits of the company. Unfortunately, the effects of these deals can lead to harm and even death to the patients taking the prescriptions. In this case, Caronia moved to dismiss the charges against him, and the court had to consider his argument about his right to free speech and the FDA's argument about its job to protect public safety.

JUDGE VITALIANO: Pursuant to the FDCA, manufacturers are restricted from marketing so-called "off-label" (i.e., non-FDA approved) uses of a drug. . . . Count one of the instant information alleges that, between March 2005 and March 2006, defendant Alfred Caronia, an Orphan sales representative, knowingly and intentionally conspired with others to misbrand a drug by marketing Xyrem for off-label uses in violation of 21 U.S.C. §§ 331(a), (k), 333(a)(1), and 18 U.S.C. § 371.

. . . In particular, the information alleges that, on October 26, 2005, Carona promoted Xyrem to a physician "John Doe" for fibromyalgia, EDS, muscle disorders, chronic pain and fatigue, which uses were for off-label indications. The information further alleges that, on November 2, 2005, Caronia introduced another physician, who was paid by Orphan, to "John Doe," and that the other physician promoted Xyrem for off-label indications, including fibromyalgia, EDS, sleepiness, weight loss and chronic fatigue.

The information supersedes a prior felony indictment against Caronia and Dr. Peter Gleason, who is the physician allegedly paid by Orphan to promote Xyrem for off-label uses. That indictment charged that Gleason and Caronia participated in a conspiracy with others to introduce a misbranded drug into interstate commerce with intent to defraud and mislead, and to make false statements in connection with the delivery of and payment for health care benefits. The indictment also charged a conspiracy to defraud public and private health care plans.

Caronia . . . argues that, assuming the lawful reach of the FDCA, he did not misbrand Xyrem within the meaning of 21 U.S.C. § 352(f) because he administered adequate warnings to the cooperating physician in October and November 2005. Somewhat confusingly, Caronia claims that no matter whether Xyrem is prescribed for on- or off-label indications, it is administered in the same manner and in the same dosage, and, therefore, the potential dangers are identical for all. Accordingly, Caronia says, his duty to provide adequate directions was satisfied when he provided the cooperating physician with the black box warning outlining the dangers and side effects of Xyrem, even if he was promoting it for off-label uses.

This argument is utterly without merit. It is well established that under the FDA's "intended use" regulations, the promotion of a drug for an off-label use by the manufacturer or its representative is prohibited regardless of what directions the manufacturer or representative may give for that use.

. . . He [also] claims (without any support whatsoever) that warnings were unnecessary because the physician to whom he promoted off-label uses of Xyrem was a confidential informant who was not going to be a user or prescriber of the drug. Yet . . . it is the mouth of the promoter not the ear or intent of the audience that controls. Promotion of off-label uses by a drug manufacturer's representative clearly falls within the broad statutory definition of the offense. On this challenge, too, count two must be sustained.

. . . Caronia's [next] argument is that the government cannot restrict truthful, non-misleading promotion by a pharmaceutical manufacturer (or its employees) to a physician of the off-label uses of an FDA-approved drug. The government rejoins that the First Amendment does not apply to Caronia's activities as alleged in the information and that, if the First Amendment does apply, the FDCA's restrictions on promotion of off-label uses are constitutional.

. . . Caronia's instant motion to dismiss appropriates an alternative First Amendment argument advanced by Gleason prior to his guilty plea. Because he was a doctor expressing his opinions about a drug he could and did prescribe, Gleason argued that his promotional activities amounted to scientific and academic speech, which resides at the core of the First Amendment and, therefore, should receive the highest constitutional protection as pure speech. Caronia, perhaps recognizing that such an argument would be of little help to him as a sales representative of the manufacturer, does not press the argument that his own speech was "pure" speech. He advances instead the alternate argument Gleason advanced that such promotional activities, if not "pure" speech, are protected at minimum as commercial speech.

. . . To determine whether a promotional activity is protectable as "commercial speech," a court must look to (1) whether the expression is an advertisement; (2) whether it refers to a specific product; and (3) whether the speaker has an economic motivation for speaking.

Regardless what else might have been covered in his discussions, Caronia's alleged speech was made on behalf of the manufacturer and clearly (1) encouraged physicians to prescribe Xyrem, (2) referred to a specific product, and (3) was economically motivated. Any such promotion by Caronia to physicians on behalf of Xyrem's manufacturer of the drug's off-label uses would be commercial speech and be "entitled to the qualified but nonetheless substantial protection accorded to commercial speech."

Finding that Caronia's alleged promotional activities in marketing Xyrem constitute commercial speech, the Court

[continued]

must now address his argument that his speech specifically is constitutionally protected. First, as a threshold matter, the Court must determine whether Caronia's commercial speech "concerns unlawful activity or is misleading." If so, then the speech is not protected. Id. If the speech concerns lawful activity and is not misleading, then the Court asks: (2) "whether the asserted government interest is substantial"; (3) whether the restriction "directly advances the government interest asserted"; and (4) whether the restriction is "not more extensive than necessary to serve that interest."

. . . Under prong one of Central Hudson, the Court finds, in harmony with the analysis in Friedman and the district court's opinion in Caputo, that promotion of the off-label uses of an FDA-approved drug concerns lawful activity and is not inherently misleading. . . . Second, the Court finds that the alleged speech is not misleading.

In line with these authorities, this Court holds that the FDCA's prohibitions on commercial speech of the kind charged in the information filed against Caronia directly advance the government's interest in subjecting off-label uses of a drug like Xyrem to the FDA's evaluation process. Central Hudson's third prong is satisfied here as well.

. . . Enter on stage the essential question—can the government satisfy the fourth prong of Central Hudson? . . . Simply put, Caronia asks this Court to extend Western States to undermine the delicate balance between ensuring the integrity of the new drug approval process while allowing patients to continue to have unfettered access to new and potentially life-saving uses for drugs and devices approved only for other purposes. As the Seventh Circuit recognized, such a result could very well leave the FDA only with options that would injure the very audience that would purportedly benefit most from the speech at issue. The Court is disinclined to do so. Quite to the contrary, the Court concludes . . . that the prohibitions on the speech which underlie the two counts in which Caronia is charged pass constitutional muster under the fourth prong of Central Hudson. Any right Caronia had as Xyrem's sales representative to express as commercial speech the truthful promotion of Xyrem's off-label uses is not unconstitutionally restricted by the misbranding provisions of the FDCA. On this ground, Caronia's motion is also denied.

SO ORDERED

CRITICAL THINKING

The Caronia case highlights a problematic relationship between pharmaceutical companies and the physicians who prescribe the medications. How could such interactions be dangerous to patients?

How, at first, did Caronia's speech fit under the umbrella of protected free speech? What reason, then, did Judge Vitaliano give for why Caronia's speech was not protected due to fulfilling the prongs of the Central Hudson test?

ETHICAL DECISION MAKING

The case mentions a physician named Gleason. Gleason was convicted in association with Orphan Pharmaceuticals prior to Caronia's case. How was Gleason acting unethically?

Business managers must sometimes decide whether to hire and fire particular employees. Their decisions will be guided by legal rules that have both ethical foundations and implications for needed legal reform.

In addition, the definition of business ethics refers to *standards* of business conduct. *It does not result in a set of correct decisions.* Business ethics can improve business decisions by serving as a reminder not to choose the first business option that comes to mind or the one that enriches us in the short run. But business ethics can never produce a list of correct business decisions that all ethical businesses will make.

At the same time that business ethics guides decisions within firms, ethics helps guide the law. Law and business ethics serve as an interactive system—informing and assessing each other. For example, our ethical inclination to encourage trust, dependability, and efficiency in market exchanges shapes many of our business laws. See Exhibit 2-2, for instance. The principles of contract law facilitate market exchanges and trade because the

COMPARING THE LAW OF OTHER COUNTRIES

BUSINESS GIFTS AND FAVORS IN CHINA

In China, the practice of using *guanxi* has become an integral part of doing business for firms already located in the country and for those interested in entering the Chinese market. *Guanxi,* which refers to a sort of relationship building, is an intricate system of interpersonal networks woven together by social ties. The concept of *guanxi* is important to individuals involved in business because having good *guanxi* means having connections that can assist you in getting things that may normally be out of reach to you or your business. The rules and regulations in China can be burdensome, but the right *guanxi,* or connections, can make many processes much easier. The *guanxi* system is built on reciprocity, and if someone does a favor for you, you'll be expected to return that favor in the future. A favor could technically be any number of things, from access to partnerships, contacts, and government officials to special consideration or useful information.

The process of creating and maintaining *guanxi* may seem somewhat taboo to westerners because businesses in the United States often have strict rules about accepting gifts, doing favors

and offering preferential treatment or consideration to clients. However, Dan Mintz, a Brooklyn native with no college degree, who is now the CEO of one of the largest advertising agencies in China, claims *guanxi* is a necessity when doing business in China. After moving to Beijing with no contacts and little experience, Mintz established his own business (Dynamic Marking Group) with two Chinese partners, Peter Xiao and Wu Bing. Both Xiao and Bing had extensive *guanxi,* networks that extended into high levels of Chinese government and banking. The trio spent their time targeting potential clients, delivering gifts, and hosting dinners as means to strengthen their *guanxi* and improve their business opportunities. Through their hard work and strong *guanxi* Mintz, Xiao, and Bing were eventually able to secure deals with some of the biggest brands in the world: Budweiser, Kraft, Audi, Volkswagen, and Nike.

Source: Flora F. Gu, Kineta Hung, and David K. Tse, "When Does Guanxi Matter? Issues of Capitalization and Its Dark Sides," *Journal of Marketing* 72 (July 2008), pp. 12–28; www.fastcompany.com/magazine/104/open_mintz.html?page=0%2C0; and www.chinasuccessstories.com/2008/02/07/dmg-chinese-advertising/.

During the past several years, ethics violations have been uncovered in the accounting practices of a number of large companies. Enron and WorldCom were two of the perpetrators in these scandals. Both companies failed to report or record billions of dollars in profit losses, which resulted in stockholders' believing that the companies were in a much better financial state than actually was the case.

Enron's tangled web involved the company's creating multiple subsidiaries and related companies. These businesses were often treated as companies independent of Enron and not shown on the accounting books. Enron used the subsidiaries to conceal debts and losses in a very complex fraud scheme. When the company went bankrupt, employees who had based their retirement plans around Enron stock lost almost everything. Additionally, Enron auditor Arthur Andersen was found guilty of shredding documents about Enron's audits.

In June 2002, shortly after the Enron bankruptcy was announced, WorldCom revealed that it also had engaged in unethical accounting practices. WorldCom's violations included counting profits twice and concealing billions of dollars in expenses when making reports to the SEC. The company thereby made itself appear profitable when it was actually losing money. In total, WorldCom had more than $7 billion in misreported debt.

These two cases, among others, left investors understandably concerned about the truthfulness of individuals who were in charge of operating large corporations. Those in charge of these companies had been awarded million-dollar bonuses while completely disregarding stockholders and employees, who lost millions of dollars when the companies collapsed.

The revelations of Enron and WorldCom suggested quite blatantly that the business world could not be allowed to regulate itself ethically. Their downfall in part led to many federal regulations designed to promote truthfulness and ethical practices among business managers. In this new business environment, there is a much greater degree of government oversight to ensure that companies maintain high standards of ethical behavior. Companies are required to make their accounting records far more transparent, to satisfy not only the federal government but their understandably wary investors.

Exhibit 2-2

Enron, WorldCom, and Shifts in Business Regulation

parties to an exchange can count on the enforceability of agreements. Legal rules that govern the exchange have been shaped in large part by our sense of commercial ethics.

Of course, different ethical understandings prevail in different countries. Thus, ethical conceptions shape business law and business relationships uniquely in each country. Increasingly, business leaders require sensitivity to the differences in legal guidelines in the various countries in which they operate. These differences are based on somewhat different understandings of ethical behavior among businesspeople in diverse countries.

As we mentioned above, business ethics does not yield one "correct" decision. So how are business managers to chart their way through the ethical decision-making process? One source of assistance consists of the general theories and schools of thought about ethics. Each ethical system provides a method for resolving ethical dilemmas by examining duties, consequences, virtues, justice, and so on. A detailed look at each of these ethical systems can be found in Appendix 2A.

Exhibit 2-2 reminds us that unethical behavior by businesses has huge costs. In the interest of providing future business managers with a practical approach to business ethics *that they can use to avoid these costs,* we suggest a three-step approach: the WPH process of ethical decision making. This approach offers future business managers some ethical guidelines, or practical steps, that provide a dependable stimulus to ethical reasoning in a business context. Appendix 2A provides the theoretical basis for the WPH approach used in this book.

The WPH Framework for Business Ethics

L03

How can we use the WPH framework for ethical business decisions?

A useful set of ethical guidelines requires recognition that managerial decisions must meet the following primary criteria:

- The decisions affect particular groups of stakeholders in the operations of the firm. The pertinent question is thus, *Whom* would this decision affect?
- The decisions are made in pursuit of a particular *purpose.* Business decisions are instruments toward an ethical end.
- The decisions must meet the standards of action-oriented business behavior. Managers need a doable set of guidelines for *how* to make ethical decisions.

The remainder of this chapter explains and illustrates this framework. See Exhibit 2-3 for a summary of the key WPH elements.

Exhibit 2-3

The WPH Process of Ethical Decision Making

1. **W—WHO (Stakeholders):**
   Consumers
   Owners or investors
   Management
   Employees
   Community
   Future generations
2. **P—PURPOSE (Values):**
   Freedom
   Security
   Justice
   Efficiency
3. **H—HOW (Guidelines):**
   Public disclosure
   Universalization
   Golden Rule

WHO ARE THE RELEVANT STAKEHOLDERS?

The stakeholders of a firm are the many groups of people affected by the firm's decisions. Any given managerial decision affects, in varying degrees, the following stakeholders:

1. Owners or shareholders.
2. Employees.
3. Customers.
4. Management.
5. The general community where the firm operates.
6. Future generations.

Exhibit 2-4 gives a portrait of General Mills' commitments to its primary stakeholders and demonstrates that General Mills is aware of the people involved in its various decisions.

When you consider the relevant stakeholders, try to go beyond the obvious. In the Case Nugget (next page), Maria's encounter with her company's vice president clearly highlights certain common interests of management and its employees. However, a useful exercise for all of us is to force ourselves to think more broadly about additional stakeholders who may be affected just as much in the long run. Then we will be less likely to make decisions that have unintended negative ethical impacts.

Maria's ethical dilemma is complex. Many of the issues in the dilemma pertain to her career and the welfare of her firm. But consider the many stakeholders whose interests were not introduced into the conversation. When we overlook important, relevant stakeholders, we are ignoring a significant component of ethical reasoning.

Consider the negative impact that results when a firm fails to show adequate respect for a major stakeholder. On December 3, 1984, a horrible catastrophe occurred at a chemical plant in Bhopal, India. The plant was a subsidiary of Union Carbide. Damage to some

Exhibit 2-4

Commitments to General Mills' Stakeholders

We share a common purpose and a common responsibility with our stakeholders. We want them to know that they can depend on us—and that they can trust us. We know too that we must depend on them. We want every stakeholder of General Mills to feel they are part of something special.

Our Consumers

Our consumers trust General Mills to deliver quality and value when they are shopping for the most important people in their lives—their families.

Our Customers

Our customers trust General Mills to deliver quality and value for their customers—the consumers of our products—and they look to us to help them grow.

Our Partners

We treat our suppliers, vendors, and other partners with respect—conducting ourselves with integrity in every aspect of every relationship.

Our Team

We are diverse, talented, committed individuals of integrity—constantly learning and growing and contributing to our communities.

Our Shareholders

Our shareholders trust General Mills to deliver superior performance and superior total investment returns.

Our Communities

We are committed to making a positive difference in people's lives by making a positive difference in our communities.

Source: www.generalmills.com/corporate/commitment/stakeholders.aspx (accessed October 30, 2008).

HYPOTHETICAL CASE NUGGET
THE MANY STAKEHOLDERS IN A BUSINESS DECISION

Maria Lopez

Maria recently became the purchasing manager of a small lawn-mower manufacturing firm. She is excited about the opportunity to demonstrate her abilities in this new responsibility. She is very aware that several others in the firm are watching her closely because they do not believe she deserves the purchasing manager position.

Her new job at the firm requires that she interact with several senior managers and leaders. One vice president in particular, Brian O'Malley, is someone she admires because he has earned the respect of the CEO on the basis of his success at making profits for the firm. Again and again, he just seems to know how to discover and take advantage of competitive opportunities that end up paying off royally for the firm.

Maria's first responsibility is to buy the motors for the assembly line. The motors constitute 30 percent of the total construction cost of the lawn mowers. Consequently, even a small error on Maria's part would have huge implications for the firm's profitability. The bids from the motor suppliers are required to be secret in order to maximize competition among the suppliers. The bids are due at 5 p.m. today.

At 3 p.m., Maria accidentally sees Brian returning the submitted bids to the locked safe where they are to be stored, according to company policy, until all bids have been submitted at 5 p.m. Then at 4:45 p.m., she notices a postal delivery of a bid from Stein's Motor Company. Her head buzzes as it hits her that Stein's president is one of Brian O'Malley's cousins.

She has no idea what to do. However, she knows she has to decide quickly.

equipment resulted in the emission of a deadly gas, methyl isocyanate, into the atmosphere. The emission of the gas caused injuries to more than 200,000 workers and other people in the neighborhood of the chemical plant. Several thousand people died.

Many factors, including worker error, faulty management decisions, equipment failures, and poor safety standards combined to cause the accident. Union Carbide was accused of not demanding the same rigorous safety standards in India as it had in the United States. Citizens of both India and the United States demanded that the corporation be held responsible for its evident neglect of safety. Union Carbide argued that it could not operate the plant if it were required to obey rigid Indian safety standards and that the economic benefits of the plant to India outweighed the risks of not following these standards. After years of litigation in both U.S. and Indian courts, Union Carbide was eventually ordered to monetarily compensate the victims of the accident. Among other factors, Union Carbide's failure to respect the interests of a major stakeholder resulted in a disaster for the firm and for the community.

After we consider stakeholders, the next step in the WPH framework is to consider the purpose of business decisions. In the next section, we look first at the parties involved, and then we explore the purposes that bring these various parties together in a common effort.

WHAT ARE THE ULTIMATE *PURPOSES* OF THE DECISION?

When we think about the ultimate reason or purpose for why we make decisions in a business firm, we turn to the basic unit of business ethics—values. Values are positive abstractions that capture our sense of what is good or desirable. They are *ideas* that underlie conversations about business ethics. We derive our ethics from the interplay of values. Values represent our understanding of the purposes we will fulfill by making particular decisions.

For example, we value honesty. We want to live in communities where the trust that we associate with honesty prevails in our negotiations with one another. Business depends on the maintenance of a high degree of trust. No contract can protect us completely against every possible contingency. So we need some element of trust in one another when we buy and sell.

When that trust is lacking, businesses fall apart. In August 2011, Maryland and Connecticut sued 16 banks for alleged rate manipulation. In the following weeks, additional banks in New York were served subpoenas, under the Martin Act, which allows investigation of businesses in New York "that may have committed deceitful practices contrary to the plain rules of common honesty." Robert Schapiro, the undersecretary of commerce for economic affairs in the Clinton administration, stated, "So long as big finance will do almost anything to goose its own profits and bonuses, self-regulation is a dangerous myth."

If we think about the definition of values for a moment, we realize two things immediately. First, there are a huge number of values that pull and push our decisions. For example, the banks mentioned above may have thought of honesty as an important value, but perhaps their desire for personal success weighed more heavily on their decision making than the need for honesty did. Second, to state that a value is important in a particular situation is to start a conversation about what is meant by that particular value. For example, some people may consider success a measure of one's character, whereas one may presume from the banks' actions that their definition of success was largely based on financial achievement.

To help make WPH useful to you as a manager, Exhibit 2-5 outlines an efficient way to apply this second step in the WPH framework. The exhibit identifies four of the most important values influencing business ethics and presents alternative meanings for each. Exhibit 2-5 should not only help clarify the importance of values in your own mind but also enable you to question others who claim to be acting in an ethical fashion.

For instance, a manager might be deciding whether to fire an employee whose performance is less than impressive. In making this decision, the manager explores alternative visions of key values such as justice and efficiency and then makes choices about which action to take. Values and their alternative meanings are often the foundation for different ethical decisions.

To avoid ambiguity, many companies summarize their values in brief statements.

Nortel Networks' statement of core values, shown in Exhibit 2-6, identifies for Nortel's stakeholders which positive abstractions guide its business decisions.

Exhibit 2-5

Primary Values and Business Ethics

VALUE	ALTERNATIVE MEANINGS
Freedom	1. To act without restriction from rules imposed by others
	2. To possess the capacity or resources to act as one wishes
	3. To escape the cares and demands of this world entirely
Security	1. To possess a large-enough supply of goods and services to meet basic needs
	2. To be safe from those wishing to interfere with your property rights
	3. To achieve the psychological condition of self-confidence to such an extent that risks are welcome
Justice	1. To receive the products of your labor
	2. To treat all humans identically, regardless of race, class, gender, age, and sexual preference
	3. To provide resources in proportion to need
	4. To possess anything that someone else is willing to grant you
Efficiency	1. To maximize the amount of wealth in society
	2. To get the most from a particular output
	3. To minimize costs

Exhibit 2-6

Core Values: A Guide to Ethical Business Practice

NORTEL NETWORKS' CORE VALUES

1. We create superior value for our customers.
2. We work to provide shareholder value.
3. Our people are our strength.
4. We share one vision. We are one team.
5. We have only one standard—excellence.
6. We embrace change and reward innovation.
7. We fulfill our commitments and act with integrity.

New ways of organizing people and work within the corporation are giving each of us more decision-making responsibility. Given the complexity and constantly changing nature of our work and our world, no book of hard-and-fast rules—however long and detailed—could ever adequately cover all the dilemmas people face. In this context, every Nortel Networks' employee is asked to take leadership in ethical decision making.

In most situations, our personal values and honesty will guide us to the right decision. But in our capacity as employees and representatives of Nortel Networks, we must also always consider how our actions affect the integrity and credibility of the corporation as a whole. Our business ethics must reflect the standard of conduct outlined in this document—a standard grounded in the corporation's values and governing Nortel Networks' relationships with all stakeholders.

HOW DO WE MAKE ETHICAL DECISIONS?

Making ethical decisions has always been one of our most confusing *and* important human challenges. In the process of meeting this challenge, we have discovered a few general, ethical guidelines to assist us. An *ethical guideline* provides one path to ethical conduct. Notice that all three ethical guidelines below reflect a central principle of business ethics: consideration for stakeholders.

The Golden Rule.   The idea that we should interact with other people in a manner consistent with the way we would like them to interact with us has deep historical roots. Both Confucius and Aristotle suggested versions of that identical guideline. One scholar has identified six ways the Golden Rule can be interpreted:

1. Do to others as you want them to gratify you.
2. Be considerate of others' feelings as you want them to be considerate of yours.
3. Treat others as persons of rational dignity like you.
4. Extend brotherly or sisterly love to others, as you would want them to do to you.
5. Treat others according to moral insight, as you would have others treat you.
6. Do to others as God wants you to do to them.

Regardless of the version of the Golden Rule we use, this guideline urges us to be aware that other people—their rights and needs—matter.

Let's return to the ethical problem outlined at the beginning of this chapter. Using the Golden Rule as your ethical guideline, how would you behave? Would you hide the information about the chemicals used to make your medications, or would you disclose the information? Put yourself in the consumer's position. As a consumer, would you want to know that your medications contained a potentially toxic chemical? Are there other

CASE NUGGET

TYSON FOODS' BRIBERY CHARGES

In 2004, memos containing information regarding illegal bribes were sent from a Tyson Foods plant manager in Mexico to corporate officials in the United States. Basically, company officials in Mexico were sending roughly $2,700 a month to the wives of two veterinarians involved in the safety and quality of the food produced at the plant. At the time, Tyson Foods was attempting to increase its national exports. However, countries involved in the importation of its products required that experts certify that the food products met certain safety and sanitary standards. Essentially, the two veterinarians were being sent extra payments so that they would sign off on the "quality" of the products produced at the plant regardless of whether the products were actually up to par with the standards imposed. This act was especially dangerous considering the relationship between poultry products and their reputation of passing on disease, including salmonella, to consumers.

The company officials in Arkansas, including the president of Tyson International and the vice president of operations, realized that bribing foreign officials, the biggest issue at hand, was a felony according to the Foreign Corrupt Practices Act. Faced with the option of investigating the allegations and bringing the illegal activities to light, the company officials instead found a way to keep sending the bribes but make the payments look legal. Two years later, Tyson officials finally hired a law firm to do an internal investigation of the bribery. In 2011, Tyson was charged with conspiracy and violating the Foreign Corrupt Practices Act. To avoid trial, Tyson was forced to pay $4 million as a criminal penalty and $1.2 million to the Securities and Exchange Commission to settle charges of maintaining illegal records.

stakeholders in the organization whose interests should be the focus of your application of the Golden Rule? The focus on others that is the foundation of the Golden Rule is also clearly reflected in a second ethical guideline: the public disclosure test.

Public Disclosure Test.   We tend to care about what others think about us as ethical agents. Stop for a moment and think of corporations that failed to apply the public disclosure test and generated negative reactions as a result. For example, in December 2012, Walgreens was ordered to pay $16.47 million to settle a lawsuit alleging that over 600 California stores had illegally handled and dumped pesticides, bleach, paint, pharmaceutical waste, and other items. Walgreens was also charged because of improper disposal of confidential medical records of customers. Walgreens denied all charges.

Walgreens would likely have behaved differently had it considered the public disclosure test before dumping toxic waste inappropriately. The company may have realized that the community would be outraged by Walgreen's disregard for the well-being of thousands of people, and the company may even have considered that its decision would cost far more money than it would save. Presumably, Walgreens would have chosen a different waste disposal option, one that would have saved its reputation, its money, and the lives of others.

Another way to think of the public disclosure test is to view it as a ray of sunlight that makes our actions visible, rather than obscured. As Exhibit 2-7 suggests, the issue of transparency of behavior is often seen as a method of improving ethical behavior. The public disclosure test is sometimes called the "television test," for it requires us to imagine that our actions are being broadcast on national television. The premise behind the public disclosure test is that ethics is hard work, labor that we might resist if we did not have frequent reminders that we live in a community. As a member of a community, our self-concept is tied, at least in part, to how that community perceives us.

Universalization Test.   A third general guideline shares with the other two a focus on the "other"—the stakeholders whom our actions affect. Before we act, the universalization test asks us to consider what the world would be like were our decision copied by everyone else. Applying the universalization test causes us to wonder aloud: "Is what I am about to do the kind of action that, *were others to follow my example,* makes the world a better place

E-COMMERCE AND THE LAW

TECHNOLOGICAL RECORDS AND ETHICS

Journalists use different technological mediums to contact and store information about confidential sources, including government whistle-blowers. One of the most important aspects of journalism is to protect confidential informants so that news sources can still enlighten the public with important and sensitive information. Here, ethical issues come up. Documents containing information about informants' identities may not be collected by the government without permission from the deputy attorney general. In other words, the First Amendment protects the privacy and individual ownership of these e-mail and phone records.

For example, in 2004, the FBI illegally obtained phone records related to the confidential informants of *The New York Times'* and *Washington Post'*s bureaus in Indonesia. The executive editors of both newspapers were called by the FBI, and both received apologies. The Justice Department looked into the illegal investigation by the FBI after the FBI went ahead with what it called "emergency"

gathering of private information related to an alleged terrorist investigation. The editors were never told why their records were needed.

Now news corporations are putting numerous security barriers and encryptions around their records so that nobody can gain access to them. In fact, Wikileaks, the organization that publicizes secret government documents on its website, has probably the strongest security procedures protecting its sources. Instant messages are expertly encrypted, as are all files passed between people. Also, the Tor Project, a tool that enables users to communicate anonymously, completely hides all servers. Other news companies are attempting to mimic such standards and adjust privacy policies to not reserve the right to release any information about a source "to law enforcement authorities or to a requesting third party, without notice."

for me and those I love?" Apply the universalization test to the Case Nugget on the previous page to get a sense of how valuable it is as an ethical guide.

In summary, business managers can apply the WPH approach to most ethical dilemmas. The WPH framework provides a practical process suited to the frequently complex ethical dilemmas that business managers must address quickly in today's society.

Exhibit 2-7

A Mandate for Ethical Behavior

THE SARBANES-OXLEY ACT

The Corporate and Criminal Fraud Accountability Act, also known as the Sarbanes-Oxley Act, was signed by President Bush in 2002 in the wake of several corporate accounting scandals. The act is intended to promote high ethical standards among business managers and employees through a series of stringent requirements and controls that regulate several different facets of corporate operation.

Among other things, the act created the Public Company Accounting Oversight Board. This board is responsible for ensuring that auditors and public accounting firms compile accurate and truthful financial reports for the companies they audit. The act also requires that companies devise a system that allows employees to report suspicions of unethical behavior within the company. The act also protects these whistle-blowers from being fired or from retaliation by their employer for reporting a possible problem within the company.

Additionally, the chief executive officer (CEO) or chief financial officer (CFO) must personally vouch that the company's financial statements are correct, meet all SEC requirements for disclosure, and represent company finances accurately. The act provides for very harsh penalties in the case of violations. If the CEO or CFO knows that the company's financial reports are incorrect but claims they are truthful, or if he or she destroys or changes financial documents, the imposed fine can run into the millions of dollars.

CASE OPENER WRAP-UP

Acne Medication and Gastrointestinal Injury

Acne medication manufacturers, as well as other firms, affect the lives of many stakeholders. A manufacturer's owners, workers, and customers are perhaps the most obvious stakeholders in decisions the manufacturer makes about its production and labeling policies. It is clear that the manufacturer's questionable decisions have potentially detrimental consequences for customers who use its acne medication, but the manufacturer's decisions may also affect the business climate among other manufacturers, which may be tempted to engage in similarly questionable business practices to increase profits. All of the manufacturer's decisions have ethical implications.

For example, in the case at hand, the courts were divided on whether Hoffman-LaRoche was responsible for listing potential illnesses such as IBD or whether it was acceptable to list only common symptoms of IBD that may occur. Issues such as these are not black and white, and often the rulings regarding these issues vary among courts.

Although, as this book was being written, no final decision had been made regarding Kendall's initial lawsuit, the court had addressed the defendant's movement to dismiss the lawsuit on the basis of untimeliness. On February 27, 2012, the court found that given that Kendall's dermatologist was unaware of, and therefore did not warn her of, the risk of IBD resulting from Accutane, a reasonable person in the plaintiff's situation would not have been aware of the potential for the medication to cause her illness. Thus, given that the plaintiff was not made aware of the connection between her illness and the medication until the 2004 lawyer's advertisement, her lawsuit against Hoffman-LaRoche was timely.

KEY TERMS

business ethics 16

ethical dilemma 16

ethical guidelines 22

ethics 16

social responsibility of
business 16

stakeholders 23

values 24

WPH process of ethical
decision making 22

SUMMARY OF KEY TOPICS

Business ethics is the application of ethics to the special problems and opportunities experienced by businesspeople.

The *social responsibility of business* consists of the expectations that the community imposes on firms doing business with its citizens.

**Business Ethics and
Social Responsibility**

Business ethics builds on business law. The law both affects and is affected by evolving ethical patterns. But business law provides only a floor for business ethics, telling business leaders the minimally acceptable course of action.

**Business Law and
Business Ethics**

Who are the relevant stakeholders? This question determines which interests (consumers, employees, managers, owners) are being pushed and prodded.

**The WPH Framework
for Business Ethics**

What are the ultimate purposes of the decision? This question determines which values (freedom, efficiency, security, and justice) are being upheld by the decision.

How do we make ethical decisions? This question leads us to apply general ethical guidelines:

- *Golden Rule:* Do unto others as you would have them do unto you.
- *Public disclosure test:* If the public knew about this decision, how would you decide?
- *Universalization test:* What would the world be like were our decision copied by everyone else?

POINT / COUNTERPOINT

Sarbanes-Oxley Act of 2002

Are the Costs Associated with the Sarbanes-Oxley Act Reason for Reform?	
NO	**YES**
Corporate and accounting scandals, such as Enron, were the reason the Sarbanes-Oxley Act of 2002 was drafted. The act promotes honesty and accountability in financial reporting, thus bringing increased security to investors. For example, corporations must now ensure the segregation of all duties related to accounting procedures.	Corporations need incentives to remain or go public. The Sarbanes-Oxley Act of 2002 is not an incentive. Although there may have been ample motivation for the development of an act that addresses accounting scandals, the costs associated with Sarbanes-Oxley are much too high. Simply purchasing and learning to use the materials needed for compliance with the act would cost approximately $3.5 million.
Although critics assert that the financial burden associated with the act is reason for reform, the compliance costs about which they speak are beginning to fall as individuals become familiar with the new systems. In addition, the Dow Jones Industrial Average is rising as a result of increased investor confidence. This confidence is the direct result of the requirement that corporations disclose information and allow for investigations by the Public Company Accounting Oversight Board.	Those who argue that the act should not be reformed often focus on the idea that every corporation is now being held to the same standards. However, as a result of the substantial economic costs associated with implementation of the guidelines, smaller businesses that would like to go public are forced to remain private to avoid the costs. Among small businesses that are already public, many are not able to gather the resources necessary to comply with the act.
Since the passing of the Sarbanes-Oxley Act, there have not been any known major accounting scandals. Without public disclosure, corporations would have little incentive to engage in rigorous evaluation of their own accounting practices. By forcing corporations to disclose information, they are being held to higher ethical standards than they were previously.	In addition to the costs associated with the act, corporations are now monitored by commissions that are appointed rather than elected. These commissions lack the accountability that is necessary to make decisions about how to regulate, tax, and punish companies and individuals that may violate the provisions of the act. Thus, the act as it is currently written does not provide an equal opportunity to all corporations and businesses.

QUESTIONS & PROBLEMS

1. How do business ethics and business law interact with each other? Is one highly ethical and the other less ethical?

2. If business ethics does not offer guidance about what is always the right thing to do, is one behavior as good as the next?

3. How does the WPH approach to ethics approach an ethical problem?

4. In December 2010, the Equal Employment Opportunity Commission filed a nationwide hiring discrimination lawsuit against the Kaplan Higher

Education Corporation. Kaplan was requiring access to applicants' credit reports and credit histories and took such information into consideration when hiring. Not only did the EEOC believe that such a requirement was discriminating against black applicants, but it also felt that during a time of financial woes for most Americans, people with damaged credit histories would have a hard time getting back into the workforce. Apparently, research showed that the reliance on credit histories significantly hurt the hiring of blacks as opposed to white applicants. The EEOC noted that the credit histories were not necessarily connected with the performance the applicant would show at the particular job being applied for. Surveys show that credit histories are required by almost half of all employers. However, states including Washington, Oregon, and Illinois have severely limited or completely banned the reliance of employers on credit histories. Because of the recession, Congress has considered imposing such restrictions or even a ban. How do you think the court ruled in this case? Do you think it is fair not only to black applicants but to all applicants that their employer bases a hiring decision on credit history? Do you think other companies will change their use of credit histories on the basis of the outcome of this case? [Civil Action No. 1:10-cv-02882 (2010).]

5. In 2011 Walmart was hit with the largest employment discrimination lawsuit in history, and the lawsuit was brought to the Supreme Court. The problems began when a female employee named Stephanie Odle found out that a male employee with the same title as hers yet less experience was earning $10,000 a year more than she was. Subsequently, she was fired when she complained about the discovery. In fact, her boss defended the salary difference, saying that the male employee should make more because he was supporting a family, even though Odle was pregnant and thus trying to save up for her family as well. The lawsuit is so large because it contains complaints from 1.5 million female Walmart employees with similar stories. However, Walmart argues that there are too many significant differences among the 1.5 million cases and that the complaints may not be brought under a single-action lawsuit. On the other hand, a group of 31 civil procedure professors created a brief saying that the women have the core point in common: Walmart discriminated against the women. In addition, because Walmart is a large corporation with an extensive litigation team and a huge amount of resources, the women need to bring their complaints to court together to stand a chance. How do you think the Supreme Court will decide? Do you think the cases among the women will be similar enough to stand under one action because there is a core ultimate problem? Do you think Walmart will win because of the resources it has as a huge corporation? [*Wal-Mart Stores, Inc. v. Betty Dukes et al.,* 131 S. Ct. 2541 (2011).]

6. Entertainment Network, Inc. (ENI), a business that provided news, entertainment, and information via the Internet, sued government officials who prohibited the company from filming the execution of Oklahoma City bomber Timothy McVeigh and selling the footage of the execution online. The government officials argued that a Justice Department regulation prohibiting audio and visual recording devices at federal executions applied in the case at hand. ENI, however, argued that the regulation violated the company's First Amendment right to free speech. How do you think the court should have ruled in this case? Do you think ENI might have altered its decision to broadcast the execution if it had applied the Golden Rule? [*Entm't Network, Inc. v. Lappin,* 134 F. Supp. 2d 1002 (2001).]

7. Ernest Price went to a doctor in 1997, seeking Oxycontin to treat pain related to sickle cell anemia. Between November 1999 and October 2000, Price sought Oxycontin prescriptions from at least ten different doctors at ten different clinics in two cities, filling the prescriptions at seven pharmacies in three cities. The doctors were notified of Price's medication-seeking behavior, and the doctors discontinued Price's treatment. Price then filed suit, claiming his doctors, pharmacies, and the pharmaceutical companies that manufactured Oxycontin had breached their duty by failing to adequately warn Price of the addictive nature of Oxycontin. How do you think the court responded to Price's claims? Think about all the stakeholders involved in such a case; how would those parties be affected by a ruling in favor of Price? In favor of the doctors and pharmaceutical companies? [*Ernest Price v. The Purdue Pharma Co.,* 920 So. 2d 479; 2006 Miss. LEXIS 67 (2006).]

8. Javier Galindo, the husband of Richard Clark's housekeeper, was sitting in his car, parked in the driveway of Clark's house, waiting to pick up his wife. While he was waiting, a leaning 80-foot tree located on an adjacent property fell on Galindo's car and killed him. Galindo's wife sued Clark, alleging that Clark

was liable for failing to notify Galindo about the danger posed by the leaning tree. Do you think that Clark had a legal responsibility to tell Galindo about the tree? Do you think Clark had an ethical responsibility to tell Galindo about the tree? Why might the answer to these questions be different? [*Galindo v. Town of Clarkstown,* 2 N.Y.3d 633 (2004).]

9. Mr. Caperton was the owner of a coal company that operated Harman mine. He sued Massey, which is a very large and powerful energy company. The suit was brought against Massey for a number of reasons. First, Massey bought another coal company called Wellmore Coal. Prior to the takeover, Wellmore Coal had bought Caperton's high-grade coal and blended that coal with its own, later selling the product to a steel company called LTV. After the takeover, Massey cut Caperton's high-quality coal out of the mix and tried to sell the cheaper product to LTV. However, LTV refused the new, low-grade coal. Thus, Massey took steps not only to make Caperton's land and business look undesirable but to ruin his business completely so that LTV had no opportunity to work with Caperton or Harman mine unless Massey owned it. Massey pushed LTV to alter contracts in ways that would financially hurt Caperton's business, and then Massey bought land around the mine to make the area unappealing to potential buyers of the mine. Massey finally offered to buy Caperton's business and mine at a huge discount. Massey told Caperton not to sue, as Massey had the resources to spend $1 million a month to fight the bankrupt company. When Caperton did sue, the lower court found Massey liable for $50 million in damages. In 2008, Massey appealed to the supreme court of appeals of West Virginia; however, the judge had special ties with the CEO of Massey. Specifically, the CEO had donated $3 million to secure Justice Benjamin's seat when he had campaigned for the supreme court of appeals.

Caperton immediately motioned for Justice Benjamin to excuse himself from the case, but the court dismissed the motion, with Benjamin voting for the majority. The court then moved to dismiss the $50 million and reverse the case. Caperton finally appealed to bring the case to the Supreme Court. What do you think the Supreme Court decided? Do you think it believed that the involvement of Justice Benjamin in the case was unethical? Do you think the CEO of Massey was contributing to the campaigns of high justices to create political ties and thus garner political support? [*Caperton v. A.T. Massey Coal Co., Inc.,* 225 W. Va. 128; 690 S.E.2d 322 (2008).]

10. Brazos Higher Education Service Corporation, Inc., was a nonprofit student loan company. Brazos allowed one of its employees to store customers' personal financial information on a laptop with an unencrypted hard drive. The laptop was subsequently stolen from the employee's home during a robbery. Brazos had no way of knowing which customers' information was contained on the laptop's hard drive or whether the information would be accessed by a third party. As a precaution, Brazos notified all of its customers that their information may have been accessed by a third party and offered each customer six months of identity-theft monitoring. One customer, Guin, brought suit against Brazos for negligence, claiming that Brazos had failed to adequately protect his financial information, thereby causing Guin harm. Guin's information was never accessed by a third party, and Guin never suffered identity theft. How might other businesses be affected if Guin's lawsuit succeeded? Do you think Brazos was wrong to store its customers' financial information on an unencrypted laptop hard drive? [*Stacy Lawton Guin v. Brazos Higher Education Service Corporation, Inc.,* 2006 U.S. Dist. LEXIS 4846 (2006).]

Looking for more review material?

The Online Learning Center at **www.mhhe.com/kubasek3e** contains this chapter's "Assignment on the Internet" and also a list of URLs for more information, entitled "On the Internet." Find both of them in the Student Center portion of the OLC, along with quizzes and other helpful materials.

APPENDIX 2A   THEORIES OF BUSINESS ETHICS

Ethical Relativism and Situational Ethics

An ethical school of thought that may seem appealing on the surface is ethical relativism. Ethical relativism is a theory of ethics that denies the existence of objective moral standards. Rather, according to ethical relativism, individuals must evaluate actions on the basis of what they feel is best for themselves. Ethical relativism holds that when two individuals disagree over a question about morality, both individuals are correct because no objective standard exists to evaluate their actions. Instead, morality is relative, and thus no one can criticize another's behavior as immoral. Many people find ethical relativism attractive because it promotes tolerance.

Ethical relativism may appear attractive at first glance, but very few people are willing to accept the logical conclusions of this theory. For example, ethical relativism requires that we see murder as a moral action as long as the murderer believes that the action is best for himself or herself. Once a person accepts the appropriateness of criticizing behavior in some situations, the person has rejected ethical relativism and must develop a more complex ethical theory.

Situational ethics is a theory that at first appears similar to ethical relativism but is actually substantially different. Like ethical relativism, situational ethics requires that we evaluate the morality of an action by imagining ourselves in the position of the person facing the ethical dilemma. But unlike ethical relativism, situational ethics allows us to judge other people's actions. In other words, situational ethics holds that once we put ourselves in another person's shoes, we can evaluate whether that person's action was ethical.

While situational ethics provides a useful rule of thumb to use when thinking about the ethical decision-making process, it does not offer specific-enough criteria to be useful in many real-world situations. Once we imagine ourselves in the position of a person facing an ethical dilemma, situational ethics does not tell us *how* to evaluate that person's actions. An alternative school of ethical thought, however, provides a much more judgmental approach to ethical dilemmas.

Absolutism

Absolutism, or *ethical fundamentalism,* requires that individuals defer to a set of rules to guide them in the ethical decision-making process. Unlike ethical relativism and situational ethics, absolutism holds that whether an action is moral does not depend on the perspective of the person facing the ethical dilemma. Rather, whether an action is moral depends on whether the action conforms to the given set of ethical rules.

Of course, people disagree about which set of rules to follow. Why should we accept and act on any one absolutist set of rules? Absolutism cannot tell us, for example, why we ought to follow the doctrines set forth in the Koran and not Hindu doctrines.

Moreover, the unquestionable nature of the rules in most absolutist repositories seems overly inflexible when applied to different situations. For instance, "Thou shalt not kill" seems to be an absolute rule, but, in practice, killing in self-defense seems to be an acceptable exception to this rule.

Consequentialism

In contrast to absolutism, consequentialism does not provide a rigid set of rules to follow regardless of the situation. Rather, as the word *consequentialism* suggests, this ethical approach "depends on the consequences." Consequentialism is a general approach to ethical dilemmas that requires that we inquire about the consequences to relevant people of our making a particular decision.

Utilitarianism is one form of consequentialism that business managers may find useful. Like many consequentialist theories of ethics, utilitarianism urges managers to take those actions that provide the greatest pleasure after having subtracted the pain or harm associated with the action in question.

Utilitarianism has two main branches: act utilitarianism and rule utilitarianism. Act utilitarianism tells business managers to examine all the potential actions in each situation and choose the action that yields the greatest amount of pleasure over pain for all involved. For example, according to act utilitarianism, a business manager who deceives an employee may be acting morally if the act of deception maximizes pleasure over pain for everyone involved.

Rule utilitarians, on the other hand, see great potential for the abuse of act utilitarianism. Instead of advocating the maximization of pleasure over pain in each individual situation, rule utilitarianism holds that general rules that *on balance* produce the greatest amount of pleasure for all involved should be established and followed in each situation. Thus, even if the business manager's decision to deceive an employee maximizes pleasure over pain in a given situation, the act probably would not be consistent with rule utilitarianism because deception does not generally produce the greatest satisfaction.

Rule utilitarianism underlies many laws in the United States. For example, labor laws prohibit employers from hiring children to do manufacturing work, even though in some situations the transaction would maximize pleasure over pain.

One form of utilitarianism commonly applied by firms and government is cost-benefit analysis. When a business makes decisions based on cost-benefit analysis, it is comparing the pleasure and pain of its optional choices, as that pleasure and pain are measured in monetary terms.

As we have shown, consequentialism is not altogether helpful because of the extreme difficulty in making the required calculations about consequences. Another issue raises an important additional objection to consequentialist thinking: Where does the important social value of justice fit into consequentialist reasoning? Many business decisions could be beneficial in their consequences for a majority of the population, but is it fair to require that a few be harmed so that the majority can be improved? Consequentialism does not provide definite answers to these questions, but an alternative ethical theory does.

Deontology

Deontology is an alternative theoretical approach to consequentialism. When you see references to *Kantian ethics*, the analysis that follows the reference will be a discussion of the most famous of the deontological approaches to business ethics. Unlike a person espousing consequentialism, a person using a deontological approach will not see the relevance of making a list of harms and benefits that result from a particular decision. Instead, deontology consists of acting on the basis of the recognition that certain actions are right or wrong, regardless of their consequences. For example, a business leader might consider it wrong to terminate a person whose spouse has terminal cancer because a firm has an obligation to support its employees when they are vulnerable, *period.*

But how are business managers to decide whether an action is right or wrong? The German deontological philosopher Immanuel Kant proposed the categorical imperative to determine whether an action is right. According to the categorical imperative, an action is moral only if it would be consistent for everyone in society to act in the same way.

Thus, for example, applying the categorical imperative would lead you to conclude that you should not cheat on a drug test, because if everyone acted in the same way, the drug test would be meaningless.

From the deontological viewpoint, the duties or obligations that we owe one another as humans are much more ethically significant than are measurements of the impacts of business decisions. For example, a person using a deontological theory of ethics may see any business behavior that violates our duty of trust as being wrong. To sell a car that one knows will probably not be usable after four years is, from this perspective, unethical. No set of positive consequences that might flow from the production decision can overcome the certainty of the deontological recognition that the sale is wrong.

The duties that we owe others imply that human beings have fundamental rights based on the dignity of each individual. This **principle of rights** asserts that whether a business decision is ethical depends on how the decision affects the rights of all involved. This principle is foundational to Western culture: The Declaration of Independence, for example, asserts that everyone has the right to "life, liberty, and the pursuit of happiness."

But just as consequentialism is incredibly complicated, deontology is difficult to apply because people disagree about what duties we owe to one another and which duties are more important than others when they conflict. For example, imagine the dilemma of a scientist working for a tobacco firm who discovers that cigarettes are carcinogenic. She owes a duty of trust to her employer, but she also has a conflicting duty to the community to do no harm. Where would a business manager find a list of relevant duties under the deontological framework, and why should we accept and act on any particular list?

In addition, as with absolutism, the absolute nature of many deontological lists of duties and rights seems overly rigid when applied to a wide variety of contexts. For instance, saying that we owe a duty to respect human life sounds absolute. In application, however, we might be forced to harm one life to preserve other life. An alternative theory of ethics, called *virtue ethics*, avoids this rigidity problem by providing us with abstract goals to pursue continually.

Virtue Ethics

Virtue ethics is an ethical system in which the development of virtues, or positive character traits such as courage, justice, and truthfulness, is the basis for morality. A morally excellent (and thus good) person develops virtues and distinguishes them from vices, or negative character traits, such as cowardice and vanity. This development of virtues occurs through practice. Virtues are the habits of mind that move us toward excellence, the good life, or human flourishing.

As a guide to business ethics, virtue ethics requires that managers act in such a way that they will increase their contributions to the good life. Virtue ethics tells them to follow the character traits that, upon introspective reflection, they see as consistent with virtue. Identifying the relevant virtues and vices requires reasoning about the kind of human behavior that moves us toward the good, successful, or happy life.

A difficulty with the application of virtue ethics is the lack of agreement about the meaning of "the good life." Without that agreement, we are not able to agree about what types of behavior are consistent with our achievement of that goal. Even so, virtue ethics is useful in reminding us that ethics is grounded in a sense of what it means to be virtuous—we need some moral beacon to call us toward a more morally excellent condition. An alternative theory of business ethics, the ethics of care, offers a clear conception of what is virtuous.

Ethics of Care

The **ethics of care** holds that the right course of action is the option most consistent with the building and maintaining of human relationships. Those who adhere to an ethic of care argue that traditional moral hierarchies ignore an important element of life: relationships. Care for the nurturing of our many relationships serves as a reminder of the importance of responsibility to others.

According to someone who adheres to an ethic of care, when one person cares for another person, the first person is acting morally. When other ethical theories emphasize different moral dimensions as a basis for resolving ethical dilemmas, they rarely consider the harm they might do to relationships; thus, from the perspective of the ethics of care, alternative theories of business ethics often encourage unethical behavior.

Ethics-of-care theorists argue that when one individual, the *caregiver,* meets the needs of one other person, the *cared-for* party, the caregiver is actually helping to meet the needs of all the individuals who fall within the cared-for party's *web of care.* Thus, by specifically helping one other individual, the caregiver is assisting numerous people.

The strength of this theoretical approach is that it focuses on the basis of ethics in general: the significance of the interests of other people. The urging to care for relationships speaks to the fundamental basis of why we are concerned about ethics in the first place. Most of us do not need any encouragement to think about how a decision will affect us personally. But ethical reasoning requires that we weigh the impact of decisions on the larger community.

Let's examine how these ethical theories are applied in real-world firms. Exhibit 2A-1 is an abridged version of the Johnson & Johnson Credo, or statement of shared corporate

Exhibit 2A-1

Johnson & Johnson's Credo

The Credo

We believe our first responsibility is to the doctors, nurses and patients, to mothers and fathers and all others who use our products and services. In meeting their needs everything we do must be of high quality. We must constantly strive to reduce our costs in order to maintain reasonable prices. Customers' orders must be serviced promptly and accurately. Our suppliers and distributors must have an opportunity to make a fair profit.

We are responsible to our employees, the men and women who work with us throughout the world. Everyone must be considered as an individual. We must respect their dignity and recognize their merit. They must have a sense of security in their jobs. Compensation must be fair and adequate, and working conditions clean, orderly and safe. We must be mindful of ways to help our employees fulfill their family responsibilities. Employees must feel free to make suggestions and complaints. There must be equal opportunity for employment, development and advancement for those qualified. We must provide competent management, and their actions must be just and ethical.

We are responsible to the communities in which we live and work and to the world community as well. We must be good citizens—support good works and charities and bear our fair share of taxes. We must encourage civic improvements and better health and education. We must maintain in good order the property we are privileged to use, protecting the environment and natural resources.

Our final responsibility is to our stockholders. Business must make a sound profit. We must experiment with new ideas. Research must be carried on, innovative programs developed and mistakes paid for. New equipment must be purchased, new facilities provided and new products launched. Reserves must be created to provide for adverse times. When we operate according to these principles, the stockholders should realize a fair return.

values. General Robert Wood Johnson, who guided Johnson & Johnson from a small, family-owned business to a worldwide enterprise, believed the corporation had social responsibilities beyond the manufacturing and marketing of products. In 1943, he wrote and published the Johnson & Johnson Credo, a document outlining those responsibilities. Does the credo depend more on ethical relativism, situational ethics, absolutism, consequentialism, deontology, virtue ethics, or the ethics of care for its ethical vision?

Exhibit 2A-2 summarizes the ethical theories discussed in this appendix.

Exhibit 2A-2
At a Glance

Theories of Business Ethics	
ETHICAL APPROACH	**DESCRIPTION**
Ethical relativism	Asserts that morality is relative.
Situational ethics	Requires that when we evaluate whether an action is ethical, we imagine ourselves in the position of the person facing the ethical dilemma.
Consequentialism	Considers the consequences (i.e., harms and benefits) of making a particular decision.
Deontology	Recognizes certain actions as right or wrong regardless of the consequences.
Virtue ethics	Encourages individuals to develop virtues (e.g., courage and truthfulness) that guide behavior.
Ethics of care	Holds that ethical behavior is determined by actions that care for and maintain human relationships.

KEY TERMS

absolutism 33	cost-benefit analysis 34	ethics of care 36	situational ethics 33
act utilitarianism 34	deontology 34	principle of rights 35	utilitarianism 34
categorical imperative 34	ethical relativism 33	rule utilitarianism 34	virtue ethics 35
consequentialism 34			

The Legal Environment of Business

The U.S. Legal System and Alternative Dispute Resolution

CASE OPENER

Questionable Jurisdiction over Caterpillar

James Lewis, a resident of Kentucky, sustained an injury while operating a Caterpillar bulldozer. He filed suit against Caterpillar, a company incorporated in Delaware but with its principal place of business in Illinois. Lewis also filed suit against the supplier of the bulldozer, Whayne Supply Company, whose principal place of business was Kentucky. Lewis filed his case in a Kentucky state court, alleging defective manufacture, negligence, failure to warn, and breach of warranty. Lewis and Whayne Supply Company agreed to settle out of court. Caterpillar then filed a motion to exercise its right of removal (its right to move the case from the state to the federal court system), arguing that the federal court had jurisdiction over the case because Caterpillar and Lewis were from different states. Lewis disagreed with Caterpillar's contention, claiming that because he had not completed his settlement with Whayne, the case still included a defendant (Whayne) from Lewis's state, Kentucky. Thus, Lewis argued, federal courts did not have jurisdiction over the case.

The court agreed with Caterpillar's argument and moved the case to a federal district court. Shortly thereafter, Lewis and Whayne finalized their settlement agreement, and the district court dismissed Whayne from the lawsuit. The federal district court granted Caterpillar a favorable judgment. Lewis, however, appealed the district court's decision, renewing his argument that the district court did not have jurisdiction over the case. The court of appeals agreed with Lewis, holding that because Whayne was a defendant in the case at the time that Caterpillar moved the case from state to federal court, the diversity of citizenship necessary to give the federal court jurisdiction over the case was absent. Thus, a state court should have resolved the dispute. Consequently, the appellate court vacated the district court's decision. Caterpillar then appealed to the U.S. Supreme Court.

1. What factors determine whether the state or federal court system hears a case?
2. If you were a businessperson with Caterpillar, why might you prefer a federal court to hear the dispute with Lewis, rather than a state court?

After reading this chapter, you will be able to answer the following questions:

LO 3-1   What types of jurisdiction must a court have to render a binding decision in a case?

LO 3-2   What is venue?

LO 3-3   What are the threshold requirements that must be met before a court will hear a case?

LO 3-4   What are the steps in civil litigation?

LO 3-5   How are the various forms of alternative dispute resolution used by businesses today?

---

trial court

A court in which most civil or criminal cases start when they first enter the legal system. The parties present evidence and call witnesses to testify. Trial courts are referred to as *courts of common pleas* or *county courts* in state court systems and as *district courts* in the federal system. Also called *court of original jurisdiction* and *court of first instance.*

appellate court

A higher court, usually consisting of more than one judge, that reviews the decision and results of a lower court (either a trial court or a lower-level appellate court) when a losing party files for an appeal. Appellate courts do not hold trials but may request additional oral and written arguments from each party; they issue written decisions, which collectively constitute case law or the common law. Also called *court of appellate jurisdiction.*

question of law

An issue concerning the interpretation or application of a law.

LO 3-1

question of fact

A question about an event or characteristic in a case.

As the Case Opener illustrates, when a dispute arises, parties in this country do not simply "go to court." They often must choose between federal and state court systems. This chapter examines these systems as well as the trial procedures that apply in civil cases.

Jurisdiction

A useful way to understand jurisdiction is to think of it as courts' power to hear cases and render decisions that bind the parties before them. A court must have several types of jurisdiction to decide any particular case.

ORIGINAL VERSUS APPELLATE JURISDICTION

Trial courts, or courts of original jurisdiction, have the power to hear and decide cases when they first enter the legal system. In these courts, the parties present evidence and call witnesses to testify. In most states, these courts are called *courts of common pleas* or *county courts.* In the federal system, these trial courts are called *federal district courts.*

Courts of appellate jurisdiction, or appellate courts, have the power to review previous judicial decisions to determine whether trial courts erred in their decisions. Appellate courts do not hold trials. Instead, appellate judges review transcripts of trial court proceedings and occasionally consider additional oral and written arguments from each party.

Appellate courts handle only questions of law, not questions of fact. A question of law is an issue concerning the interpretation or application of a law. In contrast, a question of fact is a question about an event or characteristic in the case. For example, whether a white student yelled racial slurs on a college campus is a question of fact. On the other hand, whether the First Amendment protects the student's right to utter racial slurs is a question of law.

Only judges can decide questions of law. Trial courts determine questions of fact. In a bench trial (a trial with no jury), the judge decides questions of fact; in a jury trial, the jury decides questions of fact. Appellate courts can, however, overrule trial courts' decisions on questions of fact, but only when the trial court's finding was clearly erroneous or when no trial evidence supports the trial court's finding.

JURISDICTION OVER PERSONS AND PROPERTY

In personam jurisdiction (literally, "jurisdiction over the person") is a court's power to render a decision affecting the rights of the specific persons before the court. Generally, a court's power to exercise *in personam* jurisdiction extends only over a specific geographic region. In the state court system, a court's *in personam* jurisdiction usually extends to the state's borders. In the federal system, each court's jurisdiction extends across its geographic district.

A court acquires *in personam* jurisdiction over a person (the plaintiff) when she files a lawsuit with the court. The court acquires jurisdiction over the person the plaintiff is suing (the defendant) when it gives him a copy of the complaint and a summons. The complaint specifies the factual and legal basis for the lawsuit and the relief the plaintiff seeks. The summons is a court order that notifies the defendant of the lawsuit and explains how and when to respond to the complaint.

Service of process is the procedure by which courts present these documents to defendants. Traditionally, courts used personal service: An officer of the court handed the summons and complaint to the defendant. Recently, however, courts have employed other methods of service, including *residential service,* in which a court representative leaves the summons and complaint with a responsible adult at the defendant's home, and *service by certified* or *ordinary mail.*

If the defendant is a corporation, courts generally serve either the president of the corporation or an agent whom the corporation has appointed to receive service. Most states require corporations to appoint an agent for service when they incorporate. Corporations are subject to *in personam* jurisdiction in three locations: the state of their incorporation, the location of their main offices, and the geographic areas in which they conduct business.

Courts have *in personam* jurisdiction over persons only within a specific geographic region. In the past, a state court could not acquire *in personam* jurisdiction over out-of-state defendants unless it served the defendants within the court's home state. Thus, defendants who injured plaintiffs could evade legal action by leaving the state and remaining outside its borders.

To alleviate this problem, most states have enacted long-arm statutes that enable the court to serve defendants outside the state as long as the defendant has sufficient minimum contacts within the state. Each state has its own minimum-contact requirements, but most state statutes hold that acts such as committing a tort or doing business in the state are sufficient to allow the state to serve a defendant. In the Caterpillar case, the company sold products in Kentucky, and its products caused an injury in that state. These two facts were sufficient minimum contacts to allow the Kentucky court to serve Caterpillar, even though it was an out-of-state company.

BUT WHAT IF . . .

WHAT IF THE FACTS OF THE CASE OPENER WERE DIFFERENT?

Recall that in the Case Opener, the company sold products in Kentucky, and its products caused an injury in that state. Let's say in the Case Opener that Caterpillar did not sell products in the state of Kentucky, but its products did cause an injury in that state. Could a Kentucky court still exercise *in personam* jurisdiction over Caterpillar and serve the company? Why?

Because of the increasing purchase of products over the Internet, it is sometimes difficult to know whether the court will be able to obtain *in personam* jurisdiction over the seller of a defective product. Case 3-1 illustrates how the courts are increasingly responding to this problem.

in personam jurisdiction
The power of a court to require a party (usually the defendant) or a witness to come before the court. The court must have personal jurisdiction to enforce its judgments or orders against a party. *In personam* jurisdiction extends only to the state's borders in the state court system and across the court's geographic district in the federal system.

plaintiff
The person or party who initiates a lawsuit (also known as an *action*) before a court by filing a complaint with the clerk of the court against the defendant(s). Also known as *claimant* or *complainant.*

defendant
The person or party against whom a civil or criminal lawsuit is filed in a court of law.

complaint
A formal written document that begins a civil lawsuit; contains the plaintiff's list of allegations against the defendant along with the damages the plaintiff seeks.

summons
A legal document issued by a court and addressed to a defendant that notifies him or her of the lawsuit and how and when to respond to the complaint. A summons may be used in both civil and criminal proceedings.

CASE 3-1	**ILLINOIS v. HEMI GROUP LLC** *622 F. 3d 754 (2010)*

FACTS: *Hemi Group LLC is a New Mexico–based cigarette company that was selling discounted cigarettes over the Internet to customers. The defendant company pays* *federal taxes on the cigarettes that it sells over the Internet, but in the state of Illinois, the law holds buyers accountable for paying the applicable state tax on cigarettes purchased*

(continued)

over the Internet. The plaintiff, the state of Illinois, filed suit against Hemi Group LLC, asserting that the company was failing to submit monthly reports of sales to Illinois residents as required by the Jenkins Act. The plaintiff also filed suit against the defendant company for shipping cigarettes to Illinois residents who were not licensed distributors or export warehouse operators and, last, for violating the Enforcement Act and the Consumer Fraud Act by selling brands of cigarettes to Illinois residents who were not in the Illinois Directory.

Both parties agreed that the defendant company is not a resident of Illinois and that it is not incorporated under Illinois law. Hemi Group LLC filed to dismiss the motion due to lack of personal jurisdiction. The district court denied the defendant's motion. The defendant company appealed.

ISSUE: Should a company be subject to personal jurisdiction in a state if that company's business is conducted over the Internet, and the company is not a resident of that same state?

REASONING: *If a company is involved in commercial activities over the Internet and is involved in these activities with a great number of consumers, then the company is thought to have "purposefully availed itself" of the state's jurisdiction.* In this case, the Illinois court decided to apply a test to determine whether the company had enough interactions with Illinois residents to make the company liable in that state. The court must note the legitimate concern that "premising personal jurisdiction on the maintenance of a website, without requiring some level of 'interactivity' between the defendant and consumers in the forum state, would create almost universal personal jurisdiction because of the virtually unlimited accessibility of websites across the country." Courts should be careful in resolving questions about personal jurisdiction involving online contacts to ensure that a defendant is not brought into court simply because the defendant owns or operates a website that is accessible in the forum state, even if that site is interactive.

In this case, the court decided to reference but not to apply the sliding scale test, also called the Zippo test. The Zippo test was created in *Zippo Manufacturing Co. v. Zippo Dot Com, Inc.,* 952 F. Supp. 1119 (W.D. Pa. 1997) and is now most often used as the test that determines whether a company conducting business over the Internet is subject to personal jurisdiction in a certain state. In the Zippo case, the court stated that "the likelihood that personal jurisdiction can be constitutionally exercised is directly proportionate to the nature and quality of commercial activity that an entity conducts over the Internet." In other words, if a company is involved in commercial activities over the Internet and is involved in these activities with a great number of consumers, then the company is thought to have "purposefully avail[ed] itself" of the state's jurisdiction. If the purpose of the website is to conduct business transactions, this means the company that runs the website is interacting in online commercial activities. Yet if a website is passive in that its purpose is simply to display information for online users, the company running the website will likely not be subject to personal jurisdiction.

The plaintiff provided evidence that the defendant company's contacts with Illinois were sufficient to satisfy due process. The defendant maintained commercial websites through which customers could purchase cigarettes, calculate their shipping charges by using their zip codes, and create accounts. The defendant stated that it would ship to any state in the country except New York. The defendant stood ready and willing to do business with Illinois residents. And the defendant company, in fact, knowingly did do business with Illinois residents.

DECISION AND REMEDY: The court affirmed the district court's denial of the defendant's motion to dismiss for lack of personal jurisdiction and remanded for further proceedings.

SIGNIFICANCE OF THE CASE: This case provides an illustration of the standard courts' use to determine whether a company's business over the Internet will be subject to personal jurisdiction in a given state.

CRITICAL THINKING

Why is the court reluctant to extend *in personam* jurisdiction whenever a firm with online presence offers to make a sale of products in the state in question? Why is there a reluctance to extend *in personam* jurisdiction broadly?

ETHICAL DECISION MAKING

What Illinois stakeholders are especially happy that the court extended *in personam* jurisdiction in this case?

E-COMMERCE and the Law

The Sliding-Scale Standard for Internet Transactions

Does a business that has Internet contact with a plaintiff in a different state satisfy the minimum-contacts standard?

A federal district court established the following sliding-scale standard in a 1997 case:*

> [T]he likelihood that personal jurisdiction can be constitutionally exercised is directly proportionate to the nature and quality of commercial activity that an entity conducts over the Internet. This sliding scale is consistent with well developed personal jurisdiction principles.

At one end of the spectrum are situations when a defendant clearly does business over the Internet. If the defendant enters into contracts with residents of a foreign jurisdiction that involve the knowing and repeated transmission of computer files over the Internet, personal jurisdiction is proper.

At the opposite end are situations when a defendant has simply posted information on an Internet website that is accessible to users in foreign jurisdictions. A passive website that does little more than make information available to those who are interested in it is not grounds for the exercise of personal jurisdiction.

The middle ground is occupied by interactive websites through which a user can exchange information with the host computer. In these cases, the exercise of jurisdiction is determined by examining the level of interactivity and the commercial nature of the exchange of information that occurs on the website.

* Zippo Mfg. Co. v. Zippo Dot Com, Inc., 952 F. Supp. 1119 at 1124 (1997).

If a defendant has property in a state, a plaintiff may file suit against the defendant's property instead of against the owner. For example, suppose a Utah resident had not paid property taxes on a piece of land she owned in Idaho. Idaho courts have *in rem* jurisdiction (Latin for "jurisdiction over the thing") over the property. Thus, an Idaho state court has the power to seize the property and sell it to pay the property taxes in an *in rem* proceeding.

Courts can also gain quasi *in rem* jurisdiction, or *attachment jurisdiction,* over a defendant's property that is *unrelated* to the plaintiff's claim. For example, suppose Charlie, a Massachusetts resident, ran a red light while he was vacationing in California and collided with Jessica's car. Suppose further that Jessica suffered extensive injuries from the accident and successfully sued Charlie for $200,000 in a California state court. The California court can exercise quasi *in rem* jurisdiction over Charlie's California vacation home by seizing it, selling it, and transferring $200,000 to Jessica to satisfy her judgment against Charlie. If Charlie's vacation home is worth more than $200,000, however, the court must return the excess proceeds to Charlie.

SUBJECT-MATTER JURISDICTION

Subject-matter jurisdiction is a court's power to hear certain kinds of cases. Most industrialized countries have a single court system, with courts that have the power to hear both national law cases and local law cases. In contrast, the United States has both a state and a federal court system. Subject-matter jurisdiction determines which court system may hear a particular case. Cases may fall under state jurisdiction, exclusive federal jurisdiction, or concurrent jurisdiction. Figure 3-1 illustrates the subject-matter-jurisdiction divisions.

Exclusive Federal Jurisdiction   The federal court system has exclusive jurisdiction over very few cases: admiralty cases; bankruptcy cases; federal criminal prosecutions; lawsuits in which one state; sues another state; claims against the United States; and patent, trademark, and copyright cases. Additionally, federal courts have exclusive jurisdiction over claims arising under federal statutes that specify exclusive federal jurisdiction.

State Jurisdiction   The state court system has a broad range of jurisdiction; state courts have the power to hear all cases not within the exclusive jurisdiction of the federal court system. State courts also have exclusive jurisdiction over certain cases, such as cases concerning adoption and divorce. Most cases, therefore, fall under state court jurisdiction. The Caterpillar case fell under state court jurisdiction because its subject matter—product liability and negligence—did not place the case under the exclusive jurisdiction of the federal court system.

long-arm statute
A statute that enables a court to obtain jurisdiction against an out-of-state defendant as long as the defendant has sufficient minimum contacts within the state, such as committing a tort or doing business in the state.

in rem jurisdiction
The power of a court over the property or status of an out-of-state defendant when that property or status is within the court's jurisdiction area.

quasi in rem jurisdiction
A type of jurisdiction exercised by a court over an out-of-state defendant's property that is within the jurisdictional boundaries of the court. It applies to personal suits against the defendant in which the property is not the source of the conflict but is sought as compensation by the plaintiff. Also called *attachment jurisdiction.*

subject-matter jurisdiction
The power of a court over the type of case presented to it.

Figure 3-1

Subject-Matter-
Jurisdiction
Divisions

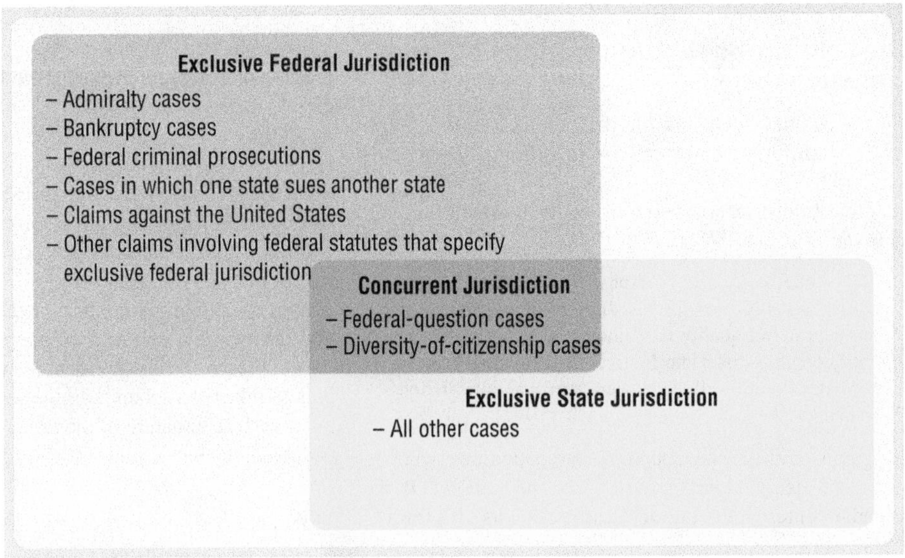

Exclusive Federal Jurisdiction

- Admiralty cases
- Bankruptcy cases
- Federal criminal prosecutions
- Cases in which one state sues another state
- Claims against the United States
- Other claims involving federal statutes that specify
  exclusive federal jurisdiction

Concurrent Jurisdiction

- Federal-question cases
- Diversity-of-citizenship cases

Exclusive State Jurisdiction

- All other cases

Concurrent Federal Jurisdiction   Concurrent federal jurisdiction means that both state and federal courts have jurisdiction over a case. Concurrent jurisdiction covers two types of cases: federal-question and diversity-of-citizenship cases. *Federal-question* cases require an interpretation of the U.S. Constitution, a federal statute, or a federal treaty. For example, suppose a plaintiff alleges that a Florida campaign-financing law violates his First Amendment free speech rights. Because this case raises a federal question, it falls under concurrent jurisdiction, and both state and federal courts have the power to hear it.

A *diversity-of-citizenship* case must satisfy two conditions: (1) The plaintiff(s) does (do) not reside in the same state as the defendant(s) and (2) the controversy concerns an amount in excess of $75,000. Courts use the location of a party's residence to determine whether diversity of citizenship exists. Most federal court cases are based on diversity of citizenship.

A business may reside in two states: the state of its incorporation and the state of its principal place of business. Thus, in the Case Opener, Caterpillar was a resident of Delaware, the state where it incorporated, and of Illinois, the state of its primary place of business.

Although the rule for determining what state a defendant is a citizen of may sound simple, determining where a corporation's principal place of business was caused a lot of controversy initially. Was it where most of the states' business activities occurred? Or was it where its headquarters was located? In Case 3-2, the Supreme Court finally clarified how courts should determine a corporation's principal place of business.

CASE 3-2

HERTZ CORPORATION v. FRIEND
UNITED STATES SUPREME COURT
130 S. Ct. 1181 (2010)

FACTS: *California employees sued their employer, Hertz Corporation, in state court, alleging violations of the state's wage and hour laws. Defendant Hertz, claiming diversity of citizenship, removed the case to the federal district court. Hertz argued that it was a citizen of New Jersey because New Jersey is its principal place of business. It is its principal place of business because Hertz has facilities in 44 states, but its leadership is at its corporate headquarters in New Jersey, and its core executive and administrative functions are primarily carried out there. Hertz also*

(continued)

stated that California accounted for only a small portion of its business activities.

The District Court concluded that it lacked diversity jurisdiction because Hertz was a California citizen under Ninth Circuit precedent, which asks whether the amount of the corporation's business activity is "significantly larger" or "substantially predominates" in one state. Finding that California was Hertz's "principal place of business" under that test because a plurality of the relevant business activity occurred there, the District Court remanded the case to state court. Hertz appealed, and the Ninth Circuit Court of Appeals affirmed. Hertz then appealed to the U.S. Supreme Court.

ISSUE: For purposes of establishing citizenship of a corporation to determine whether there is diversity of citizenship to give the federal court jurisdiction, what test should the courts use to determine a corporation's principal place of business, a nerve center test or a predominance of business activity test?

REASONING: "Principal place of business" is best read as referring to where a corporation's officers direct, control, and coordinate the corporation's activities. In practice, it should normally be where the corporation maintains its headquarters—provided that the headquarters is the actual center of direction, control, and coordination, that is, the nerve center and not simply an office where the corporation holds its board meetings.

Three reasons support use of the nerve center approach. The first is that the approach is consistent with the language of the jurisdictional statute. The statute's word "place" is singular, not plural. Its word "principal" requires the main, prominent, or most important place to be chosen. And the fact that the word "place" follows the words "State where" means that the "place" is a place within a State, not the State itself. A corporation's nerve center, usually its main headquarters, is a single place. The public often considers it the corporation's main place of business. And it is a place within a State. By contrast, the application of a more

general business activities test has led some courts to look not at a particular place within a State but incorrectly at the State itself, measuring the total amount of business activity the corporation conducts there and determining whether it is significantly larger than in the next-ranking State.

Second, administrative simplicity is desired in a jurisdictional statute. A nerve center approach, which ordinarily equates that center with a corporation's headquarters, is simple to apply, comparatively speaking.

Third, the statute's legislative history suggests that the words "principal place of business" should be interpreted to be no more complex than an earlier, numerical test that was criticized as too complex and impractical to apply. A nerve center test offers such a possibility. A general business activities test does not.

This test is relatively easier to apply and does not require courts to weigh corporate functions, assets, or revenues different in kind, one from the other. This test may produce results that seem to cut against the basic rationale of diversity jurisdiction; accepting occasionally counterintuitive results is the price the legal system must pay to avoid overly complex jurisdictional administration while producing the benefits that accompany a more uniform legal system.

DECISION AND REMEDY: For purposes of federal-court diversity jurisdiction, a corporation's principal place of business refers to the place, often called nerve center, from which the corporation's high-level officers directed, controlled, and coordinated corporation's activities. Although it appeared from the evidence that Hertz corporate offices and its nerve center are located in New Jersey, the respondents should have a fair opportunity on remand to litigate this issue in light of this holding as to the applicable rule.

SIGNIFICANCE OF THE CASE: The case settles a long-standing conflict among the circuits about what test to apply to determine where a corporation's primary place of business is.

CRITICAL THINKING

Which critical-thinking skill is the focal point of this case? Which words are not clear?

ETHICAL DECISION MAKING

What primary value can you hear in the court's reasoning?

It is important to note that diversity must be complete for a case to fall under concurrent jurisdiction. In the Caterpillar case, Lewis argued that diversity was not complete because both he and the supply company, the second defendant he originally sued, were residents of Kentucky. The appellate court agreed with his argument and overturned the district court's decision because the district court lacked subject-matter jurisdiction.

When a plaintiff files a case involving concurrent jurisdiction in state court, the defendant has a *right of removal*. This right entitles the defendant to transfer the case to federal court. Thus, either party to a case involving concurrent jurisdiction can put the case in the federal court system: The plaintiff can file the case in federal court initially; or if the case was initially filed in state court, the defendant can transfer the case to federal court by exercising her right of removal. In the Case Opener, Caterpillar exercised its right of removal, and the state trial court moved the case to a federal district court.

BUT WHAT IF . . .

Recall that in the Case Opener, Catepillar filed a motion to exercise its right of removal to move the case to federal court. If it had not filed that motion, would the case have been held in state court, even though it fell under concurrent jurisdiction?

LO 3-2

Venue

venue

(1) The place where a hearing takes place. Its geographic location is determined by each state's statutes and based on where the parties live or where the event occurred or the alleged wrong was committed. (2) A legal doctrine relating to the selection of a court with subject-matter and personal jurisdiction that is the most appropriate geographic location for the resolution of the dispute.

Once a case is in the proper court system, venue determines which trial court in the system will hear the case. Venue is a matter of geographic location that each state's statutes determine. Usually, the trial court for the county where the defendant resides is the appropriate venue. If a case involves property, the trial court where the property is located is also an appropriate venue. Finally, if the focus of the case is a particular incident, the trial court where the dispute occurred is an appropriate venue. The plaintiff initially chooses from among the appropriate venues when she files the case.

If the location of the court where the plaintiff filed the case is an inconvenience to the defendant or if the defendant believes it will be difficult to select an unbiased jury in that venue, he may request that the judge move the case by filing a motion for a change of venue. The judge has the discretion to grant or deny the motion.

The Structure of the Court System

The U.S. legal system has two parallel court structures: a federal system and a state system. Once a plaintiff files a case in one of the systems, the case remains in that system throughout the appeals process. The only exception to this rule occurs when a party to a lawsuit appeals the decision of a state supreme court to the U.S. Supreme Court.

THE FEDERAL COURT SYSTEM

The federal court system derives its power from Article III, Section 2, of the U.S. Constitution and consists of three main levels: trial courts, intermediate appellate courts, and the court of last resort. Figure 3-2 illustrates this system.

Federal Trial Courts   In the federal court system, the trial courts, or courts of original jurisdiction, are U.S. district courts. The United States has 94 districts; each district has at least one trial court of general jurisdiction. Courts of general jurisdiction have the power to hear a wide range of cases and can grant almost any type of remedy. Almost every case in the federal system begins in one of these courts.

A small number of cases, however, do not begin in trial courts of general jurisdiction. For cases concerning certain subject matter, Congress has established special trial courts of limited jurisdiction. The types of cases heard by these special trial courts include bankruptcy cases; claims against the U.S. government; and copyright, patent, and trademark cases.

In an extremely limited number of cases, the U.S. Supreme Court functions as a trial court of limited jurisdiction. These cases include controversies between states and lawsuits against foreign ambassadors.

Figure 3-2   The Federal Court System

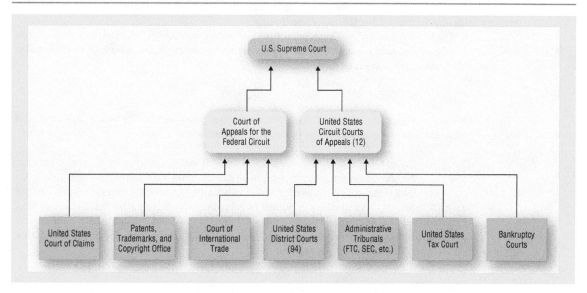

Intermediate Courts of Appeal   The U.S. circuit courts of appeal make up the second level of courts in the federal system. The United States has 12 circuits, including a circuit for the District of Columbia. Each circuit court hears appeals from district courts in its geographic area. Additionally, a federal circuit court of appeals hears appeals from government administrative agencies. Figure 3-3 illustrates the geographic circuit divisions.

Figure 3-3   The Circuits of the Federal Court System

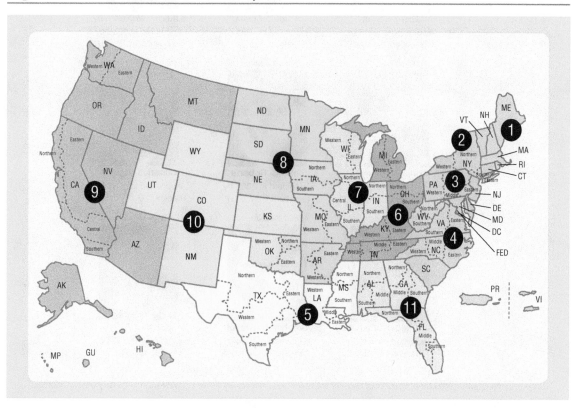

The Court of Last Resort The U.S. Supreme Court is the final appellate court in the federal system. Nine justices, who have lifetime appointments, make up the high court. Figure 3-4 identifies the nine justices on the U.S. Supreme Court.

The U.S. Supreme Court hears appeals of cases from the court of last resort in a state system. The Court will not, however, hear cases considering questions of pure state law. The Court also functions as a trial court on rare occasions.

STATE COURT SYSTEMS

No uniform state court structure exists because each state has devised its own court system, but most states have a structure similar to the federal court system's structure.

State Trial Courts In state court systems, most cases begin in a trial court of general jurisdiction. As in the federal system, state trial courts of general jurisdiction have the power to hear all cases over which the state court system has jurisdiction except those cases for which the state has established special trial courts of limited jurisdiction. Most states have a trial court of general jurisdiction in each county. The names of these courts vary by state, but most states refer to them as *courts of common pleas* or *county courts*. In some states, these courts have specialized divisions such as domestic relations and probate.

Figure 3-4

U.S. Supreme Court Justices

(All photos: Steven Petteway, Collection of the Supreme Court of the United States)

Associate Justice	*Associate Justice*	*Associate Justice*
Elena Kagan Appointed in 2010 by President Obama	**Antonin Scalia** Appointed in 1984 by President Reagan	**Anthony M. Kennedy** Appointed in 1988 by President G.H.W. Bush
Associate Justice	*Chief Justice*	*Associate Justice*
Sonia Sotomayor Appointed in 2009 by President Obama	**John G. Roberts** Appointed in 2005 by President G.W. Bush	**Clarence Thomas** Appointed in 1991 by President G.H.W. Bush
Associate Justice	*Associate Justice*	*Associate Justice*
Ruth Bader Ginsburg Appointed in 1993 by President Clinton	**Stephen G. Breyer** Appointed in 1994 by President Clinton	**Samuel Alito** Appointed in 2006 by President G.W. Bush

GLOBAL Context

The Court Structure in England

Even though we trace the roots of the U.S. legal system back to England, changes have occurred in both countries' court structures; as a result, the court structures in the United States and England share similarities but also have distinct features. The lowest criminal courts in England are the magistrates courts, which hear minor offenses. More serious cases are tried before a judge and jury in the crown court, which also hears cases appealed from the magistrates courts on factual points. The high court (in the Queen's Branch Division) hears appeals on points of law, and the court of appeal in the Criminal Division hears appeals on sentences and convictions.

Civil cases are first heard in the county courts (for minor claims) or the high court, which is divided into three divisions: Queen's Bench, Family, and Chancery. Cases may be appealed to the court of appeal (Civil Division). Cases may also be appealed from the county court to the high court.

The House of Lords is the supreme court of appeal. Its cases are heard by up to 13 senior judges known as *law lords.* In addition to the courts, there are specialized tribunals, which hear appeals on decisions made by various public bodies and government departments in areas such as employment, immigration, social security, tax, and land.

Most states also have trial courts of limited jurisdiction. Usually, these courts can grant only certain remedies. For example, small claims courts, a common type of court of limited jurisdiction in most states, may not grant damage awards larger than a specified amount. Other courts of limited jurisdiction have the power to hear only certain types of cases. For example, probate courts hear only cases about asset and obligation transfers after an individual's death.

Intermediate Courts of Appeal   Intermediate courts of appeal, analogous to federal circuit courts of appeal, exist in approximately half the states. These courts usually have broad jurisdiction, hearing appeals from courts of general and limited jurisdictions as well as from state administrative agencies. The names of these courts vary by state, but most states call them *courts of appeal* or *superior courts.*

Courts of Last Resort   Appeals from the state intermediate courts of appeal lead cases to the state court of last resort. Most states call this court the *supreme court,* although some states refer to it as the *court of appeals.* Because approximately half of the states lack intermediate courts of appeal, appeals from trial courts in these states go directly to the state court of last resort.

Threshold Requirements

LO 3-3

Before a case makes it to court, it must meet three *threshold requirements.* These requirements ensure that courts hear only cases that genuinely require adjudication. The three requirements are standing, case or controversy, and ripeness (see Figure 3-5).

STANDING

A person who has the legal right to bring an action in court has **standing** (or *standing to sue*). For a person to have standing, the outcome of a case must personally affect him or her. Thus, if you hire a landscaper to mow your lawn every week and he fails to show up every other week, you have standing to sue your landscaper. But if your friend hired the landscaper, you lack the standing to sue on your friend's behalf because you do not have a personal stake in the outcome of the case.

The reason the American legal system requires this personal stake in the outcome is the belief that the plaintiff's personal stake stimulates her to present the best possible case. The requirements for standing, according to the 2000 U.S. Supreme Court case *Friends of the Earth v. Laidlaw Environmental Services,*[1] are (1) the plaintiff must have an injury in fact that is concrete and

standing
The legal right of a party or an individual to bring a lawsuit by demonstrating to the court sufficient connection to and harm from the law or action challenged (i.e., the plaintiff has to demonstrate that he or she is harmed or will be harmed). Otherwise, the court will dismiss the case, ruling that the plaintiff "lacks standing" to bring the suit.

[1] 120 S. Ct. 923 (2000).

Figure 3-5

Threshold
Requirements

actual or imminent; (2) the injury must be fairly traceable to the challenged action of the defendant; and (3) it must be likely that the injury will be redressed by a favorable decision.[2] In applying those criteria to the Laidlaw case, the Supreme Court found that FOE members' testimony that they were afraid to fish and swim in a river they previously enjoyed satisfied the first two criteria. The Court held that although the FOE members would not directly receive money from a penalty against Laidlaw, they would benefit because the penalties would deter Laidlaw and other companies from polluting the river in the future.[3] The Court ruled in FOE's favor and assessed Laidlaw a $405,800 penalty payable to the U.S. Treasury.

CASE OR CONTROVERSY

case or controversy
A term used in the U.S. Constitution to describe the structure and requirements of conflicting claims of individuals that can be brought before a federal court for resolution. A case or controversy requires an actual dispute between parties over their legal rights that remains in conflict at the time the case is presented and that is a proper matter for judicial determination. Also referred to as *justifiable controversy.*

The case-or-controversy (or *justifiable controversy*) requirement ensures that courts do not render advisory opinions. Three criteria are necessary for a case or controversy to exist. First, the relationship between the plaintiff and the defendant must be adverse. Second, actual or threatened actions of at least one of the parties must give rise to an actual legal dispute. Third, courts must have the ability to render a decision that will resolve the dispute. In other words, courts can give final judgments that solve existing problems; they cannot provide rulings about hypothetical situations.

RIPENESS

ripeness
The readiness of a case for a decision to be made. The goal is to prevent premature litigation for a dispute that is insufficiently developed. A claim is not ripe for litigation if it rests on contingent future events that may not occur as anticipated or may not occur at all.

The case-or-controversy requirement is closely linked to the ripeness requirement. A case is *ripe* if a judge's decision is capable of affecting the parties immediately. Usually the issue of ripeness arises when one party claims that the case is moot—in other words, there is no point in the court's hearing the case because no judgment can affect the situation between the parties.

In the *Laidlaw* case, Laidlaw argued that the case was moot because by the time the case went to trial, the company had complied with the requirements of its discharge permits. The Supreme Court disagreed, ruling that the fact that a defendant voluntarily ceases a practice once litigation has commenced does not deprive a federal court of its power to determine the legality of the

[2] Ibid.
[3] Ibid.

practice, because such a ruling would leave the defendant free to return to his old unlawful practices. Thus, the Court found the case was not moot because imposing a penalty on the defendant would have an important deterrent effect.[4]

Steps in Civil Litigation

LO 3-4

The U.S. litigation system is an adversary system: A neutral fact finder—a judge or jury—hears evidence and arguments that opposing sides present and then decides the case on the basis of the facts and law. Strict rules govern the types of evidence fact finders may consider. Theoretically, fact finders make informed and impartial rulings because each party has an incentive to find all relevant evidence and make the strongest possible arguments on behalf of her or his position.

Critics of the adversary system, however, point out several drawbacks: the time and expense each lawsuit requires, the damage a suit may cause to the litigating parties' relationship, and the unfair advantage to those with wealth and experience using the court system.

THE PRETRIAL STAGE

The *rules of civil procedure* govern civil case proceedings. The Federal Rules of Civil Procedure apply in all federal courts. Each state has its own set of rules, but most states' rules are very similar to the Federal Rules of Civil Procedure. In addition, each court usually has its own set of local court rules.

Informal Negotiations The initial attempt to resolve a business dispute is usually informal: a discussion or negotiation among the parties to try to find a solution. If the parties are unable to resolve their dispute, one party often seeks an attorney's advice. Together, the attorney and client may be able to resolve the dispute informally with the other party.

Pleadings The first formal stage of a lawsuit is the *pleading stage*. The plaintiff's attorney initiates a lawsuit by filing a *complaint* in the appropriate court. The complaint states the names of the parties to the action, the basis for the court's subject-matter jurisdiction, the facts on which the plaintiff bases her claim, and the relief the plaintiff seeks. The pleadings prevent surprises at trial; they allow attorneys to prepare arguments to counter the other side's claims. Exhibit 3-1 shows a typical complaint.

Service of Process To obtain *in personam* jurisdiction over a defendant and to satisfy due process, a court must notify the defendant of the pending lawsuit. Service of process occurs when a representative of the court serves (delivers) a copy of the complaint and a summons to the defendant.

The complaint explains the basis of the lawsuit to the defendant. The summons tells the defendant that if he or she does not respond to the lawsuit within a certain period of time, the plaintiff will receive a default judgment. A default judgment is a judgment in favor of the plaintiff that occurs when the defendant fails to answer the complaint and the plaintiff's complaint alleges facts that would support such a judgment.

Defendant's Response The defendant responds to the complaint with an answer. In this document, the defendant denies, affirms, or claims no knowledge of the accuracy of the plaintiff's allegations.

A defendant uses an *affirmative defense* when his or her answer admits that the facts contained in the complaint are accurate but also includes additional facts that justify the defendant's actions and provide a legally sound reason to deny relief to the plaintiff. For example, if a woman sued a man for battery because he punched her in the face, he might claim that he hit her only because she aimed a gun at him and threatened to shoot. His claim that he was acting in self-defense is an affirmative defense.

service of process
The procedure by which a court delivers a copy of the statement of claim or other legal documents, such as a summons, complaint, or subpoena, to the defendant.

default judgment
Judgment for the plaintiff that occurs when the defendant fails to respond to the complaint.

answer
The response of the defendant to the plaintiff's complaint.

[4] Ibid.

Exhibit 3-1

A Typical Complaint

> ### THE COURT OF COMMON PLEAS
> ### OF CLARK COUNTY, NEVADA
>
> Bob Lyons and Sue Lyons, Plaintiffs
>
> v.
>
> Christine Collins, Defendant
>
> COMPLAINT FOR NEGLIGENCE
> Case No. _____
>
> Now come the plaintiffs, Bob Lyons and Sue Lyons, and, for their complaint, allege as follows:
>
> 1. Plaintiffs, Bob Lyons and Sue Lyons, both of 825 Havercamp Street, are citizens of Clark County, in the state of Nevada, and defendant, Christine Collins, 947 Rainbow Ave., is a citizen of Clark County in the state of Nevada.
> 2. On May 1, 2001, the defendant built a wooden hanging bridge across a stream that runs through the plaintiffs' property at 825 Havercamp Street.
> 3. Defendant negligently used ropes in the construction of the bridge that were not thick enough to sustain human traffic on the bridge.
> 4. At approximately 4:00 p.m., on May 20, 2001, the plaintiffs were attempting to carry a box of landscaping stones across the bridge when the ropes broke, and the bridge collapsed, causing plaintiffs to fall seven feet into the stream.
> 5. As a result of the fall, plaintiff, Bob Lyons, suffered a broken arm, a broken leg, and a skull fracture, incurring $160,000 in medical expenses.
> 6. As a result of the fall, plaintiff, Sue Lyons, suffered two broken cervical vertebrae, and a skull fracture, incurring $300,000 in medical expenses.
> 7. As a result of the fall, the landscaping stones, which had cost $1,200, were destroyed.
> 8. As a result of the foregoing injuries, plaintiff, Bob Lyons, was required to miss eight weeks of work, resulting in a loss of $2,400 in wages.
> 9. As a result of the foregoing injuries, plaintiff, Sue Lyons, was required to miss 12 weeks of work, resulting in a loss of $3,600 in wages.
>
> WHEREFORE, plaintiffs demand judgment in the amount of $467,200, plus costs of this action.
>
> Harlon Elliot
>
> Attorney for plaintiffs
>
> 824 Sahara Ave.
>
> Las Vegas, Nevada, 89117
>
> JURY DEMAND
> Plaintiffs demand a trial by jury in this matter.

motion to dismiss
A request by the defendant that asks a judge or a court in a civil case to dismiss the case because even if all the allegations are true, the plaintiff is not entitled to any legal relief. Also called *demurrer*.

motion
An application by a party to a judge or a court in a civil case requesting an order in favor of the applicant.

If the defendant plans to raise an affirmative defense, he must raise it in his answer to give the plaintiff adequate notice. If he fails to raise an affirmative defense in the answer, the judge will likely not allow him to raise it during the trial.

Upon receiving the complaint, if the defendant believes that even though all the plaintiff's factual allegations are true, the law does not entitle the plaintiff to a favorable judgment, the defendant may file a motion to dismiss, or *demurrer*. (A motion is a request by a party for the court to do something; in this instance, the request is to dismiss the case.) In deciding whether to grant a motion to dismiss, a judge accepts the facts as stated by the plaintiff and rules on the legal issues in the case. Judges generally grant motions to dismiss only when it appears beyond a doubt that the plaintiff cannot prove any set of facts to justify granting the judgment she seeks.

If the defendant believes he has a claim against the plaintiff, he includes this **counterclaim** with the answer. As Exhibit 3-2 shows, the form of a counterclaim is identical to the form of a complaint. The defendant states the facts supporting his claim and asks for relief.

If the defendant files a counterclaim, the plaintiff generally files a reply. A **reply** is an answer to a counterclaim. In the reply, the plaintiff admits, denies, or claims a lack of knowledge of the accuracy of the facts of the defendant's counterclaim. If the plaintiff plans to use an affirmative defense, she must raise it in the reply.

Pretrial Motions The early pleadings establish the legal and factual issues of the case. After the pleadings, the plaintiff or defendant may file a motion to conclude the case early, eliminate some claims, or gain some advantage. A party may move, or request, the court to do almost anything pertaining to the case. For example, if the plaintiff files a suit about the right to a piece of

counterclaim
A claim made by the defendant against the plaintiff that is filed along with the defendant's answer.

reply
A response by the plaintiff to the defendant's counterclaim.

Exhibit 3-2

Defendant's Answer and Counterclaim

THE COURT OF COMMON PLEAS
OF CLARK COUNTY, NEVADA

Bob Lyons and Sue Lyons, Plaintiffs v. Christine Collins, Defendant
ANSWER AND COUNTERCLAIM FOR BREACH OF CONTRACT
Case No. _____

Now comes the defendant, Christine Collins, and answers the complaint of plaintiffs herein as follows:

FIRST DEFENSE

1. Admits the allegations in paragraphs 1 and 2.
2. Denies the allegation in paragraph 3.
3. Is without knowledge as to the truth or falsity of the allegations contained in paragraphs 4, 5, 6, 7, 8, and 9.

SECOND DEFENSE

4. If the court believes the allegations contained in paragraph 3, which the defendant expressly denies, plaintiffs should still be denied recovery because they were informed prior to the construction of the bridge that there should be no more than one person on the bridge at one time and that no individual weighing more than 200 pounds should be allowed to walk on the bridge.

COUNTERCLAIM

5. On April 15, the parties agreed that defendant would build a wooden hanging bridge across a stream that runs through the defendant's property at 825 Havercamp Street, in exchange for which plaintiffs would pay defendant $2,000 upon completion of construction.
6. On May 1, 2001, the defendant built the agreed upon ornament, wooden, hanging bridge across a stream that runs through the defendant's property at 825 Havercamp Street, but plaintiffs failed to pay the agreed upon price for the bridge.
7. By their failure to pay, plaintiffs breached their contract and are liable to defendant for the contract price of $2,000.

WHEREFORE, defendant prays for a judgment dismissing the plaintiffs' complaint and granting the defendant a judgment against plaintiffs in the amount of $2,000 plus costs of this action.

Melissa Davenport
Attorney for Defendant
777 Decatur Ave.
Las Vegas, Nevada 89117

motion for judgment on the pleadings

In a civil case, a request made by either party, after pleadings have been entered, that asks a judge or a court to issue a judgment.

motion for summary judgment

In a civil case, a request made by either party that asks a judge or a court to promptly and expeditiously dispose of a case without a trial. Any evidence or information that would be admissible at trial under the rules of evidence, such as affidavits, interrogatories, depositions, and admissions, may be considered on a motion for summary judgment. A court may hold oral arguments or decide the motion on the basis of the parties' briefs and supporting documentation alone.

discovery

The pretrial phase in a lawsuit during which each party requests relevant documents and other evidence from the other side in an attempt to "discover" pertinent facts and avoid any surprises in the courtroom during the trial. Discovery tools include requests for admissions, interrogatories, depositions, requests for inspection, and document production requests.

interrogatories

A formal set of written questions that one party to a lawsuit asks the opposing party as part of the pretrial discovery process in order to clarify matters of evidence and help determine in advance what facts will be presented at any trial in the case. The questions must be answered in writing under oath or under penalty of perjury within a specified time. Also called *requests for further information*.

property, she may move that the court prohibit the current possessor of the land from selling it. Courts may grant or deny such motions at their discretion.

When a party files a motion with the court, the court sends a copy to the opposing attorney, who may respond to the motion, usually by requesting that the judge deny the motion. In many cases, the judge rules on the motion immediately. In other cases, the judge holds a hearing at which the attorneys for both sides argue how the judge should decide the motion.

Two primary pretrial motions are a motion for judgment on the pleadings and a motion for summary judgment. Once the parties file the pleadings, either party can file a **motion for judgment on the pleadings.** The motion is a request for the court to consider that all the facts in the pleadings are true and to apply the law to those facts. The court grants the motion if, after this process, it finds that the only reasonable decision is in favor of the moving party.

Either party can file a **motion for summary judgment** after the discovery process (described below). The motion asserts that no factual disputes exist and that if the judge applied the law to the undisputed facts, her only reasonable decision would be in favor of the moving party. The difference between this motion and a motion for judgment on the pleadings is that in a motion for summary judgment, the moving party may use affidavits (sworn statements from the parties or witnesses), relevant documents, and depositions or interrogatories (a party's sworn answers to written questions) to support his motion. The judge grants the motion if, after examining the evidence, she finds no factual disputes. If, however, she finds any factual issues about which the parties disagree, she denies the motion and sends the case to trial.

Discovery   After filing the initial pleadings and motions, the parties gather information from each other through **discovery.** The discovery process enables the parties to learn about facts surrounding the case so that they are not surprised in the courtroom. Three common discovery tools are interrogatories, requests to produce documents, and depositions.

Interrogatories are written questions that one party sends to the other to answer under oath. Frequently, a *request to admit certain facts* accompanies interrogatories. Attorneys work with their clients to answer interrogatories and requested admissions of facts. Sometimes interrogatories are called *requests for further information.*

A **request to produce documents** (or other items) forces the opposing party to produce (turn over) certain information unless it is privileged or irrelevant to the case. Parties may request documents such as photographs, contracts, written estimates, medical records, tax forms, and other government documents. In tort cases, the defendant frequently asks the plaintiff to submit a mental- or physical-examination report.

Finally, the parties may obtain testimony from a witness before trial through a **deposition.** At a deposition, attorneys examine a witness under oath. A court reporter (stenographer) records every word the witness and attorneys speak. Both parties receive a copy of the testimony in document form. Depositions provide information and may also set up inconsistencies between a witness's testimony at the deposition and his testimony at trial. If a party discovers an inconsistency in the testimony of one of the other party's witnesses, she can bring the inconsistency to the fact finder's attention to diminish the witness's credibility. The parties may also use depositions when a witness is elderly, moving, or ill and thus may be unavailable at the time of the trial.

If a party does not comply with requests for discovery, the court may admit the facts the other party sought to discover. Attorneys who feel that certain material is outside the scope of the case often argue that the material is irrelevant to the case. If the court disagrees, however, the party must supply the requested information. Although these discovery tools are important in the United States, many countries do not have a discovery process.

Pretrial Conference   A pretrial conference precedes the trial. A **pretrial conference** is an informal meeting of the judge with the attorneys representing the parties. During this conference, the parties try to narrow the legal and factual issues and possibly work out a settlement. If the parties cannot reach a settlement, the attorneys and the judge discuss the administrative details of the trial: its length, witnesses, and any pretrial stipulations of fact or law to which the parties agree.

THE TRIAL

If a plaintiff seeks at least $20 in monetary damages, the Seventh Amendment to the U.S. Constitution entitles the parties to a jury trial. The plaintiff must, however, demand a jury trial in her or his complaint. Some types of trials require 12-person juries, but 6-person juries hear most civil cases. If the plaintiff seeks an equitable remedy (an injunction or other court order) or if the parties have waived their right to a jury, a judge serves as the fact finder in the case.

Trials have six stages: jury selection, opening statements, examination of witnesses, closing arguments, conference on jury instructions, and posttrial motions. The following sections describe these stages.

Jury Selection   The jury selection process begins when the clerk of the courts randomly selects a number of potential jurors from the citizens within the court's jurisdiction. Once the potential jurors have reported for jury duty, the voir dire, or jury selection, process begins. The voir dire process selects the jurors who will decide the case as well as two or three alternate jurors who will watch the trial and be available to replace any juror who, for some legitimate reason, must leave jury duty before the trial ends.

During voir dire, the judge and/or attorneys question potential jurors to determine whether they are able to render an unbiased opinion in the case. If a potential juror's response to a question indicates that she or he may be biased, either attorney may challenge, or ask the court to remove, that potential juror "for cause." For example, a lawyer could challenge for cause a potential juror who was a college roommate of the defendant. In most states, each party has a certain number of peremptory challenges. These peremptory challenges allow a party to challenge a certain number of potential jurors without giving a reason.

Peremptory challenges, however, may lead to abuse. For example, in the past, attorneys have used peremptory challenges to eliminate a certain class, ethnic group, or gender from the jury. In the 1986 case, *Batson v. Kentucky*,[5] the U.S. Supreme Court ruled that race-based peremptory challenges in criminal cases violate the equal protection clause of the Fourteenth Amendment to the U.S. Constitution. (Chapter 4 discusses the amendments to the Constitution in more detail.) The Supreme Court later extended the ban on race-based challenges to civil cases. In Case 3-3, the U.S. Supreme Court addressed the issue of whether the equal protection clause covers gender-based challenges.

[5] 476 U.S. 79 (1986).

request to produce documents

In a lawsuit, the right of a party to examine and copy papers of the opposing party that are relevant to the case. A legal request may be made, and the categories of the documents must be stated to allow the other party to know what documents he or she must produce.

deposition

A pretrial sworn and recorded testimony of a witness that is acquired out of court with no judge present.

pretrial conference

An informal meeting of the judge with the attorneys representing the parties before the actual trial begins.

voir dire

The process of questioning potential jurors to ensure that the jury will be made up of unbiased individuals.

peremptory challenge

In a jury trial, the right of the plaintiff and the defendant in jury selection to reject, without stating a reason, a certain number of potential jurors who appear to have an unfavorable bias.

CASE 3-3	J.E.B. v. ALABAMA, EX. REL. T.B. UNITED STATES SUPREME COURT 114 S. Ct. 1419 (1994)

FACTS: *The State of Alabama filed a complaint for paternity and child support against J.E.B. on behalf of T.B., the unwed mother of a minor child. The court called a panel of 12 males and 24 females as potential jurors. Only 10 males remained after three individuals were removed for cause. The state used its peremptory challenges to remove nine male jurors, and J.E.B. removed the tenth, resulting in an all-female jury. The trial court rejected J.E.B.'s objection to the gender-based challenges, and the jury found J.E.B.*

to be the father. J.E.B. appealed, and the court of appeals affirmed the trial court's ruling that the equal protection clause of the Fourteenth Amendment does not prohibit gender-based challenges. The Alabama Supreme Court declined to hear the appeal, and J.E.B. appealed to the U.S. Supreme Court.

ISSUE: Does the equal protection clause prohibit removing possible jurors during voir dire on the basis of their gender?

(continued)

REASONING: Justice Blackmun delivered the opinion of the Court:

> Discrimination in jury selection, whether based on race or on gender, causes harm to the litigants, the community, and the individual jurors who are wrongfully excluded from participation in the judicial process. The litigants are harmed by the risk that the prejudice which motivated the discriminatory selection of the jury will infect the entire proceedings. The community is harmed by the State's participation in the perpetuation of invidious group stereotypes and the inevitable loss of confidence in our judicial system that state-sanctioned discrimination in the courtroom engenders.

As with race-based *Batson* claims, a party alleging gender discrimination must make a prima facie showing of intentional discrimination before the party exercising the challenge is required to explain the basis for the strike. When an explanation is required, it need not rise to the level of a for cause challenge; rather, it merely must be based on a juror characteristic other than gender, and the proffered explanation may not be pretextual.

Equal opportunity to participate in the fair administration of justice is fundamental to our democratic system.

It reaffirms the promise of equality under the law—that all citizens, regardless of race, ethnicity, or gender, have the chance to take part directly in our democracy. When persons are excluded from participation in our democratic processes solely because of race or gender, this promise of equality dims, and the integrity of our judicial system is jeopardized.

DECISION AND REMEDY: Yes, to remove a potential juror based solely on gender is a violation of the equal protection clause. The court of appeals decision was reversed, and the case was remanded in favor of J.E.B.

SIGNIFICANCE OF THE CASE: This case extended protection against being peremptorily removed from a jury on the basis of gender alone, thus putting gender protections on par with the protections for race and ethnicity. Although historically the extension of the Fourteenth Amendment's equal protection clause to gender has been used to protect women's equal rights, the court found that the clause was equally applicable when a man's equal rights were being violated.

CRITICAL THINKING

The defendant was contesting the removal of males from the jury. Does this fact affect your assessment of the quality of the Court's reasoning? Explain.

ETHICAL DECISION MAKING

Which ethical norm does the case decision serve?

---

mock trial

A contrived or imitation trial, with a jury recruited by a jury selection firm, that attorneys sometimes use in preparing for an actual trial to test theories, experiment with arguments, and try to predict the outcome of the real trial.

shadow jury

An unofficial jury, provided by a jury selection firm, that sits in during the actual trial and deliberates at the end of each day to evaluate for the attorneys how each side is doing.

Despite *Batson* and *J.E.B.,* it is still not easy to challenge a dismissal as being based on race or gender. And in a 2006 case, the U.S. Supreme Court said that to find a dismissal unconstitutional, there must be no alternative to a gender- or race-based reason for dismissing a juror.[6]

The voir dire process has become more sophisticated over time. In cases involving significant amounts of money, rather than relying on their instinct or experience during jury selection, attorneys use professional jury selection services to identify demographic data to help select ideal jurors. Jury selection firms also provide additional services, including mock trials, in which mock jurors who are demographically similar to the real jurors hear the arguments and give feedback prior to the case, and shadow juries, in which shadow jurors sit in during the actual trial and deliberate at the end of each day to evaluate for the attorneys how each side is doing. Critics argue that jury selection services give an unfair advantage to one side when only one party can afford these services.

Opening Statements   Once the attorneys have impaneled, or selected, a jury, the case begins with opening statements. Each party's attorney explains to the judge and jury what facts he or she

[6] *Rice, Warden et al. v. Collins,* 126 S. Ct. 969 (2006).

intends to prove, the legal conclusions to which these facts lead, and how the fact finder should decide the case based on those facts.

The Examination of Witnesses and Presentation of Evidence   Following opening statements, the plaintiff and defendant, in turn, present their cases-in-chief by examining witnesses and presenting evidence. The plaintiff has the burden of proving the case, meaning that if neither side presents a convincing case, the fact finder must rule in favor of the defendant. Thus, the plaintiff presents her case first.

The procedure for each witness is the same. First, the plaintiff's attorney questions the witness in *direct examination*. The plaintiff's attorney asks the witness questions to elicit facts that support the plaintiff's case-in-chief. Questions must relate to matters about which the witness has direct knowledge. Attorneys cannot elicit hearsay from the witnesses. *Hearsay* is testimony about what a witness heard another person say. Hearsay is impermissible because the opposing attorney cannot question the person who made the original statement to determine the statement's veracity.

The federal rules of evidence also prohibit attorneys from asking leading questions. Leading questions are questions that imply a specific answer. For example, an attorney cannot ask a witness, "Did the defendant come to your office and ask you to purchase stock from him?" Instead, attorneys must ask questions such as, "When did you first encounter the defendant?"

After direct examination, opposing counsel may *cross-examine* the witness. Opposing counsel, however, may ask only questions related to the witness's direct examination. On cross-examination, attorneys can ask leading questions. Attorneys try to show inconsistencies in the witness's testimony, cast doubt on the claims of the plaintiff's case, and elicit information to support the defendant's case.

After cross-examination, the plaintiff's attorney may conduct a *redirect examination,* a series of questions aimed at repairing damage done by the cross-examination. At the judge's discretion, opposing counsel has an opportunity to *re-cross* the witness to question her testimony on redirect examination. The parties follow this procedure for each of the plaintiff's witnesses.

Immediately following the plaintiff's presentation of her case, the defendant may move for a directed verdict. This motion is a request for the court to direct a verdict for the defendant because even if the jury accepted all the evidence and testimony presented by the plaintiff as true, the jury would still have no legal basis for a decision in favor of the plaintiff. The federal court system refers to a motion for a directed verdict as a *motion for a judgment as a matter of law.* Courts rarely grant motions for a directed verdict because plaintiffs almost always present at least *some* evidence to support each element of the cause of action.

If the court denies the defendant's motion for a directed verdict, the defendant then presents his case. The parties question the defendant's witnesses in the same manner as they questioned the plaintiff's witnesses, except that the defendant's attorney conducts direct and redirect examination and the plaintiff's attorney conducts cross-examination and recross-examination.

directed verdict
A ruling by the judge, after the plaintiff has put forward his or her case but before any evidence is put forward by the defendant, in favor of the defendant because the plaintiff has failed to present the minimum amount of evidence necessary to establish his or her claim.

Closing Arguments   After the defendant's case, the attorneys present closing arguments. In closing arguments, each attorney summarizes evidence from the trial in a manner consistent with his or her client's case. The plaintiff's attorney presents her closing argument first, followed by the defendant's attorney, and the plaintiff has the option to present a rebuttal of the defendant's closing argument.

Jury Instructions   In a jury trial, the judge "charges the jury" by instructing the jurors on how the law applies to the facts of the case. Both sides' attorneys submit statements to the judge explaining how they believe she should charge the jury. The judge's instructions are usually a combination of both sides' suggestions.

After the judge charges the jury, the jurors retire to the jury room to deliberate. Once they reach a decision, they return to the courtroom, where the judge reads their verdict and discharges them from their duty. Trial procedures in the United States are quite different from trial procedures in other countries, as the Global Context box illustrates.

GLOBAL Context

Trials in Japan

Civil procedure in Japan differs significantly from American civil procedure. The Japanese legal system has no juries and no distinct pretrial stage. Instead, a trial is a series of discrete meetings between the parties and the judge. At the first meeting, the parties identify the most critical and contested issues. They choose one and recess to gather evidence and marshal arguments on the issue.

At the next meeting, the judge rules on the chosen issue. If the judge decides against the plaintiff, the case is over. If the plaintiff wins, the process continues with the next issue. The process continues until the plaintiff loses an issue or until the judge decides all issues in the plaintiff's favor, resulting in a verdict for the plaintiff.

In addition, the discovery process in the Japanese court system is not as simple as it is in the United States. To obtain evidence, parties must convince the judge to order others to testify or produce documents. The judge can fine or jail parties who refuse to comply with such orders. Additionally, if a party does not comply with the judge's requests for discovery, the judge may admit the facts the other party sought to discover.

POSTTRIAL MOTIONS

Once the trial ends, the party who received the favorable verdict files a *motion for a judgment in accordance with the verdict.* Until the judge enters the judgment, the court has not issued a legally binding decision for the case.

The party who loses at trial has a number of available options. One option is to file a *motion for a judgment notwithstanding the verdict,* or *judgment non obstante verdicto,* asking the judge to issue a judgment contrary to the jury's verdict. To grant the motion, the judge must find that, when viewing the evidence in the light most favorable to the nonmoving party, a reasonable jury could not have found in favor of that party. In other words, as a matter of law, the judge must determine that the trial did not produce sufficient evidence to support the jury's verdict. This motion is similar to a motion for a directed verdict, except the parties cannot make this motion until *after* the jury issues a verdict. The federal court system refers to this motion as a *motion for judgment as a matter of law.*

The losing party can also file a *motion for a new trial.* Judges grant motions for a new trial only if they believe the jury's decision was clearly erroneous but they are not sure that the other side should necessarily have won the case. A judge often grants a motion for a new trial when the parties discover new evidence, when the judge made an erroneous ruling, or when misconduct during the trial may have prevented the jury from reaching a fair decision.

APPELLATE PROCEDURE

Either party may appeal the judge's decision on posttrial motions or on her or his final judgment. Sometimes, both parties appeal the same decision. For example, if a jury awarded the plaintiff $10,000 in damages, the plaintiff and the defendant may both appeal the amount of the judgment. Appellate courts, however, reverse only about 1 out of every 10 trial court decisions on appeal.

To be eligible for appeal, the losing party must argue that a *prejudicial error of law* occurred during the trial. A prejudicial error is a mistake so significant that it likely affected the outcome of the case. For example, a prejudicial error could occur if the judge improperly allowed hearsay evidence that enabled the plaintiff to prove an element of her case.

To appeal a case, the attorney for the appealing party (the appellant) files a notice of appeal with the clerk of the trial court within a prescribed time. The clerk then forwards the record of appeal to the appeals court. The record of appeal typically contains a number of items: the pleadings, a trial transcript, copies of the trial exhibits, copies of the judge's rulings on the parties' motions, the attorneys' arguments, jury instructions, the jury's verdict, posttrial motions, and the judgment order.

The appellant then files a brief, or written argument, with the court. Appellants file briefs to explain why the judgment in the lower court was erroneous and why the appeals court should reverse it. The attorney for the party who won in the lower court (the appellee) files an answering brief. The appellant may then file a reply brief in response to the appellee's brief. Generally, however, appellants do not file reply briefs.

prejudicial error
An error of law that is so significant that it affects the outcome of the case.

brief
A written legal argument, which a party presents to a court, that explains why that party to the case should prevail.

The appeals court then usually allows the attorneys to present oral arguments before the court. The court considers these arguments, reviews the record of the case, and renders a decision.

There are four possible decisions an appellate court can render. The court can accept the lower court's judgment by affirming its decision. Alternatively, the appellate court may conclude that the lower court's decision was correct but the remedy was inappropriate, in which case it modifies the remedy. If the appellate court decides that the lower court was incorrect, it reverses the lower court's decision. Finally, if the appeals court thinks the lower court committed an error but does not know how that error affected the outcome of the case, it remands the case to the lower court for a new trial.

An appellate court usually has a bench with at least three judges. Appellate courts do not have juries; rather, the judges decide the case by majority vote. One of the judges who votes with the majority records the court's decision and its reasons in the *majority opinion.* These decisions have precedential value—that is, judges use these prior appellate court decisions to make decisions in future cases. Also, these decisions establish new guidelines in the law that all citizens must follow. If a judge agrees with the majority's decision but for different reasons, she may write a *concurring opinion,* stating the reasons she used to reach the majority's conclusion. Finally, judges disagreeing with the majority may write a *dissenting opinion,* giving their reasons for reaching a contrary conclusion. Attorneys arguing that a court should change the law frequently cite dissenting opinions from previous cases in their briefs. Likewise, appellate judges who change the law often cite dissenting opinions from past cases.

For most cases, only one appeal is available. In states with both an intermediate and a final court of appeals, a losing party may appeal from the intermediate appellate court to the state supreme court. In a limited number of cases, the losing party can appeal the decision of a state supreme court or a federal circuit court of appeals to the U.S. Supreme Court.

Appeal to the U.S. Supreme Court   Every year thousands of individuals file appeals with the U.S. Supreme Court, but the Court hears, on average, only 80 to 90 cases each year. To file an appeal to the U.S. Supreme Court, a party files a petition asking the Court to issue a writ of certiorari, an order to the lower court to send to the Supreme Court the record of the case. The Court issues very few writs.

The justices review petitions and issue a writ only when at least four justices vote to hear the case (the *rule of four*). The court is most likely to issue a writ in four instances: (1) The case presents a substantial federal question that the Supreme Court has not yet addressed; (2) multiple circuit courts of appeal have decided the issue of the case in different ways; (3) a state court of last resort has ruled that a federal law is invalid or has upheld a state law that may violate federal law; or (4) a federal court has ruled that an act of Congress is unconstitutional. If the Supreme Court does not issue a writ of certiorari, the lower court's decision stands.

Alternative Dispute Resolution

Many firms find that using alternative dispute resolution (ADR) methods to resolve their legal problems offers many benefits. The term *ADR* refers to the resolution of legal disputes through methods other than litigation, such as negotiation, mediation, arbitration, summary jury trials, minitrials, neutral case evaluations, and private trials.

Why might a business prefer ADR to litigation? First, ADR methods are generally faster and cheaper. According to the National Arbitration Forum, the average time from filing a complaint to judgment through litigation is 25 months.[7] Because ADR is faster, it is usually cheaper. According to the American Intellectual Property Law Association, for cases valued in the $1 million to $25 million range, the average total cost of patent litigation for each party through the close of discovery is $1.9 million.[8] Through the end of trial, the average cost to each party is $3.5 million.

---

affirm
An appellate court decision that accepts a lower court's judgment in a case that has been appealed.

modify
An appellate court decision that grants an alternative remedy in a case; rendered when the court finds that the decision of the lower court was correct but the remedy was not.

reverse
An appellate court decision that overturns the judgment of a lower court, concluding that the lower court was incorrect and its verdict cannot be allowed to stand.

remand
An appellate court decision that returns a case to the trial court for a new trial or for limited hearing on a specified subject matter; rendered when the court decides that an error was committed that may have affected the outcome of a case.

writ of certiorari
A Supreme Court order, issued after the Court decides to hear an appeal, mandating that the lower court send to the Supreme Court the record of the appealed case.

alternative dispute resolution (ADR)
The resolution of legal problems through methods other than litigation.

---

[7] National Arbitration Forum, *Business-to-Business Mediation/Arbitration vs. Litigation: What Courts, Statistics, & Public Perceptions Show about How Commercial Mediation and Commercial Arbitration Compare to the Litigation System,* January 2005, p. 3.
[8] AIPLA, *Report of the Economic Survey,* pp. 1-109–1-110.

Thus, if a party can resolve a dispute through alternative dispute resolution, this can save a significant amount of money.

Second, a business may want to avoid the uncertainty associated with a jury decision; many forms of ADR give the participants more control over the resolution of the dispute. Specifically, the parties can select a neutral third party, frequently a person with expertise in the area of the dispute, to help facilitate resolution of the case. Third, a business may want to avoid setting a precedent through a court decision. Fourth, a business may prefer ADR because it is confidential. Fifth, because many forms of ADR are less adversarial than litigation, ADR allows the parties to preserve a business relationship.

Courts also generally support the use of ADR, which alleviates some of the pressure on the overwhelming court dockets. Congress has recognized the benefits of ADR methods through its enactment of the Alternative Dispute Resolution Act of 1998. This act requires federal district courts to have an ADR program along with a set of rules regarding the program. Additional evidence of congressional support for ADR comes from the passage of the Administrative Dispute Resolution Act, which mandates that federal agencies must create internal ADR programs.

LO 3-5 Primary Forms of ADR

NEGOTIATION

negotiation
A bargaining process in which disputing parties interact informally to attempt to resolve their dispute.

Many business managers make frequent use of negotiation, a bargaining process in which disputing parties interact informally, either with or without lawyers, to attempt to resolve their dispute. No neutral third party is involved. Thus, negotiation differs from other methods of dispute resolution because the parties maintain high levels of autonomy. Some courts require parties to negotiate before they bring their dispute to trial.

Before negotiation begins, each side must determine its goals for the negotiation. Moreover, each side must identify the information it is willing to give the other party. Because negotiation generally occurs in every case before a more formal dispute resolution method is chosen, negotiation is not necessarily considered an alternative to litigation.

MEDIATION

mediation
A type of intensive negotiation in which disputing parties select a neutral party to help facilitate communication and suggest ways for the parties to solve their dispute.

An extension of negotiation is mediation. In mediation, the disputing parties select a neutral party to help facilitate communication and suggest ways for the parties to solve their dispute. Therefore, the distinguishing feature of mediation is that the parties voluntarily select a neutral third party to help them work together to resolve the dispute. The neutral third party frequently has expertise in the area of the dispute.

Mediation begins when parties select a mediator. Each party then typically writes a mediation brief to explain why it should win. An important feature of mediation is that it allows multiple parties to participate in a dispute. The parties take turns explaining the dispute. One of the mediator's main goals is to help each party listen carefully to the opposing party's concerns. The mediator asks the parties to identify any additional concerns. The parties begin generating alternatives or solutions for the disputed points. The mediator helps the parties evaluate the alternatives by comparing the alternatives with the disputed points and interests identified earlier. Finally, the mediator assists the parties in agreeing on a solution.

The mediation concludes when the agreement between the parties is reached. The agreement is then usually put into the form of a contract and signed by the parties. The mediator may participate in the drafting of the contract. If one of the parties does not follow the agreement, that party can be sued for breach of contract. However, parties typically abide by the agreement because they helped to create it.

If mediation is not successful, the parties can turn to litigation or arbitration to resolve their dispute. However, nothing said during the mediation can be used in another dispute resolution method; the mediation process is confidential.

Advantages and Disadvantages of Mediation   The primary advantage of mediation is that it helps the disputing parties preserve their relationships; this is especially attractive for businesses with a working relationship they would like to continue. A second advantage is the possibility of finding creative solutions. The goal of mediation is to find a compromise between the needs of various parties rather than to find one party right and all the others wrong. A third advantage is the high level of autonomy mediation gives the participants. Instead of a neutral third party pronouncing a solution, the interested parties work together to create a solution, and this can make them more committed to following the agreement afterward.

These benefits can obviously be very worthwhile. However, we need to pay attention to the critics of the mediation process. One criticism of mediation is that it creates an image of equal parties working toward an equitable solution and thereby hides power imbalances that can lead to the party with greater power getting an agreement of greater benefit. A second criticism is that some people who enter mediation have no intention of finding a solution but, instead, use mediation as a tactic to draw out the dispute.

Uses of Mediation   Mediation is most commonly used in collective bargaining disputes because it allows the workers to maintain a relationship with their employer while still having their needs addressed. Under the National Labor Relations Act (NLRA), a union must contact the Federal Mediation and Conciliation Services to attempt to mediate its demands before beginning a strike to achieve higher wages or better working hours.

Similarly, the Equal Employment Opportunity Commission (EEOC) encourages the mediation of employment discrimination claims. The EEOC has a mediation program that uses mediators employed by the EEOC as well as external mediators trained in mediation and discrimination law. Mediation is also used extensively in environmental law because environmental disputes are often best served by finding a compromise between the frequently multiple parties.

ARBITRATION

One of the most frequently used methods of dispute resolution is arbitration, the resolution of a dispute by a neutral third party outside the judicial setting. Arbitration is frequently used in disagreements between employees and employers, and it is increasingly being used between consumers and businesses. Arbitration is often a voluntary process in that parties have a contractual agreement to arbitrate any disputes. This agreement may stipulate how the arbitrator will be selected and how the hearing will be administered.

Lawyers, professors, and other professionals typically serve as arbitrators. The general qualifications for being an arbitrator are honesty, impartiality, and subject-matter competence. Additionally, arbitrators are expected to follow the Arbitrator's Code of Ethics. Typically, parties choose arbitrators from the Federal Mediation and Conciliation Services (FMCS), a government agency, or the American Arbitration Association (AAA), a private, nonprofit organization.

The Arbitration Hearing   The arbitration hearing is similar to a trial. Both parties present their cases to a neutral third party; parties may represent themselves or use legal counsel. During this presentation, the parties may introduce witnesses and documentation, cross-examine the witnesses, and offer closing statements. The fact finder offers a legally binding decision. However, arbitration is also different from a trial in several ways. First, the arbitrator often takes a much more active role in an arbitration hearing than a judge takes in a trial, and the arbitrator can question witnesses. Second, no official written record of the hearing is kept in most arbitrations. Third, the rules of evidence applicable in a trial are typically relaxed in arbitration.

The Arbitrator's Award   The arbitrator typically provides a decision within 30 days of the arbitration hearing. The arbitrator's decision is called an *award,* even if no monetary compensation is awarded. The arbitrator's decision differs from a judge's decision in several ways. The arbitrator does not have to state any findings of fact, conclusions of law, or reasons to support the award, and he or she is not as bound by precedent as a judge is. Also, because the arbitrator was hired to

arbitration
A type of alternative dispute resolution in which disputes are submitted for resolution to private nonofficial persons selected in a manner provided by law or the agreement of the parties.

resolve a dispute between two parties, the arbitrator is more likely to make a compromise ruling instead of a win-lose ruling.

Unlike the case in most other forms of ADR, the arbitrator's decision is legally binding. In certain cases, a decision may be appealed to the district court. However, few of these cases are appealed. The courts give extreme deference to arbitrators' decisions.

The Federal Arbitration Act (FAA), the federal law enacted to encourage the use of arbitration, explicitly lists four grounds on which an arbitrator's award may be set aside: (1) The award was the result of corruption, fraud, or other undue means; (2) the arbitrator displayed bias or corruption; (3) the arbitrator refused to postpone the hearing despite sufficient cause, refused to hear relevant evidence, or otherwise misbehaved to prejudice the rights of one of the parties; (4) the arbitrator exceeded his or her authority or failed to use that authority to make a mutual, final, and definite award. In a 2008 decision, the U.S. Supreme Court held that these grounds are the only grounds for appeal and that the parties in an arbitration proceeding do not have the ability to give the courts additional grounds to set aside a decision.[9]

Consequently, in the United States, arbitration decisions are generally upheld. In fact, the Fifth Circuit recently held that "manifest disregard of the law and contrary to public policy are the only nonstatutory bases recognized by this circuit for the vacatur of an arbitration award."[10]

Advantages and Disadvantages of Arbitration   Arbitration may be preferable to litigation for several reasons. First, arbitration is more efficient and less expensive. Second, parties have more control over the process of dispute resolution through arbitration. They choose the arbitrator and determine how formal the process will be. Third, the parties can choose someone to serve as the arbitrator who has expertise in the specific subject matter. Fourth, the arbitrator has greater flexibility in decision making than a judge has. Unlike judges, who are bound by precedent, arbitrators generally do not have to offer reasons for their decisions.

However, arbitration is not without its critics. First, arbitration panels are being used more frequently, resulting in a loss of some of the prior advantages of arbitration, such as efficiency and lower cost. Second, because appealing an arbitration award is so difficult, some scholars argue that injustice is more likely to occur. Third, some individuals are concerned that by agreeing to give up one's right to litigate, one may be losing important civil rights or giving up important potential remedies without really understanding which rights are being given up. Fourth, some scholars are afraid that if more and more employers and institutions turn to mandatory arbitration, it will become more like litigation. Fifth, some scholars are concerned about the privacy associated with arbitration. Companies and employers are able to hide their disputes through arbitration.

Binding Arbitration Clause   Given the benefits associated with arbitration, parties may voluntarily submit their cases to arbitration. The primary method of securing arbitration is through a *binding arbitration clause,* a provision in a contract that mandates that all disputes arising under the contract must be settled by arbitration. The clause also typically states how the arbitrator will be selected. If parties have a binding arbitration agreement, the parties *must* resolve the dispute through arbitration. Both federal and state courts must uphold agreements to arbitrate. The Case Nugget illustrates the courts' willingness to enforce binding arbitration agreements.

A constraint on binding arbitration clauses is that they must be drafted in a way that ensures that the courts do not see them as unconscionable. An *unconscionable contract provision* has been defined as one in which the terms are "manifestly unfair or oppressive and are dictated by a dominant party."[11] The doctrine has been used most often to strike down binding arbitration clauses in consumer and employment contracts. Exhibit 3-3 offers tips on creating a binding arbitration clause.

binding arbitration clause
A contract provision mandating that all disputes arising under the contract must be settled by arbitration.

---

[9] *Hall Street Associates v. Mattell,* 2008 U.S. LEXIS 2911.

[10] *Kergosien et al. v. Ocean Energy, Inc.,* 390 F.3d 346 (5th Cir. 2004).

[11] *Farris v. County of Camden,* 61 F. Supp. 2d 307, 341 (D. N.J. 1999).

Exhibit 3-3

Tips for Creating a
Binding Arbitration
Clause

Overall, make sure the clause treats both parties fairly.

1. Be clear and unmistakable about what you wish to arbitrate.
2. The arbitration clause must be bilateral.
3. State explicitly which party will pay the arbitrator's fees, and make sure that it will not cost the non-drafting party more to arbitrate than it would have cost to litigate. Specify how the arbitrator will be selected.
4. Spell out the costs associated with the arbitration.
5. Avoid limitations on the remedies available to the parties.
6. Consider potential parties when determining where to hold the arbitration.

CASE Nugget

The Validity of Binding Arbitration Agreements

Preston v. Ferrer
United States Supreme Court

128 S. Ct. 978 (2008)

Under the FAA, is an administrative proceeding the same as a trial?

It has long been held that under the FAA, even if state statutes refer a state law controversy initially to a judicial forum, if the parties have agreed to submit that dispute to arbitration, the dispute must be arbitrated. Until 2008, however, the question existed of whether the same rule would apply when the state law directed that the first mode of resolution must be an administrative proceeding rather than a court hearing. In this case, the U.S. Supreme Court ruled that for purposes of the FAA, an administrative proceeding was the equivalent of a judicial proceeding. In *Preston v. Ferrer,* the two had included a binding arbitration agreement in a contract for Preston to represent Ferrer. When Preston attempted to collect his fees, a question arose about whether the matter had to be resolved by the California Labor Commission, which had jurisdiction over issues arising under the California Talent Agencies Act. The high court agreed with Ferrer that the dispute must be resolved through arbitration because the FAA preempted the state law. Even if a state law provides that an administrative forum has jurisdiction over a specific type of dispute, a binding arbitration agreement will supersede the forum declared by the state law.

Other ADR Methods

MED-ARB

Med-arb is a dispute resolution process in which the parties agree to start out in mediation and, if the mediation is unsuccessful on one or more points, to move on to arbitration. In some cases, the same neutral third party may participate in both the mediation and the arbitration. Some critics argue that if parties know that the mediator may become the ultimate decision maker, they will be less likely to disclose information during the mediation stage. Others argue that having the same neutral mediator-arbitrator offers faster resolution because the third party is familiar with the facts of the case.[12]

med-arb
A type of dispute resolution process in which both parties agree to start out in mediation and, if unsuccessful, to move on to arbitration.

---

[12] See Gerald F. Phillips, "Same Neutral Med-Arb: What Does the Future Hold?" *Dispute Resolution Journal* 60 (May–July 2005), p. 24.

SUMMARY JURY TRIAL

summary jury trial
An abbreviated trial that leads to a nonbinding jury verdict.

A summary jury trial is an abbreviated trial that leads to a nonbinding jury verdict. Two advantages are inherent in this method of dispute resolution. First, it is quick; a summary jury trial lasts only a day. Second, because a jury offers a verdict, both parties get a chance to see how their case would fare before a jury of their peers. Each judge can set his or her own rules. The judge advises the jury on the law, and each party's lawyer presents an opening statement and a limited amount of evidence before the jury. The lawyers have limited time for their presentations, and witnesses do not usually testify. The jury reaches an advisory verdict, although the jury does not know that its verdict is nonbinding. The parties then enter into a settlement conference, where they decide to accept the jury verdict, reject the verdict, or settle on some compromise. Approximately 95 percent of cases are settled at this time. However, if the case is not settled, it will go to a regular trial. At that trial, nothing from the summary jury trial is admissible as evidence.

MINITRIAL

minitrial
A type of conflict resolution in which lawyers for each side present their arguments to a neutral adviser, who then offers an opinion as to what the verdict would be if the case went to trial. This decision is not binding.

A minitrial is similar to arbitration and mediation because it involves a neutral third party. However, despite the presence of a neutral third party, business representatives of the disputing corporations participate and have settlement authority. Lawyers for each side present their arguments before these executives and the neutral adviser, who then offers an opinion as to what the verdict would be if the case went to trial. The neutral adviser's opinion, like the jury's verdict in a summary jury trial, is not binding. Next, the corporate executives discuss settlement options. If they reach an agreement, they enter into a contract that reflects the terms of the settlement.

EARLY NEUTRAL CASE EVALUATION

With *early neutral case evaluation,* the parties select a neutral third party and explain their respective positions to this neutral, who then evaluates the strengths and weaknesses of the case. The parties use this evaluation to reach a settlement. Eighteen federal district courts currently use early neutral case evaluation.[13]

PRIVATE TRIALS

private trial
An ADR method in which a referee is selected and paid by the disputing parties to offer a legally binding judgment in a dispute.

Several states allow private trials, an ADR method in which a referee is selected and paid by the disputing parties to offer a legally binding judgment in a dispute. The referees do not have to have any specific training; however, because retired judges often serve as referees, this method is often referred to as "rent-a-judge." The cases are often heard privately to ensure confidentiality. The referee writes a report and files it with the trial judge, but a dissatisfied party reserves the right to request a new trial before a trial court judge. Private jury trials with experienced jury members are becoming more popular today as well. Private trials have been criticized because they seem to provide faster and cheaper justice for those who can afford the initial fee and because they hide the trial from the public eye.

[13] Michael H. Diamant et al., *Strategies for Mediation, Arbitration, and Other Forms of Alternative Dispute Resolution,* SK074 ALI-ABA 205 (2005) [citing the CPR Institute for Dispute Resolution, www.cprador.org].

SUMMARY

Jurisdiction	*In personam jurisdiction* is the power of a court to render a decision affecting a person's legal rights.
	Subject-matter jurisdiction is the power of a court to render a decision in a particular type of case. The three forms of subject matter jurisdiction are state, exclusive federal, and concurrent.
Venue	*Venue* is the geographic location of the trial.
The Structure of the Court System	The United States has two parallel court structures: the state and federal systems. The federal structure has *district courts* (trial courts), *circuit courts of appeal,* and the *U.S. Supreme Court.* The state court structure varies by state but generally includes courts of common pleas (trial courts), state courts of appeal, and a state supreme court.

Chapter 3 The U.S. Legal System and Alternative Dispute Resolution **51**

Threshold Requirements	*Standing:* For a party to have the legal right to file a case, the outcome of the case must personally affect that party.
	Case or controversy: There must be an issue before the court that a judicial decision is capable of resolving. Parties cannot ask the judge for an advisory opinion.
	Ripeness: The case cannot be moot; it must be ready for a decision to be made.
Steps in Civil Litigation	The stages of a civil trial include the pretrial, trial, posttrial, and appellate stages.
	Pretrial includes consultation with attorneys, pleadings, the discovery process, and the pretrial conference.
	The *trial* begins with jury selection, followed by opening statements, the plaintiff's case, the defendant's case, closing arguments, jury instructions, jury deliberations, the jury's verdict, and the judgment.
	After the trial, parties may file *posttrial motions.*
	The parties may then file *appeals* to the appropriate appellate court and, in some cases, to the U.S. Supreme Court.
Alternative Dispute Resolution	*Alternative dispute resolution* is a way to settle problems without having to go to a costly and time-consuming trial.
Primary Forms of ADR	The primary forms of ADR are *negotiation, mediation,* and *arbitration.*
Other ADR Methods	Other methods of ADR include *med-arb, summary jury trials, minitrials, early neutral case evaluation,* and *private trials.*

Point/Counterpoint

Should Companies Be Allowed to Include Binding Arbitration Clauses in Consumer Contracts?	
YES	NO
Arbitration is a much faster way to resolve a likely small dispute. Through the discovery process, a defendant could draw out a case for two to three years before the case would actually go to trial. Thus, the consumer benefits from the binding arbitration clause by forcing the defendant to resolve the dispute quickly. According to a recent study by Ernst & Young, 55 percent of consumer arbitrations were resolved in the consumer's favor.* Another study suggested that 93 percent of people who participated in arbitration thought that they were treated fairly.† Consumers receive fair and fast treatment through mandatory arbitration. Consumers have a choice as to whether to purchase a good or service, and in some cases the purchase may include a requirement on how disputes will be resolved. If a consumer is opposed to a mandatory arbitration clause, the consumer can purchase the good or service from another provider. In conclusion, companies should be permitted to include binding arbitration clauses in their consumer contracts.	Arbitration may require the consumer to pay more upfront costs to begin the dispute resolution process. For example, the consumer may have to pay for the costs of the arbitrator. To file a complaint, a consumer has to pay filing fees only, which cost around $150. To file a claim through the American Arbitration Association, a consumer has to pay between $500 and $1,000, and the consumer is required to advance the arbitrator's fees. Many consumers are not likely to read all the fine print when applying for a credit card or purchasing a service. A consumer has no bargaining power to remove a mandatory arbitration clause from the contract; consequently, the consumer has no choice. It is unfair to force a consumer to submit a dispute to arbitration when she or he has no power to bargain regarding that aspect of the sales or service contract. Finally, because arbitration is secret, a company can hide its disputes from the general public. The public exposure associated with lawsuits encourages companies to respond to and resolve disputes better. In conclusion, consumers are harmed more than helped by binding arbitration clauses in consumer contracts.

* Ernst & Young, "Outcomes of Arbitration: An Empirical Study of Consumer Lending Cases," www.adrforum.com/rcontrol/documents/ResearchStudiesAndStatistics/2005ErnstAndYoung.pdf

† "Report to the Securities and Exchange Commission Regarding Arbitrator Conflict Disclosure Requirements in NASD and NYSE Securities Arbitrations," www.nyse.com/pdfs/arbconflict.pdf

Questions & Problems

1. Explain the two types of jurisdiction that a court must have to hear a case and render a binding decision over the parties.

2. Explain the differences between trial courts and appellate courts.

3. Identify and define the alternative tools of discovery.

4. Explain the three threshold requirements a plaintiff must meet before he or she can file a lawsuit.

5. The citizens of each state elect state court judges. The president, on the other hand, appoints federal court judges for lifetime positions. Why might this difference lead to different rulings on similar cases? Which method—election or appointment—do you like better? Why? What are the advantages and disadvantages of each method?

6. Missouri was International Shoe Corporation's principal place of business, but the company employed between 11 and 13 salespersons in the state of Washington, who exhibited samples and solicited orders for shoes from prospective buyers in Washington. The state of Washington assessed the company for contributions to a state unemployment fund. The state served the assessment on one of International Shoe Corporation's sales representatives in Washington and sent a copy by registered mail to the company's Missouri headquarters. International Shoe's representative challenged the assessment on numerous grounds, arguing that the state had not properly served the corporation. Is the corporation's defense valid? Why or why not? [*International Shoe Co. v. Washington,* 326 U.S. 310 (1945).]

7. The Robinsons, residents of New York, bought a new Audi car from Seaway Volkswagen Corp., a retailer that was incorporated in New York and had its principal place of business there. World-Wide Volkswagen, a company incorporated in New York and doing business in New York, New Jersey, and Connecticut, distributed the car to Seaway. Neither Seaway nor World-Wide did business in Oklahoma, and neither company shipped cars there. The Robinsons were driving through Oklahoma when another vehicle struck their Audi in the rear. The gas tank of the Audi exploded, injuring several members of the family. The Robinsons brought a product liability suit against the manufacturer, distributor, and retailer of the car in an Oklahoma state court. Seaway and World-Wide argued that the Oklahoma state court did not have *in personam* jurisdiction over them. After the state's trial court and supreme court held that the state did have *in personam* jurisdiction over Seaway and World-Wide,

they appealed to the U.S. Supreme Court. How do you think the Court decided in this case? Why? [*World-Wide Volkswagen Corp. v. Woodson,* 444 U.S. 286 (1980).]

8. Nicastro, the plaintiff, was using a metal-shearing machine in New Jersey when he hurt his hand. The machine was produced by J. McIntyre Machinery, Ltd., which manufactured the machine in England, where the company is based. However, Nicastro brought the company to court in New Jersey because that is where the injury occurred. The company argued that it could not be brought to court in New Jersey because the court did not have personal jurisdiction over it due to the company's lack of minimum contacts in the state. Nicastro also said that the company's distributor for the United States sold the equipment in the country; company officials attended trade shows in the country, even if they were not in New Jersey; and the record shows that one machine was in New Jersey. Ultimately, the company knew that its United States distributor could sell its products in any state, and any product could somehow end up in any other state. On the other hand, the company did not travel to, advertise, or contact any residents of New Jersey. Do you think the company is subject to personal jurisdiction in the state of New Jersey? How do you believe the Supreme Court ruled in this case? Why? [J. McIntyre Machinery Ltd. v. Nicastro, 131 S. Ct. 2780 (2011).]

9. Central West Virginia Energy Company, a West Virginia coal sales company, along with Massy Coal Company, a Virginia corporation, filed a lawsuit in federal district court against Mountain State Carbon and its member companies, one of which, Severstal Wheeling, was located in Wheeling, West Virginia. The plaintiffs alleged that the defendants, all of which were in the steel business, refused to accept shipments of coal in breach of their supply agreement with Central Energy. The defendants filed a motion to dismiss for lack of diversity, claiming that both Severstal and Central Energy had their principal places of business in West Virginia. The district court dismissed the complaint for lack of diversity, citing that Severstal's self-described day-to-day operations, such as "purchasing, sales, transportation, engineering, human resources, and accounting/financial functions," are all handled in Wheeling and noting Severstal's "visibility in and involvement with the Wheeling community." The plaintiffs appealed, arguing that the court misinterpreted *Hertz* and that the district court failed to consider the importance of the

fact that Severstal's officers control the company's policies and high-level decisions from the corporate offices in Dearborn, where seven of the company's eight corporate officers maintain their offices. The plaintiffs also noted that in Severstal's corporate filings with the states of Ohio, Michigan, and West Virginia, the company listed a Dearborn, Michigan, address as its principal place of business. How do you think the court ruled on the appeal? Why? [*Central West Virginia Energy Company, Inc. v. Mountain State Carbon LLC,* Case No. 10-1486, 4th Cir. Ct. of Appeals, 2011 U.S. App. LEXIS 7557.]

10. Attorneys, journalists, media, and legal and human rights organizations brought action against the Central Intelligence Agency, challenging the constitutionality of Section 702 of the Foreign Intelligence Surveillance Act (FISA). In particular, they objected to a recent change to FISA, through the FISA Amendments Act, that shifted the party-monitoring compliance with the act's limitations from the judiciary to the executive branch, eliminating the power of the judiciary to review the surveillance procedures. The government argued that the plaintiffs lacked standing to bring the case to court. The plaintiffs argued that the recent change to FISA created a reasonable fear of future injury and that they had incurred costs to avoid that future injury. How do you think the court ruled in this case? Why? [*Amnesty International United States et al. v. Clapper, Alexander, and Holder,* 2011 U.S. App. LEXIS 5699.]

11. Dakota Foundry was purchasing some equipment from Tromley Industries. According to the practice of the firm, the operations manager was supposed prepare a quote on Kloster stationery, and the back of the stationery contained its standard terms and conditions of sale, including a binding arbitration agreement. The salesman would make several copies and pass them to everyone involved for negotiations. The salesman made copies but did not include the back page, which contained the standard terms, including the binding arbitration clause. After further negotiations, Tromley issued another quotation, which stated that it was a revised quotation and had combined the December 2009 quotes "and all subsequent changes made during our meetings into one, cohesive system quote." This quote also contained the same note as the original quote, advising Dakota to "[p]lease pay particular attention to the attached copy of our Standard Terms and Conditions of Sale which are an integral part of this quotation." However, no standard terms were attached to the quote. This second quote did have a document entitled "standard payment terms" attached, but it did not include any arbitration terms. Dakota Foundry accepted the second quote.

When problems arose with the equipment, Dakota filed suit, and Tromley filed a motion to compel arbitration on grounds that the contract incorporated Tromley's Standard Terms and Conditions, which included the binding arbitration clause. Do you think the court compelled arbitration? Why or why not? [Dakota Foundry, Inc. v. Tromley Indus. Holdings, Inc., 737 F. 3d 492 (2013).]

12. Cleveland Construction Co, Inc., (CCI) was a general contractor building a grocery store in Houston, Texas. The company subcontracted the exaction and grading to Levco in a contract that contained a binding arbitration clause that mandated arbitration in Ohio of any disputes arising under the contract. When a dispute arose between the two, Levco filed suit in a Texas state court. CCI sought to compel arbitration in Ohio in accordance with the binding arbitration clause, but Levco argued that a Texas statute allowed any binding arbitration clause to be voided if it required arbitration outside the state of Texas, so the case could be litigated. Where should the case ultimately be resolved and why? [Cleveland Construction, Inc. v. Levco Construction, Inc., 359 SW 3d 843 (2012).]

PART

1

The Legal Environment of Business

CHAPTER

4

Administrative Law

CASE OPENER

Does the EPA Have an Obligation to Regulate Automobile Emissions?

On October 20, 1999, a group of 19 private organizations filed a rule-making petition asking the Environmental Protection Agency (EPA) to regulate "greenhouse gas emissions from new motor vehicles" under the Clean Air Act.[1] The petitioners cited the fact that 1998 was the "warmest year on record," that greenhouse gas emissions have significantly accelerated climate change, and that carbon dioxide is the most important man-made contribution to climate change. Fifteen months after the petition was filed, the EPA requested public comment on the issues. Then, on September 8, 2003, the EPA entered an order denying the rule-making petition, citing two reasons: (1) The Clean Air Act does not authorize the EPA to issue mandatory regulations to address global climate change; and (2) even if the agency had authority, it would be unwise to do so at this time. The case, *Massachusetts v. EPA*, eventually worked its way up to the U.S. Supreme Court, which had to decide whether the EPA was improperly failing to regulate carbon dioxide gas in automobile exhaust as a climate-changing pollutant.

1. What government entity is the final determiner of whether a particular type of rule will be issued by an agency?
2. Did the EPA err in not regulating greenhouse gases under the Clean Air Act?

[1] *Massachusetts v. EPA*, 549 U.S. 497 (2007).

LEARNING OBJECTIVES

After reading this chapter, you will be able to answer the following questions:

LO 4-1 What is administrative law?

LO 4-2 What is an administrative agency?

LO 4-3 How and why are administrative agencies created?

LO 4-4 What types of powers do administrative agencies have?

LO 4-5   What is the difference between an executive agency and an independent agency?

LO 4-6   What is the Administrative Procedures Act?

LO 4-7   How do formal, informal, and hybrid rule making differ from one another?

LO 4-8   What are the limits on agency power?

Introduction to Administrative Law

WHAT IS ADMINISTRATIVE LAW?

As a business owner or manager, you will need to be aware of regulations that affect your business. In addition to learning about laws passed by Congress, you will also need to know about rules passed by administrative agencies. Administrative law consists of the substantive and procedural rules created by administrative agencies (bodies of the city, county, state, or federal government), involving applications, licenses, permits, available information, hearings, appeals, and decision making.

An administrative agency is generally defined as any body created by the legislative branch (e.g., Congress, a state legislature, or a city council) to carry out specific duties. Agencies have three types of power: *legislative, judicial, and executive.* They may make rules for an entire industry, adjudicate individual cases, and investigate corporate misconduct. Because legislative, judicial, and executive powers have traditionally been placed in separate branches of government by the Constitution, the role of administrative agencies has led some to refer to agencies as the unofficial fourth branch of government. Although there is a semblance of truth to that characterization, administrative agencies are not in fact another branch, primarily because all their authority is simply delegated to them, and they remain under the control of the three traditional branches of government.

The first federal administrative agency, the Interstate Commerce Commission (ICC), was created by Congress near the end of the nineteenth century. Congress felt that the anticompetitive conduct of railroads could best be controlled by a regulatory body. The ICC no longer exists as a separate agency,[2] but for more than 100 years, the ICC regulated passenger and freight transportation. Following the crash of the stock market and the Great Depression of the 1930s, Congress saw a need for additional agencies to regulate business in the public interest. Since then, numerous agencies have been created whenever Congress believed an area required more intense regulation than Congress could provide. In fact, after the Enron scandal, there was talk that Congress might create a new agency to regulate the accounting industry. To date, no such agency has materialized.

WHY AND HOW ARE AGENCIES CREATED?

When Congress sees a problem that it believes needs regulation, it may create an administrative agency to deal with that problem. The idea is that the agency can be staffed with people who have special expertise in the area the agency is regulating and therefore know what types of regulations are necessary to protect the citizens in that area. Agencies typically act more swiftly than Congress in creating and enacting new laws. Today, administrative agencies actually create more rules than Congress and the courts combined.

Congress creates administrative agencies through passage of enabling legislation, which is a statute that specifies the name, functions, and specific powers of the administrative agency.

LO 4-1

administrative law
The collection of rules and decisions made by administrative agencies to fill in particular details missing from constitutions and statutes.

LO 4-2

administrative agency
Any government body created by the legislative branch (e.g., Congress, a state legislature, or a city council) to carry out specific duties.

Interstate Commerce Commission (ICC)
The first federal administrative agency; created to regulate the anticompetitive conduct of railroads.

LO 4-3

enabling legislation
A statute that specifies the name, functions, and specific powers of an administrative agency and grants the agency broad powers for the purpose of serving the public interest, convenience, and necessity.

---

[2] The functions of the ICC were transferred to the Transportation Department by Congress as part of a cost-saving measure.

Enabling statutes grant agencies broad powers for the purpose of serving the "public interest, convenience, and necessity." These broad powers include rule making, investigation, and adjudication.

BUT WHAT IF . . .

WHAT IF THE FACTS OF THE CASE OPENER WERE DIFFERENT?

In the opening case, the EPA believed it did not have enough power to make rules regarding global climate change. Let's say that a member of the EPA argued that only Congress has the power to make this type of regulation, which would directly affect the way many businesses operate. Would the EPA member be correct?

LO 4-4

Rule Making   Enabling statutes permit administrative agencies to issues rules that control individual and business behavior. These rules have the same effect as laws. If an individual or business fails to comply with agency rules, there are often civil, as well as criminal, penalties. Agencies may enact three types of rules: procedural, interpretive, and legislative.

Procedural rules are rules regarding the internal operations of an agency. *Interpretive rules* are rules that explain how the agency views the meaning of the statutes for which the agency has administrative responsibility. Finally, *legislative rules* are policy expressions that have the effect of law. The various rule-making processes are discussed later in this chapter.

subpoena

An order to appear at a particular time and place and provide testimony.

subpoena *duces tecum*

An order to appear and bring specified documents.

administrative law judge (ALJ)

A judge who presides over an administrative hearing; may attempt to get the parties to settle but has the power to issue a binding decision.

consent order

A statement in which a company agrees to stop disputed behavior but does not admit that it broke the law.

order

A binding decision rendered by a judge.

Investigation   Enabling statutes grant executive power to agencies to investigate potential violations of rules or statutes. Many times, companies cooperate with agencies and voluntarily furnish information. Other times, however, agencies must use their investigative powers, defined in their enabling legislation, to gather information. Such powers typically include the power to issue a subpoena (i.e., an order to appear at a particular time and place and provide testimony) and a subpoena *duces tecum* (i.e., an order to appear and bring specified documents).

Adjudication   Enabling statutes delegate judicial power to agencies to settle or adjudicate individual disputes that an agency may have with businesses or individuals. After investigation, the agency holds an administrative hearing before an administrative law judge (ALJ). The ALJ will try to convince the parties to reach a settlement via a consent order, but the judge also has the authority to render a binding decision (an order) after a hearing (administrative law matters are heard only by an ALJ because there is no right to a jury trial in administrative agencies). An appeal to the full commission or the head of an agency may then be filed. That decision may be appealed to the circuit court of appeals. If there are no appeals, the ALJ's initial order becomes the final order. Decisions of ALJs are typically upheld.

Example of an Administrative Problem.   The EPA administrator, using the congressional mandate under the Clean Air Act, sets forth rules governing the amount of certain hazardous air pollutants that may be emitted into the atmosphere. Using these standards, another branch of the EPA sends investigators to inspect a plant suspected of violating the act. If the inspector finds a violation and the EPA imposes a penalty, the plant operator will most likely contest the imposition of the fine, and a hearing will be held before an ALJ employed in another division of the EPA. If the matter is not settled at the hearing, the ALJ will preside over another hearing and render a binding order. That order may be appealed within the agency and finally to the federal court. The courts, however, typically defer to the expertise of the agency and the associated ALJ. In other words, most orders by an ALJ are upheld.

executive agency

An agency that is typically located within the executive branch, under one of the cabinet-level departments. The agency head is appointed by the president with the advice and consent of the Senate.

Types of Administrative Agencies

Agencies are classified as either executive or independent. The administrative head of an executive agency is appointed by the president with the advice and consent of the U.S. Senate. Executive-agency heads may be discharged by the president at any time, for any reason. When

Exhibit 4-1

Major Administrative
Agencies

INDEPENDENT AGENCIES	EXECUTIVE AGENCIES
Commodity Futures Trading Commission (CFTC)	Federal Deposit Insurance Corporation (FDIC)
Consumer Product Safety Commission (CPSC)	General Services Administration (GSA)
Equal Employment Opportunity Commission (EEOC)	International Development Corporation Agency (IDCA)
Federal Communications Commission (FCC)	National Aeronautics and Space Administration (NASA)
Federal Trade Commission (FTC)	National Science Foundation (NSF)
National Labor Relations Board (NLRB)	Occupational Safety and Health Administration (OSHA)
Nuclear Regulatory Commission (NRC)	Office of Personnel Management (OPM)
Securities and Exchange Commission (SEC)	Small Business Administration (SBA)
	Veterans Administration (VA)

a new president is elected, he will typically place his appointees in charge of executive agencies. These agencies are generally located within the executive branch, under one of the cabinet-level departments. Hence, executive agencies are referred to as *cabinet-level agencies.* Examples of traditional executive agencies are the Federal Aviation Agency (FAA), located within the Department of Transportation, and the Food and Drug Administration (FDA), located within the Department of Health and Human Services.

Independent agencies are governed by a board of commissioners, one of whom is the chair. The president appoints the commissioners of independent agencies with the advice and consent of the Senate, but these commissioners serve fixed terms and cannot be removed except for cause. No more than a simple majority of an independent agency can be members of any single political party (e.g., if the board consists of seven members, no more than four may be from the same political party). Serving fixed terms is said to make the commissioners less accountable to the will of the executive (thus the term *independent* agency). These agencies are generally not located within any department. Examples of independent agencies are the Federal Trade Commission (FTC), the Securities and Exchange Commission (SEC), and the Federal Communications Commission (FCC).

Another difference between these two types of agencies is the scope of their regulatory authority. Executive agencies tend to have responsibility for making rules covering a broad spectrum of industries and activities. Independent agencies, often called *commissions,* tend to have more narrow authority over many facets of a particular industry, focusing on such activities as rate making and licensing. Executive agencies have a tendency to focus more on *social* regulation, whereas independent agencies are more often focused on what we refer to as *economic* regulation. Exhibit 4-1 lists the major administrative agencies.

Some agencies do not fall clearly into one classification or the other. These agencies are typically referred to as hybrid agencies. Created as one type of agency, the body may share characteristics of the other. The EPA, for example, was created as an independent agency, not located within any department of the executive branch. Yet it is headed by a single administrator who serves at the whim of the president. During the early 1990s, in fact, there were discussions of the need to transform the EPA into a cabinet-level executive agency. (These initiatives did not get beyond the discussion stage.) Another example is the "independent" Federal Energy Regulation Commission (FERC), which has the typical structure of an independent agency yet is located within the Department of Energy.

How Are Agencies Run?

In 1946, Congress passed the Administrative Procedures Act (APA) as a major limitation on how agencies are run. Prior to passage of APA, agencies could decide on their own how to make rules, conduct investigations, and hold hearings and trials. Under APA, there are very specific guidelines on rule making by agencies. The two most common types of rule making are *informal* and *formal;* a third type is known as *hybrid.* Each is discussed below, along with a few exemptions.

independent agency
An agency that is typically not located within a government department. It is governed by a board of commissioners, who are appointed by the president with the advice and consent of the Senate.

LO 4-5

hybrid agency
An agency that has characteristics of both executive and independent agencies.

LO 4-6

Administrative Procedures Act (APA)
Federal legislation that places limitations on how agencies are run and contains very specific guidelines on rule making by agencies.

INFORMAL RULE MAKING

LO 4-7

informal rule making
A type of rule making in which an agency publishes a proposed rule in the *Federal Register,* considers public comments, and then publishes the final rule. Also called *notice-and-comment rule making.*

Federal Register
The government publication in which an agency publishes each proposed rule, along with an explanation of the legal authority for issuing the rule and a description of how the public can participate in the rule-making process, and later publishes the final rule.

The primary type of rule making administrative agencies use is informal rule making, or notice-and-comment rule making. Informal rule making applies in all situations in which the agency's enabling legislation or other congressional directives do not require another form. An agency initiates informal rule making by publishing the proposed rule in the *Federal Register* along with an explanation of the legal authority for issuing the rule and a description of how the public can participate in the rule-making process. The *Federal Register* is the official daily publication for rules, proposed rules, and notices of federal agencies and organizations as well as executive orders and other presidential documents.[3]

After publication, opportunity is provided for all interested parties to submit written comments. The comments may contain data, arguments, or other information a person believes might influence the agency in its decision making. Although the agency is not required to hold hearings, it has the discretion to receive oral testimony if it wishes to do so. Although the agency is not required to respond to all comments it receives, it is required to respond to comments that significantly concern the proposed rule. After considering the comments, the agency may alter the rule. It publishes the final rule, with a statement of its basis and purpose, in the *Federal Register.* This publication also includes the date on which the rule becomes effective, which must be at least 30 days after publication. Informal rule making is most often used because it is more efficient for the agency in terms of time and cost. No formal public hearing is required, and no formal record need be established. Some people believe that informal rule making is unfair because parties who are interested in the proposed rule have no idea what types of evidence the agency has received from other sources with respect to that rule. Thus, if the agency is relying on what one party might perceive as flawed or biased data, that party has no way to challenge that data.

BUT WHAT IF . . .

WHAT IF THE FACTS OF THE CASE OPENER WERE DIFFERENT?

Let's say, in the Case Opener, that the EPA decides it would like to make a rule governing the carbon dioxide emissions of new vehicles. The EPA publishes the rule in the *Federal Register* along with an explanation of the legal authority of the rule. Is this enough information for the *Federal Register?* What is the missing third prong?

FORMAL RULE MAKING

LO 4-7

formal rule making
A type of rule making that is used when legislation requires a formal hearing process with a complete transcript; consists of publication of the proposed rule in the *Federal Register,* a public hearing, publication of formal findings, and publication of the final rule if adopted.

The APA requires formal rule making when an enabling statute or other legislation mandates all regulations or rules to be enacted by an agency as part of a formal hearing process that includes a complete transcript. The first step in formal rule making is publication in the *Federal Register* of a notice of proposed rule making by the agency.

The second step is a public hearing at which witnesses give testimony on the pros and cons of the proposed rule and are subject to cross-examination. An official transcript of the hearing is kept. On the basis of information received at the hearing, the agency makes and publishes formal findings. On the basis of these findings, an agency may or may not promulgate a regulation. If a regulation is adopted, the final rule is published in the *Federal Register.* Because of the expense and time involved in obtaining a formal transcript and record, most enabling statutes do not require a formal rule-making procedure when promulgating regulations. If a statute is drafted in a manner that is at all ambiguous with respect to the type of rule making required, the court will *not* interpret the law as requiring formal rule making.

In the following case, the court had to decide whether to require formal rule making for substantive rules adopted by an agency.

[3] *Federal Register,* www.gpoaccess.gov/fr/

CASE Nugget

Do Substantive Rules Require Formal Procedure?

Alexis Perez v. John Ashcroft
U.S. District Court for the Northern District of Illinois, Eastern Division

236 F. Supp. 2d 899 (2002)

Perez, a native and citizen of Venezuela, had been a member of the Good Shepherd Church since November 1996. Beginning in December 1996, he worked as that congregation's music director, a full-time paid position. Under the law, a limited number of visas are available to an immigrant who, among other things, seeks to enter the United States to work for an organization in a professional capacity in a religious vocation or occupation. The Immigration and Naturalization Service (INS) denied Perez's visa application on the basis of his lack of religious training. Perez argued that the INS adopted the requirement of religious training in violation of the Administrative Procedures Act (APA), because it is a substantive rule adopted without the use of notice and comment or other formal rule-making procedures. Perez argued that he met all the requirements specified by the APA and INS regulations and, further, that the regulations contained no mention of a formal-religious-training requirement. INS countered that its imposition of the formal-training requirement—and its denial of Perez's visa request because he lacked that training—simply represented a reasonable interpretation of the regulations and that Perez's visa application was properly denied because he had no such training. There is no dispute that INS did not engage in any sort of formal rule-making process before adopting the requirement of formal religious training. The INS argued that the formal-training requirement was simply an interpretation of the regulations—more specifically, of the definition of "religious occupation"—and that therefore no formal rule making was necessary. The court disagreed.

All substantive rules adopted by an agency, that is, rules that create law, must be implemented through formal rule-making procedures.

HYBRID RULE MAKING

After agencies began regularly making rules in accordance with the appropriate procedures, the flaws of each type of rule making became increasingly apparent. In response to these problems, a form of hybrid rule making became acceptable to the courts and legislature. Hybrid rule making is an attempt to combine the best features of both formal and informal rule making. The starting point, publication in the *Federal Register,* is the same. Publication is followed by the opportunity for submission of written comments, and then there is an informal public hearing with a more restricted opportunity for cross-examination than that in formal rule making. The publication of the final rule is done in the same manner as it is for other forms of rule making.

Exhibit 4-2 compares formal, informal, and hybrid rule-making procedures.

EXEMPTED RULE MAKING

The APA contains an exemption from rule making that allows an agency to decide whether public participation will be allowed. Exemptions include rule-making proceedings with regard to "military or foreign affairs" and "agency management or personnel." Exemptions are also granted for rule-making proceedings relating to "public property, loans, grants, benefits, or contracts" of an agency. Military and foreign affairs often need speed and secrecy, which are incompatible with public notice and hearings. Other exemptions are becoming more difficult to justify in the eyes of the courts unless they meet one of the exemptions of the Freedom of Information Act (discussed later in this chapter).

LO 4-7

hybrid rule making
A type of rule making that combines features of formal and informal rule making; consists of publication in the *Federal Register,* a written-comment period, and an informal public hearing with restricted cross-examination.

Exhibit 4-2

Rule-Making
Procedures

PROCEDURE	Type of Rule Making		
	FORMAL	**INFORMAL**	**HYBRID**
Public hearing	Yes	No	Yes
Formal record	Yes	No	No
Publication of proposed rule in *Federal Register*	Yes	Yes	Yes
Written comments from the public and interested parties	Yes	Yes	Yes
Oral testimony and cross-examination	Yes	No (agency discretion)	Yes (limited)
Publication of final rule in *Federal Register*	Yes	Yes	Yes

Also exempted from the rule-making procedures are interpretive rules and general policy statements. An interpretive rule is a rule that does not create any new rights or duties but is merely a detailed statement of the agency's interpretation of an existing law. Interpretive rules are generally very detailed, step-by-step statements of what actions a party is to take to be considered in compliance with an existing law.

The following case demonstrates the deference federal courts give to agency interpretation of ambiguous statutes.

interpretive rule
A rule that does not create any new rights or duties but is merely a detailed statement of an agency's interpretation of an existing law, including the actions a party is to take to be in compliance with the law.

CASE Nugget

What Is the Authority of Agency Interpretation of Statutes?

Warner-Lambert Company v. United States
U.S. Court of Appeals for the Federal Circuit

425 F.3d 1381 (2005)

Warner-Lambert imports and sells lozenges in packages under the name Halls Defense™ Vitamin C Supplement Drops. The drops are composed primarily of sugar and glucose syrup, which together constitute more than 95 percent of each drop. Vitamin C constitutes just under 2 percent of each drop, with the remaining small percentage consisting of citric acid, flavors, and color. The Customs Service reclassified imported vitamin C supplement drops from their previous duty-free status as medicaments to dutiable status as sugar confectionery. As a result, the drops were subject to a duty of 6.1 percent. Warner-Lambert sued in the Court of International Trade. On appeal, the Customs Service reclassification was upheld. In a six-page detailed letter ruling, Customs explained the reasons for its action, including that its prior classification of the drops was "based upon the belief that Vitamin C imparted therapeutic or prophylactic character to the merchandise" but that "additional research indicates that Vitamin C has not been shown in the U.S. to have substances which imbue it with therapeutic or prophylactic properties or uses." The Court of International Trade held that Customs justifiably concluded that although the merchandise "may possess medical properties, it is being marketed as much for its flavor as for its medicinal value. Thus, it cannot be said that this merchandise is suitable only for medical purposes." The drops are marketed to provide users with their requirement of vitamin C, not to prevent or cure disease.

If a statute is ambiguous and if the implementing agency's construction is reasonable, the federal courts must accept the agency's construction of the statute, even if the agency's reading differs from what the court believes is the best statutory interpretation.

Policy statements are general statements about the directions in which an agency intends to proceed with respect to its rule-making or enforcement activities. Again, these statements have no binding impact on anyone; they do not directly affect anyone's legal rights or responsibilities.

A final exemption applies when public notice and comment procedures are "impracticable, unnecessary, or contrary to the public interest." This exemption is used most commonly either when the issue is so trivial that there would probably be very little, if any, public input or when the nature of the rule necessitates immediate action. Whenever an agency chooses to use this exception, it must make a good-cause finding and include in its publication of the final rule a statement explaining why there was no public participation in the process.

> **policy statement**
> A general statement about the directions in which an agency intends to proceed with respect to its rule-making or enforcement activities; has no binding impact on anyone.

REGULATED NEGOTIATION

The exceedingly high number of challenges to regulations, as well as a growing belief that structured bargaining among competing interest groups might be the most efficient way to develop rules, has stimulated interest among a number of agencies in a relatively new form of rule making, often referred to as reg-neg. Each concerned interest group and the agency itself sends a representative to bargaining sessions led by a mediator. After the parties achieve a consensus, that agreement is forwarded to the agency.

The agency is then expected to publish the compromise as a proposed rule in the *Federal Register* and follow through with the appropriate rule-making procedures. The agency, however, is not bound to do so. If it does not agree with the proposal the group negotiated, the agency is free to try to promulgate a completely different rule or a modification of the one obtained through the negotiation. The reasoning behind reg-neg is similar to that supporting the increased use of mediation. If the parties can sit down and try to work out a compromise solution together, that solution is much more likely to be accepted than one handed down by some authority. The parties who hammered out the agreement now have a stake in making it work because they helped to create it.

> **reg-neg**
> A type of rule making in which representatives of concerned interest groups and of the involved government agency participate in mediated bargaining sessions to reach an agreement, which is forwarded to the agency.

Admittedly, reg-neg is not possible in all situations. If there is an unmanageably large group of interests that would have to be represented, if any possible compromise would have to result from one group's backing away from a fundamental principle, or if two groups feel so antagonistic toward each other that they would be unable to sit down and talk rationally, reg-neg would probably not even be worth trying.

PROBLEMS ASSOCIATED WITH RULE MAKING

Agency employees are not subject to the same political pressures as legislators, but they are also not unbiased. Often the people with the necessary expertise to regulate specific areas come from the industry they will now be regulating. There is some concern that it will be difficult for regulators to ignore their past ties to industry and pass regulations that are in the public interest, especially when the regulations would increase costs to the industry or are opposed by the industry for other reasons. When people are discussing an agency in which they perceive this problem as existing, they often refer to the agency as being a captured agency. The counterargument is that those who have been deeply involved in an industry know it best. To prevent such actions during his administration, President Obama issued the *Executive Order on Ethics Commitments by Executive Branch Personnel.* The order prohibits executive-branch employees from accepting gifts from lobbyists; closes the revolving door that allowed government officials to move to and from private-sector jobs in ways that gave that sector undue influence over government; and requires government hiring to be based on qualifications, competence, and experience, not political connections.[4] Regulators must be sensitive to the role the economy plays in the public's willingness to accept or support certain regulations. When the economy is flourishing and unemployment is low, there is much greater acceptance of regulations. When unemployment is high, people are much more reluctant to accept regulations that they believe might cause some workers to lose their jobs and/or cause the prices of products to rise.

---

[4] For a full text of the executive order, see www.whitehouse.gov/the_press_office/ExecutiveOrder-EthicsCommitments/

OTHER ADMINISTRATIVE ACTIVITIES

Agencies perform a variety of less well known but equally important tasks. These include advising, conducting research, issuing permits, and managing property. One of the most common situations in which individuals come into contact with agencies occurs when an agency advises businesses and individuals on whether the agency considers an activity legal or illegal. Agencies also conduct studies of industries and markets. For example, the FTC, OSHA, and FDA conduct studies to determine, respectively, the level of economic concentration, safety in the workplace, and safety of drugs. Also, agencies provide information to the general public on various matters through hotlines, publications, and seminars. Agencies also devote much of their time to issuing licenses or permits. The EPA, for example, helps protect the environment by requiring certain environmentally sound activities before granting permits. Local agencies are responsible for issuing liquor licenses and cabaret (dancing) permits to local bars and restaurants. Finally, agencies often are responsible for managing government property.

Case 4-1 illustrates limitations on an agency's use of its powers to issue and, in this case, revoke a driver's license.

CASE 4-1

YAN JU WANG v. GEORGE VALVERDE
COURT OF APPEAL OF CALIFORNIA, SECOND APPELLATE DISTRICT
162 Cal. App. 4th 616 (2008)

FACTS: *The trial court granted plaintiff Wang's petition for a writ of administrative mandate compelling the defendant, Department of Motor Vehicles (DMV), to set aside its revocation of Wang's class C driver's license. On appeal, the DMV argued that, as a matter of law, it had the authority to revoke Wang's class C license because it allegedly caught her cheating on an examination for a class B license. Wang, the holder of a valid class C (noncommercial) driver's license, applied for a class B (commercial) driver's license. She was given a written examination to determine whether she was qualified for a class B license, but she was not permitted to complete that examination because she was allegedly cheating while taking the examination by using crib notes. Wang was never criminally prosecuted for using crib notes, under Vehicle Code section 14610.5, because the DMV determined that there was insufficient evidence to support criminal action. The only administrative action taken against Wang by the DMV was to order the revocation of her class C (noncommercial) driver's license.*

ISSUE: Does the Vehicle Code empower the state to revoke a driver's license if the driver cheated on the test for a different driver's license?

REASONING: The DMV appealed the Appeals Court's concurring opinion that "[n]o such action is authorized by the Vehicle Code." The DMV argues that, as a matter

of law, the DMV does have authority to revoke Wang's class C license because it allegedly caught her cheating on the examination for a class B license. The DMV purports to derive that authority from the Vehicle Code as follows: (1) Section 13359 provides that the DMV "may suspend or revoke the privilege of any person to operate a motor vehicle upon any of the grounds which authorize the refusal to issue a license"; (2) section 12809, subdivision (d), provides that the DMV may refuse to issue a license to any person who has "committed any fraud in any application"; (3) an examination is part of an application; (4) the use of a crib sheet in taking an examination is a fraudulent act; so (5) by using the crib sheet, Wang committed a fraud in an application, which therefore authorized refusal to issue a class B license, which therefore authorized revocation of her class C license, because any ground for refusal to issue a license is also a ground for revocation of a license.

The DMV's argument thus depends upon the DMV's contention that under section 13359, *any* ground for refusal to issue *one* license is also sufficient to justify revocation of a *different* license. The DMV cites no authority for its construction of section 13359. We have found no case on point, but we conclude that the DMV's interpretation cannot be correct because it would lead to untenable results. In general, the DMV's interpretation of the statute would authorize revocation of a class C license held by *any*

(continued)

unsuccessful applicant for a class B license. The statutory requirements for a class B license, however, are more demanding than the statutory requirements for a class C license, so statutory ineligibility for a class B license has no tendency, in itself, to show lack of statutory entitlement to a class C license. . . . Because the DMV's interpretation of section 13359 turns every unsuccessful application for a class B license into an authorization to revoke the applicant's class C license, it effectively negates the lower statutory threshold for entitlement to a class C license.

DECISION AND REMEDY: Affirmed, and respondent recovered the costs of her appeal.

SIGNIFICANCE OF THE CASE: The administrative agency is limited to the powers provided in the statute governing its operations.

CRITICAL THINKING

What facts, had they existed, would have altered this decision?

ETHICAL DECISION MAKING

Who besides the parties directly involved have interests in the results of this decision?

Limitations on Agency Powers   LO 4-8

There are four basic limits on agency power: political, statutory, judicial, and informational (see Exhibit 4-3). The hope is that these limitations will keep the agencies and their thousands of employees from abusing their discretion.

POLITICAL LIMITATIONS

As discussed earlier in this chapter, the president appoints the administrative heads of all executive agencies with the advice and consent of the Senate. If the president is unhappy with the head of such an agency, that person may be fired at any time for any (or no) reason. As such, executive agencies are particularly accountable to the executive branch. Moreover, the political slant (liberal or conservative) of the agency is significantly influenced by the president.

Congress also has significant control over agencies because the Senate must approve presidential nominees for them to become the administrative heads of agencies. Moreover, Congress has control over the budgets of all agencies. If Congress decides that a particular agency is not performing as it wishes, that agency's budget may be cut or even defunded. Just before the Enron crisis, Congress, after being heavily lobbied by the accounting industry, threatened to defund the Securities and Exchange Commission (SEC). In effect, Congress did not like the SEC's proposal that stock options should be charged as earnings. Arthur Levitt, then head of the SEC, heard the warning loud and clear and decided to walk away from his firmly held position. In later interviews, Levitt said it was his biggest regret as head of the SEC.[5]

STATUTORY LIMITATIONS

Congress has the power to create or dissolve an agency. If Congress is unhappy with an agency, it may amend the agency's enabling legislation and limit the agency's power. Moreover, in 1996, legislation was signed into law that gives Congress 60 days to review proposed agency rules.

[5] PBS video, *Bigger than Enron—How Greed and Politics Undercut America's Watchdogs,* 1999.

Congress may override those rules before they become effective. In addition, the APA (passed by Congress in 1946) sets forth guidelines that all agencies must follow when engaged in rule making.

JUDICIAL LIMITATIONS

An individual or business that believes itself harmed by an administrative rule may challenge that rule in federal court after all administrative procedures have been exhausted.[6] This is probably the biggest constraint on agency power. If a rule is subjected to judicial review, the court will consider the following:

substantial evidence
Refers to evidence that a reasonable mind could accept as adequate to support a conclusion. It is defined as "more than a scintilla but less than preponderance" and consists of "such relevant evidence as a reasonable person would accept as adequate to support a conclusion."[7]

1. *The facts of the case:* Courts typically defer to an agency's fact finding. The facts must be supported by substantial evidence.

2. *The agency's interpretation of the rule:* Once again, the courts typically defer to the expertise of the agency and uphold the agency's interpretation of the rule.

3. *The scope of the agency's authority:* Has the agency exceeded the authority granted it by its enabling legislation?

Although we typically think of judicial limitations as reining in overly zealous administrative regulators, the Case Opener illustrates that sometimes the judiciary is called on to restrict inaction by an agency. In *Massachusetts v. EPA,* the agency had resisted regulating greenhouse gases, arguing that carbon dioxide and similar gases are not pollutants under the Clean Air Act and, therefore, that the agency had no power to regulate them. When the high court reviewed the legislative mandate, however, it held that U.S. motor-vehicle emissions make a "meaningful contribution to greenhouse gas concentrations" and hence to global warming—and therefore the agency did have the authority to regulate such gases as air pollutants under the Clean Air Act.

In June 2009, the EPA granted a Clean Air Act waiver of preemption to California, allowing California to implement its own, more stringent greenhouse gas emission standards for motor vehicles beginning with model year 2009. By mid-2010, with the agreement of the auto industry, the California standard became the federal standard.[8]

The National Labor Relations Board (NLRB) is an independent administrative agency (see Exhibit 4-1). As you read the following case, Northwestern University and College Athletes Players Association, are you convinced there is *substantial evidence* that student athletes should be treated as employees under the law? Moreover, when this administrative decision is appealed to the courts, should the courts defer to the NLRB's interpretation of what it means to be an "employee?"

---

[6] In a few situations, a court may not review an agency action. These include situations involving politically sensitive issues and those in which the agency's enabling legislation prohibits judicial review.

[7] *Mareno v. Apfel,* 1999 U.S. Dist. LEXIS 8575 (S.D. Ala., Apr. 8, 1999).

[8] Tony McAdams, Nancy Neslund, and Kiren Zucker, *Law, Business, & Society,* 10th ed. (New York: McGraw-Hill, 2012), p. 745.

CASE 4-2

NORTHWESTERN UNIVERSITY AND COLLEGE ATHLETES PLAYERS ASSOCIATION (CAPA)

Case 13-RC-121359, National Labor Relations Boards (NLRB) (March 26, 2014)

FACTS: *Upon a petition duly filed under Section 9(c) of the National Labor Relations Act, as amended ("the Act"), a hearing was held before a hearing officer of the National Labor Relations Board ("the Board"). Pursuant to the provisions of Section 3(b) of the Act, the Board has delegated to the undersigned its authority in this proceeding.*

The Employer [Northwestern University] is a private, nonprofit, nonsectarian, coeducational teaching university chartered by the State of Illinois, with three campuses, including one located in Evanston, Illinois. It currently has an undergraduate enrollment of about 8,400 students. . . . The Employer maintains an intercollegiate athletic program

(continued)

and is a member of the National Collegiate Athletic Association (NCAA). The NCAA is responsible for formulating and enforcing rules governing intercollegiate sports for participating colleges. The Employer is also a member of the Big Ten Conference, and its students compete against the other 11 member schools (as well as nonconference opponents) in various sports. There are currently 19 varsity sports, which the Employer's students can participate in at the Division I level, including 83 varsity sports for men and 11 varsity sports for women. In total, there are about 500 students who compete in one of these sports each year for the Employer. . . . As part of its athletic program, the Employer has a varsity football team that competes in games against other universities. The team is considered a Football Bowl Subdivision (FBS) Division I program. Since 2006, the head football coach has been Patrick Fitzgerald, Jr., and he has been successful in taking his team to five bowl games. His football staff comprises a Director of Football Operations, Director of Player Personnel, Director of Player Development, nine full-time assistant coaches, and four graduate assistant coaches who assist him with his various duties. There are also five full-time strength coaches, two full-time video staff employees, two administrative assistants, and various interns who report to him. In turn, Head Coach Fitzgerald reports to Athletic Director James J. Phillips and President Dr. Morton Shapiro. The Employer's football team is composed of about 112 players of which there are 85 players who receive football grant-in-aid scholarships that pay for their tuition, fees, room, board, and books. The players on a scholarship typically receive grant-in-aid totaling $61,000 each academic year . . .

ISSUE: Under the Act, should student athletes who play football be deemed employees and given the legal right to bargain collectively?

REASONING: A party seeking to exclude an otherwise eligible employee from the coverage of the Act bears the burden of establishing a justification for the exclusion. Accordingly, it was the Employer's burden to justify denying its scholarship football players employee status. I find that the Employer failed to carry its burden. Section 2(3) of the Act provides in relevant part that the "term 'employee' shall include any employee. . . ." The U.S. Supreme Court has held that in applying this broad definition of "employee," it is necessary to consider the common law definition of "employee." *NLRB v. Town & Country Electric,* 516 U.S. 85, 94 (1995). Under the common law definition, an employee is a person who performs services for another under a contract of hire, subject to the other's control or right of control, and in return for payment. As a result, the Board has subsequently applied the common law test to determine whether individuals are indeed statutory employees. As the record demonstrates, players receiving scholarships to perform football-related services for the Employer under a contract for hire in return for compensation are subject to the Employer's control and are therefore employees within the meaning of the Act.

Clearly, the Employer's players perform valuable services for their Employer. Monetarily, the Employer's football program generated revenues of approximately $235 million during the nine-year period from 2003 to 2012 through its participation in the NCAA Division I and Big Ten Conference that were generated through ticket sales, television contracts, merchandise sales, and licensing agreements. The Employer was able to use this economic benefit provided by the services of its football team in any manner it chose. Less quantifiable but also of great benefit to the Employer is the immeasurable positive impact to Northwestern's reputation a winning football team may have on alumni giving and increase in number of applicants for enrollment at the University. . . . Equally important, the type of compensation that is provided to the players is set forth in a tender that they are required to sign before the beginning of each period of the scholarship. This tender serves as an employment contract and gives the players detailed information concerning the duration and conditions under which the compensation will be provided to them. Because NCAA rules do not permit the players to receive any additional compensation or otherwise profit from their athletic ability and/or reputation, the scholarship players are truly dependent on their scholarships to pay for basic necessities, including food and shelter. . . .

In the instant case, the record establishes that the players who receive scholarships are under strict and exacting control by their Employer throughout the entire year. . . . The coaches have control over nearly every aspect of the players' private lives because they must follow many rules under threat of discipline and/or the loss of a scholarship. The players have restrictions placed on them and/or have to obtain permission from the coaches before they can (1) make their living arrangements, (2) apply for outside employment, (3) drive personal vehicles, (4) travel off campus, (5) post items on the Internet, (6) speak to the media, (7) use alcohol and drugs, and (8) engage in gambling. The fact that some of these rules are put in place to protect the players and the Employer from running afoul of NCAA rules does not detract from the amount of control the coaches exert over the players' daily lives. . . . In sum, based on the entire record in this case, I find that the Employer's football players who receive scholarships fall squarely within the Act's broad definition of "employee" when one considers the common law definition of "employee."

DECISION AND REMEDY: For the reasons discussed in detail below, I find that players receiving scholarships from the Employer are "employees" under Section 2(3) of the Act. Accordingly, **IT IS HEREBY ORDERED** that an election be conducted under the direction of the Regional Director for Region 13 in the following appropriate bargaining unit: Eligible to vote are all football players receiving football grant-in-aid scholarship and not having exhausted their playing

(continued)

eligibility employed by the Employer located at 1501 Central Street, Evanston, Illinois, but excluding office clerical employees and guards, professional employees and supervisors as defined in the Act.

Peter Sung Ohr, Regional Director
National Labor Relations Board, Region 13

SIGNIFICANCE OF THE CASE: The preceding case will be appealed, potentially all the way to the U.S. Supreme Court. If the courts uphold this administrative ruling of the NLRB, colleges and universities will be required to treat students who are athletes as employees under the law, changing forever the definition of what it means to be a student athlete.[9]

CRITICAL THINKING

There is extensive listing in this decision of the various aspects of the student athlete's life that are controlled by the coaching staff. What is the purpose of that listing as justification for the eventual decision?

ETHICAL DECISION MAKING

One of the groups of stakeholders who are often ignored in an ethical decision are future generations. Those of us alive now do not know the names of future generations, have by definition never met them, and consequently have a difficult time considering them relevant when we make a decision *even when* these people are going to be affected in major ways by the decision. What groups of people in future generations will be affected by this decision? How will they be affected?

INFORMATIONAL LIMITATIONS

Agency power is limited by the Freedom of Information Act (FOIA), the Government in Sunshine Act, and the Privacy Act of 1974.

Freedom of Information Act (FOIA)

Federal legislation that mandates and facilitates public access to government information and records, including records about oneself. Sensitive information (e.g., on national security) is excluded.

Freedom of Information Act   The Freedom of Information Act (FOIA), passed in 1966, requires federal agencies to publish in the *Federal Register* places where the public can get information from the agencies. The act requires similar publication of proposed rules and policy statements. It requires agencies to make such items as staff manuals and interpretations of policies available for copying to individuals, on request. Finally, all federal government agencies must publish records electronically.

Any individual or business may make a FOIA request to a federal government agency. Information may be obtained regarding how the agency gets and spends its money. Statistics and/or information collected by the agency on a given topic is also available. Perhaps most important, citizens are entitled to any records that the government has about them. For example, you could contact the Internal Revenue Service (IRS) and request all information that it has collected about you. FOIA does not apply to Congress, the federal courts, the executive staff of the White House, state or local governments, and private businesses. Exemptions to FOIA include, but are not limited to, national security, internal agency matters (e.g., personnel issues), criminal investigations, financial institutions, and an individual's private life.

Immediately after taking office, President Obama issued a Memorandum for the Heads of Executive Departments and Agencies, indicating that FOIA should be administered with a clear presumption: In the face of doubt, openness prevails.[10] The memorandum directs that information should not be withheld simply because it is legal to do so and that if an agency cannot make full disclosure of information, it should consider making a partial disclosure. Case 4-3 demonstrates the limits of an FOIA request.

[9] For a full transcript of the NLRB's 24-page decision, go to http://www.chicagotribune.com/sports/chi-nlrb-northwestern-football-union-ruling-20140326,0,2025939.htmlpage

[10] U.S. Department of Justice, www.usdoj.gov/ag/foia-memo-march2009.pdf

CASE 4-3

ELECTRONIC PRIVACY INFORMATION
CENTER v. NATIONAL SECURITY ADMINISTRATION
795 F. Supp. 2d 85 (2011)

FACTS: *On June 25, 2009, Plaintiff Electronic Privacy Information Center (EPIC) submitted a FOIA request to the National Security Administration (NSA), seeking documents related to the Comprehensive National Cybersecurity Initiative (CNCI), an initiative established by former President George W. Bush that outlines federal cybersecurity goals. The plaintiff is a not-for-profit public interest research organization that reviews federal activities and policies to determine their possible impact on civil liberties and privacy interests. The NSA is an agency within the Department of Defense that is responsible for shielding our nation's coded communications from interception by foreign governments and for secretly intercepting intelligence communications from foreign nations.*

President Bush established the CNCI on January 8, 2008, by issuing National Security Presidential Directive 54 (NSPD 54), also known as Homeland Security Presidential Directive 23. The contents of NSPD 54 have not been released to the public. The CNCI, as described by the Senate Committee on Homeland Security and Governmental Affairs, is a "multi-agency, multi-year plan that lays out 12 steps to securing the federal government's cyber networks." The CNCI was formed "to improve how the federal government protects sensitive information from hackers and nation states trying to break into agency networks."

On June 25, 2009, the plaintiff submitted a written FOIA request to the NSA that, in its entirety, sought the following documents: the text of the National Security Presidential Directive 54 otherwise referred to as Homeland Security Presidential Directive 23; the full text, including previously unreported sections, of the Comprehensive National Cybersecurity Initiative as well as any executing protocols distributed to the agencies in charge of its implementation; and any privacy policies related to either the Directive or the Initiative, including but not limited to contracts or other documents describing privacy policies for information shared with private contractors to facilitate the Comprehensive National Cybersecurity Initiative. The NSA responded to the plaintiff's request on August 14, 2009, and produced two redacted documents that had been previously released under FOIA. The NSA referred part of the plaintiff's FOIA request to the National Security Council (NSC) because a responsive document in the NSA's possession had originated with the NSC. The plaintiff brought this lawsuit against both the NSA and NSC to compel the production of documents responsive to its FOIA request.

ISSUE: Are the NSA and NSC subject to a FOIA request?

REASONING: Congress enacted FOIA to promote transparency across the government. The Supreme Court has explained that FOIA is a means for citizens to know what their government is upto. The strong interest in transparency must be tempered, however, by the legitimate governmental and private interests that could be harmed by release of certain types of information. Accordingly, Congress included nine exemptions permitting agencies to withhold information from FOIA disclosure. The text of FOIA makes clear that the statute applies to agencies only. The statutory definition of an "agency" explicitly includes any executive department, military department, government corporation, government-controlled corporation, or other establishment in the executive branch of the government (including the Executive Office of the President). Using legislative history as its guide, however, the Supreme Court has held that "the President's immediate personal staff or units in the Executive Office whose sole function is to advise and assist the President are not included within the term 'agency' under the FOIA." The National Security Act of 1947 established the NSC to "advise the President with respect to the integration of domestic, foreign, and military policies relating to national security." This circuit has unambiguously held that the NSC is not an agency subject to FOIA. Organizations that are not an agency under FOIA are neither required to respond to a FOIA request nor subject to a FOIA lawsuit.

The plaintiff attempts to distinguish prior case law because the FOIA request in that case was made directly to the NSC, whereas in this case, the NSA referred the request to the NSC. The plaintiff contends that, by referring the FOIA request to the NSC, the NSA "treat[ed] the NSC as if it were an agency subject to the FOIA," and therefore this Court should find the NSC subject to FOIA in this case. The plaintiff's argument is unpersuasive. It is true that agencies that receive FOIA requests and discover responsive documents that were created by another agency may forward, or refer, those requests to the agency that originated the document. Here, however, the question is whether an entity *that is not an agency subject to FOIA* must respond to a FOIA request referred from an agency that is subject to FOIA. This question appears to be one of first impression in this circuit because neither the parties nor the court has located authority that directly addresses the issue. The Court finds the answer to this question to be clear-cut: The answer is no. An entity that is not subject to FOIA cannot unilaterally be made subject to the statute by any action of an agency, including referral of a FOIA request. It would defy logic and well-settled legal norms if an agency could unilaterally expand the scope of FOIA by referring requests to entities beyond FOIA's ambit.

(continued)

DECISION AND REMEDY: For the reasons previously stated, the court concludes that counts III and IV of the plaintiff's complaint should be dismissed and that the NSC should be dismissed from this action. Accordingly, the defendants' partial motion to dismiss is granted.

Beryl A. Howell United States District Judge

SIGNIFICANCE OF THE CASE: This case demonstrates that a party may not obtain documents indirectly under the FOIA that it could not obtain directly.

CRITICAL THINKING

What facts would have had to be changed for this decision to have granted the FOIA request? In other words, what facts are especially crucial to the reasoning here?

ETHICAL DECISION MAKING

Ethics requires an initial consideration of the values that are in play in this particular decision. What values would have needed to be uppermost in the judge's mind for him to have decided that with these facts, the FOIA request should have been granted?

Government in Sunshine Act   The Government in Sunshine Act requires agency business meetings to be open to the public if the agency is headed by a collegiate body. A *collegiate body* consists of two or more persons, the majority of whom are appointed by the president with the advice and consent of the Senate. This open-meeting requirement applies only when a quorum is present. The law also requires agencies to keep records of closed meetings.

Privacy Act   Under the Privacy Act of 1974, a federal agency may not disclose information about an individual to other agencies or organizations without that individual's written consent. This law guarantees three primary rights:

1. The right to see records about oneself, subject to the Privacy Act's exemptions.
2. The right to amend a nonexempt record if it is inaccurate, irrelevant, untimely, or incomplete.
3. The right to sue the government for violations of the statute, such as permitting unauthorized individuals to read your records.[11]

Exhibit 4-3

Limits on Agency Power

TYPE OF LIMIT	SPECIFIC LIMITATIONS
Political	The Senate must approve agency heads; Congress has power over agency budgets.
Statutory	Congress may create or eliminate agencies and amend enabling legislation (i.e., powers of agencies); Congress reviews and may override agency rules.
Judicial	Interested parties may challenge administrative rules in the courts, which may review the agency's finding of facts, its interpretation of the rule, and the scope of the agency's power in making the rule.
Informational	The Freedom of Information Act, Government in Sunshine Act, and Privacy Act of 1974 specify agencies' responsibilities regarding public access to information.

[11] FCIC, "Your Right to Federal Records," www.pueblo.gsa.gov/cic_text/fed_prog/foia/foia.htm

E-COMMERCE and the Law

E-Government: Changing the Relationship between the Government and Citizens

According to the United Nations, *e-government,* which is defined as the delivery of government services through digital information technologies, including the Internet, is important because it reduces the cost of government while significantly improving the quality of services and citizen access. According to the latest UN report about this topic, e-government makes public administration more proactive, efficient, transparent, and service-oriented. Annual surveys by the UN indicate that nations throughout the world have made significant progress in e-government development, with the United States and Europe being among the leaders in this development.

The UN has characterized the development of e-government into the following stages:

Stage I—Emerging: A government's online presence mainly consists of a web page and/or an official website; links to ministries or departments of education, health, social welfare, labor, and finance may or may not exist. Much of the information is static, and there is little interaction with citizens.

Stage II—Enhanced: Governments provide more information on public policy and governance. They have created links that enable citizens to access archived information such as documents, forms, reports, laws and regulations, and newsletters easily.

Stage III—Interactive: Governments deliver online services such as downloadable forms for tax payments and applications for license renewals. In addition, the beginnings of an interactive portal or website with services to enhance the convenience of citizens are evident.

Stage IV—Transactional: Governments begin to transform themselves by introducing two-way interactions between citizen and government (C to G). This includes options for paying taxes and applying for ID cards, birth certificates, passports, and license renewals

as well as similar C-to-G interactions, and it allows the citizen to access these services online 24/7.

Stage V—Connected: Governments transform themselves into a connected entity that responds to the needs of its citizens by developing an integrated back-office infrastructure. This is the most sophisticated level of online e-government initiatives, and it is characterized by:

1. Horizontal connections (among government agencies).
2. Vertical connections (central and local government agencies).
3. Infrastructure connections (interoperability issues).
4. Connections between governments and citizens.
5. Connections among stakeholders (government, private sector, academic institutions, NGOs, and civil society).

In addition, governments support and encourage e-participation and citizen engagement in the decision-making process.*

The most recent ranking of nations in terms of their progress toward development of effective e-government was as follows: (1) Sweden, (2) Denmark, (3) Norway, (4) United States, (5) Netherlands, (6) Republic of Korea, (7) Canada, (8) Australia, (9) France, and (10) United Kingdom.[†] Sadly, the United States was at the top of the list in 2001, but because the Bush administration failed to make a serious commitment to transforming the federal government through information technology and failed to develop an overall e-government plan detailing where the government wants to go and how it wants to get there, other nations have made much more rapid progress in this area than has the United States.[‡]

---

*United Nations, "E-Government Survey 2008," http://unpan1.un.org/intradoc/groups/public/documents/UN/UNPAN028607.pdf

[†] Ibid., p. 20.

[‡] Robert D. Atkinson (Progressive Policy Institute), "Unsatisfactory Progress: The Bush Administration's Performance on E-Government Initiatives," October 14, 2004, www.ppionline.org/ppi_ci.cfm?knlgAreaID=140&subsecID=290&content.ID=4252960

The Privacy Act applies only to records about individuals maintained by agencies in the executive branch of the federal government. There are 10 exemptions to the Privacy Act under which an agency can withhold certain kinds of information from you. Examples of exempt records are those containing classified information on national security and those concerning criminal investigations.[12]

---

[12] Ibid.

Federal and State Administrative Agencies

Currently, more than 100 federal agencies are in operation as well as countless state agencies. Often, when there is a federal agency, there are also comparable state agencies to which the federal agency delegates much of its work. For example, the most important federal agency affecting environmental matters is the Environmental Protection Agency. Every state has a state environmental protection agency to which the federal EPA delegates primary authority for enforcing environmental protection laws. However, if at any time the state agency fails to enforce these laws, the federal EPA will step in to enforce them.

SUMMARY

Introduction to Administrative Law	*Administrative law* consists of the substantive and procedural rules created by administrative agencies (government bodies of the city, county, state, or federal government) involving applications, licenses, permits, available information, hearings, appeals, and decision making.

An *administrative agency* is generally defined as any body created by the legislative branch (e.g., Congress, a state legislature, or a city council) to carry out specific duties.

Administrative agencies are created by Congress through passage of *enabling legislation,* which is a statute that specifies the name, functions, and specific powers of the administrative agency. Enabling statutes grant agencies broad powers for the purpose of serving the "public interest, convenience, and necessity."

An agency holds an administrative hearing before an *administrative law judge (ALJ).* The ALJ may attempt to get the parties to settle but has the power to issue a binding decision.

Types of Administrative Agencies

Executive agency: The administrative head of an executive agency is appointed by the president with the advice and consent of the U.S. Senate. Executive-agency heads may be discharged by the president at any time, for any reason. Executive agencies are generally located within the executive branch, under one of the cabinet-level departments (and thus are referred to as *cabinet-level agencies*). Examples are the Federal Aviation Agency (FAA) and the Food and Drug Administration (FDA).

Independent agency: Independent agencies are governed by a board of commissioners. The president appoints the commissioners with the advice and consent of the Senate. Commissioners serve fixed terms and cannot be removed except for cause. No more than a simple majority of an independent agency can be members of any single political party.

Hybrid agency: Hybrid agencies do not fall clearly into classification as an independent or an executive agency. Created as one type of agency, the body may share characteristics of the other type. The EPA, for example, was created as an independent agency, not located within any department of the executive branch, yet the head of the EPA serves at the whim of the president.

How Are Agencies Run?

In 1946, Congress passed the *Administrative Procedures Act (APA)* as a major limitation on how agencies are run. APA provides very specific guidelines on rule making by agencies.

- *Informal rule making:* Under APA, the proposed rule is published in the *Federal Register,* and there is opportunity for public comment.
- *Formal rule making:* All rules must be enacted by an agency as part of a formal hearing process that includes a complete transcript. The process begins with publication in the *Federal Register* of a notice of proposed rule making by the agency. Next, there is a public hearing at which witnesses give testimony on the pros and cons of the proposed rule and are subject to cross-examination. The agency makes and publishes formal findings. If a regulation is adopted, the final rule is published in the *Federal Register.*
- *Hybrid rule making:* Hybrid rule making is an attempt to combine the best features of formal and informal rule making. The starting point is publication in the *Federal Register,*

followed by the opportunity for submission of written comments and then an informal public hearing with a more restricted opportunity for cross-examination than that in formal rule making.

- *Exempted rule making:* APA contains an exemption from rule making that allows an agency to decide whether public participation will be allowed. Exemptions include rule-making proceedings with regard to military or foreign affairs, agency management or personnel, and public property, loans, grants, benefits, or contracts of an agency.

Interpretive rules are rules that do not create any new rights or duties but merely state the agency's interpretation of an existing law. They are generally very detailed, step-by-step statements of what actions a party is to take to be considered in compliance with an existing law.

In reg-neg, each concerned interest group and the agency itself sends a representative to bargaining sessions led by a mediator. If the parties achieve a consensus, that agreement is forwarded to the agency. The agency is then expected to publish the compromise as a proposed rule in the *Federal Register* and follow through with the appropriate rule-making procedures. If the agency does not agree with the proposal the group negotiated, the agency is free to try to modify or replace it.

Limitations on Agency Powers

There are four basic limits on agency power: political, statutory, judicial, and informational.

Freedom of Information Act: Passed in 1966, FOIA requires federal agencies to publish in the *Federal Register* places where the public can get information from the agencies. Any individual or business may make a FOIA request to a federal agency for information on how the agency gets and spends its money, statistics and/or information collected by the agency on a given topic, and any records the government has about the individual seeking the information. Exemptions to FOIA include, but are not limited to, national security, internal agency matters (e.g., personnel issues), criminal investigations, financial institutions, and an individual's private life.

Government in Sunshine Act: This act requires agency business meetings to be open to the public if the agency is headed by a collegiate body (i.e., two or more persons, the majority of whom are appointed by the president with the advice and consent of the Senate). The law also requires agencies to keep records of closed meetings.

Federal and State Administrative Agencies

Privacy Act: Under the Privacy Act, a federal agency may not disclose information about an individual to other agencies or organizations without that individual's written consent.

Administrative agencies exist at the federal and state levels.

Point/Counterpoint

Do Agencies Have Too Much Power?	
YES	NO
The U.S. government is founded on separation of powers. That is why we have three branches of government: executive, legislative, and judicial. Giving administrative agencies all three powers—executive, legislative, and judicial—gives the agencies power to do anything they want with virtually no oversight. Agencies hire people who formerly worked in industry. Thus, these people often view regulation skeptically, yet they are the same people who run the agencies.	Administrative agencies came into existence because Congress, as well as state and local governments, did not have the expertise, time, or resources to deal with specialized problems such as air pollution, securities regulation, and banking administration. Without administrative agencies, these problems would not be addressed. An agency employs professionals with expertise and experience in the area the agency regulates. These people understand the industry and the ways in which it needs to be regulated.

Questions & Problems

1. What is enabling legislation?

2. What are the limits on agency power?

3. What are the three main powers given to agencies?

4. List the three categories of agencies.

5. Describe the various types of rule making.

6. John and Jacqueline Stowers are the sole owners of Manna, a limited liability company registered to do business in the state of Ohio. Manna is a family-run enterprise that sells food and other products to its members. Manna operates from the family's home, specifically from the western section of the home, where its operations occupy one main room and one overflow room (the Manna rooms). Manna has approximately 100 members. To become a member, one must pay a 10-dollar initial fee, fill out an application, and complete an interview with Jacqueline Stowers. Members may order products through Manna by mail, e-mail, or phone. The products are primarily food products, although Jacqueline Stowers testified that members may also order some cleaning or personal hygiene products. The food products available to Manna members include raw chicken, turkey, beef, and eggs. The meat is typically frozen. After receiving orders from members, Manna obtains the ordered products from various suppliers. Testimony from Jacqueline and Kathryn Stowers indicated that the primary supplier from which Manna obtains products is United Natural Foods, which delivers the products to Manna from Indiana. When ordering from other suppliers, however, the Stowers will transport the products back to the Manna rooms themselves in their own unrefrigerated personal vehicles. The products are stored in refrigerators in the Manna rooms, which contain refrigerators and shelving, until members take the products from Manna. Manna has regular hours posted on the outside of the building and on its website, indicating when members may come to pick up their ordered products. Members pay Manna when they pick up their products, although the pricing is determined at the time of the order. Manna's pricelist is posted on its website. A search warrant was executed on the Manna rooms and the rest of the Stowers' home in December 2008. Manna's food products and other items were seized as part of an investigation of Manna as an unlicensed retail food establishment. Ohio law authorizes regulation of retail food establishments and requires all retail food establishments to be licensed. Appellants did not have a retail food establishment license. Should defendants be forced to obtain a food license? Why or why not? [*Stowers v. Ohio Dep't of Agric.*, (2011 Ohio 2710).]

7. Greenwood, an OSHA inspector, was driving by a construction site and thought that perhaps the site was unsafe. He got out of his car and videotaped the site, causing the foreman to ask him to leave. Greenwood also took measurements at the site and ultimately filed a report on OSHA violations of construction rules. The company running the construction site was assessed $49,000 in fines for OSHA violations. The company petitioned the court for review of the decision, arguing that an inspection by OSHA without a warrant was a violation of the right to privacy under the Fourth Amendment. How do you think the court decided? Explain your reasoning. [*Lakeland Enterprises of Rhinelander, Inc. v. Chao,* 402 F.3d 739 (7th Cir. 2005).]

8. Morales, a native and citizen of Mexico, was arrested in 1994 for entering the United States without inspection. He was released and served with a mail-out order to show cause why he should not be sent back to Mexico. Eventually, a removal hearing was scheduled, and Morales was notified by certified mail of the time and place of the hearing. When Morales failed to attend the hearing, he was ordered removed in absentia. The Immigration and Naturalization Service (INS) apprehended and removed Morales from the United States in 1998. He attempted to reenter illegally in January 2001—this time using a false border-crossing card. He was apprehended at the port of entry and was expeditiously removed. Undaunted, Morales reentered the United States undetected the following day. Sometime between his 1998 and 2001 removals, Morales married a U.S. citizen. In March 2001, Morales's wife filed an I-130 alien relative petition based on his marriage to a U.S. citizen. When Morales and his wife met with the INS in January 2003, an immigration officer served them with a denial of the I-130 petition and a notice of intent to reinstate Morales's removal order. The case came before a three-judge panel, which held that the regulation authorizing immigration officers to issue reinstatement orders is invalid, and Morales's removal order could be reinstated only by an immigration judge. Until 1997, removal orders could be reinstated only by immigration judges (i.e., not immigration officers). In 1997, the attorney general changed the applicable regulation to delegate this authority, in most cases, to immigration officers. Does the attorney general have the authority to change an INS regulation? Why

or why not? [*Raul Morales-Izuierdo v. Alberto R. Gonzales, Attorney General,* 2007 U.S. App. LEXIS 10865 (9th Cir. 2007).]

9. Six conservation organizations filed a petition in Thurston County Superior Court, asking that court to hold, pursuant to a provision in the Administrative Procedures Act (APA), that the Washington Forest Practices Board, the Washington Department of Ecology, and the Washington Department of Natural Resources (agencies) "failed to promulgate forest practice rules that advanced the environmental protection purposes and policies of the Forest Practices Act of 1974." The agencies countered by arguing that a formal petition for rule making must precede any petition for judicial review. Must an interest group exhaust administrative remedies before suing in a state or federal court? Why or why not? [*Northwest Ecosystem Alliance v. Washington Forest Practices Board,* 66 P.3d 614 (2003).]

10. Plaintiff *pro se* Wilfredo A. Golez (Golez) filed a motion to compel the work attendance records of two former coworkers who are not parties to the instant litigation. Golez states that he requires the employment records of his former coworkers to show that other employees who were late were not terminated as he was and, therefore, rebut defendants' contention that his own attendance irregularities led to termination. Plaintiff argues that he was improperly terminated during FMLA-protected absences. In addition to the rule set forth in the Privacy Act of 1974, federal courts generally recognize a privacy right that can be raised in response to discovery requests. The party whose privacy is affected may object, as defendants have done here, or seek a protective order. Resolution of a privacy objection or request for protective order requires a balancing of the need for the particular information against the privacy right asserted. Should Golez be permitted to compel production of records of his coworkers over their objections? Explain your reasoning. [*Golez v. Potter,* 18 Wage & Hour Cas. 2d (BNA) 923 (2011).]

11. On January 21, 2003, Robbins filed an application for site plan approval to construct an asphalt plant within the town limits of Hillsborough. Robbins had entered into a contract to purchase the property prior to submitting his application for site plan review, and subsequently, he purchased the property. At the time he filed his application, an asphalt plant was a permitted use in a general industrial (GI) district, subject to a site plan review. The property on which the asphalt plant was to be constructed was zoned GI. In reliance on the zoning ordinance in effect at the time of his application, Robbins spent approximately $100,000 to engineer and submit a site plan to comply with the conditional-use requirements set forth in

the ordinance and to prepare for the required public hearings before the Town of Hillsborough Board of Commissioners. Three public hearings were held. The board received evidence but reached no decision. At the close of the third hearing, the board scheduled a fourth hearing. Before the fourth hearing, the board amended the zoning ordinance to temporarily suspend review, consideration, and issuance of permits for manufacturing processes. Robbins's fourth hearing was canceled. Eventually, the suspension became a moratorium on permits until the end of the year. Robbins filed a complaint in Orange County Superior Court, alleging that he was entitled to rely on the language of the zoning ordinance in effect at the time he applied for the permit; that the board violated the law by failing to give notice of a public hearing or hold a public hearing prior to its decision to extend the moratorium; and that the defendant's decision to prohibit asphalt plants permanently was arbitrary and capricious. How should the court decide? Explain your answer. [*Robbins v. Town of Hillsborough,* 625 S.E.2d 813 (N.C. Ct. App. 2006).]

12. The county board of commissioners (the Board) entered into a memorandum of understanding (MOU) with a professional baseball team. The MOU obligated the team, among other things, to relocate to the city for spring training. The MOU called for the renovation of a stadium complex. In addition, the MOU called for renovations at the team's minor league spring training facilities. Several informational briefings for individual members of the Board were conducted privately, and e-mails were circulated among Board members, regarding the negotiations and agreement with the team. Sarasota Citizens for Responsible Government sued, alleging that the privately conducted meetings and e-mails by Board members were a violation of the Government in Sunshine Law requiring that:

> All meetings of any board or commission of any state agency or authority or of any agency or authority of any county, municipal corporation, or political subdivision, except as otherwise provided in the Constitution, at which official acts are to be taken are declared to be public meetings open to the public at all times, and no resolution, rule, or formal action shall be considered binding except as taken or made at such meeting. The board or commission must provide reasonable notice of all such meetings.

How should the court rule? Why? [*Sarasota Citizens for Responsible Gov't v. City of Sarasota,* 48 So. 3d 755 (2010).]

13. The respondent, the Public Company Accounting Oversight Board, was created as part of a series of accounting reforms in the Sarbanes-Oxley Act

of 2002. The board is composed of five members appointed by the Securities and Exchange Commission (SEC). It was modeled on private self-regulatory organizations in the securities industry—such as the New York Stock Exchange—that investigate and discipline their own members subject to SEC oversight. Unlike these organizations, however, the board is a government-created entity with expansive powers to govern an entire industry. Every accounting firm that audits public companies under the securities laws must register with the board, pay it an annual fee, and comply with its rules and oversight. The board may inspect registered firms, initiate formal investigations, and issue severe sanctions in its disciplinary proceedings. The parties agree that the board is "part of the Government" for constitutional purposes. Although the SEC has oversight of the board, it cannot remove board members at will but can do so only "for good cause shown," "in accordance with" specified procedures. The parties also agree that the commissioners, in turn, cannot themselves be removed by the president except for "inefficiency, neglect of duty, or malfeasance in office." The board inspected the petitioner accounting firm, released a report critical of its auditing procedures, and began a formal investigation. The firm and the petitioner, Free Enterprise Fund, a nonprofit organization of which the firm is a member, sued the board and its members, seeking, *inter alia,* a declaratory judgment that the board is unconstitutional and an injunction preventing the board from exercising its powers. The petitioners argued that the Sarbanes-Oxley Act contravened the separation of powers by conferring executive power on board members without subjecting them to presidential control. Is the Public Company Accounting Oversight Board constitutional? Why or why not? [*Free Enter. Fund v. Pub. Co. Accounting Oversight Bd.,* 130 S. Ct. 3138 (2010).]

CHAPTER

6 International and Comparative Law

LEARNING OBJECTIVES

After reading this chapter, you will be able to answer the following questions:

1 What is international law?

2 How is business transacted in the international marketplace?

3 What ethical considerations impact business in the international marketplace?

4 What is the General Agreement on Tariffs and Trade, and what are its important provisions?

5 What are regional trade agreements?

6 What is comparative law?

7 How does contract law differ among states?

8 How does employment law differ among states?

9 How are disputes settled in the international marketplace?

CASE OPENER

Resolving a Breach of Contract under the CISG

Chicago Prime Packers, Inc., is a Colorado corporation with its principal place of business in Avon, Colorado. Northam Food Trading Company is a Canadian corporation with its principal place of business in Montreal, Quebec, Canada. Chicago Prime and Northam are wholesalers of meat products. On March 30, 2001, Chicago Prime contracted with Northam to sell 1,350 boxes (40,500 pounds) of government-inspected fresh, blast-frozen pork back ribs, which Chicago Prime purchased from Brookfield Farms, a meat processor. The agreed-on price for the ribs was $178,200, and payment was required within seven days of the date of shipment. The ribs were stored at three different locations en route to Northam's customer Beacon Premium Meats, but at all times they were stored at or below acceptable temperatures. The ribs ultimately proved to be spoiled and were condemned by the U.S. Department of Agriculture. Nevertheless, Chicago Prime continued to demand payment from Northam. Chicago Prime brought a breach-of-contract action against Northam in U.S. federal court after Northam refused to pay for the ribs.

1. What law will the court apply to this transaction?
2. Could the parties have selected the law for the court to apply before the occurrence of their dispute?

The Wrap-Up at the end of this chapter will answer these questions.

The terms *international law* and *comparative law* are often used interchangeably, but they are quite different. International law governs the conduct of states and international organizations and their relationships with one another and with natural and juridical persons.[1]

LO1

What is international law?

A *state,* for purposes of international law, is an entity possessing territory, a permanent population, a government, and the legal capacity to engage in diplomatic relations.[2] We generally think of *international organizations* as consisting of states. The United Nations, the International Monetary Fund, the International Bank for Reconstruction and Development (World Bank), and the World Trade Organization are international organizations. The term *natural and juridical persons* refers to individuals as well as business organizations.

In contrast, comparative law is the study of the legal systems of different states. For example, a comparative legal theorist might study contracts in the American, Chinese, and French legal systems by identifying and contrasting applicable national laws. Comparative legal studies start with the examination of national sources of law embodied in constitutions, legislative enactments, administrative rules and regulations, and the decisions of judicial bodies. But where do we find principles of international law? Article 38 of the Statute of the International Court of Justice, a part of the United Nations system, identifies four sources of international law: customs, international agreements, general principles of law recognized by legal systems throughout the world (such as equity and elementary considerations of humanity), and secondary sources (such as decisions of the International Court of Justice, resolutions of the U.N. General Assembly, and scholarly writings).[3]

Legal Principle: **International law governs the conduct of states and international organizations and their relationships with one another and natural and juridical persons, while comparative law is the study of legal systems of different states.**

Most important for our purposes are customs and international agreements. *Customary international law* has two characteristics. First, in order to be deemed a custom, a practice must be general and consistent among states. Second, states must accept this general and consistent practice as binding law. The U.S. Supreme Court has held that in the absence of a governing international agreement or controlling executive or legislative act or judicial decision, U.S. courts must rely on customary international law.[4]

[1] Restatement (Third) of the Foreign Relations Law of the United States, § 101 (1987).

[2] Montevideo Convention on the Rights and Duties of States, December 26, 1933, art. 1, 165 L.N.T.S. 19, reprinted in *American Journal of International Law* 28 (Supp. 1934), p. 75.

[3] Statute of the International Court of Justice, June 26, 1945, art. 38, 59 Stat. 1055, 1060.

[4] *Paquete Habana,* 175 U.S. 677, 700 (1900).

By contrast, an *international agreement* is a written agreement made between states governed by international law that relates to an international matter.[5] International agreements can be bilateral (between two states) or multilateral (between three or more states). Regardless of their form, they do not take effect until ratified. Ratification occurs in many different ways. In the United States, it requires the advice and consent of two-thirds of the Senate after the president submits the agreement for consideration.[6]

Doing Business Internationally

L02

How is business transacted in the international marketplace?

The simplest method of entering a foreign market is through the *export* of the company's product to the foreign marketplace. A foreign sales representative is an agent who distributes, represents, or sells goods on behalf of a foreign seller and forwards orders directly to the company. The representative is usually compensated through commissions on completed transactions. Companies may also engage distributors for their products, who purchase goods from a seller for resale in a foreign market. Distributors are responsible for supporting and servicing the products they sell. Unlike the foreign sales representative, the distributor takes title to the goods and assumes the risk of being unable to resell them at a profit.

? BUT WHAT IF . . .

What if the facts of the Case Opener were different?

Recall, in the Case Opener, that both Northam and Chicago Prime were wholesalers. Let's say that Northam bought Chicago Prime meat from a distributor. The distributor picked up the meat from Chicago Prime and then made a deal with Northam to sell Northam the meat. When Northam received the meat, inspectors discovered that it was rancid. It turned out that the meat had been bad when the distributor picked it up from Chicago Prime. Who has to absorb the cost of the bad meat—Chicago Prime or the distributor?

> To see how economics and trade deficits relate to international business, please see the **Connecting to the Core** activity on the text website at www.mhhe.com/kubasek3e.

Companies seeking to enter foreign markets may also do so through franchise and licensing agreements. A franchise agreement is a contract whereby a company (known as the *franchisor*) grants permission (a license) to a foreign entity (known as a *franchisee*) to utilize the franchisor's name, trademark, or copyright in the operation of a business and associated sale of goods in a foreign state. In return for this license, the franchisee pays the franchisor, usually a percentage of the franchisee's gross or net sales. In a licensing agreement, the foreign company (known as the *licensor*) grants permission to a company in the targeted market (known as the *licensee*) to utilize the licensor's intellectual property, consisting of patents, trademarks, copyrights, or trade secrets. In return, the licensor receives royalty payments from the licensee, usually based on the licensee's gross or net sales.

Companies seeking a more permanent presence in a foreign jurisdiction have several options. A company may establish a *representative office* for limited purposes, such as market analysis or product promotion. An even more significant presence arises from a joint venture with a company in the host state, wherein the parties share profits and management responsibilities for a specific project. Companies may also establish a

---

[5] Vienna Convention on the Law of Treaties, May 23, 1969, art. 2, 1155 U.N.T.S. 331.
[6] U.S. Const., art. II, § 2, cl. 2.

foreign subsidiary, or affiliate. An affiliate is a business enterprise located in one state that is directly or indirectly owned and controlled by a company located in another state. The affiliate is usually established in conformity with the laws of the foreign state and is subject to that state's regulation.

Ethical Considerations

International businesspersons must take ethical considerations into account in the decision-making process. A company considering exporting its product for ultimate consumption by overseas consumers must resolve usage and safety issues. Foreign consumers may not fully understand risks associated with use of the product, or national safety standards may offer less protection than those applicable in the United States. Although tobacco products, for example, are subject to stringent regulation in the United States with respect to advertising, health warnings, and availability to minors, that is the exception rather than the global norm.

Ethical considerations are not limited to products. Companies must also carefully consider the location of their operations. Ethical considerations also arise from how a company does business overseas. For example, the Foreign Corrupt Practices Act (FCPA) prohibits U.S. companies from offering or paying bribes to foreign government officials, political parties, and candidates for office for the purpose of obtaining or retaining business.[7] The direct trigger for the FCPA was an investigation launched by the U.S. Securities and Exchange Commission in the 1970s that discovered 450 U.S. companies had engaged in bribery overseas totaling more than $400 million. For example, aircraft manufacturer Lockheed paid $12.6 million to Japanese officials and $10 million to Dutch, Italian, and German officials in its efforts to convince these officials to purchase Lockheed aircraft on behalf of their respective governments. The FCPA also requires that firms maintain records to fairly and accurately reflect transactions and the disposition of assets. Exhibit 6-1 summarizes recently settled cases involving alleged violations of the FCPA.

L03
What ethical considerations impact business in the international marketplace?

The General Agreement on Tariffs and Trade

There are two primary types of barriers to international trade. Tariffs are taxes levied on imported goods. They can be calculated as a percentage of the value of the imported good (*ad valorem tariff*), on the basis of the number or weight of the imported units or a flat per-unit charge (*specific tariff*), or as a combination of the two (*compound tariff*). A nontariff

L04
What is the General Agreement on Tariffs and Trade, and what are its important provisions?

---

[7] 15 U.S.C. §§ 78dd-1–78ff (2010).

COMPANY	STATE	CONTRACT	FINE (MILLIONS)
Baker Hughes	Kazakhstan	Oil and gas	$ 44.0
Kellogg, Brown & Root	Nigeria	Natural gas	579.0
Siemens	China, Russia, and 7 other states	Equipment, service, and construction	$1,600.0
Titan Corporation	Benin	Telecommunications	28.5
Willbros Group	Nigeria	Oil services	32.0

Exhibit 6-1
Summary of Recent Settlements of FCPA Cases

barrier is any impediment to trade other than tariffs, including quotas, embargoes, and indirect barriers. *Quotas* are limits on imported goods, usually imposed for national economic reasons or for the protection of domestic industry. An *embargo* is a ban on trade with a particular state or on the sale of specific products, usually on the basis of foreign policy or national security. *Indirect barriers* are laws, practices, customs, and traditions that limit or discourage the sale and purchase of imported goods.

The General Agreement on Tariffs and Trade (GATT) is a comprehensive multilateral trading system designed to achieve distortion-free international trade by minimizing tariffs and removing artificial barriers. GATT is a legacy of the Great Depression and World War II. Originally conceived as a temporary measure, it became effective on January 1, 1948, and included the United States as one of 23 signing countries. Since then it has undergone numerous changes as a result of eight different negotiating rounds. The most recently completed round is the Uruguay Round, which was completed in 1994 and took effect on January 1, 1995. Thus, the most recent version of GATT is known as *GATT 1994*. The most recent round of GATT, the Doha Development Agenda, has been under negotiation for several years, and negotiations for its completion are presently stalled.

The Uruguay Round established the World Trade Organization (WTO). The WTO facilitates international cooperation in opening markets and provides a forum for future trade negotiations and the settlement of international trade disputes. WTO membership presently consists of 157 states, thereby making the WTO the most comprehensive trading system in world history.

GATT established several general principles of trade law. Article I addresses the principle of *most-favored-nation* relations, a principle now known as normal trade relations. This principle requires that WTO member states treat like goods coming from other WTO member states on an equal basis. WTO member states are specifically prohibited from discriminating against like products on the basis of their country of origin. National treatment is set forth in Article III. It prohibits WTO member states from regulating, taxing, or otherwise treating imported products any differently from domestically produced products. Article XI prohibits quantitative restrictions that limit the importation of certain products on the basis of number of units, weight, or value, for national economic reasons, or for the protection of domestic industry.

Legal Principle: **As a general rule, GATT and the WTO prohibit discrimination against imported goods on the basis of their country of origin and also prevent quantitative restrictions on such imports.**

BUT WHAT IF . . .

What if the facts of the Case Opener were different?

Let's say, in the Case Opener, that Northam, the Canadian company, was trying to sell products to Chicago Prime, the American company. To import the products, Chicago Prime had to pay an extra .06 percent tax on the products. Also, Chicago Prime could purchase only 200 pounds of Northam's meat products. Which impediment is a tariff, and which is a nontariff barrier? What is the reasoning behind imposing such barriers?

Article VI relates to dumping and subsidies. Dumping is the practice wherein an exporter sells products in a foreign state for less than the price charged for the same or comparable goods in the exporter's home market. Article VI condemns dumping if it causes or threatens to cause material injury to an established industry. Government authorities usually make this determination by examining the volume of imports, their effect on prices, and their impact on the industry. After investigation, the remedy for dumping is the assessment of *antidumping duties,* tariffs equal to the difference between the export and domestic prices.

A subsidy is a government payment to a specific industry or enterprise. Subsidies can be direct transfers of funds, such as loans and grants; loan guarantees; tax credits; government procurement; and price supports. There are three basic types. *Actionable subsidies* are illegal under Article VI. They include subsidies payable to domestic manufacturers either on the basis of export performance or for the use of domestic, rather than imported, input in the manufacturing process. Actionable subsidies are remedied through the imposition of countervailing duties, special tariffs imposed on subsidized goods to offset the benefit of the illegal subsidy. *Nonactionable subsidies* are expenditures on research and development, aid to underdeveloped regions within a state, and aid to foster compliance with environmental standards. *Domestic subsidies* are generally not actionable unless they are not part of the government's legitimate responsibility of directing industrial growth and funding social programs and they cause material injury to other WTO member states.

Legal Principle: As a general rule, GATT and the WTO prohibit dumping and subsidies that are based on export performance or the use of domestic rather than imported input in the manufacturing process.

The Dispute Settlement Understanding allows recognized governments of WTO member states to bring an action alleging a violation. After an aggrieved state files a complaint, the states that are parties to the dispute consult with one another in an attempt to resolve the dispute. The states may also ask a trade expert to mediate. If these efforts are unsuccessful, the WTO Secretariat establishes a panel of three to five trade experts to hear oral arguments and review the written submissions of the parties. The panel then drafts and ultimately adopts a report determining the merits of the claims. Aggrieved states have the right to contest the panel's decision before the WTO's appellate body. The panel and the appellate body may only recommend that a state found in violation of its obligations cease and desist from such practices within a reasonable time. Failure to comply may lead to the imposition of sanctions, usually consisting of the suspension of concessions by the injured state. Such sanctions may impose only an equivalent burden on the noncomplying state and can be imposed only for as long as the trade barrier remains in place.

Regional Trade Agreements

There are three basic types of regional trade agreements: multilateral free trade agreements, customs unions, and bilateral free trade agreements. In a multilateral free trade agreement, three or more states agree to reduce and gradually eliminate tariffs and other trade barriers. The North American Free Trade Agreement (NAFTA) between the United States, Canada, and Mexico is a multilateral free trade agreement. In effect since January 1, 1994, NAFTA mirrors many of the provisions set forth in GATT but accords favorable treatment only to goods of "North American origin." NAFTA also reduces barriers to direct foreign investment and ensures the free flow of capital. Disputes between NAFTA members are resolved through a dispute resolution process coordinated by the Free Trade Commission. This process includes attempts to reach a negotiated settlement, the convocation of dispute resolution panels to hear evidence and determine the existence of a violation, and enforcement of orders through the authorization of retaliation in the event of noncompliance. Unlike the WTO system, NAFTA addresses environmental and workers' rights issues. Its three members pledge to cooperate in protecting the environment

L05

What are regional trade agreements?

and developing common environmental standards. They also recognize basic labor rights, including freedom of association, the right to engage in collective bargaining and strikes, prohibitions on forced labor and child labor, freedom from employment discrimination, the right to receive equal pay for work of equal value, and the right to minimum acceptable working conditions and occupational safety and health. The United States is also a party to the Central American Free Trade Agreement (CAFTA) with El Salvador, Guatemala, Nicaragua, Honduras, Costa Rica, and the Dominican Republic.

A *customs union* is a free trade area with the additional feature of a common external tariff on products originating outside the union. The European Union (EU) is a customs union. It is a loose association of states with a basis in international law formed for the purpose of forging closer ties among the peoples of Europe. The modern EU had its inception in three treaties between Belgium, France, Italy, Luxembourg, the Netherlands, and West Germany (now Germany) in the 1950s. These treaties integrated industrial sectors within the states, eradicated internal tariffs, created a common external tariff for goods originating in nonmember states, and strove to create a common market through the free movement of people, services, goods, and capital. Subsequent rounds of expansion added Austria, Denmark, Finland, Greece, Ireland, Portugal, Spain, Sweden, and the United Kingdom. Expansion in 2004 added 10 more states: Cyprus, the Czech Republic, Estonia, Hungary, Latvia, Lithuania, Malta, Poland, Slovakia, and Slovenia. This expansion created the largest regional trading bloc in the world, containing more than 500 million people. The most recent expansions in 2007 and 2013 added Bulgaria, Romania, and Croatia.

States may also enter into bilateral free trade agreements, which relate to trade between two states. The United States has several bilateral free trade agreements, including those with Australia, Bahrain, Chile, Colombia, Israel, Jordan, Korea, Morocco, Oman, Panama, Peru, and Singapore.

Comparative Law

LO6

What is comparative law?

What are the benefits of comparing the laws and legal systems of different states? First, we gain a better understanding of the general purpose of law by studying other legal systems and their goals. Second, we can better develop a critical viewpoint on our own legal system as just one of many alternatives. Third, the specific laws you will encounter will likely be different from U.S. laws. After thinking critically about alternative laws, you might decide your own state should adopt the other state's law or method of resolving a dispute.

What do comparative legal scholars actually study? What kinds of questions do they ask? Generally they ask two types: questions about the system and its procedures and questions about substantive law. Below we look at different legal systems and procedures. Then we consider substantive law by comparing contract law and employment law in a variety of states. The chapter concludes with a look at dispute resolution between private parties.

Legal Systems and Procedures

CIVIL LAW SYSTEMS

Many *civil law systems* are derived from Roman law. Other civil law systems were strongly influenced by the French Civil Code of 1804 and the German Civil Code of 1896. Other legal systems fashioned their own laws around a mixture of these. The codes generally covered areas of private law such as property, contracts, torts, and family law and tended to reflect preferences for the protection of private property, individual freedom, and freedom of contract.

Today, codes in civil law systems serve as the sole official source of law. Secondary sources include custom and general principles of law; precedent is not an important source of civil law. The civil law system is the most common legal system in the world. We find examples in most European nations, the People's Republic of China, and Japan. Louisiana, because of its French roots, has a "mixed" legal system.

Civil law systems assume a separation of powers, but it is unlike the U.S. system of checks and balances. In civil law systems, the legislative branch has ultimate authority. Remember, the ultimate source of law in a civil law system is the code. The judicial branch interprets the code and applies it to resolve disputes. However, the judicial branch cannot create its own law. Thus, the separation of powers refers to the limitations on the judicial branch and the superiority of the codes.

Judges in the civil law system typically assume the role early in their careers, following a training period and examination. At the highest judicial levels they are typically professors or experienced practitioners.

After the pleadings have entered the legal system, the evidence period—a series of meetings and hearings—begins. The judge is primarily responsible for developing evidence by asking witnesses questions and introducing legal theories. Neither the parties nor the judge is required to formally admit evidence to the court, and hearsay and opinion are acceptable.

Judges in the civil law system have primary responsibility for determining and applying the correct legal principles. However, the judge responsible for deciding the case may not be the same one who helped gather evidence. In fact, several judges might serve on a panel to decide the case.

COMMON LAW SYSTEMS

Common law systems originated in the English legal system. English common law began in 1066, when William the Conqueror assumed the English throne. The centralization of government that followed paved the way for a centralized court system.

In the common law system, the courts develop rules governing areas of law. In addition to relying on constitutions, legislation, and regulations, they are guided by precedent, or *stare decisis;* thus, if a higher court has created a precedent, a lower court is bound by that precedent. However, if a court cannot find a precedent to guide its reasoning, it may offer its own rule. Both the emphasis on precedent and the judge's ability to create rules are important characteristics of common law systems. Common law systems exist in Australia, India, the United Kingdom, and the United States.

Unlike civil law judges who are trained and tested, judges in the common law system are typically appointed. In the United States, some judges are elected.

Because common law judges have opportunities to make law through their decisions, they are relatively well known and the public perceives them as powerful. Some in the United States have been criticized for being "activists" and going beyond the bounds of their roles.

The common law system is an *adversarial system,* in which two opposing sides present their arguments before a neutral fact finder who determines which side has presented the most credible evidence or met its burden of proof. The adversarial method leads to procedures that differ from those in civil law systems. First, after the advocates enter pleadings in the common law system, there is a period in which discovery is conducted. Second, the judge typically does not become significantly involved in the case until trial. Third, in the common law system, the judge is not responsible for gathering any evidence; the parties themselves bear this responsibility. Fourth, common law systems often rely on juries as fact finders; civil law systems do not use juries. Fifth, as a consequence of the use of juries, common law systems have extensive rules governing admissibility of evidence.

OTHER LEGAL SYSTEMS

Although the civil and common law systems are predominant, other legal systems deserve mention. *Socialist legal systems,* such as exist in Cuba and North Korea, are based on the premise that the rights of society as a whole outweigh the rights of the individual. In such systems, law does not act as a limit on the exercise of government power. Traditionally, the state owns the means of production and property in a socialist legal system.

An *Islamic legal system* is based on the fundamental tenet that law is derived from and interpreted in harmony with *Shari'a* ("God's law") and the Koran. The preeminent concern is moral conduct, such as honoring agreements and acting in good faith. However, there are many interpretations of Islamic law, as evidenced by the differences between the legal systems in Iran, Pakistan, and Saudi Arabia and that practiced by the former Taliban regime in Afghanistan.

Substantive Law

COMPARATIVE CONTRACT LAW

L07

How does contract law differ among states?

The U.S. businessperson in the global marketplace should give careful thought to the question of what law may be applicable to the interpretation and enforcement of his or her contracts. Anyone who assumes all applicable laws are identical, or similar enough that differences do not matter, is likely to be unpleasantly surprised. This section reviews the sources of contract law in the international marketplace and notes some of the similarities and differences between these sources.

The Lex Mercatoria and National Contract Codes. One potential source of contract law is the *lex mercatoria,* literally the "law of merchants." This is the body of customs or trade usages merchants developed to facilitate business transactions. Its sources are public international law, uniform laws, general principles of contract law, rules of international organizations, custom and usage, standard form contracts, and arbitral decisions.

Another source of law applicable to international contracts is *national laws.* In the United States, these laws are embodied in the common law of contracts and, for contracts relating to the sale of goods, in the Uniform Commercial Code. Given the predominance of the civil law system, most nations' contract laws are set forth in codes. These codes have many similarities to U.S. law. For example, Section 2-615 of the Uniform Commercial Code excuses delays in the delivery of goods or nondelivery in the event performance has been rendered "impracticable by the occurrence of a contingency the nonoccurrence of which was a basic assumption on which the contract was made." In a similar fashion, the Civil Code of the Russian Federation excuses nonperformance if it is the result of an unanticipated "essential change of circumstances" that could not be avoided through the exercise of reasonable care. A similar excuse for nonperformance exists in the Unified Contract Law of the People's Republic of China and in the Principles of European Contract Law. Under China's national contract code, a nonperforming party is excused from liability if its inability to perform was the result of *force majeure* ("superior force"). Force majeure is a "situation which, on an objective view, is unforeseeable, unavoidable and is not able to be overcome." The Principles of European Contract Law excuse nonperformance if it is due to an impediment that is not "reasonably expected" and is beyond the control of the nonperforming party.

BUT WHAT IF . . .

What if the facts of the Case Opener were different?

Let's say that products from Northam were being shipped to Russia, China, and the United States. The plane was to make a stop in all three countries and had delivery contracts with all three stating the shipment would arrive no later than the following week. However, the plane encountered an unforeseeable tropical storm and was unable to deliver the products by the date stated in the contracts. According to clauses in the contract laws of the countries, how would China, Russia, and the United States respond?

Despite their similarities, the differences between U.S. law and national contract codes may be very pronounced. The Principles of European Contract Law provide that a contract is concluded only when the acceptance reaches the offeror. The principles further require that the parties give reasons for terminating contract negotiations. In the United States, parties do not owe one another a duty to negotiate in good faith and may terminate negotiations in bad faith without liability unless the other party relied on the likelihood of a final agreement. Furthermore, the European Principles do not require that the contract be in writing. Rather, a contract can be proved by any means. Contracts are subject to interpretation utilizing the totality of the circumstances surrounding the transaction, including statements made by the parties before entering into the contract.

Even in the areas where U.S. law and national contract codes converge, international businesspeople must be aware of differences. Despite having writing requirements like those in the United States, China's Unified Contract Law provides, in addition, that all written contracts must state the name and residence of each party, subject matter of the contract, quantity and quality of the subject matter, price, time, place and methods of contractual performance, liability for breach, and methods of dispute resolution.

Legal Principle: **Despite numerous similarities among contract laws, international businesspersons must be aware of significant differences between U.S. and other national contract laws.**

The Convention on the International Sale of Goods. The Convention on the International Sale of Goods (CISG) applies to the commercial sale of goods. A *commercial sale of goods* is the exchange of tangible personal property between merchants in return for consideration. A *merchant* is a person engaged in the transfer of goods in the ordinary course of business.

The CISG was adopted in 1980 and has been ratified by the majority of states in the developed world, including Australia, Canada, China, Korea, Mexico, Russia, most nations of Western Europe, and the United States, where it became effective in 1988. Notable states that have not adopted the CISG include Brazil, India, Pakistan, Saudi Arabia, and the United Kingdom.

Two sets of laws govern the sale of goods in the United States, the CISG and the Uniform Commercial Code (UCC). The UCC applies when both parties to the sales transaction are residents of the United States. The CISG is applicable when one party is a U.S. resident and the other is a resident of a jurisdiction that has ratified the CISG. Nevertheless, the parties are always free to opt out of the CISG and select another law to apply to their transaction. In the absence of such a selection, the CISG applies to the sale of goods between merchants residing in different states that have ratified the CISG. The CISG also applies if national conflict-of-law rules direct the court or arbitral body to apply the law of a state that has ratified the CISG. Finally, the CISG may serve as evidence of trade usage and customs. National contract law applies in areas not covered by the CISG, such as services, real estate, and intellectual property.

How do U.S. businesspeople determine which set of rules they want to apply to their international contracts? There are numerous similarities between the UCC and CISG. For example, both recognize express warranties and implied warranties of merchantability and fitness for a particular purpose arising from the sale of goods.[8] Both the UCC and the CISG limit damages to those that were foreseeable at the time of the formation of the contract. Furthermore, only damages that can be proved with some degree of certainty may be awarded. The nonbreaching party has a duty to mitigate damages, and damage awards can be reduced to the extent that the loss could have been prevented or minimized through mitigation.

However, the differences between the UCC and CISG are substantial in many areas. Exhibit 6-2 summarizes some of these differences.

COMPARATIVE EMPLOYMENT LAW

L08

How does employment law differ among states?

The employment relationship in the United States is governed by the *employment-at-will standard.* This standard means either the employer or the employee may terminate the employment relationship at any time. Furthermore, both parties are free to determine the conditions of employment. If an express employment agreement exists, however, and either party breaks it, the other can sue for breach of contract.

Although the employment-at-will doctrine remains predominant in the United States, the nature of the employment relationship has changed. Federal, state, and local government restrictions protect workers in the areas of minimum wages, unemployment and workers' compensation, occupational health and safety, employment discrimination, and termination. These restrictions vary significantly when a U.S. firm seeks to hire employees outside the United States where the employment-at-will standard does not apply.

This section discusses two such differences, minimum-wage laws and termination. We conclude with a look at the effect of international labor standards on the employment relationship.

Exhibit 6-2

Some Differences between the UCC and the CISG

RULE OR DOCTRINE	UCC PROVISION	CISG PROVISION
Mailbox rule	Acceptance is generally effective upon mailing.	Acceptance is generally effective only upon receipt.
Statute of frauds	Requires that contracts for the sale of goods in excess of $500 be in writing.	No required writing.
Parol evidence rule	Prevents introduction of preliminary negotiations to alter an unambiguous written contract.	No parol evidence rule.
Notice of nonconforming goods	Specific description of nonconformity is generally not required.	Specific description of nonconformity is required.
Additional time to perform contract	None unless specified in contract.	*Nachfrist*—allows additional time for performance of a contract upon notice to the other party.

[8] Compare UCC §§ 2-313–316 with CISG art. 35.

National Regulation of the Employment Relationship

Minimum-Wage Laws. Under the Fair Labor Standards Act (FLSA), all U.S. employers are required to pay a minimum wage to employees.[9] The current federal minimum wage under the act is $7.25 per hour, as of summer 2013. States are free to adopt minimum-wage laws in excess of the federal rate, and many have done so.[10]

The U.S. businessperson seeking to hire employees overseas will find a wide variety of frequently changing laws relating to the payment of minimum wages. Some states, such as the People's Republic of China, have no national minimum-wage laws. Minimum wages are established by provincial and municipal government officials. A similar method of regulation exists in Canada, which also lacks a national minimum-wage law. Minimum wages are established individually by the provinces. Thus, the hourly minimum wage is C$11 (Canadian dollars) in Nunavut, C$10.25 in Ontario, but only C$9.75 in Alberta. In other states that lack national minimum-wage laws, such as Denmark, Finland, Germany, Italy, and Sweden, industrial collective agreements establish minimum wages.

Some states with minimum wages vary them depending on the age of the worker. In Ireland, employers are required to pay no less than €8.65 (euros) per hour. However, employers are permitted to reduce this amount by 30 percent for employees under the age of 18. A 20 percent reduction is permitted for employees over the age of 18 but in their first year of employment since turning 18. The permitted reduction is 10 percent for workers in their second year of employment since turning 18.

Other states calculate minimum wages on the basis of weekly earnings. Australia requires that employers pay at least A$606.40 (Australian dollars) per week. States may also require the payment of minimum wages calculated on the basis of monthly earnings. In the Russian Federation, national law establishes the minimum wage as R4,330 (rubles) per month. Some states have a combination of minimum-wage requirements. For example, in January 2012, Taiwan adopted a law raising the minimum monthly wage to NT$18,780 (new Taiwan dollars) and the minimum hourly wage to NT$103. Other states use different combinations. For example, Greece has a monthly minimum wage of €683.76, but this amount may vary depending on whether the worker is employed in a white- or blue-collar position, the length of the worker's service, and his or her marital status.

Employment Termination Laws. The employment-at-will doctrine has been modified over the years by federal and state laws prohibiting the termination of employment on the basis of certain statuses such as race, gender, age, and disability.[11] Termination for whistle-blowing is also prohibited.[12] Finally, the ability to terminate employment may be impacted by statements contained within employment manuals.[13]

The employment-at-will doctrine has been rejected in many states throughout the world. In some states, employment is viewed as a property right or a lifetime entitlement. These jurisdictions sharply restrict the ability of the employer to terminate the relationship. The German Termination Protection Act of 2004 provides that, in the absence of detrimental behavior, employees of "works" with more than 10 employees can be terminated

---

[9] 29 U.S.C. § 206(a)(1) (2010).

[10] The states are Alaska, Arizona, California, Colorado, Connecticut, Florida, Illinois, Maine, Massachusetts, Michigan, Missouri, Montana, Nevada, New Mexico, Ohio, Oregon, Rhode Island, Vermont, and Washington. Washington currently has the highest minimum wage in the United States, $9.19 per hour.

[11] 29 U.S.C. § 623(a)(1) (2010) (age discrimination); 42 U.S.C. § 2000e-2(a)(1) (2010) (race, national origin, gender, and religion); Americans with Disabilities Act of 1990, Pub. L. No. 101-336, 104 Stat. 327.

[12] Whistleblower Protection Act of 1989, Pub. L. No. 101-12, 103 Stat. 16.

[13] See, e.g., *Litton v. Maverick Paper Co.*, 354 F. Supp. 2d 1209 (D. Kan. 2005); *Continental Airlines, Inc. v. Keenan*, 731 P.2d 708 (Colo. 1987); *Gaudio v. Griffin Health Servs. Corp.*, 733 A.2d 197 (Conn. 1999); *O'Brien v. New England Tel. & Tel. Co.*, 664 N.E.2d 843 (Mass. 1996); *Bobbitt v. The Orchard, Ltd.*, 603 So. 2d 356 (Miss. 1992); *Wuchte v. McNeil*, 505 S.E.2d 142 (N.C. App. 1998); *Thompson v. St. Regis Paper Co.*, 685 P.2d 1081 (Wash. 1984).

for operational reasons only if the termination is "socially justified." Social justification depends on the worker's age, years of service, disability, and number of dependents. The employer must provide notice of four weeks to seven months, depending on the employee's years of service. Termination also must be coordinated with the appropriate works councils. Employers must pay severance equal to one-half month's gross salary for every year of service.

Termination laws are similar in other jurisdictions. France's Labor Code states that termination of employment by companies with more than 20 employees on economic grounds other than *faute grave* (serious fault or gross negligence on the part of the employee) or elimination or transformation of the job requires written notice in French, a pretermination meeting with the employee, consultation with the appropriate works committee, and a required waiting period. Redundancies (layoffs for economic reasons) require the existence of severe economic constraints and notice to the government. China's Labor Contract Law recognizes three separate grounds for termination. First, the occurrence of certain events such as expiration of the term, death of the employee, or bankruptcy of the employer may cause termination of the employment agreement. Second, the employee may terminate the agreement upon 30 days' written notice unless the termination occurs under "extreme circumstances." Third, the employer may terminate the agreement for the employee's failure to satisfy the conditions of employment during any probationary period, material breach of contract, serious dereliction of duty, corruption, conflict of interest, criminal activity, or inability to perform the work due to a nonwork-related injury or illness or for a major change in the employer's circumstances (upon 30 days' notice or payment of one month's wages). Mass layoffs are defined as termination of 20 or more employees or 10 percent of the total number of employees. Such layoffs are only permitted in the event of bankruptcy, "serious difficulties" in production or operations, changes that require layoffs (such as technological innovation), or "major change in objective economic circumstances." The employer must explain the circumstances to affected labor unions and workers no less than 30 days in advance. Such employers may also be required to retain "priority persons" such as employees with long fixed-term or open-ended contracts and those who are the only employed members of a family containing elderly persons or minors.

International Labor Standards.   Employers must ensure that their employment practices conform to international labor standards. This concern is particularly acute in the developing world, where national labor protections are lax or nonexistent, enforcement attitudes vary widely, and the temptation to exploit local populations is significant.

International labor standards arise from general human rights instruments that apply across a broad spectrum of areas and from specialized documents that focus exclusively on labor. The Universal Declaration of Human Rights of 1948, often referred to as the basis for modern human rights law, prohibits slavery and grants everyone the right to free choice of employment, just and favorable conditions of work, reasonable limitation of working hours, and compensation adequate to provide for the worker's health and that of his or her family.[14] The International Covenant on Economic, Social and Cultural Rights also recognizes these rights, as well as fair wages and safe and healthy working conditions.[15]

Many of the specialized instruments that focus exclusively on labor rights are based on norms developed by the International Labor Organization (ILO). Established in 1919 by the Treaty of Versailles, the ILO operates under the principle that "labor should not

---

[14] Universal Declaration of Human Rights, G.A. Res. 217A (III), U.N. GAOR, 3d Sess., at 71, arts. 4, 23–25, U.N. Doc. A/810 (1948).

[15] International Covenant on Economic, Social and Cultural Rights, G.A. Res. 2200A (XXI), 21 U.N. GAOR, 21st Sess., Supp. No. 16, arts. 6–7, 11, U.N. Doc. A/6316 (1966).

PERSONAL JURISDICTION AND THE INTERNET

Pebble Beach Company v. Caddy
453 F.3d 1151 (9th Cir. 2006)

Pebble Beach Company is a well-known golf course and resort located in Monterey County, California. The golf resort has used "Pebble Beach" as its trade name since 1956. Caddy ran a three-room bed and breakfast, restaurant, and bar located on a cliff overlooking the pebbly beaches of England's south shore, in a town called Barton-on-Sea. The name of Caddy's operation was "Pebble Beach." Caddy advertised his services, which did not include a golf course, at his website, www.pebblebeach-uk.com. Caddy's website included information about the accommodations, lodging rates, a menu, and a wine list. The website did not have a reservation system and did not allow potential guests to book rooms or pay for services online. Pebble Beach sued Caddy for infringement and dilution of its "Pebble Beach" trademark in the U.S. District Court for the Central District of California. Caddy moved to dismiss the complaint for lack of personal jurisdiction. The district court granted Caddy's motion, and Pebble Beach appealed to the U.S. Court of Appeals for the Ninth Circuit.

The court of appeals affirmed the dismissal of the lawsuit for lack of personal jurisdiction. Pebble Beach failed to identify any conduct by Caddy that took place in California or in the United States that could be considered purposeful availment. All of Caddy's actions identified by Pebble Beach took place in the United Kingdom. Alternatively, Pebble Beach claimed that Caddy expressly aimed conduct at California through his website and domain name. The court rejected this contention as the website was passive in nature. The court held that an Internet domain name and passive website alone are not enough to subject a party to jurisdiction. The fact that the name "Pebble Beach" was a famous mark known worldwide was of little practical consequence to the determination of whether an action was directed at a particular forum via the Internet. Such aiming also could not be supported by the fact that Caddy's business was located in an area frequented by Americans and that Americans often were guests at the establishment. Although vacationing Americans may have stopped at Caddy's business, there was no evidence that this patronage was related to Caddy's choice of a domain name or the posting of a passive website.

be regarded merely as a commodity or article of commerce." In 1998, the ILO issued its Declaration on Fundamental Principles and Rights at Work. This statement enumerated a number of "core labor standards," including freedom of association, the right to engage in collective bargaining, and the elimination of all forms of forced or compulsory labor, child labor, and employment discrimination.[16] Many of the ILO's instruments relate to specific labor practices. For example, the Convention Concerning Forced or Compulsory Labor and the Abolition of Forced Labor Convention obligate states to prohibit the utilization of forced or compulsory labor, including labor for the benefit of private individuals, companies, or associations.[17]

Dispute Settlement in an International Context

Disputing parties to international transactions can resolve their differences in two ways. Assuming settlement negotiations, mediation, conciliation, or some other form of nonadversarial dispute resolution fails, they can resort to litigation or arbitration. However, each of these methods has disadvantages of which an international businessperson must be aware.

L09

How are disputes settled in the international marketplace?

LITIGATION

The first step in litigation is determining whether the selected court has jurisdiction, specifically, the power to hear the case and resolve the dispute. Judgments entered by a court without jurisdiction are null and void. There are two primary types of jurisdiction. A court must possess subject-matter jurisdiction, which is power over the type of case presented to it. In the United States, subject-matter jurisdiction is based on the type of case (such as civil, criminal, probate, or domestic relations) or the amount of money at issue.

[16] ILO, Declaration on Fundamental Principles and Rights at Work, art. 2(a–d) (1998).

[17] Abolition of Forced Labor Convention (ILO No. 105), art. 1, 320 U.N.T.S. 291 (1957); Convention Concerning Forced or Compulsory Labor (ILO No. 29), arts. 1–2, 4–5, 39 U.N.T.S. 55 (1930).

In contrast, **personal jurisdiction** is the power of the court over the persons appearing before it. **General personal jurisdiction** permits adjudication of any claims against a defendant regardless of whether the claim has anything to do with the forum, or location, where the claim is filed. To obtain general personal jurisdiction, the defendant must maintain some presence in the forum. For a court to exercise **specific personal jurisdiction**, the defendant must have purposefully availed itself of the protections of the forum, and the selected forum must be reasonable.[18] Merely placing a product into the stream of commerce is not sufficient unless the product was designed specifically for the forum or the defendant provided regular advice to customers or maintained a distributor in the forum.

Case 6-1 demonstrates the application of these jurisdictional rules.

[18] *Asahi Metal Indus. v. Superior Court,* 480 U.S. 102, 109, 113 (1987).

CASE 6-1   GOODYEAR DUNLOP TIRES OPERATIONS, S.A. v. BROWN
UNITED STATES SUPREME COURT
131 S. CT. 2846 (2011)

Two North Carolina teenagers were fatally injured when the bus upon which they were riding overturned on a roadway outside Paris, France. The parents of the decedents brought a lawsuit in North Carolina state court against Goodyear Tire and Rubber Company and its subsidiaries based in Luxembourg, Turkey, and France, alleging that the accident was caused by negligent design and production of the bus tires. The plaintiffs alleged that the subsidiaries placed their tires into the stream of commerce and some of these tires ended up in North Carolina. The subsidiaries alleged that there was no personal jurisdiction as the mere placement of a product in the stream of commerce is an insufficient basis for the assertion of personal jurisdiction especially when the accident had no connection with the forum other than the residence of the decedents. Additionally, the mere placement of tires into the stream of commerce did not constitute a continuous and systematic presence in North Carolina as to subject the subsidiaries to personal jurisdiction. The North Carolina state courts disagreed and exercised personal jurisdiction over the subsidiaries. The subsidiaries appealed to the U.S. Supreme Court.

ASSOCIATE JUSTICE GINSBURG: This case concerns the jurisdiction of state courts over corporations organized and operating abroad. We address, in particular, this question: Are foreign subsidiaries of a United States parent corporation amenable to suit in state court on claims unrelated to any activity of the subsidiaries in the forum State?

A state court's assertion of jurisdiction exposes defendants to the State's coercive power, and is therefore subject to review for compatibility with the Fourteenth Amendment's Due Process Clause. *International Shoe Co.* v. *Washington,* 326 U.S. 310, 316 (1945). Opinions in the wake of the pathmarking *International Shoe* decision have differentiated between general or all-purpose jurisdiction, and specific or case-linked jurisdiction. *Helicopteros Nacionales de Colombia, S. A.* v. *Hall,* 466 U.S. 408 (1984).

A court may assert general jurisdiction over foreign (sister-state or foreign-country) corporations to hear any and all claims against them when their affiliations with the State are so "continuous and systematic" as to render them essentially at home in the forum State. See *International Shoe,* 326 U.S., at 317. Specific jurisdiction, on the other hand, depends on an "affiliatio[n] between the forum and the underlying controversy," principally, activity or an occurrence that takes place in the forum State and is therefore subject to the State's regulation. In contrast to general, all-purpose jurisdiction, specific jurisdiction is confined to adjudication of issues deriving from, or connected with, the very controversy that establishes jurisdiction.

We granted certiorari to decide whether the general jurisdiction the North Carolina courts asserted over petitioners is consistent with the Due Process Clause of the Fourteenth Amendment.

The Due Process Clause of the Fourteenth Amendment sets the outer boundaries of a state tribunal's authority to proceed against a defendant. The canonical opinion in this area remains *International Shoe* in which we held that a State may authorize its courts to exercise personal jurisdiction over an out-of-state defendant if the defendant has "certain minimum contacts with [the State] such that the maintenance of the suit does not offend traditional notions of fair play and substantial justice." *Id.* at 316.

Endeavoring to give specific content to the "fair play and substantial justice" concept, the Court in *International Shoe* classified cases involving out-of-state corporate defendants. First, as in *International Shoe* itself, jurisdiction

[continued]

unquestionably could be asserted where the corporation's in-state activity is "continuous and systematic" and *that activity gave rise to the episode-in-suit.* Further, the Court observed, the commission of certain "single or occasional acts" in a State may be sufficient to render a corporation answerable in that State with respect to those acts, though not with respect to matters unrelated to the forum connections. The heading courts today use to encompass these two *International Shoe* categories is "specific jurisdiction." Adjudicatory authority is "specific" when the suit arises out of or relates to the defendant's contacts with the forum.

International Shoe distinguished from cases that fit within the "specific jurisdiction" categories, "instances in which the continuous corporate operations within a state [are] so substantial and of such a nature as to justify suit against it on causes of action arising from dealings entirely distinct from those activities." Adjudicatory authority so grounded is today called "general jurisdiction." For an individual, the paradigm forum for the exercise of general jurisdiction is the individual's domicile; for a corporation, it is an equivalent place, one in which the corporation is fairly regarded as at home.

In only two decisions postdating *International Shoe* has this Court considered whether an out-of-state corporate defendant's in-state contacts were sufficiently "continuous and systematic" to justify the exercise of general jurisdiction over claims unrelated to those contacts: *Perkins* v. *Benguet Consol. Mining Co.,* 342 U.S. 437 (1952) (general jurisdiction appropriately exercised over Philippine corporation sued in Ohio, where the company's affairs were overseen during World War II); and *Helicopteros,* 466 U.S. 408 (helicopter owned by Colombian corporation crashed in Peru; survivors of U.S. citizens who died in the crash, the Court held, could not maintain wrongful-death actions against the Colombian corporation in Texas, for the corporation's helicopter purchases and purchase-linked activity in Texas were insufficient to subject it to Texas court's general jurisdiction).

To justify the exercise of general jurisdiction over petitioners, the North Carolina courts relied on the petitioners'

placement of their tires in the "stream of commerce." The stream-of-commerce metaphor has been invoked frequently in lower court decisions permitting "jurisdiction in products liability cases in which the product has traveled through an extensive chain of distribution before reaching the ultimate consumer." Typically, in such cases, a nonresident defendant, acting *outside* the forum, places in the stream of commerce a product that ultimately causes harm *inside* the forum.

The North Carolina court's stream-of-commerce analysis elided the essential difference between case-specific and all-purpose (general) jurisdiction. Flow of a manufacturer's products into the forum, we have explained, may bolster an affiliation germane to *specific* jurisdiction. But ties serving to bolster the exercise of specific jurisdiction do not warrant a determination that, based on those ties, the forum has *general* jurisdiction over a defendant.

Helicopteros concluded that "mere purchases [made in the forum State], even if occurring at regular intervals, are not enough to warrant a State's assertion of [general] jurisdiction over a nonresident corporation in a cause of action not related to those purchase transactions." *Id.* at 418. We see no reason to differentiate from the ties to Texas held insufficient in *Helicopteros,* the sales of petitioners' tires sporadically made in North Carolina through intermediaries. Under the sprawling view of general jurisdiction urged by respondents and embraced by the North Carolina Court of Appeals, any substantial manufacturer or seller of goods would be amenable to suit, on any claim for relief, wherever its products are distributed.

Measured against *Helicopteros* and *Perkins,* North Carolina is not a forum in which it would be permissible to subject petitioners to general jurisdiction. Petitioners are in no sense at home in North Carolina. Their attenuated connections to the State fall far short of "the continuous and systematic general business contacts" necessary to empower North Carolina to entertain suit against them on claims unrelated to anything that connects them to the State.

For the reasons stated, the judgment of the North Carolina Court of Appeals is reversed.

CRITICAL THINKING

What were the factual and legal grounds for the Court's refusal to find personal jurisdiction in this case? Was the Court correct in its conclusion? Should it be foreseeable to any modern multinational corporation engaged in manufacturing that its products may end up anywhere in the world and thus become the subject matter of litigation? What policy reasons may underlie the Court's decision in this case?

ETHICAL DECISION MAKING

The result in this case requires the plaintiffs to proceed in a court outside the United States with respect to claims against Goodyear Dunlop's foreign subsidiaries despite the fact that some of their tires entered the U.S. marketplace and, in particular, the North Carolina marketplace. Does this result strike you as fair and reasonable? Should non-U.S. companies that place their goods into the U.S. stream of commerce be responsible under all circumstances when those products cause harm in the United States?

The reasonableness of the selected forum is determined by balancing the burden on the defendant, the interest of the forum in resolving the dispute, the plaintiff's interest in obtaining relief in the forum, and foreign policy concerns. For example, the forum may be unreasonable if the majority of the evidence and witnesses are located outside the forum or the case involves an occurrence that is of little relevance to the jurors that might decide the case. The Case Nugget on page 137 addresses the issue of asserting personal jurisdiction over a foreign defendant on the basis of the defendant's presence in the jurisdiction through the Internet.

Legal Principle: **For a U.S. court judgment to be fully enforceable, the court must possess power over the type of case (subject-matter jurisdiction) and the people appearing before it (personal jurisdiction), which may be obtained by the defendant's presence in the forum (general personal jurisdiction) or purposeful availment of the protection of the forum (specific personal jurisdiction).**

There are numerous defenses available to the exercise of jurisdiction. The Foreign Sovereign Immunities Act is a federal statute that denies subject-matter jurisdiction and grants immunity from civil actions to foreign states and their political subdivisions, agencies, and instrumentalities.[19] One important exception to foreign sovereign immunity is a situation in which the immune entity engages in a commercial activity. A commercial activity is defined as a regular course of commercial conduct or a particular commercial transaction with a U.S. nexus.

There are also several instances when a court may refuse to exercise existing jurisdiction. *The act of state doctrine* has been defined as "a nonjurisdictional, prudential doctrine based on the notion that the courts of one country will not sit in judgment on the acts of the government of another state done within its own territory."[20] The *political question doctrine* may be invoked when there has been a demonstrable constitutional commitment of an issue to a coordinate political department; there is a lack of judicially discoverable and manageable standards; it is impossible to decide the case without resolving an issue appropriate for nonjudicial discretion or without demonstrating lack of respect for coordinate branches of government; there is an unusual need for unquestioning adherence to a political decision already made; and there is the potential of embarrassment from multiple pronouncements by various departments on one question.[21] *Comity* has been defined as the "recognition which one nation allows within its territory to the legislative, executive or judicial acts of another nation."[22]

Forum non conveniens is a doctrine that permits courts to decline to exercise jurisdiction where there is a more convenient forum to hear the case.[23] This determination is based on judicial analysis of the adequacy of the alternative forum and the balance of private- and public-interest factors. Public-interest factors include court congestion, the unfairness of imposing jury duty on a community with no relation to the litigation, the interest of the community in having localized controversies decided at home, and the avoidance of problems associated with conflict of laws and the application of foreign law. Private-interest factors include ease of access to evidence, the cost for witnesses to attend trial, and the availability of compulsory process.

Case 6-2 demonstrates the application of the doctrine of forum non conveniens in the context of product liability litigation.

---

[19] 28 U.S.C. §§ 1602–1611 (2010).

[20] *Underhill v. Hernandez*, 168 U.S. 250, 252 (1897).

[21] *Baker v. Carr*, 369 U.S. 186, 217 (1962).

[22] *Hilton v. Guyot*, 159 U.S. 113, 164 (1895).

[23] *Piper Aircraft Co. v. Reyno*, 454 U.S. 235, 254 n.22 (1981); and *Gulf Oil Corp. v. Gilbert*, 330 U.S. 501, 507 (1947).

GONZALES v. CHRYSLER CORP.
U.S. COURT OF APPEALS FOR THE FIFTH CIRCUIT

In 1995, while in Houston, the plaintiff, Jorge Luis Machuca Gonzalez ("Gonzalez") saw several magazine and television advertisements for the Chrysler LHS. The advertisements sparked his interest, and Gonzalez visited Houston car dealerships. Convinced by these visits that the Chrysler LHS was a high-quality and safe car, Gonzalez purchased a Chrysler LHS upon returning to Mexico.

On May 21, 1996, Gonzalez's wife was involved in a collision with another moving vehicle while driving the Chrysler LHS in Atizapan de Zaragoza, Mexico. The accident triggered the passenger-side air bag. The force of the air bag's deployment instantaneously killed Gonzalez's three-year-old son, Pablo.

CIRCUIT JUDGE E. GRADY JOLLY: Gonzalez brought suit in Texas district court against (1) Chrysler, as the manufacturer of the automobile; (2) TRW, Inc. and TRW Vehicle Safety Systems, Inc., as the designers of the front sensor for the air bag; and (3) Morton International Inc., as designer of the air bag module. Gonzalez asserted claims based on products liability, negligence, gross negligence, and breach of warranty. Texas, however, has a tenuous connection to the underlying dispute. Neither the car nor the air bag module was designed or manufactured in Texas. The accident took place in Mexico, involved Mexican citizens, and only Mexican citizens witnessed the accident. Moreover, Gonzalez purchased the Chrysler LHS in Mexico (although he shopped for the car in Houston, Texas). Because of these factors, the district court granted the defendants' motions for dismissal on the ground of forum non conveniens. Gonzalez now appeals.

The primary question we address today involves the threshold inquiry in the forum non conveniens analysis: Whether the limitation imposed by Mexican law on the award of damages renders Mexico an inadequate alternative forum for resolving a tort suit brought by a Mexican citizen against a United States manufacturer.

The forum non conveniens inquiry consists of four considerations. First, the district court must assess whether an alternative forum is available. An alternative forum is available if the entire case and all parties can come within the jurisdiction of that forum. Second, the district court must decide if the alternative forum is adequate. An alternative forum is adequate if the parties will not be deprived of all remedies or treated unfairly, even though they may not enjoy the same benefits as they might receive in an American court. If the district court decides that an alternative forum is both available and adequate, it next must weigh various private interest factors. If consideration of these private interest factors counsels against dismissal, the district court moves to the fourth consideration in the analysis. At this stage, the district court must weigh numerous public interest factors. If these factors weigh in the moving party's favor, the district court may dismiss the case.

The heart of this appeal is whether the alternative forum, Mexico, is adequate.

The jurisprudential root of the adequacy requirement is the Supreme Court's decision in *Piper Aircraft Co. v. Reyno*, 454 U.S. 235 (1981). The dispute in *Piper Aircraft* arose after several Scottish citizens were killed in a plane crash in Scotland. A representative for the decedents filed a wrongful death suit against two American aircraft manufacturers. The Court noted that the plaintiff filed suit in the United States because U.S. laws regarding liability, capacity to sue, and damages are more favorable to her position than are those of Scotland. The Court further noted that Scottish law does not recognize strict liability in tort. The Court held that although the relatives of the decedent may not be able to rely on a strict liability theory, and although their potential damage award may be smaller, there is no danger that they will be deprived of any remedy or treated unfairly in Scotland. Thus, the Court held that Scotland provided an adequate alternative forum for resolving the dispute, even though its forum provided a significantly lesser remedy.

Gonzalez contends that a Mexican forum would provide a clearly unsatisfactory remedy because (1) Mexican tort law does not provide for a strict liability theory of recovery for the manufacture or design of an unreasonably dangerous product and (2) Mexican law caps the maximum award for the loss of a child's life at approximately $2,500 (730 days' worth of wages at the Mexican minimum wage rate). Thus, according to Gonzalez, Mexico provides an inadequate alternative forum for this dispute.

Gonzalez's first contention may be quickly dismissed based on the explicit principle stated in *Piper Aircraft*. There is no basis to distinguish the absence of a strict products liability cause of action under Mexican law from that of Scotland. Accordingly, we hold that the failure of Mexican law to allow for strict liability on the facts of this case does not render Mexico an inadequate forum.

Gonzalez's second contention—that the damage cap renders the remedy available in a Mexican forum "clearly unsatisfactory"—is slightly more problematic. We start from basic principles of comity. Mexico, as a sovereign nation, has made a deliberate choice in providing a specific remedy for this tort cause of action. In making this policy choice, the Mexican government has resolved a trade-off among the competing objectives and costs of tort law, involving interests of victims, of consumers, of manufacturers, and of various other economic and cultural values. In

[continued]

resolving this trade-off, the Mexican people, through their duly-elected lawmakers, have decided to limit tort damages with respect to a child's death. It would be inappropriate—even patronizing—for us to denounce this legitimate policy choice by holding that Mexico provides an inadequate forum for Mexican tort victims. In short, we see no warrant for us, a United States court, to replace the policy preference of the Mexican government with our own view of what is a good policy for the citizens of Mexico.

Having concluded that Mexico provides an adequate forum, we now consider whether the private and public interest factors nonetheless weigh in favor of maintaining this suit in Texas. The district court found that almost all of the private and public interest factors pointed away from Texas and toward Mexico as the appropriate forum. It is clear to us that this finding does not represent an abuse of discretion. After all, the tort victim was a Mexican citizen, the driver of the Chrysler LHS (Gonzalez's wife) is a Mexican citizen, and the plaintiff is a Mexican citizen. The accident took place in Mexico. Gonzalez purchased the car in Mexico. Neither the car nor the air bag was designed or manufactured in Texas. In short, there are no public or private interest factors that would suggest that Texas is the appropriate forum for the trial of this case.

For the foregoing reasons, the district court's dismissal of this case on the ground of forum non conveniens is affirmed.

CRITICAL THINKING

Given the cap on damages in Mexican law for the loss of a child and the cost of litigation, is it likely that Gonzales will file a lawsuit in Mexico? Does Mexico offer an inadequate forum because it does not make economic sense for Gonzalez to file his lawsuit in Mexico? Why or why not?

ETHICAL DECISION MAKING

Would the universalization principle or the Golden Rule provide any strong argument against the ruling made by Judge Jolly?

Businesses can minimize some of the uncertainties associated with personal jurisdiction by carefully selecting the forum and inserting choice-of-law clauses in international agreements. A forum selection agreement allows the parties to choose where disputes between them will be resolved. In the United States, such clauses are presumptively valid and will be disregarded only if they are unreasonable.[24] Grounds for ignoring a forum selection clause include fraud or coercion in its procurement, unconscionability, lack of notice, or serious inconvenience posed by the selected forum. A choice-of-law clause lets the parties to a contract choose the law of a certain state to apply to the interpretation of the contract or in the event of a dispute. Choice-of-law clauses are generally enforceable as long as there is a reasonable relation between the transaction and the law of the selected jurisdiction.

Legal Principle: **The parties to an international contract may select the forum in which disputes are to be resolved and the applicable law within the terms of their agreement.**

The plaintiff must also select the proper venue for the litigation. Proper venue is the court with subject-matter and personal jurisdiction that is the most appropriate geographic location for the resolution of the dispute. With respect to federal litigation in the United States, the Alien Venue Statute provides that aliens may be sued in any federal judicial district but makes an exception for suits against foreign sovereigns, which may be initiated only in the U.S. District Court for the District of Columbia.[25]

There are other problems with litigation as a method of international dispute resolution. Methods of discovery used in civil litigation in the United States may be ineffective if used to obtain evidence located abroad. Although the Hague Evidence Convention, a

---

[24] *M/S Bremen v. Zapata Off-Shore Co.*, 407 U.S. 1, 15 (1972).

[25] 28 U.S.C. § 1391(d) (2010).

multilateral convention establishing procedures for transnational discovery between private persons in different states, attempts to resolve such problems, it has been ratified by only 47 states. Furthermore, judgments obtained in foreign courts may not be enforceable in other states. For example, in the United States, foreign judgments are not entitled to full faith and credit but are only evidence of the justice of the plaintiff's claims.[26] U.S. courts may ignore the results of foreign proceedings under numerous circumstances, including lack of fairness, jurisdiction, or timely notice; fraud; and inconsistency with U.S. public policy. Foreign states take similar views with respect to U.S. judgments. Courts in such states may refuse to enforce U.S. civil judgments deemed to be criminal or penal in nature (such as taxes and fines) and awards of punitive damages.

ARBITRATION

Arbitration is a type of alternative dispute resolution by private, nonofficial persons selected in a manner provided by law or the agreement of the parties. The New York Convention,[27] an international agreement governing the arbitration of private international disputes, has been ratified by 148 states to date, including the United States. The convention applies when an award is made and one party seeks enforcement in the territories of the contracting states. It requires that each state recognize written arbitration agreements and recognize arbitral awards as enforceable in its national courts.

Arbitration as a means of dispute resolution has many advantages over litigation. It is cheaper and faster, and it is a nonpublic procedure. Arbitration also permits the parties to select the forum and the presiding party. Concerns regarding the enforceability of a judicial decision entered in one state but sought to be enforced in another state are also minimized. However, the ability of parties in arbitration to conduct discovery of the opposing party's case may be limited, as well as the ability to appeal an adverse decision. Furthermore, arbitrators' decisions may not serve as precedent in future cases. Any company contemplating the use of arbitration as a means of dispute resolution must carefully balance these disadvantages with the benefits of the arbitral process.

[26] Restatement (Third) of the Foreign Relations Law of the United States, § 481 (1987).

[27] Convention on the Recognition and Enforcement of Foreign Arbitral Awards, June 10, 1958, 21 U.S.T. 2517, 330 U.N.T.S. 38.

CASE OPENER WRAP-UP

Resolving a Breach of Contract under the CISG

In the case of *Chicago Prime Packers, Inc. v. Northam Food Trading Co.,*[28] the district court held that the transaction was governed by the CISG. The CISG was applicable as Chicago Prime was a U.S. resident and Northam Food Trading was a resident of a jurisdiction that had ratified the CISG. The court held that because the contract did not contain an inspection provision, the requirement under Article 38 of the CISG that the buyer examine the goods, or cause them to be examined, "within as short a period as is practicable in the circumstances" was controlling. Decisions under the CISG indicated that the buyer bears the burden of proving that the goods were inspected within a reasonable time. Northam did not present any evidence as to why the ribs, or a portion of the ribs, were not and could

[28] 320 F. Supp. 2d 702 (N.D. Ill. 2004).

not have been examined by Northam, Beacon, or someone acting on their behalf when the shipment was delivered to Beacon or within a few days thereafter.

Northam also failed to prove that it gave notice to Chicago Prime within a reasonable time after it ought to have discovered the alleged lack of conformity. Article 39 of the CISG states that "[a] buyer loses the right to rely on a lack of conformity of the goods if he does not give notice to the seller specifying the nature of the lack of conformity within a reasonable time after he has discovered it or ought to have discovered it." A buyer bears the burden of showing that notice of nonconformity has been given within a reasonable time. The court further noted that when defects are easy to discover by a prompt examination of the goods, the time of notice must be reduced. The putrid condition of the meat was apparent even in its frozen state. Because the court found that Northam failed to examine the shipment of ribs in as short a period of time as was practicable, it followed that Northam also failed to give notice within a reasonable time after it should have discovered the alleged nonconformity.

As a result, the court entered a judgment in favor of Chicago Prime Packers, Inc., and against Northam Food Trading Company in the amount of $178,200 plus $27,242.63, representing prejudgment interest calculated at a rate of 5 percent from May 1, 2001, for a total payment of $205,442.63.

Before their dispute arose, the parties could have selected the law for the court to apply through a choice-of-law clause, which permits the parties to a contract to choose the law of a certain state to apply to the interpretation of the contract in the event of a dispute. Choice-of-law clauses are generally enforceable as long as there is a reasonable relation between the transaction and the law of the selected jurisdiction. The same rules apply with respect to the CISG. The parties are always free to opt out of the CISG and select another law to apply to their transaction. Thus, the parties could have selected U.S. or Canadian sales law to apply to the resolution of disputes arising from their transaction. In the absence of such a selection, the CISG applied to this transaction.

KEY TERMS

affiliate   127

arbitration   143

bilateral free trade agreement   130

choice-of-law clause   142

comparative law   125

Convention on the International Sale of Goods (CISG)   133

Dispute Settlement Understanding   129

distributor   126

dumping   128

Foreign Corrupt Practices Act (FCPA)   127

foreign sales representative   126

foreign subsidiary   127

forum selection agreement   142

franchise agreement   126

free trade agreement   129

General Agreement on Tariffs and Trade (GATT)   128

general personal jurisdiction   138

Hague Evidence Convention   142

international law   125

joint venture   126

jurisdiction   137

lex mercatoria   132

licensing agreement   126

national treatment   128

New York Convention   143

nontariff barrier   127

normal trade relations   128

North American Free Trade Agreement (NAFTA)   129

personal jurisdiction   138

quantitative restriction   128

specific personal jurisdiction   138

subject-matter jurisdiction   137

subsidy   129

tariff   127

venue   142

World Trade Organization (WTO)   128

SUMMARY OF KEY TOPICS

International law refers to the laws governing the conduct of states and international organizations and their relations with one another and natural and juridical persons.

Doing Business Internationally

Firms participating in international markets have special ethical considerations, including whether to do business with repressive governments, whether to provide products for the poor at reduced prices, and whether to treat workers according to local custom or to international standards of humane treatment.

Ethical Considerations

GATT is a comprehensive multilateral trading system designed to achieve distortion-free international trade through the minimization of tariffs and removal of artificial barriers. It established several general principles of trade law:

The General Agreement on Tariffs and Trade

- *Article I:* Addresses the principle of *most-favored-nation relations,* now known as *normal trade relations;* requires that WTO member states treat like goods coming from other WTO member states on an equal basis, specifically prohibiting member states from discriminating against like products on the basis of their country of origin.
- *Article III:* Sets forth the principle of *national treatment,* which prohibits WTO member states from regulating, taxing, or otherwise treating imported products any differently than domestically produced products.
- *Article VI:* Prohibits certain types of *dumping* and *subsidies.*
- *Article XI:* Prohibits *quantitative restrictions* on imports (e.g., limits on importation of certain products on the basis of number of units, weight, or value for national economic reasons or the protection of domestic industry).

Free trade agreement: Two or more states agree to reduce and gradually eliminate tariffs and other trade barriers [e.g., North American Free Trade Agreement (NAFTA)].

Regional Trade Agreements

Customs union: States in a free trade area agree on a common external tariff on products originating outside the union (e.g., European Union).

Bilateral trade agreement: Two states agree on issues relating to trade between them (e.g., United States–Australia agreement).

Comparative law is the study of the legal systems of different states. This study provides a better understanding of the general purpose of law, assists in the development of a critical viewpoint of one's own legal system, and demonstrates that one's own legal system is only one of many alternatives. After thinking critically about alternative laws, one might decide that one's own state should adopt the other state's law or method of resolving a dispute.

Comparative Law

Civil law systems constitute the majority of the world's legal systems and are based on detailed national legal codes, which serve as the sole official source of law. *Common law* systems derive from the British and American models and are based on constitutions, legislation, regulations, and their interpretation by courts of law. *Socialist law* systems are based on the premises that the rights of society as a whole outweigh individual rights and that the state owns the means of production and property. *Islamic law* systems are based on the tenet that law is derived from and interpreted in conformance with *Shari'a* ("God's Law") and the Koran.

Legal Systems and Procedures

If the parties to international transactions are unable to resolve their dispute through nonadversarial methods, the parties may use litigation or arbitration to resolve their differences.

Dispute Settlement in an International Context

POINT / COUNTERPOINT

Should U.S. Courts Refer to Foreign Law in Their Decisions?	
NO	**YES**
Reference to foreign law fails to recognize the exceptional nature of the U.S. legal system and experience. Such reference is an unnecessary surrender of sovereignty and abdication of the judiciary's responsibility to interpret and apply the national laws of the land. The U.S. Constitution and statutes enacted in accordance with it should be interpreted according to the framers' original intent and congressional intent. Reference to foreign law in U.S. courts fails to recognize that only domestic law should serve the American people. Additionally, foreign legislative bodies that adopt laws and the courts that interpret them are not accountable to the American people. Utilization of such laws and decisions expands judicial discretion in the United States beyond that which is desirable. Finally, there is little need for uniformity in many areas of the law.	Reference to foreign law in U.S. court decisions recognizes that the United States is a member of the family of nations and demonstrates respect for the legal systems of other states. Foreign law may serve as a source of inspiration for U.S. courts, enriches legal thinking, enhances judicial creativity, and strengthens democratic ties and the foundations of different legal systems. U.S. judges could learn from their brethren in other states. Reference to foreign law promotes uniformity and predictability, which is extremely important in international business transactions. State courts already reference foreign law when they cite the decisions of courts in other states, the results of which are persuasive authority at best. In any event, foreign law is not binding on U.S. courts, and there is no danger that such law could serve as precedent or mandate an outcome in a particular case.

QUESTIONS & PROBLEMS

1. Spain divided unroasted nondecaffeinated coffee into five separate classifications. A 7 percent tariff was imposed on three of these classifications. The other two classifications were duty-free. Brazil, the principal supplier of the coffee subject to the tariff, alleged that the Spanish classification regime failed to extend most-favored-nation treatment to like products originating from Brazil, thus violating GATT. Spain defended the classifications on the basis that the products were not like products due to differences resulting from geographic factors, cultivation methods, processing, and genetics. The GATT panel rejected these arguments. The panel noted that most coffees are blends, coffee is universally regarded as a well-defined and single product intended for drinking, and no other state maintained a similar classification scheme. The panel thus concluded that the classification system discriminated against like products in violation of GATT's most-favored-nation requirement. Do you agree with this decision? Is coffee a single universal product regardless of where it is grown, how it is processed, or what the cost is to consumers? [*Spain—Tariff Treatment of Unroasted Coffee,* 1981 GATTPD LEXIS 5 (1981).]

2. Italy adopted a law that permitted the government to extend credit to Italian farmers in order to finance the purchase of agricultural machinery. Farmers purchasing machinery manufactured in Italy were entitled to a loan of up to 75 percent of the value of the machinery for a term of five years at a 3 percent interest rate. Farmers purchasing machinery not manufactured in Italy were also entitled to loans but at an interest rate of 10 percent. The United Kingdom claimed that the Italian loan program violated GATT's national treatment obligation by modifying the conditions of sale between imported and domestically produced machinery. Italy defended the loan program on the basis that national treatment applied only to sales in the context of international trade and not to internal conditions of sale. Italy also claimed that national treatment was not applicable to economic development initiatives such as the loan program. The GATT panel disagreed and held that the national treatment requirement applied to internal conditions impacting domestic sales. The panel also concluded that economic development initiatives were required to be consistent with the principle of national treatment.

Based on this decision, are there any limits to the concept of national treatment? How might a state undertake an economic development initiative without violating national treatment? [*Italy— Imported Agricultural Machinery,* GATT Report L/833-7S/60 (1958).]

3. Nicastro was severely injured at his workplace in New Jersey by an industrial metal-shearing machine manufactured by J. McIntyre Machinery, Ltd., an English company. Nicastro filed a product liability claim against McIntyre in New Jersey state court. McIntyre denied that the New Jersey state courts had personal jurisdiction. McIntyre had no office in New Jersey, and it did not pay taxes, own property, advertise, or maintain employees in New Jersey. McIntyre's only contact with New Jersey was the presence of the metal-shearing machine at Nicastro's workplace. The New Jersey Supreme Court held that state courts could exercise personal jurisdiction with respect to Nicastro's claim. McIntyre appealed this decision to the U.S. Supreme Court. Do the New Jersey courts have personal jurisdiction over McIntyre arising from Nicastro's injuries? [*J. McIntyre Machinery, Ltd. v. Nicastro,* 131 S. Ct. 2780 (2011).]

4. In *Asahi Metal Industries v. Superior Court,* the U.S. Supreme Court held that the mere placement of a product in the stream of commerce is not sufficient to subject the manufacturer to the personal jurisdiction of a California state court in the absence of "purposeful availment," such as designing a product specifically for the forum, maintaining a distributor in the forum, or providing regular advice to customers in the forum. Is this reasoning still valid in the modern global marketplace, where goods routinely cross international boundaries? Why or why not? [*Asahi Metal Industries v. Superior Court,* 480 U.S. 102 (1987).]

5. Seung was a passenger on the M/S *Paul Gauguin* cruise ship owned by Regent Seven Seas Cruises. The cruise ship operated exclusively in French Polynesia. Seung's ticket contained a forum selection clause that designated Paris, France, as the sole location for any lawsuit that might be filed arising from passenger injuries on cruises that did not include a U.S. port. Seung was injured on her cruise and filed a lawsuit in the U.S. District Court for the Southern District of Florida. Regent Seven Seas Cruises moved to dismiss the lawsuit on the basis of the forum selection clause. Seung claimed that the clause was unfair as she was financially and medically unable to bring a lawsuit in Paris and that Paris was a "remote alien forum" designated for the sole purpose of discouraging passengers from bringing legitimate claims. The district court dismissed Seung's lawsuit, and she appealed to the U.S. Court of Appeals for the 11th Circuit. Is the forum selection clause as drafted enforceable against Seung barring her lawsuit in the United States? Why or why not? [*Seung v. Regent Seven Seas Cruises, Inc.,* 2010 U.S. App. LEXIS 17449 (11th Cir., August 19, 2010).]

6. Juliette Shulof Furs (JSF) was a New York corporation that had been in the fur-dealing business for 15 years. George Shulof, an officer of JSF, attended two auctions conducted by Finnish Fur Sales (FFS) in Finland in 1987. He purchased more than $1.2 million worth of skins at the auctions. Shulof attended each auction and was the actual bidder. The conditions of sale were listed in the auction catalog in English. Section 4 of "Conditions of Sale" provided that "[a]ny person bidding at the auction shall stand surety as for his own debt until full payment is made for purchased merchandise. If he has made the bid on behalf of another person, he is jointly and severally liable with the person for the purchase." Section 15 of "Conditions of Sale" provided that "[t]hese conditions are governed by Finnish law." JSF paid for the majority of the skins purchased, leaving an unpaid balance of $202,416.85. FFS brought an action to recover the contract price of the skins from Shulof, claiming he was personally liable for payment under Finnish law. Shulof responded that he was acting only as the agent for JSF and that under New York law he was not personally responsible for the contracts of the corporation he represented at the auction. He also claimed that the choice of Finnish law was invalid, and its application would lead to a result contrary to the public policy of the state of New York. Is the choice-of-law clause valid? Would the imposition of personal liability upon Shulof be in violation of New York public policy? What are the reasons for your answers? [*Finnish Fur Sales Co., Ltd. v. Juliette Shulof Furs, Inc.,* 770 F. Supp. 139 (S.D.N.Y. 1991).]

7. In an interview published in the *New York Times* in February 1976, former Lockheed president A. Carl Kotchian defended the payment of bribes by the company as follows:

> Some call it gratuities. Some call them questionable payments. Some call it extortion. Some call it grease. Some call it bribery. I look at these payments as necessary to sell a product. I never felt I was doing anything wrong.

More than 30 years later, Reinhard Siekaczek, an accountant employed by Siemens who oversaw an annual budget for questionable payments in excess of $50 million, stated:

> I never thought I would go to jail for my company. . . . We thought we had to do it. Otherwise, we'd ruin the company. . . . People will only say about Siemens that they were unlucky and that they broke the Eleventh Commandment. The Eleventh Commandment is "Don't get caught."

Given these attitudes, is the Foreign Corrupt Practices Act likely to result in a change in corporate culture at multinational businesses? Is the FCPA a success or a failure to the extent that its prohibitions are not taken seriously, as demonstrated by the above statements?

8. A construction company submitted a bid to build a municipal swimming pool in the Netherlands. The mayor and his municipal councilors found this bid to be the best and to be within the municipality's budget for the project. However, the town council rejected the bid and awarded the contract to another firm. The construction company sued the town for expenses incurred in preparing the bid and damages suffered as a result of loss of the contract. The court held that, under Dutch law, there are three stages of contract negotiation. In the initial stage, either party may break off negotiations without incurring liability. In the second or continuing stage, either party may break off the negotiations but is liable to the other party for expenses. In the final stage, the parties are prohibited from terminating negotiations without incurring liability for damages resulting from loss of the contract. Parties enter the third stage of negotiations when they have a mutual and reasonable expectation that a contract will result from the negotiations. In this case, the court concluded the parties were in the continuing-negotiation stage and awarded the construction company the expenses incurred in preparing its bid proposal. Is such an approach to contract negotiations realistic? How would you define the different stages of negotiation created by the court? [*Plas v. Valburg*, 18-6 Netherlandse Jurisprudentie 723 (1983).]

9. A U.S. software manufacturer sold software for processing credit card charges to a U.S. limited liability company that was a wholly-owned subsidiary of a German corporation. The software did not function properly. The U.S. buyer and its German parent sued the software manufacturer for breach of contract. The plaintiffs asserted that the CISG was applicable to the transaction as the head of the German parent company signed the purchase and sales contract. The software manufacturer alleged that the CISG was inapplicable as the contract was addressed to the U.S. limited liability company and the purchase price was paid with a check tendered by the U.S. purchaser. Is the CISG applicable to this transaction? Why or why not? [*American Mint LLC v. GOSoftware, Inc.*, 2006 U.S. Dist. LEXIS 1569 (M.D. Pa. 2006).]

Looking for more review material?

The Online Learning Center at **www.mhhe.com/kubasek3e** contains this chapter's "Assignment on the Internet" and also a list of URLs for more information, entitled "On the Internet." Find both of them in the Student Center portion of the OLC, along with quizzes and other helpful materials.

The Legal Environment of Business

PART

1

CHAPTER

7

Tort Law

Plastic Surgeon Defamation

Dr. Walter Sullivan was one of several plastic surgeons in Las Vegas whom Julie Jones visited. Jones, an exotic dancer, sought plastic surgery to improve her ability to make money in her profession. After visiting Sullivan for a consultation, she then visited Dr. Joseph Bongiovi, Jr. During her consultation with Bongiovi, Jones mentioned her earlier visit with Sullivan. Bongiovi then told her that a patient of Sullivan's died the previous week during the same procedure Jones sought. Bongiovi told her the death was the direct result of Sullivan's negligence.

Despite Bongiovi's allegations, Jones saw Sullivan again and scheduled the surgery with him. Jones did, however, attend a prescheduled appointment with Bongiovi. During the appointment, at Jones's prompting, Bongiovi confirmed what he had said before—that Sullivan had recently been responsible for a patient's death during the same procedure Jones sought.

On the basis of the confirmation from Bongiovi, Jones called to cancel her surgical appointment with Sullivan. When Sullivan's office manager asked why she was canceling the appointment, Jones said she had been told that Sullivan was under investigation for a patient's death. When Sullivan learned of the cancellation, he called Jones to find out who had made the statements; he was unsuccessful in obtaining a name. After speaking with Sullivan, Jones again called Bongiovi's office to receive confirmation about the allegation. Bongiovi's assistant confirmed that the statements were true.

When Sullivan eventually learned the identity of Bongiovi, he filed suit for defamation. According to Sullivan, Bongiovi's statements were slanderous per se. At the conclusion of a trial, a jury found in favor of Sullivan and awarded him $250,000 in compensatory damages and $250,000 in punitive damages. Bongiovi appealed, arguing that the jury should have been instructed that actual malice was the standard because Sullivan was a public figure. Furthermore, Bongiovi argued that the compensatory and punitive damages awarded were exorbitant.

1. What defenses, if any, could Bongiovi have presented to prevent the damage awards?
2. Under which ethical system, if any, should Bongiovi be required to pay damages to Sullivan? Why?

After reading this chapter, you will be able to answer the following questions:

LO 7-1   How are torts classified?

LO 7-2   What are some of the most common intentional torts, and what are the elements needed to prove these torts?

LO 7-3   What are the elements that must be proved to win a negligence case?

LO 7-4   What are the doctrines that help a plaintiff win a negligence case?

LO 7-5   What defenses are available in a negligence case?

LO 7-6   How does a party prove a strict-liability case?

LO 7-7   What types of damages are available in tort cases?

tort

A violation of another person's rights or a civil wrongdoing that does not arise out of a contract or statute; primary types are intentional, negligent, and strict-liability torts.

As a future business manager, you will likely be involved in a situation in which one party believes he or she has been injured by the actions of another party, in the same way Dr. Sullivan believed he had been injured by Dr. Bongiovi's allegations about the death of one of Dr. Sullivan's patients due to the doctor's negligence. Wrongs such as these are often referred to as *torts*. A tort is commonly defined as a wrong or injury to another, other than a breach of contract. In fact, *tort* is a French word meaning "wrong." This chapter first examines the goals of tort law and the three primary classifications of torts. Next, the chapter examines each of the categories of torts. It concludes by discussing damages that may be available in tort cases.

Introduction to Tort Law

Chapter 5 introduced criminal law and explained the punishment individuals may receive for committing crimes. Most of the actions that give rise to criminal prosecutions also provide the basis for a tort claim by the victim of the crime.

Although the primary objectives of criminal law are to punish wrongdoers and preserve order in society, the primary objective of tort law is to provide compensation for injured parties. Tort law also contributes to maintaining order in society because it discourages private retaliation by injured persons and their friends. After all, we do not want to live in a community where vigilantes with tempers are roaming about righting some harm they believe has occurred to them.

A third objective of tort law is to give citizens a sense that they live in a just society. Our collective sense of right and wrong suggests that someone who creates harm should make things right by compensating those who were harmed. The recognition that one will have to pay for the personal injuries she or he causes may also serve to deter the commission of torts.

Although this chapter discusses torts as if they were the same everywhere, tort law is primarily state law, so states may have slightly different definitions of each tort. In describing torts, this chapter uses the definitions common in most states, noting when there seems to be a significant difference in the way certain states define the tort.

Despite the public impression of a tort litigation explosion often conveyed by the media, because tort law is state law, no entity regularly compiles and publishes an annual report of the total number of tort cases filed nationwide. Writers for a legal publication, *Lawyer's Weekly USA*, however, do keep track of the top 10 jury verdicts every year. What they have found is that after years of decline since 2000, the top 10 jury verdicts rose dramatically in 2008 and increased by a smaller number in 2009, with the average of the top 10 jury verdicts increasing from $112 million to nearly $145 million. But the very top award in 2009 was slightly lower, at $370 million, versus $388 million in 2008. In 2010, the average increased less than the prior year, however, rising from nearly $145 million to just under $157 million, but the top award was significantly higher in 2010. A Las Vegas attorney won a judgment of $505 million, with $500 million being punitive damages, against a manufacturer and distributor whose oversized vials of a drug led to an outbreak of hepatitis C at outpatient surgical centers.[1] Given what we do know about tort litigation and damages, we know that potential tort liability should concern a competent business manager.

Classification of Torts

LO 7-1

Torts are most commonly classified as intentional, negligent, or strict-liability torts. Each category differs in terms of the elements needed to prove the tort, the available damages, the available defenses, and the degree of willfulness of the actor. Intentional torts occur when the defendant takes an action intending that certain consequences will result or knowing certain consequences are likely to result. Negligent torts occur when the defendant acts in a way that subjects other people to an unreasonable risk of harm. In other words, the defendant is careless to someone else's detriment. Finally, strict-liability torts occur when the defendant takes an action that is inherently dangerous and cannot ever be undertaken safely, no matter what precautions the defendant takes. It is important to remember that when we discuss these classifications, we are referring to their use in the United States. The Chinese legal system, for example, narrowly defines the activities actionable under tort law.

intentional tort
A civil wrong resulting from an intentional act committed on the person, property, or economic interest of another. Intentional torts include assault, battery, conversion, false imprisonment, intentional infliction of emotional distress, trespass to land, and trespass to chattels.

Intentional Torts

Intentional torts are the most willful of torts. Intentional torts are predicated on the common element of intent. The intent at issue is not intent to harm but, rather, to engage in a specific act, which ultimately results in an injury, physical or economic, to another. In fact, one does not need to establish a motive when proving liability in an intentional tort case. Moreover, in tort law, it is assumed that people intend what could be considered the normal consequences of their actions. For example, if Rob throws a rock toward a group of people, it would be assumed under the law that he intended to hit someone with the rock and that the person hit would be hurt, regardless of Rob's intention merely to scare the group of people.

negligent tort
A civil wrong that occurs when the defendant acts in a way that subjects other people to an unreasonable risk of harm (i.e., the defendant is careless, to someone else's detriment). Negligence claims are usually used to achieve compensation for accidents and injuries.

As a general rule, each specific intentional tort has a set of elements that must be proved to establish the tort, along with specific defenses that can be raised against each tort. However, not all harms intentionally committed will fall neatly into an existing category of torts. Therefore, a general theory of intentional tort liability has been created to aid judges in their decision making. In Section 870 of the Restatement (Second) of Torts, the general theory is explained this way:

strict-liability tort
A civil wrong that occurs when the defendant takes an action that is inherently dangerous and cannot ever be undertaken safely, no matter what precautions the defendant takes. In such situations, a defendant is liable for the plaintiff's damages without any requirement for the plaintiff to prove that the defendant was negligent.

> One who intentionally causes injury to another is subject to liability to the other for that injury, if his conduct is generally culpable and not justifiable under the circumstances. This liability may be imposed although the actor's conduct does not come within a traditional category of tort liability.

Intentional torts are divided into the following three categories: (1) torts against persons, (2) torts against property, and (3) torts against economic interests. The following sections discuss a number of specific torts that fall into each category, along with the defenses for each.

INTENTIONAL TORTS AGAINST PERSONS

LO 7-2

Torts against persons are intentional acts that harm an individual's physical or mental integrity. There are a significant number of these torts. Assault and battery are two of the most common. Imagine that after searching for a parking space for 20 minutes, you finally pull into a spot.

---

[1] Lawyers USA Online, "Top Ten Jury Verdicts of 2010," http://lawyersusaonline.com/free-white-paper-top-ten-jury-verdicts-of-2010

However, as soon as you turn off your car, a man who looks like Mike Tyson starts pounding on your car window. He angrily yells, "You took my spot! If you don't move your car now, I'm going to hit you so hard you won't remember what your car looks like!" The man has just assaulted you.

assault

A civil wrong that occurs when one person intentionally and voluntarily places another in fear or apprehension of an immediate, offensive physical harm. Assault does not require actual contact.

An **assault** occurs when one person places another in fear or apprehension of an immediate, offensive bodily contact. Therefore, in the above example, if you think the man is just joking and you start laughing, no assault has taken place because there is no fear or apprehension. Not only must you feel fear or apprehension, but that feeling must be reasonable under the circumstances.

An assault is often, but not always, followed by a **battery,** an intentional, unwanted, offensive bodily contact. Almost any unwanted, intentional contact constitutes a battery. Even contacts that are harmless, if unwanted, are batteries. And even if a touch is intended as a joke, if the reasonable person would be offended, the contact is deemed offensive.[2] To return to the example of the parking-space incident, if the man actually hit you, his action would constitute a battery. In contrast, if you both happened to be getting out of your respective cars at the same time and consequently bumped into each other, no battery would have occurred because there was no *intentional* bodily contact.

battery

A civil wrong that occurs when one person intentionally and voluntarily brings about a non-consented harmful or offensive contact with a person or something closely associated with him or her. Battery requires an actual contact.

BUT WHAT IF . . .

WHAT IF THE FACTS OF THE CASE OPENER WERE DIFFERENT?

Recall in the Case Opener that Dr. Sullivan sued Dr. Bongiovi because of the false statement he made. What if, instead, Dr. Sullivan had called Dr. Bongovi and said, "If you ever tell a potential client a lie like that about me again, I will slit your throat!" Would Dr. Sullivan have committed an assault or battery? Why or why not?

A limited number of defenses are available to an action for a battery. A party charged with a battery may argue that the offended party consented to the contact. *Consent,* as a defense, mitigates the element of unwanted. A person cannot commit a battery if the contact was consented to and therefore wanted.

The most common defense to battery is *self-defense,* responding to the force of another with comparable force to defend oneself. In our parking-space example, if the man took a swing at you and you shoved him to try to keep him from hitting you, causing him to fall backward and hit his head on the street, he would not succeed in a case against you for battery because you could raise the defense of self-defense. To use this defense, you cannot use a greater level of force than is being used against you.

A third defense, *defense of others,* allows you to defend another by using the same degree of force that you could use to defend yourself. A final defense, *defense of property,* allows you to use reasonable force to defend your property from an intruder. The use of deadly force in defense of property is rarely, if ever, considered justified.

defamation

A false statement or an action that harms the reputation or character of an individual, business, product, group, government, or nation.

The tort alleged in this chapter's opening case was **defamation,** which is the intentional publication (communication to a third party) of a false statement harmful to an individual's reputation. In addition to the person who publishes a false statement, anyone who republishes, or in any manner repeats, a defamatory statement is also liable for defamation, even if he or she cites the original source of the defamation.

If the defamation is published in a permanent form, such as printed in a magazine or newspaper, it is known as *libel.* Defamation through television and radio broadcasts is also considered libel because the broadcasts are permanently recorded. In the case of libel, general damages are presumed. Thus, the victim would be entitled to compensation for the damages

---

[2] Restatement (Second) of Torts, sec. 19.

that are presumed to flow from defamation yet are hard to prove, such as the humiliation the victim would feel.

If the defamation is made orally, it is *slander.* To recover damages in a case of slander, the plaintiff must prove special damages; that is, the plaintiff must show specific monetary loss that resulted from the defamatory statements. Although libel is contained in a permanent form, slander, by virtue of being spoken, is not. It is the lack of permanence that gives way to the special damages involved with slander. If the people who heard the slander do not act in a way to cause harm to the slandered person, there is no cause for compensation, which is one of the main goals of tort law.

One exception to the requirement of special damages occurs if the false statements constitute *slander per se.* Slander per se statements are considered so inherently harmful that general damages are presumed. The kinds of statements considered slander per se are claims that an individual (1) has a loathsome, communicable disease (traditionally, venereal disease or leprosy); (2) has committed a crime for which imprisonment is a possibility; (3) is professionally incompetent; or (4) if a woman, has engaged in sexual misconduct.

If you say your boss is a tyrant or your roommate is a slob, are you in danger of being sued for defamation? You probably are not because such statements are not really statements of fact; rather, they are opinions, and subjective opinions that cannot be proven are generally not actionable.

One of the important elements of defamation is that the defamatory statement must be damaging to someone's reputation. For example, when a convicted criminal serving three life sentences attempted to sue a journalist for alleged errors in an article detailing his criminal history, the journalist filed a motion to dismiss on grounds that the defendant was libel-proof as a matter of law regarding claims about his criminal background. Upholding the dismissal, the court said the plaintiff's public reputation at the time the articles were published was so diminished with respect to a specific subject (his kidnapping and murder convictions) that he could not be further injured by allegedly false statements on that subject.[3]

BUT WHAT IF . . .

WHAT IF THE FACTS OF THE CASE OPENER WERE DIFFERENT?

Recall in the Case Opener that Dr. Bongiovi knew Jones was contemplating going to Dr. Sullivan for treatment, and he wanted her business, so he told her negative stories about Dr. Sullivan. What if Dr. Bongiovi had no idea Jones had ever heard of Dr. Sullivan and was telling her the story just as a reminder that no surgery is completely risk-free?

The increase in communication over the Internet has presented new questions for the law of defamation to answer. First, does a false statement made over this information network constitute defamation? Second, who can be held liable if defamation does exist?

The court first attempted to answer these issues in the case of *Cubby v. CompuServ.*[4] In that case, CompuServ was sued because of defamatory statements published on one of the forums available through its online information service. In holding that CompuServ could not be held liable, the court made an analogy between an online information service provider such as CompuServ and bookstores, saying, "CompuServ's CIS product is in essence an electronic, for profit library." The court went on to say that once CompuServ decides to carry a given publication such as a news forum, it has little or no editorial control over that forum. It would therefore be no more feasible for CompuServ to examine every publication it carries for defamatory material than it would be for libraries or booksellers to do so.

---

[3] *Thomas P. Lamb v. Tony Rizzo,* 391 F.3d 1133 (2004).
[4] 77b F. Supp. 135 (1991).

Since *Cubby* was decided, the Communications Decency Act of 1996 was passed. One section of this act gives immunity to providers of interactive computer services for liability they might otherwise incur because of material they disseminate but others create.

A person who is accused of defamation can raise two defenses: truth and privilege. *Truth* is frequently considered an absolute defense. That is, one cannot be held liable for defamation, regardless of whether damages result, if the statement made was the truth. If I say Bill is a convicted felon, and he is, I have not committed defamation. Under ordinary circumstances, the fact that you *thought* a statement was true is not a defense. So if I honestly believe Bill is a convicted felon and I tell others he is, but he is not, then I have committed slander.

Privilege is an affirmative defense in a defamation action. An affirmative defense occurs when the defendant admits to the accusation but argues that there is a reason he should not be held liable. A privilege is either absolute or conditional. When an absolute privilege exists, one cannot be sued for defamation for any false statements made, regardless of intent or knowledge of the falsity of the claim. Absolute privilege arises in only a limited number of circumstances. The speech and debate clause of the U.S. Constitution gives an absolute privilege to individuals speaking on the House and Senate floors during congressional debate. This privilege exists because Congress wants to get to the truth of matters before it, and if people testifying before Congress had to fear they might be sued, they might be afraid to testify. Absolute privilege also arises during a judicial proceeding. Again, we do not want people to be afraid to testify in court, so we prohibit them from being sued for whatever occurs within the courtroom. As the following Case Nugget illustrates, the concept of a judicial proceeding can extend beyond a traditional courtroom.

Conditional privilege is the second type. Under a conditional privilege, a party will not be held liable for defamation unless the false statement was made with actual malice. A statement is made with actual malice if it is made with *either* knowledge of its falsity or reckless disregard for its truth. Businesspersons should be most concerned about the conditional privilege that arises with respect to job recommendations. To encourage employers to give honest assessments of their former employees, this privilege protects an employer who makes a false statement about a former worker: The employer will not be held liable as long as the statement was made in good faith and was made only to those who had a legitimate interest in the information being communicated.

Another conditional privilege is the public figure privilege. Public figures are individuals who are in the public eye, typically politicians and entertainers. Because these individuals have a significant impact on our lives, we want to encourage free discussion about them, so we do not hold people liable for making false statements about them as long as the statements were not made with malice. This privilege does not seem to place an unfair burden on the public figure because such an individual can easily respond publicly to any false claims, given that he or she is already in the public eye and has appropriate outlets available for giving his or her opinion. In the opening scenario, Bongiovi argued on appeal that Sullivan was a public figure by nature of his profession. If Bongiovi could establish that Sullivan was a public figure, Sullivan would have to show that Bongiovi acted with actual malice while making the statements to the patient.

There are those who believe a conditional privilege should apply when the defamatory statement is posted somewhere on the Internet. The reasoning behind application of the privilege in this context is that the person who has been defamed over the Internet can respond to the defamatory remarks in the same forum with minimal effort. Thus, there is less need for the stronger legal protection we ordinarily give to private parties who are defamed. In addition, we want to encourage free expression and the exchange of ideas on the Internet. One way to do so is to allow people to respond openly to criticisms on the Internet. When people are overly concerned about making errors, free exchange is hindered. Relaxing defamation standards in regard to the Internet can encourage people to speak their minds freely. Thus far, however, no such privilege has been established. And when a person is found to have committed defamation on an online bulletin board or website, the damages can be significant. For example, a jury awarded $3 million to a university professor who sued a former student who had accused him of being a pedophile on a website she maintained.

absolute privilege

A special right, immunity, permission, or benefit given to certain individuals that allows them to make any statements about someone without being held liable for defamation for any false statement made, regardless of intent or knowledge of the falsity of the claim.

conditional privilege

A special right, immunity, permission, or benefit given to certain individuals that allows them to make any statements about someone without being held liable for defamation for any false statement made without actual malice.

actual malice

In defamation, either a person's knowledge that his or her statement or published material is false or the person's reckless disregard for whether it is false.

public figure privilege

A special right, immunity, or permission given to people that allows them to make any statements about public figures, typically politicians and entertainers, without being held liable for defamation for any false statement made without malice.

CASE Nugget

The Applicability of an Absolute Privilege

Hartman and Swinehart v. Keri
Supreme Court of Indiana

2008 Ind. LEXIS 265, 883 N.E.2d 774

On May 12, 2003, graduate students Virginia Hartman and Suzanne Swinehart filed formal complaints alleging sexual harassment by Dr. Gabe Keri, an assistant professor at Indiana University–Purdue University Fort Wayne (IPFW) from whom they had taken courses. IPFW charged Dr. Elaine Blakemore with the task of investigating the allegations; Blakemore submitted a report on June 30, 2003, that concluded Hartman and Swinehart's allegations were credible and commended their willingness to report the behavior. Furthermore, Blakemore suggested Keri be immediately removed from teaching positions. These findings and recommendations were further investigated by a three-person panel and Chancellor Wartell. Blakemore's report was supported and Keri was given a 100 percent research position with no use of his university office.

Keri appealed to the president of Purdue, who upheld the chancellor's decision. In response, Keri filed suit against Hartman and Swinehart in the Allen Superior Court, claiming libel, slander, and malicious interference. Hartman and Swinehart moved for summary judgment, claiming their statements were protected by absolute privilege. This motion was denied. Hartman and Swinehart appealed.

In finding that the students' statements were entitled to absolute privilege, the state supreme court judges explained that administrative proceedings that are quasi-judicial in nature are entitled to absolute protection. They applied the factors courts use to determine whether a proceeding is quasi-judicial in nature. These factors include whether the body has the power to (1) exercise judgment and discretion; (2) hear and determine or to ascertain facts and make decisions; (3) make binding orders and judgments; (4) affect the personal or property rights of private persons; (5) examine witnesses and hear the litigation of issues on a hearing; or (6) enforce decisions or impose penalties.

One final tort against persons is the tort of intentional infliction of emotional distress. Sometimes called the tort of outrage, intentional infliction of emotional distress occurs when someone engages in outrageous, intentional conduct likely to cause extreme emotional distress to another party. For example, if a person calls his former employer and falsely says her son was just arrested for a double homicide after a botched robbery attempt, most courts would find that behavior outrageous enough to satisfy the first element of the tort.

Before damages are awarded in some jurisdictions, the plaintiff must demonstrate injury through physical symptoms directly related to the emotional distress. For instance, in the preceding example, if the employer fainted upon hearing the news, hitting her head on the table and cutting it as she passed out, she would have physical symptoms sufficient to justify a recovery. Other physical symptoms from emotional distress include headaches, a sudden onset of high blood pressure, hives, chills, inability to sleep, and inability to get out of bed.

Businesses frequently find themselves sued for this type of tort when they terminate someone's employment or fail to provide a service that a consumer expected. Many of these actions, like the one in Case 7-2, are unsuccessful, primarily because the bar for what is considered outrageous is high, as are the standards for emotional distress.

CASE 7-1

AARON OLSON, APPELLANT, v. CENTURYLINK, RESPONDENT
COURT OF APPEALS OF MINNESOTA
No. A12–0884 (UNPUBLISHED OPINION, February 4, 2013)

FACTS: *On December 14, 2011, appellant Aaron Olson contracted to receive telephone service from respondent, CenturyLink, and applied for reduced-rate services that CenturyLink provides through Minnesota's Telephone Assistance Plan (TAP), a statewide program established to reduce telephone rates for low-income households.*

The respondent did not apply the reduced rate to Olson's first bill but attached a blank copy of the TAP application. Olson completed the application and mailed it to the respondent, but his next bill also did not reflect a reduced rate. Olson called the respondent and learned that the company had not received his application. Olson then faxed another application to the respondent. A few days later, he contacted the respondent company, but could not confirm whether his application had been received.

On January 31, 2012, the respondent company disconnected Olson's telephone service. When Olson called the respondent to resolve the dispute, the company representatives repeatedly hung up on him.

In April 2012, Olson filed suit, claiming that the respondent company violated the Minnesota Human Rights Act (MHRA) and committed intentional infliction of emotional distress. Because he did not have the money for filing fees, Olson also filed a petition to proceed in forma pauperis (IFP). The district court denied the petition, determining that the action was frivolous because the claims had no basis in law. Olson appealed.

ISSUE: When should a defendant be held liable in tort for intentional infliction of emotional distress?

REASONING: To prevail on this tort, a plaintiff must establish that the defendant's conduct (1) was extreme and outrageous, (2) was intentional or reckless, (3) caused emotional distress, and (4) the distress was severe. Extreme and outrageous conduct is behavior that is "so atrocious that it passes the boundaries of decency and is utterly intolerable to the civilized community." Furthermore, to hold a party liable in tort for intentional infliction of emotional distress, the emotional distress must be so severe "that no reasonable man could be expected to endure it."

In this case, the respondent's acts of failing to process Olson's application, disconnecting his telephone service, and hanging up on him during telephone conversations are not so atrocious that they pass the boundaries of decency. For example, previous case law *Langeslag v. KYMN Inc.* states that "insults, indignities, annoyances, petty oppressions, and other trivialities do not constitute extreme and outrageous conduct." The evidence provided by the appellant regarding the acts against him by the respondent mirror the acts cited by *Langeslag* that were previously determined not to constitute extreme and outrageous conduct.

DECISION AND REMEDY: The court affirmed the denial of the petition by the district court in favor of the defendant.

SIGNIFICANCE OF THE CASE: This case outlines the standards that must be met for a defendant to be held liable in tort for intentional infliction of emotional distress.

CRITICAL THINKING

Notice that case law can, as in this case, serve as a restriction on our emotional response to a case. Many of us have had trouble with our phone carrier. The alleged behavior of CenturyLink is at minimum annoying, but case law lays out standards that determine the availability of remedies in cases like these. Reading the case law, describe behavior that CenturyLink would have had to engaged in for the plaintiff to have prevailed.

ETHICAL DECISION MAKING

What value is the court upholding in finding against the plaintiff?

INTENTIONAL TORTS AGAINST PROPERTY

Because businesses own property, anyone who manages a business should be concerned about torts against property. The most common torts a businessperson might be involved with are trespass to realty, nuisance, trespass to personalty, and conversion.

Trespass to Realty   The tort of trespass to realty, also called *trespass to real property,* occurs when a person intentionally (1) enters the land of another without permission; (2) causes an object to be placed on the land of another without the landowner's permission; (3) stays on the land of another when the owner tells him to depart; or (4) refuses to remove something he placed on the property that the landowner asked him to remove.

It is no defense for a person to argue that she thought she had a legal right to be on the property or she thought the land belonged to someone else. The intent refers to intentionally being on that particular piece of land. In a recent, unusual case heard in a small claims court in Westchester County, a plaintiff sued the defendant for trespass to realty when the defendant entered the plaintiff's property to serve the plaintiff with a reply affidavit for another legal action. The defendant had previously been barred from entering the plaintiff's property. The plaintiff argued that the defendant could not dictate how legal papers are served. The plaintiff sued for $3,000 in compensatory, nominal, and punitive damages. Although the court ruled that the defendant committed trespass to realty, it awarded only nominal damages in the sum of $1.

Because guests are welcomed onto one's property, they are not considered trespassers. However, if a guest is asked to leave and he or she refuses, the person immediately becomes a trespasser and no longer maintains a right to be on the property in question. If charges were brought against such a person, that person could not raise the defense that he or she was a guest.

Also, when a trespasser is on someone's property, the trespasser is liable for damages she or he might cause to the property. Furthermore, under common law, a trespasser cannot hold an owner of property liable for damages the trespasser sustains while on the property. However, as of late, courts have been shifting away from this common law rule. Now, courts typically maintain that owners owe a reasonable duty to anyone who may end up on their property. The specifics of the duty vary by jurisdiction as well as by the status of the parties. In some jurisdictions, it is possible, although rare, for owners to be liable for trespassers who were injured while trying to steal property from the owners.

trespass to realty
A tort that occurs when someone goes on another's property without permission or places something on another's property without permission.

Private Nuisance   A private nuisance occurs when a person uses her property in an unreasonable manner that harms a neighbor's use or enjoyment of his property. Using one's property in a manner that caused the neighbor to be subjected to flooding, vibrations, excessive noise, or smoke could lead to a nuisance claim.

private nuisance
A nuisance that affects only a single person or a very limited number of individuals.

Trespass to Personal Property   A person commits trespass to personal property, also called *trespass to personalty,* by temporarily exerting control over another's personal property or interfering with the true owner's right to use the property. Under trespass to personal property, the trespasser is responsible for damages caused to the property as well as for damages caused to the owner related to the trespasser's wrongful possession of the property. For example, if I take someone's bike from his garage and use it for a week, I have committed trespass to personalty. If I return the bike after it has a flat tire, I will have to compensate the owner for the cost of repairing the tire and any other expenses that resulted from my having the bike for a week. Also, if the bike was the only means the person had for getting to work, I would be responsible for the person's lost wages resulting from the missed work, because I took the person's means of transportation.

trespass to personal property
Temporary interference with another's use or enjoyment of his or her personal property.

Conversion   Conversion occurs when a person permanently removes personal property from the owner's possession and control. When conversion occurs, the true owner can no longer regain the property. The owner usually recovers damages for the full value of the converted item plus any additional damages that resulted from the loss.

It is not a defense to conversion for a person to argue that she believed she had a legal claim to the goods. For example, if Brittany accidentally takes Melvin's suitcase believing it to be hers and

conversion
Permanent interference with another's use and enjoyment of his or her personal property.

then loses it, she is still liable for conversion. Moreover, the possession of stolen goods also makes a person liable for conversion. Therefore, buying goods in good faith without knowledge of any impropriety also is not a defense to conversion. Even if a person bought the goods believing the purchase was legal, the person with the stolen goods is liable to the legal owner of the goods.

An illustration of conversion comes from a recent case heard in the Westchester County Supreme Court. An amateur race-car driver left her race car at a service station. While the car was in the possession of the service station, an employee of the station, with a known drinking problem, apparently drove the car, wrecked it, and totally destroyed it. The car could never be returned in the condition it was in when brought to the station. The owner sued for conversion and recovered the value of the car in damages.

INTENTIONAL TORTS AGAINST ECONOMIC INTERESTS

All businesspersons should be familiar with the torts against economic interest. The five most common torts against economic interests, frequently referred to as "business torts," are disparagement, intentional interference with contract, unfair competition, misappropriation, and fraudulent misrepresentation. The first tort, disparagement, is similar to defamation, but it is a business's or product's reputation that has been tarnished.

The plaintiff in a disparagement case must prove that the defendant published a false statement of a material fact about the plaintiff's product or service that resulted in a loss of sales. When such statements are criticisms of the quality, honesty, or reputation of the business or product, the tort is sometimes called slander of quality (if spoken) or trade libel (if in printed form). If the statements relate to the ownership of the business property, the term slander of title is used.

Damages for disparaging are ordinarily based on a decrease in profits that can be linked to the publication of the false statement. An alternative, although less common, way to prove damages is to demonstrate that the plaintiff had been negotiating a contract with a third party but the third party lost interest shortly after the publication of the false statement. The profits the plaintiff would have made on the contract would be the damages.

Some interesting variations of the tort of disparagement have developed. For example, in 2007, California became the thirteenth state to recognize the tort of food disparagement, which critics call veggie libel. Such laws provide ranchers and farmers with a cause of action when someone knowingly makes false, damaging statements about a food product. The California law was drafted in response to an incident during 2006 in which Taco Bell executives wrongly identified green onions grown at Boskovich Farms in Oxnard as the source of an *E. coli* outbreak that sickened 70 of the fast-food chain's customers.

A second tort against economic interests is the tort of intentional interference with contract. To bring a claim of intentional interference with contract successfully, the plaintiff must prove that (1) a valid and enforceable contract between the two parties existed; (2) the defendant party knew of the existence of the contract and its terms; (3) the defendant intentionally undertook steps to cause one of the parties to breach the contract; and (4) the plaintiff was injured as a result of the breach.[5]

When a contract exists, clear liability is placed on third parties for inducing a party to the contract to breach the contract. However, when a prospective contract exists, a third party might be liable for inducing a party to pull out of the contract before it is formed. Because the essence of business involves competition, simply offering a better deal is not enough to create liability when a prospective contract exists. However, if a party uses illegal means to cause another party not to enter into a contract, the party who acted illegally is liable for interfering with contractual relations.[6]

The most common situation involving intentional interference with a contract in the business context occurs when one employer tries to lure an employee away from another employer. Liability in such a situation, however, is limited to when the employee has a contract for a set period of time and the prospective employer actually knows of the contract.

disparagement
A business tort that occurs when a statement is intentionally used to defame a business product or service.

slander of quality
A business tort that occurs when false spoken statements criticize a business product or service and result in a loss of sales.

trade libel
A business tort that occurs when false printed statements criticize a business product or service and result in a loss of sales.

slander of title
A business tort that occurs when false published statements are related to the ownership of the business property.

food disparagement
A tort that provides ranchers and farmers with a cause of action when someone spreads false information about the safety of a food product.

intentional interference with contract
The tort that occurs when someone intentionally takes an action that will cause a person to breach a contract that she or he has with another.

---

[5] Restatement (Second) of Torts, sec. 766.

[6] Restatement (Second) of Torts, sec. 766B.

When a third party interferes with a contract, injured parties may recover damages for what was directly lost through the breached contract. They may also recover any losses suffered related to the breached contract, in addition to damages for emotional distress and harm to reputation.[7]

A third tort against economic interests, **unfair competition,** exists because of American views about the purpose of a business. Americans believe a business is intended to make a profit, and the law protects businesses acting on this profit motive. Therefore, when someone enters a business with the sole intent of driving another firm out of business, the law punishes this act as unfair competition. For example, if there is only one jewelry store in town, Mark cannot come in and set up a store that makes no profits, just to drive the other store out of business so that an acquaintance of his can then move in and open up a legitimate jewelry store once the competition has been eliminated.

A fourth tort against economic interests is **fraudulent misrepresentation,** which occurs when one uses intentional deceit to facilitate personal gain. To establish that a fraudulent misrepresentation exists, a party must demonstrate all the following:

1. A party knowingly, or with reckless disregard for the truth, misrepresented material facts and conditions.
2. The party intended to have other parties rely on the misrepresentations.
3. The injured party reasonably relied on the misrepresentations.
4. The injured party suffered damages because of relying on the misrepresentations.
5. A direct link exists between the injuries suffered and a reliance on the misrepresentations.[8]

As in the criminal act of fraud, in the civil act of fraudulent misrepresentation, a party materially misrepresents something and thereby causes another party to suffer damages. Typically, fraudulent misrepresentation applies only to the misrepresentation of material facts. However, when a party with expert knowledge regarding a specific matter states an opinion, any party reasonably relying on the statement, although it is an opinion and not fact, may recover damages under the tort of fraudulent misrepresentation.

> **unfair competition**
> The act of competing with another not to make a profit but for the sole purpose of driving that other out of business.

> **fraudulent misrepresentation**
> The tort that occurs when a misrepresentation is made with the intent to facilitate personal gain and with the knowledge that it is false.

Negligence

LO 7-3

Negligence is behavior that creates an unreasonable risk of harm to others. Unlike intentional torts, which result from a person willfully taking actions that are likely to cause injury, negligent torts involve the failure to exercise reasonable care to protect another's person or property.

Sometimes, however, harm occurs because an individual suffers an unfortunate accident, an incident that simply could not be avoided, even with reasonable care. For example, suppose Jonathan is driving on the highway when he suffers a stroke. Because of the stroke, he crashes into two other vehicles. He is not, however, liable for damages caused by the accident because he was not negligent. Yet if Jonathan had some type of warning that the stroke was going to occur, he might be liable for the accident.

To win a negligence case, the plaintiff must prove four elements: (1) duty, (2) breach of duty, (3) causation, and (4) damages (see Exhibit 7-1). A plaintiff who cannot establish all four of these elements will be denied recovery.

> **negligence**
> Behavior that creates an unreasonable risk of harm to others.

DUTY

The plaintiff must first establish that the defendant owes a *duty* to the plaintiff. In some particular situations, the law specifies the duty of care one individual owes to another. In most cases, however, the courts use the reasonable person standard to determine the defendant's duty of care. The **reasonable person standard** is a measurement of the way members of society expect an individual

> **reasonable person standard**
> A measurement of the way members of society expect an individual to act in a given situation.

---

[7] Restatement (Second) of Torts, sec. 774A.
[8] Restatement (Second) of Torts, sec. 525.

Exhibit 7-1

Elements of
Negligence

To prove negligence, a plaintiff must demonstrate:

1. Duty
2. Breach of duty
3. Causation—actual and proximate
4. Damages

to act in a given situation. To determine the defendant's duty of care, the judge or jury must determine the degree of care and skill that a reasonable person would exercise under similar circumstances. The judge or jury then uses this standard to evaluate the actions of the individual in the case.

When courts attempt to determine whether a reasonable person would have owed a duty to others, they consider four questions:

1. How likely was it that the harm would occur?
2. How serious was the potential harm?
3. How socially beneficial was the defendant's conduct that posed the risk of harm?
4. What costs would have been necessary to reduce the risk of harm?

In many situations, it is far from clear what a reasonable person would do. For example, if a reasonable person saw an infant drowning in a shallow swimming pool, what would she do? In most situations like this one, the law holds that individuals have no duty to rescue strangers from perilous situations.

In some cases, however, the courts hold that individuals have a duty to aid strangers in certain types of peril. For example, if Sam negligently hits Janice with his car and, as a result, Janice is lying in the street, Sam has a duty to remove her from that dangerous position. Similarly, employers have a special duty to protect their employees from dangerous situations.

The courts generally hold that landowners have a duty of care to protect individuals on their property. Similarly, businesses have a duty of care to customers who enter business property. It is important, therefore, for future business managers to be knowledgeable about this duty. Businesses should warn customers about risks they may encounter on business property. Some risks, however, are obvious, and businesses need not warn customers about them. For example, a business need not inform customers that they could get a paper cut from the pages of a book.

The courts generally hold that businesses have a duty of care to protect their customers against foreseeable risks about which the owner knew or reasonably should have known. For example, in *Haywood v. Baseline Construction Company,* a woman who tripped over lumber on the front porch of the House of Blues restaurant in Los Angeles sued for negligence. The business's attempt to warn customers by marking the lumber with yellow construction tape was insufficient to avoid the determination of negligence; the woman was awarded $91,366 in damages.

The liability of businesses grew out of the traditional common law, under which the duty of owners and occupiers of real property depends primarily on the status of the injured party. The injured party may be an invitee, a person who enters another's premises as a result of an express or implied invitation of the owner for their mutual benefit, with a business invitee being one who is invited onto the property for the purpose of doing business; a licensee, a person who enters another's premises with the occupier's consent for his or her benefit alone; or a trespasser, one who is on the property without the owner's or occupier's permission, as described earlier in this chapter. Under this approach, the owner owes the greatest duty to the invitee, a duty to inspect the premises to ensure that they are reasonably safe and to warn of any hidden dangers. The owner has a duty to a licensee to warn of any hidden dangers of which he knows but has no affirmative duty to inspect for hidden problems. The owner owes no duty to trespassers except to do them no intentional harm.

In 1968, however, the California Supreme Court rejected this rigid division,[9] substituting a general duty of reasonable care in its place, under which a duty of reasonable care is owed any

---

[9] Rowland, 443 P.2d 561 (Cal. 1968).

E-COMMERCE and the Law

Negligence on the Internet

A commonly offered explanation for the increasing occurrence of violence is the increased violence portrayed in the media. Some plaintiffs try to hold owners of certain websites liable under negligence theories for violent acts committed by teenagers. For example, in *James v. Meow Media,* a 14-year-old boy took six guns to school and shot three of his classmates to death. The parents of the deceased classmates brought suit against several Internet websites and the creators and distributors of various video games. The parents argued that these defendants had a duty of ordinary care to the slain girls.

The courts have been consistent, however, in finding that it was not foreseeable that a boy who played certain video games and viewed certain websites would murder three of his classmates. In similar cases, courts have ruled that defendants (such as website owners, creators and distributors of video games, and directors and producers of movies) do not have a duty to protect a person from the criminal acts of a third party unless there is a special relationship that requires the defendant to act with that duty.

Although it appears that website owners, manufacturers, and producers will not be held liable, plaintiffs continue to bring suits against these groups of people. Can you think of an argument for why these groups of people might owe a duty of care to these plaintiffs?

---

entrant onto the land, regardless of status. More than 25 states have now moved to this standard, with a few using this standard for both the invitees and the licensees, while maintaining the traditional approach to trespassers. The trend is toward the use of this unitary standard, but given the lack of uniformity among the states, it is important to know which approach is being used by the state in which you live and do business.

Professionals have more training than ordinary people. Thus, when professionals are serving in their professional capacity, courts generally hold that they have a higher duty of care to clients than does the ordinary person. A professional cannot defend against a negligence suit by claiming ignorance of generally accepted principles in her or his field of expertise. Clients who feel that they have suffered damages as a result of a professional's breach of her duty of care can bring a negligence case against her. These actions are frequently referred to as *malpractice cases.*

BREACH OF DUTY

Once the plaintiff has established that the defendant owes her a duty of care, she must prove that the defendant's conduct violated that duty. This violation is called a *breach of duty.* For example, the driver of an automobile owes the other passengers in his car a duty of care to obey traffic signs. If he fails to stop at a stop sign, he has violated his duty to follow traffic signs and has therefore breached his duty of care.

CAUSATION

Causation is the third element of a successful negligence claim, and it has two elements: actual cause and proximate cause. The plaintiff must prove both elements of causation to be able to recover damages.

The first element, actual cause (also known as *cause in fact*), is the determination that the defendant's breach of duty resulted directly in the plaintiff's injury. The courts commonly determine whether a breach of duty actually caused the plaintiff's injury by asking whether the plaintiff would have been injured if the defendant had fulfilled his or her duty. If the answer is no, then the actual cause of the plaintiff's injury was the defendant's breach. Actual cause is sometimes referred to as but-for causation because the plaintiff argues that the damages she suffered would not have occurred *but for* (except because of) the actions of the defendant.

Proximate cause, sometimes referred to as *legal cause,* refers to the extent to which, as a matter of policy, a defendant may be held liable for the consequences of his actions. In most states, proximate cause is determined by foreseeability. Proximate cause is said to exist only when both the plaintiff and the plaintiff's damages were reasonably foreseeable at the time the defendant breached his duty to the plaintiff. Thus, if the defendant could not reasonably foresee

actual cause
The determination that the defendant's breach of duty resulted directly in the plaintiff's injury.

proximate cause
The extent to which, as a matter of policy, a defendant may be held liable for the consequences of his or her actions. In the majority of states, proximate cause requires the plaintiff and the plaintiff's damages to have been foreseeable at the time of the accident. In the minority of states, proximate cause exists if the defendant's actions led to the plaintiff's harm.

GLOBAL Context

Negligence in Germany

German law is concerned with the defendant's ability to foresee, understand, and avoid danger. Both mental and physical capabilities are taken into account. For example, the duty-of-care standard stipulates that "physical and mental disabilities or defects, panic, or confusion" exempt the defendant from being found negligent. Also, although the distinction is not recognized by a statute, the courts distinguish between conscious and unconscious negligence. *Conscious negligence* requires knowledge that the offense is about to occur and that it is an actual offense. *Unconscious negligence* occurs when the defendant is either unaware that the act constitutes an offense or unaware that the act is occurring at all. In such cases, the defendant is found not liable by reason of unconscious negligence.

the damages that the plaintiff suffered as a result of his action, the plaintiff's negligence claim will not be sustained because it lacks the element of proximate causation.

You must be able to foresee that either the plaintiff himself or herself or a person in the plaintiff's position would be hurt. If you are running a red light, it is foreseeable that a person will be crossing with the light. If you hit a person crossing with the light, we say the person hit was foreseeable. If it makes more sense, we could say "both a person in the plaintiff's position" and the "plaintiff's damages," but most people refer simply to "the plaintiff and the plaintiff's damages."

For example, if a defective tire on a vehicle blows out, it is foreseeable that the driver may lose control and hit a pedestrian. It is not foreseeable, however, that the pedestrian may be a scientist carrying a briefcase full of chemicals that may explode on impact, causing a third-floor window to shatter, injuring an accountant at his desk. In most states, the accountant would not succeed if he sued the tire manufacturer for negligence. The tire failure is not considered a proximate cause of the accountant's injury because the contents of the pedestrian's briefcase were highly unusual. The pedestrian, however, would be eligible to recover damages from the tire manufacturer because hitting a pedestrian is a foreseeable consequence of tire failure. Thus, the defect in the tire is a proximate cause of the pedestrian's injury.

Palsgraf v. Long Island Railroad Company is a well-known case in which the majority opinion set forth the rule of foreseeability in determining proximate cause. The dissent, however, set forth an alternative definition of proximate cause that is accepted today in a small minority of states. Courts following the minority definition do not distinguish actual cause from proximate cause. In these states, if the defendant's action constitutes an actual cause, it is also considered the proximate cause. Therefore, in these few states, both the pedestrian-scientist and the third-floor accountant would be able to recover damages from the tire manufacturer in the previous example.

DAMAGES

compensatory damages
Money awarded to a plaintiff as reimbursement for her or his losses; based on the amount of actual damage or harm to property, lost wages or profits, pain and suffering, medical expenses, disability, and so on.

Damages are the final required element of a negligence action. The plaintiff must have sustained compensable injury as a result of the defendant's actions. Because the purpose of tort law is to compensate individuals who suffer injuries as a result of another's action or inaction, a person cannot bring an action in negligence seeking only nominal damages. Rather, a person must seek compensatory damages, or damages intended to reimburse a plaintiff for her or his losses.

punitive damages
Compensation awarded to a plaintiff that goes beyond reimbursement for actual losses and is imposed to punish the defendant and deter such conduct in the future.

In typical negligence cases, courts rarely award punitive damages or *exemplary damages,* which are imposed to punish the offender and deter others from committing similar offenses. Instead, courts usually award punitive damages in cases in which the offender has committed gross negligence, an action committed with extreme reckless disregard for the property or life of another person.

gross negligence
An action committed with extreme reckless disregard for the property or life of another person.

LO 7-4

Plaintiff's Doctrines

The plaintiff has the burden of proving all four elements of a negligence case. Direct evidence of negligence by the defendant, however, is not always available. For example, there may have been no witnesses to the negligent conduct, and other evidence may have been destroyed. Therefore, two doctrines have been adopted by courts to aid plaintiffs in establishing negligence claims: *res ipsa loquitur* and negligence per se.

RES IPSA LOQUITUR

Res ipsa loquitur literally means "the thing speaks for itself." The plaintiff uses this doctrine to allow the judge or jury to infer that, more likely than not, the defendant's negligence was the cause of the plaintiff's harm, even though there is no direct evidence of the defendant's lack of due care. To establish *res ipsa loquitur* in most states, the plaintiff must demonstrate that:

1. The event was a kind that ordinarily does not occur in the absence of negligence.
2. Other responsible causes, including the conduct of third parties and the plaintiff, have been sufficiently eliminated.
3. The indicated negligence is within the scope of the defendant's duty to the plaintiff.

> **res ipsa loquitur**
> A doctrine that allows the judge or jury to infer that, more likely than not, the defendant's negligence was the cause of the plaintiff's harm, even though there is no direct evidence of the defendant's lack of due care.

Proof of these three elements does not require a finding of negligence, however; it merely permits it. Once the plaintiff has demonstrated these three elements, the burden of proof shifts to the defendant, who must prove that he was not negligent to avoid liability.

One of the earliest uses of *res ipsa loquitur* was the case of *Escola v. Coca Cola*.[10] In that case, the plaintiff, a waitress, was injured when a bottle of Coca-Cola that she was removing from a case exploded in her hand. From the facts that (1) bottled soft drinks ordinarily do not spontaneously explode and (2) the bottles had been sitting in a case, undisturbed, in the restaurant for approximately 36 hours before the plaintiff simply removed the bottle from the case, the jury reasonably inferred that the defendant's negligence in the filling of the bottle resulted in its explosion. The plaintiff therefore recovered damages without direct proof of the defendant's negligence. Plaintiffs in numerous accident cases have subsequently used the doctrine when there has been no direct evidence of negligence. The defendant's best response to this doctrine is to demonstrate other possible causes of the accident. Case 7-2 illustrates the use of this doctrine.

[10] 24 Cal. 2d 453, 150 P.2d 436 (1944).

CASE 7-2

SANDRA MORRIS v. WALMART STORES, INC.
U.S. COURT OF APPEALS FOR THE SIXTH DISTRICT
330 F.3d 854 (2003)

FACTS *On September 27, 1998, the Plaintiff and her husband, Michael Morris, were shopping in the defendant's Sam's Club when the plaintiff slipped and fell on a substance thought to be water next to a small portable freezer known as a spot box. After the fall, some of the defendant's employees approached to lend the Plaintiff assistance. At this point, the Plaintiff noticed that her clothes were soaked in what she believed to be water from the nearby freezer. When the store manager arrived at the scene, he ordered the water to be cleaned up. He pointed out to the Plaintiff and her husband that the plug in the bottom of the freezer was out. The Plaintiff testified that the store*

manager additionally said that the spot box was new and that he feared it might not be functioning properly. As a result of her injury, the Plaintiff was severely bruised and advised to stay in bed and off of her feet for a week.

The Plaintiff subsequently filed suit against the defendant in Shelby County, Tennessee. The defendant removed the matter to District Court on the basis of diversity of citizenship. Following the Plaintiff's case-in-chief, the defendant moved for a judgment as to law, arguing that the Plaintiff failed to provide evidence that the defendant had notice of the water, and that the Plaintiff could not rely upon the doctrine of res ipsa loquitur. *The Plaintiff argued*

(continued)

that she was not attempting to and could not show notice. She claimed instead that she provided evidence that the defendant created a dangerous condition by placing the new spot box out without a plug in it, and that the doctrine of res ipsa loquitur applied. The District Court granted the defendant's motion. The Plaintiff appealed.

ISSUE: Should a plaintiff be allowed to use *res ipsa loquitur* to recover from injuries suffered by a defendant's malfunctioning product?

REASONING: A plaintiff should be allowed to use *res ipsa loquitur* to allow the jury to infer negligence when the plaintiff can demonstrate two conditions. First, the plaintiff was injured by an instrumentality that was within the defendant's exclusive control; second, the injury would not ordinarily have occurred in the absence of negligence.

To satisfy the first condition, Tennessee courts require that establishing "exclusive control" involves proving the defendant had a duty of care over the instrument that caused the harm. This standard should not be applied strictly because then the standard would become overly restrictive. Instead, showing that the negligence was more likely than not that of the defendant and not another person will satisfy this condition. The second condition would be satisfied if the plaintiff proves that the injury more likely than not occurred because of some negligent conduct. This standard does not require all possible alternatives to be disproved.

The defendant moved for a judgment as to law, which required the trial court to look at the evidence in the most favorable light possible to the nonmoving party, the plaintiff. If a reasonable jury could find in favor of the plaintiff after evaluating all the evidence, then the trial court's granting of the motion was in error.

In this case, the plaintiff provided evidence that the manager believed that the freezer was malfunctioning and subsequently wanted to remove it from the public space, that the freezer did not have a plug properly installed, and that the substance that she slipped on was likely water emanating from the freezer. The evidence regarding where the liquid was from was corroborated by the plaintiff's written statement at the scene as well as the testimony of the employee tasked with cleaning the liquid, who said that the water was about 10 inches in diameter and "right there under the drain of the freezer." This evidence would be sufficient to allow a reasonable jury to find both elements of *res ipsa loquitur* satisfied and infer negligence on the part of the defendant.

DECISION AND REMEDY: The court reversed the trial court's granting of summary judgment in favor of the defendant and ordered a new trial at which *res ipsa loquitur* may be used.

SIGNIFICANCE OF THE CASE: This case provides an illustration of the type of conditions that can lead a jury to infer negligence.

CRITICAL THINKING

Given a negligence action like this one, what evidence could the defendant provide that might convince a jury not to find the defendant negligent?

ETHICAL DECISION MAKING

How does the court's ruling demonstrate that the law is based on the ethical concern for future customers of business firms?

NEGLIGENCE PER SE

negligence per se
A doctrine that allows a judge or jury to infer duty and breach of duty from the fact that a defendant violated a criminal statute that was designed to prevent the type of harm that the plaintiff incurred.

Negligence per se (literally, "negligence in or of itself") is another doctrine that helps plaintiffs succeed in negligence cases. Negligence per se applies to cases in which the defendant has violated a statute enacted to prevent a certain type of harm from befalling a specific group to which the plaintiff belongs. If the defendant's violation causes the plaintiff to suffer from the type of harm that the statute intends to prevent, the violation is deemed negligence per se. The plaintiff does not have to show that a reasonable person would exercise a certain duty of care toward the plaintiff. Instead, the plaintiff can offer evidence of the defendant's violation of the statute to establish proof of the negligence.

For example, if Ohio passes a statute prohibiting the sale of alcohol to minors, and a minor runs a red light and kills two pedestrians while driving under the influence of alcohol sold to him illegally, the liquor store's violation of the statute prohibiting the sale of alcohol to minors establishes negligence per se on the part of the store. The families of the pedestrians do not need to establish that a reasonable person would have a duty not to sell alcohol to a minor. The Case Nugget provides another illustration of negligence per se.

Defenses to Negligence

LO 7-5

The courts' doctrines of *res ipsa loquitur* and negligence per se help the plaintiff in a negligence case, but the courts permit certain defenses that relieve the defendant from liability even when the plaintiff has proved all four elements of negligence. Defendants can successfully rebut negligence claims with contributory negligence, comparative negligence, assumption of the risk, and other special negligence defenses.

CASE Nugget

A Clear Illustration of Negligence per se

O'Guin v. Bingham County
Superior Court of Idaho

122 P.3d 308 (Sup. Ct. Id. 2005)

Shaun and Alex O'Guin cut across a field on their way home from school and entered the back of a landfill that was not fenced off, despite a law that required it to be fenced. A portion of a wall of the landfill collapsed, killing the boys. The boys' parents sued the county that operated the landfill, alleging that failure to have the landfill properly fenced constituted negligence per se.

The court agreed, explaining that the following four elements of negligence per se had been met: (1) The statute or regulation clearly defines the required standard of conduct, (2) the statute or regulation must have been intended to prevent the type of harm the defendant's act or omission caused, (3) the plaintiff must be a member of the class of persons the statute or regulation was designed to protect, and (4) the violation must have been the proximate cause of death.

CONTRIBUTORY NEGLIGENCE

Contributory negligence, a defense once available in all states but replaced today in some states by the defense of comparative negligence (discussed in the next section), applies in cases in which both the defendant and the plaintiff were negligent. The defendant must prove that (1) the plaintiff's conduct fell below the standard of care needed to prevent unreasonable risk of harm and (2) the plaintiff's failure was a contributing cause of the plaintiff's injury. How can defendants use contributory negligence in a case? Some defense lawyers argue that if a plaintiff involved in a car accident failed to wear her seat belt, that failure constitutes contributory negligence because her action contributed to her injuries.

If the defendant successfully proves contributory negligence, no matter how slight the plaintiff's negligence, the plaintiff will be denied any recovery of damages. Because this defense seems unfair, many states have adopted the **last-clear-chance doctrine.** This doctrine allows the plaintiff to recover damages despite proof of contributory negligence as long as the defendant had a final clear opportunity to avoid the action that injured the plaintiff.

contributory negligence
A defense to negligence whereby the defendant can escape all liability by proving that the plaintiff failed to act in a way that would protect him or her from an unreasonable risk of harm and that the plaintiff's negligent behavior contributed in some way to the plaintiff's accident.

last-clear-chance doctrine
A doctrine used by the plaintiff when the defendant establishes contributory negligence. If the plaintiff can establish that the defendant had the last opportunity to avoid the accident, the plaintiff may still recover, despite being contributorily negligent.

For example, suppose that Samantha and Nicole, in their cars, are facing each other while stopped at a red light. The light turns green, and Nicole starts to turn left at the intersection. Samantha sees Nicole start to turn, but she still continues to travel straight through the intersection and crashes into Nicole's car. Although Samantha had the right-of-way at the intersection, she could have avoided hitting Nicole's car by braking or swerving. Thus, according to the last-clear-chance doctrine, Nicole could recover damages.

COMPARATIVE NEGLIGENCE

pure comparative negligence
A defense accepted in some states whereby the defendant is not liable for the percentage of harm that he or she can prove is due to the plaintiff's own negligence.

modified comparative negligence
A defense accepted in some states whereby the defendant is not liable for the percentage of harm that he or she can prove is due to the plaintiff's own negligence if the plaintiff's negligence is responsible for less than 50 percent of the harm; if the defendant establishes that the plaintiff's negligence caused more than 50 percent of the harm, the defendant has no liability.

assumption of the risk
A defense whereby the defendant must prove that the plaintiff voluntarily assumed the risk the defendant caused.

Most states have replaced contributory negligence with comparative negligence because the adoption of the last-clear-chance doctrine still left many situations in which an extremely careless defendant can cause a great deal of harm to a plaintiff who is barred from recovery due to minimal contributory negligence. There are two forms of comparative negligence: pure and modified. According to a pure comparative negligence defense, the court determines the percentage of fault of the defendant. The defendant is then liable for that percentage of the plaintiff's damages.

Courts calculate damages according to modified comparative negligence in the same manner, except that the defendant must be more than 50 percent at fault before the plaintiff can recover.

Twenty-eight states have adopted modified comparative negligence, 13 have adopted pure comparative negligence, and 9 have adopted contributory negligence. Every state has adopted one of these three defenses. Thus, the parties to a negligence suit cannot choose among them.

ASSUMPTION OF THE RISK

Another defense available to defendants facing negligence claims is called assumption of the risk. To use this defense successfully, a defendant must prove that the plaintiff voluntarily and unreasonably encountered the risk of the actual harm the defendant caused. In other words, the plaintiff willingly assumed as a risk the harm she suffered. There are two types of this defense. *Express assumption of the risk* occurs when the plaintiff expressly agrees (usually in a written contract) to assume the risk posed by the defendant's behavior. In contrast, *implied assumption of the risk* means that the plaintiff implicitly assumed a known risk.

The most difficult part of establishing this defense is showing that the plaintiff assumed the risk of the *actual* harm she suffered. A 1998 case against the Family Fitness Center illustrates an unsuccessful attempt to use assumption of the risk as a defense against a negligence claim.[11] In that case, the plaintiff was injured when a sauna bench on which he was lying collapsed beneath him at the defendant's facility. The trial court granted summary judgment in favor of the defendant on the basis of assumption of the risk. The plaintiff had signed a contract that included the following provision: "Buyer is aware that participation in a sport or physical exercise may result in accidents or injury, and Buyer assumes the risk connected with the participation in a sport or exercise and represents that Member is in good health and suffers from no physical impairment which would limit their use of FFC's facilities." The appellate court overturned the trial court's decision because the type of injury the plaintiff suffered was not the type of risk he had assumed. The court held that anyone signing a membership agreement could be deemed to have waived any hazard known to relate to the use of the health club facilities, such as the risk of a sprained ankle due to improper exercise or overexertion, a broken toe from a dropped weight, injuries due to malfunctioning exercise or sports equipment, or injuries from slipping in the locker room shower. No patron, however, could be charged with realistically appreciating the risk of injury from simply reclining on a sauna bench. Because the collapse of a sauna bench, when properly used, is not a known risk, the court concluded that the plaintiff did not assume the risk of this incident as a matter of law.

---

[11] *Leon v. Family Fitness Center, Inc.,* 61 Cal. App. 4th 1227 (1998).

SPECIAL DEFENSES TO NEGLIGENCE

Many states have additional ways to defend against a claim of negligence. For example, laws in some states hold that people in peril who receive voluntary aid from others cannot hold those offering aid liable for negligence. These laws, commonly called Good Samaritan statutes, attempt to encourage selfless and courageous behavior by removing the threat of liability.

The defendant in a negligence suit can also avoid liability by establishing a superseding cause. A *superseding cause* is an unforeseeable event that interrupts the causal chain between the defendant's breach of duty and the damages the plaintiff suffered. For example, suppose Jennifer is improperly storing ammonia in her garage when a meteor strikes her garage, spilling the ammonia into a stream nearby. Will, living downstream, drinks water from the stream and becomes dangerously ill. Because the meteor was unforeseeable, Jennifer is not liable for Will's injuries, even though she breached her duty of care to Will. Superseding causes allow the defendant to avoid liability because they are evidence that the defendant's breach of duty was not the proximate cause of the plaintiff's injuries. In other words, superseding causes disprove the causation element necessary to sustain a negligence claim.

Good Samaritan statute

A statute that exempts from liability a person, such as a physician passerby, who voluntarily renders aid to an injured person but negligently, but not unreasonably negligently, causes injury while rendering the aid.

Strict Liability

LO 7-6

Strict liability is liability without fault. The law holds an individual liable without fault when the activity in which she engages satisfies three conditions: (1) it involves a risk of serious harm to people or property; (2) it is so inherently dangerous that it cannot ever be safely undertaken; and (3) it is not usually performed in the immediate community. Instead of banning such activities, the law allows people to engage in these activities but holds them liable for all resulting harm.

Inherently dangerous activities include dynamite blasting in a populated area and keeping animals that have not been domesticated. If an animal has shown a vicious propensity, strict liability applies and the owner of the animal is responsible for any injuries suffered in an attack by the animal. If an individual keeps an animal that has shown vicious propensity, he has a duty to warn and protect individuals who come into contact with the animal. Today, the theory of strict liability is used most commonly when the plaintiff is claiming to have been injured by a product that was unreasonably dangerous.

strict liability

Liability in which responsibility for damages is imposed regardless of the existence of negligence. Also called *liability without fault*.

Damages Available in Tort Cases

LO 7-7

There are three types of damages available in tort cases: compensatory, nominal, and punitive (see Exhibit 7-2). You will see this system of classifying damages again when we talk about damages in other contexts, such as in cases involving the breach of a contract.

TYPE	PURPOSE	AMOUNT
Compensatory	To make the plaintiff whole again.	An amount equivalent to all losses caused by the tort, including compensation for pain and suffering, but not attorney fees.
Nominal	To recognize that the defendant committed a tort against the plaintiff.	A trivial amount, typically $1 to $5.
Punitive	To punish the defendant and deter future wrongdoers.	An amount based on two factors: the severity of the wrongful conduct and the wealth of the defendant.

Exhibit 7-2

Types of Tort Damages

COMPENSATORY DAMAGES

tortfeasor

A person who commits an intentional or through-negligence tort that causes a harm or loss for which a civil remedy may be sought.

Because the primary objective of tort law is to compensate victims, the primary type of damages are *compensatory damages,* damages designed to compensate the victim for all the harm caused by the person who committed the tort, often referred to as the tortfeasor. Although we seem to hear a lot about runaway jury awards, there does not seem to be evidence of a trend toward increasingly huge jury awards. The overall median jury award for personal injury cases from 1998 to 2004 was $35,298; that amount actually fell from $37,086 in 2003 to $35,000 in 2004.[12] In 2010, the median jury verdict award in personal injury cases was $40,000, which is not a huge jump over a six-year time span.[13]

Compensatory damages are typically awarded for pain and suffering, costs of repairing damaged property, medical expenses, and lost wages. In the case opener, Dr. Bongiovani argued on appeal that the compensatory damages were excessive, but the appellate court upheld them, noting that when one is defamed in their line of business, they are entitled to general damages for harm to their reputation. In light of the fact that after the allegations, the number of exotic dancers seeking Dr. Sullivan's services declined, the amount did not seem unreasonable to the court. Surprisingly, attorney fees are *not* recoverable as compensatory damages, despite the fact that most plaintiffs could not bring an action against the tortfeasor without hiring an attorney. Because the plaintiffs in personal injury cases must usually pay their attorneys anywhere from one-third to one-half of their recovery, some argue that compensatory damages fail to meet the intended goal of properly compensating victims. Others point out that one of the ways plaintiffs can, in essence, recover their attorney fees is by increasing their pain and suffering damages enough to cover these expenses.

NOMINAL DAMAGES

nominal damages

Monetary damages awarded to a plaintiff in a very small amount, typically $1 to $5, to signify that the plaintiff has been wronged by the defendant even though the plaintiff suffered no compensable harm.

Nominal damages are a small amount of money given to recognize that a defendant did indeed commit a tort in a case in which no compensable damages were suffered by the plaintiff. A plaintiff may receive nominal damages by simply failing to prove actual damages.

PUNITIVE DAMAGES

Punitive damages are awarded to punish the defendant. They are given only when the defendant's conduct is extremely outrageous. The purposes of punitive damages are both to punish the defendant and to deter him and others who are similarly situated from engaging in that kind of activity again. In awarding punitive damages, juries usually consider the egregiousness or willfulness of the tort and the wealth of the defendant. Obviously, the more wrongful the nature of the defendant's act, the greater the desire to send a message that such behavior will not be tolerated; and the greater the wealth of the defendant, the higher the damages must be to actually punish the defendant.

Although the threat of large punitive damages is seen by many groups, including consumer advocates, as a good method for encouraging manufacturers to produce the safest possible products, others disagree. They believe that no threat beyond compensatory damages is required; and they argue that the main effect of punitive damages is to discourage innovation because manufacturers will be afraid of the risk of producing a defective product, which could cost them millions in punitive damages.

Since the late 1970s, insurance companies and tort reform groups have been trying to limit the amount of punitive damages that can be assessed, using both the legislative process and the courts. The 1994 case of *Honda Motor Company v. Oberg*[14] provided tort reformers with their first judicial victory. In this case, the U.S. Supreme Court finally struck down a punitive-damage award as being a violation of due process. *Oberg,* however, was a limited victory because of two unique aspects of the case. First, the punitive damages were over 500 times the amount of the compensatory damages, which is extraordinarily rare. Second, the state law under which the

---

[12] JVR news release, www.juryverdictresearch.com/Press_Room/Press_releases/Verdict_study/verdict_study41.html (accessed October 10, 2006).

[13] Indiana Jury Verdicts, Accident and Injury Lawyer Blog, www.accidentinjurylawyerblog.com/2011/08/indiana_jury_verdicts.html, August 8, 2011.

[14] 114 S. Ct. 2331 (1994).

GLOBAL Context

Punitive Damages in Canada and Japan

Those who believe the U.S. tort system is in need of reform with respect to its treatment of punitive damages may look to their Canadian neighbors with envy. Punitive-damage awards in Canada are both rare and small.

A study in 1990 reported on punitive-damage awards in Ontario. The researchers found that the highest award was $50,000. The majority of punitive-damage awards were less than $25,000; the median award was approximately 20 percent of the compensatory-damage award in the particular case.

Following English common law, Canadian courts have traditionally restricted punitive damages to two situations: cases involving oppressive, arbitrary, or unconstitutional actions by government servants and cases in which the defendant's conduct was calculated to have made a profit in excess of compensatory damages. In 1989, the Canadian Supreme Court recognized that punitive damages could also be awarded for conduct deserving punishment because of its "harsh, vindictive, reprehensible, and malicious manner."

Two reasons seem to explain the differences in Canadian and American treatment of punitive damages. First, Canadians see something undignified about the flamboyant punitive-damage awards in the United States. Second, civil juries are much less common in Canada, and, in general, judges tend to be much more conservative than juries in making punitive-damage awards.

Another country that would be even more heroic to those opposed to punitive damages is Japan. Several times, the Japanese Supreme Court ruled that punitive damages violated Japan's public policy. Recently, following the lead of the courts, the Japanese legislature forbade the acceptance of punitive damages, even those awarded by foreign courts.

damages were awarded was the only state law in the country that had no provision for judicial review of the amount of punitive-damage awards, and it was the denial of this safeguard that violated the due process clause. Because of its unusual facts, *Oberg* did not provide much guidance about when punitive damages were so excessive that they violated due process.

A few years later, however, in *BMW v. Gore*,[15] the Supreme Court set forth a test that a number of commentators thought would substantially curb punitive-damage awards. The Court said three factors should be considered in determining whether an award was grossly excessive: "the degree of reprehensibility of the nondisclosure; the disparity between the harm or potential harm suffered by [the plaintiff] and his punitive damages award; and the difference between this remedy and the civil penalties authorized or imposed in comparable cases." However, a 1999 study found that the year after *BMW v. Gore*, punitive-damage awards across the country were not reduced any more frequently than they had been the year before the decision.[16]

Since *BMW v. Gore*, the Supreme Court has continued to encourage the courts to scrutinize punitive-damage awards carefully. In the 2001 case of *Cooper Industries, Inc. v. Leatherman Tool Group, Inc.*,[17] the high court ruled that appellate courts must review the trial court's decision on the constitutionality of an award *de novo*, meaning they should no longer give deference to the trial court's determination that the jury award was not unconstitutionally excessive and uphold it unless there was a clear abuse of discretion on the part of the trial court judge.

In the 2003 case *State Farm v. Campbell*,[18] the Supreme Court once again addressed the issue of how to determine punitive damages properly. The Campbells had won a jury verdict for $1 million in compensatory damages and $145 million in punitive damages after State Farm failed to settle what was clearly a valid claim. The high court ruled that punitive-damage awards should bear some relationship to the actual harm caused and should not focus on the wealth of the defendants. Although refusing to draw a firm line about what ratio of compensatories to punitives was acceptable, the Court did say that "in practice, few awards exceeding a single-digit ratio between punitive and compensatory damages, to a significant degree, will satisfy due process."[19] The Court also stated that damages should not focus on deterrence based on wealth or on actions unrelated to the case at hand. Case 7-3 demonstrates how the courts are applying these guidelines today.

[15] *BMW of North America v. Ira Gore, Jr.*, 116 S. Ct. 1589 (1995).

[16] James Dam, "Large Punitives Mostly Upheld, but $5B Award Overturned," *Lawyer's Weekly*, November 12, 2001, p. A1.

[17] 532 U.S. 424 (2001).

[18] 123 S. Ct. 1513 (2003).

[19] Ibid., p. 1524.

CASE 7-3

CLARK v. CHRYSLER CORPORATION
U.S. COURT OF APPEALS FOR THE SIXTH CIRCUIT
2006 U.S. App. LEXIS 2435

FACTS: *Charles Clark was fatally injured in an automobile accident when he pulled into an intersection in front of an oncoming vehicle and collided with it. He was not wearing a seat belt and was consequently ejected from his vehicle. His wife sued Chrysler, claiming that its pickup truck was defectively and negligently designed.*

After a three-day trial, the jury rendered a unanimous verdict in favor of Mrs. Clark on claims of strict liability, negligence, and failure to warn. The jury found Chrysler and Mr. Clark each 50 percent at fault, returning a verdict of $471,258.26 in compensatory damages and $3 million in punitive damages. The court entered a judgment against Chrysler for $3,235,629.13, reflecting 50 percent of the compensatory damages plus the $3 million punitive damages award. After a series of appeals, the last being an appeal of the trial court's motion to deny the defendant's motion to send the case back to the district court for a reduction of damages, the case finally landed at the circuit court of appeals on the issue of whether the jury verdict was constitutionally excessive.

ISSUE: Should the plaintiff's $3 million punitive-damage award be struck down as constitutionally excessive when the amount of the compensatory damages is $471,258.26?

REASONING: Application of the *Gore* guideposts to this case renders the punitive-damage award excessive. According to *Gore,* five criteria are used to determine the reprehensibility of the defendant's conduct: (1) The harm caused was physical as opposed to economic; (2) the tortious conduct evinced an indifference to or a reckless disregard for the health or safety of others; (3) the target of the conduct had financial vulnerability; (4) the conduct involved repeated actions or was an isolated incident; and (5) the harm was the result of intentional malice, trickery, or deceit or mere accident. In this case, the physical harm suffered by Mr. Clark weighed strongly in favor of finding Chrysler's conduct reprehensible, but considering the four other factors leads to the conclusion that the factors as a whole show that Chrysler's conduct was not sufficiently reprehensible to warrant a $3 million punishment.

The second guidepost is the disparity between the actual or potential harm inflicted on the plaintiff and the punitive-damage award. Because the compensatory-damage award here is relatively small, a 1:1 ratio is inappropriate; but because of the lack of reprehensibility, a ratio higher than 2:1 would be unwarranted.

The third guidepost is the difference between the punitive-damage award and the civil or criminal penalties that could be imposed for comparable misconduct. Given *State Farm*'s focus on civil penalties, a $3 million punitive-damage award is excessive in light of comparable civil penalties.

DECISION AND REMEDY: The damage award was excessive. Chrysler's motion was reversed and remanded, with instructions to enter a punitive-damage award in the amount of $471,258.26.

SIGNIFICANCE OF THE CASE: This case gives the courts a little more guidance about when punitive damages may be considered excessive.

CRITICAL THINKING

Which of the criteria used by the judge seems ambiguous? How might that ambiguity have affected the outcome of the case?

ETHICAL DECISION MAKING

What values are guiding the judge's decision that the punitive-damage award was excessive? Do you think that the values promoted by the decision are appropriate for the situation? Why or why not?

SUMMARY

Introduction to Tort Law	*Tort:* A civil wrong giving the injured party the right to bring a lawsuit against the wrongdoer to recover compensation for the injuries.
Classification of Torts	Torts are classified as intentional, negligent, and strict liability.
Intentional Torts	*Torts against persons* include assault, battery, and defamation.
	Torts against property include trespass to realty, private nuisance, trespass to personal property, and conversion.
	Torts against economic interest include disparagement, intentional interference with contract, unfair competition, misappropriation, and fraudulent misrepresentation.
Negligence	The plaintiff must prove four elements: duty, breach of duty, causation (actual and proximate), and damages.
Plaintiff's Doctrines	Doctrines used to establish negligence: • *Res ipsa loquitur* • Negligence per se
Defenses to Negligence	• Contributory negligence • Modified comparative negligence • Pure comparative negligence • Assumption of the risk
Strict Liability	Persons who engage in activities that are so inherently dangerous that no amount of due care can make them safe are strictly liable, regardless of the degree of care they used when undertaking the activity.
Damages Available in Tort Cases	*Compensatory damages* to make the plaintiff whole again
	Punitive damages to punish the defendant and deter future wrongdoers
	Nominal damages to recognize that the defendant committed a tort against the plaintiff

Point/Counterpoint

Should Punitive Damages Be More Strictly Limited?

YES	NO
Excessive punitive damages are fundamentally unfair.	**The *BMW* standard for excessive punitive damages strikes a fair balance, protecting the interests of both consumers and firms.**
Punitive damages are not a normal part of the tort system. Tort law is supposed to be a way to compensate victims. Punitive damages are almost quasi-criminal in nature; they are designed to punish the defendant, and they reward a plaintiff with, in some cases, riches far beyond what any reasonable person would see as compensation. Tort cases, with the possibility of huge punitive-damage awards, have turned into nothing but litigation lotteries, which have nothing to do with the purposes of our tort system.	In the 20 years prior to the *BMW* case, courts handed down a number of huge punitive-damage awards, some even exceeding $100 million. However, in the years since the *BMW* case, we have seen that the court's three-pronged test has resulted in reducing punitive-damage awards, generally staying below a 9:1 ratio of punitive to compensatory damages. They now appear to be much more reasonable and to fulfill their necessary function. If we examine the top

The possibility of a huge punitive-damage award causes people to bring all sorts of loony lawsuits in hopes of striking it rich. If punitive damages were more reasonable, you would not see people, for example, suing the phone company for publishing false information about a physician that led to a botched liposuction or suing NBC for millions because a *Fear Factor* episode that involved eating rats made a viewer "dizzy and lightheaded and caused him to vomit and run into a doorway."

Besides, unfair punitive-damage awards can ruin a defendant's good name and, in some cases, run target companies out of business. We must bring fairness back to our tort system by limiting punitive damages. Sure, damage awards have fallen since the *BMW* and *State Farm* cases, but they were so exorbitant that they could hardly have gone any higher! Besides, the fact that they have fallen does not mean that they have fallen to reasonable levels.

We need more stringent standards for punitive damages to bring predictability, efficiency, and fairness to our civil justice system. We must all work together for these necessary changes.

10 jury verdicts of 2005, the awards are significantly lower than those of 2004 and previous years. There is no longer any need to limit punitive damages further because they are now reasonably related to the harm the defendant has caused, and they are still large enough to deter behavior.

Punitive damages, in their current manifestation, fulfill two important functions. First, they represent an important way for a significantly harmed plaintiff to recover costs and attorney fees. Without the possibility of large punitive-damage awards, the plaintiff may not actually be compensated for his or her losses because so much of the recovery goes to the attorneys and costs of litigation.

Second, punitive damages perform a necessary deterrence function. If corporations no longer have to fear punitive-damage awards that will hurt them, they will lose some of their motivation to produce safe products and behave as responsible citizens.

With the *BMW* rule, as clarified by *State Farm*, we now have a system in which punitive damages can serve their intended purpose without posing an unreasonable risk to potential defendants.

Questions & Problems

1. Distinguish the three types of damages available in tort cases.

2. Explain why some people see punitive damages as a necessary aspect of our tort system, whereas others want to restrict their availability.

3. List five intentional torts and explain the elements needed to prove each.

4. List and define the elements that are necessary to prove a case of negligence.

5. Explain the differences between contributory and comparative negligence.

6. Explain the relationship between negligence per se and *res ipsa loquitur.*

7. Kerns, a home owner, sued defendant contractor Sealy for negligence, breach of contract, wantonness, and *res ipsa loquitur* in connection with a fire that occurred during the contractor's application of foam installation in the plaintiff's attic. The contractor knew that applying the foam at a thickness over 2 inches created a risk of fire, and he applied the foam at a thickness exceeding 4 inches. He then left the scene for lunch. When he returned, Sealy discovered a haze indicative of fire and attempted to remove the foam. At trial, the defendant made a motion of summary judgment to dismiss all charges. Which charges,

if any, do you think survived summary judgment in district court? [*Kerns et al. v. Sealy et al.,* 496 F. Supp. 2d 1306 (2007).]

8. Former Major League Baseball player and radio game announcer Bob Uecker sought an injunction against Ann Ladd, alleging a six- or seven-year pattern of harassment. Ladd, who claimed to be a devoted fan, was charged with felony stalking. An injunction was issued against her bothering Uecker, but the stalking charge was dropped when she agreed to cooperate. Later, Ladd sued Uecker for defamation, claiming that Uecker defamed her in the material he filed in support of his application for the injunction. The trial court dismissed her suit, and she appealed. What do you think the outcome of her appeal was and why? [*Ladd vb. Uecker,* 780 N.W.2d 216 (Ct. App., Wisc., 2010).]

9. Vernon Hendrickson, an inmate at an Indiana correctional facility, sued correctional officer Scott Cooper for violation of the Eighth Amendment protections against cruel and unusual punishment after Cooper threw Hendrickson against a wall, slammed him onto the concrete floor of his housing unit, and then pressed his knees against Hendrickson's back while another officer cuffed Hendrickson. The jury found Cooper liable for excessive force and awarded

Hendrickson $75,000 in compensatory damages and an additional $125,000 in punitive damages. Cooper appealed the decision, arguing that the jury did not have enough evidence to make its finding of excessive force and that the damage awards were excessive. Using the analysis discussed in this chapter, do you think that the punitive damages awarded to Hendrickson were excessive? What other facts might help inform your decision? [*Hendrickson v. Cooper*, 589 F.3d 887 (2009).]

10. At 2:08 a.m., on Friday, December 29, 2006, the defendant received by e-mail the Lake in the Hills police department Daily Bulletin, and it reported that Carolene Eubanks had been charged with theft and obstruction of justice. As it normally does, the newspaper placed the information from the report in an article and then placed the article in line for publication in the upcoming issue of the newspaper. The article was eventually printed before 6 a.m. on January 2, 2007, and appeared in the defendant's newspaper on the same date.

The Lake in the Hills police department had also sent a second e-mail on December 29, 2006, at 10:25 p.m., that said to remove the name of Carolene Eubanks and replace it with the name of Barbara Bradshaw. Because the employee who posted the article had already gone home, and it was a long holiday weekend, no one was in when the second e-mail arrived, so it wasn't read until January 2, 2007, at 10:17 a.m.

Consequently, the January 2, 2007, edition of the defendant's newspaper, printed before 6 a.m. on that date, published the article indicating that the plaintiff had been arrested and charged with theft and attempted obstruction of justice. The defendant published a retraction of the article in its January 3, 2007, newspaper, stating that the plaintiff was not the one charged with those crimes.

On June 15, 2007, the plaintiff filed her complaint for defamation based on the January 2, 2007, publication. The trial court granted the defendant's motion for summary judgment based on its exercise of a privilege. Plaintiff appealed. What privilege do you think the court relied on? What do you think the outcome

of the appeal was and why? [*Eubanks v. Northwest Herald Newspapers,* 397 Ill.App.3d 746, 922 N.E.2d 1196 (2010).]

11. The Bank of New York (BONY) sued the defendant insurance company, Fremont General Corporation, for intentional interference with contract and conversion. BONY sought to recover damages from the defendant's withdrawal of $14 million from BONY, which BONY alleged interfered with the New York Insurance Company's ability to pay claims of its policyholders. BONY had a valid contract with Fremont Indemnity, a compensation fund that was managed by the defendant. The defendant was aware of the contract between Fremont Indemnity and BONY. By transferring $14 million to another bank, the defendant breached the custodian agreement. The district court granted Fremont General's motion for summary judgment on both claims. BONY appealed the decision, arguing that it had met the evidentiary standards required to prove both claims. Do you agree with the district court? What additional information might alter your decision? [*Bank of New York v. Fremont General Corporation,* 523 F.3d 902 (2008).]

12. In 2008, Wayne Singleton and his eight-year-old son, Jaron, were traveling on a bus for a school field trip to Six Flags. Wayne fell asleep on the way, and while he was asleep, the bus became airborne and drove off the road into a wooded area. The bus eventually collided with a tree. Singleton was asleep when the bus went off the road but woke up for the collision. Jaron was awake the whole time but did not understand the situation. Wayne sued the District of Columbia for the negligence of its employee. At the trial, only Wayne and his son were presented as witnesses. They did not call the bus driver or any other passenger or driver as a witness to provide evidence for why the bus went off the road. Due to this lack of evidence, Wayne invoked *res ipsa loquitur* to infer evidence for the negligence of the driver. The trial court disagreed and granted the District's motion for summary judgment. How do you think the case was ultimately decided on appeal? Why? [*District of Columbia v. Wayne Singleton* et al., No. 77. Court of Appeals of Maryland. (2012).]

Product Liability

LEARNING OBJECTIVES

After reading this chapter, you will be able to answer the following questions:

1 What are the theories of liability in product liability cases?

2 What is market share liability?

CASE OPENER

Is Human Sperm Subject to Product Liability Laws?

Many single women and married couples use donated sperm to conceive children each year. Pennsylvania resident Donna Donovan decided to use donated sperm from Idant Laboratories, a New York sperm bank that emphasized (1) its screening process far exceeded mandated standards and (2) its rigorous screening process ensured that donors had a good genetic history. After using sperm from Idant Laboratories, Donovan gave birth to a girl, Brittany. Donovan began noticing abnormalities in Brittany's development, and Brittany was soon diagnosed as a Fragile X baby. Fragile X is a genetic mutation that causes a range of mental and physical impairments, such as learning disabilities, mental retardation, and behavior disorders. A genetic test for Fragile X was developed two years before Donovan used the sperm from Idant Laboratories. Two years after Brittany's birth, genetic tests showed that the sperm from Idant Laboratories was the carrier of the Fragile X defect. Donovan and Brittany brought suit against Idant Laboratories for selling defective sperm.

1. What do you think the outcome of Donovan's case was?
2. Should the sale of sperm be considered the sale of a product?
3. How do product liability issues affect you?

The Wrap-Up at the end of the chapter will answer these questions.

Breast implants, Ford Explorers, cigarettes, pet food, fast food, fingers in fast food—all of these topics have been the subject of product liability suits. According to the U.S. Department of Justice's Bureau of Justice Statistics, approximately 5 percent of state tort trials in 2005 involved product liability issues.[1] Approximately 25 percent of these trials addressed toxic substances, such as asbestos, tobacco, chemicals, and other toxic substances. The median award to plaintiffs in state court product liability cases that went to trial was $500,000. Each year, juries award hundreds of millions of dollars to plaintiffs bringing suit against companies offering products. If a company manufactures or sells a product, it should expect to be a party to a product liability lawsuit.

In this chapter, we examine the legal theories commonly used by plaintiffs in product liability cases, along with some of the defenses that are used against these cases. By understanding the law of product liability, you may be less likely to take actions that would lead you and your company into costly litigation.

Theories of Liability for Defective Products

L01

What are the theories of liability in product liability cases?

Product liability law is based primarily on tort law. There are three commonly used theories of recovery in product liability cases: negligence, strict product liability, and breach of warranty. A plaintiff may bring a lawsuit based on as many of these theories of liability as apply to the plaintiff's factual situation. While a plaintiff must establish different elements under each of these theories, the plaintiff must generally show two common elements: (1) that the product is defective, and (2) that the defect existed when the product left the defendant's control.

How might a product be defective? Suppose you select a glass bottle of Diet Coke at the grocery store. When you grab the bottle, it shatters in your hand and severely cuts your thumb. Most bottles of soda do not shatter when touched; thus, there must have been a problem in the manufacture of this particular bottle. When an individual product (e.g., the shattered Diet Coke bottle) has a defect making it more dangerous than other identical products (the 200 other Diet Coke bottles at the grocery store), this individual product has a **manufacturing defect.**

Given your severe cut from the Diet Coke bottle, you get into your car to drive to the hospital. Unfortunately, someone rear-ends your car; the crash causes your driver's seat to bend backward such that you hit your head on the backseat and suffer a serious neck injury. The design of the driver's seat allowed the seat to bend backward, and all driver's seats in this type of car have the same design. When all products of a particular design are defective and dangerous, these products have a **design defect.**

Because of the pain associated with your neck injury and lacerated thumb, you take a new over-the-counter pain reliever. You read and follow the instructions on the box and take two pills. However, you begin to feel incredibly ill. You rush to the hospital and discover that you are experiencing negative side effects from the pain reliever because it has interacted with some of your other medications. You had carefully read the instructions and warnings, but you did not see anything about drug interactions. A product may be defective as a result of the manufacturer's **failure to provide adequate warnings** about potential dangers associated with the product.

The product examples above (Diet Coke bottle, driver's seat in a car, pain reliever) are tangible items. However, can an intangible "product" be subject to product liability claims? See the Case Nugget "What Is a Product?"

---

[1] Bureau of Justice Statistics, "Civil Justice Survey of State Courts: Tort Breach and Jury Trials in State Courts, 2005," November 2009, http://bjs.ojp.usdoj.gov/content/pub/pdf/tbjtsc05.pdf.

Radford v. Wells Fargo Bank
2011 WL 1833020 (D. Haw. 2011)

Plaintiff Richard Radford brought a suit against Wells Fargo Bank alleging that he was enticed into purchasing a defective product and claiming an intentional or negligent failure to warn of a defective product (i.e., his mortgage loan). The district court held that a mortgage is not a "product" that can be subject to product liability claims for at least three reasons. First, "[p]roducts liability covers products that are reasonably certain to place life and limb in peril and may cause bodily harm if defective. The language of products liability law reflects its focus on tangible items." Second, the Restatement (Second) of Torts provides examples of items covered by product liability claims, and a mortgage loan does not appear on the list. Finally, there was no case law in Hawaii supporting Radford's contention that a loan is a product.

In summary, a product may be defective because of a manufacturing defect, a design defect, or inadequate warnings. As you read the chapter, think about how these types of defects fit in with the three theories of liability: negligence, strict liability, and breach of warranty.

NEGLIGENCE

To win a case based on negligence, the plaintiff must prove the four elements of negligence explained in Chapter 9: (1) The defendant manufacturer or seller owed a duty of care to the plaintiff; (2) the defendant breached that duty of care by supplying a defective product; (3) this breach of duty caused the plaintiff's injury; and (4) the plaintiff suffered actual injury.

Prior to the landmark 1916 case of *MacPherson v. Buick Motor Co.*, negligence was rarely used as a theory of recovery for an injury caused by a defective product because of the difficulty of establishing the element of duty. Until that case, the courts said that a plaintiff who was not the purchaser of the defective product could not establish a duty of care, because one could not owe a duty to someone with whom one was not "in privity of contract." Being *in privity of contract* means being a party to a contract. Because most consumers do not purchase goods directly from the manufacturers, product liability cases against manufacturers were rare before the *MacPherson* case.

Following *MacPherson,* any foreseeable plaintiff can sue a manufacturer for its breach of duty of care. Foreseeable plaintiffs include users, consumers, and bystanders. Moreover, foreseeable plaintiffs can bring a case against retailers, wholesalers, and manufacturers. However, retailers and wholesalers can satisfy their duty of care by making a cursory reasonable inspection of a product when they receive it from the manufacturer.

Negligent Failure to Warn. To bring a successful case based on negligent failure to warn, the plaintiff must demonstrate that the defendant knew or should have known that without a warning, the product would be dangerous in its ordinary use, or in any *reasonably foreseeable* use, yet the defendant still failed to provide a warning. For example, the 10th Circuit recently affirmed a trial court decision in which a smoker was awarded approximately $200,000 from R. J. Reynolds Tobacco, which before 1969 had negligently failed to warn smokers of the harm associated with smoking cigarettes. No duty to warn exists for dangers arising either from unforeseeable misuses of a product or from obvious dangers. A producer of razor blades, for example, need not give a warning that a razor

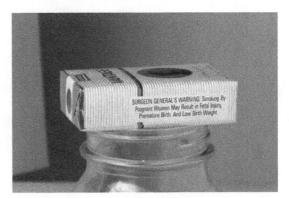

Prior to these required warning labels on cigarette packages, one basis for suing the tobacco industry was failure to warn.

CASE NUGGET

MCDONALD'S COFFEE IS HOT!

**Liebeck v. McDonald's Corp.
No. D-202 CV-93-02419**

One of the most famous product liability cases is the McDonald's coffee-cup case. Stella Liebeck, a 79-year-old woman, spilled a cup of McDonald's coffee in her lap. She sued McDonald's, and in 1994, a jury awarded her almost $3 million in damages. Many people cite the case as an example of the need for product liability law reform; however, they either intentionally or inadvertently omit a discussion of the facts of the case:

- Liebeck spilled the entire cup of coffee in her lap. McDonald's required that its franchises serve coffee at 180 to 190 degrees Fahrenheit. Liquid at this high temperature causes third-degree burns in two to seven seconds. Liebeck suffered third-degree burns on her skin that required skin grafting. She was in the hospital for eight days and required two years of treatment for the burns.

- Liebeck asked McDonald's to cover her medical costs and settle the case for $20,000; McDonald's offered $800. She filed the lawsuit after McDonald's refused to raise its offer from $800.

- Through documents produced by McDonald's, Liebeck discovered that between 1982 and 1992, McDonald's had received over 700 complaints about the temperature of the coffee. Some of these complaints discussed burns in varying degrees of severity, and McDonald's had previously received claims arising from burn complaints for over $500,000.

- Before the beginning of the jury trial, a retired judge, who was serving as a mediator, recommended that the parties settle the case for $225,000. McDonald's refused.

- While the jury awarded Liebeck $200,000 in compensatory damages and $2,700,000 in punitive damages, the court reduced the damages award to $160,000 in compensatory damages (finding Liebeck 20 percent at fault in the spill) and $480,000 in punitive damages. The parties ultimately settled the case for an undisclosed amount under $600,000.

How do these facts affect your thinking about product liability law?

blade may cut someone. For example, in *Ward v. Arm & Hammer,*[2] after being convicted on criminal charges for distribution of crack cocaine, the plaintiff brought suit against Arm & Hammer, arguing that the company should have included a warning on its package of baking soda of the criminal consequences of using the baking soda to make cocaine. The court emphasized that the manufacturer of a raw component that is not in itself dangerous has no duty to warn the public of the dangers associated with combining that component in a dangerous or criminal manner. Courts often consider the likelihood of the injury, the seriousness of the injury, and the ease of warning when deciding whether a manufacturer was negligent in failing to warn. To the extent that a company is aware of potential harm associated with reasonably foreseeable uses of its products, the safest course of action for the company is to identify this harm to the consumers as a warning.

When providing a warning, the manufacturer must ensure that the warning will reach those who are intended to use the product. For example, if parties other than the original purchaser will be likely to use the product, the warning should be placed directly on the product itself, not just in a manual that comes with the product. Picture warnings may be required if children, or those who are illiterate, are likely to come into contact with the product and risk harm from its use.

Products such as drugs and cosmetics are often the basis for actions based on negligent failure to warn because the use of these products frequently causes adverse reactions. When the user of a cosmetic or an over-the-counter drug has a reaction to that product, many courts find that there is no duty to warn unless the plaintiff proves that (1) the product contained an ingredient to which an appreciable number of people would have an adverse reaction; (2) the defendant knew or should have known, in the exercise of ordinary care, about the existence of this group; and (3) the plaintiff's reaction was due to his or her membership in this abnormal group.

[2] 341 F. Supp. 2d (D.N.J. 2004).

CASE NUGGET

FAILURE TO WARN ABOUT FOOD

Pelman v. McDonald's
237 F. Supp. 2d 512 (S.D.N.Y 2003)

Consumers have recently been bringing cases that attempt to hold others liable for their health problems allegedly caused by unhealthy food. In *Pelman v. McDonald's*, the plaintiffs alleged that McDonald's failed to warn customers of the "ingredients, quantity, qualities and levels of cholesterol, fat, salt and sugar content and other ingredients in those products, and that a diet high in fat, salt, sugar and cholesterol could lead to obesity and health problems." Judge Sweet originally dismissed the plaintiffs' claims, stating his decision was guided by the principle that legal consequences should not attach to the consumption of hamburgers and other fast-food fare unless consumers are unaware of the dangers of eating such food. He determined that consumers know, or should reasonably know, the potential negative health effects associated with eating fast food. The plaintiffs filed an amended complaint, asserting that McDonald's engaged in a scheme of deceptive advertising that in effect created the impression that McDonald's food products were nutritionally beneficial and part of a healthy lifestyle. In September 2006, Judge Sweet refused to dismiss the plaintiffs' claims, and as of February 2010, the case was still moving forward as a class action.

Similarly, in *Gorran v. Atkins Nutritionals, Inc.*, Jody Gorran argued that he developed heart disease by following the Atkins diet, which encourages dieters to limit carbohydrates such as bread, rice, and pasta while increasing meat, cheese, eggs, and other high-protein (and high-fat) foods.* According to Gorran's complaint, Atkins Nutritionals promoted the health benefits of its diet while knowing that some people were "fat-sensitive" and subject to adverse health effects, yet Atkins failed to warn the public. The court determined that as long as the food was sold in a condition anticipated by the consumer, it was not a defective product simply because it could negatively affect the consumer's health.

* "Judge Rebuffs Atkins' Second Bid to Dismiss Dieter's Lawsuit," *Andrews Product Liability Litigation Reporter* 16, no. 1 (2005), p. 2.

Other courts, however, use a balancing test to determine negligence in such cases. They weigh the degree of danger to be avoided with the ease of warning. For example, in 1994, a jury awarded over $8.8 million to a man who suffered permanent liver damage as a result of drinking a glass of wine with a Tylenol capsule (the award was reduced to $350,000 due to a statutory cap). As early as 1977, the company knew that combining a normal dose of Tylenol with a small amount of wine could cause massive liver damage in some people, but the company failed to put a warning to that effect on the label because such a reaction was rare. Through the balancing test, the court found that the degree of potential harm was substantial and that it would have been relatively easy to place a warning on the product label.

Furthermore, some courts have permitted a "sophisticated-user" defense, which acts as a complete defense to failure-to-warn claims. For example, in a 2008 case, the Supreme Court of California adopted the sophisticated-user defense, noting that a user's knowledge of certain dangers is equivalent to notice. In that case, the plaintiff was a trained and certified heating, ventilation, and air-conditioning (HVAC) technician who alleged that he suffered harm from exposure to a certain gas frequently used in air-conditioning systems. Because the training and certification for HVAC taught about the harm related to this gas, the court determined that the technician, as a sophisticated or educated user, could not recover.

Negligence Per Se. As you know from Chapter 9, a statute violation that causes the harm that the statute was enacted to prevent constitutes *negligence per se*. This doctrine is also applicable to product liability cases based on negligence. When a law establishes labeling, design, or content requirements for products, the manufacturer has a duty to meet these requirements. Failure by the manufacturer to meet those standards means that the manufacturer has breached its duty of reasonable care. If the plaintiff can establish that the failure to meet such a standard caused injury, the plaintiff can recover under negligence per se.

Damages. Damages that are recoverable in negligence-based product liability cases are the same as those in any action based on negligence: compensatory damages and punitive damages. As you should recall from Chapter 8, *compensatory damages* are those designed to make the plaintiff whole again; they cover items such as medical bills, lost wages, and compensation for pain and suffering. While this list of recoverable harms may seem "obvious" to us, not all countries allow such extensive recovery. For example, in German product liability cases, consumers do not have a right to recover damages for pain and suffering or for emotional distress. *Punitive damages* are meant to punish the defendant for extremely harmful conduct. The amount of the punitive-damage award is determined by the wealth of the defendant and the maliciousness of the action.

In 2009–2011, Toyota announced that millions of its cars would be recalled due to acceleration and braking problems. As of February 2010, dozens of product liability lawsuits had been filed against Toyota. In many of these cases, plaintiffs were seeking damages for personal injuries or wrongful death due to the alleged acceleration and braking problems. Some of these cases were claims against Toyota to recover damages for the reduced value of their cars. Specifically, before the recall, Toyota owners claim that they could resell their cars at a certain price; after the recall, this price was several thousand dollars lower. In fact, the *Kelley Blue Book* reported that the resale value of Toyota models fell 1 to 3 percent in just one week following certain recalls.[3]

In December 2012, Toyota agreed to pay over $1 billion to settle the class action litigation regarding the loss-of-economic-value claims related to the recalls.[4] The National Highway Traffic Safety Administration fined Toyota more than $60 million for failing to inform regulators of internal information Toyota had regarding the sudden acceleration.

Legal Principle: **The plaintiff in a product liability case may recover compensatory damages, designed to provide compensation for provable losses, and punitive damages, an amount awarded to punish the defendant.**

Defenses to a Negligence-Based Product Liability Action.   The defenses to negligence discussed in the previous chapter are available in product liability cases based on negligence. A common defense in such cases is that the plaintiff's own failure to act reasonably contributed to the plaintiff's own harm. This negligence on the part of the plaintiff allows the defendant to raise the defense of *contributory, comparative,* or *modified comparative negligence,* depending on which defense is accepted by the state where the case arose. Remember, in a state that allows the contributory negligence defense, proof of any negligence by the plaintiff is an absolute bar to recovery. In a state where the defense of pure comparative negligence is allowed, the plaintiff can recover for only that portion of the harm attributable to the defendant's negligence. In a modified comparative negligence state, the plaintiff can recover the percentage of harm caused by the defendant as long as the jury finds the plaintiff's negligence responsible for less than 50 percent of the harm.

A closely related defense is *assumption of the risk.* This defense arises when a consumer knows that a defect exists but still proceeds unreasonably to make use of the product, creating a situation in which the consumer has voluntarily assumed the risk of injury from the defect and thus cannot recover. To decide whether the plaintiff did indeed assume the risk, the trier of fact may consider such factors as the plaintiff's age, experience, knowledge, and understanding, as well as the obviousness of the defect and the danger it poses. When a plaintiff knows of a danger but does not fully appreciate the magnitude of the risk, the applicability of the defense is a question for the jury to determine.

Another common defense is *misuse* of the product. The misuse must be unreasonable or unforeseeable. When a defendant raises the defense of product misuse, the defendant is really arguing that the harm was caused not by the defendant's negligence but by the plaintiff's failure to properly use the product.

---

[3] Nick Bunkley, "Some Toyota Owners Voice an Eroding Loyalty," *The New York Times,* February 7, 2010.

[4] Bill Vlasic, "Toyota Agrees to Settle Lawsuit Tied to Accelerations," *New York Times,* December 26, 2012.

COMPARING THE LAW OF OTHER COUNTRIES

PRODUCT MISUSE IN JAPAN

Like the United States, Japan also addresses situations in which the consumer misuses a defective product. In Japan, such a situation is called *comparative negligence*. The negligence of both the defendant and the plaintiff is taken into account when determining the distribution of damages. The leading case of comparative negligence is that of *Miyahara v. Matsumoto Gas Company*. In this case, the defendant purchased a gas stove from Matsumoto.

A faulty rubber nose valve caused the stove to start a fire, resulting in extensive damage to Miyahara's home. An investigation after the fire, however, showed that Miyahara had failed to close the valve before going to sleep the evening of the fire. Consequently, both he and the gas company were found negligent. The cost of the damages was split between the two parties.

The *state-of-the-art defense* is used by a defendant to demonstrate that his alleged negligent behavior was reasonable, given the available scientific knowledge existing at the time the product was sold or produced. If a case is based on the defendant's negligent defective design of a product, the state-of-the-art defense refers to the technological feasibility of producing a safer product at the time the product was manufactured. In cases of negligent failure to warn, the state-of-the-art defense refers to the scientific knowability of a risk associated with a product at the time of its production. This is a valid defense in a negligence case because the focus is on the reasonableness of the defendant's conduct. However, the state of scientific knowledge at the time of production, and the lack of a feasible way to make a safer product, does not always preclude liability. The court may find that the defendant's conduct was still unreasonable because even in its technologically safest form, the risks posed by the defect in the design so outweighed the benefits of the product that the reasonable person would not have produced a product of that design.

Suppose a defendant designs a product to comply with federal safety regulations regarding that product. That defendant may attempt to argue that *compliance with federal laws* is a defense to state tort law because the state tort law is preempted by a federal statute designed to ensure the safety of a particular class of products. The Supreme Court recently issued a ruling on whether a state tort claim was preempted because the FDA had approved the drug label (see Case 10-1).

Each preemption case requires careful scrutiny of the purpose of the statute. For example, in *Tebbetts v. Ford Motor Co.*, the plaintiff argued that the 1988 Ford Escort was defectively designed because it did not have a driver's side air bag. Ford raised the preemption defense, arguing that it had complied with federal safety regulations under the National Traffic and Motor Vehicle Safety Act (NTMVSA). Consequently, Ford argued that its compliance preempted recovery under state product liability laws. After considering the legislative history and the law, the court discovered a clause in the law stating that "[c]ompliance with any Federal motor vehicle safety standard issued under this act does not exempt any person from any liability under common law." Thus, the court ruled that the Tebbetts were not preempted from bringing their product liability action.

Similarly, oil companies have argued that their compliance with the Clean Air Act should not subject them to tort liability for MTBE contamination in groundwater. Through the Clean Air Act, Congress required that oil companies include an oxygenate in gasoline to allow the gasoline to burn more cleanly and thus to improve air quality. MTBE, or methyl tertiary butyl ether, is one type of oxygenate. While everyone expected MTBE to help improve air quality, widespread use of this oxygenate had a negative consequence: It contaminated water. A very small amount of MTBE affects the smell and taste of water. Given these extreme negative consequences, numerous states banned MTBE. Moreover, cities and individuals have sued oil companies to pay for the costs, in the millions of dollars, that will be incurred to clean the drinking water. While a few courts have agreed with

CASE 10-1   WYETH v. LEVINE
UNITED STATES SUPREME COURT
555 U.S. 555, 2009, 129 S. CT. 1187 (2009)

Diana Levine, a professional musician, sought treatment for her migraine headaches and was given an injection of Wyeth's antinausea drug, Phenergan. While the drug was supposed to be injected directly into Levine's vein through a method called the IV-push method, the drug entered an artery instead. Consequently, Levine developed gangrene and had to have her right hand and entire forearm amputated. She incurred substantial medical expenses and could no longer perform as a professional musician. At trial, Levine argued that Wyeth's labeling was defective because although it warned of the danger of gangrene and amputation following inadvertent intra-arterial injection, it failed to instruct clinicians to use the IV-drip method of intravenous administration instead of the higher-risk IV-push method. The jury agreed with Levine. Wyeth argued that the judge should overturn the jury verdict because Levine's claim was preempted because the drug's label had been approved by the Food and Drug Administration. The judge rejected Wyeth's argument, and the Vermont Supreme Court upheld that ruling, holding that the federal regulations created a floor and not a ceiling and Wyeth could have warned against IV-push administration. Wyeth appealed to the U.S. Supreme Court, making 2 arguments: (1) it was impossible to comply with both its state and federal law obligations and (2) Levine's common-law claims stand as an obstacle to the accomplishment of Congress' purposes in the Food, Drug and Cosmetic Act (FDCA).

JUSTICE STEVENS: The . . . question presented is whether federal law preempts Levine's claim that Phenergan's label did not contain an adequate warning about using the IV-push method of administration. Wyeth first argues that Levine's state-law claims are preempted because it is impossible for it to comply with both the state-law duties underlying those claims and its federal labeling duties. The FDA's premarket approval of a new drug application includes the approval of the exact text in the proposed label. Generally speaking, a manufacturer may only change a drug label after the FDA approves a supplemental application. There is, however, an FDA regulation that permits a manufacturer to make certain changes to its label before receiving the agency's approval. Among other things, this "changes being effected" (CBE) regulation provides that if a manufacturer is changing a label to "add or strengthen a contraindication, warning, precaution, or adverse reaction" or to "add or strengthen an instruction about dosage and administration that is intended to increase the safe use of the drug product," it may make the labeling change upon filing its supplemental application with the FDA; it need not wait for FDA approval.

Wyeth argues that the CBE regulation is not implicated in this case because a 2008 amendment provides that a manufacturer may only change its label "to reflect newly acquired information." Resting on this language, Wyeth contends that it could have changed Phenergan's label only in response to new information that the FDA had not considered.

Wyeth could have revised Phenergan's label even in accordance with the amended regulation. As the FDA explained in its notice of the final rule, "newly acquired information" is not limited to new data, but also encompasses "new analyses of previously submitted data." The rule accounts for the fact that risk information accumulates over time and that the same data may take on a different meaning in light of subsequent developments. Levine . . . present[ed] evidence of at least 20 incidents prior to her injury in which a Phenergan injection resulted in gangrene and an amputation. After the first such incident came to Wyeth's attention in 1967, it notified the FDA and worked with the agency to change Phenergan's label. In later years, as amputations continued to occur, Wyeth could have analyzed the accumulating data and added a stronger warning about IV-push administration of the drug.

[A]bsent clear evidence that the FDA would not have approved a change to Phenergan's label, we will not conclude that it was impossible for Wyeth to comply with both federal and state requirements.

Impossibility preemption is a demanding defense. On the record before us, Wyeth has failed to demonstrate that it was impossible for it to comply with both federal and state requirements. The CBE regulation permitted Wyeth to unilaterally strengthen its warning, and the mere fact that the FDA approved Phenergan's label does not establish that it would have prohibited such a change.

Wyeth also argues that requiring it to comply with a state-law duty to provide a stronger warning about IV-push administration would obstruct the purposes and objectives of federal drug labeling regulation. Levine's tort claims, it maintains, are preempted because they interfere with "Congress's purpose to entrust an expert agency to make drug labeling decisions that strike a balance between competing objectives." We find no merit in this argument, which relies on an untenable interpretation of congressional intent and an overbroad view of an agency's power to preempt state law.

Wyeth contends that the FDCA establishes both a floor and a ceiling for drug regulation. Wyeth relies . . . on the preamble to a 2006 FDA regulation governing the content and format of prescription drug labels. In that preamble, the FDA declared that the FDCA establishes "both a 'floor' and a 'ceiling,'" so that "FDA approval of labeling . . . preempts conflicting or contrary State law." It further stated that

[continued]

certain state-law actions, such as those involving failure-to-warn claims, "threaten FDA's statutorily prescribed role as the expert Federal agency responsible for evaluating and regulating drugs." . . .

[T]he FDA's 2006 preamble does not merit deference. When the FDA issued its notice of proposed rulemaking in December 2000, it explained that the rule would "not contain policies that have federalism implications or that preempt State law." In 2006, the agency finalized the rule and, without offering States or other interested parties notice or opportunity for comment, articulated a sweeping position on the FDCA's preemptive effect in the regulatory preamble. The agency's views on state law are inherently suspect in light of this procedural failure.

In short, Wyeth has not persuaded us that failure-to-warn claims like Levine's obstruct the federal regulation of drug labeling. Congress has repeatedly declined to preempt state law, and the FDA's recently adopted position that state tort suits interfere with its statutory mandate is entitled to no weight. Although we recognize that some state-law claims might well frustrate the achievement of congressional objectives, this is not such a case.

We conclude that it is not impossible for Wyeth to comply with its state and federal law obligations and that Levine's common-law claims do not stand as an obstacle to the accomplishment of Congress' purposes in the FDCA. Accordingly, the judgment of the Vermont Supreme Court is affirmed.

AFFIRMED.

CRITICAL THINKING

What are the reasons for the Court's conclusion that Levine's product liability claims are not preempted?

ETHICAL DECISION MAKING

Recall the WPH process for ethical decision making. Who are the relevant stakeholders affected by this decision?

the oil companies, most cases have held that the Clean Air Act does not preempt tort cases because the oil companies had a choice of oxygenates to use. Moreover, the courts state that the problem of water contamination is too far removed from the problem that Congress was trying to address through the Clean Air Act regulations; thus, there is no preemption.

Certain statutory defenses are also available in negligence-based product liability cases. To ensure that there will be sufficient evidence from which a trier of fact can make a decision, states have *statutes of limitations* that limit the time within which all types of civil actions may be brought. In most states, the statute of limitations for tort actions, and thus for negligence-based product liability cases, varies between one and four years from the date of injury.

Statutes of repose provide an additional statutory defense by barring actions arising more than a specified number of years after the product was purchased. Statutes of repose are usually much longer than statutes of limitations, generally running at least 10 years.

STRICT PRODUCT LIABILITY

The requirements for proving strict product liability can be found in Section 402A of the Restatement (Second) of Torts. This section reads as follows:

1. One who sells any product in a defective condition, unreasonably dangerous to the user or consumer or his family is subject to liability for physical harm, thereby, caused to the ultimate user or consumer, or to this property, if
   a. the seller is engaged in the business of selling such a product, and
   b. it is expected to and does reach the consumer or user without substantial change in the condition in which it was sold.
2. The rule stated in Subsection (1) applies although
   a. the seller has exercised all possible care in the preparation and sale of his product, and
   b. the user or consumer has not bought the product from or entered into any contractual relation with the seller.

Under **strict product liability,** courts may hold liable the manufacturer, distributor, or retailer to any reasonably foreseeable injured party. Any reasonably foreseeable injured party includes the buyer; the buyer's family, guests, and friends; and foreseeable bystanders. The actions of the manufacturer or seller are not relevant; rather, strict product liability focuses on the *product.* Thus, duty is irrelevant. Courts focus on whether the product was in a "defective condition, unreasonably dangerous" when sold. To succeed in a strict-liability action, the plaintiff must prove three things:

1. The product was defective when sold.
2. The product was so defective that the product was unreasonably dangerous.
3. The product was the cause of the plaintiff's injury.

As stated earlier, a product may be defective because of (1) a flaw in its manufacturing that led to its being more dangerous; (2) a defective design; or (3) missing or inadequate instructions or warnings that could have reduced or eliminated foreseeable risks posed by the product.

Plaintiffs usually prove that a defect exists by means of (1) experts who testify as to the type of flaw in the product that led to the plaintiff's injury and/or (2) evidence of the circumstances surrounding the accident that would lead the jury to infer that the accident must have been caused by a defect in the product. Exhibit 10-1 describes how expert opinion is used in product liability cases. Case 10-2 illustrates how circumstances can provide a reasonable basis for such an inference.

Exhibit 10-1

The Battle of the Experts

EXPERT OPINION IN PRODUCT LIABILITY CASES

Plaintiffs use experts in product liability cases to show the existence of a flaw or to show that a flaw caused the plaintiff's injuries. To rebut the plaintiff's expert opinion, the defense usually hires an expert to show that there is no defect or that the product did not cause the plaintiff's injuries. These experts frequently battle over the scientific evidence regarding causation.

Expert testimony is used in various types of litigation: drugs, breast implants, automobile accidents, and pollution. Expert opinion is generally admissible in a trial if two conditions are met:
1. The subject matter is one in which scientific, technical, or other specialized knowledge would help the finder of fact, and the knowledge is relevant and reliable.
2. The expert offering the testimony is qualified as an expert.

Juries, or even judges, have sometimes been persuaded by an "expert" advocating "junk science." Junk science may be "biased data, spurious inferences, and logical legerdemain, patched together by researchers whose enthusiasm for discovery and diagnosis outstrips their skill. It is a catalog of every conceivable kind of error: data dredging, wishful thinking, truculent dogmatism, and now and again, outright fraud."* In an attempt to reduce the use of junk science in the courtroom, the Supreme Court, in *Daubert v. Merrell Dow Pharmaceutical,* determined that judges are responsible for assessing expert opinion. It identified four considerations for relevant and reliable opinions:
1. Did the expert use the scientific method?
2. Has the expert's theory or technique been subjected to peer review and publication?
3. Does the particular technique have a significant rate of error?
4. Is the methodology generally accepted in the scientific community?

Expert-witness fees may range from $100 to $1,000 an hour. Experts are usually deposed during litigation, so their time preparing for depositions and trial can easily run into hundreds of hours, which can be quite costly for clients.

* Peter Huber, *Galileo's Revenge: Junk Science in the Courtroom* (New York: Basic Books, 1991).

CASE 10-2   WELGE v. PLANTERS LIFESAVERS CO.
COURT OF APPEALS FOR THE SEVENTH CIRCUIT

17 F.3D 209 (7TH CIR. 1994)

Richard Welge, who boarded with Karen Godfrey, liked peanuts on his ice cream sundaes. Godfrey bought a 24-ounce vacuum-sealed plastic-capped jar of Planters peanuts for Welge at K-Mart. To obtain a $2 rebate, Godfrey needed proof of her purchase from the jar of peanuts. She used an Exacto knife to remove the part of the label that contained the bar code and placed the jar on top of the refrigerator for Welge. A week later, Welge removed the plastic seal from the jar, uncapped it, took some peanuts, replaced the cap, and returned the jar to the top of the refrigerator. A week after that, he took down the jar, removed the plastic cap, spilled some peanuts into his left hand to put on his sundae, and replaced the cap with his right hand. As he pushed the cap down on the open jar, the jar shattered. His hand was severely cut, and became permanently impaired.

Welge filed product liability actions against K-Mart, the seller of the product; Planters, the manufacturer of the peanuts; and Brockway, the manufacturer of the glass jar. Defendants filed a motion for summary judgment after discovery. The district judge granted the motion on the ground that the plaintiff had failed to exclude possible causes of the accident other than a defect introduced during the manufacturing process. The plaintiff appealed.

JUSTICE POSNER: No doubt there are men strong enough to shatter a thick glass jar with one blow. But Welge's testimony stands uncontradicted that he used no more than the normal force that one exerts in snapping a plastic lid onto a jar. So the jar must have been defective. No expert testimony and no fancy doctrine are required for such a conclusion. A nondefective jar does not shatter when normal force is used to clamp its plastic lid on. The question is when the defect was introduced. It could have been at any time from the manufacture of the glass jar by Brockway (for no one suggests that the defect might have been caused by something in the raw materials out of which the jar was made) to moments before the accident. But testimony by Welge and Godfrey . . . excludes all reasonable possibility that the defect was introduced into the jar after Godfrey plucked it from a shelf in the K-Mart store. From the shelf she put it in her shopping cart. The checker at the check out counter scanned the bar code without banging the jar. She then placed the jar in a plastic bag. Godfrey carried the bag to her car and put it on the floor. She drove directly home, without incident. After the bar code portion of the label was removed, the jar sat on top of the refrigerator except for the two times Welge removed it to take peanuts out of it. Throughout this process it was not, so far as anyone knows, jostled, dropped, bumped, or otherwise subjected to stress beyond what is to be expected in the ordinary use of the product. Chicago is not Los Angeles; there were no earthquakes. Chicago is not Amityville either; no supernatural interventions are alleged. So the defect must have been introduced earlier, when the jar was in the hands of the defendants.

. . . [I]t is always possible that the jar was damaged while it was sitting unattended on the top of the refrigerator, in which event they are not responsible. Only if it had been securely under lock and key when not being used could the plaintiff and Karen Godfrey be certain that nothing happened to damage it after she brought it home. That is true—there are no metaphysical certainties—but it leads nowhere. Elves may have played ninepins with the jar of peanuts while Welge and Godfrey were sleeping; but elves could remove a jar of peanuts from a locked cupboard. The plaintiff in a product liability suit is not required to exclude every possibility, however fantastic or remote, that the defect which led to the accident was caused by someone other than one of the defendants. The doctrine of *res ipsa loquitur* teaches that an accident that is unlikely to occur, unless the defendant was negligent, is itself circumstantial evidence that the defendant was negligent. The doctrine is not strictly applicable to a product liability case because, unlike an ordinary accident case, the defendant in a products case has parted with possession and control of the harmful object before the accident occurs. . . . But the doctrine merely instantiates the broader principle, which is as applicable to a products case as to any other tort case, that an accident can itself be evidence of liability. . . . If it is the kind of accident that would not have occurred but for a defect in the product, and if it is reasonably plain that the defect was not introduced after the product was sold, the accident is evidence that the product was defective when sold. The second condition (as well as the first) has been established here, at least to a probability sufficient to defeat a motion for summary judgment. Normal people do not lock up their jars and cans lest something happens to damage these containers while no one is looking. The probability of such damage is too remote. It is not only too remote to make a rational person take measures to prevent it; it is too remote to defeat a product liability suit should a container prove dangerously defective.

. . . [I]f the probability that the defect which caused the accident arose after Karen Godfrey bought the jar of Planters peanuts is very small—and on the present state of the record we are required to assume that it is—then the probability that the defect was introduced by one of the defendants is very high.

. . . The strict-liability element in modern product liability law comes precisely from the fact that a seller, subject to that law, is liable for defects in his product even if those defects were introduced, without the slightest fault of his own for failing to discover them, at some anterior stage of production. . . . So the fact that K-Mart sold a defective jar of peanuts to Karen Godfrey would be conclusive of K-Mart's

[continued]

liability, and since it is a large and solvent firm there would be no need for the plaintiff to look further for a tortfeasor.

. . . Here we know to a virtual certainty (always assuming that the plaintiff's evidence is believed, which is a matter for the jury) that the accident was not due to mishandling after purchase, but to a defect that had been introduced earlier.

REVERSED and REMANDED in favor of the plaintiff.

CRITICAL THINKING

What are Justice Posner's reasons for reversing the decision? Do you find his reasons compelling?

ETHICAL DECISION MAKING

Suppose that the defect had been introduced by Brockway and that corporate management had been aware of the defect but believed the chances of someone's being hurt were small enough to be negligible. Therefore, Brockway did not inform Planters of the defect. Should it have informed Planters?

In Case 10-2, the product had a manufacturing defect, which was fairly straightforward to prove. However, it is sometimes more difficult to prove that a design is defective. States are not in agreement as to how to establish a design defect, and two different tests have evolved to determine when a product is so defective as to be unreasonably dangerous. The first test, set out in the Restatement (Second) of Torts, is the *consumer expectations test:* Did the product meet the standards that would be expected by the reasonable consumer? This test relies on the experiences and expectations of the ordinary consumer, and thus it is not answered by the use of expert testimony about the merits of the design. See Exhibit 10-2 for an analysis of the difference between the second and third Restatement of Torts.

Exhibit 10-2

Impact of the Restatement (Third) of Torts

Section 402A of the Restatement (Second) of Torts is generally the foundation of modern product liability law, but that section has been subject to considerable criticism. In 1998, the criticisms led the American Law Institute to adopt the "Restatement of the Law (Third), Torts: Product Liability," which is intended to replace Section 402A.

Under the Restatement (Third):

[O]ne engaged in the business of selling or otherwise distributing products who sells or distributes a defective product is subject to liability for harm to persons or property caused by the defect.

The section departs from the Restatement (Second) by holding the seller to a different standard of liability, depending on whether the defect in question is a manufacturing defect, a design defect, or a defective warning.

It is only a manufacturing defect that results in strict liability. A manufacturing defect arises when "the product departs from its intended design," and liability is imposed regardless of the care taken by the manufacturer.

The Restatement (Third) applies a reasonableness standard to design defects, stating:

[A] product is defective in design when the foreseeable risks of the harm posed by the product could have been reduced or avoided by the adoption of a reasonable alternative design by the seller . . . and the omission of the alternative design renders the product not reasonably safe.

Comments in the Restatement (Third) list a number of factors the court can use to determine whether a reasonable alternative design renders the product not reasonably safe, including:

(continued)

the magnitude and probability of the foreseeable risks of harm, the instructions and warnings accompanying the product, and the nature and strength of consumer expectations regarding the product, including expectations arising from product portrayal and marketing, . . . the relative advantage and disadvantages of the product as designed and as it alternatively could have been designed, . . . the likely effects of the alternative design on product longevity, maintenance, repair and esthetics, and the range of consumer choice among products.

Thus, the Restatement (Third) has in effect shifted to a risk-utility test.

The Restatement (Third) has likewise adopted a reasonableness standard for defective warnings:

A product is defective because of inadequate instructions or warnings when the foreseeable risks of harm posed by the product could have been reduced or avoided by the provision of reasonable instructions or warnings by the seller . . . and the omission of the warnings renders the product not reasonably safe.

The potential effects of changes brought about by the newest Restatement have yet to be fully felt. As of 2001, the Restatement (Third) had not been widely adopted by the states.

Exhibit 10-2
Continued

The second is the *feasible alternatives test,* sometimes referred to as the *risk-utility test.* In applying this test, the court focuses on the usefulness and safety of the design and compares it to an alternative design. The exact factors that the court examines are detailed in Case 10-3, which makes explicit the differences between the two tests.

CASE 10-3 · SPERRY–NEW HOLLAND, A DIVISION OF SPERRY CORPORATION v. JOHN PAUL PRESTAGE AND PAM PRESTAGE
SUPREME COURT OF MISSISSIPPI
617 SO. 2D 248 (1993)

Mr. Prestage's foot and lower leg were caught in a combine manufactured by defendant Sperry–New Holland. He and his wife sued defendant for damages arising out of the accident. Their first cause of action was based on the theory of strict product liability. A jury awarded John $1,425,000 for his injuries and Pam $218,750 for loss of consortium (the ability to engage in sexual relations with one's spouse). Defendant appealed.

JUDGE PRATHER: . . . Two competing theories of strict liability in tort can be extrapolated from our case law. While our older decisions applied a "consumer expectations" analysis in products cases, recent decisions have turned on an analysis under "risk-utility." We today apply a "risk-utility" analysis and write to clarify our reasons for the adoption for that test.

Section 402A is still the law in Mississippi. How this Court defines the phrases "defective conditions" and "unreasonably dangerous" used in 402A dictates whether a "consumer expectations" analysis or a "risk-utility" analysis will prevail. Problems have arisen because our past decisions have been unclear and have been misinterpreted in some instances.

"Consumer Expectations" Analysis

. . . In a "consumer expectations" analysis, "ordinarily the phrase 'defective condition' means that the article has something wrong with it, that it did not function as expected." Comment g of Section 402A defines "defective condition" as "a condition not contemplated by the ultimate consumer, which will be unreasonably dangerous to him." Thus, in a "consumer expectations" analysis, for a plaintiff to recover, the defect in a product which causes his injuries must not be one which the plaintiff, as an ordinary consumer, would know to be unreasonably dangerous to him. In other words, if the plaintiff, applying the knowledge of an ordinary consumer, sees a danger and can appreciate that danger, then he cannot recover for any injury resulting from that appreciated danger.

"Risk-Utility" Analysis

In a "risk-utility" analysis, a product is "unreasonably dangerous" if a reasonable person would conclude that the danger-in-fact, whether foreseeable or not, outweighs the utility of the product. Thus, even if a plaintiff appreciates the danger of a product, he can still recover for any injury resulting from the danger, provided that the utility of the product is

[continued]

outweighed by the danger that the product creates. Under the "risk-utility" test, either the judge or the jury can balance the utility and danger-in-fact, or risk, of the product.

A "risk-utility" analysis best protects both the manufacturer and the consumer. It does not create a duty on the manufacturer to create a completely safe product. Creating such a product is often impossible or prohibitively expensive. Instead, a manufacturer is charged with the duty to make its product reasonably safe, regardless of whether the plaintiff is aware of the product's dangerousness. . . . In balancing the utility of the product against the risk it creates, an ordinary person's ability to avoid the danger by exercising care is also weighed.

Having here reiterated this Court's adoption of a "risk-utility" analysis for product liability cases, we hold, necessarily, that the "patent danger" bar is no longer applicable in Mississippi. Under a "risk-utility" analysis, the "patent danger" rule does not apply. In "risk-utility," the openness and obviousness of a product's design is simply a factor to consider in determining whether a product is unreasonably dangerous.

There is sufficient evidence to show that Prestage tried his case under a "risk-utility" analysis. It is also clear from the record that the trial court understood "risk-utility" to be the law in Mississippi and applied that test correctly.

AFFIRMED in favor of plaintiff.

CRITICAL THINKING

Why was the risk-utility test viewed as the best method of evaluating this case?

ETHICAL DECISION MAKING

The risk-utility test allows products to pose a danger to consumers as long as they are reasonably safe. Under which ethical theory would producing such a product be ethical? Under which theory would such production not be ethical?

Some states require that one of these tests must be used. For example, in South Carolina, the risk utility test is the exclusive test.[5] Other states permit use of either the consumer expectations test or the risk utility test (e.g., Illinois).[6]

Legal Principle: **A product liability case based on the theory of strict product liability may be brought when a person is injured by a product with a manufacturing defect that caused that product to be unreasonably dangerous.**

Liability to Bystanders. We have been looking thus far at liability to those who are in lawful possession of the defective product. The question arises as to whether strict product liability can be used by someone other than the owner or user of the product. The Bystanders Case Nugget provides the rationale of one court that chose to allow recovery by a bystander.

Various companies involved in manufacturing and selling products may be named as defendants in product liability cases. However, some states restrict which companies may be named as defendants. See the Case Nugget "Who Is the Proper Defendant?"

Defenses to a Strict–Product Liability Action. Most of the defenses to a negligence-based product liability claim are available in a strict–product liability case. These defenses include product misuse, assumption of the risk, and the lapse of time under statutes of limitations and statutes of repose.

One defense that may not be available in all states, however, is the state-of-the-art defense. Courts have rejected the use of this defense in most strict-liability cases, reasoning

---

[5] *Peters-Martin v. Navistar Intern. Transp. Corp.*, 2011 WL 462657 (4th Cir. 2011).
[6] 659 F.3d 584 (7th Cir. 2011).

STRICT LIABILITY FOR BYSTANDERS

James A. Peterson, Adm'r of the Estate of Maradean Peterson et al. v. Lou Backrodt Chevrolet Co.
Appellate Court of Illinois
307 N.E.3d 729 (1974)

A car dealer sold an automobile with a defective brake system. When the defective brakes failed, the driver struck two minors, killing one and injuring the other. The deceased minor's estate brought a product liability action against the car dealer. The court relied on a statement by the California Supreme Court in *Elmore v. American Motors Corp.* to allow recovery by bystanders:

If anything, bystanders should be entitled to greater protection than the consumer or user where injury to bystanders from the defect is reasonably foreseeable. Consumers and users, at least, have the opportunity to inspect for defects and to limit their purchases to articles manufactured by reputable manufacturers and sold by reputable retailers, whereas the bystander ordinarily has no such opportunities. In short, the bystander is in greater need of protection from defective products which are dangerous, and if any distinction should be made between bystanders and users, it should be made . . . to extend greater liability in favor of the bystanders.

that the issue in such cases is not what the producers knew at the time the products were produced but whether the product was defective and whether the defect caused it to be unreasonably dangerous. For example, the supreme court of Missouri, in a case involving an asbestos claim, said that the state of the art has no bearing on the outcome of a strict-liability claim because the issue is the defective condition of the product, not the manufacturer's knowledge, negligence, or fault.

The refusal of most courts to allow the state-of-the-art defense in strict-liability cases is consistent with the social policy reasons for imposing strict liability. A reason for imposing strict liability is that the manufacturers or producers are best able to spread the cost of the risk; this risk-spreading function does not change with the availability of scientific knowledge. The counterargument is that if the manufacturer has indeed done everything as safely and carefully as available data allow, it seems unfair to impose liability on the defendant. After all, how else could the company have manufactured the product?

WARRANTY

Another theory of liability for defective products is *breach of warranty.* Unlike negligence and strict-liability theories, breach of warranty stems from contract theory rather than tort theory. This theory of liability is established through the Uniform Commercial Code (UCC). A warranty is a guarantee or a binding promise regarding a product. Generally, the product (or the product's performance) does not meet the manufacturer's or seller's promises.

Warranties may be either *express* (clearly stated by the seller or manufacturer) or *implied* (automatically arising out of a transaction). Either type may give rise to liability. Two types of implied warranties may provide the basis for a product liability action: warranty of merchantability and warranty of fitness for a particular purpose.

Express Warranty. When a seller makes an affirmative representation about a product, this representation—an express warranty—becomes part of the bargain. The representation may be a written or verbal guarantee about the product. For example, a car dealer may make an express statement that the car will work perfectly for the first 30,000 miles. In contrast, a car dealer may engage in vague sales talk (e.g., "This car runs well") that does not constitute an express warranty.

Determining whether a statement is a warranty may be a difficult task. In one case, for example, the court considered whether advertising statements constituted a warranty:

> To see how total quality management relates to prevention of product liability cases, please see the **Connecting to the Core** activity on the text website at www.mhhe.com/kubasek3e.

WHO IS THE PROPER DEFENDANT?

Block v. Toyota Motor Corporation
2011 WL 6306689 (8th Cir. 2011)

Angela Block filed a strict-liability suit after her son was killed and her daughter was seriously injured in a collision with a Toyota vehicle that allegedly improperly suddenly accelerated. Block filed suit in Minnesota state court against Toyota (the manufacturer of the vehicle), its affiliates, and Brooklyn Park Motors, the automobile dealership that had originally sold the Toyota vehicle 10 years earlier. The defendants removed the case to federal court, and the plaintiff argued that removal of the case to federal court was improper because the automobile dealership was a Minnesota resident. Minnesota has a "seller's exception statute" that requires the dismissal of strict-liability claims against nonmanufacturers when

the nonmanufacturer provides the identity of the manufacturer unless the plaintiff shows that the nonmanufacturer falls into one of three exceptions:

1. The defendant has exercised some significant control over the design or manufacture of the product or provided instruction or warnings to the manufacturer.
2. The defendant had actual knowledge of the defect in the product that caused the injury, death, or damage.
3. The defendant created the defect in the product that caused the injury, death, or damage. The district court concluded that the auto dealership fell under the seller's exception statute and dismissed all claims with prejudice against the dealership. On appeal, the Eighth Circuit upheld the dismissal.

When a consumer was deciding whether to buy a luxury yacht, the seller gave him a brochure with a picture of the yacht along with the following caption: "Offering the best performance and cruising accommodations in its class, the 3375 Esprit offers a choice of either stern drive or inboard power, superb handling and sleeping accommodations for six." The buyer argued that on the basis of express representations about the yacht in this brochure, he chose to purchase the $150,000 yacht. Later, the yacht had mechanical and electrical problems. The supreme court of Utah concluded that an express warranty is a promise or affirmation of fact. "[T]he photograph and caption contained in Cruisers' brochure are not objective or specific enough to qualify as either facts or promises; the statements made in the caption are merely opinions, and the photograph makes no additional assertions with regard to the problems of which Boud has complained." Thus, the court ruled there was no express warranty.

To establish a claim for breach of express warranty, the plaintiff must show that (1) the representation was the basis of the bargain and (2) there was a breach of the representation. Generally, the plaintiff simply has to demonstrate a breach of warranty; she does not have to prove that the occurrence of the breach was the defendant's fault.

Implied Warranty of Merchantability. When a seller sells a particular kind of goods, there is an implied warranty of merchantability. *Merchantability* means that the particular goods would be accepted by others who deal in similar goods. Thus, an implied warranty of merchantability means that the goods are fit for the purpose for which they are sold and used. This warranty is found in Article 2, Section 314(2), of the UCC. Under the UCC, for goods to be merchantable, they must meet six conditions:

a. Pass without objection in the trade under the contract description.
b. In the case of fungible goods, be of fair average quality within the description.
c. Be fit for the ordinary purposes for which such goods are used.
d. Run, within the variations permitted by the agreement, of even kind, quality and quantity within each unit and among all units involved.
e. Be adequately contained, packaged, and labeled as the agreement may require.
f. Conform to the promises or affirmations of fact made on the container or label, if any.

E-COMMERCE AND THE LAW

USER GUIDES ON THE INTERNET

In a footnote in the Sperry–New Holland case, the court relied on Professor John Wade's article "On the Nature of Strict Tort Liability for Products"* to list seven factors a trial court may find helpful when balancing a product's utility against the risk the product creates:

1. The usefulness and desirability of the product—its utility to the user and to the public as a whole.
2. The safety aspects of the product—the likelihood that it will cause injury and the probable seriousness of the injury.
3. The availability of a substitute product that would meet the same need and not be as unsafe.
4. The manufacturer's ability to eliminate the unsafe character of the product without impairing its usefulness or making it too expensive to maintain its utility.
5. The user's ability to avoid danger by the exercise of care in the use of the product.
6. The user's anticipated awareness of the dangers inherent in the product and their avoidability, because of general public knowledge of the obvious condition of the product or of the existence of suitable warnings or instructions.
7. The feasibility, on the part of the manufacturer, of spreading the loss by setting the price of the product or carrying liability insurance.

With regard to factor 6, the court's analysis considered whether warnings included in an owner's manual were suitable to warn Prestage of the danger of the combine. One of Sperry's expert witnesses testified: "Warnings are a third-rate way of preventing accidents. . . . [W]arnings are something that . . . operators read once, and forget."

Query: Is it possible that as owner's and user's manuals become available online, judges and experts will be less sympathetic to the owner or user who says he read the warnings once but then forgot about them? Have you ever misplaced an owner's or user's manual and later looked for it online when you needed information about a product? If so, are you more likely to review safety information than you may have been in the past, when it was easy to misplace manuals?

* *Mississippi Law Journal* 44 (1973), p. 825.

For example, a consumer purchased an "unbreakable" baseball bat that developed cracks after the repeated use of hitting baseballs. The consumer brought suit against the retailer that sold the bat. Given that the bat could not be used for the purpose for which it was intended (i.e., hitting baseballs), the judge relied on the implied warranty of merchantability to determine that the consumer was entitled to a refund.[7]

One of the requirements of this provision is that the seller of the good must be a "merchant with respect to goods of that kind" [UCC Section 2–314(1)]. Thus, the seller must deal with the goods in question on a regular or continuous basis. For example, a private individual who places an advertisement in the paper to sell her personal car is not a seller of goods under this section of the UCC.

Contracts for sales of goods frequently contain numerous disclaimers, and one of these disclaimers includes the implied warranty of merchantability. If the disclaimer uses the word *merchantability,* the disclaimer will be upheld for economic losses but not personal injuries.

Implied Warranty of Fitness for a Particular Purpose. When a customer purchases a product for a particular purpose and the seller is aware of this purpose, an implied warranty of fitness for a particular purpose arises. This warranty is found in Article 2, Section

Here's a dilemma. Should the disclaimer for our client's new sleeping pill read, "May cause drowsiness" or "May <u>not</u> cause drowsiness"?

stus.com

---

[7] *Dudzik v. Klein's All Sports,* 158 Misc. 2d 72 (N.Y. Just. Ct. 1993).

CASE NUGGET

WHEN MIGHT YOUR COMPANY UNEXPECTEDLY BE CONSIDERED A SELLER OF GOODS?

Nutting v. Ford Motor Company
180 A.D.2d 122 (N.Y.A.D. 1992)

Catherine Nutting was driving her 1984 Mercury Marquis station wagon when the engine stalled, and the car collided with another vehicle. Nutting brought suit against Ford Motor Company, the car manufacturer, and Hewlett-Packard (HP), a manufacturer and seller of computer products. Why HP? HP had purchased the car at issue in this case from Ford through a program where HP purchased approximately 3,200 cars for use by HP employees. After about one and a half years, HP disposed of the cars through an auction conducted by its agent. Hi-Way Motors, a used-car dealership owned by Nutting's father, purchased the car at auction and transferred titled to Nutting. When Nutting brought suit against HP for breach of implied warranty of merchantability, HP argued that it was an occasional seller of surplus vehicles. The court disagreed, finding that HP was in the regular business of a used-car dealer and thus was a seller and merchant within the meaning of UCC Section 2-314. You may want to examine the way that your business regularly disposes of surplus equipment or other products to consider whether you could unexpectedly be considered a seller of goods.

315, of the UCC. The buyer is relying on the seller's skill and judgment to select the particular goods. Thus, to succeed on a claim for breach of implied warranty of fitness for a particular purpose, the plaintiff would need to show (1) knowledge—the seller had knowledge of the customer's specific purpose; and (2) reliance—the customer relied on the seller's skill and judgment. Unlike the implied warranty of merchantability, which requires that the seller be a merchant of the goods involved, the implied warranty of fitness for a particular purpose applies to a sale of goods regardless of whether the seller qualifies as a merchant.

Exhibit 10-3 summarizes the three theories of product liability.

Exhibit 10-3   Summary of Product Liability Theories

THEORIES OF LIABILITY	WHO CAN SUE	WHO CAN BE LIABLE	DEFENSES	DAMAGES
Negligence	Any foreseeable plaintiff	Any commercial supplier in the distribution chain (Retailers and sellers can satisfy their duty by a cursory reasonable inspection.)	Assumption of the risk Comparative/contributory negligence	Personal injuries Property damages No recovery solely for economic damages
Strict liability	Anyone harmed (buyer, user, bystander)	Any commercial supplier in the distribution chain	Assumption of the risk Product misuse	Personal injuries Property damages No recovery solely for economic damages
Warranty	Privity required (Injured party must be the buyer, the buyer's family, or the buyer's guest.)	Any seller	Assumption of the risk Product misuse Disclaimer	Recovery solely for economic damage

Market Share Liability

L02
What is market share liability?

In most cases, the plaintiff can identify the manufacturer of a defective product that caused the injury at issue. Sometimes, however, some plaintiffs may not learn of their injuries until years after the injury occurs. By this time, plaintiffs cannot trace the product to any particular manufacturer. Often, a number of manufacturers produced the same product, and the plaintiff would have no idea whose product had been used. A plaintiff may have even used more than one manufacturer's product.

Before the 1980s, plaintiffs in this situation would have been unable to gain any sort of recovery for their injuries. However, recovery may be possible today because of the market share theory, created by the California Supreme Court in the case of *Sindell v. Abbott Laboratories.*

In *Sindell,* the plaintiffs' mothers had all taken a drug known as diethylstilbestrol (DES) during pregnancies that had occurred before the drug was banned in 1973. Because DES had been produced 20 years before the plaintiffs suffered any effects from the drug their mothers had taken, it was impossible to trace the defective drug back to each manufacturer that had produced the drug causing each individual's problems. To balance the competing interests of the victims, who had suffered injury from the drug, and the defendants, who did not want to be held liable for a drug they did not produce, the court allowed the plaintiffs to sue all the manufacturers that had produced the drug at the time that the plaintiffs' mothers had used the drug. Then the judge apportioned liability among the defendant-manufacturers on the basis of the share of the market they had held at the time that the drug had been produced.

This theory has since been used by some other courts, primarily in drug cases. Courts using the market share theory generally require that the plaintiff prove that (1) all defendants are tortfeasors; (2) the allegedly harmful products are identical and share the same defective qualities; (3) the plaintiff is unable to identify which defendant caused her injury, through no fault of her own; and (4) the manufacturers of substantially all the defective products in the relevant area and during the relevant time are named as defendants.

Some states have modified the approach of *Sindell.* At least one court has held that the plaintiff need sue only one maker of the allegedly defective drug. If the plaintiff can prove that the defendant manufactured a drug of the type taken by the plaintiff's mother at the time of the mother's pregnancy, that defendant can be held liable for all damages. However, the defendant may join other defendants, and the jury may apportion liability among all defendants.

While the utility of this theory for drug cases is evident, plaintiffs have not been as successful in extending the theory to products other than drugs. For example, in 2001, plaintiffs who were unable to identify the maker of the guns that were used to kill their family members were unsuccessful in their attempt to sue a group of manufacturers for negligent marketing under the theory of market share liability. However, at least one court has extended the theory to lead carbonate to permit market share liability for lead poisoning.

A related issue is product liability insurance. Start-up companies often have difficulty obtaining product liability insurance because they frequently cannot meet the insurance company's requirements, such as sales totaling a certain amount per year. The cost of the insurance will depend on the purpose of the product. If the product is related to safety or product performance, the product will be more expensive to insure than a product related to a decorative function. Insurance premiums for start-up products could range from $2,500 to $10,000 per year.[8]

---

[8] Karen Klein, "When You Can't Secure Product Liability Insurance," *BusinessWeek,* June 9, 2009, www.businessweek.com/smallbiz/content/jun2009/sb2009069_307233.htm.

COMPARING THE LAW OF OTHER COUNTRIES

COLLECTIVE INSURANCE IN SCANDINAVIA

The Scandinavian countries of Sweden, Finland, Denmark, and Norway share a unique feature: the role of collective insurance groups in product liability. Manufacturers, producers, and importers of similar products form cooperative groups and obtain an insurance policy. For example, in Finland, a voluntary insurance policy group headed by the Finnish Pharmaceutical Insurance Pool enlists pharmaceutical companies as members. To hear the appeals of those seeking damages, the pool appoints a board. The board follows the basic liability principle of insurance groups, which is that causation, rather than fault or defectiveness, determines compensation.

Pharmaceutical companies find this principle especially appealing because they can admit liability without damaging the name of their products as a whole. Supporters of the insurance system also point out that elimination of the defectiveness requirement enables product developers to concentrate on improving their products, as opposed to being tied up with product liability cases.

CASE OPENER WRAP-UP

Is Human Sperm Subject to Product Liability Laws?

Donovan's case was the first decision to hold that a sperm bank could be sued under product liability theories for the sperm it provides.[9] One of the issues was whether Pennsylvania or New York law applied to the sale of the sperm. (Donovan and Brittany were Pennsylvania residents, and the sperm came from New York.) Many states, including Pennsylvania and New York, have enacted "blood shield" statutes that prohibit product liability suits based on donated blood. Pennsylvania's blood shield statute included human tissue other than blood, but New York's statute shielded blood and its derivatives only. Therefore, Donovan could have a product liability claim in New York but not in Pennsylvania. The court decided that because the screening of the sperm and the formation of the contract occurred in New York, New York law would apply in Donovan's case and thus, under New York law, the suit could move forward. Another issue was whether Idant provided a service or a product. The court again referred to the blood shield statute and stated that "[u]nder New York law, the sale of sperm is a product and is subject to strict liability."

The court's decision did not find that the sperm actually was defective; it simply found that a New York sperm bank could be sued under product liability laws. However, the case raises some interesting questions: Should a laboratory be held responsible for genetic diseases for which there are no tests? Do the same standards apply to donated eggs? Suppose Brittany Donovan had children who had the same genetic effects. Would they have any claim against the sperm bank?

[9] *Donovan v. Idant Laboratories,* Case No. 08-4075, Memorandum and Order (E.D. Pa., Mar. 31, 2009).

KEY TERMS

design defect 236
express warranty 249
failure to provide adequate
   warnings 236

implied warranty of fitness for
   a particular purpose 251
implied warranty of
   merchantability 250

manufacturing defect 236
market share theory 253

strict product liability 244
warranty 249

SUMMARY OF KEY TOPICS

Theories of Liability For Defective Products

Negligence: Plaintiff must show that (1) the defendant manufacturer or seller owed a duty of care to the plaintiff; (2) the defendant breached that duty of care by supplying a defective product; (3) this breach of duty caused the plaintiff's injury; and (4) the plaintiff suffered actual injury.

Strict product liability: Plaintiff must show that (1) the product was defective when sold; (2) the product was so defective that the product was unreasonably dangerous; and (3) the product was the cause of the plaintiff's injury.

Express warranty: The plaintiff must show that (1) the representation was the basis of the bargain and (2) there was a breach of the representation.

Implied warranty of merchantability: The plaintiff must show that the goods are fit for the purpose for which they are sold and used.

Implied warranty of fitness for a particular purpose: The plaintiff must show that the customer purchased a product for a particular purpose and the seller was aware of this purpose.

Market Share Liability

When plaintiffs cannot trace a product to any particular manufacturer and a number of manufacturers produced the same product, a court may use the theory of market share liability to impose a portion of fault on a number of manufacturers.

POINT / COUNTERPOINT

Should Companies Be Held Strictly Liable for Their Products?	
YES	NO
Companies, rather than individual consumers, are in the best position to absorb the risk of their products. The manufacturer is in the best position to anticipate the harm the product might cause and has more information regarding the product. If a company manufactures and sells a product that seriously harms large numbers of individuals (both consumers and bystanders), the company, rather than the individuals should be responsible for these costs. The company receives all the rewards of selling the product (i.e., the profit) and should thus bear the risks associated with selling the product.	The cost of product liability insurance is so high that companies need to add this cost to the price of the product. Consequently, consumers have to pay unnecessarily higher prices for products, and this creates inefficiency in the market. Similarly, manufacturers waste time and resources creating unnecessary warnings on labels (e.g., "Do not eat" warnings on nonfood products). Furthermore, strict liability discourages companies from developing and testing new products because of the fear that the product could be faulty. Finally, strict–product liability law incentivizes consumers to improperly use products.

QUESTIONS & PROBLEMS

1. Explain the elements one would have to prove to bring a successful product liability case based on negligence, and identify the available defense.

2. Why would a defendant prefer to be found to have produced a product that was defectively manufactured rather than defectively designed?

3. Explain the defenses available in a case based on a theory of strict product liability.

4. The plaintiff suffered a carotid artery tear that left him partially paralyzed after being tackled during a high school football scrimmage. While he was on the field, his coaches removed his helmet, which was then lost. The plaintiff's mother filed suit against the helmet manufacturers, alleging that the helmet's liner and foam padding were defectively designed. The district court granted summary judgment to the defendants because the plaintiff could not produce the specific helmet at issue and thus could not prove the helmet was defective. The plaintiff appealed, arguing that the fact that she could not produce the specific helmet was irrelevant as she was arguing that all of the helmets were defective due to their design. Do you think the appellate court agreed that the specific helmet need not be produced?

[*A.K.W. v. Easton-Bell Sports, Inc., et al.,* No. 11-60293, 2011 U.S. App. LEXIS 21108 (5th Cir. 2011).]

5. The plaintiff's son was given St. Joseph's Aspirin for Children when he had the flu. The aspirin triggered Reye's syndrome, leaving the child a quadriplegic, blind, and mentally retarded. The aspirin contained a warning, approved by the Food and Drug Administration, about the dangers of giving aspirin to children with the flu. The product was advertised in Spanish in the Los Angeles area, but the warning was not in Spanish. The child's guardians could not read English. Do you believe the court imposed liability on the company for failure of its duty to warn? Why or why not? [*Ramirez v. Plough, Inc.,* 25 Cal. Rptr. 2d (1993).]

6. Plaintiff Darren Traub was playing a pickup game of basketball on his college campus and tried to dunk the ball, but his hand hit the rim and he fell down, hurting both wrists. He sued the basketball hoop manufacturer and the university, claiming that the rigid rim caused his injury or made it worse. The defendants filed a motion for summary judgment. Do you think it should have been granted? [*Traub v. Cornell,* 1998 WL 187401 (N.D.N.Y. 1998).]

7. In 1991, three-year-old Douglas Moore was playing with one of BIC's lighters. While playing with the lighter, he started a fire that severely injured his 17-month-old brother. BIC Manufacturers Inc. included several child-safety warning labels on their lighters. These labels identified the risk of fire or injury as a result of misusing the product. The lighter provided warnings to adults to "keep out of reach of children" or "keep away from children." The BIC Corporation had knowledge that its lighters could be manipulated by children, but it felt that including safety features would significantly increase the cost of the lighter. The Moore family brought a strict-liability suit against BIC. Explain why strict liability should or should not be applicable in this case. [*Price v. BIC Corp.,* 702 A.2d 330 (Sup. Ct. N.H. 1997).]

8. The federal Organic Foods Production Act and National Organic Program create uniform federal standards for organic labeling. Under these federal programs, producers of products can become certified as organic. Aurora's Milk, sold by Aurora Dairy Corp., was certified as organic under these programs. In 2007, the USDA produced a report regarding alleged violations in Aurora's organic operations, but Aurora's organic certification was not revoked. The plaintiffs brought suit against Aurora Dairy Corp. for false certification. The defendants argued that the plaintiffs' claims were preempted. Do you think the defendants were successful in their preemption argument? [*Aurora Dairy Corp. Organic Milk Marketing and Sales Practices Litigation,* Case No. 08-md-01907 (E.D. Mo. 2009).]

9. Three men were riding in a pickup truck when the tire tread separated on a rear wheel. The driver lost control of the truck, which rolled over. The two passengers in the truck were killed, and the estate of one of the passengers brought suit against Cooper Tire, the manufacturer of the tire. The plaintiff argued that the tire was defective in design and had a manufacturing defect. During the discovery portion of the case, the plaintiff sought information regarding all tires manufactured by the defendant; specifically, the plaintiff was seeking information to show that Cooper Tire had notice of a tread separation problem in its other tires. Cooper Tire refused to produce that information, arguing that information regarding other tires that it manufactured but were not at issue in the case was irrelevant. What arguments, if any, could the plaintiff use to establish that the information regarding other tires is relevant? [*Mario Alvarez v. Cooper Tire & Rubber Co.,* 75 So. 3d 789 (Fla. Dist. Ct. App., 4th Dist. 2011).]

10. Chris Hill ran a red light while talking on his cell phone. He crashed into a car driven by Linda Doyle, who was killed in the collision. Doyle's estate brought suit against Sprint/Nextel Corp., arguing that Sprint was negligent in failing to warn Hill that it was dangerous to use a cell phone while driving. Sprint moved to dismiss the case, arguing that it had no duty to noncustomer automobile drivers to warn customers of the dangers of talking on the phone while driving. Do you think the court agreed with Sprint? [*Estate of Doyle v. Sprint/Nextel Corp.,* 248 P.3d 947 (Okla. Civ. App. 2010).]

Looking for more review materials?

The Online Learning Center at **www.mhhe.com/kubasek3e** contains this chapter's "Assignment on the Internet" and also a list of URLs for more information, entitled "On the Internet." Find both of them in the Student Center portion of the OLC, along with quizzes and other helpful materials.

Introduction to Contracts

LEARNING OBJECTIVES

After reading this chapter, you will be able to answer the following questions:

1 What is a contract?

2 What are the sources of contract law?

3 How can we classify contracts?

4 What are the rules that guide the interpretation of contracts?

CASE OPENER

A Questionable Contract

Mary Kay Morrow began working for Hallmark in 1982. At the beginning of 2002, Hallmark adopted the "Hallmark Dispute Resolution Program," which required, among other things, that claims against the company be resolved in binding arbitration rather than litigation. Hallmark assumed that employees who remained at Hallmark after the policy became effective were bound by the new company policy. Additionally, Hallmark reserved the right to modify the program at any time and excluded claims it brought from the arbitration requirement.

Fifteen months after the policy became effective, Hallmark terminated Morrow's employment. Morrow filed a claim against Hallmark, claiming that she had not been fired for just cause but, rather, had been terminated because of age discrimination and retaliation resulting from her earlier complaints about company policies. In response to the suit, which was filed in the circuit court of Jackson County, Hallmark filed a motion to stay the litigation and compel arbitration in accordance with its Dispute Resolution Program. The court granted Hallmark's motion.

After several additional failed attempts to get the circuit court to hear the case, Morrow proceeded with the only route she had left—arbitration. The arbitrator dismissed Morrow's claims for lack of timeliness and ruled that the program constituted a valid contract and was not unconscionable. In yet another effort to have the case heard, Morrow went back to the trial court with a motion to vacate the arbitrator's ruling. The motion was denied. Morrow appealed the case to the Missouri Court of Appeals on the grounds that the Dispute Resolution Program did not constitute an enforceable contract.

1. By what standard would the courts determine whether a contract existed?
2. Did each party to the supposed contract make a valid promise that would support the existence of the contract?

The Wrap-Up at the end of the chapter will answer these questions.

The Definition of a Contract

LO1

What is a contract?

This part of the text focuses on contracts, but what is a contract? The Restatement (Second) of Contracts defines a contract as "a promise or set of promises for the breach of which the law gives a remedy or the performance of which the law in some way recognizes a duty."[1] Another way to think of a contract is as a set of legally enforceable promises. Contracts play a fundamental role in business; after all, almost all business relationships are created by contracts.

One of the most important business relationships, the relationship that exists between employers and employees, is often created through contracts. Typically, during the hiring process, an employer will establish an employment contract, which lists the terms and obligations a new employee must agree to before starting work. One particular type of employment contract is a covenant not to compete. Covenants not to compete restrict what an employee may do after leaving a company, and they often dictate where, when, and with whom an employee may work. Employers justify the use of covenants not to compete by saying they are necessary to protect their trade secrets, talent, and proprietary information.

Noncompete contracts are especially common in industries such as technology and sales, where possession of cutting-edge information or client lists can greatly affect the competition between companies. For example, in 2008, IBM and Apple found themselves in a court battle over employee Mark Papermaster. Apple had hired Papermaster away from his high-level position at IBM and wished to put him in charge of Apple's iPhone and iPod division. In turn, IBM argued that Papermaster's move to Apple violated his covenant not to compete, which stated that he would not work for a competitor during the year after he left IBM. Former employer IBM also argued that because Papermaster had been a top executive at IBM, he was in possession of confidential and proprietary information that could be valuable to Apple. The court agreed with IBM and thus issued an injunction barring Papermaster from starting work at Apple until after a trial had taken place. Apple and IBM opted to reach an agreement out of court, and Papermaster was cleared to start work at his new position in April 2009.[2] Covenants not to compete are discussed in greater detail in Chapter 16 of this text.

ELEMENTS OF A CONTRACT

We can flesh out the definition of a contract by examining the four elements that are necessary for it to exist. These elements are the agreement, the consideration, contractual capacity, and a legal object. The agreement consists of an offer by one party, called the *offeror,* to enter into a contract and an acceptance of the terms of the offer by the other party, called the *offeree* (see Exhibit 13-1). This first element is discussed in detail in Chapter 14.

The second element of the contract is the consideration, the bargained-for exchange or what each party gets in exchange for his or her promise under the contract. We discuss consideration in Chapter 15.

---

[1] Restatement (Second) of Contracts, sec. 1.
[2] See www.networkworld.com/community/node/37835 and http://library.findlaw.com/2003/Feb/5/132530.html.

BUT WHAT IF . . .

WHAT IF THE FACTS OF THE CASE OPENER WERE DIFFERENT?

To fulfill the element of consideration, both parties to a contract must make promises to the other. Recall that, in the Case Opener, Hallmark made no promises to the employees who had to agree to the program. In fact, Hallmark stipulated that it could "modify or discontinue" the program at any time. But what if Hallmark promised raises to each employee who agreed to abide by the rules of the program? Do you see any potential problems with such an agreement?

Exhibit 13-1   The Formation of a Contract

This exhibit illustrates the first element of the contract, the agreement. For a contract to exist, the parties also must have legal capacity to enter into a contract, exchange valid consideration, and be entering into a contract with a legal purpose. The contract is formed as soon as the second party makes his or her promise.

E-COMMERCE AND THE LAW

CONTRACT FORMATION AND E-COMMERCE

Contract law operates on the Internet, with adjustments for special issues that range from jurisdiction to payment. Which state's or country's laws apply if the parties to an e-contract end up in a dispute? What happens if an online company engages in fraud by using a customer's credit card information in ways the customer never intended?

Contract formation via the Internet is especially important. Issues regarding contract formation range from timing to contract terms. For instance, given the speed with which e-mails go back and forth between parties, it is sometimes difficult to know when the parties have created a contract. Once a contract is formed, additional questions arise: What specific terms does the contract include? Can a company post standard terms on a website rather than in a document or on a ticket?

Fortunately, legislators have drafted and implemented key pieces of legislation that clarify issues related to contract formation and e-commerce. Two examples of e-commerce legislation are the Electronic Signatures in Global and National Commerce (ESIGN) Act and the Uniform Electronic Transactions Act (UETA).

Congress passed ESIGN to facilitate the use of electronic records and signatures in e-commerce. The federal law affirms e-contracts as legally valid. This law makes it clear that documents produced electronically are as valid as documents produced on paper. Congress did not write or pass UETA. Instead, the National Conference of Commissioners on Uniform State Laws proposed this piece of legislation, which almost every state has adopted. UETA's intent was similar to Congress's intent regarding ESIGN. In addition to affirming electronic contracts as legally valid, UETA attempts to make state laws consistent regarding topics such as the validity of signatures created online.

The third element is contractual capacity. Capacity is the legal ability to enter into a binding agreement. Most adults over the age of majority have capacity; those under the age of majority, people suffering from mental illness, and intoxicated persons do not. Chapter 16 explains further cases that limit or prohibit capacity.

Chapter 16 also discusses the fourth element of a binding legal contract, legal object. This means that to be enforceable, the contract cannot be either illegal or against public policy.

Legal Principle: **A legally binding contract requires four elements: agreement, consideration, capacity, and legal object.**

DEFENSES TO THE ENFORCEMENT OF A CONTRACT

Sometimes a contract appears to be legally binding because all four elements of a contract are present, but one of the parties may have a defense to its enforcement. Such defenses fall into two categories. The first is a lack of genuine assent (Chapter 17). A contract is supposed to be entered into freely by both parties, but sometimes the *offeror* (the party proposing the contract) secures acceptance of the agreement through improper means such as fraud, duress, undue influence, or misrepresentation. In these situations, there is no genuine assent to the contract, and the *offeree* (the person who agreed to or accepted the contract) may be able to raise that lack of genuine assent as a defense to enforcement of the agreement.

BUT WHAT IF . . .

WHAT IF THE FACTS OF THE CASE OPENER WERE DIFFERENT?

Recall that, in the Case Opener, Hallmark made it company policy for employees to participate in the dispute Resolution Program when a dispute arose. Employees were bound to the program through employment documents. But what if the facts were different? Let's say that company managers told employees they would be immediately terminated if they did not sign a contract agreeing to the program. Would the contract be valid? If not, on what grounds would the contract be invalid?

The second defense, discussed in Chapter 18, is that the contract lacks the *proper form,* which typically means it lacks a writing. As Chapter 18 will explain, the contract itself does not have to be in writing, but a writing meeting certain criteria that confirms the existence of the contract must exist.

Exhibit 13-2 summarizes the requirements of an enforceable contract.

Legal Principle: **Two defenses to the enforcement of a contract are lack of genuine assent and lack of proper form.**

THE OBJECTIVE THEORY OF CONTRACTS

Contract law is based on an *objective theory of contracts,* which means we base the existence of a contract on the parties' outward manifestations of intent and we base its interpretation on how a reasonable person would interpret it. Thus, the subjective intent of the parties is not usually relevant; what matters is how they represented their intent through their actions and words.

The subjective intent may be relevant, however, under a limited number of circumstances. As Chapter 17 explains in its discussion of mistake, if a mutual misunderstanding between the parties exists, and if as a result they did not really come to a meeting of the minds, there is no contract. The courts may then look at how each party subjectively interpreted the situation to determine whether the parties really reached an agreement.

Legal Principle: **In determining whether parties intended to enter into a contract, the courts look at their objective words and behavior and do not try to figure out what they might have been secretly intending.**

Sources of Contract Law

The two most important sources of contract law are case law and the Uniform Commercial code (UCC). A third source of law, which has become more important with increasing globalization, is the Convention on Contracts for International Sales of Goods (CISG). In this part of the book we focus primarily on the law of contracts as established by common law. (Part Three, "Domestic and International Sales Law," focuses more on the law as set out by the UCC and CISG.)

L02

What are the sources of contract law?

COMMON LAW

Today's law of contracts actually originated in judicial decisions in England, later modified by early courts in the United States. Since then, contract law has been further modified by U.S. legislatures and court rulings. The law of contracts is primarily common law. Therefore, to find out what the law is, we could go to the Reporters and read the decisions,

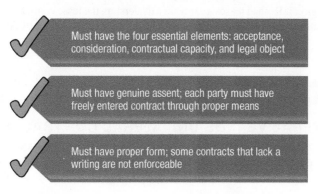

Must have the four essential elements: acceptance, consideration, contractual capacity, and legal object

Must have genuine assent; each party must have freely entered contract through proper means

Must have proper form; some contracts that lack a writing are not enforceable

Exhibit 13-2

Requirements of an Enforceable Contract

COMPARING THE LAW OF OTHER COUNTRIES

CHINA

Countries outside the United States have slightly different laws for different types of contracts. China, for example, has seven chapters of general provisions for contracts but also has chapters with special provisions for 15 different types of contracts governing sales, leases, loans, donations, construction projects, storage, and transportation.

but it is easier to go to the Restatement (Second) of the Law of Contracts. Prominent legal scholars, recruited by the American Law Institute, organized the principles of the common law of contracts into the original *Restatement of the Law, Contracts.* The compilation has been revised and published as *Restatement of the Law Second, Contracts.* The case in the opening scenario is governed by common law.

The Restatement (Second) is not actually the law itself, although judges frequently cite it because it is an authoritative statement of what the law is. As the common law of contracts evolved, not all states interpreted all aspects of it in the same way, so while we can make generalizations about the law of contracts, you will always want to know exactly what the law at issue is in your own state. In the Restatement (Second), the drafters often explain what the law about a particular matter is in the majority of states and then provide alternative approaches other states have adopted.

UNIFORM COMMERCIAL CODE

Having different laws governing contracts in different states did not make interstate commerce flow smoothly. To remedy some of the difficulties created by a patchwork of different laws governing commercial transactions, the National Conference of Commissioners on Uniform State Laws and the American Law Institute drafted a set of commercial laws that could be applicable to all states. This effort was called the Uniform Commercial Code (UCC). The UCC became law in each state that adopted it in whole or in part as an element of its state code. Thus, if a firm enters into a contract governed by the Uniform Commercial Code in Ohio, it will be operating under the Ohio Uniform Commercial Code.

Legal Principle: **All contracts are governed by either common law or the Uniform Commercial Code (UCC). If the contract is for the sale of a good, it falls under Article 2 of the UCC; if it is for anything else, it falls under common law.**

The part of the Uniform Commercial Code relevant to contracts is Article 2, which governs contracts for the sale (exchange for a price) of goods (tangible, movable objects). In this part of the book we will sometimes point out important differences between the UCC and common law, but we discuss contracts governed by the UCC primarily in Part Three. Also relevant to contract law is UCC Article 2A, which governs contracts for the lease of goods. For instance, if Rashad leases a car from a dealership, the lease contract is governed by Article 2A. If Rashad purchases the car, the purchase contract is governed by Article 2 of the UCC.

Classification of Contracts

L03

How can we classify contracts?

Contracts are classified in a number of different ways. Different classifications are useful for different purposes. This section describes the primary ways by which we classify contracts.

BILATERAL VERSUS UNILATERAL CONTRACTS

All contracts are either unilateral or bilateral. Knowing whether a contract is unilateral or bilateral is important because that classification determines when the offeree is legally bound to perform. Exhibit 13-3 highlights the difference between unilateral and bilateral contracts.

A PROMISE + A PROMISE = A *BILATERAL* CONTRACT

A PROMISE + A REQUESTED ACTION = A *UNILATERAL* CONTRACT

Exhibit 13-3
Bilateral vs. Unilateral
Contracts

If the offeror wants a promise from the offeree to form a binding contract, the contract is a bilateral contract, commonly defined as a promise in exchange for a promise. As soon as the promises are exchanged, a contract is formed and the parties' legal obligations arise. When Shannon promises to pay Gary $1,000 in exchange for his promise to paint her car on July 1, they have a bilateral contract. If either party fails to perform, the other may sue for breach. In the opening scenario, Hallmark wanted its employees to promise to submit any claims against it to arbitration rather than litigation. At issue in this case is, among other things, the question of whether Hallmark promised anything in return.

Another example of a bilateral contract can be found in the bidding process used by eBay. When an auction on eBay's website has closed, a bilateral contract exists between the seller and the individual who made the highest bid. The seller has promised to send the item (which needs to be comparable to the item described in the listing) to the bidder. The bidder has promised to make payment to the seller in the full amount of his or her bid. Should either party fail to perform, the other party may seek legal remedy according to the terms and conditions set forth by eBay's seller-bidder agreements.

In a bilateral contract, it is crucial that both parties are in fact making binding promises. In Case 13-1, you can see that one party wanted to argue that there was a bilateral agreement, when in fact that party was not binding itself to anything.

CASE 13-1   **IN RE ZAPPOS.COM INC., CUSTOMER DATA SECURITY BREACH LITIGATION**
2012 WL 4466660 (D. NEV., SEPT. 27, 2012)

Zappos.com is a popular website known mainly for its discounted shoe sales. In 2012, a hacker hacked into the Zappos website in an effort to obtain the personal account information of Zappos shoppers. After releasing news of the breach, Zappos faced numerous lawsuits from unhappy customers. Subsequently, Zappos moved to compel arbitration as mandated in its terms of use listed on its website. Zappos argued that it and its customers were in a bilateral agreement stating that arbitration must be used in the event of a dispute between the two parties, as supported by its customer terms of use. However, also in the terms of use, Zappos stipulated that it could change its terms of use and all of its agreements anytime at its own discretion. Hence, customers argued that the agreement was not bilateral and was in fact unfairly unilateral. Specifically, customers argued that Zappos was not actually agreeing to anything and made no promise to its customers regarding dispute resolution. Therefore, customers argued that they should not have to use arbitration and instead should be able to file their class action lawsuit against Zappos.

JUDGE JAMES: . . . The first paragraph of the Terms of Use provides [a] relevant part: "We reserve the right to change this Site and these terms and conditions at any time." The Priera Plaintiffs argue that because the Terms of Use grants Zappos the unilateral right to revise the Arbitration Clause, the contract is illusory and therefore unenforceable. In other words, Plaintiffs argue that the Arbitration Clause is illusory because Zappos can avoid the promise to arbitrate simply by amending the provision, while Zappos.com users are simultaneously bound to arbitration.

Most federal courts that have considered this issue have held that if a party retains the unilateral, unrestricted right to terminate the arbitration agreement, it is illusory and unenforceable, especially where there is no obligation to receive consent from, or even notify, the other parties to the contract.

. . .The Terms of Use gives Zappos the right to change the Terms of Use, including the Arbitration Clause, at any time without notice to the consumer. On one side, the Terms of Use purportedly binds any user of the Zappos.com website to mandatory arbitration. However, if a consumer sought

[continued]

to invoke arbitration pursuant to the Terms of Use, nothing would prevent Zappos from unilaterally changing the Terms and making those changes applicable to that pending dispute if it determined that arbitration was no longer in its interest. In effect, the agreement allows Zappos to hold its customers and users to the promise to arbitrate while reserving its own escape hatch. By the terms of the Terms of Use, Zappos is free at any time to require a consumer to arbitrate and/or litigate anywhere it sees fit, while consumers are required to submit to arbitration in Las Vegas, Nevada. Because the Terms of Use binds consumers to arbitration while leaving Zappos free to litigate or arbitrate wherever it sees fit, there exists no mutuality of obligation. We join those other federal courts that find such arbitration agreements illusory and therefore unenforceable.

A court cannot compel a party to arbitrate where that party has not previously agreed to arbitrate. The arbitration provision found in the Zappos.com Terms of Use purportedly binds all users of the website by virtue of their browsing.

However, the advent of the Internet has not changed the basic requirements of a contract, and there is no agreement where there is no acceptance, no meeting of the minds, and no manifestation of assent. A party cannot assent to terms of which it has no knowledge or constructive notice, and a highly inconspicuous hyper link buried among a sea of links does not provide such notice. Because Plaintiffs did not assent to the terms, no contract exists, and they cannot be compelled to arbitrate. In any event, even if Plaintiffs could be said to have consented to the terms, the Terms of Use constitutes an illusory contract because it allows Zappos to avoid arbitration by unilaterally changing the Terms at any time, while binding any consumer to mandatory arbitration in Las Vegas, Nevada. We therefore decline to enforce the arbitration provision on two grounds: there is no contract, and even if there was, it would be illusory and therefore unenforceable.

IT IS, THEREFORE, HEREBY ORDERED that Defendant Zappos.com, Inc.'s Motion to Compel Arbitration and Stay Action (#3) is DENIED.

CRITICAL THINKING

Is there enough ambiguity with the word *agreement* that Zappos could argue that it had an agreement with its customers? If Zappos could change any rule or promise it made to a customer at any time, how could Zappos argue that it was agreeing to anything?

ETHICAL DECISION MAKING

When a court makes a decision in a contract case, what values is it elevating? In other words, the court is anchoring its reasoning on a preference for a particular value or set of values. What is that value or set of values in a contract case?

In a **unilateral contract,** the offeror wants the offeree to *do* something, not to promise to do something. Perhaps the most common kind of unilateral offer is a reward. If Jim loses his dog, he may post a sign saying, "$50 reward for the safe return of my Poodle, Frenchie." When Michiko calls Jim and says, "Don't worry, I'll find your dog," she is not making a contract because the unilateral offer calls for an action, not a promise.

Just as the offeree is under no obligation to actually perform the act called for by the offeror, the offeror may revoke the offer at any time before performance. Initially this situation created problems because a person could be halfway through the performance and the offeror could revoke the offer. Because of the unfairness of such a scenario, today the courts hold that once an offeree begins performance, the offeror must hold the offer open for a reasonable time to allow the offeree to complete it.

BUT WHAT IF . . .
WHAT IF THE FACTS OF THE CASE OPENER WERE DIFFERENT?

Recall that, in the Case Opener, Hallmark's contract with its employees involved an employee promise to settle disputes with the company through arbitration. What if, instead, the contract said that if employees settled disputes with the company through arbitration, all fees resulting from the dispute would be covered by Hallmark? Which scenario is bilateral? Which is unilateral?

EXPRESS VERSUS IMPLIED CONTRACTS

We can classify contracts as express or implied depending on how they are created. The terms of express contracts are all clearly set forth in either written or spoken words. In the opening scenario, Hallmark contended that the Dispute Resolution Program constituted an express contract because it had laid out the terms for the contract in a writing received by its employees. Implied contracts, in contrast, arise not from words but from the conduct of the parties. If you have a dental emergency and the dentist pulls your severely infected tooth without prior negotiation about payment, or even any mention of payment, you have an implied contract for payment for her services. However, if you go to the dentist's office, ask how much it will cost to whiten your teeth, and sign a written agreement that stipulates exactly what the process will entail and how much you will pay, you have an express contract.

Apple's iTunes store provides another example of express contracts. Apple has several express contracts with music labels and television stations to sell music and television shows online. As a result of each sale, Apple retains a percentage of the profit and submits the remainder to the music label or television station. Should Apple, or the label, not receive the appropriate percentage of the sale, a breach-of-contract suit could be filed.

As a general rule, three conditions must be met for the courts to find an implied, or *implied-in-fact,* contract. First, the plaintiff provided some property or service to the defendant. Second, the plaintiff expected to be paid for such property or service, and a reasonable person in the position of the defendant would have expected to pay for it. Third, the defendant had an opportunity to reject the property or service but did not. In Case 13-2, the court had to decide whether the facts gave rise to an implied-in-fact contract.

CASE 13-2   PACHE v. AVIATION VOLUNTEER FIRE CO.
SUPREME COURT OF NEW YORK, APPELLATE DIVISION, THIRD DEPARTMENT
20 A.D.3D 731, 800 N.Y.S.2D 228 (2005)

Mr. Pache was the fire chief of the Aviation Volunteer Fire Company, which serves several neighborhoods in the Bronx. Mr. Pache suffered a fatal heart attack at the scene of a fire. His widow applied for Workers' Compensation, and was ultimately granted benefits by the Workers' Compensation Board. The decision was based on a finding that there was an implied contract between Aviation and the City of New York giving rise to the City's liability pursuant to the Volunteer Fireman's Benefit Law. The City appealed.

MERCURE, J.: . . . The City initially contended that claimant was not a covered employee within the meaning of Volunteer Firefighters' Benefit Law because the City had no written contract with Aviation. In relevant part, Volunteer Firefighters' Benefit Law § 30(2) provides:

> If at the time of injury the volunteer fire[fighter] was a member of [an incorporated] fire company . . . and located in a city, . . . protected under a contract by the fire department or fire company of which the volunteer fire[fighter] was a member, any benefit under this chapter shall be a city . . . charge.

Having conceded at oral argument that an implied contract against the City is a legal possibility, the City argues that it was error to find an implied contract in this case because there was no evidence that the Commissioner of the Fire Department of the City of New York (hereinafter FDNY) ever approved such a contract and there was insufficient proof of the elements of formation of an implied contract. We find both contentions to be unavailing.

In general, "it is well settled that a contract may be implied in fact where inferences may be drawn from the facts and circumstances of the case and the intention of the parties as indicated by their conduct." . . . However, there cannot be a valid implied contract with a municipality when the Legislature has assigned the authority to enter into contracts to a specific municipal officer or body or has prescribed the manner in which the contract must be approved, and there is no proof that the statutory requirements have been satisfied.

Here, the City relies on several provisions of the City Charter for the proposition that the Commissioner of the FDNY has the exclusive authority to enter into contracts on behalf of the FDNY (New York City Charter §§ 16-389, 17-394, 19-487). To the extent that this argument—explicitly

[continued]

asserted for the first time before this Court—is properly before us, it is unpersuasive because these provisions, individually and in conjunction, do not include an express assignment of exclusive contracting authority to the Commissioner.

The City further contends that there was insufficient evidence to support the Board's finding of an implied-in-fact contract because there was no evidence of assent by the City to the alleged contract. While acknowledging the absence of direct evidence on the issue of assent, we conclude that the Board's finding of an implied contract between the City and Aviation should not be disturbed. The Board was presented with evidence that Aviation had been in existence since 1923, and that it worked "hand in hand" with the local FDNY company to fight fires. There was evidence that the local fire company occasionally called Aviation to request its assistance. A representative of the City provided evidence that the City was aware of Aviation, and knew that it fought

fires in conjunction with the FDNY. If Aviation arrived at the scene of a fire before the local FDNY company, Aviation would be in charge of a fire scene until the FDNY company arrived and would thereafter continue working under its supervision. There was no evidence that City officials or the local fire company ever objected to or rejected the services of Aviation. Moreover, although the City was directed to produce an employee from the local FDNY company with knowledge of the relationship between the local fire company and Aviation as well as other facts relevant to the implied contract issue, it failed to do so. . . . Inasmuch as the Board was entitled to draw reasonable and adverse inferences from the City's failure to produce a knowledgeable employee, we are satisfied that substantial evidence supports the Board's determination that an implied-in-fact contract existed between the City and Aviation.

AFFIRMED in favor of Plaintiff.

CRITICAL THINKING

Do you agree that enough evidence has been considered in establishing an implied-in-fact contract? If so, what makes the evidence strong; and if not, what further evidence do you feel is necessary to make a confident claim?

Can you find an appreciable body of evidence in this case in support of an opposite contention? What is it?

ETHICAL DECISION MAKING

Justify the decision reached by the court by using different guidelines for ethical decision making. Which guideline fits most strongly with the case data? Why?

What values might the court be attempting to uphold with this ruling? What values are necessarily sacrificed to these interests? Can you justify this preference, and if so how?

QUASI-CONTRACTS

Quasi-contracts are sometimes called *implied-in-law contracts,* but they are not actually contracts. Rather, in order to prevent one party from being unjustly enriched at the expense of another, the courts impose contractual obligations on one of the parties *as if* that party had entered into a contract.

Assume Diego hears a noise in his driveway. He looks out and sees a group of workers apparently getting ready to resurface it. The doorbell rings, but he does not answer it. He goes down to his basement office and stays there until the workers have gone and he has a resurfaced driveway. When he receives a bill from the paving company, Diego refuses to pay on the grounds that he did not ask to have the driveway paved. In such a case, where the defendant knew the company was getting ready to bestow on him a benefit to which he was not entitled, the court will probably impose a quasi-contract, requiring that Diego pay the paving company the fair market value of the resurfacing. Imposing such a duty prevents him from being unjustly enriched at the expense of the paving company.

There are limits to the doctrine, however; specifically, the enrichment must be unjust. Sometimes a benefit may be conferred on you simply because of a mistake by the other party, and the courts will not make people pay for others' mistakes. Had Diego been out of town when his driveway was repaved, he would have just gotten lucky. The courts are not going to make him pay for the pavers' mistake when he could have done nothing to prevent the benefit from being bestowed on him.

A defendant, however, does not need to acknowledge the subcontractor's role, as was the case in Case 13-3, for a quasi-contract to exist.

CASE 13-3	REISENFELD & CO. v. THE NETWORK GROUP, INC.; BUILDERS SQUARE, INC.; KMART CORP.

U.S. COURT OF APPEALS FOR THE SIXTH CIRCUIT
277 F.3D 856 U.S. APP. (2002)

Network Group ("Network") was contracted by BSI to assist in selling or subleasing closed Kmart stores in Ohio. A few years later, Network entered into a commission agreement with Reisenfeld, a real estate broker for Dick's Clothing and Sporting Goods ("Dicks"). Dicks then subleased two stores from BSI. According to executed assignment and assumption agreements signed in November of 1994, BSI was to pay a commission to Network. Network was then responsible, pursuant to the commission agreement with Reisenfeld, to pay a commission of $1 per square foot to Reisenfeld. There was no direct agreement made between BSI and Reisenfeld.

During this time, Network's sole shareholder was defrauding BSI. This shareholder was convicted of several criminal charges stemming from his fraudulent acts. Network was ordered by the district court to disgorge any commissions received from BSI, and BSI was relieved of any duty to pay additional commissions to Network. As such, Reisenfeld never received his commission related to the Dicks sublease.

Reisenfeld sued in state court for the $160,320 in commissions he had not been paid. In addition to suing Network, Reisenfeld also named BSI as a defendant. The suit alleged, among other things, that based on a theory of quasi-contracts, BSI was jointly and severally liable for the commission.

JUDGE BOOGS: . . . A contract implied-in-law, or "quasi-contract," is not a true contract, but instead a liability imposed by courts in order to prevent unjust enrichment. . . . Under Ohio law, there are three elements for a quasi-contract claim. There must be: (1) a benefit conferred by the plaintiff upon the defendant; (2) knowledge by the defendant of the benefit; and (3) retention of the benefit by the defendant under circumstances where it would be unjust to do so without payment. . . .

There is no disagreement as to the first two requirements. It is clear that Reisenfeld's work as broker benefited BSI and that BSI was aware of the work Reisenfeld was doing. The disagreement rests on the third requirement—whether it would be unjust for BSI to retain the benefit it received without paying Reisenfeld for it. . . . Unreported Ohio Court of Appeals cases support the proposition that, in the contractor/subcontractor context, when the subcontractor is not paid by the contractor and the owner has not paid the contractor for the aspect of the job at issue, the subcontractor can look to the owner for payment under a theory of unjust enrichment. . . . Further, another Ohio case, in dicta, supports the proposition that nonpayment by the owner would make payment on an unjust enrichment theory appropriate. . . .

[H]ere, BSI has not paid Network on this contract, and the losses suffered by BSI at Network's hands were "soft" losses of additional profits Network might have made, rather than quantifiable losses (due, for example, to theft) that might be held to constitute payment. . . . Therefore, though not controlling of this matter, the Ohio contractor/subcontractor cases involving property owners who have not paid the contractors provide persuasive support for the proposition that Reisenfeld may hold BSI accountable on a theory of quasi-contract for the benefits it provided to BSI, and for which it was not compensated by Network. . . .

Of course, liability under quasi-contract does not necessarily imply liability for the amount of money promised Reisenfeld under its contract with Network. Instead, the proper measure of liability is the reasonable value of the services Reisenfeld provided to BSI. We must therefore vacate the district court's order and remand the case for a determination of value.

REMANDED for consideration of damages.

CRITICAL THINKING

What words or phrases important to the reasoning of this decision might be ambiguous? What alternate definitions are possible? How does this ruling appear to be defining the words or phrases? Would another choice affect the acceptability of the conclusion?

Provide an example of one piece of new evidence that might lead Judge Boggs to a different conclusion, and explain how this information changes the consideration.

ETHICAL DECISION MAKING

Does this ruling establish a positive precedent in terms of the potential effect on future participants in disputes of this sort?

Does this decision appear to follow the Golden Rule guideline? Why or why not? How is this question particularly relative to the person making the judgment, and what sorts of interpersonal differences might lead to a variety of responses?

Legal Principle: **Recovery in quasi-contract may be obtained when (1) a benefit is conferred by the plaintiff upon the defendant; (2) the defendant has knowledge of the benefit that is being bestowed upon her; and (3) the defendant retains the benefit under circumstances in which it would be unjust to do so without payment.**

VALID, VOID, VOIDABLE, AND UNENFORCEABLE CONTRACTS

What everyone hopes to enter into, of course, is a valid contract, one that contains all the legal elements set forth in the beginning of this chapter. As a general rule, a valid contract is one that will be enforced. However, sometimes a contract may be valid yet unenforceable when a law prohibits the courts from enforcing it. The statute of frauds (Chapter 18) requires that certain contracts must be evidenced by a writing before they can be enforced. Similarly, the statute of limitations mandates that an action for breach of contract must be brought within a set period of time, thereby limiting enforceability.

A void contract is in effect not a contract at all. Either its object is illegal or it has some defect so serious that it is not a contract. If you entered into a contract with an assassin to kill your business law professor, that contract would be void because it is obviously illegal to carry out its terms.

A contract is voidable if one or both parties has the ability to either withdraw from the contract or enforce it. If the parties discover the contract is voidable after one or both have partially performed, and one party chooses to have the contract terminated, both parties must return anything they had already exchanged under the agreement so that they will be restored to the condition they were in at the time they entered into it.

Certain types of errors in the formation of a contract can make it voidable. Typically, the person who can void the contract is the person the court is attempting to protect, or the party the court believes might be taken advantage of by the other. For example, contracts by minors are usually voidable by the minor (Chapter 16). Contracts entered into as a result of fraud, duress, or undue influence, as described in Chapter 17, may be voided by the innocent party. In the opening scenario, Morrow attempted to prove that the Dispute Resolution Program was a voidable contract because it did not include mutual promises, could be changed at any time without approval, and lacked genuine assent from the employees.

EXECUTED VERSUS EXECUTORY CONTRACTS

Once all the terms of the contract have been fully performed, the contract has been executed. As long as some of the terms have not yet been performed, the contract is executory. If Randolph hires Carmine to paint his garage on Saturday for $800, with $200 paid as a down payment and the balance due on completion of the job, the contract becomes executory as soon as they reach agreement. When Randolph makes the down payment and Carmine's work is half complete, it is still executory. Once the painting has been finished and the final payment made, the contract is an executed contract. In the opening scenario, Hallmark assumed that any employee who remained at the company had executed the contract.

FORMAL VERSUS INFORMAL CONTRACTS

Contracts can be formal or informal. Formal contracts have a special form or must be created in a specific manner. The Restatement (Second) of Contracts identifies the following

COMPARING THE LAW OF OTHER COUNTRIES

A SPECIAL KIND OF CONTRACT IN IRAQ

While most foreign states recognize the marriage contract, a different kind of marriage contract, sanctioned by Shiite clerics, is legal in Iraq. Called *muta'a* ("contract for a pleasure marriage"), it can last anywhere from an hour to 10 years and is renewable. Under the contract, the male typically receives sexual intimacy, in exchange for which the woman receives money. For a one-hour contract, she can generally expect the equivalent of $100; for a longer-term arrangement, $200 a month is typical, although she might receive more. The couple agrees to not have children, and if the woman does get pregnant, she can have an abortion but then must pay a fine to a cleric. The male can usually void the contract before the term ends, but the female can do so only if such a provision is negotiated when the contract is formed.

Muta'as originally developed as a way for widows and divorced women to earn a living and for couples whose parents would not allow a permanent marriage to be together. Many women's rights advocates, however, see these contracts as exploiting women and are opposed to their increased popularity after the fall of Saddam Hussein in 2003. But as the aftermath of the war in Iraq continues to produce greater numbers of widows, increasing numbers of them are turning to this method of putting food on the table for themselves and their children.

Source: Rick Jervic, "'Pleasure Marriages' Regain Popularity in Iraq," *USA Today,* May 5, 2005, p. 8A; Bobby Caina Calvin, "In Shiite Iraq, Temporary Marriage May Be Rising," *McClatchy News,* www.mcclatchydc.com/103/story/21584.html (accessed June 9, 2009).

---

four types of formal contracts: (1) contracts under seal, (2) recognizances, (3) letters of credit, and (4) negotiable instruments.

When people hear the term *formal contract,* what often comes to mind is a *contract under seal,* named in the days when contracts were sealed with a piece of soft wax into which an impression was made. Today, sealed contracts may still be sealed with wax or some other soft substance, but they are more likely to be simply identified with the word *seal* or the letters *L.S.* (an abbreviation for *locus sigilli,* which means "the place for the seal") at the end. Preprinted contract forms with a printed seal can be purchased today, and parties using them are presumed, without evidence to the contrary, to be adopting the seal for the contract.

U.S. states today do not require that contracts be under seal. However, 10 states still allow a contract without consideration to be enforced if it is under seal.

A recognizance arises when a person acknowledges in court that he or she will perform some specified act or pay a price upon failure to do so. A bond used as bail in a criminal case is a recognizance. The person agrees to return to court for trial or forfeit the bond.

A letter of credit is an agreement by the issuer to pay another party a sum of money on receipt of an invoice and other documents. The Uniform Commercial Code governs letters of credit.

Negotiable instruments (discussed in detail in Chapters 26 and 27) are unconditional written promises to pay the holder a specific sum of money on demand or at a certain time. The most common negotiable instruments are checks, notes, drafts, and certificates of deposit. They are governed primarily by the UCC.

Any contract that is not a formal contract is an informal contract, also called a simple contract. Informal contracts may in fact be quite complex, but they are called "simple" because no formalities are required in making them. Even though informal, or simple, contracts may appear less official, they are just as important and legally binding as their more formal counterparts. One particular case, *Baum v. Helget Gas Products, Inc.,* proved that something as basic as handwritten notes can be considered an enforceable employment contract in a court of law.

In *Baum v. Helget Gas Products, Inc.,*[3] Robert Baum alleged that a series of handwritten notes, which were compiled during his interview with Helget Gas Products, constituted a three-year employment contract with the company. The notes Baum took during the interview process outlined three years' worth of salary, bonuses, benefits, and vacation time as discussed in the meetings. After being hired by the company, Baum also added "contract with Helget Gas Products St. Louis Mo. Market" to the top of the notes and had a Helget executive sign the document. Helget countered by saying that Baum, a salesman for the company, knew that he must meet certain performance goals each month or risk being fired. Thus, Helget's decision to fire Baum, based on his poor performance only a year after being hired, was legitimate. Helget further said that the itemizations produced by Baum in his notes were simply specifications of what Baum would receive if he remained employed by the company for the duration of three years and were not the components of an employment contract.

BUT WHAT IF . . .

In 2012, a hospital in Pennsylvania communicated with Republic Bank through e-mails about purchasing medical equipment from the bank. In the series of e-mails, the hospital agreed to purchase the equipment for stipulated prices. The bank agreed to the terms. However, the hospital never followed through with the deal. The bank sued the hospital, claiming there was a breach of contract. What kind of contract could the e-mails be labeled as?

Initially, the district court agreed with Helget Gas Products and ruled against Baum on his breach-of-contract claim. However, Baum appealed, and the U.S Court of Appeals for the Eighth Circuit reversed the district court's judgment on the breach-of-contract claim. For business students, *Baum v. Helget Gas Products, Inc.,* demonstrates the importance of being aware of what you are agreeing to when you sign a document, regardless of how informal, or simple, it may seem.

For a summary of contract classification, see Exhibit 13-4.

Interpretation of Contracts

L04

What are the rules that guide the interpretation of contracts?

Perhaps the best-known rule of interpretation is the plain-meaning rule, which states that if a writing, or a term in question, appears to be plain and unambiguous on its face, we must determine its meaning from just "the four corners" of the document, without resorting to outside evidence, and give the words their ordinary meaning.

Although parties try to draft contracts as clearly as possible, sometimes they disagree about exactly what their obligations are under the agreement. Over time, the courts have developed some general guidelines to aid them in interpreting contracts and ascertaining the intentions of the parties:

- A judge should interpret a contract so as to give effect to the parties' intentions at the time they entered into the contract and to ensure the agreement makes sense as a whole. If possible, the court should ascertain the parties' intentions from the writing.

[3] 440 F.3d 1019; 2006 U.S. App. (accessed on Lexis Nexis, April 4, 2009).

Exhibit 13-4   Classification of Contracts

BILATERAL	or	UNILATERAL
Consists of a promise in exchange for a promise		Requires a performance by the offeree to form a contract

EXPRESS	or	IMPLIED
The terms of the contract are clearly formed either in written or spoken words		Arises from the conduct of the parties rather than their words

EXECUTED	or	EXECUTORY
A contract whose terms have been fully performed		A contract in which not all the duties have been performed

FORMAL	or	INFORMAL
Contracts created in a specific manner: contracts under seal, recognizances, letters of credit, and negotiable instruments		Simple contracts that require no formalities in making them; payment can be demanded by the payee at any time (e.g., checks)

VALID	or	VOID	or	UNENFORCEABLE	or	VOIDABLE
A contract that has all the legal elements of a contract and thus can be enforced		Not a contract because either its object is illegal or it has a serious defect		A valid contract that can't be enforced because some law prohibits it		A contract in which one or both parties has the ability to either withdraw from or enforce the contract

- If multiple interpretations are possible, the court should adopt the interpretation that makes the contract lawful, operative, definite, reasonable, and capable of being carried out.
- If the contract contains ambiguity, the judge should interpret it against the interests of the drafter. After all, the drafter is the one who could have prevented the ambiguity in the first place.
- If there is a conflict between preprinted and handwritten terms, the handwritten ones prevail. If numerals and numbers written out in words conflict, the written words prevail. If there is a conflict between general terms and specific ones, the specific terms apply.
- The court should interpret technical words in a contract as they are usually understood by persons in the profession or business to which they relate, unless clearly used in a different sense.

The Case Nugget on page 320 illustrates how some of these principles can be important in determining the outcome of a case.

CASE NUGGET

A QUESTION OF INTERPRETATION

Davco Holding Co. v. Wendy's International
2008 U.S. Dist. LEXIS 27108

Plaintiff Davco Holding Co., a franchisee of Wendy's, sued the company for breach of the franchise agreement for refusing to allow Davco to sell Pepsi from an unapproved supplier. The franchise agreement permits franchisees desiring to purchase products from an unapproved supplier to submit a written request to Wendy's for approval to do so. In response to Davco's written request to obtain beverage syrup from unapproved Pepsi, Wendy's informed Davco that CCF was the only approved supplier for fountain beverages and, further, that Pepsi syrup was not even an equivalent to Coke syrup because the drinks were made from two different secret formulas. The plaintiff alleged that Wendy's failed to adequately consider its request to solicit bids from Pepsi or to investigate Pepsi as a potential supplier and that this failure resulted in a breach by Wendy's of the franchise agreement.

The paragraph discussing the request for using an unapproved supplier contained the following language:

> Franchisor shall have the right to require that Franchisor be permitted to inspect the supplier's facilities, and that samples from the supplier be delivered, either to Franchisor or to an independent laboratory designated by Franchisor for testing. . . . Franchisor reserves the right to reinspect the facilities and products of any such approved

supplier and to revoke its approval upon the supplier's failure to continue to meet any of Franchisor's then-current criteria. Nothing in the foregoing shall be construed to require Franchisor to approve any particular supplier, nor to require Franchisor to make available to prospective suppliers, standards and specifications for formulas that Franchisor, in its sole discretion, deems confidential.

The plaintiff claimed that Wendy's breached the agreement because it didn't inspect the facilities of Pepsi, request samples, or make its criteria available to Pepsi.

In interpreting the contract, the court said that where the terms of an existing contract are clear and unambiguous, the court "cannot create a new contract by finding an intent not expressed in the clear and unambiguous language of the written contract," and that a written agreement that appears complete and unambiguous on its face will not be given a construction other than that which the plain language of the contract provides.

As the court pointed out in dismissing the plaintiff's claims, the clause gives Wendy's the right to inspect a potential supplier, but giving someone a right to do something is not imposing a duty to do so. Thus, Wendy's failure to inspect cannot be a breach. Likewise, the terms of the clause clearly state that approval of another supplier lies within the sole discretion of Wendy's and that Wendy's does not have to share its criteria with the potential supplier.

CASE OPENER WRAP-UP

A Questionable Contract

The main issue in the Hallmark case was whether a valid contract existed. Hallmark argued that by staying with the company beyond the effective date of the program, employees were agreeing to the terms of the contract. To Hallmark, the bargained-for exchange was continued employment in exchange for a promise to submit to arbitration in lieu of litigation. The circuit court sent the case to arbitration, where the arbitrator found that the program constituted a valid contract.

The appellate court, however, using the objective standard for determining whether a contract existed, found that there was not a valid contract. For a valid, bilateral contract to exist, both sides would have to be making a valid promise. Hallmark was not binding itself to anything. The program did not require Hallmark to submit its claims to arbitration or in any way bind the company to keep any other promise mentioned in the Dispute Resolution Program (DRP). Further, Hallmark had reserved the right to "modify or discontinue the DRP at any time."

In response to the claim that continued employment was given to the employees in exchange for their promise to submit all disputes to arbitration, the court found that no such promise had been made by Hallmark. The employees to be bound by the program were at-will employees. As such, employment could be terminated at any time by Hallmark. Thus, the employees were receiving no rights in regard to employment that they did not already have. Because no mutually binding promises were exchanged, the appellate court ruled that the trial court had erred in accepting the arbitrator's award. In other words, because there was no consideration from Hallmark, there was no binding contract to submit disputes to arbitration. The case was remanded for further proceedings on Morrow's discrimination and retaliation claims.[4]

KEY TERMS

acceptance 306	executed 316	letter of credit 317	unenforceable 316
agreement 306	executory 316	negotiable instruments 317	Uniform Commercial Code (UCC) 310
bilateral contract 311	express contracts 313	offer 306	
consideration 306	formal contracts 317	plain-meaning rule 318	unilateral contract 311
contract 306	implied contracts 313	quasi-contracts 313	valid 316
contractual capacity 308	informal contract 317	recognizance 317	void 316
covenant not to compete 306	lack of genuine assent 308	simple contract 317	voidable 316

SUMMARY OF KEY TOPICS

Contracts at their simplest level are legally enforceable agreements. A *valid contract* is generally one that has the following elements:

The Definition of a Contract

- *Agreement,* which is made up of the offer and the acceptance.
- *Consideration,* which is the bargained-for exchange.
- *Legal object,* which means that the subject matter does not violate the law or public policy.
- *Parties with contractual capacity,* which means they are at least the age of majority and do not suffer from any defect that renders them unable to understand the nature of the contract or their obligations under it.

The two most important sources of contract law are state common law and the Uniform Commercial Code. The Uniform Commercial Code, in Article 2, governs contracts for the sale of goods. All other contracts are also governed by the UCC.

Sources of Contract Law

Contracts may be classified in a number of ways. Every contract is either unilateral or bilateral; express or implied; valid, voidable, void, or enforceable; executed or executory; and formal or informal.

Classification of Contracts

- A *unilateral contract* requires a performance in order to form a contract.
- A *bilateral contract* consists of a promise in exchange for a promise.
- An *express contract* has all the terms clearly set forth in either written or spoken words.
- An *implied contract* arises from the conduct of the parties rather than their words.

[4] *Mary Kaye Morrow v. Hallmark Cards,* 273 S.W.3d 15, 2008 Mo. App. LEXIS 908.

- A *valid contract* is one that contains *all* the legal elements of a contract (agreement, consideration, contractual capacity, and legal object).
- A contract is *void* when either its object is illegal or it has some defect so serious that it is not actually a contract.
- A contract is *unenforceable* when some law prohibits the court from enforcing an otherwise valid contract.
- A contract is *voidable* if one or both of the parties has the ability to withdraw from the contract or to enforce it.
- *Executed contracts* are those whose terms have been fully performed.
- A contract is considered *executory* when some of the duties have not yet been performed.

Interpretation of Contracts

Courts have established rules to help interpret contracts so that they can ascertain and enforce the intent of the agreement.

The *plain-meaning rule* requires that if a writing, or a term in question, appears to be plain and ambiguous, its meaning must be determined from the instrument itself, with the words given their ordinary meaning.

POINT / COUNTERPOINT

Should the Distinction between Sealed and Unsealed Contracts Be Abolished?	
NO	**YES**
The distinction between sealed and unsealed contracts was drawn for several reasons, many of which are still relevant. As such, the distinction should remain intact despite the many attempts to have it abolished.	Advocates of abolishing the distinction between sealed and unsealed contracts argue that the distinction has become unnecessary and outdated. Sealed contracts can be dated back to medieval England when a substantial portion of the population was illiterate and many people were unable to sign their own names. As a result, each party to a sealed contract was responsible for impressing on the physical document a wax seal or some other mark bearing his or her individual sign of identification. The seals, in place of signatures, became proof of the parties' identities as well as the authenticity of the document.
Sealed contracts, at common law, did not require consideration. In many instances today, consideration is not a necessary part of the agreement. These instances include releases, modifications and discharges, promises to keep offers open, promises based on past consideration, and promises to make gifts. In these instances, one party is offering to give something without consideration. For example, an individual wishing to make a charitable donation could enter into a binding agreement to make the donation without receiving any consideration in return. By sealing the contract, the charitable organization receiving the donation would be protected against lawsuits arising from a lack of consideration. In this instance, the distinction between a sealed and unsealed contract would be the difference between a judgment in favor of the charitable organization despite the lack of consideration and an outright dismissal.	The practice of actually affixing a seal to a document is no longer necessary. Today, the parties to a sealed contract need only write the words "under seal" or "sealed" or the letters "L.S" (*locus sigilli*) for the document to be given the privileged status of a sealed document.
Additionally, sealed contracts are often accompanied by an increased statute of limitations. In instances when there are potentially long-term ramifications tied to the signing of a contract, a sealed contract would provide a much longer period in which the parties could sue than would be the case if the contract were left unsealed.	In response to those who argue that sealed contracts are necessary to bind contracts that do not contain consideration, abolishment advocates argue that there are other, and perhaps more meaningful, methods of accomplishing this. Instead of sealing a contract, one could (1) require that the promise without consideration be explicitly referenced and agreed to in the text itself; or (2) require that witnesses be present at the signing of the contract (as is the practice with regard to wills); or (3) simply rewrite the contract to provide for consideration.

(Continued)

Given the protections offered by sealed contracts, abolishing them would be irresponsible. Moreover, the elimination of the sealed-unsealed distinction would necessarily result in the creation of another method of enforcement. Why should we abolish a technique that provides protection to the parties involved in the making of a contract only to turn around and create a similar distinction under a different name?

The practice of sealing contracts is outdated and irrelevant. Parties to contracts lacking consideration could be more protected from lawsuits by using different methods of enforcement. The sealed contract should be abolished in all states (as has already been done in several states).

QUESTIONS & PROBLEMS

1. What are the elements of a valid contract?

2. What is the difference between an offer for a unilateral contract and an offer for a bilateral contract? Why might that difference be important to understand?

3. Explain how a valid contract differs from one that is void or voidable.

4. What is the objective theory of contracts?

5. What must a party prove to recover under the theory of quasi-contract?

6. What is the difference between a formal and an informal contract?

7. What is the plain-meaning rule?

8. AES was formed in 1996 and hired eight employees. At a meeting in 1997, these employees expressed concern that the company might not survive as it was using outdated equipment. At that meeting, a company executive asked the employees to remain with the firm and stated that the company was likely to merge with another firm and, if it did, the original eight employees would receive 5 percent of the value of the sale or merger as a reward for staying. In 2001, the firm was bought by another firm, and the seven employees who had stayed sought to collect their 5 percent. The company refused to pay on grounds there was no contract. Did the company and employees have a bilateral or a unilateral contract? Explain. [*Vanegas v. American Energy Services*, 302 S.W.3d 299, 2009 WL 4877734 (Sup. Ct. Tex., 2009).]

9. R.J. Reynolds Tobacco Company (RJR) operated a customer rewards program, called Camel Cash, from 1991 to 2007. Under the terms of the program, RJR urged consumers to purchase Camel

cigarettes, to save Camel Cash certificates included in packages of Camel cigarettes, to enroll in the program, and, ultimately, to redeem their certificates for merchandise featured in catalogs distributed by RJR.

The plaintiffs were 10 individuals who joined the Camel Cash program by purchasing RJR's products and filling out and submitting signed registration forms to RJR. RJR sent each plaintiff a unique enrollment number that was used in communications between the parties. These communications included catalogs RJR distributed to the plaintiffs containing merchandise that could be obtained by redeeming Camel Cash certificates.

From time to time, RJR issued a new catalog of merchandise offered in exchange for Camel Cash, which it either sent on request or mailed to consumers enrolled in the program. The number of Camel Cash certificates needed to obtain merchandise varied from as few as 100 to many thousands, and this encouraged consumers to buy more packages of Camel cigarettes and also to save Camel Cash certificates to redeem them for more valuable items.

RJR honored the program from 1991 to 2006, and during that time Camel's share of the cigarette market nearly doubled, from approximately 4 percent to more than 7 percent. In October 2006, however, RJR mailed a notice to program members announcing that the program would terminate on March 31, 2007. The termination notice stated: "As a loyal Camel smoker, we wanted to tell you our Camel Cash program is expiring. C–Notes will no longer be included on packs, which means whatever Camel Cash you have is among the last of its kind. Now this isn't happening overnight—there'll be plenty of time to redeem your C–Notes before the program ends. In fact, you'll have from OCTOBER '06 though MARCH '07 to go to camelsmokes. com to redeem your C–Notes. Supplies will be limited, so it won't hurt to get there before the rush."

Beginning in October 2006, however, RJR stopped printing and issuing catalogs and told consumers that it did not have any merchandise available for redemption. Several of the plaintiffs attempted, without success, to redeem C–Notes or obtain a catalog during the final six months of the program. The plaintiffs had saved hundreds or thousands of Camel Cash certificates that they were unable to redeem.

In November 2009, the plaintiffs filed a class action complaint against RJR. They alleged breach of contract and promissory estoppel, among other claims, because RJR's actions had made the plaintiffs' unredeemed certificates worthless.

The Defendant argued that it had no bilateral contract to breach because the plaintiffs had not promised to do anything. The trial court agreed and dismissed the complaint. The plaintiffs appealed.

How do you think the appellate court ruled, and why? [*Sateriale v. R.J. Reynolds Tobacco Co., 697 F.3d 777, C.A.9 (Cal. 2012).*]

10. An oral agreement was made among multiple parties to put together some money and open a bar and restaurant. The men had to first create a joint company. However, one potential owner was not able to provide his share of the funding at the time of the company formation and was subsequently pushed out of the deal by the other owners, who formed the company without him. The man then sued the owners. In response, the defendants argued that the plaintiff had no documentation to support a cause of action. The court had to decide whether the plaintiff's complaint and statement of fact could support a breach-of-contract claim when no contract seemed to exist. Furthermore, the court considered the idea that a theory of quasi-contract could maintain a cause of action that could consist of the theft of ownership opportunity and/or breach of fiduciary duty. How do you think the court ultimately decided? [*Don v. Broger,* Index No. 6826/12 (Sup. Ct. Kings Cnty., Oct. 10, 2012).]

Looking for more review materials?

The Online Learning Center at **www.mhhe.com/kubasek3e** contains this chapter's "Assignment on the Internet" and also a list of URLs for more information, entitled "On the Internet." Find both of them in the Student Center portion of the OLC, along with quizzes and other helpful materials.

Agreement

14

LEARNING OBJECTIVES

After reading this chapter, you will be able to answer the following questions:

1 What are the elements of a valid offer?

2 How may an offer terminate?

3 What are the elements of an acceptance?

CASE OPENER

The Problematic Promotion

A Pepsi promotion encouraged consumers to collect "Pepsi points" and redeem them for merchandise. If they did not have quite enough points for the prize they wanted, they could buy additional points for 10 cents each; however, at least 15 original Pepsi points had to accompany each order.

In an early commercial for the promotion, which can be viewed on the web at www.youtube.com/watch?v=U_n5SNrMaL8, three young boys are sitting in front of a high school, one reading his Pepsi Stuff catalog while the others drink Pepsi. All look up in awe at an object rushing overhead as the military march in the background builds to a crescendo. A Harrier Jet swings into view and lands by the side of the school building, next to a bicycle rack. Several students run for cover, and the velocity of the wind strips one hapless faculty member down to his underwear. The voice-over announces: "Now, the more Pepsi you drink, the more great stuff you're gonna get."

A teenager opens the cockpit of the fighter and can be seen, without a helmet, holding a Pepsi. He exclaims, "Sure beats the bus," and chortles. The military drumroll sounds a final time as the following words appear: "Harrier Fighter 7,000,000 Pepsi Points." A few seconds later, the following appears in more stylized script: "Drink Pepsi—Get Stuff."

A 21-year-old student named John Leonard decided to accept what he believed was Pepsi's offer of the Harrier fighter jet for 7 million Pepsi points. He quickly realized it would be easier to raise the money to buy points than to collect 7 million points. In early March 1996, he filled out an order form requesting the jet and submitted it to Pepsi, along with 15 Pepsi points and a check for $700,000.

In response, Pepsi sent him a letter saying, "The item that you have requested is not part of the Pepsi Stuff collection. It is not included in the catalogue or on the order form, and only catalogue merchandise can be redeemed under this program." Leonard sued for breach of contract.

1. Did Pepsi offer to sell the Harrier jet for 7 million points?
2. Did Leonard's submission of the order form constitute an acceptance of an offer?

The Wrap-Up at the end of the chapter will answer these questions.

The plaintiff in the opening scenario hoped to obtain a jet like this one.

Elements of the Offer

LO1

What are the elements of a valid offer?

The first element of a contract is the agreement, which is made up of an offer and an acceptance, as shown in Exhibit 14-1. Formation of the agreement begins when the party initiating the contract, called the *offeror*, makes an offer to another party, called the *offeree*. The elements of an offer are (1) serious intent by the offeror to be bound to an agreement, (2) reasonably definite terms, and (3) communication to the offeree. Remember, this chapter focuses on the elements of a contract under the common law. Some of these elements have been modified under the UCC for contracts for the sale of goods, and we discuss these changes in Chapter 21.

> ### ? BUT WHAT IF . . .
> #### WHAT IF THE FACTS OF THE CASE OPENER WERE DIFFERENT?
> Recall that, in the Case Opener, the Pepsi commercial shows a fighter jet jokingly dropping a boy off at school. But what if the Pepsi commercial featured a man fully capable of owning and operating a fighter jet who turned in an appropriate and realistic number of Pepsi points and Pepsi Company officials subsequently handed him the keys and deeds to such a prize? What if the commercial announcer turned to the viewers and seriously announced that such a prize was included in the prize catalog and could be theirs? Do both scenarios constitute a realistic offer, or does neither scenario, or only the second scenario constitute such an offer?

INTENT

The first element of the offer is **intent.** The offeror must show intent to be bound by the offeree's acceptance. As explained in Chapter 13, we interpret contracts using an objective standard, meaning the courts are concerned only with the party's outward manifestations of intent, not internal thought processes. The courts interpret the parties' words and actions the way a reasonable person would interpret them.

Exhibit 14-1

The Formation of an Agreement

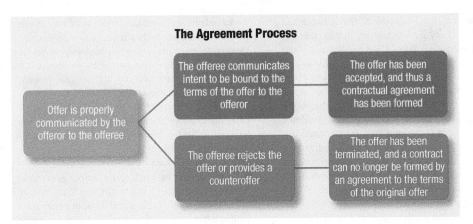

The Agreement Process

Thus, if Jude is clearly joking or speaking in anger, a reasonable person would not think Jude seriously intended to make an offer and the courts will not treat his words as an offer. If someone tries to accept Jude's offer, the courts will find a contract has not been made.

Sometimes an offeror may try to avoid being bound to a contract by later claiming she was only joking when she made the offer, but the courts are not interested in her hidden intent. As Case 14-1 demonstrates, if you joke too well, you may find yourself in an unwanted contract.

CASE 14-1   **LUCY v. ZEHMER**
SUPREME COURT OF APPEALS OF VIRGINIA
196 VA. 493, 84 S.E.2D 516 (1954)

Plaintiffs W. O. and J. C. Lucy had wanted to purchase Ferguson Farm from the Zehmers for at least eight years. One night, Lucy stopped by the establishment the Zehmers operated and said that he bet Zehmer wouldn't accept $50,000 for the place. Zehmer replied that he would, but he bet that Lucy wouldn't pay $50,000 for it. Over the course of the evening, the parties drank whiskey and engaged in casual conversation, with the talk repeatedly returning to the sale of Ferguson Farm. Eventually Lucy got Zehmer to draw up a contract for the sale of the farm for $50,000.

When Lucy later attempted to enforce the agreement, Zehmer refused to complete the sale, arguing that he had been drunk, and that the agreement to sell the property had been made in jest. Lucy sued to enforce the agreement. The trial court found for the defendants and the plaintiffs appealed.

JUSTICE BUCHANAN: If it be assumed, contrary to what we think the evidence shows, that Zehmer was jesting about selling his farm to Lucy and that the transaction was intended by him to be a joke, nevertheless the evidence shows that Lucy did not so understand it but considered it to be a serious business transaction and the contract to be binding on the Zehmers as well as on himself. The very next day he arranged with his brother to put up half the money and take a half interest in the land. The day after that he employed an attorney to examine the title. The next night, Tuesday, he was back at Zehmer's place and there Zehmer told him for the first time, Lucy said, that he wasn't going to sell, and he told Zehmer, "You know you sold that place fair and square." After receiving the report from his attorney that the title was good, he wrote to Zehmer that he was ready to close the deal.

Not only did Lucy actually believe, but the evidence shows he was warranted in believing, that the contract represented a serious business transaction and a good faith sale and purchase of the farm.

In the field of contracts, as generally elsewhere, "We must look to the outward expression of a person as manifesting his intention rather than to his secret and unexpressed intention. 'The law imputes to a person an intention corresponding to the reasonable meaning of his words and acts.'"

[continued]

At no time prior to the execution of the contract had Zehmer indicated to Lucy by word or act that he was not in earnest about selling the farm. They had argued about it and discussed its terms, as Zehmer admitted, for a long time. Lucy testified that if there was any jesting it was about paying $50,000 that night. The contract and the evidence show that he was not expected to pay the money that night. Zehmer said that after the writing was signed he laid it down on the counter in front of Lucy. Lucy said Zehmer handed it to him. In any event there had been what appeared to be a good faith offer and a good faith acceptance, followed by the execution and apparent delivery of a written contract. Both said that Lucy put the writing in his pocket and then offered Zehmer $5 to seal the bargain. Not until then, even under the defendants' evidence, was anything said or done to indicate that the matter was a joke. Both of the Zehmers testified that when Zehmer asked his wife to sign he whispered that it was a joke so Lucy wouldn't hear and that it was not intended that he should hear.

The mental assent of the parties is not requisite for the formation of a contract. If the words or other acts of one of the parties have but one reasonable meaning, his undisclosed intention is immaterial except when an unreasonable meaning which he attaches to his manifestations is known to the other party.

The law, therefore, judges of an agreement between two persons exclusively from those expressions of their intentions which are communicated between them.

An agreement or mutual assent is of course essential to a valid contract but the law imputes to a person an intention corresponding to the reasonable meaning of his words and acts. If his words and acts, judged by a reasonable standard, manifest an intention to agree, it is immaterial what may be the real but unexpressed state of his mind.

So a person cannot set up that he was merely jesting when his conduct and words would warrant a reasonable person in believing that he intended a real agreement. . . .

Whether the writing signed by the defendants and now sought to be enforced by the complainants was the result of a serious offer by Lucy and a serious acceptance by the defendants, or was a serious offer by Lucy and an acceptance in secret jest by the defendants, in either event it constituted a binding contract of sale between the parties.

Defendants contend further, however, that even though a contract was made, equity should decline to enforce it under the circumstances. These circumstances have been set forth in detail above. They disclose some drinking by the two parties but not to an extent that they were unable to understand fully what they were doing. There was no fraud, no misrepresentation, no sharp practice and no dealing between unequal parties. The farm had been bought for $11,000 and was assessed for taxation at $6,300. The purchase price was $50,000. Zehmer admitted that it was a good price. There is in fact present in this case none of the grounds usually urged against specific performance.

REVERSED and REMANDED in favor of Plaintiff.

CRITICAL THINKING

How can someone be held to have made a contract when the necessary acceptance was "in secret jest"? In other words, why must a joke be visibly a joke to a reasonable observer for there to be no acceptance?

ETHICAL DECISION MAKING

What stakeholders are being protected by this ruling? What value is playing the largest role in shaping this ruling?

Legal Principle: **In determining intent to enter into a contract, the court looks at the person's objective manifestation of intent and does not try to interpret what the person may have been secretly thinking.**

Preliminary Negotiations. An invitation to negotiate or an expression of possible interest in an exchange is not an offer because it does not express any willingness to be bound by an acceptance. For example, if Rachael asked Bill whether he would sell his car for $5,000, she is not making an offer; she is just inquiring about his potential willingness to sell. Likewise, when a firm or government entity requests bids for a construction project, the request is just an invitation for contractors to make offers. The bids, however, would be offers.

While it may seem easy to distinguish an offer from an invitation to negotiate, whether an offer in fact existed is a question of fact and sometimes ends up being litigated. When

CASE NUGGET

WHEN IS AN AD AN OFFER?

Lefkowitz v. Great Minneapolis Surplus Store, Inc.
251 Minn. 188, 86 N.W.2d 689 (1957)

Great Minneapolis Surplus Store published a newspaper announcement stating: "Saturday 9 AM Sharp, 3 Brand New Fur Coats, Worth up to $1,000.00, First Come First Served $1 Each." Morris Lefkowitz arrived at the store, dollar in hand, but was informed that under the defendant's "house rules," the offer was open to ladies but not gentlemen. The court ruled that because the plaintiff had fulfilled all the terms of the advertisement, and the advertisement was specific and left nothing open for negotiation, a contract had been formed.

From this case came the often-quoted exception to the rule that advertisements do not create any power of acceptance in potential offerees: an advertisement that is "clear, definite, and explicit, and leaves nothing open for negotiation." In that circumstance, "it constitutes an offer, acceptance of which will complete the contract." Unlike the illustration of the invitation for an offer in the text (below), where the store obviously could not give every person who came to the store a rocking chair, in the Lefkowitz case, it was very clear that there were three new fur coats and the first three people who showed up with $1 would receive them. There was nothing indefinite or unclear about how to accept the offer.

you are either making an offer or attempting to begin negotiations about a possible contract, you should use very precise language that clearly expresses your intent.

Advertisements.   Another illustration of an offer to make an offer is the advertisement. If a custom furniture maker places an advertisement in the paper that reads, "Old-fashioned, hand-crafted cedar rocking chairs only $250 the first week in May," the store is merely inviting potential customers to come to the store and offer $250 for a rocker. Because no reasonable person would expect the store to be able to sell a rocking chair to every person who might see the ad, the court will interpret the intent of the store as being to invite readers to make an offer.

Under limited circumstances, however, an ad can be treated as an offer. If it appears from the wording that the store did, in fact, intend to make an offer, that is, the ad specifies a limited quantity and provides a specific means by which the offer can be accepted, the courts will treat the ad as an offer, as demonstrated by the Case Nugget at top of this page.

John Leonard, the plaintiff in the case described in the opening scenario, tried to rely on the *Lefkowitz* decision to argue that the Pepsi commercial was an offer because it was "clear, definite, explicit, and left nothing to negotiation." After all, the commercial clearly stated that 7 million points earned a Harrier jet, and the catalog provided an additional means of buying the points for cash.

The court, however, found that the commercial could not be regarded as sufficiently definite because it specifically reserved the details of the offer to a separate writing, the catalog. Also, the commercial itself made no mention of the steps a potential offeree would be required to take to accept the alleged offer of a Harrier jet.

The court further found that the only offer in this scenario was the plaintiff's letter of March 27, 1996, along with the order form and appropriate number of Pepsi points. Since Pepsi rejected this offer with its letter, there is no contract.

Sometimes, however, unlike in the opening scenario, the advertiser's intent does appear to be to enter into a contract, even though that is not what the advertiser subjectively had in mind. A good example of such a situation occurred when Cathy McGowan called in to a U.K. radio station to enter a contest and win the advertised prize: a brand new car. The radio DJ told McGowan that to win the new car, a Renault Clio, she would have to identify a scrambled version of a song. McGowan did correctly identify the song and was told that she could come down to the radio station to collect her prize. It was not until she arrived at the radio station that McGowan became aware that she was going to receive not an actual new car but, instead, a toy version of the Renault Clio.

An upset McGowan took her case to court and argued that the radio station broadcasters gave no indication to their listeners that the contest prize was actually a toy version of the car. A Derby crown court judge agreed with McGowan and ruled that the radio station had a legal contract to provide the contest winner with a new car. The judge further said that after reviewing the broadcast, he saw nothing that suggested the radio DJ was joking or intended to award contest winners with toy cars. Cathy McGowan was thus awarded £8,000, the cost of a new Renault Clio. The case, although from the United Kingdom, still has important implications for U.S. business students. In many respects U.K. contract laws are very similar to those of the United States, and had this case occurred on U.S. soil, a similar outcome would have been reached.[1]

To prevent possible "bait-and-switch" advertising that would appear as offers, some states have consumer protection laws requiring advertisers to state in their ads either that quantities of the item are limited to the first X number of people or that rain checks will be available if the item sells out.

Auctions.   Another situation in which what seems to be an offer may not be is the auction. When Janine places a good with an auctioneer for sale by auction, is she making an offer, or is Kevin, who bids on it? It depends on what kind of auction is taking place.

If nothing is stated to the contrary in the terms of the auction, an auction is presumed to be *with reserve,* which means that the seller is merely expressing intent to receive offers. The auctioneer may withdraw the item from auction at any time before the hammer falls, signaling the acceptance of the bid. The bidder may also revoke the bid before that point.

In an auction *without reserve,* the seller is treated as making an offer to accept the highest bid and therefore must accept it. Not surprisingly, very few auctions are without reserve.

Legal Principle: **If an auction is without reserve, the auctioneer must accept the lowest bid; if it is with reserve, the auctioneer may refuse to sell the item if he or she is not satisfied with the size of the highest bid.**

DEFINITE AND CERTAIN TERMS

Under the common law, the terms of the offer must be definite and certain. In other words, all the material terms must be included.[2] The material terms allow a court to determine damages in the event that one of the parties breaches the contract. They include the subject matter, price, quantity, quality, and parties.

Sometimes an offer contains not the material term itself but a method for determining it. For example, Hampton's Construction Company is building a new garage for Jones, and the parties want to make it possible for Jones to pay one-third of the price of the garage in advance, one-third upon completion, and one-third in 12 monthly payments, with interest, beginning a month after completion. Rather than stipulating an interest rate to be charged on the monthly payments, the contract might specify an external standard according to which the interest rate would be set through the course of the 12-month payment period.

The question of whether the terms of an alleged offer were adequate for the formation of a valid contract often arises when one party believes a contract has been formed and the other believes the terms were not definite enough. That issue is the focus of Case 14-2.

[1] www.dailymail.co.uk/news/article-40153/8-000-Clio-winner-handed-toy.html.

[2] See UCC § 2-204 or Chapter 21 of this text for the modification of this element for sale-of-goods contracts.

CASE 14-2	ANDRUS v. STATE, DEPARTMENT OF TRANSPORTATION, AND CITY OF OLYMPIA

WASHINGTON STATE APPELLATE COURT
117 P.3D 1152 (WASH. APP. 2005)

Scott Andrus applied for a position as a building inspector with the city of Olympia. He received a call from Tom Hill, an engineering supervisor with the city. Hill stated, "You're our number one choice, and I'm offering you the job." Andrus responded "Great" and "Yes." Hill did not discuss the specifics of the job, so Andrus asked Hill to fax him those details. The city never sent such a fax or a written job offer and request for acceptance.

On the same day that Andrus received the call from Hill, the city checked Andrus's employment references, including his current employer (the Washington Department of Transportation), which proved unsatisfactory. Hill called Andrus the next day, informing him that the city had withdrawn the job offer because of further reference checks.

Andrus sued the city and the DOT, claiming wrongful discharge and arguing that the phone call from Hill offering the position was an employment contract. He also alleged the

DOT was liable for defamation for providing a bad employment reference to the city. The superior court granted the city's request to dismiss his claims without a trial, and he appealed only the breach of contract claim against the city.

JUSTICE QUINN-BRINTNALL: An enforceable contract requires, among other things, an offer with *reasonably certain* terms. Restatement (Second) of Contracts §33 (1979) ("The fact that one or more terms of a proposed bargain are left open or uncertain may show that a manifestation of intention is not intended to be understood as an offer or as an acceptance"). Hill's "job offer" contained no starting date, salary, or benefit information. Moreover, it was to be followed by a written offer and request for acceptance. Under these facts, the July 13 phone conversation did not form an employment contract.

AFFIRMED in favor of the city.

CRITICAL THINKING

How could the original phone call from Hill be considered an employment contract? What would have to be included in the conversation? What could be left out? How different do you think the call would have needed to be to qualify as an employment contract between the plaintiff and the city? Why?

ETHICAL DECISION MAKING

How well does this decision hold up under examinations of ethicality, such as the public disclosure test and the universalization test? Do you think Justice Quinn-Brintnall took such examinations into account in reaching this decision? Why or why not?

COMMUNICATION TO THE OFFEREE

The third element of the offer is communication. The offer must be communicated to the offeree or the offeree's agent. Only the offeree (or his agent acting on his behalf) can accept the offer. If Bill overhears Sam offer to sell his car to Helen for $5,000, Bill cannot walk over and form a contract with Sam by accepting the offer to Helen. If he says to Sam, "I'll give you $5,000 for your car," he is not accepting the offer but, rather, is making a new offer.

Legal Principle: **To have a valid offer under the common law, you need (1) the intent to be bound by an acceptance, (2) definite and certain terms, and (3) communication to the offeree.**

Termination of the Offer

Offers, once made, do not last forever. At some point in time they terminate. When an offer is terminated, the offeree can no longer accept it to form a binding contract. Termination of an offer can occur in one of five ways: revocation by the offeror, rejection or counteroffer

L02

How may an offer terminate?

by the offeree, death or incapacity of the offeror, destruction or subsequent illegality of the subject matter of the offer, or lapse of time or failure of other conditions stated in the offer. Each method is discussed below and summarized in Exhibit 14-2.

REVOCATION BY THE OFFEROR

To see how the six components of communication relate to the making of an agreement, please see the **Connecting to the Core** activity on the text website at www.mhhe.com/kubasek3e.

The offeror is said to be the "master of his or her offer" and, as such, can revoke it at any time, even if the offer states it will be open for a specified period of time. If Jim sends Carol a letter offering to mow her yard every week during the summer for the price of $20 per week as long as she responds to his offer within the next month, he can still change his mind and tell her at any time before she responds that he is no longer interested in working for her, thereby revoking his offer.

As a general rule, a revocation is effective when the offeree receives it. If it is really important to the offeror that the offeree know the offer has been revoked, the offeror should deliver the revocation personally.

Exceptions to the Revocability of the Offer. An offeree who wishes to ensure that an offer will in fact be held open for a set period of time may do so by entering into an option contract with the offeror. In an option contract the offeree gives the offeror a piece of consideration in exchange for holding the offer open for the specified period of time.

There is no requirement as to the value of the consideration. If it is money, the parties may agree that if the offer is eventually accepted and a contract is formed, the consideration will become part of the offeree's payment under the contract. This situation frequently arises in real estate contracts. Jose may be considering opening a restaurant and would like to have the option of purchasing a lot owned by Simone, so he gives her $1,000 for a 30-day option to purchase, with the provision that she will deduct the $1,000 from the purchase price if Jose purchases the property. If he does not, Simone will keep the $1,000.

Detrimental reliance on the offer may also form the basis for the court's not allowing the offeror to revoke an offer. If the offeree had reasonably relied on the offeror's promise to hold the offer open and had taken action in reliance on the offer, the courts may use the doctrine of promissory estoppel to estop, or prevent, the offeror from revoking his offer.

Detrimental reliance also comes into play to prevent a party who made a unilateral offer from revoking the offer once the offeree has begun performance of the action necessary to accept the unilateral offer. While the contract cannot be considered formed until the action requested has been completed, most courts recognize that to allow the offeror to revoke her offer after the offeree has expended significant amounts of time or money in

Exhibit 14-2

Ways an Offer Can Be Terminated

Revocation	The offeror can revoke the offer at any time unless the offeree entered into an option contract with the offeror.
Rejection	The offeree can reject the offer.
Counteroffer	If the offeree offers a counteroffer, the original offer is terminated.
Death or incapacity	If the offeror becomes incapacitated or dies, the offer immediately terminates.
Illegality	If the subject matter of the offer becomes illegal, the offer immediately terminates.
Lapse of time	The offer will expire after a reasonable amount of time, which depends on the subject matter of the offer, unless a specific time condition is given.

reliance on the offer would be to allow an unjustifiable injustice to occur. Therefore, once significant partial performance in reliance has begun, most courts require that the offeror give the offeree a reasonable amount of time to complete performance.

BUT WHAT IF . . .

In 1985, two New York couples went to court over an adopted two-year-old girl. The girl's adopted parents had reared the girl since she was five days old, yet when the girl was 15 weeks old her biological parents decided they wanted her back. In other words, the biological parents wanted to revoke their offer for their baby to be adopted. The biological parents argued that a revocation time frame for revocation had not been made sufficiently clear. However, New York State adoption law clearly stipulates that parents have only 30 days to revoke their consent for adoption, and the parents in this case had signed an "irrevocable consent" form. Would the parents be able to get their biological daughter back? Why or why not?

REJECTION OR COUNTEROFFER BY THE OFFEREE

The second means by which an offer can be terminated is rejection by the offeree. Regardless of how long the offer was stated to be open, once the offeree rejects it, it is terminated. In our earlier illustration, if Carol calls Jim and says she is not interested in his working for her this summer or any summer because of the poor quality of his work but then she calls him back an hour later to say she has changed her mind and would like to hire him in accordance with his proposed terms, it is too late. There is no offer for her to accept because her rejection terminated it.

In the same illustration, if Carol tells Jim she would indeed like him to cut her grass every week this summer but will pay him only $15 each week, she has made a counteroffer, defined by the Restatement as "an offer made by an offeree to his offeror relating to the same matter as the original offer and proposing a substituted bargain differing from that proposed by the original offer."[3] A counteroffer terminates the original offer, and so Carol's counteroffer terminates Jim's original offer. Thus, if you receive an offer that you might want to accept but you are wondering whether you can get better terms, you should inquire about how set the offeror is on the terms proposed before you make a counteroffer. For example, Carol might have simply asked Jim whether he would consider doing the job at any other price.

DEATH OR INCAPACITY OF THE OFFEROR

An offer terminates immediately if the offeror dies or loses the legal capacity to enter into the contract, even if the offeree does not know of the terminating event. If the parties had already entered into an option contract to hold the offer open for a set period of time, however, the administrator of the offeror's estate or the guardian of the offeror must hold the offer open until it expires in accordance with the option contract.

DESTRUCTION OR SUBSEQUENT ILLEGALITY OF THE SUBJECT MATTER

If the subject matter of the offer is destroyed or becomes illegal, the offer immediately terminates. For example, if Jamie offers Mercedes a job managing the riverboat casino he plans to open on January 1 but, before Mercedes accepts the offer, the state decides to no longer allow riverboat casinos to operate, the offer of employment terminates.

[3] Restatement (Second) of Contracts, sec. 39 (1981).

CASE NUGGET

THE IMPORTANCE OF CONDITIONS IN OFFERS

Adone v. Paletto
2005 NY Slip Op 50196U; 6 Misc. 3d 1026A;
800 N.Y.S.2d 341

On July 26, 2004, the defendants' counsel made an "Offer to Compromise" and settle the action in the amount of $500,000, plus costs accrued to that date, which represented the entire available coverage under the defendants' insurance policy. Part of the offer stated:

> If within ten days thereafter the claimant serves a written notice that he accepts the offer, either party may file the summons, complaint, and offer, with proof of acceptance, and thereupon the clerk shall enter judgment accordingly. If the offer is not accepted and the claimant fails to obtain a more favorable judgment, he shall not recover costs from the time of the offer, but shall pay costs from that time. An offer of judgment shall not be made known to the jury.

On August 9, 2004, the parties appeared before the court for a settlement conference in which the plaintiffs' counsel made a demand of $700,000 to settle the case. This demand was clearly not an acceptance of the offer to compromise; instead, it was a counteroffer that rejected that $500,000 offer.

The plaintiffs' $700,000 demand was not acceptable to the defendants, and the case was not settled. On September 24, 2004, the plaintiffs' counsel sent a letter to the defendants accepting the $500,000 judgment offered two months earlier, which was to include interest from the date of the summary judgment and costs. On September 28, the defendants rejected the acceptance in writing because it was not within 10 days of the offer.

The plaintiffs' motion for a judgment to enforce the offer to compromise was denied because the acceptance was not within the 10-day time frame.

LAPSE OF TIME OR FAILURE OF ANOTHER CONDITION SPECIFIED IN THE OFFER

We've noted that the offeror has the power to revoke the offer at any time, even if the offer states that it will be held open for a set period. But if the offer states that it will be held open for only a certain time, it terminates when that time expires. In the absence of such a time condition, the offer will expire after the lapse of a reasonable amount of time. What constitutes a reasonable amount of time varies, depending on the subject matter of the offer. An offer by a retailer to purchase seasonal goods from a wholesaler would lapse sooner than an offer to purchase goods that could be easily sold all year long. The Case Nugget above illustrates the consequences of not paying attention to the time or other limiting conditions specified in an offer, and see again a summary of the ways a contract can be terminated can be found in Exhibit 14-2.

The Acceptance

L03

What are the elements of an acceptance?

Once an offer has been made, the offeree has the power to accept that offer and form a contract. Under the common law, the basic requirements for a valid acceptance parallel those for a valid offer. There should be a manifestation of intent to be bound by the acceptance to the contract, agreement to the definite and certain terms of the offer, and communication to the offeror.

MANIFESTATION OF INTENT TO BE BOUND TO THE CONTRACT

In general, there are two ways an offeree can manifest intent to enter into the contract: by performance or by a return promise. The offeree must either do or say something to form the contract.

Recall, from Chapter 12, the distinction between a bilateral and a unilateral contract. If the offer is for a unilateral contract, the offeree can accept only by providing the requested performance. If Bill offered to pay $500 to anyone who returned his lost dog to him, Mary could accept the offer only by returning the dog. Bill did not want her promise, and if she called and promised to return the dog to him, that promise would have no legal effect because the only way to accept a unilateral offer is by performance.

BUT WHAT IF . . .

WHAT IF THE FACTS OF THE CASE OPENER WERE DIFFERENT?

Recall that, in the Case Opener, PepsiCo required that a customer mail in Pepsi points before the company would mail the customer a prize. But what if the Pepsi-points contract required that the customer only send in a signed statement that they had the requisite number of points and would be subsequently sending in the Pepsi points on a certain date and that PepsiCo would send the prize upon receipt of the statement? Would this scenario create a unilateral or a bilateral contract?

Remember from the previous section that the offeror has the right to revoke the offer at any time before it has been accepted. This rule is slightly modified with respect to unilateral offers so that if one party has begun performance, the offeror must give the offeree a reasonable time to complete it.

In a bilateral contract, what the offeror wants is not performance but, rather, a return promise. Sometimes, however, it is not clear what the offeror wants. Then the offeree has the option of either performing or making a return promise.

Silence as a Form of Acceptance.   Silence, as a general rule, cannot be used to form a contract. Lisa and Marie both work at a local diner where the manager is very flexible about their hours and lets them trade shifts. Marie leaves Lisa a voice-mail message saying, "I can't work my three night shifts this week. If you can cover them for me, I'll pay you an extra $40 on top of the money you'll receive from the boss for working my shifts. If I don't hear from you by 7 p.m. tomorrow, I'll assume we have a deal. Thanks so much!" If Lisa does not call back, no contract has been formed because silence under these circumstances will not constitute acceptance.

There are, however, a few situations in which silence *can* mean acceptance. In the most common, the parties, by their previous course of dealing with each other, have established a pattern of behavior whereby it is reasonable to assume silence communicates acceptance. If a wholesaler and a retailer have a long-standing relationship in which the retailer will reject a shipment that does not meet his needs, when a shipment is not sent back it is reasonable for the wholesaler to assume that the retailer means to accept it.

Silence can also be acceptance when the offeree receives the benefits of the offered services with reasonable opportunity to reject them and knowledge that some form of compensation is expected yet remains silent. In this case, an implied-in-fact contract is created. Because many unscrupulous businesspersons once took advantage of this rule and sent unordered merchandise to people, stating the goods could be returned or be kept on payment of a set price, most states have passed laws providing that unsolicited merchandise does not have to be returned and the recipient may keep it as a gift, with no contract being formed.

A third situation occurs when the parties agree that silence will be an acceptance. For example, a person may join a book club whose contract provides that a new book will be sent every month if the member does not send notification rejecting the month's selection.

COMPARING THE LAW OF OTHER COUNTRIES

CONTRACTS IN JAPAN

The Japanese tend to view contracts as ongoing relationships in which parties work with each other to smooth out any problems that arise in performance of the contract. Often suspicious of long, detailed contracts, they have a distinct preference for short, flexible agreements that leave a number of terms to be decided later.

ACCEPTANCE OF DEFINITE AND CERTAIN TERMS: THE MIRROR-IMAGE RULE

When a bilateral contract is being formed under the common law, the mirror-image rule applies to the acceptance. The **mirror-image rule** says that the terms of the acceptance must mirror the terms of the offer. If they do not, no contract is formed. Instead, the attempted acceptance is a counteroffer.[4]

COMMUNICATION TO THE OFFEROR

An offeror has the power to control the means by which the acceptance is communicated, so if the offeror specifies that only a certain means of communication will be accepted, then only an acceptance by that means forms a valid contract. Suppose Jennifer offers to paint Rashad's car for $500 but says he must accept the offer by telephone before midnight on Thursday. If Rashad sends Jennifer an e-mail Thursday morning accepting her offer, there is no contract. Even though e-mail might be a valid means of accepting a contract offer if no means is specified, when the offer is limited to a specific means of communicating the acceptance, only that means results in a valid contract. Thus, Rashad's attempted acceptance was simply a new offer.

BUT WHAT IF . . .

WHAT IF THE FACTS OF THE CASE OPENER WERE DIFFERENT?

Recall that, in the Case Opener, PepsiCo stipulated that customers must mail in Pepsi points. What if, instead, the company required that contestants fax in photos of their collected Pepsi points. If Leonard mailed his Pepsi points to the company, would that count as a valid acceptance of the offer?

If no means of communicating the acceptance is specified, any reasonable means is generally acceptable. Telephone, mail, fax, and e-mail are all valid means of accepting an offer, as is accepting it in person. When drafting an offer, if a person wishes acceptance to be only by a particular means, the offer must make it clear that only certain means are allowed. As Case 14-3 illustrates, courts will carefully interpret provisions specifying the means of acceptance.

The Mailbox Rule. Because not all acceptances are made in person, the courts needed a rule to determine the point at which an acceptance made through the mail became effective. They settled on the **mailbox rule**, which provides that an acceptance is valid when the offeree places it in the mailbox, whereas a revocation is effective only when the offeree receives it. The mailbox rule is not applicable when there is instantaneous communication, such as over the phone, in person, or by telex.

---

[4] See UCC § 2-207 and Chapter 21 for an explanation of how the UCC modifies the mirror-image rule for contracts for the sale of goods.

| CASE 14-3 | **ALEXANDER v. LAFAYETTE CRIME STOPPERS, INC.** |

COURT OF APPEALS OF LOUISIANA, THIRD CIRCUIT
28 SO. 3D 1253 (LA. APP. 3 CIR., 2010)

In the summer of 2002, after several South Louisiana women had been murdered, the Multi Agency Homicide Task Force (Task Force) was established to investigate these murders, which they believed were being committed by the individual referred to as the South Louisiana Serial Killer. In April 2003, the Baton Rouge Crime Stoppers (BRCS) began publicizing a reward offer in newspapers, television stations, and billboards around the Baton Rouge area regarding the South Louisiana Serial Killer. A short time later, Lafayette Crime Stoppers (LCS) also publicized a reward offer. Both reward offers included an expiration date of August 1, 2003.

On July 9, 2002, Dianne Alexander was attacked in her home in St. Martin Parish. Her son came home during the attack and chased the attacker away. Ms. Alexander reported the attack to local police, and, later, both Ms. Alexander and her son described the attacker to the St. Martin Sheriff's Department.

The lead investigator on Ms. Alexander's attack began to suspect that Ms. Alexander's attacker could be the South Louisiana Serial Killer, so in May 2003, he shared information regarding Ms. Alexander's attack with the Lafayette Sheriff's Department, which then shared it with the Task Force.

On May 22, 2003, Ms. Alexander was interviewed by an FBI agent assisting the Task Force. Based upon that interview, a composite sketch was drawn and released to the public on May 23, 2003. Investigators believed the composite sketch matched the description of a possible suspect in an investigation being handled by the Louisiana Attorney General's Office and the Zachary Police Department. On May 25, 2003, Ms. Alexander, in a photo lineup, identified her attacker as the same man suspected in the Zachary investigation.

Around August 14, 2003, Ms. Alexander contacted LCS and sought to collect the advertised award, but was told she was ineligible to receive the award. In 2006, Ms. Alexander and her son sued BRCS and LCS, alleging that the defendants owed them $100,000 and $50,000, respectively, for the information they provided to the defendants. The defendants filed motions for summary judgment asserting there was no genuine issue of material fact because the plaintiffs would be unable to prove that a contract ever existed between the parties. The trial court granted the motions. The plaintiffs appealed, asserting that there is a genuine issue of material fact over whether LCS and BRCS offers contained a requirement that acceptance of the reward must be done through the Crime Stoppers' tip line.

JUDGE AMY: . . . The defendants filed motions for summary judgment asserting that a valid contract never existed between the parties. Specifically, the defendants argued that the plaintiffs never provided information to Crime Stoppers via the tipster hotline and thus did not comply with the "form, terms, or conditions required by the Crime Stoppers offers[.]" The trial court granted the defendants' motions for summary judgment, finding that the offer from Crime Stoppers was conditioned on the information being provided to the defendant entities rather than law enforcement. . . .

Louisiana Civil Code Article 1927 provides:
A contract is formed by the consent of the parties established through offer and acceptance.

Unless the law prescribes a certain formality for the intended contract, offer and acceptance may be made orally, in writing, or by action or inaction that under the circumstances is clearly indicative of consent.

Unless otherwise specified in the offer, there need not be conformity between the manner in which the offer is made and the manner in which the acceptance is made.

"Louisiana jurisprudence has recognized that an advertisement may constitute an offer susceptible of giving rise to a binding contract upon acceptance in instances where a prize is offered or where the terms of a contest are announced." . . . Once a plaintiff performs all of the requirements of the offer in accordance with the published terms, it creates a valid and binding contract, under which one is entitled to the promised rewards. . . . '68 So. 2d (1953)

The offer made by LCS in a May 14, 2003, press release, reads as follows:

The Greater Lafayette Chamber of Commerce has joined with Lafayette Crime Stoppers to offer a reward of $50,000 for information relating to the murders of five south Louisiana women. A $25,000 reward offer by Lafayette Crime Stoppers has been matched through commitments from Chamber members.

In order to qualify for the reward, the tipster must provide information which leads to the arrest, DNA match, and the formal filing of charges against a suspect through grand jury indictment or Bill of Information. In addition, the qualifying tip must be received prior to midnight, August 1, 2003. Investigators with the Serial Killer Task Force have expressed optimism that a large enough reward might provide the impetus for someone with knowledge of the killings to come forward. By stipulating a deadline, investigators hope to expedite receipt of the information.

All callers the Crime Stoppers Tips line remain anonymous. A code number is issued as the only means of identification. Tips can be submitted 24 hours a day at 232–TIPS or toll free at 1–800–805–TIPS.

[continued]

The offer from BRCS, as published in the *Morning Advocate,* reads as follows:

> Crime Stoppers, Inc. $100,000 reward for information on the South Louisiana Serial Killer. A $100,000 reward will be given for information leading to the arrest and indictment of the South Louisiana Serial Killer. Call today and help make Baton Rouge a safer place for you and your family. All calls remain anonymous. 334–STOP or 1–877–723–7867. Reward expires August 1, 2003.

Both LCS and BRCS offers were irrevocable offers because they specified a period of time for acceptance. La. Civil Code Article 1934 provides that "acceptance of an irrevocable offer is effective when received by the offeror." Acceptance is received when it comes into the possession of a person authorized by the offeror to receive it, or when it is deposited in a place the offeror has indicated as the place where communications of that kind are to be deposited for him.

The plaintiffs argue that there is a genuine issue of material fact as to whether they accepted the Crime Stoppers' reward offers; however, the plaintiffs admit that they did not contact either Crime Stopper organization before August 1, 2003. The plaintiffs argue that they accepted the offers by performance when they provided information about the serial killer to law enforcement. Further, the plaintiffs

contend that this performance is a customary manner of accepting reward offers from Crime Stopper organization.

In the present matter, the plaintiffs' acceptance of the reward offers must have been received by the defendants (offerors) by the time prescribed in the offer (August 1, 2003) in the place where communications of that kind were to be deposited (the phone number cited in the offers). The record contains no evidence indicating the defendants were notified by the plaintiffs in the time and manner indicated in the offer. While the plaintiffs may have provided information related to the arrest or indictment of Derrick Todd Lee to local law enforcement and the Task Force, there is no indication in the offer that either of those parties were the offerors of the reward or persons authorized to receive acceptance on their behalf.

The plaintiffs argue that they accepted the offers by performance when they provided information about the serial killer to law enforcement. Further, the plaintiffs contend that this performance is a customary manner of accepting reward offers from Crime Stopper organization. While acceptance may be valid if customary in similar transactions, according to La.Civ.Code art. 1936, it must be "customary in similar transactions at the time and place the offer is *received.*" As indicated above, there is no evidence in the record that the defendants received any acceptance of the offer. Accordingly, no contract was formed between the parties.

Summary Judgment in favor of Defendants, AFFIRMED.

CRITICAL THINKING

What is ambiguous about the concept of acceptance? How does the law act to clarify the potential liability?

ETHICAL DECISION MAKING

How might the public disclosure test give false guidance to the ethics of this decision? Do you think that the public's attitude toward the interaction between Crime Stoppers and the people who helped solve a crime might have resulted in a different decision had the public disclosure principle been used to resolve the case?

Since the mailbox rule does not apply to instantaneous communications, when are faxes, text messages, and e-mail effective? Are these instantaneous forms of communication? Text messages seem the easiest to answer yes to. There is still some disagreement among jurisdictions as to whether faxes and e-mail should be effective on dispatch or receipt. The majority rule with respect to faxes appears to be that faxes are instantaneous transmissions and therefore effective on receipt, but some jurisdictions have applied the mailbox rule to them. There seems to be greater split among the jurisdictions over how to treat e-mail transmissions. The Uniform Electronic Transactions Act seems to create an electronic version of the mailbox rule, providing that an e-mail is sent when properly addressed to an information processing system designated by the recipient, in a form capable of being processed by that system, and enters an information processing system out of

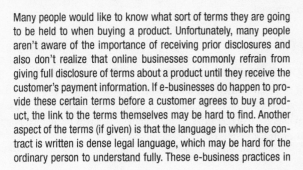

E-COMMERCE AND THE LAW

DISCLOSURE OF DEFINITE AND CERTAIN TERMS

Many people would like to know what sort of terms they are going to be held to when buying a product. Unfortunately, many people aren't aware of the importance of receiving prior disclosures and also don't realize that online businesses commonly refrain from giving full disclosure of terms about a product until they receive the customer's payment information. If e-businesses do happen to provide these certain terms before a customer agrees to buy a product, the link to the terms themselves may be hard to find. Another aspect of the terms (if given) is that the language in which the contract is written is dense legal language, which may be hard for the ordinary person to understand fully. These e-business practices in regard to disclosure of terms can be very deceptive. A customer may inadvertently agree to a contract when the customer is only given some information about it. This situation would be similar to one in which a student were given a page of text that appeared to be whole and complete, and the student had completed an entire report on the text before being given an additional 50 pages that were also a part of the text. Customers who shop online should be aware of the potential for deception with online sellers and should use caution when making purchases.

Source: http://digitalcorpora.org/corp/nps/files/govdocs1/021/021056.pdf.

the control of the sender. It is considered received when it enters the information processing system designated by the recipient.

Authorized Means of Acceptance. The means by which the offeree can communicate acceptance to the offeror may either be expressly stated in the offer, which is called an *express authorization,* or be implied from the facts and circumstances surrounding the communication of the offer to the offeree. If the offer specifies that acceptance must be communicated by a specific mode, that mode is the only means for accepting the offer, and once the acceptance is dispatched, the contract has been formed. If any other attempted means of acceptance is used, there is no valid contract. For example, if the offer says acceptance must be by certified mail, then as soon as the acceptance is taken to the post office, there is a valid contract. If the offeree instead faxes an acceptance, there is no contract.

According to the Restatement, if no mode of communication is specified in the offer, any reasonable means of acceptance is valid. To determine the reasonableness of the means, courts look at such factors as the means by which the offer was communicated and the surrounding circumstances.

Effect of an Unauthorized Means of Acceptance. As noted above, when an offer specifies that acceptance must be communicated by a particular mode, no other form of acceptance is valid. However, if the offer merely authorizes certain modes of acceptance but does not condition acceptance on the use of those modes, use of an unauthorized means of acceptance is acceptable but the contract is not formed until the acceptance is received by the offeror. For example, if Beth sends an offer to Joe via a fax, saying in the offer that acceptance may be via fax or e-mail, and Joe accepts her offer by overnight mail, his acceptance is valid but it is effective only on receipt.

If the offeree makes a mistake and sends the acceptance to the wrong address, there is no acceptance on dispatch. However, if a correction is made and the letter eventually reaches the offeror, the acceptance is valid on receipt, assuming the offer was still open.

The Effect of an Acceptance after a Rejection. We've seen that if an acceptance is received after a rejection, the acceptance is not valid because the rejection terminated the offer. However, sometimes a rejection is dispatched, but before it is received, the acceptance is communicated to the offeror. In that case, a valid contract has been formed because the rejection is not effective until it is received. Suppose Brenda e-mails an offer to Harry, and he puts a rejection in the mail; then, before it is received, Harry calls Brenda and tells her he accepts. A valid contract has been formed, and the rejection will have no

340   Part 2   Contracts

effect when Brenda receives it. However, if Harry telephoned after Brenda had received the rejection, there could be no contract.

BUT WHAT IF . . .

WHAT IF THE FACTS OF THE CASE OPENER WERE DIFFERENT?

What if Leonard had sent in a certain number of Pepsi points to receive a corresponding prize but at the last minute e-mailed the company to reject the prize because he wanted to save his points for a bigger prize. If the company receives his mailed points before his e-mailed rejection, is his rejection valid?

CASE OPENER WRAP-UP

The Problematic Promotion

Much to the plaintiff's dismay, the court in the Pepsi case found that the commercial could not be regarded as sufficiently definite to be an offer, because it specifically reserved the details of the offer to a separate writing, the catalog.[5] Also, the commercial itself made no mention of the steps a potential offeree would be required to take to accept the alleged offer of a Harrier jet. As in most cases where a consumer attempts to place an order for an advertised item, the court regarded the plaintiff's purported acceptance as an offer. And it was an offer that Pepsi obviously rejected. And while the court did not specifically mention this factor, common sense should have indicated to the plaintiff and his family that Pepsi did not really intend to give a harrier jet as one of the promotional prizes.

KEY TERMS

acceptance 334	definite and certain terms 330	material terms 330	rejection 333
communication 331	intent 326	mirror-image rule 336	revocation 332
counteroffer 333	mailbox rule 336	option contract 332	termination 331

SUMMARY OF KEY TOPICS

Elements of the Offer   A valid offer requires (1) the manifestation of the offeror's intent to be bound, (2) definite and certain terms, and (3) communication to an offeree.

Termination of the Offer   An offer can be terminated by revocation by the offeror; rejection or counteroffer by the offeree; death or incapacity of the offeror; destruction or subsequent illegality of the subject matter of the offer; or lapse of time or failure of other conditions stated in the offer.

The Acceptance   An acceptance is valid when a manifestation of intent to be bound to the terms of the offer is communicated to the offeror by the offeree.

[5] *Leonard v. Pepsico*, 210 F.3d 88, 2000 U.S. App. LEXIS 6855.

POINT / COUNTERPOINT

Should Internet Click-Wrap and Browse-Wrap Agreements Be Treated as Legally Binding Contacts?	
YES	**NO**
Nearly all computer users have, at some point, encountered form contracts while browsing the Internet. Whether they pertain to downloading software, signing up for a free e-mail service, or making an online purchase, many online forms are designed to protect the host company or retail store's interests. To protect these companies and ensure continued online commerce, these contracts *must* be viewed as legally binding.	Nearly all computer users have agreed to and proceeded beyond click-wrap agreements. Many of these computers users have used websites that have browse-wrap agreements embedded within their pages. But the mere existence of these agreements does not mean that they are valid contracts under existing contract laws; they should not.
The two types of Internet contracts are click-wrap and browse-wrap contracts. A click-wrap contract requires that users read all terms and conditions before clicking an "I Agree" button. Such contracts give users the ability to *choose* whether to accept the conditions and proceed or decline and withdraw. This process includes an offer by the offeror (the terms and conditions as listed) and acceptance by the offeree (clicking the "I Agree" button). The contract includes a clear manifestation of the offeree's intent to be bound when he or she clicks the accept button.	In both click-wrap and browse-wrap agreements, the terms are decided prior to the user even installing the software or visiting the site. The user is not given an opportunity to negotiate the terms; in essence, there is no meeting of the minds. If the user wishes to use the website, software, or e-mail system, he or she must accept the prewritten terms.
In the second type of Internet contract, the browse-wrap agreement, the user is not required by the site to click any button but is seen under the law as having accepted the terms by viewing the website. In such instances, the site provides its terms and conditions via a hyperlink at the top of a web page. By posting the link, the website has provided users with notice that there are terms and conditions associated with the site and that users who continue making use of the site should be bound by those terms. By viewing the site (the performance), the user is bound to the terms (the offer).	Click-wrap agreements have become so prevalent throughout recent years that Internet users often ignore the text of the agreement and simply click the "I Agree" box. Without reading and understanding the terms of the agreement, lawyers, consumers, and companies are left to wonder whether the user lacked genuine assent.
Given the large quantity of transactions occurring over the Internet, browse-wrap and click-wrap agreements offer an efficient means for governance. In an effort to protect companies and ensure compliance by consumers, these agreements *must* be treated as legally binding contracts.	Browse-wrap agreements, unlike click-wrap agreements, are not even located on the general web page. In order to view the terms and conditions of use, the user must find the hyperlink on a page, click on it, read the terms, and then decide whether or not to continue reading the web page. The site owners cannot be certain that users will find, read, or understand the terms and conditions of use before they browse the site. Without knowledge, Internet users should not be bound to the terms and conditions.
	Finally, when paper contracts are signed, one can be certain whom the relevant parties are. With electronic contracts, that certainty quickly dissipates. Even though a click-wrap agreement is offered and accepted, without proper verification, one cannot be certain who was using the computer at the time the contract was formed. If, for example, a friend uses your computer while visiting your dorm room and enters into a click-wrap agreement, which you later violate unknowingly, who is accountable? Can you prove you were not the one who agreed to the terms? Identifying the parties associated with electronic contracts would be more difficult than identifying those associated with paper contracts.

QUESTIONS & PROBLEMS

1. What is the mirror-image rule?

2. What is the mailbox rule?

3. In July 2012, the six adult cast members of the hit television show *Modern Family* filed a joint lawsuit against Twentieth Century Fox Television in an attempt to void their contracts. The lawsuit claimed that their contracts were illegal, in that the contracts broke California's "7-year rule." The 7-year rule stipulates that contracts regarding personal services may not span longer than seven years. Yet the actors' contracts guaranteed their services from 2009 to 2016. A big incentive for the actors to file the lawsuit was to increase the amount they each were paid per episode, which for most of them was $65,000 an episode. If a contract is illegal, may it be voided even if the actors knowingly signed to the terms of the contract? How do you think the judge should have decided this case, and why? [*Vergara et al. v. Twentieth Century Fox International Television, Inc.* BC488786 (Sup. Ct. L.A. 2012).]

4. Michael and Laurie Montgomery negotiated with Norma English with regard to the potential sale of the Montgomerys' home. English submitted a bid for $272,000, but she included a request to purchase some of the Montgomerys' personal property and expressed that an "as-is" provision was not applicable to the sale. When the Montgomerys received the offer, they deleted the personal property provision, deleted provisions related to latent defects and a building inspection, and added a specific as-is rider. English's agent then delivered the counteroffer to English, who initialed many, but not all, of the Montgomerys' modifications, such as the deletion of the personal property provision. The Montgomerys refused to proceed with the sale, so English filed suit for specific performance of the contract. Under the mirror-image rule, did a contract exist between the Montgomerys and English? Why or why not? [*Montgomery v. English*, 2005 Fla. App. LEXIS 4704.]

5. Nutritional Sciences LLC sponsored the "Quarter Million Dollar Challenge," a contest requiring contestants to use the company's nutritional products and training plans to lose weight and get in shape during a 13-week period. A panel of judges would select a number of winners based on their success in the program. Contest rules stipulated that "all winners must agree to the regulations outlined specifically for winners before claiming championship or money." Next to this statement was an asterisk. The note linked to the asterisk reserved the right of Nutritional Sciences to cancel the contest or alter its terms at any time. Donna Englert learned that she was chosen female runner-up in her age group, and she expected to receive the advertised prize of $1,500 cash and $500 worth of products. When she went to sign the agreement to claim her prize, she found that the company had changed the cash prize to $250, so she refused to sign and sued for breach of contract. The trial court initially dismissed her case, and she appealed. How do you think the court of appeals decided the case and why? [*Englert v. Nutritional Sciences, LLC*, 2008 WL 44 4416597 (Ohio App. 2008).]

6. The Pennsylvania Department of Transportation (PennDOT) issued a Request for Bid Proposal for Vending Machine Services for rest areas on highways in the state. ATI submitted the lowest bid for the sites. PennDOT selected ATI for a contract for 35 vending sites. Enclosed with the notice of award sent to ATI was a service purchase contract to be executed by ATI, by PennDOT, by the commonwealth comptroller, and by PennDOT's attorney. Also, "if required," signature lines for the Office of General Counsel and the Attorney General's Office were provided. The award notice indicated that the contract would become effective "after all approvals have been received from the administrative and fiscal personnel in Harrisburg" and further stated that no activities may be performed until the contract is fully executed. ATI returned an executed contract to PennDOT. PennDOT's director of the Bureau of Maintenance and Operations and a representative from its legal department executed the agreement. The comptroller and Office of General Counsel subsequently signed the contract; however, the Attorney General's Office refused to execute the agreement. The Attorney General's Office subsequently filed criminal charges, related to sales tax issues, against ATI's president. As a result, the Attorney General's Office notified PennDOT it would not approve the contract.

PennDOT never returned an executed contract to ATI or provided a notice-to-proceed to ATI. Instead, PennDOT notified ATI it would not enter into the contract because it determined ATI is not a responsible contractor. ATI filed a complaint alleging PennDOT breached a valid contract. After the hearing, the board determined that PennDOT never delivered an acceptance of the offer to ATI and, as a result, a contract was never formed. ATI appealed, arguing that the board erred in finding a contract did not exist because PennDOT's representatives, who signed the contract, intended to bind PennDOT to the terms of the contract. How did the court rule on appeal? Did the documents contain a proper acceptance? [*Makoroff v. DOT,* 938 A.2d 470 (Pa. Commw. Ct. 2007).]

7. Plaintiff Business Systems Engineering, Inc., was one of several subcontractors that agreed to provide technical consultants for defendant IBM's work on a transit project. In a "plan of utilization" provided by IBM to the transit authority, IBM had listed Business Systems as one of its intended subcontractors, with $3.6 million listed on that document under the heading "contract amount." The terms of the arrangement between IBM and its subcontractors for the job were that when IBM needed technical consultants for a part of the project, the subs would submit bids and when the subcontractor's bid was accepted, the subcontractor would receive a specific statement of work detailing the scope of the specific project, the time frame, the conditions under which the task would be deemed complete, and the hourly wage, followed by a work authorization. The transit authority retained the authority to reject any individual consultant who was selected by the subcontractor, and the contract between the subcontractors and IBM incorporated by reference the contract between IBM and the transit authority. Work was not to begin until a final work authorization was issued. At the end of the project, 38 work authorizations had been issued to the plaintiff by the defendant for a total of $2.2 million, rather than the $3.6 million that had been projected in the original estimate IBM had provided to the transit authority. IBM had paid the plaintiff the $2.2 million for the work done on the work authorizations, but the plaintiff argued that it should have been entitled to the full $3.6 million contained in the estimate that was incorporated by reference in

the contracts between IBM and the subcontractors. The plaintiff argued that it had a contract with IBM for the full $3.6 million. The district court granted summary judgment for the defendant. What do you think the plaintiff's argument was on appeal? What do think the outcome of the appeal was and why? [*Business Systems Engineering, Inc. v. International Business Machines Corp.,* 547 F.3d 883, 2008 U.S. App LEXIS 23682.]

8. Plaintiff VanHierden injured his thumb and finger at work and had it surgically repaired. He later developed a persistent pain at the base of his thumb. He went to see the defendant about having a sympathectomy to alleviate his pain. The defendant told the plaintiff, "We're going to get rid of your pain and get you back to work." The plaintiff then signed a written consent form to have the surgery, which included the following:

The procedure listed under paragraph 1 has been fully explained to me by Dr. Swelstad and I completely understand the nature and consequences of the procedure(s). I have further had explained to me and discussed available alternatives and possible outcomes, and understand the risk of complications, serious injury or even death that may result from both known and unknown causes. I have been informed that there are other risks that are adherent to the performance of any surgical procedure. I am aware that the practice of medicine and surgery is not an exact science and I acknowledge that no guarantees have been made to me concerning the results of the operation or procedure(s).

The defendant performed the sympathectomy, but it did not alleviate the plaintiff's pain; nor was he able to return to work, so he sued the defendant for breach of a contract to cure the pain. The district court granted summary judgment for the defendant, finding that no contract had been formed as a matter of law. On appeal, do you believe the court found a valid agreement between the parties? Why or why not? [*Ronald VanHierden v. Jack Swelstad, MD,* 2010 Wis. App. 16, 2009 Wis. App. LEXIS 1013.]

9. In 2008, a lawyer for Mutual Life Insurance e-mailed Dr. Miles regarding the settlement of a lawsuit that he had filed against the insurance company. The e-mail that the attorney sent contained proposed settlement terms. Dr. Miles's attorney sent an e-mail back explicitly stating that Dr. Miles accepted the terms the company was offering. After

the trial was canceled in light of the settlement, the company's attorney sent Dr. Miles a written settlement that was different from the terms contained in the e-mail. Thus, Dr. Miles rejected the offer, and the company subsequently claimed that there was no settlement. Dr. Miles then took the company to court a second time regarding whether a contract was created through the e-mail that proposed specific settlement terms. If the e-mail seemed to contain all the essential terms of an offer, how do you think the judge decided? [*Miles v. Northwestern Mutual Life Insurance Company,* 677 F. Supp. 2d 1312, U.S. Dist. LEXIS 123597 (2009).]

10. Sarah and Eddie Hogan wanted to sell 2.5 acres of land through their real estate agent, Darita Richardson. On December 10, 2001, Warren Kent offered to purchase the land for $52,500. An "Agreement to Buy or Sell" was created, which Kent signed right away. One term of the agreement was that the offer would expire on December 11, 2001, at 3 p.m., and it stated additionally, "Time is of the essence and all deadlines are final except where modifications, changes, or extensions are made in writing and signed by all parties." Although Richardson scheduled a meeting on December 11, 2001, at 2 p.m. with the Hogans, the Hogans failed to appear. However, the parties agreed to a two-day extension, lasting until December 13, 2001, at 3 p.m., and the extension was binding and irrevocable according to the "Addendum to Agreement to Purchase or Sell." The Hogans signed both documents at 9 a.m. on December 13, 2001. At about 11 a.m., Kent also signed the addendum. However, neither Kent's agent nor Richardson contacted the Hogans before 3 p.m. about Kent's acceptance. After 3 p.m., Richardson realized that the Hogans had not placed the date and time next to their signatures. When she met with the Hogans, the Hogans placed the date and the time as 4:48 p.m., informing Richardson that they, the Hogans, had changed their minds about the sale. Kent sued for specific performance of the contract. What effect, if any, did the failure to communicate the acceptance of the offer before 3 p.m. have in terms of whether a contract was formed? What was the appellate court's reasoning? [*Kent v. Hogan,* 2004 La. App. LEXIS 2539.]

Looking for more review material?

The Online Learning Center at **www.mhhe.com/kubasek3e** contains this chapter's "Assignment on the Internet" and also a list of URLs for more information, entitled "On the Internet." Find both of them in the Student Center portion of the OLC, along with quizzes and other helpful materials.

Consideration

LEARNING OBJECTIVES

After reading this chapter, you will be able to answer the following questions:

1 What is consideration?

2 What are the rules regarding consideration?

3 What is promissory estoppel, and when can it be used?

4 What is an illusory promise?

5 What is the difference between a liquidated debt and an unliquidated debt?

6 What is an accord and satisfaction?

CASE OPENER

Upper Deck—Contract Liability or Gift?

In 1988 the Upper Deck Company was a company with an idea for a better baseball card: one that had a hologram on it. By the 1990s the firm was a major corporation worth at least a quarter of a billion dollars.

In 1988, however, its outlook hadn't been so bright. Upper Deck lacked the funds for a $100,000 deposit it needed to buy some special paper by August 1. Without that deposit its contract with the Major League Baseball Players Association would have been jeopardized.

Upper Deck's corporate attorney, Anthony Passante, Jr., loaned the company the money. That evening, the directors of the company accepted the loan and, in gratitude, agreed to give Passante 3 percent of the firm's stock. Passante never sought to collect the stock, and later the company reneged on its promise. Passante sued for breach of oral contract.[1]

1. If you were on the jury, how would you decide the case? Was the offer of 3 percent of the firm's stock legal consideration for the loan? Or was it a mere gift?

2. Does Upper Deck have a moral obligation to give Passante the stock? If so, is this obligation legally enforceable?

The Wrap-Up at the end of the chapter will answer these questions.

[1] *Passante v. McWilliam,* 53 Cal. App. 4th 1240 (1997).

What is Consideration?

L01

What is consideration?

Consideration is required in every contract. It is what a person will receive in return for performing a contract obligation. Suppose Dan agrees to purchase Marty's car for $1,000. Dan's payment of $1,000 is the consideration Marty will receive for the car. Title to and possession of the car are the consideration Dan will receive in exchange. Consideration can be anything, as long as it is the product of a bargained-for exchange. In a business context it is often (but not always) money. Exhibit 15-1 provides other examples of consideration.

Rules of Consideration

L02

What are the rules regarding consideration?

The key to understanding consideration is understanding the rules that govern it and their exceptions. We explore them below.

LACK OF CONSIDERATION

A court will enforce one party's promise only if the other party promised some consideration in exchange. For example, in a bilateral contract (a promise for a promise), the consideration for each promise is a return promise. Suppose Nicole promises to pay Mike $2,000 tomorrow for his car. Mike promises to sell Nicole his car tomorrow for $2,000. There is an oral contract between them. Nicole's promise is her consideration to Mike. Mike's promise is his consideration to Nicole. There has been a mutual exchange of something of value.

An example of a bilateral contract, or a promise for a promise, occurred when the U.S. government seized control of insurance giant American International Group (AIG). The government agreed to lend AIG up to $85 billion in exchange for nearly 80 percent of AIG's stock. The consideration AIG received was the promise of up to $85 billion in U.S. government loans. The consideration the government received was a promise of almost 80 percent of AIG's stock.[2]

In a unilateral contract (a promise for an act), one party's consideration is the promise and the other party's consideration is the act. Suppose your professor made the following statement in class: "If any student shows up at my house on Saturday and does the gardening, I will pay that student $100." You show up and do the gardening. The professor's consideration to you is the promise of the payment of $100 on completion of the gardening, and your consideration to the professor is the act of completing the gardening. Once again, there has been a mutual exchange of something of value.

Exhibit 15-1

Examples of Consideration

TYPE OF CONSIDERATION	EXAMPLE
A benefit to the promisee	A promise to stay in a job until a particular project is complete (this is a benefit to the employer)
A detriment to the promisor	A promise to your football coach to refrain from riding your motorcycle during football season even though you love riding it
A promise to do something	A promise to cook dinner for your roommate for the next six months
A promise to refrain from doing something	A promise to stop staying out late at night during exam week

[2] "U.S. Seizes Control of AIG with $85 Billion Emergency Loan," *Washington Post*, September 17, 2008, www.washingtonpost.com/wp-dyn/content/article/2008/09/16/AR2008091602174 (accessed May 25, 2009).

TYPE OF CONTRACT	PROMISOR	PROMISEE
Bilateral	A promise	A promise
Unilateral	A promise	An act

Exhibit 15-2
Type of Consideration Based on Type of Contract

See Exhibit 15-2 for an explanation of bilateral and unilateral contracts.

Legal Principle: **For a promise to be enforced by the courts, there must be consideration.**

One exception to the rule requiring consideration is promissory estoppel. Promissory estoppel occurs when three conditions are met:

L03

What is promissory estoppel, and when can it be used?

- One party makes a promise and either knows or should know that the other party will reasonably rely on it.
- The other party does reasonably rely on the promise.
- The only way to avoid injustice is to enforce the promise.

How does promissory estoppel work? Suppose upon graduation from college, Amanda receives a job offer across the country. She gives up her apartment, cancels all her other job interviews, and moves all her possessions. Upon arriving, she rents a new apartment and shows up for work. Amanda is then told there is no job! May she sue the employer? The answer in most states is yes, under the theory of promissory estoppel. Amanda may be able to recover her *reliance damages* (money she spent in "reliance" on the job offer). Promissory estoppel is not awarded regularly, but in the right case it can provide a remedy where no other remedy exists.

In a recent case, the Ninth Circuit Court of Appeals held that Yahoo's promise to remove a nude photo from its website was subject to a claim of promissory estoppel. In that case, the plaintiff learned that her ex-boyfriend, pretending to be her, had posted nude photos of her on Yahoo. He also included all her contact information and an invitation for men to contact her for sexual purposes.[3] The plaintiff contacted Yahoo (in accordance with its established policies) and requested that the photo be removed. Yahoo agreed but, despite repeated requests, did not remove the photo for six months. The court held that Yahoo's promise to depost the profile meant that Yahoo had a duty to the plaintiff. As such, the plaintiff's claim of promissory estoppel could be maintained. If the plaintiff is able to prove that she reasonably relied on Yahoo's promise to her detriment, she may well prevail on her claim for damages.

BUT WHAT IF . . .

WHAT IF THE FACTS OF THE CASE OPENER WERE DIFFERENT?

Recall, in the Case Opener, that the attorney for the Upper Deck Company was a very wealthy attorney who invested $100,000 in the company for a 3 percent share. But what if the attorney was not very wealthy, invested in the company at extreme financial risk to himself, and was promised a quick return on the money, which did not get returned. If the attorney could prove that he reasonably relied on the promise of the company to his detriment, could promissory estoppel be awarded?

[3] "Do Interactive Websites Have a Legal Duty to Remove Malicious Content?" http://writ.news.findlaw.com/scripts/printer_friendly.pl?page5/ramasastry/20090519.html (accessed May 25, 2009) [discussing *Barnes v. Yahoo, Inc.*, 2009 U.S. App. LEXIS 10940 (9th Cir. 2009)].

CASE NUGGET

PROMISSORY ESTOPPEL

Double AA Builders, Ltd. v. Grand State Construction L.L.C.
114 P.3d 835 (Ariz. Ct. App. 2005)

In anticipation of submitting a bid for the construction of a Home Depot Store in Mesa, Arizona, Double AA solicited bids from subcontractors for various portions of the work. Grand State faxed a written but unsigned bid to Double AA in the amount of $115,000 for installation of the exterior insulation finish system (EIFS) on the project. The proposal stated: "Our price is good for 30 days." Double AA relied on several subcontractor bids, including Grand State's, in preparing its overall price for the project.

On December 21, 2001, Home Depot advised Double AA it was the successful bidder for the project. On January 11, 2002, within the 30-day "price is good" period, Double AA sent a subcontract for the EIFS work to Grand State to be signed and returned. Grand State advised Double AA it would not sign the subcontract or perform on the project. Double AA subsequently entered into a subcontract with a replacement subcontractor to install the EIFS at a cost of $131,449, which exceeded Grand State's quoted price

by $16,449. Double AA demanded that Grand State pay the difference between its bid and Double AA's ultimate cost to perform the same work. After Grand State refused, Double AA filed suit based on promissory estoppel.

When a general contractor prepares an overall bid for a competitively bid construction project, it receives bids and quotes from subcontractors for portions of the work. The general contractor uses the bids in preparing its overall price for the project. A subcontractor's refusal to honor its bid can be financially disastrous for the general contractor, because the general contractor will typically be bound by the bid price it submitted to the project owner.

Promissory estoppel may be used to require that the subcontractor perform according to the terms of its bid to the contractor if the contractor receives the contract award, because the contractor has detrimentally relied on the subcontractor's bid and must perform for a price based on that reliance. Double AA prevailed. Nonperformance by the subcontractor resulted in damages equal to the difference between what the contractor had to pay and what it would have paid had the subcontractor performed.

A second exception to the rule requiring consideration is a *contract under seal.* In the past, contracts were sealed with a piece of soft wax into which an impression was made. Today, sealed contracts are typically identified with the word *seal* or the letters *L.S.* (an abbreviation for *locus sigilli,* which means "the place for the seal") at the end. Consumers may also purchase contract forms with a preprinted seal. The parties using them are presumed, without evidence to the contrary, to be adopting the seal for the contract. States in the U.S. no longer require that contracts be under seal. However, 10 states still allow a contract without consideration to be enforced if it is under seal.

Legal Principle: **Promissory estoppel and contracts under seal are two exceptions to the common law rule requiring consideration.**

ADEQUACY OF CONSIDERATION

The court does not weigh whether you made a good bargain. Suppose Donna purchases a flat-screen TV from Celia, a friend in her business law class. Donna pays $500 for the TV but later realizes it is worth less than $100! May Donna sue Celia? Typically, the answer is no. It is Donna's responsibility to do her research and determine what price she should pay. The court will not set aside the sale because she made a bad deal. Conversely, if the court believes fraud or undue influence occurred, the court may look at adequacy of consideration. (For example, suppose a person divests himself of all his assets for pennies on the dollar and then declares bankruptcy—the court would likely review the consideration paid to determine whether there was fraud by the debtor against the creditors.)

BUT WHAT IF . . .

WHAT IF THE FACTS OF THE CASE OPENER WERE DIFFERENT?

Recall, in the Case Opener, that the company attorney Passante invested $100,000 into the Upper Deck Company so that it could produce hologram baseball cards. In return, Passante received a 3 percent share of the company. What if the hologram baseball cards were not successful and the company filed for bankruptcy? If Passante made a bad investment and did not receive a return on his money, could he sue the company for damages?

Legal Principle: **The court seldom considers adequacy of consideration.**

Is a promise to refrain from something you are legally entitled to do appropriate consideration for a contract? See Case 15-1.

CASE 15-1   HAMER V. SIDWAY
COURT OF APPEALS OF NEW YORK
124 N.Y. 538 (1891)

Plaintiff sought to enforce against the defendant estate a promise made by his now-deceased uncle to pay plaintiff a sum of money if plaintiff refrained from the use of alcohol and tobacco for a period of years. Plaintiff so refrained and sought recovery of the sum promised.

J. PARKER: In 1869, William Story, 2d, promised his nephew that if he refrained from drinking liquor, using tobacco, swearing, and playing cards or billiards for money until he was 21 years of age, then he would pay him the sum of $5,000. William Story, the nephew, agreed and fully performed.

The defendant (the deceased uncle's estate) now contends that the contract was without consideration to support it, and, therefore, invalid. He asserts that the nephew, by refraining from the use of liquor and tobacco, was not harmed but benefited; that that which he did was best for him to do independently of his uncle's promise, and insists that it follows that unless the nephew was benefited, the contract was without consideration. This contention, if well founded, would seem to leave open for controversy in many cases whether that which the promisee did or omitted to do was, in fact, of such benefit to him as to leave no consideration to support the enforcement of the promisor's agreement.

Such a rule could not be tolerated, and is without foundation in the law. Consideration means not so much that one party is profiting as that the other abandons some legal right in the present or limits his legal freedom of action in the future. Now, applying this rule to the facts before us, the promisee used tobacco, occasionally drank liquor, and he had a legal right to do so. He abandoned that right for a period of years based upon the promise of his uncle that for such forbearance he would give him $5,000. We need not speculate on the effort which may have been required to give up the use of those stimulants. It is sufficient that he restricted his lawful freedom of action within certain prescribed limits upon the faith of his uncle's agreement. Now, having fully performed the conditions imposed, it makes no difference whether such performance was actually a benefit to the promisor, and the court will not inquire into it. Even if it were a proper subject of inquiry, we see nothing in this record that would permit a determination that the uncle was not benefited in a legal sense. It is deemed established for the purposes of this appeal, that on January 31, 1875, defendant's testator was indebted to William E. Story, 2d, in the sum of $5,000. All concur.

The order reversing the trial court judgment in favor of plaintiff is reversed on the grounds that plaintiff's promise to abandon his legal right to use tobacco and alcohol was sufficient consideration to enforce the contract.

CRITICAL THINKING

What difference would it have made in this case had the nephew not had the legal right to drink or smoke? Why is this question crucial to the decision?

ETHICAL DECISION MAKING

William Story, 2d, may well have thought that he should win the case on moral grounds. He is applauding his nephew's behavior in recognition that the behavior the nephew stopped was behavior that was harming his nephew. So, since his nephew is now in better condition than he was before their exchange of views, why does the court put itself in the position of requiring William Story, 2d, to pay the $5,000?

350   Part 2   Contracts

In Case 15-2, the court had to consider whether $1 plus "love and affection" was adequate consideration for the transfer of property.

CASE 15-2   THELMA AGNES SMITH V. DAVID PHILLIP RILEY
COURT OF APPEALS OF TENNESSEE,
EASTERN SECTION, AT KNOXVILLE
2002 TENN. APP. LEXIS 65 (2002)

The plaintiff, Thelma Agnes Smith, lived with the defendant out of wedlock for several years. When the relationship ended, she sued the defendant, seeking to enforce two written agreements with him regarding the sale and assignment of property to her. The trial court enforced the agreements and divided the parties' property. The defendant appealed, arguing the agreements lacked consideration and were void as against public policy.

JUDGE CHARLES D. SUSANO: . . . Thelma Agnes Smith and David Phillip Riley, both of whom then resided in Florida, separated from their respective spouses in 1997 and began a romantic relationship. In early 1998, the two moved to Tennessee and began cohabitating. . . . Smith and Riley opened a joint checking account in March, 1998. Over time, Smith deposited into that account $9,500—the proceeds from an insurance settlement and monies received when her divorce later became final; she also deposited her monthly social security check of $337 into the same account. Smith continued to deposit her social security check in the joint account until December, 1998, when she opened her own checking account. Riley also contributed to the joint account. He placed a settlement of $84,000 from the Veteran's Administration into the account. In addition, he deposited his monthly pension check of $2,036 into the same account. . . .

On July 31, 1998, Riley entered into a lease with Jerry Strickland and Wanda Strickland with respect to a residence owned by them; the lease was accompanied by an option to purchase. Almost four months later, on November 20, 1998, Smith and Riley returned to their attorney's office, at which time the attorney prepared a bill of sale and an assignment. In the bill of sale, Riley transferred [to Smith] a one-half undivided interest in seven items of personal property. . . . Riley also assigned to Smith a one-half undivided interest in the lease and option to purchase with the Stricklands, which interest included a right of survivorship in the one-half interest retained by Riley as well. The property Riley sold and assigned to Smith in the two agreements was stated in each to be "for and in consideration of the sum of One Dollar ($1.00) and other and good and valuable consideration, the sufficiency of which is hereby acknowledged. . . ."

When Smith and Riley separated in April, 1999, Smith filed suit against Riley in the trial court, seeking the dissolution of their "domestic partnership." Smith alleged that she and Riley had been living together for several years without the benefit of marriage and had acquired both real and personal property, some of which Riley had assigned to her. As a result, she asked the court to award her 50 percent of the "partnership" assets, leaving the other 50 percent to Riley. . . . [The trial court ruled in favor of Smith and Riley appealed.]

Riley first argues that the trial court erred in finding that the bill of sale and assignment are supported by valid consideration. Specifically, Riley relies on Smith's statements at trial that she considered their pending engagement and the funds she deposited into their joint account to be consideration for their agreements.

It is a well-settled principle of contract law that in order for a contract to be binding, it must, among other things, be supported by sufficient consideration. [Citations omitted.] In expounding on the adequacy of consideration, the Tennessee Supreme Court has stated that it is not necessary that the benefit conferred or the detriment suffered by the promisee shall be equal to the responsibility assumed. Any consideration, however small, will support a promise. In the absence of fraud, the courts will not undertake to regulate the amount of the consideration. The parties are left to contract for themselves, taking for granted that the consideration is one valuable in the eyes of the law. . . .

Quoting the United States Supreme Court, the Tennessee Supreme Court went on to state that "[a] stipulation in consideration of $1 is just as effectual and valuable a consideration as a larger sum stipulated for or paid." [Citations omitted.] Indeed, the consideration of love and affection has been deemed sufficient to support a conveyance. . . .

Both the bill of sale and the assignment recite that they are undertaken "for and in consideration of the sum of One Dollar ($1.00) and other and good and valuable consideration, the sufficiency of which is hereby acknowledged. . . ." Facially, the documents are therefore supported by sufficient consideration, as clearly recognized by the Supreme Court. . . . Moreover, Smith's "society and consortium"—a concept comparable to the love and affection . . . is further evidence of sufficient consideration to support these conveyances.

Riley calls our attention to Smith's statement at trial that she considered the funds she deposited into their joint

[continued]

account to be consideration for the conveyances. If this were the only consideration involved in this case, Riley's argument regarding past consideration supporting a present transaction might have some merit. However, the recitals of nominal consideration that are present in both agreements, as well as the consideration of Smith's love and affection, are adequate consideration and will support the conveyances represented by the assignment and bill of sale....

Judgment affirmed in favor of Plaintiff.

CRITICAL THINKING

What is the reasoning of the appellant in terms of why the consideration was not adequate to cause the contracts to be enforceable? What key rule of law did this reasoning overlook?

ETHICAL DECISION MAKING

What values are being advanced by the logic of the relevant rule of law in this case? In other words, what values prevent the rule of law from being that "consideration must be in an amount similar in value to the item or services being transferred in order for the contract to be enforceable"?

ILLUSORY PROMISE

What is an illusory promise? Suppose Shawn offers to sell Molly his skis for $300. Molly responds, "I'll look at them in the morning, and if I like them, I'll pay you." At this point, Molly has not committed to doing anything. The law considers this an illusory promise—it is not a promise at all.

L04

What is an illusory promise?

> Legal Principle: **An illusory promise is not consideration.**

BUT WHAT IF . . .
WHAT IF THE FACTS OF THE CASE OPENER WERE DIFFERENT?

Let's say that, in the Case Opener, Passante was approached by executives of the Upper Deck Company and they asked him to invest money into their company so that they could purchase hologram baseball cards. In response, Passante told them, "That sounds like a good idea. I'll have my financial adviser call you for more details." Is Passante making a contractual promise to the company? What is the term for his type of response in this situation?

PAST CONSIDERATION

For a court to enforce a promise, both sides must offer consideration. Imagine you graduate from college and get a great job. After five years, your boss says to you, "Because you have done such a great job the last five years, I am going to give you 5 percent of the company stock." Six months later, you still have not received the stock. May you sue your boss to enforce the promise? The answer is no. For a promise to be enforceable, there must be bargaining and an exchange. Because your work has already been performed, you have given nothing in exchange, and the court will not enforce the promise. A promise cannot be based on consideration provided before the promise was made. You are at the mercy of your boss's goodwill.

> Legal Principle: **Past consideration is no consideration at all.**

As you have probably guessed by now, there is an exception to this rule. Under the Restatement (Second) of Contracts (a persuasive, though not binding, authority), promises

COMPARING THE LAW OF OTHER COUNTRIES
CONTRACT ENFORCEMENT IN CHINA

Every year the World Bank publishes its Doing Business rankings, which rate 181 countries by ease of doing business (the rankings can be found at **www.doingbusiness.org/rankings**). In the category "Enforcing Contracts," China is rated number 10. This means that China has one of the best systems in the world for enforcement of contracts. Compare that with India, which is rated 180 out of 181

countries, or Brazil, which is rated at 100. China is actually rated better than the United Kingdom, which comes in at 23, and better than Japan, which comes in at 21. It is therefore a serious mistake to place China in the same category as some of its developing country competitors.

Source: Dan Harris, "Enforcing Contracts in China: Way, Way Better Than You Think," July 13, 2009, www.chinalawblog.com/2009/07/enforcing_contracts_in_china_w.html.

based on past consideration may be enforceable "to the extent necessary to avoid injustice." In some cases, if past consideration was given with expectation of future payment, the court may enforce the promise.

In Case 15-3, the court must decide whether the promise to pay a friend for coming up with a merchandising idea is compensable when the promise to pay was made after the idea was given.

CASE 15-3 JAMIL BLACKMON V. ALLEN IVERSON
U.S. DISTRICT COURT FOR THE EASTERN DISTRICT OF PENNSYLVANIA
324 F. SUPP. 2D 602 (2003)

The defendant, Allen Iverson, was a professional basketball player. The plaintiff, Jamil Blackmon, was a family friend. In July of 1994, Mr. Blackmon suggested that Mr. Iverson use "The Answer" as a nickname in the summer league basketball tournaments in which Mr. Iverson would be playing. Mr. Blackmon told Mr. Iverson that Mr. Iverson would be "The Answer" to all of the National Basketball Association's ("NBA's") woes. Mr. Blackmon and Mr. Iverson also discussed the fact that the nickname "The Answer" had immediate applications as a label, brand name, or other type of marketing slogan for use in connection with clothing, sports apparel, and sneakers. The parties also discussed using "The Answer" as a logo. Later that evening, Mr. Iverson promised to give Mr. Blackmon twenty-five percent of all proceeds from the merchandising of products sold in connection with the term "The Answer." The parties understood that in order to "effectuate Mr. Iverson's agreement to compensate" Mr. Blackmon, Mr. Iverson would have to be drafted by the NBA.

Mr. Blackmon thereafter began to invest significant time, money, and effort in the refinement of the concept of "The Answer." Mr. Blackmon continued to develop and refine the marketing strategy for the sale of merchandise, such as athletic wear and sneakers, in connection with the term "The Answer." He retained a graphic designer to develop logos bearing "The Answer" as well as conceptual drawings for sleeveless T-shirts, adjustable hats, and letterman jackets for sale in connection with "The Answer." In 1994 and 1995, during Mr. Iverson's freshman year at Georgetown University and the summer thereafter, there were

numerous conversations between Mr. Blackmon and Mr. Iverson regarding Mr. Blackmon's progress in refining the marketing concept for "The Answer." In 1996, just prior to the NBA draft, during which Mr. Iverson was drafted by the Philadelphia 76ers, Mr. Iverson advised Mr. Blackmon that Mr. Iverson intended to use the phrase "The Answer" in connection with a contract with Reebok for merchandising of athletic shoes and sports apparel. Mr. Iverson repeated his promise to pay Mr. Blackmon twenty-five percent of all proceeds from merchandising goods that incorporated "The Answer" slogan or logo. . . . Despite repeated requests and demands from Mr. Blackmon, Mr. Iverson has never compensated Mr. Blackmon and continues to deny Mr. Blackmon twenty-five percent of the proceeds from the merchandising of products incorporating "The Answer."

Mr. Blackmon is now suing Mr. Iverson, seeking damages for claims alleging [among others] . . . breach of contract . . . arising out of the basketball player's use of "The Answer," both as a nickname and as a logo or slogan. The defendant filed a motion to dismiss this complaint.

JUDGE MARY A. MCLAUGHLIN: . . . The essence of . . . the plaintiff's claim is that the defendant took and used the plaintiff's ideas without compensating the plaintiff.

. . . The plaintiff claims that he entered into an express contract with the defendant pursuant to which he was to receive twenty-five percent of the proceeds that the defendant received from marketing products with "The Answer" on them. The defendant argues that there was not a valid contract because the claim was not timely filed under the Pennsylvania

[continued]

statute of limitations, the terms of the contract were not sufficiently definite, and there was no consideration alleged. Because the Court has determined that the claim should be dismissed for failure to allege proper consideration, the Court need not address the defendant's other arguments about the statute of limitations and definiteness of terms. . . .

According to the facts alleged by the plaintiff, he made the suggestion that the defendant use "The Answer" as a nickname and for product merchandising one evening in 1994. This was before the defendant first promised to pay; according to the plaintiff, the promise to pay was made later that evening. The disclosure of the idea also occurred before the defendant told the plaintiff that he was going to use the idea in connection with the Reebok contract in 1996, and before the sales of goods bearing "The Answer" actually began in 1997. Regardless of whether the contract was formed in 1994, 1996, or 1997, the disclosure of "The Answer" idea had already occurred and was, therefore, past consideration insufficient to create a binding contract. **Motion granted in favor of Defendant.**

CRITICAL THINKING

What key fact would have had to be different for Mr. Blackmon to have received a favorable ruling in this case?

ETHICAL DECISION MAKING

Most people reading this case probably feel some sympathy for Mr. Blackmon. He put in a lot of time in reliance on a promise he was made by Iverson. He received nothing for that time even though Iverson benefited from some of it. What stakeholders in a contract are being protected by strict adherence to the need for consideration that the court used to form its conclusion?

PREEXISTING DUTY

There are two parts to the preexisting duty rule. *Performance of a duty you are obligated to do under the law is not good consideration.* Part of a police officer's sworn public duty is catching suspected criminals. If someone offers a reward for the capture of a suspect, the police officer may not collect it, as he or she was already obligated to apprehend the suspect. Moreover, *performance of an existing contractual duty is not good consideration.* Gene decides to have a pool built in his backyard. Under the existing contract, the pool is to be completed by June 1, just in time for summer. The pool contractor then explains that due to a shortage of workers, the completion date cannot be met; however, if Gene were to pay an extra $5,000, additional workers could be hired and the pool completed on time. Gene tells the contractor he will pay the $5,000. On June 1, the pool is completed and the contractor asks for the additional payment. Is Gene legally obligated to pay? The answer is no. The pool contractor had a preexisting contractual duty to complete the pool by June 1. Gene is under no obligation to pay the additional money.

Legal Principle: **A promise to do something that you are already obligated to do is not valid consideration.**

BUT WHAT IF . . .

WHAT IF THE FACTS OF THE CASE OPENER WERE DIFFERENT?

Recall that, in the Case Opener, Passante agreed to invest $100,000 in the Upper Deck Company so that he could own 3 percent of it. But what if the company told Passante that its sales were sinking and that if he didn't agree to invest another $50,000, the company would go bankrupt and Passante would receive no return on his investment? Suppose Passante agrees. If a month later the company came to collect the $50,000, does Passante legally have to pay the extra money because he told the company he would?

Exceptions to the Preexisting Duty Rule.   There are exceptions to the preexisting duty rule: unforeseen circumstances, additional work, and UCC Article 2 (sale of goods).

If *unforeseen circumstances* cause a party to make a promise regarding an unfinished project, that promise is valid consideration. Suppose the pool contractor has been building pools in Gene's neighborhood for the last 20 years and has never had any problem with rocks—until now. While bulldozing the hole for the pool in Gene's backyard, the pool contractor hits solid rock. It will cost an additional $5,000 to clear the rock with jackhammers, possibly even dynamite. The contractor says unless Gene agrees to pay the additional money, he will not be able to finish the pool. Gene agrees to pay. When the pool is completed, the contractor asks for the additional $5,000. Will a court enforce Gene's promise? The answer is yes. Even though the contractor is completing only what he was obligated to do under the contract, neither party knew of the solid rock. The contractor has given additional consideration (removal of the rock) and Gene will be held to his promise to pay the additional money.

If a party to a contract agrees to do *additional work* (more than the contract requires), the promise to do it is valid consideration. If the contractor asks Gene for an additional $10,000 but agrees to add a waterfall and a deck to the pool, the promise to do the additional work is consideration. If Gene agrees to pay the $10,000, that is his consideration. Both parties are now bound.

Partial Payment of a Debt

L05

What is the difference between a liquidated debt and an unliquidated debt?

Partial payment of a debt may or may not be valid consideration, depending on whether the debt is liquidated or unliquidated. In a liquidated debt, there is no dispute that money is owed or how much. Natalie calls her credit card company and explains she is a poor student and cannot afford to pay the entire $3,000 she owes. The credit card company agrees to accept $2,000 as payment in full. The following month, Natalie receives her new credit card statement showing she owes the remaining $1,000. May the credit card company collect the additional $1,000? Yes! A creditor's promise to accept less than owed, when the debtor is already obligated to pay the full amount, is not binding.

The exception to the rule regarding liquidated debt occurs when the debtor offers different performance. Suppose Natalie offered the credit card company her car in full settlement of the $3,000 debt. If the credit card company accepts, regardless of the value of the car, the debt is paid in full and the credit card company may not sue Natalie for any additional money.

L06

What is an accord and satisfaction?

In an unliquidated debt, the parties either disagree about whether money is owed or dispute the amount. They can settle for less than the full amount if they enter into an accord and satisfaction, which must meet three requirements to be enforceable:

1. The debt is unliquidated (the amount or existence of the debt is in dispute).
2. The creditor agrees to accept as full payment less than it claims is owed.
3. The debtor pays the amount they have agreed on.

Under these circumstances, the debt is fully discharged. The *accord* is the new agreement to pay less than the creditor claims is owed. The *satisfaction* is the debtor's payment of the reduced amount. It pays to keep your word: If the debtor fails to pay the new amount, the creditor may sue for the full amount of the original debt. Exhibit 15-3 clarifies the accord-and-satisfaction process.

Legal Principle: **When a debt is unliquidated, the parties may enter into an accord and satisfaction.**

Debtors sometimes attempt to create an accord and satisfaction by sending the creditor a check with "paid in full" written on it. Under the common law, in many states this did

Exhibit 15-3   Accord and Satisfaction

DEBT DISPUTED?	STATUS OF DEBT	PAYMENT?	CREATE AN ACCORD?	CREATE A SATISFACTION?
Yes—*amount* of debt in dispute	Unliquidated	Debtor offers to pay less money than creditor believes is owed as full payment, and creditor agrees.	Yes	Yes. Once debtor pays the money agreed to, the debt is satisfied and the creditor may not collect any additional money.
Yes—*existence* of debt in dispute	Unliquidated	Debtor offers to pay a sum of money as full payment when debtor does not believe anything is owed, and creditor agrees.	Yes	Yes. Once the debtor pays the money agreed to, the debt is satisfied and the creditor may not collect any additional money.
No dispute over amount of debt or existence of debt	Liquidated	Debtor offers to pay less money than is owed as full payment, and creditor agrees.	No	No. Even if the debtor pays the money agreed to, the creditor may still sue for the balance it believes is owed.
No dispute over amount of debt or existence of debt	Liquidated	Debtor offers a *different* payment (e.g., her car) as full payment.	Yes	Yes. Once the debtor makes a *different* payment, the debt is satisfied and the creditor may not collect anything else.

create an accord and satisfaction, and if the creditor cashed the check, he or she was bound to accept the lesser amount as payment in full. The UCC (introduced in Chapter 13) has reduced the scope of this rule, however. Under UCC Section 3-311, effective in 30 states, the rule has two major exceptions.

First, business organizations can receive thousands of checks each day. To protect themselves, they may notify their debtors that any offer to settle a claim for less than the amount owed must be sent to a particular address and/or person. If you check the terms printed on your credit card statement, you will likely find language directing you to send such payments to a different address and person than regular payments are sent to. This safeguard protects businesses from inadvertently creating accord-and-satisfaction agreements. Below is a typical clause you might find on any credit statement regarding conditional payments:

> *Conditional Payments:* Any payment check or other form of payment that you send us for less than the full balance that is marked "paid in full" or contains a similar notation, or that you otherwise tender in full satisfaction of a disputed amount, must be sent to [address omitted]. We reserve all rights regarding these payments (e.g., if it is determined that there is no valid dispute or if any such check is received at any other address, we may accept the check and you will still owe any remaining balance).[4]

In the second exception, if a business does inadvertently cash a "paid-in-full" check, it has 90 days to offer the debtor repayment in the same amount. For example, if John owed his credit card company $3,000 and sent a $2,000 check marked "paid in full" to the correct address and person, the credit card company has 90 days to offer to repay John the $2,000. Once the business has made that offer, no accord and satisfaction exists.

To see how an accord and satisfaction relates to income taxation, please see the **Connecting to the Core** activity on the text website at www.mhhe.com/kubasek3e.

[4] From Chase Visa statement.

CASE NUGGET

ACCORD AND SATISFACTION

Thomas v. CitiMortgage, Inc.
2005 U.S. Dist. LEXIS 14641 (Dist. Ct. Ill. 2005)

In November 1979, Thomas assumed an existing mortgage, which CitiMortgage now holds, that required him to make a payment on the first of each month. Beginning in April 1996, his payments became sporadic. On December 16, 1996, Thomas sent a letter to CitiMortgage. He wrote:

> My primary concern is the effect on my credit rating and the fact that I have an application to refinace [*sic*] the mortgage which cannot be finalized, at great cost to me, unless this matter is resolved and my credit cleared up. I have enclosed a check in the amount of the monthly payment on condition that it be applied to tha [*sic*] May payment and that it will allow you to remove the negative material relative to my credit rating.

CitiMortgage cashed the check enclosed with the December 16 letter and credited it to Thomas's account. At CitiMortgage as of 1996, mail was sorted in a central mail room. The persons processing checks lacked the authority either to accept conditions on payments or to change credit reports. In his breach-of-contract claim, Thomas asserted that he and CitiMortgage had entered an agreement whereby he would make a payment on his mortgage in exchange for CitiMortgage's agreement to "remove the negative material" from his credit rating. He further claimed that CitiMortgage accepted the contract when it cashed the check he enclosed with his December 16 letter. Whether Thomas's claim was considered an accord and satisfaction or a simple contract, he could not prevail unless he established that consideration supported the agreement.

Consideration can consist of a promise, an act, or a forbearance. The preexisting duty rule provides, however, that when a party does what it is already legally obligated to do, there is no consideration because there has been no detriment. Thomas claimed that the payment he made with his December 16 letter constituted consideration for the agreement. As of that date, however, he was already two months in arrears on his mortgage payment. Thus, he was already legally obligated—under the terms of the mortgage—to make the payment he enclosed with the letter. Accordingly, that payment could not be consideration for an additional agreement to "remove the negative material" from his credit rating.

CASE OPENER WRAP-UP

Upper Deck—Contract Liability or Gift?

As you know from the Case Opener, Passante sued Upper Deck for breach of oral contract. At trial, the jury awarded him close to $33 million—the value of 3 percent of Upper Deck's stock at the time of the trial in 1993. Upper Deck appealed.

As a matter of law, any claim by Passante for breach of contract is necessarily based on the rule that consideration must result from a bargained-for exchange. In this case, the appellate court held that if the stock promised was truly bargained for, then Passante had an obligation to give Upper Deck the opportunity to have separate counsel represent it in the course of that bargaining. The legal profession has certain rules regarding business transactions with clients. Bargaining between the parties might have resulted in Passante's settling for just a reasonable finder's fee.

All Passante's services in arranging the $100,000 loan for Upper Deck had already been rendered (even though the board had not formally accepted the loan) before the idea of giving him stock came up. There was no evidence he had any expectation of receiving stock in return. If there is no expectation of payment by either party when services are rendered, the promise is a mere promise to make a gift and not enforceable. The promise of 3 percent of the stock represented a moral obligation but was legally unenforceable.

KEY TERMS

accord and satisfaction   354   illusory promise   351   preexisting duty   353   unliquidated debt   354

consideration   346   liquidated debt   354   promissory estoppel   347

SUMMARY OF KEY TOPICS

Consideration is something of value given in exchange for something else of value; it must be the product of a mutually bargained-for exchange. **What Is Consideration?**

The key to understanding consideration is understanding the various rules: **Rules of Consideration**

- For a promise to be enforced by the courts, there must be consideration.
- *Exception: Promissory estoppel* occurs when one party makes a promise knowing the other party will rely on it, the other party does rely on it, and the only way to avoid injustice is to enforce the promise even though it is not supported by consideration.
- The court seldom considers adequacy of consideration.
- An *illusory promise* is not consideration.
- Past consideration is no consideration at all.
- A promise to do something you are already obligated to do is not valid consideration. (This is the *preexisting duty rule*.)

In a *liquidated debt*, there is no dispute that money is owed or the amount. In an *unliquidated debt*, the parties dispute either the fact that money is owed or the amount. **Partial Payment of a Debt**

To be enforceable, an *accord and satisfaction* must meet three requirements: (1) The debt is unliquidated (the amount or existence of the debt is in dispute); (2) the creditor agrees to accept as full payment less than the creditor claims is owed; and (3) the debtor pays the amount they agree on.

POINT / COUNTERPOINT

Should the Courts Require Consideration to Create a Binding Contract?	
YES	**NO**
The rules of consideration have been established for many years and precedent should be followed.	All promises should be enforced, eliminating the need to distinguish between binding and nonbinding promises.
Requiring consideration gives the court a way to distinguish between binding and nonbinding promises, or between a promise made as a gift and a promise made as part of a contract.	If a person makes a promise, its timing should not make a difference. If Barbara's grandmother promises her $50,000 for "all you have done for me these last five years," why should Barbara be denied the money because it was based on acts she did in the past? The right thing, ethically and morally, is to enforce this promise whether or not Barbara acted with expectation of payment. Under current law, some states can use the moral-obligation exception to reward those who expect something when they do good and punish those who do the right thing with no expectation of reward.
We have enough exceptions to the rule requiring consideration to make enforcement fair. If a promise was made and there was expectation of economic benefit, some courts will permit enforcement under the moral-obligation exception.	
If we suddenly did not require consideration to create binding contracts, the courts would fill with civil cases of people trying to enforce all kind of promises.	

QUESTIONS & PROBLEMS

1. List the four types of consideration described in the text.

2. What is required to prove promissory estoppel when consideration is missing?

3. Can $1 be adequate consideration? Why or why not?

4. List and describe the three exceptions to the preexisting duty rule.

5. List the three elements of accord and satisfaction.

6. The plaintiff is Amir Peleg, a gay Jewish male of Israeli national origin. He worked at the Neiman Marcus store in Beverly Hills from December 28, 2005, to February 21, 2008. The store is owned by the defendant, Neiman Marcus Group, Inc. Peleg worked in the fragrances department and performed his duties in an exemplary manner. Peleg alleges that on February 21, 2008, he was discharged because of his national origin, religion, and sexual orientation in violation of the California Fair Employment and Housing Act (FEHA). Neiman Marcus responded to the complaint with a motion to compel arbitration of the entire case. The company established that, at the time of hire, Peleg was given its "Mandatory Arbitration Agreement." Peleg asserted that the agreement was illusory and unenforceable in light of the following provision:

> This Agreement to arbitrate shall survive the termination of the employer-employee relationship between the Company and any Covered Employee, and shall apply to any covered Claim whether it arises or is asserted during or after termination of the Covered Employee's employment with the Company or the expiration of any benefit plan. This Agreement can be *amended, modified, or revoked in writing by the Company at anytime,* but only upon thirty (30) days' advance notice to the Covered Employee of that amendment, modification, or revocation. However, any amendment, modification, or revocation will have *no effect on any Claim that was filed for arbitration prior to the effective date* of such amendment, modification, or revocation.

Plaintiff alleges that the arbitration agreement is illusory. Do you agree? Why or why not? [*Peleg v. Neiman Marcus Group, Inc.,* 204 Cal. App. 4th 1425 (2012).]

7. Joana Perez began working for Datamark in January 2005. She received two booklets at orientation, the "Non-Staff Employee Handbook" and the "Summary Plan Description." She did not read either one of them. According to the human resource director, Perez also received the "Problem Resolution Program" booklet (the PRP) that described company dispute resolution policies and procedure. Perez denied receiving it, but she did sign the "Receipt and Arbitration Acknowledgment," which was maintained in her personnel file. Her signature acknowledged that she had received and read (or had the opportunity to read) both the "Summary Plan Description" and the PRP. She also acknowledged that an arbitration policy required the submission of all employee-related disputes to an arbitrator in accordance with the procedures described in the PRP. Datamark reserved the right to revoke or modify the PRP in writing at any time as long as the writing was signed by an officer of the company and articulated an intent to revoke or modify a policy. Perez learned she was pregnant in August 2005. While employed full-time, she began to miss work due to pregnancy difficulties. She was discharged on October 21, 2005, and she filed suit alleging unlawful discrimination because of her gender and/or pregnancy. Perez also alleged that Datamark intentionally or recklessly engaged in extreme and outrageous behavior that caused her severe emotional distress. Datamark filed a motion to compel arbitration. In her response to the motion, Perez alleged that the arbitration agreement was illusory because Datamark could unilaterally change or terminate the agreement without prior notice to the employees. Do you believe the agreement to arbitrate is illusory? Why or why not? [*In re Datamark, Inc., Relator,* 296 S.W.3d 614, 2009 Tex. App. LEXIS 794 (2009).]

8. On February 1, 2004, Zhang entered into a contract to buy former realtor Frank Sorichetti's Las Vegas home for $532,500. The contract listed a March closing date and a few household furnishings as part of the sale. On February 3, Sorichetti told Zhang that he was terminating the sale "to stay in the house a little longer" and that Nevada law allows the rescission of real property purchase agreements within three days of contracting. Sorichetti stated that he would sell the home, however, if Zhang paid more

money. Zhang agreed. Another contract was drafted, reciting a new sales price, $578,000. This contract added to the included household furnishings drapes that were not listed in the February 1 agreement, and it set an April, rather than March, closing date. The primary issue before the court was whether a real property purchase agreement is enforceable when it is executed by the buyer only because the seller would not perform under an earlier purchase agreement for a lesser price. Should the court enforce the second contract? Why or why not? [*Zhang v. The Eighth Judicial District Court of the State of Nevada,* 103 P.3d 20 (Sup. Ct. Nev. 2004).]

9. Charles Houser began working for the appellee, 84 Lumber Company, L.P., in 1985. In 1998, Houser became an outside salesman with 84 Lumber, and his compensation changed from a set salary to commission based on his sales. At that time, Houser signed a noncompete agreement, which prohibited him from engaging in sales activities with a competitor of 84 Lumber within a 25-mile radius of 84 Lumber's Macedonia store for a two-year period following the conclusion of his employment with 84 Lumber. In June 2008, Houser signed a contract providing a set weekly draw and yet another noncompete agreement. In March 2009, Houser left 84 Lumber and, almost immediately thereafter, began working for Carter Lumber, a competitor of 84 Lumber. 84 Lumber filed a lawsuit alleging that Houser had violated the noncompete agreement. The essential question is whether the 2008 noncompete agreement was supported by adequate consideration. "[A] restrictive covenant is enforceable if supported by new consideration, either in the form of an initial employment contract or a change in the conditions of employment." 84 Lumber Company argued that Houser's continued employment was adequate consideration for the new noncompete agreement. Do you agree? Why or why not? [*84 Lumber Co., L.P. v. Houser,* 2011 Ohio 6852 (2011).]

10. Five employees of American Electric Power (AEP) Service Corp. invented a new product. "In consideration of the sum of One Dollar (1.00), and of other good and valuable consideration paid to the undersigned Assignor," each employee signed an agreement giving AEP exclusive patent rights to the invention. Some of the employees sued, alleging that there was no contract because AEP never paid the one dollar. How do you think the court ruled? Explain your reasoning. [*Bennett et al. v. American Electric Power Service Corporation,* 2001 Ohio App. LEXIS 4357 (Ohio Ct. App. 2001).]

Looking for more review materials?

The Online Learning Center at **www.mhhe.com/kubasek3e** contains this chapter's "Assignment on the Internet" and also a list of URLs for more information, entitled "On the Internet." Find both of them in the Student Center portion of the OLC, along with quizzes and other helpful materials.

PART 2   CONTRACTS

CHAPTER

16 Capacity and Legality

LEARNING OBJECTIVES

After reading this chapter, you will be able to answer the following questions:

1   What is the legal effect of a lack of capacity on a person's ability to enter into a contract?

2   Under what circumstances would a party have limited capacity to enter into a contract?

3   What is the legal effect of entering into a contract for an illegal purpose?

CASE OPENER

Apple's Questionable Contracts

Parents of minors took Apple to court in 2012 for supplying game applications, on iPhones, that were "free" but through which users could purchase in-game currencies. Apparently, parents would log on to the games, but within a subsequent 15-minute time frame, the minors using the game would rack up bills ranging from $99.99 to $338.72 "at a time."

Apple stated that while minors were downloading these applications and in-game currency, the contract in question was actually the Terms of Service between the parents and Apple. According to the Terms of Service, any unauthorized log-in on one's account or unauthorized purchases by anyone on the account were the responsibility of the account holder. On the other hand, the parents argued that all in-game purchases made by minors were separate contracts that may be disaffirmed by a parent or guardian. Apple also argued that a "contract" as the parents were describing it could not legally exist in that, as the parents described the scenario, the contractual offer was made to parents in the Terms of Service, yet accepted by the children, and consideration was provided by the parents (the original offerees).[1]

1. Do the individual purchases made by the minors indeed qualify as separate contracts between Apple and the minors?

2. Even if the purchases were contracts between the minors and Apple, could the parents void these contracts?

The Wrap-Up at the end of the chapter will answer these questions.

[1] *In re Apple In-App Purchase Litigation*, 5:11-CV-1758 (N.D. Cal., Mar. 31, 2012).

Capacity

Capacity is the third element of a legally binding contract. A person who has legal capacity has the mental ability to understand his or her rights and obligations under a contract and therefore presumably to comply with the terms. *Incapacity*, or *incompetence* as it is sometimes called, is the possession of a mental or physical defect that prevents a natural person from being able to enter into a legally binding contract. Depending on the nature and extent of the defect, a person may have either no capacity, the complete inability to enter into contracts, or limited capacity, the ability to form only voidable contracts.

Historically, people with limited or no capacity included married women, minors, and insane persons. Other categories were added by statutes, such as people for whom guardians had been appointed, including habitual drunkards, narcotic addicts, spendthrifts, the elderly, and convicts. Today, married women have been removed from the category of those lacking contractual capacity, although in a few states their capacity to enter into certain kinds of contracts is still limited. In this section of the chapter, we explain the current law limiting the capacity of some categories of persons to enter into legally binding agreements.

MINORS

One of the oldest limitations on capacity is the fact that minors may enter into only voidable contracts. Today, in all but three states, a *minor* is someone under the age of 18.[2] In most states, however, a person is given full legal capacity to enter into contracts when he or she becomes emancipated before reaching the age of majority. *Emancipation* occurs when a minor's parents or legal guardians give up their right to exercise legal control over the minor, typically when the minor moves out of the parents' house and begins supporting himself or herself. Often the minor will petition the court for a declaration of emancipation. In most cases, when a minor marries, she or he is considered emancipated.

Legal Principle: **As a general rule, any contract entered into by a minor is voidable by the minor until he or she reaches the age of majority or a reasonable time thereafter.**

Disaffirmance of the Contract.   Because their contracts are voidable, minors have the right, until a reasonable time after reaching the age of majority, to disaffirm or void their contracts. Note that it is only the minor who has the right to disaffirm, never the adult with whom the minor entered into the agreement. No formalities are required to disaffirm the contract; the minor need only show an intention to rescind it, either by words or actions. However, the minor must void the entire contract; he or she cannot choose to disaffirm only a portion of it.

> ## BUT WHAT IF . . .
> WHAT IF THE FACTS OF THE CASE OPENER WERE DIFFERENT?
>
> Let's say, in the Case Opener, that the court decided that all of the purchases made by the minors were indeed contracts between the minors and Apple. Let's say that the parents attempted to void the contracts themselves because the parents are technically the minors' legal guardians. Would such a move be effective? Why or why not?

[2] In Alabama, Nebraska, and Wyoming, full capacity to contract does not arise until the person reaches the age of 19, which is the age of majority in those states. In Mississippi, the age of majority is still 21.

L01
What is the legal effect of a lack of capacity on a person's ability to enter into a contract?

L02
Under what circumstances would a party have limited capacity to enter into a contract?

COMPARING THE LAW OF OTHER COUNTRIES
THE AGE OF MAJORITY IN GREAT BRITAIN

People in the United States take the idea of an "age of majority" for granted; the only question is whether it should be 18, 19, or 21. Yet in Great Britain there is no magical age at which a young person suddenly acquires the legal capacity to enter into a contract. British courts will not enforce contracts with immature minors. However, they make the decision of whether a person is too immature to enter into a contract on a case-by-case basis. If the courts consider a person under 18 to be able to look out for his or her own interests, the contract will be enforced. If not, it will be void. A key factor is often the fairness of the agreement. If the agreement is one-sided and favors the adult, the young person is usually considered to lack the maturity to enter into it.

The minor's obligations on disaffirmance vary from state to state. Traditionally, most states simply required the minor to notify the competent party and return any consideration received, regardless of its condition. If the consideration had been damaged or destroyed, the other party had no recourse against the minor. For instance, if William, a minor, purchased a flat-screen TV from Sound Systems, Inc., under a six-month contract and dropped the TV a week after he took it home, he could return it in its broken condition and tell the store owner he wished to rescind the contract. He would be entitled to the return of his down payment and would owe no further obligations to the store.

The traditional rule makes sense if we view minors as innocents in need of protection from competent adults who would otherwise take advantage of them. However, it is not going to encourage competent parties to enter into contracts with minors, and some argue that it allows a knowledgeable and unethical minor to take advantage of a competent party. Thus, a number of states have modified the duty of the minor on disaffirmance, holding that the minor has a duty of restitution, requiring that she or he place the competent party back in the position that party was in at the time the contract was made. In these states, William would have a duty of restoration that would require him to compensate the store owner for the difference between the value of the TV when he got it and its value when he returned it.

The disaffirmance must occur before or within a reasonable time of the minor's reaching the age of majority. What constitutes a reasonable time is determined on a case-by-case basis. But even when the courts scrutinize the cases individually, the laws created to protect minors from being victimized by competent adults do not necessarily protect competent adults from being taken advantage of by knowledgeable and unethical minors. Thus, individuals operating or working in businesses subject to laws requiring that their customers be the age of majority or older must familiarize themselves with the laws pertaining to minors, because often the responsibility of making sure that a business is dealing with people who are of legal age falls on the employees and the owner. However, since some minors use false identification or misrepresent themselves as adults, it is difficult for business owners and employees to recognize which customers are truly of age.

For example, as CEO of Girls Gone Wild (GGW), Joe Francis runs a business that requires he be familiar with the laws surrounding minors. In fact, Francis has said that GGW has very specific procedures in place to prevent filming underage girls and even teaches its camera crew ways to ensure that the girls the crew is selecting to appear in GGW spring break videos are of age. During the selection procedure, the GGW camera crew is required to check the IDs of girls wanting to be filmed, obtain signed written

GGW has very specific procedures in place to prevent filming underage girls and even teaches its camera crew ways to ensure that the girls the crew is selecting to appear in GGW spring break videos are of age. During the selection procedure, the GGW camera crew is required to check the IDs of girls wanting to be filmed, obtain signed written release forms in which the girls give their consent to be filmed, and videotape the girls' IDs as well as the actual process of signing the release forms. Regardless of his company's strict policies, Francis found himself in the middle of a heated legal battle in 2003 when seven girls claimed that they were underage when the GGW camera crew filmed them on vacation in Panama City, Florida. Francis fought back, saying that the girls misrepresented themselves, knowingly sought out the GGW crew and wanted to exploit the company in order to obtain a monetary settlement. After four years of court proceedings and intense media coverage, Francis reached an undisclosed settlement with the women, who reportedly wanted a total of $70 million.[3]

Exceptions to the Minor's Right to Disaffirm the Contract. The minor's right to disaffirm is designed to protect the minor from competent parties who might otherwise take advantage of him or her. But primarily for public policy reasons, in most states, courts or state legislatures have determined that the minor should *not* have the right to disaffirm contracts for life insurance, health insurance, psychological counseling, the performance of duties related to stock and bond transfers and bank accounts, education loan contracts, child support contracts, marriage contracts, and enlistment in the armed services.

Most of these exceptions apply in most, but not all, states. Another issue on which the states disagree is what should happen when a minor misrepresents his or her age. While the majority rule is that a minor's misrepresentation of age does not affect the minor's right to disaffirm the contract, some states hold that when a minor who appears to be of the age of majority misrepresents his or her age and a competent party relies on that misrepresentation in good faith, the minor gives up the right to disaffirm the agreement and can be treated as an adult. One justification for this rule is that any minor who is going to misrepresent his or her age does not need the protection that disaffirmance is designed to provide.

Other states have compromised, either by requiring that the minor restore the competent party to that party's precontract position before allowing the disaffirmance or by allowing the minor to disaffirm but then giving the competent party the right to sue the minor in tort and recover damages for fraud.

> To see how marketing research relates to the legal system's protection of minors, please see the **Connecting to the Core** activity on the text website at www.mhhe.com/kubasek3e.

Liability of Minors for Necessaries. A necessary is a basic necessity of life, generally including food, clothing, shelter, and basic medical services. Technically, minors can disaffirm contracts for necessaries, but they will still be held liable for the reasonable value of the necessary. The purpose of this limitation on the minor's right to disaffirm is to ensure that sellers will not be reluctant to provide minors the basic necessities of life when their parents will not provide them.

Food, clothing, shelter, and basic medical services are clearly necessaries, but it is sometimes difficult to determine whether something is in fact a necessary. Some courts define a necessary as what a minor needs to maintain his or her standard of living and financial and social status, but this can lead to a problem when an item considered a necessary for a child of upper-income parents is a luxury to a child of lower-income parents. Whether an item is considered a necessary also depends on whether the minor's parents are

---

[3]www.meetjoefrancis.com/legalstory/;www.associatedcontent.com/article/280397/two_florida_women_sue_girls_gone_wild.html?cat=17; and www.usatoday.com/life/people/2007-06-13-joe-francis_N.htm.

willing to provide it. Clearly, the games in the opening scenario would not be considered necessaries!

Ratification.   Once a person reaches the age of majority, he or she may ratify, or legally affirm, contracts made as a minor. Once ratified, the contract is no longer voidable. Ratification may be either express or implied (see Exhibit 16-1).

An *express ratification* occurs when, after reaching the age of majority, the person states orally or in writing that he or she intends to be bound by the contract entered into as a minor. For example, when she is 17, Marcy enters into an agreement to purchase an automobile from Sam for 10 monthly payments of $1,000. After making the fifth payment, Marcy turns 18 and decides to move out of state. She e-mails Sam and tells him not to worry because even though she is moving, she still intends to make her monthly payments to purchase the car. Marcy has expressly ratified the contract.

An *implied ratification* occurs when the former minor takes some action after reaching the age of majority consistent with intent to ratify the contract. Going back to the previous example, if the day after she turns 18 Marcy enters into an agreement with Joe to sell him the car in six months, that action is obviously consistent with intent to finish purchasing the car, so she has impliedly ratified the contract with Sam. Most courts find that continuing to act in accordance with the contract, such as continuing to make regular payments after reaching the age of majority, constitutes ratification. So, if (without the agreement with Joe) Marcy continued using the car and making payments on it for several months after reaching the age of majority, the courts would probably find that she had ratified the contract.

Parents' Liability for their Children's Contracts, Necessaries, and Torts.   As a general rule, parents are not liable for contracts entered into by their minor children. Thus, merchants are often reluctant to enter into contracts with minors unless some competent person is willing to cosign and become legally bound to perform if the minor no longer wishes to live up to the terms of the contract. Parents do, however, have a legal duty to provide their children with the basic necessities of life, such as food, clothing, and shelter. Thus, they may be held liable in some states for the reasonable value of necessaries for which their children enter into contracts.

In most states, minors, not their parents, are liable for a minor's personal torts. In many states, however, parents may be liable when a child causes harm if it can be proved that the parent failed to properly supervise the child, thereby subjecting others to an unreasonable risk of harm.

Exhibit 16-1
Ratifying a Contract

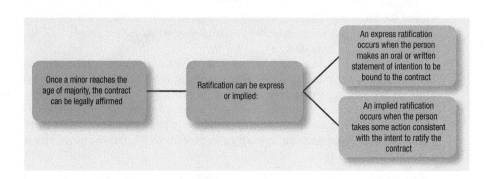

MENTALLY INCAPACITATED PERSONS

Persons suffering from a mental illness or deficiency may have full, limited, or no legal capacity to enter into a binding contract, depending on the nature and extent of their deficiency. If a person suffers from mental problems yet still understands the nature of the contract and the obligations it imposes, that person may enter into a binding, legal agreement. Suppose Gina suffers from the delusion that she is a rock star. When an encyclopedia salesperson comes to her door, she buys a set from him because she believes it is important to be knowledgeable to set a good example for her fans. As long as she understands that she is binding herself through a contract to make monthly payments for two years, Gina is bound to the contract. If, after making a year of payments, she no longer suffers from her delusions and wishes to disaffirm the contract, she will not be able to do so because her delusions had not affected her understanding of what she was legally agreeing to do when she entered into the contract.

However, a person has only limited capacity to enter into a contract if she suffers from a mental illness or deficiency that prevents her from understanding the nature and obligations of the transaction. If, in the above scenario, Gina's delusions persuaded her that she was giving the salesperson her autograph when she signed the contract, the contract is voidable. She may disaffirm it at any time until a reasonable time after she no longer suffers from the mental deficiency. Once the deficiency has been removed, Gina may also choose to ratify the contract.

As with contracts of minors, a contract for necessaries by a person suffering from a mental deficiency can be enforced for the reasonable value of the necessary.

If a person has been adjudicated insane and has a guardian appointed, that person has no capacity to enter into contracts and any contract he does attempt to enter into is void. Guardians may also be appointed for persons who have been adjudicated habitual drunkards and for those whose judgment has been impaired because of a condition such as Alzheimer disease. The guardian has the sole legal capacity to enter into contracts on such a person's behalf.

Legal Principle: **Contracts of a person with limited mental capacity can be valid, voidable, or void, depending on the extent of the mental incapacity. If a person suffers from delusions that may impair his judgment but he can still understand that he is entering into a contract and understand his obligations under the contract, his contract is valid; if his delusions prevent him from understanding that he is entering into a contract or the nature and extent of his obligations under the contract, his contract is voidable; and if he has been adjudicated insane, his contract is void.**

BUT WHAT IF . . .

WHAT IF THE FACTS OF THE CASE OPENER WERE DIFFERENT?

Let's say, in the Case Opener, that it was not children making a purchase but a mentally disabled person named Chloe, who was convinced that she owned a dog even though she didn't. And let's say that instead of purchasing in-game currencies on an iPhone, she ordered $1,000 worth of dog food. How would you describe Chloe's legal capacity? Could she avoid liability under her contract if she were subsequently treated by a therapist, no longer had her delusions, and realized that she had no need for the dog food? What if Chloe had been adjudicated insane and committed to a mental institution, but was staying with her sister on a weekend visitation pass when she made the purchase using her sister's computer?

The degree of intoxication is crucial when determining the capacity to agree to a legal contract.

INTOXICATED PERSONS

For purposes of determining capacity, intoxicated persons include those under the influence of alcohol or drugs. Most states follow the Restatement of Contracts, Section 16, which provides that contracts of an intoxicated person are voidable if the other party had reason to know that intoxication rendered the person unable to understand the nature and consequences of the transaction or unable to act in a reasonable manner in relation to the transaction. If the intoxication merely causes someone to exercise poor judgment, the person's capacity is not affected unless the other party unfairly capitalizes on this impaired judgment. Exhibit 16-2 presents the key points regarding contracts made by intoxicated persons.

Recall the case of *Lucy v. Zehmer,* discussed in Chapter 14. Another argument Zehmer tried to make in that case was that he was "high as a Georgia pine" when he signed the agreement and that the transaction was "just a bunch of two doggoned drunks bluffing to see who could talk the biggest and say the most."[4] Lucy, however, testified that while he felt the drinks, he was not intoxicated and that, from the way Zehmer handled the transaction, he did not think Zehmer was either. Zehmer's discussion of the terms of the agreement made it clear that he did in fact understand the nature of the transaction and thus could not claim a lack of capacity due to intoxication.

Similarly, if one party had no way of knowing that the other was intoxicated and if the agreement is a fair one, most courts will uphold it. Suppose Lisa e-mails Rob and offers to buy his antique car for $8,000. Rob has been drinking all day and immediately responds with a yes. Lisa has no way of knowing Rob is intoxicated, so they would have a valid contract in most states.

Exhibit 16-2
Intoxicated Individuals

Generally, contracts made by intoxicated persons are voidable. However, there are exceptions:

1. If the intoxication just causes the person to exercise poor judgment, the contract is not voidable unless the other party unfairly capitalized on the impaired judgment.

2. When the intoxicated person becomes sober, the contract can be ratified or disaffirmed; however, the courts will fairly liberally interpret behavior that seems like ratifying the contract once the intoxicated person becomes sober.

---

[4] *Lucy v. Zehmer,* 84 S.E.2d 516 (1954).

Once sober, the previously intoxicated person has the ability to either ratify or disaffirm the contract. Because public policy does not favor intoxication, the courts tend to not be sympathetic to intoxicated parties and will fairly liberally interpret behavior that seems like ratification as ratifying the contract. If Jim became intoxicated at a bar one evening and Randi took advantage by getting him to sign a contract to sell her his 2010 SUV for $8,000, any act Jim takes consistent with ratification after becoming sober will result in a binding contract. If Randi appears at his house the next morning with the cash, shows him the contract drafted on a napkin he signed, and asks for the keys and the title, by giving her the keys and saying, "I knew I shouldn't have drunk that much," Jim has entered into a binding contract.

If the contract is disaffirmed on the basis of intoxication, each party must return the other to the condition he or she was in at the time they entered into the contract. And, just as with contracts of minors and mentally incapacitated persons, the courts will enforce an intoxicated person's contract for necessaries for their reasonable value.

Exhibit 16-3 summarizes the general rules on incapacity and contracts.

TYPE OF INCAPACITY	CONSIDERATIONS	IF THE ANSWER IS YES, THE GENERAL RULE IS:
*I*nfancy	Is the person under the age of majority (a minor)?	The contract is voidable.
*I*nsanity	Is the person suffering from mental deficiencies that prevent him from understanding his legal obligations under the contract he is entering into?	The contract is voidable.
	Does the person's mental deficiency simply impair her judgment about the desirability of the contract but not prohibit her from understanding her obligations under it?	The contract is valid.
	Is the person adjudicated insane?	The contract is void.
*I*ntoxication	Is the sober party aware that the intoxicated person is so impaired that he is unable to understand his legal obligations under the contract he is entering into?	The contract is voidable.
	Is the intoxication such that it impairs only the intoxicated person's judgment but not her understanding of her contractual obligations?	The contract is valid.
	Has the intoxicated person been adjudicated a habitual drunkard?	The contract is void.

Exhibit 16-3

The Three *I*'s of Incapacity: General Rules

Legality

L03

What is the legal effect of entering into a contract for an illegal purpose?

To be enforceable, contracts must have legal subject matter and must be able to be performed legally. They cannot violate either state or federal law. A contract overturned for illegal subject matter or for being illegal to perform is generally declared void. A contract need not be in violation of a statute to be illegal; agreements against generally accepted public policy are also illegal and unenforceable.

Contracts that are made for an illegal purpose or that cannot be carried out by legal means are made void for two main reasons: First, making them void clearly indicates that such agreements are not socially acceptable, and, second, doing so prevents the legal system's being used to promote agreements that are harmful to society.

CONTRACTS THAT VIOLATE STATE OR FEDERAL STATUTES

There are any number of ways in which contracts can violate a state or federal statute. Some of the more common ones are discussed below and summarized in Exhibit 16-4.

Agreements to Commit a Crime or Tort.   Again, contracts cannot be for illegal purposes or require illegal acts for performance. Any agreement to commit a crime or tort is illegal and unenforceable. However, should a legal contract be formed and its subject later become illegal under a new statute, the contract is considered to be discharged by law. Suppose Jim agrees to paint Hiroki's house and, in exchange, Hiroki agrees to be a poker dealer at Jim's casino, starting in two weeks. Before Hiroki can begin work, however, the state amends its gaming statute, making all games of chance other than slot machines illegal. Because it is now illegal for Jim's casino to offer poker, it would be illegal for Hiroki to perform the contract. Because a change in the law has made the subject matter of the contract illegal, both parties are discharged from their obligations under the contract.

Licensing Statutes.   All 50 states have statutes requiring that people in certain professions obtain a license before practicing their craft. For example, doctors of all varieties, plumbers, cosmetologists, lawyers, electricians, teachers, and stockbrokers are all required to obtain a license before practicing. While this list is far from exhaustive, it demonstrates how widespread the licensing requirement can be. For most of these licensed professions, licenses are typically issued only after extensive schooling, training, and/or demonstrating some degree of competence. These requirements reflect the value society places on proper performance of duties in the licensed professions.

Licensing statutes have three main purposes in addition to indicating this value. The first is to give the government some control over which people, and how many people, can perform certain jobs. Second, by charging for licenses, the government can obtain revenue.

Exhibit 16-4

Contracts That Violate State or Federal Statutes

Agreements to commit a crime or tort are illegal in all states.

Agreements made for the purpose of protecting the public's health, safety, or welfare by a party unlicensed to do so are typically illegal in all states.

Agreements regarding usurious loans may be illegal in some states.

Agreements regarding gambling are illegal in most states.

Agreements that violate Sabbath or Sunday laws are illegal in some states.

The third purpose of licensing statutes, the protection of the public's health, safety, and welfare, is related to the public interest. By imposing legal standards on a profession, the government can try to prevent harm to public health, safety, and welfare due to substandard work. For instance, it is not in the public's best interest to allow an unqualified person to perform the delicate and complicated process of medical surgery. To limit the number of people who might be harmed during surgery, the government requires that prospective surgeons, even after extensive schooling, obtain a license.

Given these different reasons for licensing various professionals, different outcomes can result when someone enters into an agreement with a person who is unlawfully unlicensed, depending on the purpose of the licensing statute. The state in which the unlicensed person is practicing is relevant, because many licensing statutes occur at the state level and thus vary from state to state. In some states the rule is "no license, no contract." These states will not enforce any agreement with an unlawfully unlicensed professional.

However, in other states the courts typically consider the purpose of licensing. If it is to provide government control over the profession or generate revenue, most states allow enforcement of the contract. Although the unlicensed professional is acting in violation of the law and is usually required to pay a fine for working without a license, there are no grave reasons the contract should not be carried out.

If the licensing statute is intended to protect the public's health, safety, and welfare, however, the agreement is typically deemed illegal and unenforceable. For example, the public would not be made safer if the government allowed unlicensed people to perform surgery. Therefore, a person cannot enter into a contract for professional service with an unlicensed professional when the law requires a license out of intent to protect the public.

Case 16-1 illustrates how failure to obtain a license can preclude a party from suing to enforce a contract.

CASE 16-1   KING v. RIEDL
ALABAMA CIVIL COURT OF APPEALS
58 SO. 3D 190 (2010)

Roseann and Bryan Riedl entered into a contract with Jim King d/b/a King Home Services to make improvements to the Riedls' house. The improvements entailed work throughout the entire property, including work to the yard and demolition and installation work to the house. The Riedls paid King a total of $14,075 for some, but not all, of the work specified in the contract. King was not at any time a licensee of the Alabama Home Builders Licensure Board.

The Riedls were unsatisfied with the work contracted for and performed by King. Consequently, Roseann filed a small-claims complaint in the small-claims division of the Madison District Court, alleging that King had damaged her house. Roseann sought compensation for repair work performed by other parties. In response, King filed an action in the Madison Circuit Court against the Riedls, alleging a number of claims, including breach of contract. In the district court, King requested that the district-court action be consolidated with the circuit-court action. After the Riedls also requested consolidation, the district-court action was transferred to the circuit court, and the two actions were consolidated.

The Riedls filed a motion for a summary judgment in the circuit court, asserting that King lacked standing to institute the circuit-court action against them because he was an unlicensed home builder. In response, King claimed that he did not need a license in order to enforce his contract with the Riedls. After a hearing, the circuit court entered a summary judgment in favor of the Riedls, dismissing all King's claims against them. King filed an appeal of the summary judgment entered in the circuit-court action.

JUDGE THOMAS:

I. Breach of Contract Claim

Section 34–14A–5, Ala.Code 1975, requires all home builders to be licensed by the Alabama Home Builders Licensure Board. A residential home builder is defined by § 34–14A–2(10), Ala.Code 1975, as follows:

(10) Residential home builder. One who constructs a residence or structure for sale or who, for a fixed price, commission, fee, or wage, undertakes or offers to undertake the construction or superintending of the construction, or who manages,

[continued]

supervises, assists, or provides consultation to a homeowner regarding the construction or superintending of the construction, of any residence or structure which is not over three floors in height and which does not have more than four units in an apartment complex, or the repair, improvement, or reimprovement thereof, to be used by another as a residence *when the cost of the undertaking exceeds ten thousand dollars ($10,000).* Nothing herein shall prevent any person from performing these acts on his or her own residence or on his or her other real estate holdings. Anyone who engages or offers to engage in such undertaking in this state shall be deemed to have engaged in the business of residential home building.

. . . Thus, whether a license is required depends on the cost of the undertaking.

King argues that the cost of the undertaking in the present case was less than $10,000 because, he contends, work done to the Riedls' porch, "doggie doors," and fence should not be included in calculating the cost of the undertaking. King further argues that the Riedls had full control over the subcontractors and, thus, that he is exempted from obtaining a license by § 34–14A–6(5). Also, King contends that he did not have sufficient control over the subcontractors and materials for the amounts paid to those subcontractors and for those materials to contribute toward the cost of the undertaking. Finally, King argues that he was compensated for his work by periodic payments of less than $10,000 each, and, thus, he argues, he was not required to have a license.

Two of King's arguments are raised for the first time on appeal: King's argument that work done to the porch, "doggie doors," and fence should be considered separately from work performed on the house in calculating the total cost of the undertaking and his argument that he did not have sufficient control over the subcontractors and, thus, falls within an exemption to the licensing scheme. . . . Arguments not presented to the trial court are not proper arguments for appeal. . . . Accordingly, we consider all the work performed by King to be work performed on a house, which requires a license if the cost of the undertaking is greater than $10,000.

King argues that there remains a genuine issue of fact regarding whether the cost of the undertaking was more than $10,000. The Riedls note that King's admission that the costs of the undertaking exceeded $10,000 in his response to an interrogatory is in conflict with his affidavit filed in response to the Riedls' motion for a summary judgment. King's contradictory assertions in his response to an interrogatory and in his affidavit filed in response to the motion for a summary judgment do not create a genuine issue of a material fact regarding the cost of the undertaking. The Riedls' seventh interrogatory to King stated:

Regarding the contract alleged to have been breached by [the Riedls] within [King's] Complaint, provide the total amount to be paid for said work and services under the terms of said contract, including any and all estimated or fixed costs for materials provided.

King answered that the cost of the undertaking, under the terms of the contract, was "[i]n excess of $10,000.00." However, King submitted affidavit testimony in opposition to the motion for a summary judgment that stated that "at no time was I contracted to receive in excess of $10,000.00 as payment for my services." This contradiction cannot be used to create a genuine issue of material fact. . . .

King argues on appeal that payments made through him for the countertop and carpet were ultimately controlled by the Riedls. Contrary to his argument on appeal, however, the evidence submitted in support of and in opposition to the motion for a summary judgment does not indicate that King was hired to install carpet or to install the countertop. King produced no evidence indicating that the payments he received were intended to pay for either of those tasks, or for the materials involved in those tasks. The evidence indicates that King provided "turnkey" construction and supervision to the Riedls for an amount over $10,000.

The Riedls made periodic payments to King as he worked on the property, which, King contends, represent separate transactions. Thus, King argues, the contracted amount never exceeded $10,000. We have rejected this argument before, albeit in a case concerning a licensing statute pertaining to general contractors that is similar to § 34–14A–14. . . . "[A] contrary holding would encourage unscrupulous contractors to avoid the requirements of the licensing statute by designating payments to subcontractors and suppliers incident to 'separate contracts.' ". . . Similarly, allowing King to avoid licensure requirements by classifying a series of periodic payments as pertaining to separate contracts would render the residential home builder licensing statute meaningless. Thus, we conclude that there is no genuine issue of material fact on this issue and that the cost of the undertaking was over $10,000.

King violated § 34–14A–14 because he performed work, under his direct control and supervision, for more than $10,000. A residential home builder who fails to maintain a license with the Alabama Home Builders Licensure Board is statutorily barred from bringing or maintaining "any action to enforce the provisions of any contract for residential home building which he or she entered into in violation of this chapter." . . . King admitted that he was not a licensed residential home builder before, during, or after the construction work on the Riedls' house. Furthermore, the cost of the undertaking was more than $10,000. Therefore, King violated § 34–14A–14, and, thus, he has no standing to bring his breach-of-contract claim.

Summary Judgment affirmed in favor of the Reidls.

CRITICAL THINKING

When a judge or judicial panel makes a decision, the judge or panel must do so on the basis of the information available. What is an illustration of a fact that, were it true, would have caused this case to have provided King standing with respect to his breach-of-contract action? What fact was especially important in moving the decision in the direction of summary judgment?

ETHICAL DECISION MAKING

The statute spelling out the need for a residential home builder license has an exemption for small contracts. What stakeholders are being especially advantaged by the exemption?

Legal Principle: **If the licensing statute is intended simply to generate revenue, then the contract of an unlicensed person is valid; if the purpose of the licensing statute is to protect the public's health, safety, and welfare, however, the agreement of an unlicensed person is typically deemed illegal and unenforceable.**

Usury. Almost as widespread as licensing statutes, statutes prohibiting usury are found on the books of nearly every state. Usury occurs when a party gives a loan at an interest rate exceeding the legal maximum. The legal maximum interest rate varies from state to state, but it is easy to determine the rate of any given state.

While usury statutes act as a ceiling on rates, there are a few legal exceptions whereby loans may exceed the predetermined maximum. To facilitate business transactions and keep the economy healthy, for example, most states with usury statutes allow corporations willing to pay more to lend and borrow at rates exceeding the maximum. The rationale behind the corporation exception is that if a business needs money to expand and is willing to pay the higher interest rate, the corporation should be afforded the opportunity to borrow. The converse is that if a corporation is willing to borrow at a high interest rate, parties should be allowed to lend at that rate for corporations only. The intent is to facilitate business transactions in order to keep the economy in a healthy state.

Many states also allow parties to make small loans at rates above the maximum to parties that cannot obtain a needed loan at the statutory maximum. The belief is that if people need money and the statutory maximum is not inducing others to lend, certain parties will make the necessary loans at a higher rate as long as the loan is "small." This exception allows cash advance institutions to operate.

If no exception allows a usurious loan, the legal outcome varies by state. A few states declare all usurious loans void, which means the lender is not entitled to recover either interest or principal from the borrower. A larger number of states allow lenders to recover the principal but no interest. States most favorable toward lenders allow recovery of the principal as well as interest up to, but not exceeding, the statutory maximum.

Gambling. All states regulate gambling. As used in this chapter, the term gambling refers to agreements in which parties pay consideration (money placed during bets) for the chance, or opportunity, to obtain an amount of money or property. Industry officials, however, prefer to use the term *gaming*.

While gambling is illegal in most states, some allow casino gambling, notably Nevada, New Jersey, and Louisiana. Some allow certain other types of gambling, either intentionally or through legal loopholes. For example, given California's definition of gambling, betting on draw poker is legal. Some states make other exceptions, such as for horse tracks, casinos on Native American reservations, or state-run lotteries, which, although most people do not consider them to be such, are a form of gambling.

E-COMMERCE AND THE LAW

OBSERVING SABBATH DAYS ONLINE

Sabbath days stem from the religious traditions that were so widespread in America's early days. Among the religions that still practice observing Sabbath days today is Judaism, which has very strict laws in relation to refraining from conducting business on the Sabbath. This prohibition even extends to the online realm. Not only are those of the Jewish faith told to abstain from conducting online transactions on the day of the Sabbath, but it is also prohibited to make transactions online on the Sabbath even if the individual in question has no awareness of doing so. For example, if an individual schedules to pay for an item when it ships and the item happens to be shipped on the day of the Sabbath, it is considered that the individual has broken Sabbath law. Laws against conducting certain types of business are still active even today, though they may not be rigidly enforced.

Source: http://belogski.blogspot.com/2008/03/must-your-online-shop-shut-on-shabbat.html.

Sabbath Laws.   A large number of states still have *Sabbath, Sunday,* or *blue* laws on the books. Sabbath laws limit the types of business activities in which parties can legally engage on Sundays. In Colonial times, these laws prohibited store operations and all work on the "Lord's day" (Sunday). Today these laws vary by state. Most prohibit the sale of all alcohol, or specific types, either all day or at particular times on Sundays. Some Sabbath laws also make it illegal to enter into any contract on a Sunday. However, an executed, or fully performed, contract created on a Sunday cannot be rescinded.

There are exceptions to Sabbath laws. Most states allow the performance of charity work on Sundays. In addition, the laws typically do not apply to contracts for obtaining "necessities," including prescription medication, food, and anything else related to health or survival.

Regardless of how widespread Sabbath laws are, the vast majority of states do not enforce some or all of their Sabbath laws. In fact, some have been held to violate the First Amendment. If they are on the books, however, they can be applied, and some states do apply them. Prudent businesspersons should always find out whether Sabbath laws exist in their state and whether authorities enforce them.

AGREEMENTS IN CONTRADICTION TO PUBLIC POLICY

Some types of agreements are not illegal per se, as they are not in violation of any statute or legal code, but are nevertheless unenforceable because courts have deemed them to be against public policy. Public policy involves both the government's concern for its citizens and the beliefs people hold regarding the proper subject of business transactions. The focus is what is "in society's best interest."

Contracts in Restraint of Trade.   It is a widely held belief in economics, and in U.S. culture in general, that competition drives down prices, which is good for consumers. Thus, agreements that restrain trade, called *anticompetitive agreements,* are viewed as being harmful to consumers and against public policy. They also frequently violate antitrust laws. See Chapter 47 for an in-depth discussion of antitrust law.

When courts determine a restraint on trade is reasonable, however, and the restraint is part of a subordinate, or ancillary, clause in the contract, the restraint is typically allowed. Such restraints are known as covenants not to compete, or *restrictive covenants.* There are two types.

The first enforceable type of restrictive covenant is one made in conjunction with the sale of an ongoing business. The public policy argument in favor of supporting restrictions regarding the sale of a business involves the fairness of the sale, as illustrated by the following hypothetical: Suppose you purchase a jewelry store from Ann, a well-respected member of the community, whose business has been around for many years. The people in the community know the store, and they trust Ann to provide fair exchanges. As a well-informed businessperson, you know about Ann's good reputation and it made the purchase more appealing.

Now suppose a month later Ann opens another jewelry store a block away. Ann's loyal customers are likely to go to her new store because they still trust her. In the meantime, Ann's good name is no longer associated with your store, and your business suffers accordingly. You entered into the sales agreement thinking you would benefit from Ann's good name, but in the end you overpaid for a business that lacks that benefit, because Ann took her name with her when she went into competition with your store. In the interest of fairness, courts are willing to impose restrictions preventing Ann, or others in her position, from going into immediate competition with you, or others in your position. Public policy requires fairness in business transactions, which does not occur when people profit from the sale of a business and then start a new business that destroys the one they just sold.

Remember, if the covenant not to compete is an integral part of the main agreement, not subordinate, the agreement is typically considered unenforceable and void, because it goes against public policy by creating unreasonable restraints on trade. When the covenant is subordinate, however, the specific noncompetition clause can be removed and the agreement can go forward as planned. In Case 16-2, the court had to determine the reasonableness of a covenant not to compete that was included in a separation agreement.

CASE 16-2   WILLIAM CAVANAUGH v. MARGARET McKENNA
SUPERIOR COURT OF MASSACHUSETTS, AT MIDDLESEX
22 MASS. L. REP. 694; 2007 MASS. SUPER. LEXIS 298

Defendant entered into a separation agreement with the plaintiff at the time of their divorce. The agreement provided in part that defendant would not accept full-time employment or open her own funeral business in Wilmington so long as the plaintiff maintained his funeral business. The trial court found that plaintiff had breached the agreement by competing with defendant by working for, and later owning, Nichols Funeral Home. On appeal, the defendant argued that the covenant not to compete was unenforceable as a restraint of trade that violated public policy.

JUSTICE SMITH: A covenant to not compete must be reasonable in time and scope, serve to protect a party's legitimate business interest, be supported by consideration, and be consonant with the public interest. . . . While most covenants not to compete arise either in the context of an employment relationship or the sale of a business, there are situations which do not "fit neatly into existing standards for reviewing

such covenants" which require analogy. *Boulanger v. Dunkin' Donuts, Inc.,* . . . (2004) (finding covenant in franchise agreement akin to that of covenant in sale of business). With the sale of a business, "courts look less critically at covenants not to compete because they do not implicate an individual's right to employment to the same degree as in the employment context." . . . Courts will consider whether the parties were represented by counsel in making the agreement and entered the agreement without compulsion. . . .

The reasonableness of a covenant not to compete must be determined by the facts of each case. . . . Factors considered in determining the reasonableness of a restriction as to time include: 1) the nature of the business; 2) the type of employment involved; 3) the situation of the parties; 4) the legitimate business interests; and 5) a party's right to work and earn a livelihood. . . . Legitimate business interests include trade secrets, confidential business information, and good will. *Id.,* 779–80.

[continued]

Here, the covenant not to compete contained within the separation agreement is most analogous to the sale of a business. While McKenna worked at Cavanaugh Funeral Home before her divorce, she was not considered to be an employee. Her relinquishment of the right to operate a competing funeral home is akin to her sale of an asset. As such, the covenant not to compete should be construed more liberally. Also important in this consideration is the fact that McKenna was represented by counsel when she agreed to the noncompete provision, and there is no allegation that she was in any way coerced.

The Court finds that her covenant not to compete in the funeral business in the town of Wilmington for as long as Cavanaugh operates his funeral home there is reasonable in time and space. The restriction only applies to the town of Wilmington. Nothing prevents McKenna from entering the funeral business in another town (in fact, she worked for a funeral business in the town of Newton previously). In addition, it is important to note that there are only two funeral homes in Wilmington, Cavanaugh's and Nichols Funeral Home, and the defendant's utilization of the personal relationships forged while working at the plaintiff's funeral home would, in effect, misappropriate the good will of the plaintiff's business.

As part of the separation agreement, Cavanaugh gave up his right to the marital home and assumed the mortgage, and, in the modification, agreed to make weekly support payments, obtaining protection for the good will of his business in return. Allowing McKenna to compete in the same town while soliciting his clientele can be expected to eviscerate the good will of his business, the protection of which he received in return for his contractual undertakings.

In these circumstances, the Court finds that her covenant not to compete is enforceable. . . . Accordingly, the Court grants summary judgment to the plaintiff on Count I, leaving the issue of damages for trial.

AFFIRMED in favor of Plaintiffs.

CRITICAL THINKING

Provide an example of a piece of evidence that the defendant could have provided to indicate the unreasonableness of the scope of the covenant in this case. How does your example weigh in comparison to the evidence provided to the contrary? Do you think it would or should be sufficient to change the conclusion of the court? Defend your answer.

ETHICAL DECISION MAKING

What values are in conflict in this case? Which are supported by the ruling, and which are not? How well can the ethical stance taken by the court in this area be defended, and what ethical guidelines might be used in the effort to do so?

Legal Principle: **Covenants not to compete in conjunction with the sale of a business are generally enforceable if they are for a reasonable length of time and involve a reasonable location.**

The second category of permissible restraints on trade is covenants not to compete in employment contracts. The employee is agreeing, in the event of her leaving, not to compete with her boss (by starting her own company or working for competitors) for a designated period of time within a designated geographic area. These covenants are not unusual. In fact, many middle or upper-level managers enter into them.

Covenants not to compete in employment contracts are legal in most states, but they must protect a legitimate business interest. They must also apply to a period of time and geographic area that are reasonable for that purpose and not unlawfully impinge on the employee's rights. Not surprisingly, the enforceability of covenants not to compete in employment contracts varies from state to state. California does not allow any covenants not to compete. Texas requires that the employee gain or be given a specific benefit beyond employment before its courts will enforce even a reasonable covenant not to compete.

Employers and employees may therefore attempt to file suit or have their cases heard in the location that can provide them with the most favorable legal environment given their situation. Thus, business owners who create covenants not to compete may prefer to file suit in a location that is more tolerant of covenants not to compete, and employees may wish to have their cases heard in a location, such as California, that generally prohibits the enforceability of covenants not to compete.

For example, when executive Kai-Fu Lee left his job with Microsoft to join rival Google, Microsoft filed suit in the state of Washington, alleging that Lee's decision was in violation of his noncompete contract. Google fought back by filing suit against Microsoft in California, the state where Google is based, saying that under California laws Lee's noncompete contract was unenforceable. Both companies fought one another in court to have the case heard in the state where one or the other had the best chance of winning. In the end, a district court judge ruled that the case would first be tried in Washington, and if Google wanted to pursue the case further in California, it could do so after the trial. Early decisions made by the judge in Washington state court seemed to fall in Microsoft's favor, and Lee was initially barred from doing certain tasks for Google until after the trial. However, before the trial could end, the two companies reached a private settlement agreement.[5]

Unconscionable Contracts or Clauses.   When courts are asked to review contracts, fairness is not usually high on their list of things to look for. Instead, they typically assume that the contracting parties are intelligent, responsible adults who enter into contracts because they want to. Nevertheless, some agreements are so one-sided that the courts will not make the innocent party be harmed by fulfilling his or her contractual duties. These heavily one-sided agreements are known as unconscionable agreements. The term *unconscionable* refers to the fact that the agreement in question is so unfair that it is void of conscience.

The common law would not enforce contracts the courts deemed unconscionable. Now rules against unconscionable contracts exist in both the Restatement (Second) of Contracts and the Uniform Commercial Code. UCC Section 2-302 states:

> (1) If the court as a matter of law finds the contract or any clause of the contract to have been unconscionable at the time it was made, the court may refuse to enforce the contract, or it may enforce the remainder of the contract without the clause, or it may so limit the application of any unconscionable clause as to avoid any unconscionable result; (2) When it is claimed or appears to the court that the contract or any clause thereof may be unconscionable, the parties shall be afforded a reasonable opportunity to present evidence as to its commercial setting, purpose, and effect to aid the court in making the determination.

Every state except California and Louisiana has incorporated this section into its UCC. Section 208 of the Restatement also incorporates the above section.

There are two main types of unconscionable agreements, procedural and substantive. Procedural unconscionability describes conditions that impair one party's understanding of a contract, as well as the integration of terms into a contract. These conditions can be anything from tiny, hard-to-read print on the back of an agreement to excessive use of legalese (unnecessarily technical legal language) or even a person's inability to fully read a contract and ask questions before being required to sign.

Procedural unconscionability usually arises in an adhesion contract, an agreement presented on a take-it-or-leave-it basis or as the only chance the presented party (the *adhering party*) will have to enter into it. While adhesion contracts are legal, they do raise red flags for courts, which will try to determine how voluntary the agreement really was.

---

[5] http://news.cnet.com/Kai-Fu-Lees-California-case-put-on-hold/2100-1022_3-5918672.html; www.forbes.com/2005/12/23/gates-microsoft-google-cx_cn_1223autofacescan02.html; and http://news.cnet.com/Microsoft-sues-over-Google-hire/2100-1014_3-5795051.html.

Substantive unconscionability occurs when an agreement is overly harsh or lopsided. Courts would find the following, for example, to be substantively unconscionable: large differences between cost and price in a sales agreement; agreements in which one party gains vastly more than the other; agreements in which one party is prevented from having equal benefit or has little to no legal recourse; and portions of an agreement unrelated to either party's business risk.

Exculpatory Clauses. An exculpatory clause releases one of the contracting parties from all liability, regardless of who is at fault or what injury is suffered. Because tort law attempts to return the wronged party to a state he or she was in before the wrong occurred, anything preventing this corrective mechanism is against public policy. It does not benefit society to allow some parties to get away with not having to pay for wrongs they commit simply because they state they will not be liable in various contracts. In fact, the patently unfair nature of an exculpatory clause is closely tied to the idea of unconscionable contracts.

Exculpatory clauses frequently show up in rental agreements for commercial or residential property. It does not serve the public's interest to allow landlords, especially of residential property, to disavow in advance all liabilities for injuries due to carelessness, negligence, or other wrongdoing. If they were allowed to do so, nothing would require them to fix problems in their rental units, including potentially lethal problems like faulty wiring or the presence of lead-based paint.

A basic test to determine whether an exculpatory clause is enforceable is to see whether the enforcing party engages in a business directly related to the public interest, as does a bank, transportation provider, or public utility. Courts believe it is against the public interest to allow businesses engaging in work in the public's interest *not* to be held accountable to the public they are serving.

Businesses serving the public interest can also possess unfair bargaining power in negotiating a contract; they could simply demand that all customers accept the exculpatory clause, thereby escaping all liability. Worse, there would then be no financial motive for them to conduct operations carefully, and the potential for increased accidents would be great. Obviously, it is not in the public's interest to have unsafe businesses not be accountable to the public. Thus, these businesses cannot enforce exculpatory clauses.

Case 16-3 details a court's determination that an illegal exculpatory clause existed.

CASE 16-3   ERIC LUCIER AND KAREN A. HALEY v. ANGELA AND JAMES WILLIAMS, CAMBRIDGE ASSOCIATES, LTD., AND AL VASYS

SUPERIOR COURT OF NEW JERSEY, APPELLATE DIVISION
841 A.2D 907 (2004)

Eric Lucier and Karen A. Haley, a young married couple, were first-time home buyers. They contracted with the Williamses to purchase a single-family residence. Lucier and Haley engaged the services of Cambridge Associates, Ltd. (CAL), to perform a home inspection. Al Vasys had formed CAL and was its president. Lucier dealt directly with Vasys, and Vasys performed the inspection and issued the home inspection report on behalf of CAL.

The home inspection agreement contains a provision limiting CAL's liability to "$500, or 50% of fees actually paid to CAL by Client, whichever sum is smaller." This provision,

like several others in the form agreement prepared by CAL, was followed by a line for the clients' initials. Lucier initialed this provision. The fee for the home inspection contract was $385, which Lucier paid to CAL.

Lucier claims when he began to read the agreement, in Vasys' presence, he felt some of the language was unfair and confusing. According to Lucier, Vasys stated he would not change any provisions, that it was a standard contract based upon home inspections done in New Jersey, and Lucier would have to sign the agreement "as is" or not at all. Vasys does not dispute this but relies upon Lucier's signing the

[continued]

agreement and initialing the limitation of liability clause. Likewise, Lucier does not deny signing the contract or initialing that clause.

Lucier and Haley obtained title to the property from the Williamses. Shortly after, they noticed leaks in the house. They engaged the services of a roofing contractor and found the roof was defective. Lucier and Haley argue Vasys should have observed and reported the problem to them. The cost of repair was about $8,000 to $10,000.

Lucier and Haley brought suit against the Williamses, CAL, and Vasys, seeking damages to compensate them for the loss occasioned by the alleged defect. CAL and Vasys moved for partial summary judgment seeking a declaration that the limit of their liability in the action, if any, was one-half the contract price, or $192.50. The motion for partial summary judgment was granted. Lucier and Haley then filed this appeal, seeking review of the partial summary judgment order.

JUDGE LISA: There is no hard and fast definition of unconscionability. As the Supreme Court explained in *Kugler v. Romain,* unconscionability is "an amorphous concept obviously designed to establish a broad business ethic." The standard of conduct that the term implies is a lack of "good faith, honesty in fact and observance of fair dealing."

In determining whether to enforce the terms of a contract, we look not only to its adhesive nature, but also to "the subject matter of the contract, the parties' relative bargaining positions, the degree of economic compulsion motivating the 'adhering' party, and the public interests affected by the contract." Where the provision limits a party's liability, we pay particular attention to any inequality in the bargaining power and status of the parties, as well as the substance of the contract.

We also focus our inquiry on whether the limitation is a reasonable allocation of risk between the parties or whether it runs afoul of the public policy disfavoring clauses which effectively immunize parties from liability for their own negligent actions. To be enforceable, the amount of the cap on a party's liability must be sufficient to provide a realistic incentive to act diligently.

Applying these principles to the home inspection contract before us, we find the limitation of liability provision unconscionable. We do not hesitate to hold it unenforceable for the following reasons: (1) the contract, prepared by the home inspector, is one of adhesion; (2) the parties, one a consumer and the other a professional expert, have grossly unequal bargaining status; and (3) the substance of the provision eviscerates the contract and its fundamental purpose because the potential damage level is so nominal that it has the practical effect of avoiding almost all responsibility

for the professional's negligence. Additionally, the provision is contrary to our state's public policy of effectuating the purpose of a home inspection contract to render reliable evaluation of a home's fitness for purchase and holding professionals to certain industry standards.

This is a classic contract of adhesion. There were no negotiations leading up to its preparation. The contract was presented to Lucier on a standardized preprinted form, prepared by CAL, on a take-it-or-leave-it basis, without any opportunity for him to negotiate or modify any of its terms.

The bargaining position between the parties was grossly disparate. Vasys has been in the home inspection business for twenty years. He has inspected thousands of homes. He has an engineering degree. He has served as an expert witness in construction matters. He holds various designations in the building and construction field. He advertises his company and holds it and himself out as possessing expertise in the home inspection field. Lucier and Haley, on the other hand, are unknowledgeable and unsophisticated in matters of home construction. They are consumers. They placed their trust in this expert. They had every reason to expect he would act with diligence and competence in inspecting the home they desired to purchase and discover and report major defects. The disparity in the positions of these parties is clear and substantial.

The foisting of a contract of this type in this setting on an inexperienced consumer clearly demonstrates a lack of fair dealing by the professional. The cost of homes in New Jersey is substantial.

The limitation of liability clause here is also against public policy. First, it allows the home inspector to circumvent the state's public policy of holding professional service providers to certain industry standards. Second, it contravenes the stated public policy of New Jersey regarding home inspectors.

With professional services, exculpation clauses are particularly disfavored. The very nature of a professional service is one in which the person receiving the service relies upon the expertise, training, knowledge and stature of the professional. Exculpation provisions are antithetical to such a relationship.

In summary, the limitation of liability provision in this contract is unconscionable and violates the public policy of our State. The contract is one of adhesion, the bargaining power of the parties is unequal, the impact of the liability clause is negligible to the home inspector while potentially severe to the home buyer, and the provision conflicts with the purpose of home inspection contracts and our Legislature's requirement of accountability by home inspectors for their errors and omissions.

REVERSED and REMANDED.

[continued]

CRITICAL THINKING

In this decision, does Judge Lisa make any assumptions regarding the facts of the case without proper evidence to support them as a reasoning step? For instance, what evidence supports her characterization of Lucier? Is it possible he is significantly different from the way he has been presented? How might such differences affect the acceptability of the conclusion? Can you locate any other assumptions in this ruling? How do they affect the reasoning?

ETHICAL DECISION MAKING

Examine the actions of each party leading up to this dispute. Who behaved in a blameworthy fashion, and who in a praiseworthy fashion? What facts from the case and what ethical theories or guidelines support your claim?

Now consider each party's stance in the legal dispute. Does either one appear more or less ethical, relative to that party's earlier actions? Why or why not?

While businesses closely linked to the public interest cannot enforce exculpatory clauses, not all such clauses are unlawful. To prevail, the party seeking enforcement must be a private business or individual *not* important to the public interest. These private businesses or individuals provide nonessential services and thus do not have the same bargaining power as the previously discussed groups, such as banks, utilities, or airlines. Given their lack of huge bargaining power, courts assume such businesses and individuals will enter a contract voluntarily and on relatively equal terms.

Private businesses that *can* enforce exculpatory clauses thus include skiing facilities such as resorts or rental places, private gyms or health clubs, any business offering sky diving or bungee jumping, and amusement parks, to name a few. Because their services and those of others in this category are not related to the public interest and are not activities in which people *must* engage, these parties are allowed to deny liability if the other party agrees to the exculpatory clause. Just because these parties *might* be able to enforce an exculpatory clause, however, does not mean the clause is always automatically enforceable.

EFFECT OF ILLEGAL AGREEMENTS

When an agreement is deemed illegal, courts will usually label it void. The reason is the legal principle of *in pari delicto,* which means both parties are equally responsible for the illegal agreement. In that case, it does not make sense for the courts to attempt to salvage the agreement or reward either party. Therefore, neither party can enforce the agreement, and neither is entitled to recovery.

But what if both parties are *not* at fault? What if one is significantly more culpable? Then it sometimes makes sense to allow one party to an illegal agreement to recover various damages.

The first exception to the general rule occurs when a member of a protected class is party to an agreement that contradicts a statute intended to protect the specific class. That party is allowed to sue for performance. The reasoning is that a statute intended to protect a specific class should not be allowed to harm those in the class.

For example, a work agreement between Diego and his employer may specify that Diego gets paid for the number of hours he works as a truck driver. Yet certain statutes limit the number of hours truck drivers may drive in a given time period. If Diego accidentally drives more than the allowable hours, he has technically violated a statute. However, this violation does not allow his employer to refuse to pay him for the extra hours. Rather, Diego may sue his employer to enforce the work agreement.

The second exception to the voiding of illegal agreements occurs when *justifiable ignorance of facts* leaves one party unaware of a provision of the agreement that would

DETERMINING THE LEGALITY OF AN ARBITRATION CLAUSE

Buckeye Check Cashing, Inc. v. Cardegna et al.
United States Supreme Court
126 S. Ct. 1204, 163 L. Ed. 2d 1038 (2006)

The respondents, Cardegna et al., entered into a number of deferred-payment transactions with Buckeye Check Cashing. Each agreement they signed contained a provision requiring binding arbitration to resolve disputes arising out of the agreement. The respondents filed a class action suit against Buckeye in Florida state court, alleging that Buckeye charged usurious interest rates and that the agreement violated various Florida laws, rendering it illegal on its face. The trial court denied Buckeye's motion to compel arbitration, holding that a court rather than an arbitrator should resolve a claim that a contract is illegal and void *ab initio*. A state appellate court reversed, but its decision was in turn reversed by the Florida Supreme Court, which reasoned that enforcing an arbitration agreement in a contract challenged as unlawful would

violate state public policy and contract law. The case was appealed to the U.S. Supreme Court to determine whether the courts or an arbitrator should determine the legality of a potentially illegal contract containing a binding arbitration clause.

The Court answered this question by relying on three established propositions. First, as a matter of substantive federal arbitration law, an arbitration provision is severable from the remainder of the contract. Second, unless the challenge is to the arbitration clause itself, the issue of the contract's validity is considered by the arbitrator in the first instance. Third, this arbitration law applies in state as well as federal courts. Applying these propositions to the case, the high court concluded that when an agreement as a whole, but not specifically its arbitration provisions, is challenged, the arbitration provisions are enforceable apart from the remainder of the contract. The challenge to the legality of the contract itself should therefore be considered by an arbitrator, not a court.

make it illegal. While ignorance of the law does not excuse illegal behavior, not knowing that the other party intended to fulfill the agreement through illegal means does function as an excuse.

When one party is relatively innocent, the court may give back any consideration that party gave or may require exchange for partial performance such that both parties can be returned to the positions they were in before they entered into the agreement. If one party is completely innocent of any illegality and has completed his or her portion of the contract, then—depending on the reason the contract is considered illegal and which state's laws are in question—the court might enforce the entire agreement.

A third exception to the general rule occurs when one of the parties withdraws from an illegal agreement. The key to any recovery is that the party must have withdrawn before any illegality occurred. The party may then recover value for whatever partial or full performance has been completed. However, a party involved in the illegal activity in any way cannot recover at all.

Severable Contracts.

Severable contracts, also known as *divisible contracts*, contain multiple parts that can each be performed separately and for which separate consideration is offered. In essence, a severable contract

What happened to you?!?!

stus.com

The court severed my illegal provision. Man, it hurts.

is like numerous contracts in one. An *indivisible contract,* on the other hand, requires complete performance by both parties, even if it appears to contain multiple parts.

With respect to illegality, severable contracts have a huge advantage: If they have both legal and illegal portions, the court can void only the illegal sections and enforce the rest as long as they represent the main purpose of the original agreement. Indivisible contracts must be enforced or rejected in their entirety. If declaring parts of a contract void substantially alters it, the court is not likely to enforce the remaining portions. Courts ultimately want to facilitate business transactions and enforce the legal wishes of parties, and severable contracts enable them to do so.

Legal Principle: **If the court can sever the illegal part of a contract from the legal part, it will generally do so and enforce only the legal part; if the contract is indivisible, then it generally will be unenforceable.**

CASE OPENER WRAP-UP

Apple's Questionable Contract

The U.S. District Court for the Northern District of California denied Apple's motion to dismiss the lawsuit. The court stated that the complaint could not be dismissed because no case law was provided to prove that Apple's Terms of Service served as a contract for all subsequent transactions. Apple then constructed a settlement with all the plaintiffs in the class action lawsuit that had to be court-approved.

First, Apple would have to immediately send notices to 23 million customers with iTunes accounts, notifying the customers of parental controls that can block extra purchases. Second, customers in the lawsuit were to receive a $5 credit for use at the iTunes store. Customers whose children spent $30 or more would be entitled to a cash refund instead of credits. Finally, Apple would pay $1.3 million in attorney fees.

KEY TERMS

adhesion contract 375	exculpatory clause 376	procedural	substantive
capacity 361	gambling 371	unconscionability 375	unconscionability 376
covenants not to	*in pari delicto* 378	Sabbath laws 372	unconscionable 375
compete 372	indivisible contract 380	severable contracts 379	usury 371

SUMMARY OF KEY TOPICS

Natural persons over the age of majority are presumed to have the full legal capacity to enter into binding legal contracts.

Capacity

A person has only limited capacity to enter into a legally binding contract, and therefore can enter into only voidable contracts, if the person is either:

- A minor.
- Suffering from a mental deficiency that prevents the person from understanding the nature and obligations of contracts.
- Intoxicated.

A person has no capacity to enter into a contract if the person either:

- Has been adjudicated insane.
- Has been adjudicated a habitual drunkard.
- Has had a legal guardian appointed to enter into contracts on his or her behalf.

Necessaries: Even if a party has the ability to disaffirm a contract, if the contract is for a necessary—something like food, clothing, or shelter—the party cannot completely disaffirm the contract; she will be held liable for the reasonable value of the necessary.

Contracts that do not have a legal object are not valid.

Legality

Contracts that lack a legal object because they violate a statute or violate public policy are not valid.

When a contract is partly legal and partly illegal, if the illegal part can be severed, then the legal part will still be enforced, but if the contract is indivisible, it will be void and not enforced.

POINT / COUNTERPOINT

Should the Age at Which Minors Have Full Capacity to Enter into Binding Contracts Be Lowered to 16?	
YES	**NO**
Given the rights and responsibilities currently granted to 16-year-olds, lowering the age at which minors can enter into legally binding contracts seems logical. One of the most widely argued reasons given against lowering the age requirement pertains to a teenager's ability to fully understand a contract and comprehend the consequences associated with it. In response, proponents argue that society has already given children responsibilities and rights that are associated with long-term consequences; 16-year-olds are viewed, in the eyes of the law, as being able to consent to a sexual relationship. Along with this right comes the responsibility of understanding the potential for pregnancy and/or disease (which are *extremely* long-term consequences).	Under the law, teenagers are not viewed as adults until they have reached the age of majority. In nearly every state, the age of majority is at least 18. The age at which teenagers can enter into binding contracts should *not* be lower than the age of majority. At the age of 16, teenagers are still in the process of completing high school. They have not taken courses in financial management and have not been adequately introduced to contracts through life experiences. As such, these youths lack the ability to fully understand or comprehend the nature of or consequences associated with entering into contracts.

Perhaps as a result of their ability to consent to sexual relationships, 16-year-olds are often able to marry if the female is pregnant. Marriage is, by definition, a contract. These teenagers are already able, albeit in a limited fashion, to enter into binding contracts.

Furthermore, at the age of 16, a teenager can request a work permit and begin employment. As a result of this employment, the teenager is able to earn an income and make purchases. By maintaining the current age at which teenagers are seen as having the legal capacity to enter into a contract, society is, in effect, limiting the teenager's ability to make transactions he or she would otherwise be able to make. This limitation not only restricts teenagers' freedoms but also reduces commerce in this country. Society *should* lower the age requirement to 16.

Additionally, at the age of 16, nearly all teenagers are still residing within the home of a parent and/or guardian. Parents are held liable for many actions and decisions of their children. To cite but one potential example, if a child under the age of majority entered into a cell phone contract and was eventually unable to pay the related bills, it is possible that under parental liability law the parents will be held responsible for the funds owed. In short, society could prevent this undue burden from being placed on parents by keeping the age at which youths have the capacity to enter into contracts equal to, or greater than, the age of majority. Parents should have the ability to decide whether or not they wish to sign a contract on their child's behalf if it is potentially they who will ultimately be held responsible.

QUESTIONS & PROBLEMS

1. How does the concept of the age of majority differ in Great Britain from that in the United States?

2. Explain the obligations of a minor who chooses to disaffirm a contract.

3. Go back to the discussion of contracts that cannot be disaffirmed by minors, and explain the policy reasons that support each of the exceptions. Can you make an argument for any additional kinds of contracts that should not be subject to disaffirmance by minors?

4. If all you know about a man is that his neighbors think he is crazy, you do not know whether the contract he entered into was valid, voidable, or void. Why not?

5. What factors determine whether a covenant not to compete is legal or illegal?

6. What is the relationship between contracts in restraint of trade and unconscionable contracts?

7. Three salesmen worked for Sentient Jet, a small luxury airline charter service. They signed a noncompete agreement, promising to not go to work for a competing employer within a year after working for Sentient and also agreeing to not take any confidential information with them when they left the firm. When there was a change in the CEO of their firm, and talk of the company's possibly being bought out, the employees left the firm and went to work for Apollo Jets, a competitor, and allegedly took proprietary information with them that allowed them to solicit former Sentient clients. The plaintiff sought an injunction to ban the employees from working for a competitor for a year and also sought damages. The defendants argued that material changes in circumstances should have made the agreement not to compete unenforceable. How do you think the jury decided in this case? [*Sentient Jet v. MacKenzie,* Massachusetts Superior Court, January 2013 non-reported case. Discussed at http://www.hrwlawyers.com/pdfs/MLW-Non-Compete-Article-1-21-2013-(A121154).pdf.]

8. Paul Stewart and Ellen Chalk bought a wireless LAN PC card, manufactured by Sony, to connect wirelessly to the Internet through service provided by T-Mobile. Stewart and Chalk also signed a one-year service agreement with T-Mobile. The service agreement mandated arbitration and prohibited class action lawsuits. For approximately three weeks after the purchase of the card, Stewart and Chalk were able to insert it into their IBM ThinkPad laptop and connect to the Internet without any difficulty. They then did not attempt to use the card again for a few months, at which time they were unable to insert the card into their ThinkPad. They contacted T-Mobile technical support several times and received refurbished cards on three separate occasions. None of the refurbished cards fit into the ThinkPad. After Stewart and Chalk were unable to insert the third card, staff from T-Mobile technical support informed them that they would have to pursue the issue at the T-Mobile store where they purchased the original card. At the store, a Sony representative attempted to insert the card, but he failed as well. He then promised to contact them about how to solve the problem. They never heard back from him, despite multiple e-mail inquiries.

Ultimately, Stewart and Chalk filed a class action lawsuit against T-Mobile and Sony. The complaint alleged that Sony and T-Mobile knew or should have known that the card "was not compatible and/or did not fit into the IBM ThinkPad laptop" computers and that Sony and T-Mobile allowed customers to purchase cards and enter into long-term service contracts from which consumers would receive no benefit without a compatible card. Sony and T-Mobile filed a motion to compel arbitration. Stewart and Chalk opposed the motion, contending that the arbitration clause was unconscionable and therefore unenforceable. The district court ruled in favor of Sony and T-Mobile. Stewart and Chalk appealed. Is the arbitration agreement unconscionable? If you were an attorney for Stewart and Chalk, would you argue that the arbitration clause was procedurally unconscionable, substantively unconscionable, or both? Why? [*Chalk v. T-Mobile, USA, Inc.,* 560 F.3d 1087 (2009).]

9. Washington State resident Patty Gandee entered into a debt adjustment contract with Freedom Enterprises. She subsequently sought to file a class action against Freedom for violations of the state debt adjusting act and the Consumer Protection Act. The company sought to compel arbitration based on a binding arbitration clause she had signed. The clause provided that any disputes under the contract were to be submitted to arbitration that would take place in Orange County, California, under American Arbitration Association rules, and the prevailing party would be entitled to reasonable legal fees and costs, including attorney fees. Both the trial court and the Washington Supreme Court refused to enforce the binding arbitration clause. Explain why they would not enforce the clause. [*Patty J. Gandee v. LDL Freedom Enterprises,* Case No. 87674-6 (Wash. Sup. Ct., Feb. 7, 2013) (available at http://lawyersusaonline.com/wp-files/pdfs-5/gandee-v-ldl-freedom-enterprises.pdf).]

10. The Finches hired Inspectech to perform a home inspection of property they were purchasing. The contract they signed included a clause that read:

It is understood and agreed that the COMPANY [Inspectech] is not an insurer and that the inspection and report are not intended to be construed as a guarantee or warranty of the adequacy, performance or condition of any structure, item or system at the property address. The CLIENT [the Finches] hereby releases and exempts the COMPANY and its agents and employees of and from all liability and responsibility for the cost of repairing or replacing any unreported defect or deficiency and for any consequential damage, property damage or personal injury of any nature. In the event the COMPANY and/or its agents or employees are found liable due to breach of contract, breach of warranty, negligence, negligent misrepresentation, negligent hiring or any other theory of liability, then the liability of the COMPANY and its agents and employees shall be limited to a sum equal to the amount of the fee paid by the CLIENT for the inspection and report.

After the inspection, which reported no significant defects, the Finches purchased the house. Within one week of closing, the Finches discovered water damage; prior repairs to correct the water damage; and water infiltration in the basement of their new home, as well as structural problems affecting the house's foundation. The Finches alleged that these defects were not obviously visible because of the location of a workbench owned by the sellers. They sued to recover the $39,000 they had to spend to repair the water and structural damage.

On the basis of the contractual language, the circuit court awarded summary judgment to Inspectech, concluding that the release prohibited the Finches from asserting their claims against Inspectech for damages they claimed were occasioned by Inspectech's failure to identify and disclose various defects in their new home. The court concluded that the clause was unambiguous and conspicuously placed in the contract and that the Finches had specifically agreed to its terms and its inclusion in the parties' Inspection Agreement contract. On what grounds do you think the West Virginia Supreme Court overturned the granting of summary judgment to Inspectech? [*David Finch and Shirley Finch v. Inspectech, LLC,* Case No. 11-0278 (W. Va. Sup. Ct. App., May 24, 2012) (available at http://lawyersusaonline.com/wp-files/pdfs-4/finch-v-inspectech.pdf).]

Looking for more review materials?

The Online Learning Center at **www.mhhe.com/kubasek3e** contains this chapter's "Assignment on the Internet" and also a list of URLs for more information, entitled "On the Internet." Find both of them in the Student Center portion of the OLC, along with quizzes and other helpful materials.

17 Legal Assent

LEARNING OBJECTIVES

After reading this chapter, you will be able to answer the following questions:

1 Why is legal assent important?

2 What are the elements of mistake?

3 What are the elements of misrepresentation?

4 What are the elements of undue influence?

5 What are the elements of duress?

6 What are the elements of unconscionability?

CASE OPENER

A Disagreement over an Agreement

In spring 1989, Michael Jordan and the Chicago Bulls were in Indianapolis, Indiana, to play against the Indiana Pacers. At the same time, Karla Knafel was singing with a band at a hotel in Indianapolis. After Knafel's performance, a National Basketball Association referee approached her and introduced her to Jordan via telephone. Knafel and Jordan began a long-distance telephone relationship that continued for several months.

In December 1989, Knafel traveled to Chicago to meet with Jordan, where the couple had unprotected sex for the first time. In November 1990, the couple had unprotected sex again while in Phoenix, Arizona. Shortly after this second meeting, Knafel learned that she was pregnant. Knafel was "convinced that she was carrying Jordan's baby" despite having had sex with other male partners. Later, during spring 1991, Knafel informed Jordan "she was pregnant with his child."

As a result of several conversations about the baby, Knafel alleged that the two had agreed that Jordan would pay her $5 million when he retired from professional basketball. In return, Knafel promised she would not file a paternity suit against him and would keep their relationship a secret.

In July 1991, the baby was born. Jordan paid some hospital bills and medical costs, and he paid Knafel $250,000 for "her mental pain and anguish arising from her relationship with him." Knafel continued to keep the relationship and paternity a secret.

After Jordan retired from professional basketball, a lawsuit arose between the parties in 2000. Jordan sought declaratory judgment and an injunction against Knafel, who had been approaching him for the $5 million. Knafel filed a counterclaim for Jordan's alleged breach of contract. The trial court dismissed all claims, but the appellate court remanded Knafel's claim for breach of contract. Although Jordan had originally denied the existence of the agreement, on remand he did not contest the existence of the alleged settlement agreement. Instead, Jordan argued that the alleged agreement was not enforceable because it either was fraudulently induced or was based on a mutual mistake of fact. In support of his argument, Jordan produced the affidavit of Dr. Storm, who, after DNA testing, concluded that Jordan was not the child's father.

In response to Jordan's argument, Knafel claimed that the paternity of the child was irrelevant to the enforceability of the alleged agreement. An obstetrician had told Knafel that the baby was conceived on November 19 or 20, 1990 (while she was in Phoenix with Jordan). As a result of this information, Knafel believed that the baby was Jordan's. Additionally, Knafel asserted that the paternity was irrelevant because Jordan entered into the agreement knowing that she had been having sex with other men.

The trial court ruled in favor of Jordan, finding that "as a result of Knafel's fraudulent misrepresentation to Jordan that he was the child's father or, alternatively, as a result of a mutual mistake of fact, the alleged settlement contract is voidable and is therefore unenforceable against Jordan." Knafel appealed.

1. Imagine you are the judge in this case. Do you think that both parties were able to legally assent to the agreement?
2. Under which ethical system, if any, should Knafel be able to recover the $5 million for breach of contract?

The Wrap-Up at the end of the chapter will answer these questions.

The Importance of Legal Assent

When two people talk in the hope that an exchange will take place between them, all kinds of things can go wrong. Yet global business needs dependability. Imagine what transactions would be like if "Yes" meant "Maybe"! Deals would be closed only to be reopened again and again. The costs of all purchases would soar. Businesses would be forced to charge extra to pay for all the extra time they had to spend to finally get to the point where "Yes" really meant "Yes."

L01

Why is legal assent important?

To make business transactions smoother and more dependable, courts have developed rules about when an assent to do something is a legal assent, that is, a promise the courts will require the parties to obey.

The courts see some forms of assent as more genuine or real than others. It is important for businesspeople to know the differences among the various kinds of assent. Why do the differences matter? Jamal may think he has sold his tutoring services to Harrison. However, without legal assent the contract may be voidable, a circumstance that can cost a business large profits when the transaction is significant. A voidable contract can be rescinded, or canceled, permitting the person who canceled the contract to require the return of everything she gave the other party. She must herself return whatever she has received. An enormous waste of time and an unnecessary cost of doing business may be the result.

The major theme of this chapter is that *best-practice firms aim for legal assent in their contracts*. This chapter shows you how to achieve legal assent. It explains the major obstacles to legal assent: mistake, misrepresentation, undue influence, duress, and unconscionability. By knowing about these potential problems, you will be in a good position to avoid them.

Mistake

LO2

What are the elements of mistake?

When people agree to buy or sell, they do so with a particular understanding about the nature of the good or service they are about to exchange. However, one or both parties may think they consented to exchange a particular thing only to find out later that no meeting of the minds had occurred. People may misunderstand either some fact about the deal or the value of what is being exchanged. We focus on misunderstandings about facts, because they are the only issues that raise the potential of rescission (the rescinding of a contract) in U.S. courts. Mistaken beliefs about the subjective value of an item do not affect the validity of the contract.

In contract law a mistake of fact is an erroneous belief about the facts of the contract *at the time the contract is concluded*. Legal assent is absent when a mistake of fact occurs. Later in this chapter, when we discuss misrepresentation, our focus will be on incorrect beliefs about the facts of the contract caused by the other party's untrue statements. Mistakes in contract law do *not* result from these untrue statements.

Mistakes can be unilateral, the result of an error by *one* party about a material fact, that is, a fact that is important in the context of the particular contract. Or mistakes can be mutual, shared by both parties to the agreement. As we see next, this distinction is important in determining which contracts are voidable.

The insurance companies are fighting about "mutual mistake." I thought they were talking about the accident, but it's actually about the wording of the insurance documents.

stus.com

COMPARING THE LAW OF OTHER COUNTRIES

THE EUROPEAN VIEW ABOUT MISTAKES ABOUT VALUE

European courts take a different approach to mistakes about the *value of performance* of the contract. In general, they agree with the reluctance of U.S. courts to interfere with a contract just because the value of the item in question has changed since the agreement. The parties are assumed to have accepted the risk that the value might change after they made the contract. However, European courts permit rescission of the contract for a mistake of value when the mistake involves more than 50 percent of the value at the time of the contract.

UNILATERAL MISTAKE

Because courts are hesitant to interfere when one of the parties has a correct understanding of the material facts of the agreement, a unilateral mistake does not generally void a contract. For instance, a widow seeking to rescind her and her husband's election to have his retirement benefits paid out over *his* life was not permitted to receive survivor's pension benefits. The court held that representatives of the retirement system had provided sufficient information to the plaintiff and her husband before they elected that particular form of payout.[1] The Case Nugget on the next page provides another illustration of a failed attempt to argue that a unilateral mistake was present.

On rare occasions, however, rescission *is* permitted for unilateral mistakes. Because our economic well-being depends so heavily on reliable contracts, we want to be fully aware of the circumstances under which unilateral mistakes permit rescission. Any of the following conditions would permit a court to invalidate a contract on grounds of unilateral mistake:

1. One party made a mistake about a material fact, and the other party knew or had reason to know about the mistake.
2. The mistake was caused by a clerical error that was accidental and did not result from gross negligence.
3. The mistake was so serious that the contract is unconscionable, that is, so unreasonable that it is outrageous.

These situations are rare, but it is important to be aware of them because any rescission can be costly in terms of time and lost opportunities.

MUTUAL MISTAKE

When both parties are mistaken about a current or past material fact, either can choose to rescind the contract. Rescission is fair because any agreement was an illusion: Ambiguity prevented a true meeting of the minds.

The famous story of the ship *Peerless*[2] has taught generations of students the importance of being very clear in defining material facts in any contract. The parties in the case had agreed that the vessel *Peerless* would deliver the cotton they were exchanging. Unfortunately for them, there were two ships named *Peerless*. So when the deal was made, one party had one *Peerless* in mind while the other meant the second. The times the ships sailed were materially different, so the court rescinded the contract. *Warning:* Anticipate ambiguity in material facts, and clarify them in advance to save yourself headaches later.

---

[1] *Ricks v. Missouri Local Government Employees Retirement System,* 1999 WL 663217 (Mo. App. WD).

[2] *Raffles v. Wichelhaus,* 159 Eng. Rep. 375 (1864).

CASE NUGGET

A QUESTIONABLE "MISTAKE"

Mary W. Scott (Respondent-Appellant) v. Mid-Carolina Homes, Inc. (Appellant-Respondent)
Court of Appeals of South Carolina
293 S.C. 191 (1987)

Mary Scott signed a contract to purchase a repossessed 1984 mobile home from Mid-Carolina Homes, Inc., for $5,644 to be paid in full before delivery. Scott gave the salesperson a check for $2,913.71, and agreed to pay the balance before the end of the month. Within the next week, the salesman called Scott and told her that according to the standards of the South Carolina Manufactured Housing Board he could not sell her the home because it had a bent frame. Scott offered to buy it as is and sign a waiver, but the salesman said that would not be legal. A few weeks later, Mid-Carolina sold the mobile home to another couple for $9,220. Scott sued and was awarded $3,600 actual damages, $6,400 punitive damages for breach of contract accompanied by a fraudulent act, and $3,000 actual damages for violation of a state consumer protection law. The appeals court upheld the award.

On appeal, Mid-Carolina argued that it was entitled to rescind the contract because the salesperson was acting under a mistake of fact when he gave Scott the sales price. In upholding the award, the state supreme court explained that a contract may be rescinded for unilateral mistake only when the mistake has been induced by fraud, deceit, misrepresentation, concealment, or imposition of the party opposed to the rescission, without negligence on the part of the party claiming rescission, or when the mistake is accompanied by very strong and extraordinary circumstances that would make it a great wrong to enforce the agreement. Mid-Carolina had not demonstrated the presence of any of these. The salesperson was in the superior bargaining position to know the price, and the buyer's reliance on a salesperson's representation of the price was reasonable.

For a mutual mistake to interfere with legal consent, all the following must be present:

1. A basic assumption about the subject matter of the contract.
2. A material effect on the agreement.
3. An adverse effect on a party who did not agree to bear the risk of mistake at the time of the agreement.

Courts will not void contracts for reason of mutual mistake if even one of these conditions is missing. (See Exhibit 17-1.) Let's see why they matter.

To rise to the level of a basic assumption, a mistake must be about the existence, quality, or quantity of the items to be exchanged. To be material, condition 2, the mistake must affect the essence of the agreement. A fact is material when it provides a basis for a person's agreeing to enter into the contract. Neither party can void the contract simply by falsely claiming that the item to be exchanged is not the one he intended.

The third condition protects those who bargain with someone who agreed, at the time of the agreement, to bear the risk of mistake but then later wishes to avoid that risk when the contract does not work out as well as he or she had planned. This situation might arise, for instance, if the adversely affected party had agreed in the contract to accept items "as is" but later felt they were not worth the price paid. In the opening scenario, had Jordan agreed to pay Knafel the $5 million regardless of the outcome of any future paternity tests, the

Exhibit 17-1

Enforceability of a Mutual Mistake

Before a contract can be voided for a mutual mistake, you must answer each of the following questions with a yes:

1. Is the mistake about a basic assumption that affects the subject matter of the contract?
2. Does the mistake have a material effect on the agreement?
3. Would enforcement of the contract have an adverse effect on the party who did not agree to bear the risk of mistake at the time of the agreement?

outcome of the case would have been very different. Instead, Jordan had allegedly agreed to pay Knafel the money on the basis of misinformation that the child was definitely his. Upon learning that the child was not his, Jordan wanted to have the contract rescinded on the basis, partly, of the mutual mistake made between himself and Knafel. Case 17-1 provides an illustration of an unsuccessful attempt to avoid a contract on the basis of mutual mistake.

CASE 17-1   SIMKIN v. BLANK
COURT OF APPEALS OF NEW YORK
19 N.Y.3D 46 (2012)

When Steven Simkin and Laura Blank divorced in 2006, they split their $13.5 million in assets. Most of Simkin's $5.4 million share of the settlement was invested in Bernie Madoff's Ponzi scheme, whereas Blank received a cash settlement. Then, in 2008, Simkin thought the terms of the divorce contract should be renegotiated because he lost almost all of his divorce proceeds when it came to light that his investment in Madoff's business turned out to be a fraud and Madoff's business turned out to be a huge Ponzi scheme. Simkin argued that both he and his ex-wife had shared in the mistake of investing funds into Madoff's project, yet only Simkin received the invested funds in the divorce settlement and Blank received cash. Simkin also argued that because his funds never existed as an "investment" as they had already vanished in the Ponzi scheme, he never really received an equal share of their existing assets. Thus, he asked Ms. Blank if the two could renegotiate the contract. When she refused, he sued. A lower court granted Simkin the right to sue, but the case moved on to the Court of Appeals of New York.

JUDGE GRAFFEO: Marital settlement agreements are judicially favored and are not to be easily set aside. Nevertheless, in the proper case, an agreement may be subject to rescission or reformation based on a mutual mistake by the parties. Similarly, a release of claims may be avoided due to mutual mistake. Based on these contract principles, the parties here agree that this appeal turns on whether husband's amended complaint states a claim for relief under a theory of mutual mistake.

We have explained that the mutual mistake must exist at the time the contract is entered into and must be substantial. Put differently, the mistake must be "so material that . . . it goes to the foundation of the agreement" ["The parties must have been mistaken as to a basic assumption of the contract. . . . Basic assumption means the mistake must vitally affect the basis upon which the parties contract"]. Court-ordered relief is therefore reserved only for "exceptional situations." The premise underlying the doctrine of mutual mistake is that "the agreement as expressed, in some material respect, does not represent the meeting of the minds of the parties."

Although we have not addressed mutual mistake claims in the context of marital settlement agreements, the parties cite a number of Appellate Division cases that have analyzed this issue. Husband relies on True v True . . . where the settlement agreement provided that the husband's stock awards from his employer would be "divided 50-50 in kind" and recited that 3,655 shares were available for division between the parties. After the wife redeemed her half of the shares, the husband learned that only 150 shares remained and brought an action to reform the agreement, arguing that the parties mistakenly specified the gross number of shares (3,655) rather than the net number that was actually available for distribution. The Second Department agreed and reformed the agreement to effectuate the parties' intent to divide the shares equally, holding that the husband had established "that the parties' use of 3,655 gross shares was a mutual mistake because it undermined their intent to divide the net shares available for division, 50-50 in kind."

Other cases relied on by husband involve marital settlement agreements that were set aside or reformed because a mutual mistake rendered a portion of the agreement impossible to perform. In Banker v Banker . . . the Third Department reformed a provision of a marital settlement that required the subdivision of a parcel of real property because the parties were unaware of a restrictive covenant against further subdivision.

Applying these legal principles, we are of the view that the amended complaint fails to adequately state a cause of action based on mutual mistake. As an initial matter, husband's claim that the alleged mutual mistake undermined the foundation of the settlement agreement, a precondition to relief under our precedents, is belied by the terms of the agreement itself. Unlike the settlement agreement in True that expressly incorporated a "50-50" division of a stated number of stock shares, the settlement agreement here, on its face, does not mention the Madoff account, much less evince an intent to divide the account in equal or other proportionate shares. To the contrary, the agreement provides that the $6,250,000 payment to wife was "in satisfaction of [her] support and marital property rights," along with her release of various claims and inheritance rights. Despite the fact that the agreement permitted husband to retain title to his "bank, brokerage and similar financial accounts" and

[continued]

enumerated two such accounts, his alleged $5.4 million Madoff investment account is neither identified nor valued. Given the extensive and carefully negotiated nature of the settlement agreement, we do not believe that this presents one of those "exceptional situations" warranting reformation or rescission of a divorce settlement after all marital assets have been distributed.

Even putting the language of the agreement aside, the core allegation underpinning husband's mutual mistake claim—that the Madoff account was "nonexistent" when the parties executed their settlement agreement in June 2006—does not amount to a "material" mistake of fact as required by our case law. The premise of husband's argument is that the parties mistakenly believed that they had an investment account with Bernard Madoff when, in fact, no account ever existed. In husband's view, this case is no different from one

in which parties are under a misimpression that they own a piece of real or personal property but later discover that they never obtained rightful ownership, such that a distribution would not have been possible at the time of the agreement. But that analogy is not apt here. Husband does not dispute that, until the Ponzi scheme began to unravel in late 2008—more than two years after the property division was completed—it would have been possible for him to redeem all or part of the investment. In fact, the amended complaint contains an admission that husband was able to withdraw funds (the amount is undisclosed) from the account in 2006 to partially pay his distributive payment to wife. Given that the mutual mistake must have existed at the time the agreement was executed in 2006, the fact that husband could no longer withdraw funds years later is not determinative.

REVERSED in favor of defendant Blank.

CRITICAL THINKING

When Simkin claimed that the contract terms should be altered on the basis of a "mutual mistake" when the two entered into the divorce contract, he referenced their "mistake" being that the settlement terms allocated to him were nonexistent due to the Ponzi scheme. Should Simkin have defined his use of "nonexistent" according to a time frame? The funds were nonexistent two years after the divorce settlement, but the funds were existent in 2006 during the divorce.

ETHICAL DECISION MAKING

Could a decision in favor of Simkin's altering the terms of the marriage contract create copycat suits? Courts typically leave divorce terms intact except in rare circumstances, but many couples could attempt to claim that an outside force affected their divorce settlement assets.

Misrepresentation

L03

What are the elements of misrepresentation?

Misrepresentations are similar to mistakes in that at least one of the parties is in error about a fact material to the agreement. But a misrepresentation is an untruthful assertion by one of the parties about that material fact; it prevents the parties from having the mental agreement necessary for a legal contract. They only *appeared* to agree, so their contract lacked legal assent.

The courts insist on a meeting of the minds for a valid contract. Thus, they might rescind a contract even though the person making the false assertion was entirely innocent of any intentional deception.

The topic of misrepresentation should be particularly important to future business professionals, especially those interested in marketing or advertising careers, as it may one day be your job to develop promotional materials for a company's products. Marketing and advertising professionals must exercise special care when developing product labels, packaging, and advertisements because consumers often depend on the information provided by a company when deciding whether to purchase a product. Thus, if the marketing materials created by a company are seen as being inaccurate or appear to misrepresent what a product truly is or what benefits the product offers, consumers may attempt to take legal action.

For example, in 1991 a Michigan man, Richard Overton, filed suit against Anheuser-Busch, claiming that the company's commercials made untrue statements and misrepresentations that caused him to continually buy and consume the company's beer. More specifically, Overton alleged that Anheuser-Busch was liable for creating advertisements that falsely suggested drinking its beer would result in fantasies coming to life (tropical settings, beautiful women, and happiness). Overton sought to recover $10,000 in damages from Anheuser-Busch for causing him physical and mental injury as well as emotional distress and financial loss. A circuit court granted summary judgment in favor of the defendant. Richard Overton appealed, and the Michigan Court of Appeals affirmed the lower court's ruling.[3] While the company won the case, it still had the expense of defending its actions. It is always better to try to avoid being sued in the first place.

INNOCENT MISREPRESENTATION

An innocent misrepresentation results from a false statement about a fact material to an agreement that the person making it believed to be true. The person had no knowledge of the claim's falsity. We say he or she lacked scienter (from the Latin root of the word meaning "knowledge").

Innocent misrepresentations permit the misled party to rescind the contract. However, because the other party had no intent to mislead, the aggrieved party cannot sue for damages. The reasoning in these cases resembles the arguments in a mutual mistake case, as you might expect.

BUT WHAT IF . . .
WHAT IF THE FACTS OF THE CASE OPENER WERE DIFFERENT?

Let's say that, in the Case Opener, Knafel was incorrectly told by her doctor that the baby was Jordan's. She then told Jordan that she indeed was carrying his baby. Thus, Jordan signed the contract and paid Knafel a large sum of money. Later, the two found out the baby was not Jordan's. What kind of misrepresentation occurred? Can Jordan sue for damages?

NEGLIGENT MISREPRESENTATION

In some contract negotiations, one party makes a statement of material fact that he thinks is true. If he could have known the truth by using reasonable care to discover or reveal it, his statement is a negligent misrepresentation.

Even though he had no intent to deceive, in contract law the party is treated as if he did. If this standard seems unfair to you, remember that the courts find negligent misrepresentation only when the party making the false statement should have known the truth using the skills and competence required of a person in his position or profession. The impact of negligent misrepresentation is identical to that of fraudulent misrepresentation, discussed next.

FRAUDULENT MISREPRESENTATION

Any fraud on the part of a party to a contract provides a basis for rescission. The parties cannot be said to have assented when one of the parties was tricked into the "agreement"

---

[3] 205 Mich. App. 259, 517 N.W.2d 308 (case summary accessed on Lexis Nexis May 25, 2009).

by a fraudulent misrepresentation. Thus, the agreement was not voluntary and can be rescinded on the ground that there was no meeting of the minds.

Even in countries trying to encourage joint ventures and global commercial activity, such as the People's Republic of China, fraudulent claims can end the country's hospitality to agreements with outsiders.[4] In China, accusations of outsiders' fraudulent misrepresentation have resulted in heavy fines and even refusals to allow the fraudulent party to enter into any more agreements with Chinese firms. In most, if not all, cultures, little judicial sympathy exists for those who consciously mislead others in commercial activities.

A fraudulent misrepresentation is a consciously false representation of a material fact intended to mislead the other party. It is also referred to as intentional misrepresentation. Here scienter is clear: The party making the misrepresentation either knows or believes that the factual claim is false or knows there is no basis for it.

To understand the requirements for a finding of fraudulent misrepresentation, start with the two elements from the definition:

1. *A false statement about a past or existing fact that is material to the contract.*
2. *Intent to deceive,* which can be inferred from the particular circumstances.

Then add a third necessary element:

3. *Justifiable reliance on the false statement by the innocent party to the agreement:* Justifiable reliance is generally present unless the injured party knew, or should have known by the extravagance of the claim, that the false statement was indeed false. For example, a homeowner could not justifiably rely on a claim by a gardener that if she will pay him to apply a special fertilizer to her trees once a week, the trees would never die.

Finally, if damages are sought, the defrauded party must have been injured by the misrepresentation.

In the opening scenario, Jordan claimed that he had been the victim of a fraudulent misrepresentation made by Knafel. To meet the three requirements, Jordan argued that Knafel told him that he was definitely the child's father despite her knowledge that she had been having sexual relationships with other men during the same time period. According to Jordan, Knafel had reason to believe that her representation could be false and still made it with certainty in an effort to deceive him. Finally, it was based on the assertion that he was the father that Jordan allegedly agreed to pay Knafel $5 million. Hence, according to Jordan, he had proved that the statement qualified as a fraudulent misrepresentation. Does Knafel's representation that Jordan was the child's father amount to a fraudulent misrepresentation?

Each of the three aforementioned elements can become a source of debate in any attempt to rescind a contract on grounds of fraudulent misrepresentation. Thus, it is your responsibility as a person who will be involved with dozens of contracts in your business activities to know these elements. A rescinded contract is a time-consuming and expensive business opportunity that has gone wrong. And don't forget that you can collect damages only from parties you can locate.

Before we go into greater detail about the elements of fraudulent misrepresentation, please consider Case 17-2. Follow the court's reasoning as it works through the elements of the attempt to rescind a contract.

---

[4] Charles D. Paglee, "Contracts and Agreements in the People's Republic of China," www.qis.net/chinalaw/explan1.htm, updated March 6, 1998.

CASE 17-2 GARY W. CRUSE AND VENITA R. CRUSE v. COLDWELL BANKER/ GRABEN REAL ESTATE, INC.
SUPREME COURT OF ALABAMA
667 SO. 2D 714 (1995)

Mr. and Mrs. Cruse sued Mr. and Mrs. Harris, Coldwell Banker, and Graben Real Estate, Inc., alleging defective workmanship in the construction of a house they had bought from the Harrises and fraudulent misrepresentation and/or suppressed material facts about the condition of the house.

When the Cruses began looking for a home, they contacted Graben Real Estate, and a Graben agent took them to see the Harrises' house. Randy Harris, a building contractor, had built the house for sale, and he and his wife were occupying it at that time. Graben listed the house as "new" in its advertisements, and the agent told the Cruses it was new. She also told them it was comparable to, or even better than, other houses in the neighborhood, that it was a good buy, and that if they purchased it they could look forward to years of convenient, trouble-free living.

The Cruses signed a contract on November 11, 1992, to purchase the house from the Harrises. When they told the agent they wanted to hire an independent contractor to assess its condition, she told them it was not really necessary to do so because Randy Harris was a contractor and the house was well-built.

The Cruses signed an "Acceptance Inspection Contract," which stated that they had inspected the property or waived the right to do so, accepted it in "as-is" condition, and based their decision to purchase on their own inspection and not on any representations by the broker.

Plaintiffs took possession of the residence in mid-December 1992 and soon began noticing many defects in the structure and electrical wiring. They contacted Graben Real Estate, which sent an agent to remedy the problems. The defects continued and multiplied, so the Cruses sued. At the trial, defendants moved for summary judgment, which was granted. Plaintiffs appealed.

JUSTICE BUTTS: To establish fraudulent misrepresentations, the Cruses are required to show that Graben Real Estate made a false representation concerning a material fact and that they relied upon that representation, to their detriment. The Cruses contend that Graben Real Estate represented to them that the house was new; that, in reliance on that representation, they decided not to hire a contractor to inspect the house and discover its defects; and that reliance resulted in damage to them.

The unequivocal term "new," when applied to real estate, is not merely descriptive. It is a definite legal term that carries with it the implied warranty of habitability and prevents the realtor from invoking the protection of the doctrine of caveat emptor. Graben Real Estate marketed the house as "new," both in print and in direct response to the Cruses' queries. In so doing, Graben Real Estate made statements that went beyond the patter of sales talk and became representations of material fact. Moreover, Gary Cruse testified . . . that he relied upon this representation in failing to hire a contractor to inspect the house before he bought it.

Graben Real Estate argues that even if it did misrepresent the newness of the house, the Cruses could not have justifiably believed the misrepresentation and relied upon it to the point that they would not closely inspect the house before buying it. Graben Real Estate relies heavily on the fact that the Cruses knew that the house was being occupied by the Harrises at the time of the sale, and concludes that this alone should have proved to the Cruses that the house was not actually new. . . . We do not agree that the mere knowledge of the Harrises' prior occupancy so wholly contradicted the printed and spoken representations of Graben Real Estate that the Cruses could not, as a matter of law, have justifiably relied upon them.

Graben Real Estate also argues that, regardless of whether the house was new or was used, the Cruses cannot recover because they signed an "as-is" agreement at the time of the sale, thereby, Graben Real Estate says, accepting the condition of the house without a prior inspection. Graben Real Estate relies on Hope v. Brannan, wherein this Court held that buyers of a 58-year-old house who signed a statement accepting the house "as-is," without independently inspecting it for defects, could not maintain an action for fraud arising from the seller's statements concerning the condition of the house.

Graben Real Estate's reliance on Hope is misplaced; in Hope, the house was not new, nor was it represented to be new. A buyer's failure to inspect the premises of a 58-year-old house before signing an "as-is" agreement is hardly the equivalent of the Cruses' failure to inspect the premises of a house that their realtor had represented to be new.

The evidence establishes that Graben Real Estate misrepresented a material fact and creates a jury question as to whether the Cruses could have justifiably relied upon this misrepresentation in deciding not to closely inspect the house before buying it. The fact that the Cruses knew the house was occupied by a third party before they bought it, along with the fact that they signed an "as-is" agreement, separate from the purchase contract, for a house they claim to have regarded as new, are elements for the jury to consider.

REVERSED and REMANDED.

[continued]

CRITICAL THINKING

Several key points in the reasoning of this decision rely on personal testimony. On the basis of your life experience and any knowledge you may have accumulated through your educational career, how reliable do you think witness testimony is as a form of evidence in legal disputes? What are some of the ways that this testimonial evidence might be flawed? What are its particular strengths? In this case, do you think the testimonies are valid? Why or why not?

ETHICAL DECISION MAKING

What general values might the court be interested in protecting in this ruling? How are they similar to values upheld by other cases in this chapter? How are they different? What opposing values are less important in these rulings?

The elements of fraudulent misrepresentation become more complicated in the context of actual disagreements. Let's revisit them for more insight.

False Assertion of Fact.   For fraudulent misrepresentation to be the basis for a contract rescission, the statement of fact need not be an actual assertion. It can also be an act of concealment or nondisclosure. Concealment is the *active* hiding of the truth about a material fact, for example, removing 20,000 miles from the odometer on your car before selling it. Nondisclosure is a failure to provide pertinent information about the projected contract. The courts have until recently been hesitant to use nondisclosure as a basis for rescinding a contract because it is a passive form of misleading conduct. Under ordinary situations associated with a legal bargain, it is not the obligation of one party to bring up any and all facts he or she might possess. Each individual is, to a large extent, treated as a responsible decision maker.

However, courts will now find nondisclosure as having the same legal effect as an actual false assertion under certain conditions:

1. *A relationship of trust exists between the parties to the contract.* In this situation the relationship provides a reasonable basis for one person's expectation that the other would never act to defraud him or her.
2. *There is failure to correct assertions of fact that are no longer true.* Caroline's failure to inform Vito of the recent outbreak of rust on her "rust-free" car that Vito agreed to purchase next month is nondisclosure.
3. *A statute requires the disclosure,* such as mandatory disclosures under residential real estate sales laws.
4. *The nondisclosure involves a dangerous defect,* such as bad brakes in a car that is being sold.

Nondisclosure is especially likely to provide the basis for rescission when one party has information about a basic assumption of the deal that is unavailable to the other party. Sellers thus have a special duty to disclose because they know more about the structural makeup of the item being purchased.

? BUT WHAT IF . . .
WHAT IF THE FACTS OF THE CASE OPENER WERE DIFFERENT?

Let's say that, in the Case Opener, Knafel had Jordan sign a contract that stipulated he must make monthly payments to her for the baby they both believed was genetically theirs together. Then, after signing, Knafel discovered the baby was not in fact Jordan's but did not relay the information to him. What kind of misrepresentation occurred here?

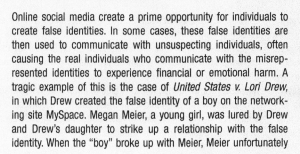

E-COMMERCE AND THE LAW

FRAUDULENT MISREPRESENTATION IN SOCIAL MEDIA

Online social media create a prime opportunity for individuals to create false identities. In some cases, these false identities are then used to communicate with unsuspecting individuals, often causing the real individuals who communicate with the misrepresented identities to experience financial or emotional harm. A tragic example of this is the case of *United States v. Lori Drew,* in which Drew created the false identity of a boy on the networking site MySpace. Megan Meier, a young girl, was lured by Drew and Drew's daughter to strike up a relationship with the false identity. When the "boy" broke up with Meier, Meier unfortunately committed suicide. The prosecution of Drew was unsuccessful. A major issue with the prosecution was that there was no federal statute against cyberbullying, and the judge did not feel comfortable relying on a breach-of-contract premise that would make this case of fraudulent misrepresentation equivalent to a case of computer hacking. As the likelihood of fraudulently misrepresenting an individual increases, misrepresentation must be addressed in such a way that all possible aspects in which fraudulent misrepresentation could occur are covered by statutes.

Source: www.wired.com/threatlevel/2009/07/drew_court/.

Intent to Deceive.   *Scienter* is present when the party making the fraudulent assertion believed it was false or had no regard for whether it was true or false. *Intent to deceive* occurs when the party making the false statement claims to have or implies having personal knowledge of its accuracy. Any resulting assent is not legal because the injured party was not allowed to join the mind of the deceiving party. The party with scienter or intent to deceive wanted the contract to be fulfilled on the basis of a falsehood.

Justifiable Reliance on the False Assertion.   What responsibilities does the injured party have in a case of false assertion? As we've said, the injured party has no justifiable claim of fraud after relying on assertions whose falsity should have been obvious. Anyone who pays for a house in reliance on the claim that it was "built before the founding of our country" cannot later rescind the contract on grounds of fraudulent misrepresentation.

Nor can parties successfully claim they justifiably relied on a false assertion when its falsity would have been clear to anyone who inspected the item. However, the duty to inspect is declining in modern contract law, and courts are giving increasing responsibility to the person who made the erroneous assertion.

As you might infer from the foregoing discussion, the process of determining whether intentional misrepresentation has occurred can be an extremely difficult task. This process can become even more complex when the defendant believes that the other party was never misled in the first place. Such was the case when several individuals involved in the movie *Borat* filed suit against Sacha Baron Cohen and Twentieth Century Fox for fraudulent and negligent misrepresentation as well as other various claims. The plaintiffs in the case were lawyers who represented the locals of the Romanian village of Glod, where the opening scenes of the movie were filmed. In their suit, the villagers alleged that Cohen and Twentieth Century Fox convinced them that they were taking part in a documentary film about poverty in Romania, not a blockbuster movie set in Kazakhstan. Further, the lawsuit asserted that Cohen and Twentieth Century Fox "used their superior educational background, stature, influence and economic position" to exploit the villagers and that the company also encouraged villagers to sign documents that they did not understand and that had not been fully explained.

Twentieth Century Fox defended its film and claimed that the villagers of Glod knew they were participating in a movie and not a documentary. The company further defended its position by stating that the villagers were paid more than the average going wage for movie extras. Eventually, the lawsuit was thrown out by a U.S district court judge who stated that the allegations against Sacha Baron Cohen and Twentieth Century Fox needed to be more specific. The lawyers of the Glod villagers said that they intended to file a new suit in the future.[5]

[5] http://news.bbc.co.uk/2/hi/europe/7686885.stm; and http://74.125.113.132/search?q=cache:jQ0M5aR16wUJ:www.courthouse-news.com/onpoint/borat_NY.pdf+Twentieth+century+fox+v+michael+witti+and+ed+fagan&cd=1&hl=en&ct=clnk&gl=us.

COMPARING THE LAW OF OTHER COUNTRIES

CONSUMER CONTRACTS LAW IN JAPAN

In 1997, after studying the application of civil law in the country, the Japanese Social Policy Council, an advisory body to the prime minister, recognized that the consumer environment was growing more diversified and that a significant gap existed between consumers and businesses in their access to information and knowledge and their negotiating power. Because it cannot honestly be said that consumers and businesses are equal, as contracting parties are presumed to be under the country's Civil Code, the council developed a special Consumer Contracts Law. This legislation is considered to place consumers and businesses on a more equal footing in transactions.

Under the Consumer Contracts Law, a consumer may cancel the contract whenever a business (1) fails to provide information about the contents of the contract, (2) fails to provide information necessary for the consumer to decide to enter into the contract, or (3) makes misrepresentations. In many such cases, the consumer would not have been entitled to relief under the Civil Code because of its strict requirements for the application of fraud.

To see how certain aspects of marketing relate to misrepresentation, please see the **Connecting to the Core** activity on the text website at www.mhhe.com/kubasek3e.

Before we conclude this section about misrepresentation, consider what would have happened if Karla Knafel, in the opening scenario, had told Jordan there was a strong probability that the child was his. Would Jordan have been able to claim that their contract lacked assent because of Knafel's misrepresentation?

Legal Principle: **The effect of both a negligent misrepresentation and a fraudulent misrepresentation is that the victim can either rescind the contract or keep the contract and sue for damages, whereas if the mistake is innocent, the victim can seek only rescission.**

Undue Influence

LO4

What are the elements of undue influence?

When legal assent is present, the courts assume both parties have made their own choices based on complete freedom to accept or reject the terms of the bargain. However, many factors can work to make our choices anything but free. Undue influence refers to those special relationships in which one person takes advantage of a dominant position in a relationship to unfairly persuade the other and interfere with that person's ability to make his or her own decision. When people bargain with their attorney, doctor, guardian, relative, or anyone else in a relationship that includes a high degree of trust, they are susceptible to being persuaded by unusual pressures unique to that relationship. Consequently, the assent that results may not be legal consent. The courts may see the undue influence of the relationship as interfering with the free choice required for an enforceable contract. Whatever contracts result from undue influence are voidable.

Are all contracts in which undue influence might arise likely to be rescinded? Not necessarily. The courts look to the mental condition of the person relying on the guidance of the dominant person. Courts look to the extent to which the dominant person used the persuasive powers of his or her dominance to secure assent.

Factors that enter into the finding of undue influence are the following:

1. Was the dominant party rushing the other party to consent?
2. Did the dominant party gain undue enrichment from the agreement?
3. Was the nondominant party isolated from other advisers at the time of the agreement?
4. Is the contract unreasonable because it overwhelmingly benefits the dominant party?

The more of these factors present, the more likely a court is to rescind the contract on grounds of undue influence. The Case Nugget on the next page provides an illustration of undue influence.

CASE NUGGET

A CASE OF UNDUE INFLUENCE

**Evan Rothberg v. Walt Disney Pictures
1999 U.S. App. 1472**

Robert Jahn was a senior executive at Walt Disney Pictures until he died of complications from AIDS. Within days before his death, a Disney official visited him at the hospital and convinced him to sign a release that waived his rights to approximately $2 million in employee benefits, including life insurance, stock options, bonuses, and deferred compensation. After his death, his estate sued to recover the benefits waived in the release. Disney received a motion for summary judgment, and the plaintiff appealed. In reversing the motion for summary judgment, the court ruled that the question of

whether the release had been procured by undue influence was a question for a jury. The court pointed out that undue influence requires (1) undue susceptibility on the part of the weaker party and (2) application of excessive pressure by the stronger party. In this case, the first fact was self-evident. The defendant was in the hospital and was fearful that Disney would expose information that would destroy his reputation. Regarding the second element, however, the court noted that in most undue-influence cases, and this case was no exception, direct evidence is rarely obtainable and thus the jury must decide the issue on the basis of inferences drawn from all the facts and circumstances. Thus, the court said that summary judgment was improper.

Legal Principle: **The essential element of undue influence is the existence of a dominant-subservient relationship, so if you are going to enter into a contract with someone with whom you have such a relationship, to ensure that the agreement will be enforced in the future, make sure that the person in the subservient position has independent advice before entering into the contract.**

BUT WHAT IF . . .
WHAT IF THE FACTS OF THE CASE OPENER WERE DIFFERENT?

Let's say that, in the Case Opener, Jordan was married at the time of his affair with Knafel and he did not want his wife or the public to know about the affair or the baby. Furthermore, let's say that Knafel threatened to make the information public (among other information about Jordan) if he did not sign her contract. Would such a scenario constitute undue influence?

Duress

Duress is a much more visible and active interference with free will than is undue influence. Duress occurs when one party is forced into the agreement by the wrongful act of another.

The wrongful act may come in various forms. Any of the following would trigger a successful request for rescission on grounds of duress:

- One party threatens physical harm or extortion to gain consent to a contract.
- One party threatens to file a criminal lawsuit unless consent is given to the terms of the contract. (Threats to bring civil cases against a party to a lawsuit do not constitute duress unless the suit is frivolous.)
- One party threatens the other's economic interests (this is known as *economic duress*). For instance, a person refuses to perform according to a contract unless the other person either signs another contract with the one making the threat or pays that person a higher price than specified in the original agreement.

L05

What are the elements of duress?

COMPARING THE LAW OF OTHER COUNTRIES

DURESS IN AUSTRALIA

Australia recognizes a special category called *duress of goods*, which occurs whenever one party makes an illegitimate threat to hold goods unless another party makes payment or enters into an agreement. Note that this is different from a situation in which someone legitimately holds goods when money is owed on them or the goods have been used as security for a loan.

Australia also recognizes economic duress, which is the unacceptable use of economic power to leave someone with no practical alternative but to submit to the accompanying demand.

To prove economic duress, a plaintiff must establish that (1) pressure was used to procure his or her assent to an agreement

or to the payment of money, (2) the pressure was illegitimate in the circumstance, (3) the pressure in fact contributed to the person's assenting to the transaction, and (4) the person's assent to the transaction was reasonable in the circumstances.

Just as with economic duress in the United States, it is often unclear when pressure is illegitimate. A threat to do something unlawful is almost always undue pressure. A threat to use the civil legal process is usually considered lawful, unless the contemplated legal action would clearly be an abuse of process. "Driving a hard bargain" or refusing to do any more business with someone in the future is generally not regarded as economic duress.

The injured party makes the case for duress by demonstrating that the threat left no reasonable alternatives and that the free will necessary for legal consent was removed by the specifics of the threat.

Legal Principle: **When one party is forced to enter into a contract by the wrongful threat of another, the contract is voidable by the innocent party due to duress.**

BUT WHAT IF . . .

In 2009, a humane society officer named William Sandstrom confiscated Miles Thomas's dog due to certain violations of the state's animal cruelty laws. Thomas signed a release form for the humane society to take ownership of the dog. Later, Thomas claimed the release form was unenforceable because he was under duress when he signed it. Specifically, he claimed he was under duress at the time because he was sad about his dog. Does Thomas's account of his signing the release form actually fulfill the requirements of duress? Is the release form unenforceable?

Unconscionability

L06

What are the elements of unconscionability?

A final way to question the appropriateness of consent arises when one of the parties has so much more bargaining power than the other that he or she dictates the terms of the agreement. Such an agreement can be rescinded on grounds of unconscionability (as discussed in Chapter 4). The disproportionate amount of power possessed by one party to the contract has made a mockery of the idea of free will, a necessity for legal consent. The resulting contract is called an adhesion contract.

Although unconscionability has traditionally been limited to the sale of goods under the Uniform Commercial Code, many courts have not followed that tradition. When they see contracts written by one party and presented to the other with the threat to "take it or leave it," they sometimes extend the idea of unconscionability beyond the sale of goods.

Follow the judge's reasoning in Case 17-3 to review the type of reasoning that makes up a claim for unconscionability.

CASE 17-3   **ORVILLE ARNOLD AND MAXINE ARNOLD, PLAINTIFFS v. UNITED COMPANIES LENDING CORPORATION, A CORPORATION, AND MICHAEL T. SEARLS, AN INDIVIDUAL, DEFENDANTS**
SUPREME COURT OF APPEALS OF WEST VIRGINIA
1998 WL 8651015

On September 17, 1996, Michael Searls came to the residence of Orville and Maxine Arnold, an elderly couple, and offered to arrange a loan for them, acting as a loan broker. He procured a loan for them. From the loan proceeds, a mortgage broker fee of $940.00 was paid to Searls and/or Accent Financial Services, with which Searls was affiliated.

At the loan closing, United Lending had the benefit of legal counsel, while the Arnolds apparently did not. During the course of the transaction, the Arnolds were presented with more than twenty-five documents to sign. Among these were a promissory note, reflecting a principal sum of $19,300.00 and a yearly interest rate of 12.990%; a Deed of Trust, giving United Lending a security interest in the Arnolds' real estate; and a two-page form labeled "Acknowledgment and Agreement to Mediate or Arbitrate," which stated that all legal controversies arising from the loan would be resolved through nonappealable, confidential arbitration, and that all damages would be direct damages, with no punitive damages available. However, this agreement not to arbitrate did not limit the lender's right to pursue legal actions in a court of law relating to collection of the loan.

On July 10, 1997, the Arnolds filed suit against United Lending and Searls, seeking a declaratory judgment adjudging the arbitration agreement to be void and unenforceable. On August 11, 1997, United Lending moved to dismiss the entire action on the basis of the compulsory arbitration agreement. The circuit court certified three questions to the state supreme court.

JUSTICE McCUSKEY: We reformulate the question as follows: Whether an arbitration agreement entered into as part of a consumer loan transaction containing a substantial waiver of the consumer's rights, including access to the courts, while preserving for all practical purposes the lender's right to a judicial forum, is void as a matter of law.

The drafters of the Uniform Consumer Credit Code explained that the [basic test] of unconscionability is whether . . . the conduct involved is, or the contract or clauses involved are, so one-sided as to be unconscionable under the circumstances existing at the time the conduct occurs or is threatened or at the time of the making of the contract. . . . [T]his Court stated:

["W]here a party alleges that the arbitration provision was unconscionable, or was thrust upon

him because he was unwary and taken advantage of, or that the contract was one of adhesion, the question of whether an arbitration provision was bargained for and valid is a matter of law for the court to determine by reference to the entire contract. . . ." A determination of unconscionability must focus on the relative positions of the parties, the adequacy of the bargaining position, the meaningful alternatives available to the plaintiff, and "the existence of unfair terms in the contract."

Applying the rule . . . leads us to the inescapable conclusion that the arbitration agreement between the Arnolds and United Lending is "void for unconscionability" as a matter of law. . . . The relative positions of the parties, a national corporate lender on one side and elderly, unsophisticated consumers on the other, were "grossly unequal." In addition, there is no evidence that the loan broker made any other loan option available to the Arnolds. In fact, the record does not indicate that the Arnolds were seeking a loan, but rather were solicited by defendant Searls. Thus, the element of "a comparable, meaningful alternative" to the loan from United Lending is lacking. Because the Arnolds had no meaningful alternative to obtaining the loan from United Lending, and also did not have the benefit of legal counsel during the transaction, their bargaining position was clearly inadequate when compared to that of United Lending.

Given the nature of this arbitration agreement, combined with the great disparity in bargaining power, one can safely infer that the terms were not bargained for and that allowing such a one-sided agreement to stand would unfairly defeat the Arnolds' legitimate expectations.

Finally, the terms of the agreement are "unreasonably favorable" to United Lending. United Lending's acts or omissions could seriously damage the Arnolds, yet the Arnolds' only recourse would be to submit the matter to binding arbitration. At the same time, United Lending's access to the courts is wholly preserved in every conceivable situation where United Lending would want to secure judicial relief against the Arnolds. The wholesale waiver of the Arnolds' rights together with the complete preservation of United Lending's rights "is inherently inequitable and unconscionable because in a way it nullifies all the other provisions of the contract."

Judgment in favor of Plaintiffs.

[continued]

CRITICAL THINKING

This case highlights the importance of language in the legal system. Phrases quoted from the law are subject to significant judicial discretion, which allows rulings like this to be possible. Using the contextual clues found in the information given, choose two descriptions in quotes and write your idea of how the judge must be defining the relevant phrase. Then come up with some other ways these phrases could have been defined. Would the use of your alternatives significantly affect the reasonableness of the conclusion?

ETHICAL DECISION MAKING

Does this case lend itself very well to considerations of ethicality? What sort of theoretical approach do you see the court taking with this ruling?

On the basis of other decisions you have encountered in this book, what do you think is probably the most common ethical framework U.S. courts use in guiding their rulings? How well does this case fit with larger trends? Support your answer.

CASE OPENER WRAP-UP

A Disagreement over an Agreement

The trial court agreed with Michael Jordan's argument regarding a mutual mistake or fraudulent misrepresentation in the contract. Knafel appealed, and the court affirmed the lower court's decision. The court held that Knafel's representation to Jordan that he was the father met the requirements of being (1) a material fact, (2) made for the purpose of inducing Jordan to act, (3) that either was known by Knafel to be false or was not actually believed by her on reasonable grounds to be true, but Jordan reasonably believed it to be true, and (4) that was relied on by Jordan to his own detriment. Thus, the appellate court found that Knafel's representation that Jordan *was* the father constituted fraud. The agreement can be rescinded because Jordan would not have entered into the agreement but for the fraudulent representation made by Knafel. Even if Knafel did not act fraudulently, at the time the agreement was created both parties believed that the child was Jordan's. After the paternity tests revealed that the baby was *not* Jordan's, the agreement could still be rescinded based on a mutual mistake of fact.

KEY TERMS

adhesion contract   398
concealment   394
duress   397
fraudulent
   misrepresentation   392
innocent
   misrepresentation   391

intentional
   misrepresentation   392
legal assent   385
misrepresentation   390
mistake
   of fact   386
mutual   386

negligent
   misrepresentation   391
nondisclosure   394
rescinded   385
scienter   391
unconscionability   398
undue influence   396

unilateral   386
voidable   385

SUMMARY OF KEY TOPICS

If assent is not genuine, or legal, a contract may be voidable.

The Importance of Legal Assent

Mistakes are erroneous beliefs about the material facts of a contract at the time the agreement is made. They may be either unilateral or mutual. Only under certain rare conditions are unilateral mistakes a basis for rescinding a contract. However, if both parties to a contract are mistaken about a material fact, either can opt to rescind it. The agreement was not based on a meeting of the minds, a basic criterion for a legal assent.

Mistake

Misrepresentation is an intentional untruthful assertion by one of the parties about a material fact. An innocent misrepresentation occurs when the party making the false assertion believes it to be true. The misled party may then rescind the contract. When a misrepresentation is fraudulent, any assent is gained by deceit and the courts permit rescission. In addition to requiring a false assertion and intent to deceive, fraudulent misrepresentation also requires the innocent party's justifiable reliance on the assertion.

Misrepresentation

Undue influence is the persuasive efforts of a dominant party who uses a special relationship with another party to interfere with the other's free choice of the terms of a contract. Any relationship in which one party has an unusual degree of trust in the other can trigger concern about undue influence.

Undue Influence

Duress occurs when one party threatens the other with a wrongful act unless assent is given. Such assent is not legal assent because coercion interferes with the party's free will. For the courts to rescind the agreement, the injured party must demonstrate that the duress left no reasonable alternatives to agreeing to the contract.

Duress

Unconscionability may be a basis for avoiding a contract if one party has so much relative bargaining power that he or she in effect dictates the terms. The resulting agreement is an adhesion contract.

Unconscionability

POINT / COUNTERPOINT

Are Payday Loans, and the Accompanying Interests Rates, Unconscionable?	
YES	**NO**
The consumers who take out payday loans are often desperate and lack other methods of obtaining a loan. For these consumers, getting a loan from a bank is impossible due to their poor credit ratings or lack of necessary collateral. The companies that offer these consumers payday loans are preying on a vulnerable population by exploiting their lack of bargaining power. Payday loans are unconscionable.	The companies that supply payday loans offer short-term solutions to difficult financial situations. For consumers who find themselves strapped and in dire need of cash, payday loans provide a means to repair a broken-down car, pay the rent, or pay other accumulating bills. Although the interest rates are high, these loans do not violate any laws and the consumers' loan agreements are not unconscionable.
Regardless of the amount of advertising a lender may provide, consumers who find themselves in need of payday loans lack the necessary bargaining power to make these loans conscionable. For a loan to be unconscionable, one of the parties has to have so much more bargaining power than the other that he or she dictates the terms of the agreement; in payday loans it is the lender that has the power to dictate the terms. Desperate consumers often feel that they are left with no choice but accepting the terms offered by the payday lenders.	When consumers approach a payday lender for a loan, they are greeted by a plethora of signs indicating relevant interest rates. Before signing the loan documents, the consumer is given numerous documents containing the interest rates. Additionally, many states require that the lender verbally state the interest rates to consumers. These consumers have numerous opportunities to walk away from the lender if they are unwilling to accept the high interest rates.

Additionally, payday loans exploit the financial hardships experienced by consumers and often result in increased hardship. A typical bank loan is usually capped at an APR of 35 percent; payday loans average an APR of 530 percent. The consumers' ability to pay back the loans is often limited by the individuals' impoverished situation, and, as a result, these loans will often roll over, making it impossible for consumers to recover. As a result of the consumers' limited bargaining power, payday loans trap disadvantaged populations in high–interest rate loans they cannot afford. Thus, payday loans are *inherently unconscionable*.

In response to those who argue that these loans are unconscionable, supporters argue that consumers still have the free will to choose whether or not to enter into the loan agreement. These loans do not involve any coercion or enticing.

Furthermore, the high interest rates tied to payday loans are the reason these lenders are able to make small (often between $100 and $500) loans to otherwise risky consumers. Without the ability to raise interest rates, these companies would not be able to offset their own risk in providing the loans. Therefore, these loans are *not unconscionable*.

QUESTIONS & PROBLEMS

1. Explain the difference between a unilateral mistake and a mutual mistake.

2. Explain when a unilateral mistake can lead to a contract's being voidable.

3. Distinguish innocent misrepresentation from fraudulent misrepresentation.

4. Explain how nondisclosure can be treated as misrepresentation.

5. Explain the primary differences between duress and undue influence.

6. After a collision involving Alston and Alexander, Alston was diagnosed with chest problems and was prescribed a number of medications. During the time of her treatment and release on the day of the accident, she did not make note of any pain in her neck or back. Instead, she argued that she developed neck and back pain between one and two days after her original treatment. Later, Alston signed a release for her injury compensation check, which is standard insurer procedure. However, Alston later testified that she did not read the insurance release and her compensatory check and that the check from the insurance company did not contain compensation for her injuries that occurred later. Alston sued on the grounds of mutual mistake. Specifically, the check did not make light of all of her injuries, and she did not read the check release. Thus, she claimed the release was invalidated. The superior court upheld the validity of a general release signed by Alston and granted summary judgment in Alexander's favor on that basis. Alston appealed. With whom do you think the state's supreme court agreed and why? [*Alston v. Alexander,* Del. Sup. Ct. LEXIS 384 (2012).]

7. Audrey Vokes was a 51-year-old widow who wanted to become an "accomplished dancer." She was invited to attend a "dance party" at J. P. Davenports' School of Dancing, an Arthur Murray franchise. She subsequently signed up for dance classes, at which she received elaborate praise. Her instructor initially sold her eight half-hour dance lessons for $14.50 each, to be used one each month. Eventually, after being continually told that she had excellent potential and that she was developing into a beautiful dancer—when, in fact, she was not developing her dance ability and had no aptitude for dance—she ended up purchasing a total of 2,302 hours' worth of dance lessons for a total of $31,090.45. When it finally became clear to Vokes that she was not developing her dance skills, in part because she had trouble even hearing the musical beat, she sued Arthur Murray. What would be the basis of her argument? Her case was initially dismissed by the trial court. What do you think the result of her appeal was? [*Okes v. Arthur Murray,* 212 So. 2d 906 (1968).]

8. In 1998, the governor of New York, George Pataki, formulated a $185 million plan to update old Amtrak trains. The purpose of the project was to make the old trains faster than the more current Amtrak trains. Such a reconstruction would allow for a high-speed rail system between Albany and New York City. Unfortunately, Amtrak produced only one train, and although millions of dollars were poured into the company to fund the project, auditing showed that the company showed little spending on the trains. Problems stemmed in part from the lack of engineering expertise of the Steel Company that was picked to work on the

trains. Also, the state's Department of Transportation was not experienced in overseeing projects of this type, so little oversight was given to Amtrak. Additionally, unforeseen problems arose such as air-conditioning malfunctions and the removal of asbestos from train cabins. After the plan seemed as though it would never be successful and Amtrak was extremely low on money due to normal operations, the company tried to settle with the state to escape the project. However, the state filed a lawsuit against Amtrak. Amtrak's defense was that both parties made a unilateral mistake because neither party foresaw the problems or extra costs associated with the project that made it unrealistic. How do you think the court decided? [*New York v. Amtrak,* 2007 U.S. Dist. LEXIS 13045 (N.D.N.Y, Feb. 23, 2007).]

9. The Winklers were interested in purchasing a home in the Valleyview Farms housing development. They contacted the developer, Galehouse, and selected a lot that cost $57,000. They asked the developer to show them plans for houses for which the construction costs would range from $180,000 to $190,000, indicating this was the price they would be willing to spend for construction only and wasn't to include the lot price. The developer gave them several books and plans to look at.

After the Winklers had several conversations with Galehouse, the developer drafted plans for a 2,261-square-foot house and gave the Winklers a quote of $198,000 for construction. The lot price was not included. After several months of adding options and upgrades to the plan, the cost rose to $242,000, excluding the lot. The parties then engaged in a couple of weeks of negotiations regarding the price of the construction and lot. Eventually they reached a compromise price of $291,000 ($243,000 for the construction and $48,000 for the lot).

Galehouse prepared a written contract to reflect the parties' agreement, but the developer forgot to include the lot price. The Winklers paid Galehouse $48,000, the lot price, as a deposit on the contract. When the construction was completed, and the Winklers were finalizing their loan from the bank, the parties discovered the drafting error. Galehouse sued to have the contract reformed to reflect the agreed-on price. Should the contract be reformed? Why or why not? [*Galehouse v. Winkler,* 1998 WL 312527.]

10. Vincent Concepcion sued AT&T mobile in 2006, claiming that the company had deceptively advertised a free phone with a wireless plan. After the suit evolved into a class action suit, the company claimed that in accordance with their contracts, the plaintiffs must settle through individual arbitration processes. Yet the district court ruled that California law banned parties from creating contracts that excused them from an infraction based on certain clauses—specifically, clauses like the AT&T clause disallowing class action suits although the damages to the individual are small and not worth the time or money required to engage in an individual arbitration process. Thus, the district court refused to dismiss the suit. The company then appealed to the Ninth Circuit Court of Appeals and finally the Supreme Court, arguing that the Federal Arbitration Act should trump state law. However, unconscionability doctrines and substantial consumer protection laws are created under state law. Thus, the justices questioned, "Are we going to tell the State of California what it has to consider unconscionable?" How do you think the justices decided? [*AT&T Mobility LLC v. Concepcion,* 2011 U.S. LEXIS 3367.]

Looking for more review materials?

The Online Learning Center at **www.mhhe.com/kubasek3e** contains this chapter's "Assignment on the Internet" and also a list of URLs for more information, entitled "On the Internet." Find both of them in the Student Center portion of the OLC, along with quizzes and other helpful materials.

CONTRACTS   PART 2

CHAPTER

18 Contracts in Writing

LEARNING OBJECTIVES

After reading this chapter, you will be able to answer the following questions:

1   What is the purpose of the statute of frauds?

2   Which kinds of contracts require a writing to satisfy the statute of frauds?

3   What must a writing contain to be sufficient to satisfy the statute of frauds?

4   What is the purpose of the parol evidence rule?

CASE OPENER

Admissibility of an Oral Contract in Court

Monroe Bradstad borrowed $100,000 from his aunt, Jeanne Garland, to purchase farmland. Both parties subsequently signed a promissory note stipulating that interest would be accrued prior to or on January 1, 1992. After that, payments and interest would be made on January 1 of each following year, with the final balance due on January 1, 2010. The land was used as security for the note; thus Branstad executed a mortgage. Branstad paid a total of $33,000 from 1993 to 1997. In 1998, Branstad and Garland had a falling out, and Garland served Branstad with a notice to pay $43,998 in past-due interest. However, Branstad and his wife claimed that they had made a subsequent oral agreement with Garland that they would manage and spend money on her other properties in lieu of paying interest. Garland argued that there was no oral agreement and that any oral evidence would be inadmissible in court due to the parol evidence rule. Branstad argued that the oral agreement was made after the written contract was created, not before or during, and thus the oral contract was a separate contract and not subject to the parol evidence rule.

1. Does it matter when the oral contract was made in relation to when the written contract was created?
2. Why might it be ethically important for the court to hear the subsequent oral agreement made between Branstad and Garland?

The Wrap-Up at the end of the chapter will answer these questions.

Written contracts provide certain advantages oral contracts lack. Disputes about the specifics of the terms in an oral contract are easier to settle when the terms are solidified in writing. The moment of writing also allows both parties to reconsider their terms and ensure that they are advocating what they desire in the contract. In general, written contracts smooth the conduct of business transactions. Some contracts thus require a writing.

This idea actually comes from an English law, the Act for the Prevention of Frauds and Perjuries passed by Parliament in 1677. To correct a problem in the common law, the act required that specific types of contracts be in writing and be signed by both parties to ensure enforceability.

Although the law frequently references the *statute of frauds,* the term is somewhat misleading. There is no federal legislation entitled "Statute of Frauds." Rather, the statute exists as legislation at the state level. In fact, almost every state has created its own version of the 1677 English act, adopting it in total or in part. The exceptions are Louisiana, which has no such legislation, and New Mexico and Maryland, which follow statutes of frauds created by judicial decision and not the legislature. Interestingly enough, the English have repealed almost all their requirements for writing, while U.S. states and courts are still expanding the requirements for what falls within the statute of frauds.

Before entering into a contract one needs to know whether its subject matter requires a writing.

In addition to the statute's not being a unitary government act, the name "statute of frauds" is misleading in another way. It does not relate to fraudulent contracts, nor does it address the issue of illegal contracts. Rather, it addresses the enforceability of contracts that fail to meet the requirements set forth in it. Furthermore, the statute serves to protect promisors from poorly considered oral contracts by requiring that certain contracts be in writing.

This chapter addresses some commonalities of the statutes of frauds of different states; in it, we refer to the "statute of frauds" as if it were a unitary law. We examine which contracts need to be in writing, as well as exceptions to the rule. Then we look at the parol evidence rule, which discusses which types of oral evidence are admissible and when, as related to contracts within the scope of the statute of frauds.

Statute of Frauds

LO1

What is the purpose of the statute of frauds?

The **statute of frauds** has three main purposes. First, it attempts to ease contractual negotiations by requiring sufficiently reliable evidence to prove the existence and specific terms of a contract. When a contract is deemed important enough that being in writing is required under the statute of frauds, the statute specifies what is considered reliable evidence.

The second main purpose of the statute of frauds is to prevent unreliable oral evidence from interfering with a contractual relationship. By requiring that a contract be in writing, the statute precludes the admittance of oral evidence denying the existence of a contract or claiming additional terms that would substantially alter the contract from its agreed-on written form. This chapter further discusses the admissibility or denial of oral evidence later, in the section on the parol evidence rule.

The third main purpose of the statute of frauds is to prevent parties from entering into contracts with which they do not agree. That is, it provides some degree of cautionary protection for the parties, who must carefully consider the terms, agree to them, write them out, and finally sign the contract. The law assumes that these steps will allow time for careful consideration. Thus, the statute works to prevent hasty, improperly considered contracts.

Contracts Falling within the Statute of Frauds

L02

Which kinds of contracts require a writing to satisfy the statute of frauds?

As previously mentioned, only specific types of contracts are within the scope of the statute of frauds and thus required to be evidenced by a writing. They are (1) contracts whose terms prevent possible performance within one year, (2) promises made in consideration of marriage, (3) contracts for one party to pay the debt of another if the initial party fails to pay, and (4) contracts related to an interest in land. Although required to be in writing under the Uniform Commercial Code (UCC), and not the statute of frauds, a related fifth category is contracts for the sale of goods totaling more than $500.[1]

CONTRACTS WHOSE TERMS PREVENT POSSIBLE PERFORMANCE WITHIN ONE YEAR

Contracts whose performance, based on the terms of the contract, could not possibly occur within one year fall within the statute of frauds and therefore must be in writing.[2] Note that the one-year period begins the day after the contract is created, *not* when it is scheduled to begin.

For example, Roberto enters into a contract with Elise to work for her for one year starting October 1. If the contract is created on the preceding September 15, it cannot be completed in one year from September 16; therefore, it must be in writing. However, if the contract is scheduled to start immediately, it *can* be completed in one year and need not be in writing because it is not within the statute of frauds.

It's technically possible that you could finish this deal within a year, so let's just shake on it.

stus.com

The test for compliance with the one-year rule does not consider the likelihood of completing the contract within one year. Rather, it considers the *possibility* of completing the contract in one year. While Roberto and Elise's contract is within the statute because, according to its terms, it cannot be performed within one year, a contract for lifetime employment does not need to be in writing.

If Roberto contracts with Elise for lifetime employment, they do not have to write and sign the agreement because it is possible for the contract to be completed within one year: Robert *could* die after two days of work. Moreover, if oral, their contract would be enforceable, because it is not within the statute of frauds. The possibility that a contract's terms could be performed within one year removes the contract from the statute's written requirements.

[1] UCC § 2-201.

[2] Restatement (Second) of Contracts, sec. 130.

AURIGEMMA V. NEW CASTLE CARE, LLC

2006 Del. Super. LEXIS 337, June 12, 2006

Dr. Ralph M. Aurigemma filed suit against New Castle Care, LLC, alleging breach of an oral contract. New Castle Care operated the Arbors Rehabilitation Center, the facility where Aurigemma worked. Aurigemma claimed that after the medical director for the Arbors unexpectedly died, he and many other doctors expressed an interest in filling the newly vacant position. Aurigemma stated that individuals from New Castle Care made him interim medical director and, on September 4, 2003, created an oral contract under which he agreed to serve as permanent medical director from October 1, 2003, until October 1, 2004.

New Castle Care claimed that it made no such oral contract with Aurigemma and stated that even if it had, Aurigemma's oral contract would not be enforceable because the terms of the contract, which was created on September 4, 2003, and intended to go until October 1, 2004, could not possibly be completed within a year. Therefore, New Castle Care claimed that Aurigemma's alleged oral contract fell within the statue of frauds and thus required a writing to be enforceable. Additionally, New Castle Care claimed it had been clear that the company had not intended to have

Aurigemma act as permanent medical director, and it cited a written contract it had created with another doctor on September 15, 2003, as proof that no oral contract existed.

Aurigemma countered by saying that because he began to assume the duties of medical director, he had already partially performed the terms of the contract. Thus, because partial performance sometimes creates an exception to the statue of frauds, Aurigemma argued that the oral contract did not need to be in writing.

On June 15, 2006, New Castle Care filed a motion for summary judgment; shortly after, a Delaware superior court granted summary judgment in favor of the company on both counts. In conclusion, the court stated that New Castle Care was correct in its argument. Because the terms of the oral contract were for a time period of more than a year, the oral contract would have had to have been in writing in order to have been valid. The court also pointed out that in Delaware the partial-performance exception to the statute of frauds does not apply to oral contracts incapable of being performed within a year. Therefore, Aurigemma's alleged oral contract was not included in the partial-performance exception to the statute of frauds and was accordingly unenforceable.

Similarly, contracts for complex construction projects need not be in writing because, theoretically, they can be completed within one year if a sufficiently large crew works around the clock every day, even if the scenario is highly unlikely.

Legal Principle: **If a contract can possibly be performed within a year, even if such performance is highly unlikely, then the contract does not need a writing to be enforceable.**

BUT WHAT IF . . .

WHAT IF THE FACTS OF THE CASE OPENER WERE DIFFERENT?

Let's say, in the Case Opener, that the promissory note was issued when Branstad had purchased a tractor for a price of $475 from Garland and both parties agreed on April 15, 2012, that Branstad would pay Garland back in full on or before March 30, 2013. Would such an agreement require a writing according to the statute of frauds?

The above Case Nugget illustrates how important the facts are when ascertaining whether a contract cannot be performed within a year.

PROMISES MADE IN CONSIDERATION OF MARRIAGE

Agreements regarding marriage in which one party is gaining something other than a return on his or her promise to marry are within the statute of frauds and must be in writing.[3] In other words, when one party promises something to the other as part of an offer of marriage, the contract must be in writing to be enforceable.

[3] Ibid., sec. 124.

For example, Ed and Jeanie want to get married. Ed promises Jeanie he will buy her a new car every other year if she will marry him. To be enforceable, Ed and Jeanie's agreement must be in writing because Jeanie stands to benefit, by way of new cars, if she marries Ed.

Mutual promises to marry do not fall within the statute of frauds. If Ed and Jeanie promise each other they will get married, this agreement does not need to be in writing because neither party is gaining anything other than a return on his or her promise to marry; thus the agreement does not fall within the statute.

While mutual promises to marry do not fall within the statute of frauds, prenuptial agreements do. A **prenuptial agreement** is an agreement two parties enter into before marriage that clearly states the ownership rights each party enjoys in the other party's property. For these agreements, writing is required, although not sufficient, to establish enforceability. Furthermore, although consideration is *not* legally required, courts tend to privilege prenuptial agreements that include it. Consideration offers evidence that both parties understand and agree to all the terms of the agreement and that the agreement is not biased in favor of one party.

Legal Principle: **Contracts in which one party promises something in exchange for another's promise to marry must have a writing to be enforceable, but mutual promises to marry do not require a writing.**

CONTRACTS FOR ONE PARTY TO PAY THE DEBT OF ANOTHER IF THE INITIAL PARTY FAILS TO PAY

The contracts within the statute of frauds that concern promises to pay a debt are of a very limited kind. Known as *secondary obligations,* they are also called *secondary promises, collateral promises,* or *suretyship promises.* A secondary obligation occurs when a party outside a primary agreement promises to fulfill one of the original party's (primary debtor's) obligations if the original party fails to fulfill it. For example, Helen enters into a contract with Tomas to sell him her car. Subsequently, Rina agrees to pay Tomas's debt if he fails to pay Helen the money he owes her. To be enforceable, Rina's promise needs to be in writing because it is a secondary obligation and therefore falls within the statute.

The distinction between primary and secondary obligations determines when the statute requires a written agreement. *Primary obligations* are debts incurred in an initial contract. Using our car-sale example, the primary obligation is Tomas's promise to pay Helen for the car. Primary obligations are not within the statute of frauds and, therefore, need not be in writing to be enforceable. Secondary obligations, as we've seen, are within the statute and need to be in writing.

A specific instance of a secondary obligation involves the administrator or executor of an estate. Administrators and executors of estates are responsible for paying off the debts of an estate and then dividing the remaining assets appropriately among the heirs. While an agreement to pay the estate's debts with these funds need not be in writing, promises the administrator or executor makes to do so personally are within the statute of frauds and must be in writing. Because the administrator or executor is promising to pay with his or her own money, and not the estate's, the promise must be in writing to be enforceable; the administrator or executor has assumed a secondary obligation.

There is an exception under which a secondary obligation need *not* be in writing: the *main-purpose rule.* If the main purpose for incurring a secondary obligation is to obtain a personal benefit, the promise does not fall within the statute and does not have to be in writing.[4] The assumption is that a party attempting to achieve a personal benefit will not

---

[4] Ibid., sec. 116.

back out of the promise, therefore eliminating the need of a written record of the promise. The court's job is to use the context surrounding the agreement to determine the third party's main purpose for entering the agreement, which will determine whether a writing is required for the agreement to be enforceable.

Legal Principle: **Primary obligations do not require a writing, but secondary obligations do unless the main reason a person makes a secondary promise is to obtain a personal benefit.**

BUT WHAT IF . . .
WHAT IF THE FACTS OF THE CASE OPENER WERE DIFFERENT?

Let's say that Branstad buys a tractor from Garland. Branstad makes an agreement to pay Garland back in full, but his father makes a promise to pay for the tractor in case Branstad fails to complete his payments. Garland says that there needs to be a written contract explaining the father's promise according to the statute of frauds. Is Garland correct?

     Case 18-1 is an example of a court's consideration of a suretyship promise in its attempt to determine whether the promise falls within the statute of frauds.

CASE 18-1   POWER ENTERTAINMENT, INC., ET AL. v. NATIONAL FOOTBALL LEAGUE PROPERTIES, INC.
U.S. COURT OF APPEALS FOR THE FIFTH CIRCUIT 151 F.3D 247 (1998)

Pro Set had a licensing agreement with NFLP, which allowed Pro Set to market NFL cards bearing the statement "official card of the National Football League." Pro Set filed for bankruptcy owing NFLP approximately $800,000 in unpaid royalties from card sales. Representatives of Power Entertainment met with NFLP to discuss taking over the licensing agreement between NFLP and Pro Set. Power Entertainment alleges NFLP orally agreed to transfer Pro Set's license to Power Entertainment in return for Power Entertainment's agreement to assume Pro Set's debt to NFLP. NFLP subsequently refused to transfer the licensing agreement to Power Entertainment.

Power Entertainment then brought a breach of contract suit against NFLP seeking damages for amounts spent in reliance on the alleged agreement and for lost profits. The district court granted NFLP's motion to dismiss, holding Power Entertainment's contract claim failed as a matter of law because it was not in writing and Power Entertainment had failed to plead facts sufficient to support an estoppel claim. Power Entertainment filed timely notice of appeal.

JUDGE BENAVIDES: In granting NFLP's motion to dismiss, the district court concluded the "suretyship" statute of frauds rendered the alleged oral agreement between NFLP and Power Entertainment unenforceable because Power

Entertainment promised to assume Pro Set's debt to NFLP as part of the alleged oral agreement. The relevant statute of frauds provision under Texas law provides "a promise by one person to answer for the debt, default, or miscarriage of another person" must be in writing. As the Supreme Court of Texas has explained, the suretyship statute of frauds serves an evidentiary function:

> Probably the basic reason for requiring a promise to answer for the debt of another to be in writing is the promisor has received no direct benefit from the transaction. When the promisor receives something, this is subject to proof and tends to corroborate the making of the promise. Perjury is thus more likely in the case of a guaranty where nothing but the promise is of evidentiary value. The lack of any benefit received by the promisor not only increases the hardship of his being called upon to pay but also increases the importance of being sure that he is justly charged.

These evidentiary concerns do not pertain, however, if "the promise is made for the promisor's own benefit and not at all for the benefit of the third person. . . ." Consistent with this common-sense approach, the Texas courts have

[continued]

adopted the "main purpose doctrine," which, broadly speaking, removes an oral agreement to pay the debt of another from the statute of frauds "wherever the main purpose and object of the promisor is not to answer for another, but to subserve some purpose of his own. . . ."

In applying the main purpose doctrine under Texas law, this court has articulated the three factors used by Texas courts to determine whether the main purpose doctrine applies:

(1) [Whether the] promisor intended to become primarily liable for the debt, in effect making it his original obligation, rather than to become a surety for another;

(2) [Whether there] was consideration for the promise; and

(3) [Whether the] receipt of the consideration was the promisor's main purpose or leading object in making the promise; that is, the consideration given for the promise was primarily for the promisor's use and benefit.

Applying these factors to the facts alleged by Power Entertainment, it is apparent Power Entertainment may be able to show the alleged oral agreement falls outside of the statute of frauds. Consistent with the allegations in its complaint, Power Entertainment may be able to adduce facts that would prove Power Entertainment intended to create primary responsibility on its part to pay Pro Set's $800,000 debt to NFLP, rather than merely acting as a surety for Pro Set's obligation. According to Power Entertainment's complaint, Pro Set had already declared bankruptcy and defaulted on its royalty obligations to NFLP, and there is no indication Pro Set was involved in any way in the negotiations between NFLP and Power Entertainment.

Further, the licensing agreement constituted valuable consideration for Power Entertainment's agreement to pay Pro Set's debt. Finally, Power Entertainment apparently agreed to pay Pro Set's debt to NFLP not to aid Pro Set, but to induce NFLP to transfer Pro Set's licensing agreement to Power Entertainment for Power Entertainment's use and benefit. Under these circumstances, we conclude Power Entertainment may be able to prove a set of facts that would allow a jury to find the alleged oral agreement is not barred by the statute of frauds. Thus, the district court erred in dismissing Power Entertainment's complaint based on the statute of frauds.

REVERSED and REMANDED.

CRITICAL THINKING

Why do you think that the judge describes a certain approach to verbal contracts as "common sense," and what is that approach? How strong is the argument for the commonsense approach? What assumptions are probably shared by most people who accept this argument as common sense?

ETHICAL DECISION MAKING

The judge seems to think that in some circumstances a verbal agreement could facilitate unethical behavior. What ethical theory does the judge seem to assume most people use in ethical decision making? Why might it be wise to use the judge's assumption when making business decisions?

CONTRACTS RELATED TO AN INTEREST IN LAND

Within the statute of frauds, "land" encompasses not only the land and soil itself but anything attached to the land, such as trees or buildings. Because the statute requires a writing as evidence of the contract, a claim to an oral contract for the sale of land is not enough to prove such a contract existed.

Contracts transferring other interests in land are also within the statute of frauds. Mortgages and leases are within the statute because they are considered transfers of interest in land.

Determining exactly what constitutes an "interest in land" within the statute of frauds is difficult. A number of things that seem as if they are interests in land do not fall within the statute. For example, promises to sell crops annually, agreements between parties for profit sharing from the sale of real property, and boundary disputes that have been settled through the use of land are all outside the statute of frauds and, therefore, do not require evidence in writing. The nearby Case Nugget presents a case related to land in which the parties disagreed as to whether a writing was needed.

CASE NUGGET

WHAT IS AN "INTEREST IN LAND"?

Shelby's, Inc. v. Sierra Bravo, Inc. 68 S.W.3d 604 (2002)

Shelby's, Inc., and Sierra Bravo entered into a written agreement that granted Sierra permission to use Shelby's land as a disposal site for waste and debris Sierra removed as part of the construction of a new highway. Shelby's claimed the parties also entered into an oral contract for Sierra to construct a waterway and building pad on Shelby's property. Sierra never completed the construction and denied that an oral contract existed. Shelby's sued, and the jury found in its favor.

Sierra appealed on the basis that the oral agreement was within the statute of frauds and therefore unenforceable. Sierra saw the alleged oral agreement as specifying a sale of an interest in land, which is within the statute of frauds. Therefore, the agreement, to be enforceable, would have had to be in writing. The court firmly disagreed with Sierra's argument, stating:

We agree with the well-reasoned argument of Respondent [Shelby's]. The contract in this case was not a "sale," much less a sale of an interest in lands. . . . Here, there was no transfer of ownership or title. The written agreement gave Appellant [Sierra] permission to deposit debris and soil on Respondent's land, not the right to do so. The oral contract was for the construction of a waterway and building pad and passed no interest in the land. . . . We decline to create a new category to which the statute of frauds applies, that of a contract for services for the deposit of dirt and soil on land. The trial court did not err in denying Appellant's motion for judgment notwithstanding the verdict. Appellant's point is denied and the judgment of the trial court is affirmed.

CONTRACTS FOR THE SALE OF GOODS TOTALING MORE THAN $500

Agreements for a sale in which the total price is $500 or more are required by the UCC, Section 2-201, to be recorded in a written contract or a memorandum. This writing need only state the quantity to be sold; buyer, seller, price, and method of payment do not need to be included. In fact, terms other than quantity can be inexact or left out of the writing as long as what is written does not contradict the parties' agreement about them. The contract will be enforceable for the stated quantity and not a unit more. Furthermore, for the contract to be enforceable, both the UCC and the statute of frauds require that the party against whom action is sought must have signed the written document.

Suppose Donnie and Gretchen enter into a sales contract. Donnie wrote the agreement, and Gretchen was the only party to sign. Later, Donnie attempts to enforce the agreement against Gretchen for the agreed-to quantity. Because Gretchen signed it, Donnie can bring suit against her. However, because Donnie did not sign the agreement, Gretchen can neither sue nor countersue him.

Other situations under the UCC that require contracts in writing are the lease of goods and the sale of securities[5] and personal property[6] if the price is greater than $5,000.

FURTHER REQUIREMENTS SPECIFIC TO CERTAIN STATES

Because the statute of frauds is actually state law, certain states have various requirements not found in others. In some states, under the **equal dignity rule** contracts that would normally fall under the statute and need a writing if negotiated by the principal must be in writing even if negotiated by an agent. For example, Luke appoints Sanjeev to act as his agent. Sanjeev enters into an agreement for Luke with Carrie that cannot be completed within one year according to the contractual terms. Had Luke contracted directly with Carrie, the agreement would be within the statute and require a writing. Therefore, Sanjeev's contract, which is on behalf of Luke, must also be in writing according to the equal dignity rule.

[5] UCC § 8-319.
[6] UCC § 81-206.

A few states have special provisions in matters related to promises to pay debt. To be enforceable, a promise to pay a debt that has already been discharged because of bankruptcy must be in writing, to prevent the promisor from hiding behind the fact that the debt has been discharged. Another example is a promise to pay a debt when collection is barred by a statute of limitations. The logic here is the same as that in the first example. If the agreement is not in writing, the promisor can easily claim he or she does not need to pay. Therefore, the statute of frauds in certain states requires that both of these types of promises be in writing to be enforceable.

One last example of rules that hold only in some states occurs when the contract cannot be performed in the promisor's lifetime. For example, Heather promises to give $10,000 to Misha's charity on Heather's death. According to the terms of the promise, the agreement cannot be carried out within Heather's lifetime. In some states, Heather's promise would fall within the statute of frauds and would therefore have to be in writing. The intent here is to offer estates some protection from claims made on the basis of alleged oral contracts.

Exhibit 18-1 summarizes the contracts that fall within the statute of frauds and presents a mnemonic for remembering them.

Exhibit 18-1
A Mnemonic for Remembering Which Contracts Fall within the Statute of Frauds

	Circumstances in Which the Statute of Frauds Applies (MY LEGS)	
M	Marriage	Contracts made in consideration of marriage
Y	Year	Contracts whose terms prevent possible performance within one year
L	Land	Contracts related to an interest in land
E	Executor	Contracts in which the executor promises to pay the debt of an estate with the executor's own money
G	Goods	Contracts for the sale of goods totaling more than $500
S	Suretyship	Contracts involving secondary obligations or suretyships

L03

What must a writing contain to be sufficient to satisfy the statute of frauds?

Sufficiency of the Writing

There are no specific requirements for the form of a written contract under the statute of frauds. In fact, one or several documents can together make up the written agreement under the statute, although certain elements need to be present for a writing to constitute proper evidence of a written contract under the statute (see Exhibit 18-2).

Required elements include the identification of the parties to the contract, the subject matter of the agreement, the consideration (if any), and any pertinent terms. The contract

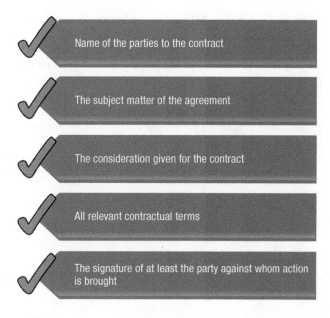

must be signed, but the signature need not be at the end. In fact, it need not be a full signature; a mark, such as an initial, is permissible as long as it is intended as a signature. While it is standard for both parties to sign the agreement, because the writing is being offered as proof of an agreement, only the party against whom action is sought needs to have signed it. If only one party signed, it is possible to have an agreement enforceable against that party but not the other. In some states oral testimony regarding an invoice for products sold is enough to meet the requirements under the statute if an actual invoice is not produced. The required elements in a writing can be contained in a memorandum, a document, or a compilation of several documents.

As you might gather from the information provided above, the statute of frauds can be particularly helpful to individuals involved in business transactions because it requires that certain important elements be present when a contract is in writing. In a way, the statute of frauds may help eliminate, or reduce, the ambiguity involved with contracts by requiring that certain conditions be met for a written document to constitute an enforceable contract. For example, when Medical Research Consultants (MRC) hired Michael Gallagher as a sales representative, the company required that he sign an employee handbook that outlined the terms of his employment. In signing the employee handbook, Gallagher acknowledged that he was an at-will employee of the company and could potentially be let go by MRC at any time. After Gallagher signed the handbook, a human resource representative for MRC faxed him a draft of an employment agreement which stated that Gallagher would work for a period of three years. Over the next several months, while Gallagher was working for MRC, he altered the draft that was faxed to him by MRC; Gallagher changed the number of years under the noncompete clause from two years to one year, and he wrote "3 weeks paid vacation" in a blank space on the draft (even after being told on more than one occasion that he was to receive two weeks' unpaid vacation). Then, after being employed by MRC for approximately four months, Gallagher faxed the draft with his signature back to the company. An attorney for MRC promptly responded to Gallagher and stated in an e-mail that "the draft sent to you . . . was for discussion purposes only. MRC never agreed to an employment contract with you and will not enter into one." Soon after, Gallagher was terminated from employment at MRC.

Gallagher filed suit against MRC, alleging breach of his three-year employment contract, which he maintained was created both orally during his early negotiations with MRC and also through the signed employment agreement draft. The court, however, found that even if MRC had orally agreed to a three-year contract with Gallagher, it would not have been enforceable because the statute of frauds dictates that agreements incapable of being completed within a year must be in writing. Further, according to the statute of frauds, the draft that Gallagher faxed back to MRC was also unenforceable because the party being charged must have signed the document and MRC clearly had not.[7]

Case 18-2 demonstrates how judges go about determining what constitutes a writing and when a writing is sufficient under the statute of frauds.

> To see how effective writing principles relate to contracts under the statute of frauds, please see the **Connecting to the Core** activity on the text website at www.mhhe.com/kubasek3e.

[7] *Michael J. Gallagher v. Medical Research Consultants, LLP,* Civil Action No. 04-236 (case summary accessed on LexisNexis May 26, 2009).

CASE 18-2   STEWART LAMLE v. MATTEL, INC.
U.S. COURT OF APPEALS FOR THE FEDERAL CIRCUIT
394 F.3D 1355 (2005)

Steward Lamle is the inventor of Farook, a board game. Lamle obtained two patents for Farook from the United States Patent and Trademark Office and negotiated with Mattel, Inc., regarding the licensing of Farook by Mattel. Early in these negotiations, Lamle signed Mattel's standard Product Disclosure Form, which contained the following provision:

> *I understand that . . . no obligation is assumed by [Mattel] unless and until a formal written contract is agreed to and entered into, and then the obligation shall be only that which is expressed in the formal, written contract.*

The negotiations advanced, and a meeting was held on June 11 where the parties discussed the terms of a licensing agreement. Mattel and Lamle there agreed on many terms of a license including a three-year term, the geographic scope, the schedule for payment, and the percentage royalty. Mattel asked Lamle to "draft a formal document memorializing 'The Deal'" and "promised [that] it would sign a formal, written contract before January 1, 1998."

Mattel employee Mike Bucher sent Lamle an email entitled "Farook Deal" on June 26 that substantially repeated terms agreed to at the June 11 meeting. The email stated the terms "have been agreed in principal [sic] by . . . Mattel subject to contract." The salutation "Best regards Mike Bucher" appeared at the end of the email.

On October 8, Mattel notified Lamle of its decision not to go ahead with the production of Farook. Lamle filed action asserting, among other things, a claim of breach of contract. The district court granted summary judgment in favor of Mattel on all claims. The Court of Appeals vacated that grant of summary judgment and remanded the case to the district court. The district court on remand again granted summary judgment in favor of Mattel on all claims. Lamle appealed again.

JUDGE DYK: Mattel contends, and the district court held, any oral agreement made during the June 11 meeting cannot be enforced because of the California Statute of Frauds.

There is no question the alleged oral agreement for a three year license was one that, by its terms, could not be "performed within a year from the making thereof." The only question, therefore, is whether there is a writing to evidence the agreement or an applicable exception to the Statute of Frauds. To satisfy the Statute of Frauds, a writing must contain all the material terms of the contract. The writing must also be signed by the party against whom enforcement is sought. Lamle argues the June 26 email from Bucher satisfied both requirements.

The June 26 email specified the term of the license, the geographic scope, the percentage royalty, and the total advance and minimum amount to be paid under the contract. Bucher stated these terms had "been agreed in principal [sic] by [his] superiors at Mattel subject to contract" and the email message "covers the basic points."

California law is clear that "a note or memorandum under the statute of frauds need not contain all of the details of an agreement between the parties." Rather, the statute only requires "every material term of an agreement within its provisions be reduced to written form." "If the court, after acquiring knowledge of all the facts concerning the transaction which the parties themselves possessed at the time the agreement was made, can plainly determine from the memorandum the identity of the parties to the contract, the nature of its subject matter, and its essential terms, the memorandum will be held to be adequate." What is an essential term

[continued]

"depends on the agreement and its context and also on the subsequent conduct of the parties."

Mattel correctly points out the June 26 email does not contain all the terms that Lamle asserts are part of the oral contract. In particular, Mattel correctly notes Lamle alleges Mattel (1) guaranteed to sell 200,000 units of Farook each year; (2) promised to sell Farook units to Lamle at cost; and (3) promised Lamle the right to approve or disapprove the design and packaging of Farook units. None of these terms appears in the June 26 email. Again, we think there is a genuine issue of material fact as to the materiality of these terms. The Ninth Circuit, interpreting California law, has stated "the subject matter, the price, and the party against whom enforcement is sought" are the "few terms deemed essential as a matter of law by California courts." A jury could well conclude these omitted terms allegedly agreed to at the meeting but not reflected in the writing were not material.

There also remains the issue of whether an email is a writing "subscribed by the party to be charged or by the party's agent." The party to be charged in this case is Mattel, and the June 26 email was written by Bucher, an employee of Mattel, and his name appears at the end of the email, which concludes with "Best regards Mike Bucher." Mattel has not disputed the agency authority of Bucher to bind it. Therefore, the only question is whether Bucher's name on an email is a valid writing and signature to satisfy the Statute of Frauds.

California law does provide, however, typed names appearing on the end of telegrams are sufficient to be writings under the Statute of Frauds. California law also provides that a typewritten name is sufficient to be a signature. We can see no meaningful difference between a typewritten signature on a telegram and an email. Therefore, we conclude under California law the June 26 email satisfies the Statute of Frauds, assuming there was a binding oral agreement on June 11 and the email includes all the material terms of that agreement.

To prove a contract with Mattel, Lamle must prove the parties objectively intended to be immediately bound by an oral contract on June 11; the June 26 email contains the material terms of that oral contract; and Bucher had actual or apparent authority to sign for Mattel. Reviewing the record, Lamle has presented sufficient evidence to create genuine issues of material fact on these points. This is not to say Lamle should prevail at trial. Indeed, among other things, Lamle faces a difficult burden persuading the jury, despite Mattel's stating it would sign a formal contract later, the objective intention of both parties was to be immediately bound by the oral contract, and to abrogate a prior written agreement to the contrary.

Therefore, we vacate the grant of summary judgment with respect to the breach of contract claim and remand for further proceedings consistent with this opinion.

VACATED-IN-PART and REMANDED.

CRITICAL THINKING

The judge makes an argument about what constitutes a signature by referring to precedent and drawing an analogy between e-mails and telegrams. How strong is this analogy? Outline an argument against it. Explain.

ETHICAL DECISION MAKING

When Mattel's agents in charge of buying or rejecting games were negotiating with Lamle, they may have considered the ethical aspects of their decisions. If you were Mattel's agent, what ethical guidelines and values would you want to consider while evaluating the ethicality of terminating Mattel's relationship with Lamle? What ethical considerations would you find the most important?

Exceptions to the Statute of Frauds

Like most legal rules, the statute of frauds allows certain exceptions. These exceptions are (1) admission, (2) partial performance, and (3) promissory estoppel. There are also exceptions under the UCC. All these exceptions are summarized in Exhibit 18-3.

ADMISSION

An **admission** is a statement made in court, under oath, or at some stage during a legal proceeding in which a party against whom charges have been brought admits that an oral contract existed, even though the contract was required to be in writing.[8]

---

[8] Restatement (Second) of Contracts, sec. 133.

Exhibit 18-3

Exceptions to the
Statute of Frauds

Admission	The party against whom charges have been brought admits during legal proceedings that an oral contract existed, even though the contract was supposed to be in writing.
Partial performance	A buyer of land, in alleged contract, has paid a portion of the sales price, has begun permanently improving the land, or has taken possession of it; these actions prove the existence of a contract.
Promissory estoppel	One party was detrimentally reliant on the contract, and this reliance was for seeable by the other party.
Exceptions under the UCC	1. Oral contracts between merchants selling goods to one another need not be in writing.
	2. Oral contracts for customized goods are enforceable, even if they would normally have to be in writing.

Sinead enters into an agreement with Jin for the sale of a plot of land. The parties fail to write down their agreement but proceed as if it were finalized. Jin changes his mind and does not go through with the transaction. Sinead then sues him. If Jin admits during trial that there was an oral contract between him and Sinead, the courts would uphold the contract for the sale of land. Without this admission, the agreement between Sinead and Jin for the sale of interest in land would need to be in writing to be enforceable.

All states except Louisiana and California allow the admission exception. To the extent that the statute of frauds is intended to require proper evidence of agreements, the admission exception is well reasoned. However, to the extent that the statute is intended to encourage care and caution in establishing the specific details of agreements, the admission exception seems to unnecessarily punish honest parties while rewarding dishonest ones.

Like the statute of frauds, the UCC makes an exception when parties admit to the existence of an oral contract. However, it provides that a contract required to be in writing but admitted to in court will be enforceable only for the quantity admitted.[9]

BUT WHAT IF . . .

WHAT IF THE FACTS OF THE CASE OPENER WERE DIFFERENT?

Let's say that Branstad buys $1,000 worth of products from Garland. Such an agreement requires a writing, yet the two parties never made a written contract for the agreement. In court, both parties admit to making an oral agreement encompassing the same terms. Would the court be able to view such an agreement as being a valid contract?

PARTIAL PERFORMANCE

Although the statute of frauds requires a writing for sales of interests in land, under the partial-performance exception, if the buyer in an alleged contract for the sale of land has paid any portion of the sale price, has begun to permanently improve the land, or has taken possession of it, the courts will consider the contract partially performed and this partial performance will amount to proof of the contract.

[9] UCC § 2-201(3)(b).

Accordingly, partial performance can override the statute's requirement for a written agreement. The logic here is that the actions of both parties demonstrate the existence of their agreement, so the agreement no longer needs to be in writing to be enforceable. Under similar sections of the UCC, an oral contract is enforceable by the buyer or seller to the extent that he or she accepts payment or delivery of the goods in question.[10]

BUT WHAT IF . . .

WHAT IF THE FACTS OF THE CASE OPENER WERE DIFFERENT?

Let's say that Branstad bought land from Garland. Although such an agreement requires a writing, the two parties made only an oral agreement. Shortly after the agreement, Branstad began making payments and fixing up the land. Garland subsequently denied any agreement being made. Could some of Branstad's actions following the agreement be proof of the agreement? Could the court recognize the oral agreement as a valid contract?

PROMISSORY ESTOPPEL

Under certain circumstances, when a party relies on an oral contract that within the statute of frauds is required to be in writing, the reliance can create a situation in which the contract is nevertheless enforceable. Promissory estoppel is the legal enforcement of an otherwise unenforceable contract due to a party's detrimental reliance on the contract.

For promissory estoppel to be in effect, the party's reliance must be to her own detriment. Furthermore, the reliance must have been reasonably foreseeable; that is, the party who did not rely on the contract should have known the other party was going to rely on it.[11]

Suppose you enter into a contract to buy a house after having accepted an offer on your current house. The new house costs more than the price you are getting for your old house, and the person from whom you are buying knows about the sale of your old house and the difference in prices. To come up with the price difference, you sell your collection of rare coins. Unfortunately, however, you forget to create a written contract for your purchase of the new house, and the other person refuses to sell it to you. You are now homeless and have sold off your only real assets. Because the other person reasonably should have known you were relying on the contract, and because you did so to your own detriment, under promissory estoppel you could win performance of the sales contract.

This argument is not an easy one to make, however. For example, when Cheesecake Factory tried to argue that it should have been entitled to rely on a bank's oral representation that a loan would be approved, the court said that the firm's reliance on such representations was not reasonable. Further, the time between the representation and the firm's discovery that it would not receive the loan was so brief that the reliance could not have been that detrimental.[12]

EXCEPTIONS UNDER THE UCC

Exceptions also exist under the UCC. For instance, oral contracts between merchants need not be in writing to be enforceable. If one merchant agrees to sell goods to another, the contract is enforceable even if it is not in writing.

---

[10] UCC § 2-201(3)(c).

[11] Restatement (Second) of Contracts, sec. 139.

[12] *Classic Cheesecake Company, Inc., et al., v. JPMorgan Chase Bank, N.A.*, 546 F.3d 839, 2008 U.S. App. LEXIS 21632.

E-COMMERCE AND THE LAW

THE STATUTE OF FRAUDS AND LEGALLY BINDING ELECTRONIC TRANSACTIONS

An issue that comes up again and again in e-commerce is the lack of precedents or statutes applicable to situations arising in the new environment. Until rather recently, there weren't any statutes that specifically addressed the nature of electronic transactions. This situation requires that judges rely on their good judgment when interpreting traditional contract law and applying it to e-commerce. For some transactions to be viewed as legally valid under the statute of frauds, there must be written copies of the contract that are then signed by at least one of the parties. In 2000, the Uniform Electronic Transactions Act was proposed by the National Conference of Commissioners on Uniform State Laws. It was subsequently adopted as

law in 49 states plus the District of Columbia, Puerto Rico and the U.S. Virgin Islands. This act circumvents the former requirements of the statute of frauds regarding the validity of online transactions. The act reflects the decision that particular electronic transactions may constitute a "written copy" and therefore have legal significance, despite the fact that the electronic transaction is not technically a written document. These statutory changes ensure that business owners are assured of the validity of an online contract.

Source: Uniform Electronic Transactions Act, National Conference of State Legislatures, http://www.ncsl.org/issues-research/telecom/uniform-electronic-transactions-acts.aspx.

Likewise, oral contracts for customized goods are enforceable even if they would normally have to be in writing. The reasoning is that customized goods are not likely to be salable to a general audience, so the party that did not back out of the agreement probably incurred unreasonable costs under the contract.

L04

What is the purpose of the parol evidence rule?

Parol Evidence Rule

A problem arises with written contracts when a party asserts that the writing is in some way deficient. To smooth transactions by limiting the types of evidence admissible in such claims, the courts rely heavily on the **parol evidence rule.** This common law rule makes oral evidence of an agreement inadmissible if it is made before or at the same time as a writing that the parties intend to be the complete and final version of their agreement.[13] *Parol* in "parol evidence rule" means speech or words, specifically words outside the original writing.

The purpose of the parol evidence rule is to prevent evidence that substantially contradicts the agreement in its written form. Therefore, evidence of prior agreements and negotiations, as well as contemporaneous agreements and negotiations, is typically excluded under the parol evidence rule. A written agreement is assumed to be complete, and evidence contradicting it usually impedes business transactions, which is why the rule exists.

However, when a court determines that the written agreement does *not* represent a complete and final version of the agreement, evidence to further the court's understanding may be admissible. The additional evidence is limited to elements missing from the writing but consistent with it. These may be terms typically included in similar transactions or separate agreements in which consideration had been offered.

Note, however, that parol evidence applies first and foremost to spoken and written words extrinsic to the original writing. The parol evidence rule is also *not* a rule of evidence; rather, it relates to the substantive legal issue of what constitutes a legally binding agreement and how we know what that agreement is. Finally, the parol evidence rule is not a unitary concept or rule but an amalgamation of different rules and conditions.

Although the parol evidence rule applies to writings created at the same time as the written agreement, these writings tend to be treated differently than prior or contemporaneous oral agreements. That is, the writings are more readily admitted as part of the written agreement than is oral evidence regarding conditions or terms in the final agreement. As long as contemporaneous written documents do not substantially contradict what is in the final

---

[13] Restatement (Second) of Contracts, sec. 213.

writing, judges can use their discretion to deem these other writings part of that agreement. Consequently, the parol evidence rule does not usually exclude extrinsic written evidence.

Sometimes parties take the initiative and, in a merger clause, attempt to signal to judges that the written contract is intended to be the final and complete statement of their agreement. In essence, a merger clause seeks to blend other agreements either into the final agreement or into something explicitly identified as being outside the final agreement. Not all courts consider merger clauses to be conclusive proof of a contract. Where they are accepted, however, merger clauses greatly reduce the amount of guesswork courts must do in determining what is the final statement of the agreement.

Legal Principle: **Once a fully integrated agreement has been written, no oral evidence of any prior or contemporaneous agreement can be admitted in court to change the terms of the agreement.**

BUT WHAT IF . . .

WHAT IF THE FACTS OF THE CASE OPENER WERE DIFFERENT?

Recall that, in the Case Opener, Garland and Branstad's alleged oral agreement regarding interest payments was made after the completion of the written agreement. What if the oral agreement had been made before the two parties completed the written agreement? Would the oral agreement be admissible in court under the parole evidence rule?

Exceptions to the Parol Evidence Rule

Like the statute of frauds, the parol evidence rule admits some exceptions in which parol evidence, normally excluded, may be admissible in court. These exceptions are (1) contracts that have been subsequently modified, (2) contracts conditioned on orally agreed-on terms, (3) contracts that are not final as they are part written and part oral, (4) contracts with ambiguous terms, (5) incomplete contracts, (6) contracts with obvious typographical errors, (7) voidable or void contracts, and (8) evidence of prior dealings or usage of trade. (See Exhibit 18-4.)

Exhibit 18-4

Summary of Parol Evidence Rule

Parol Evidence Rule
Oral evidence of an agreement is inadmissible if it is made before or at the same time as a writing that the parties intend to be the complete and final version of the agreement.

Exceptions to the Rule

- Contract has been subsequently modified.
- Written agreement was based on an orally agreed-on condition.
- Contract is nonfinalized in that it is partly written and partly oral.
- Contract contains ambiguous terms that significantly affect its interpretation.
- Contract is incomplete in that it is missing critical information.
- Contract contains obvious typographical errors.
- Contract is void or voidable.
- Evidence about past business transactions will clarify missing information or ambiguities in the contract.

COMPARING THE LAW OF OTHER COUNTRIES

CIVIL LAW COUNTRIES AND THE PAROL EVIDENCE RULE

A number of our European allies, such as Germany and France, are civil law rather than common law countries and have a different approach to many of the legal doctrines the United States follows. For example, German law does not have a parol evidence rule. Instead, German courts tend to allow what U.S. courts call *parol evidence*. The logic is that such information is important for knowing the parties' intent when they entered into the contracts.

Unlike Germany, France does have a parol evidence rule, albeit a very limited one that does not apply to commercial contracts. The

French court system thus attempts to facilitate business exchanges by allowing parol evidence to clarify all points related to terms of a contract or what a party thought he or she was agreeing to.

Interestingly enough, the parol evidence rule, a long-standing tradition in the common law, actually came to U.S. law by way of French law, just as the statute of frauds came through English common law. Yet the United States applies both rules to more cases than does either of the countries where these rules originated.

CONTRACTS THAT HAVE BEEN SUBSEQUENTLY MODIFIED

Although parol evidence contradictory to the final terms is inadmissible, evidence regarding a contract's subsequent modification *is* admissible. The modification must have been made after the writing, and the evidence must clearly indicate this later modification.

Despite the allowance of evidence to demonstrate modifications, not all evidence of modification is admissible. If the agreement is required to be in writing because it is within the statute of frauds, oral modifications are unenforceable. However, oral evidence of a subsequent written agreement is admissible. In addition, if the contract's terms require that modification be in writing, oral modifications are inadmissible and unenforceable.[14]

CONTRACTS CONDITIONED ON ORALLY AGREED-ON TERMS

The parol evidence rule does not prevent parties from introducing evidence proving the written agreement was conditioned on terms agreed to orally. The reason is that the evidence being elicited does not substantially modify the written agreement. Rather, what is at issue with such evidence is the enforceability of the contract as written. No terms are altered, so the parol evidence rule does not apply.

When an entire contract is conditioned on something else's occurring first, that first event is known as a condition precedent. Evidence of the existence of a condition precedent agreed to orally is admissible, as stated previously, because the contract is not modified by such evidence; rather, its enforceability is called into question. Since the statute of frauds is concerned primarily with the enforceability of agreements, it logically follows that the parol evidence rule does not apply to evidence of condition precedents.

NONFINALIZED, PARTIALLY WRITTEN AND PARTIALLY ORAL CONTRACTS

When a contract consists of both written and oral elements, judges tend to treat it as non-finalized and assume that the parties do not intend to have the written part represent the entire agreement. Therefore, oral evidence related to the contract is admissible because the written document is not the complete and final representation of the agreement.

CONTRACTS CONTAINING AMBIGUOUS TERMS

A contract that contains what the court deems to be ambiguous terms presents a dilemma in interpretation. To reach the most accurate interpretation of the original agreement, the

---

[14] UCC § 2-209(2),(3).

court allows evidence, even if it is oral, for the sole purpose of clarifying, *not* changing, ambiguous contractual terms. As with the evidence regarding orally agreed-on condition precedents, evidence used to clarify ambiguity is believed not to modify the contract but, rather, to clarify, and therefore it is admissible.

INCOMPLETE CONTRACTS

When a contract is fundamentally flawed because it is missing critical information, typically related to essential terms, courts can allow parol evidence to fill in the missing parts while not modifying the written agreement in any substantial way. Parol evidence is here used to facilitate business transactions, not to force the parties to enter into a new, complete agreement.

CONTRACTS WITH OBVIOUS TYPOGRAPHICAL ERRORS

Whenever a written agreement under the statute of frauds contains a serious, and obvious, typographical error (typo), parol evidence is admissible to demonstrate that it was a typo, as well as to set forth the proper term. This admission does not fundamentally alter the written agreement because the typo is not an accurate reflection of the parties' agreement.

VOID OR VOIDABLE CONTRACTS

Certain conditions can make an otherwise valid contract void or voidable. (Refer to Chapter 13 for an in-depth discussion of what makes a contract void or voidable.) While the contract does not list these conditions, the courts allow parol evidence to demonstrate them. Like most exceptions to the parol evidence rule, this one does not fundamentally alter the terms of the contract but, rather, addresses its enforceability. Furthermore, evidence of a defense against a contract (discussed in Chapter 16) is admissible to prove a contract is void or voidable.

EVIDENCE OF PRIOR DEALINGS OR USAGE OF TRADE (UCC)

This final exception actually falls under the UCC and not the statute of frauds. According to the UCC, parol evidence is admissible for the sake of clarification if it addresses prior dealings between the parties or usages of trade in the business they are in.[15] Evidence related to past dealings can help clarify missing or ambiguous terms by demonstrating how the parties have previously interacted; the assumption is that they will continue to interact in a similar manner. Therefore, if a term is missing or ambiguous, the courts rely on evidence of what the parties did in the past to gauge what they intended in the contract in question.

Similarly, when a contract is ambiguous or incomplete, the courts examine standard practices in the business, assuming the parties intend to engage in these practices even if they are not included in the agreement. Once again, an exception is made to allow parol evidence to clarify a contract, as opposed to changing any material terms.

Integrated Contracts

Integrated contracts are written contracts intended to be the complete and final representation of the parties' agreement. When the courts deem a contract integrated, with the exception of the above exceptions, parol evidence is inadmissible. In partially integrated contracts, parol evidence is admissible to the extent that it clarifies part of the contract or

---

[15] UCC §§ 1-205 and 2-202.

CASE NUGGET

A CLEAR ILLUSTRATION OF THE NEED FOR A WRITING

Scalisi et al. v. New York University Medical Center
805 N.Y.S.2d 62 (N.Y. App. Div., 1st Dept., Dec. 6, 2005)

The plaintiffs in this breach-of-contract action learned the importance of getting guarantees in writing. They allegedly entered into an oral agreement with the Medical Center for an in vitro fertilization procedure that would not result in the birth of an autistic child. Subsequently, the parties signed a written contract stating that a certain percentage of children are born with physical and mental defects and the occurrence of such defects is "beyond the control of the physician." The document also stated that the Medical Center and its physicians would not "assume responsibility for the physical and mental characteristic or hereditary tendencies" of any child born as a result of the in vitro procedure.

When one of the twins conceived as a result of the in vitro procedure was born with "autistic traits," the parents sued for breach of the oral agreement, alleging that they had entered into it for the purpose of having offspring free of autism. The lower court granted the hospital summary judgment, holding that the written agreement signed by the parents barred the admissibility of the oral agreement. The state court of appeals affirmed, finding that even if the alleged oral promises had been made, they were inadmissible in light of the existence of the subsequent written agreement directly contradictory to them.

addresses its enforceability.[16] Therefore, the easiest test to determine the admissibility of parol evidence is to check whether the written contract, within the statute of frauds, is an integrated contract.

We've seen that one way parties can indicate their desire to create an integrated contract is through the use of a merger clause. A merger clause explicitly states that the written contract is intended to be the complete and final version of the contract between the parties and that other possible agreements between the parties, besides the one in question, are not part of the final written agreement. Most states will allow a merger clause to constitute the stated intent of the parties unless one party offers proof of a personal defense against the contract. However, some states consider merger clauses to be recommendations, not necessarily binding on the parties.

CASE OPENER WRAP-UP

Admissibility of an Oral Contract in Court

The district court found for Branstad after seeing evidence that Branstad and his wife had not only managed Garland's other properties until 1998 but had spent their own money on the properties' upkeep. Additionally, in accordance with Branstad's account of the oral agreement, the payments Branstad had made to Garland were listed in payment and tax records as noninterest payments. Such information showed that Garland had made no attempt to collect interest payments until the two had a falling out in 1998. Furthermore, the court determined that the parol evidence rule did not apply to the oral agreement in question because the agreement was made after the completion of the written contract, not before or during. Ultimately, the court determined that the oral contract existed as a separate agreement and not as part of the original written agreement.[17]

[16] Restatement (Second) of Contracts, sec. 216.

[17] *Garland v. Brandstad*, 648 NW 2d 65 (2002).

KEY TERMS

admission   415

condition precedent   420

equal dignity rule   411

integrated contracts   421

merger clause   419

parol evidence rule   418

partial performance   416

prenuptial agreement   408

promissory estoppel   417

statute
of frauds   405

SUMMARY OF KEY TOPICS

The term *statute of frauds* refers to various state laws modeled after the 1677 English Act for the Prevention of Frauds and Perjuries. These state laws are intended to (1) ease contractual negotiations by requiring sufficient reliable evidence to prove the existence and specific terms of a contract, (2) prevent unreliable oral evidence from interfering with a contractual relationship, and (3) prevent parties from entering into contracts with which they do not agree.

Statute of Frauds

Contracts falling within the statute of frauds:

1. Contracts whose terms prevent possible performance within one year.
2. Promises made in consideration of marriage.
3. Contracts for one party to pay the debt of another if the initial party fails to pay.
4. Contracts related to an interest in land.
5. Under the Uniform Commercial Code, contracts for the sale of goods totaling more than $500.

Contracts Falling within the Statute of Frauds

A sufficient writing under the statute of frauds must clearly indicate (1) the parties to the contract, (2) the subject matter of the agreement, (3) the consideration given for the contract, (4) all relevant contractual terms, and (5) the signature of at least the party against whom action is brought.

Sufficiency of the Writing

Under the UCC, writing must clearly indicate (1) the quantity to be sold and (2) the signature of the party being sued.

Under both the statute of frauds and the UCC, a writing may consist of multiple documents as long as they explicitly reference one another.

Exceptions to the requirement of a writing under the statute of frauds:

1. Admission that an oral agreement exists.
2. Partial performance of the contract.
3. Promissory estoppel (legal enforcement due to a party's detrimental reliance on the contract).
4. Various exceptions under the UCC.

Exceptions to the Statute of Frauds

The *parol evidence rule* is a common law rule stating that oral evidence of an agreement made prior to or contemporaneously with the written agreement is inadmissible when the parties intend to have a written agreement be the complete and final version of their agreement.

Parol Evidence Rule

Exceptions to the parol evidence rule:

1. Contracts that are subsequently modified.
2. Contracts conditioned on orally agreed-on terms.
3. Contracts that are not final because they are partly written and partly oral.
4. Contracts with ambiguous terms.
5. Incomplete contracts.

Exceptions to the Parol Evidence Rule

6. Contracts with obvious typographical errors.

7. Voidable or void contracts.

8. Evidence of prior dealings or usage of trade.

Integrated Contracts   *Integrated contracts* are written contracts within the statute of frauds intended to be the complete and final representation of the parties' agreement, thus precluding the admissibility of parol evidence other than in the exceptions listed above.

POINT / COUNTERPOINT

Does the United States Still Benefit from Having a Statute of Frauds?	
YES	NO
The statute of frauds provides great benefit as a social lubricant aiding U.S. business transactions. By requiring that certain types of contracts be in writing, we ensure that they either will have enough evidence to prove the existence and terms of the contract or will be unenforceable. Because only certain contracts are required to be in writing, the rule does not preclude oral contracts, but it ensures that the most important contracts can be enacted without complications. Another way in which the statute of frauds benefits U.S. business is by preventing unreliable evidence from being used in court. Human memories are notoriously weak and faulty, and it does not make sense to base important legal decisions on what someone says he or she remembers. Furthermore, people with a vested interest can change their testimony on the basis of changed circumstances in pursuit of personal gain. However, with the requirement that certain contracts be in writing, the parties are bound by what they wrote. Finally, the act of writing gives people time to pause for reflection. No one benefits when parties hastily rush into an agreement they later regret. Thoughtful reflection prevents parties from entering into contracts with which they do not agree, and this means fewer cases are brought due to one party's entering an unfair, or otherwise defective, agreement.	The statute of frauds acts as an impediment to contractual agreements, and the states should repeal the relevant sections of their laws. When parties agree, why should they be subjected to unnecessary formalities? The written requirements of the statute of frauds get in the way of business transactions more often than they help. Furthermore, the required writing frequently imposes additional costs on the parties. When even simple agreements in which neither party contests the terms must be written, more time is spent *not* conducting other business. Frequently, the parties have to hire attorneys to write their contracts, imposing still more costs and helping decrease whatever benefit the parties might have gained from the original agreement before the writing took place. In addition, although most parties enter agreements in good faith, it is not uncommon for parties to seek a way out of contracts they cannot perform. The writing requirements are not always accurately fulfilled, and unethical parties can exploit minor technicalities to have a contract declared void. In the end, the innocent party is harmed by the writing requirement, and the unethical party escapes a bad situation with little to no harm.

QUESTIONS & PROBLEMS

1. Describe the contents of a writing that would be sufficient to satisfy the statute of frauds under the common law.

2. List the kinds of contracts that require a writing under the statute of frauds.

3. Identify the exceptions to the parol evidence rule, and explain why some people might argue that the rule is not very effective.

4. The McCartheys controlled Salt Lake City's largest daily newspaper, *The Salt Lake Tribune,* through their

collective ownership of shares in the Kearns-Tribune (KT) Corporation, a holding company for the newspaper. In 1997, KT merged with Tele-Communications, Inc. (TCI). The McCartheys originally opposed the merger but later agreed to it. In 1999, TCI and AT&T merged, and AT&T sold the *Tribune* to MediaNews in 2001. The McCartheys argue that according to an oral agreement reached in 1997, at the time of the original merger that they opposed, the McCartheys have the opportunity to buy back the *Tribune* after five years (in 2002) for a fair market price but that MediaNews tried to block any attempt at a sale. The McCartheys filed suit to enforce the oral agreement. MediaNews moved for a declaratory judgment that the McCartheys have no independent rights in the *Tribune*. The district court granted the defendant's motions as to all claims. The McCartheys appealed. Under what conditions would the McCartheys' claim be successful? As a judge, what evidence would help you decide whether the oral agreement constituted a valid contract? [*MediaNews Group, Inc. v. McCarthey,* 494 F.3d 1254 (2007).]

5. Antwun Echols, a professional boxer, signed a promotional agreement with Banner Promotions Inc. The agreement gave Banner the right to be Echols's sole representative in negotiations for all fights. Banner's major obligation under the agreement was to "secure, arrange and promote" not less than three bouts for Echols during each year of the contract. Banner was to pay Echols not less than a contractually stated minimum amount for each bout in which he appeared, with the amount of the minimum depending on where the bout was televised and whether Echols appeared as a champion. However, Banner had the option to renegotiate the amounts if Echols lost a fight, which he did one month into the contract; afterward, Banner chose to negotiate Echols's compensation on a bout-by-bout basis. After several fights under the new agreement, Echols became dissatisfied with the situation, arguing that Banner had made him "take it or leave it" offers for what he believed was below-market compensation. Echols sued Banner, arguing that the variable amounts made the contract vague and therefore unenforceable. Did the agreement constitute a valid contract? Why or why not? [*Echols v. Pelullo,* 377 F.3d 272 (2004).]

6. Sunkist Growers Inc. brought Nabisco to court, claiming that under the companies' mutually agreed-on license agreement, Nabisco was causing Sunkist to engage in improper practices. Nabisco claimed that, under the license agreement, the companies had to settle the dispute through arbitration. However, Sunkist claimed that it was a nonsignatory to the contract and thus did not have to settle through arbitration. Nabisco claimed that Sunkist was legally compelled to settle through arbitration, even though Sunkist had not signed the document, because the two parties admitted to the license agreement being an agreement between them and both companies' actions had been based on the agreement. How do you think the court decided? [10 F. 3d 753 (Ga. CA 11, 1993).]

7. The plaintiff investor sued the defendant investment company for breach of an oral agreement on the part of the defendant to recommend hedge funds for the plaintiff and exercise due diligence with respect to the recommendations, in exchange for which the plaintiff would pay a 1 percent fee for every year the defendant held the fund. The suit arose when the plaintiff found out that the hedge fund the company recommended was a ponzi scheme. The district court dismissed the case on the grounds that the contract was an ongoing one that would not be completed within a year and therefore required a writing to be enforceable. The plaintiff appealed. How do you think the appellate court ruled on this issue, and why? [*South Cherry Street, LLC v. Hennessee Group LLC,* 573 F.3d 98, 2009 U.S. App. LEXIS 15467.]

8. In 1995, Schaefer was in a car accident, and his vehicle was damaged. His insurance company looked at his vehicle and gave him money to repair it. However, even with the repairs, Schaefer's vehicle's overall value dropped almost $3,000 due to the accident. Schaefer's interpretation of the insurance company's written policy was that the company would return the vehicle to its original value before the accident. On the other hand, the insurance company interpreted the written policy as meaning that the company would pay the lesser option of either replacing the vehicle with one of a similar value or paying for repairs. How do courts usually resolve cases of ambiguity in contracts? How did the court decide this case? [*Am. Mfrs. Mut. Ins. Co. v. Schaefer,* 124 S.W.3d 154, 2003 Tex. LEXIS 472, 47 Tex. Sup. Ct. J. 40 (Tex. 2003).]

9. In 2004, real estate broker Richard Davis called an A&E television executive about partnering on a

new reality show called *Flip This House.* Davis said he would undertake the financial risks of purchasing and later reselling the real estate and he and the network would split the net profits. Davis received confirmation from the network director over the phone and later with three other executives. The network never paid Davis and claimed no agreement was made. The district court found on behalf of Davis, and the network appealed. The appellate court stipulated that two facts must be true to find on behalf of Davis: first, that Davis reasonably believed that an agreement was made during the phone conversations and, second, that such a belief would be made by an objectively reasonable person. How do you think the court decided? [*Davis v. A&E Television,* 422 Fed. Appx. 199, 2011 U.S. App. LEXIS 7382.]

10. Benito Brino owned real property that he leased to Salvatore and Linda Gabriele. During the lease, the Gabrieles attempted to purchase the property from Brino. Both parties agreed on a purchase price of $565,000 with a closing date of September 15, 2001. However, the Gabrieles were not able to obtain the full amount in loan financing from the bank, so they made a counteroffer to purchase for $450,000, which Brino rejected. The Gabrieles later obtained the full $565,000 from another lending institution and drafted an addendum to the July sales agreement that altered the closing date to May 5, 2002. Brino orally accepted the terms of the agreement, but the document was not signed until May 16, 2002, after the closing date. Consequently, the bank refused to acknowledge the addendum's validity. Thereafter, the Gabrieles drafted a second sales agreement with the same terms as the July agreement, except that the second agreement did not include a closing date but stated that the effective date would be the signing date. Both parties signed the agreement on June 16, 2002, and the bank accepted the agreement and agreed to provide the loan. The Gabrieles informed Brino that they were ready to close, but Brino did not convey title of the property to the Gabrieles. The Gabrieles brought suit against Brino, seeking specific performance, but Brino argued that the agreement was not enforceable as it did not satisfy the statute of frauds, primarily because the agreement did not designate the seller. In response, the Gabrieles claimed that their obtaining financing was partial performance of the agreement. How did the court resolve this issue with regard to the statute of frauds? [*Gabriele v. Brino,* 2004 Conn. App. LEXIS 428.]

Looking for more review materials?

The Online Learning Center at **www.mhhe.com/kubasek3e** contains this chapter's "Assignment on the Internet" and also a list of URLs for more information, entitled "On the Internet." Find both of them in the Student Center portion of the OLC, along with quizzes and other helpful materials.

CHAPTER

20

Discharge and Remedies

LEARNING OBJECTIVES

After reading this chapter, you will be able to answer the following questions:

1 What are the primary methods of discharging a contract?

2 What are the primary legal remedies available for a breach of contract?

3 What are the primary equitable remedies available for a breach of contract?

CASE OPENER

Impossible Wine Bottles

The Anchor Glass Container Corporation and its parent company, Consumers Packaging, Inc. (CPI), entered into a series of agreements with Encore Glass, Inc., to supply glass containers of a specific type and quality for the wine industry. On June 24, 1999, Encore entered into an amended agreement with Anchor and CPI. In the amended agreement, the parties agreed that the products would be manufactured at CPI's Lavington plant. Additionally, the amended agreement gave Encore a generous rebate schedule ranging from 1 to 2.5 percent and a new discount schedule.

In May 2001, CPI filed for bankruptcy. As a result of the bankruptcy proceedings, the Lavington plant was sold in August 2001. The new owners of the Lavington plant did not assume CPI's obligations under the amended agreement. The Lavington plant could no longer be used to supply the glass containers to Encore. As a result of the sale, Anchor notified Encore on October 12, 2001, that it considered itself relieved of its obligations under the agreement due to its impossibility to perform. Encore took its business to another company, which did not offer the same rebates and discounts as had Anchor.

When Anchor filed for bankruptcy in 2002, Encore filed a claim to recover the $6,102,912.60 it lost when Anchor stopped providing it with rebates and discounts under the contract. The bankruptcy court ruled against Encore, finding that it was impossible for Anchor to perform after the Lavington plant was sold. Encore appealed.

1. Should Anchor be required to honor the contract despite the loss of the Lavington plant? Why or why not?
2. What ethical system, if any, would permit Encore to recover the lost rebates and discounts?

The Wrap-Up at the end of the chapter will answer these questions.

Methods of Discharging a Contract

L01

What are the primary methods of discharging a contract?

The previous seven chapters focus primarily on how parties enter into a legally binding agreement. Once a party has entered into a binding agreement, how does the party terminate his or her obligation under the contract? That question is the focus of this chapter. When a party's obligations under a contract are terminated, the party is said to be discharged. There are a number of ways by which a party's contractual obligations can be terminated and the party thereby discharged. The first, and the one most parties hope to secure from the other when they enter into an agreement, is performance. The others are the happening of a condition or its failure to occur, material breach by one or both parties, agreement of the parties, and operation of law. This chapter explains each of these methods.

CONDITIONS

Under ordinary circumstances, a party's duty to perform the promise agreed to in a contract is absolute. Sometimes, however, a party's duty to perform may be affected by whether a certain condition occurs. Contracts containing conditions affecting the performance obligations of the parties are called conditional contracts. The conditions may be either implied by law or expressly inserted into the contract by the parties.

Discharge by Conditions Precedent, Subsequent, and Concurrent.   There are three types of conditions: condition precedent, condition subsequent, and concurrent conditions (see Exhibit 20-1). A condition precedent is a particular event that must occur in order for a party's duty to arise. If the event does not occur, the party's duty to perform does not arise. Frequently, real estate contracts are conditioned on an event such as the buyer's being able to sell his current home by a certain date. If the home does not sell, the condition does not arise. Thus, the parties have no duty to perform and are discharged from the contract.

Another common example of a contract containing a condition precedent is an insurance contract. If Bill purchases a life insurance contract, he is obligated to pay the monthly premiums specified in the contract but the insurance company's obligation to perform arises only when he dies. His death is the condition that triggers the company's duty to pay his beneficiary.

A condition subsequent is a future event that terminates the obligations of the parties when it occurs. For example, Joan may enter into an agreement to lease an apartment for five years, conditioned on her not being called to active duty in the National Guard. If she is called to serve, her obligation to be bound by the lease is discharged.

We're suing for breach of contract because we almost fulfilled our end of the bargain.

Come back if you can get rid of the "almost."

stus.com

Exhibit 20-1
Conditional Contracts:
Types of Conditions

Condition precedent	The party's duty to perform arises after a particular event occurs; if the event never occurs, the party's duty to perform never arises and the parties are thus discharged from the contract.
Condition subsequent	The party has a duty to perform until a future event occurs that discharges the party from the obligation.
Condition concurrent	The party's duty to perform requires that each party perform for the other at the same time. If one party offers to perform his duty and the other party does not, he can sue the other for nonperformance.
Express conditions	Conditions in the contract that are usually preceded by words such as *provided that, if,* or *when.* If these conditions are not met, a party could be discharged from the contract.
Implied conditions	Conditions that are inferred from the nature and language of the contract and are not explicitly stated. If the implied conditions are met, the party could be discharged from the contract.

Legal Principle: **A condition precedent exists when a condition must occur before a party's duty to perform arises, whereas a condition subsequent exists when the occurrence of the condition extinguishes a party's duty to perform.**

Concurrent conditions occur when each party's performance is conditioned on the performance of the other. They occur only when the parties are required to perform for each other simultaneously. For example, when a buyer is supposed to pay for goods on delivery, the buyer's duty to pay is impliedly conditioned on the seller's duty to deliver the goods, and the seller's duty to deliver the goods is impliedly conditioned on the buyer's duty to pay for the goods. The legal effect of a contract's being concurrently conditioned is that each party must offer to perform before being able to sue the other for nonperformance.

Legal Principle: **Concurrent conditions exist when the parties are to perform their obligations for each other simultaneously.**

Express and Implied Conditions. Conditions in contracts are also described as being express or implied. Express conditions are explicitly stated in the contract and are usually preceded by words such as *conditioned on, if, provided that,* or *when.* For example, in a situation involving a potential sale of a house, the offer expressly required that the buyer make a deposit of $1,000 "on acceptance." The buyer wrote "accepted" on the offer and returned it but did not include the deposit. No deposit of money was ever made. The seller then canceled the transaction. Several weeks later, the buyer attempted to tender payment to the seller. The court found that under the terms of the contract, payment of the $1,000 was an express condition of acceptance and since the acceptance was incomplete, there was no contract.[1]

Implied conditions are those that are not explicitly stated but are inferred from the nature and language of the contract. For example, if one enters into a contract with a builder to replace the windows in one's house, there is an implied condition that the builder will be given access to the home so that she may fulfill her obligations under the contract.

---

[1] *Smith v. Holmwood,* 231 Cal. App. 2d 549 (1965).

Legal Principle: **An express condition is clearly stated, whereas an implied condition is not stated but can be inferred from the nature and language of the contract.**

? BUT WHAT IF . . .

WHAT IF THE FACTS OF THE CASE OPENER WERE DIFFERENT?

Let's say, in the Case Opener, that the contract between Encore and Anchor included a clause that stated that the two companies would owe duties to each other as long as CPI was not bankrupt and was involved in the relationship. What kind of a condition would that be? Would Encore have been able to sue Anchor?

DISCHARGE BY PERFORMANCE

In most situations, parties discharge their obligations by doing what they respectively agreed to do under the terms of the contract; this is called *discharge by performance*. Parties also discharge their duty by making an offer to perform and being ready, willing, and able to perform. This offer of performance is known as a tender. If a painter shows up at Sam's house with his paint and ladders and is ready to start painting the garage, he has tendered performance. If Sam refuses to let him start, the painter has now discharged his duties under the contract by his tender of performance and he may sue Sam for material breach (discussed later in this chapter).

Types of Performance. There are two primary kinds of performance: complete performance and substantial performance. Performance may also be conditioned on the satisfaction of a party to the contract or of a third party.

Complete performance occurs when all aspects of the parties' duties under the contract are carried out perfectly. In many instances, complete performance is difficult, if not impossible, to attain, and courts today generally require only substantial performance.

Substantial performance occurs when the following conditions have been met: (1) completion of nearly all the terms of the agreement, (2) an honest effort to complete all the terms, and (3) no willful departure from the terms of the agreement. Substantial performance discharges the party's responsibilities under the contract, although the court may require that the party compensate the other party for any loss in value caused by the failure to meet all the standards set forth in the contract. For example, if a contract called for all bedrooms of a house to be painted blue but one was inadvertently painted green, the court may require that the contractor compensate the buyer by the amount that it will cost the buyer to have that room repainted. Of course, it is sometimes difficult to determine whether in fact there has been substantial performance, which is why there is litigation over this issue.

Performance Subject to Satisfaction of a Contracting Party. Sometimes the performance of the contract is subject to the satisfaction of one of the contracting parties. In such a case, a party is not discharged from the contract until the other party is satisfied. Satisfaction is considered an express condition that must be met before the other party's obligation to pay for the performance arises.

Satisfaction may be judged according to either a subjective or an objective standard. When the judgment involved is a matter of personal taste, such as when a woman is having a dress custom made for her, the courts apply a subjective satisfaction standard. As long as the person, in good faith, is not satisfied, the other party is deemed to have not met the condition.

If the performance is one related to a mechanical or utility standard, the objective satisfaction standard applies. Also, if the contract does not clearly specify that the satisfaction is to be personal, the objective standard applies. When an objective standard is used, the courts ask whether a reasonable person would be satisfied with the performance.

Sometimes the contract is conditioned on the satisfaction of a third party. Usually, such provisions arise in construction contracts specifying that before a buyer accepts a building, an architect must provide a certificate stating that the building was constructed according to the plans and specifications.

DISCHARGE BY MATERIAL BREACH

A *breach* occurs whenever a party fails to perform her obligations under the contract. If the breach is a minor one, it may entitle the nonbreaching party to damages but it does not discharge the nonbreaching party from the contract.

A *material breach,* however, discharges the nonbreaching party from his obligations under the contract. A material breach occurs when a party unjustifiably fails to substantially perform his obligations under the contract. It is often difficult to know when the court is going to determine that a breach is material. For example, auto racing fans thought that a contract between them and Formula One and the Indianapolis Speedway, created by their purchase of tickets to a recent car race, had been materially breached when a race that was scheduled to feature 20 cars ended up having only 6. The reduction in the number of cars occurred when it was discovered that a flaw in the tires of a number of cars made it too dangerous for those cars to be in the race and there was not enough time to find replacement vehicles. Regulations explicitly provide that races may be canceled when fewer than 12 cars are available, but the organizers chose to go ahead and hold the race. The court found that the contract was for the event and that no fan would reasonably expect that organizers were specifically guaranteeing a set number of participants.[2] Case 20-1 demonstrates the analysis a court may use to determine whether a defendant's behavior constitutes material breach.

[2] *Larry Bowers, Alan G. Symons, Carey Johnson, et al., v. Federation Internationale de l'Automobile, Formula One Administration Limited, Indianapolis Motor Speedway Corporation, et al.,* 489 F.3d 316 (2007).

CASE 20-1	**HAMILTON v. STATE FARM FIRE & CASUALTY INSURANCE COMPANY**

U.S. COURT OF APPEALS FOR THE FIFTH CIRCUIT
2012 U.S. APP. LEXIS 8744

When the Hamiltons' home was ruined by a hurricane, the couple moved out of the home to other residences. The couple provided their insurance company with several documents and submitted an insurance claim. However, the couple refused to allow representatives from the insurance agency to inspect their other homes and refused to give the company other vital documents proving the damage of certain assets. Thus, the insurance company denied the Hamiltons' insurance claim, saying that the couple materially breached the contract because they did not comply with the terms of the policy. The appellate court found that the couple could not recover under the insurance policy because they materially breached the contract by not complying with the cooperation clause.

JUDGES BENAVIDES, STEWART, AND HIGGINSON:
Louisiana law provides that an insurance policy is a contract between the parties and should be construed by using the general rules of interpretation of contracts set forth in the Louisiana Civil Code. "If the policy wording at issue is clear and unambiguously expresses the parties' intent, the insurance contract must be enforced as written."

"In an insurance contract, the insured's duty to provide information ordinarily arises only under the express policy obligations." Cooperation clauses in insurance contracts "fulfill the reasonable purpose of enabling the insurer to obtain relevant information concerning the loss while the information is fresh." "Compliance with insurance policy provisions are conditions precedent to recovery under that

[continued]

policy, which must be fulfilled before an insured may proceed with a lawsuit." "[F]ailure of an insured to cooperate with the insurer has been held to be a material breach of the contract and a defense to suit on the policy." Such failure may be "manifested by a refusal to submit to an examination under oath or a refusal to produce documents."

"[T]he purpose of the oral examination of the insured is to protect the insurer against fraud, by permitting it to probe into the circumstances of the loss, including an examination of the insured[.]" The defendant must also show that it has been prejudiced by the failure of the plaintiffs to submit to examinations under oath. "The burden is on the insurer to show actual prejudice."

In this case, the Hamiltons reported the alleged theft to local law enforcement, submitted their claim to State Farm, and returned the PPIFs to State Farm as requested; the Hamiltons failed to provide most of the supporting documentation of their loss as requested by State Farm, with the exception of a few duplicate receipts. When asked for the additional documentation, the Hamiltons simply provided their sworn statements as to the losses claimed, without providing the additional supporting documentation requested.

The Hamiltons' failure to comply with State Farm's request to examine the separate residences in which they lived, while not expressly required under the policy's cooperation clause, appears from the record to have been the event which prompted State Farm to request the examinations under oath. The Hamiltons, however, failed to respond to State Farm's multiple verbal and written requests for examinations under oath. Their failure to

do so was in direct violation of the policy's cooperation clause provision, Section 1 - Conditions, (2)(d)(3)(b), and is thus considered a "material breach of the contract." The Hamiltons concede in their brief that they failed to respond to State Farm's request for their examinations under oath but submit that State Farm was not prejudiced by their refusals because they would have consented to depositions to be taken later in the litigation. This argument is not persuasive. The underlying purpose of a cooperation clause is to allow the insurer to obtain the material information it needs from the insured to adequately investigate a claim of loss prior to the commencement of litigation proceedings.

Without the additional requested documentation in support of their loss or their sworn statements under oath, State Farm had nothing but the Hamiltons' original recorded statements, which often conflicted with each other factually, and several duplicated receipts to process their claim of over $120,000 in losses. Consequently, it is clear that State Farm's investigation into the claim was prejudiced from the Hamiltons' failure to comply with the terms of the cooperation clause.

Because the Hamiltons materially breached the terms of the policy by failing to comply with the terms of the cooperation clause, they were precluded from recovering under the policy. Additionally, considering that State Farm's denial of the claim was due to the Hamiltons' material breach of the policy, the Hamiltons are also precluded from recovering penalties and attorney fees.

AFFIRMED in favor of State Farm.

CRITICAL THINKING

What kind of evidence would have persuaded State Farm that the Hamiltons had a legitimate insurance claim? What is the reasoning of the court in supporting State Farm's expectations under the cooperation clause in the policy?

ETHICAL DECISION MAKING

How would the universalization principle have aided the Hamiltons in understanding the logic being used by State Farm?

? **BUT WHAT IF . . .**
WHAT IF THE FACTS OF THE CASE OPENER WERE DIFFERENT?
Recall, in the Case Opener, that CPI manufactured Encore's products in its factory. Let's say that CPI simply stopped allowing the products in the factory. Would Encore be able to be discharged from the contract, or would Encore have to stay in the contract and find some sort of resolution?

Anticipatory Repudiation. Sometimes a contracting party may decide not to complete the contract before the actual time of performance. This situation often arises when market conditions change and one party realizes that it will not be profitable to carry out the terms of the contract. The breaching party may convey the anticipatory breach to the nonbreaching party either by making an express indication of her intent to no longer perform or by taking an action that would be inconsistent with her ability to carry out the contract when performance was due.

Once the contract has been anticipatorily repudiated, the nonbreaching party is discharged from his obligations under the contract. He is free to go ahead and sue for breach, as well as find another similar contract elsewhere. However, if the nonbreaching party wishes, he may decide to give the party who repudiated the opportunity to change her mind and still perform.

DISCHARGE BY MUTUAL AGREEMENT

Sometimes the parties to a contract agree to discharge each other from their obligations. They may do so through four primary means: discharge by mutual rescission, discharge by a substituted contract, discharge by accord and satisfaction, or discharge by novation. (See Exhibit 20-2.)

Mutual Rescission.   Parties may agree that they simply wish to discharge each other from their mutual obligations and therefore rescind or cancel the contract. For example, if James had agreed to cater a graduation reception for Bill's son but it appeared that the child was not going to graduate when planned, James could agree to no longer hold Bill responsible for paying him the agreed-on cost for the catering in exchange for Bill's agreement to no longer expect James to cater a reception.

> To see how techniques of group problem solving relate to mutual rescission, please see the **Connecting to the Core** activity on the text website at www.mhhe.com/kubasek3e.

Substituted Contract.   Sometimes, instead of canceling the contract and terminating their relationship, the parties wish to substitute a new agreement in place of the original. The substituted contract immediately discharges the parties from their obligations under the old contract and replaces those obligations with the new obligations imposed by the substituted contract.

In the opening scenario, the amended agreement between Anchor and Encore is a substituted contract. In their original contract, the parties were silent about where the wine bottles would be produced and Anchor provided Encore with a rebate discount schedule ranging from 1 to 2.5 percent. Their substituted contract (the amended agreement) discharged the parties from the previous requirements, specified the Lavington facility as the production location, and increased the rates associated with the discount schedule.

Mutual rescission	Parties mutually agree to discharge each other from the contract.	
Substituted contract	Parties mutually agree to discharge each other from the contract by substituting a new agreement.	
Accord and satisfaction	Parties agree that one party will perform her or his duty differently from the performance specified in the original agreement; after the new duty is performed, the party's duty under the original contract becomes discharged.	
Novation	The original parties and a third party all agree that the third party will replace one of the original parties and that the original party will then be discharged.	

Exhibit 20-2

Ways to Discharge by Mutual Agreement

Accord and Satisfaction.   An accord and satisfaction is used when one of the parties wishes to substitute a different performance for his or her original duty under the contract. The promise to perform the new duty is called the *accord,* and the actual performance of that new duty is called the *satisfaction.* The party's duty under the contract is not discharged until the new duty is actually performed. Thus, it is the satisfaction that discharges the party.

Novation.   Sometimes the parties to the agreement want to replace one of the parties with a third party. This substitution of a party is called a novation. The original duties remain the same under the contract, but one party is discharged and the third party now takes that original party's place. All three parties must agree to the novation for it to be valid.

DISCHARGE BY OPERATION OF LAW

Sometimes a contract may be discharged not by anything the parties do but, rather, by operation of law. Alteration of the contract, bankruptcy, tolling of the statute of limitations, impossibility, commercial impracticability, and frustration of purpose are all situations in which a contract may be discharged by operation of law.

Alteration of the Contract.   The courts wish to uphold the sanctity of contracts. Therefore, if one of the parties materially alters a written contract without the knowledge of the other party, the courts have held that such alteration allows the innocent party to be discharged from the contract. For example, if a seller, without knowledge of the buyer, changes the price of the contract, the buyer can treat the contract as terminated.

Bankruptcy.   When a party files bankruptcy, the court allocates the assets of the bankrupt among the bankrupt's creditors and then issues the party a discharge in bankruptcy. Once the assets have been distributed, all of the bankrupt's debts are discharged. (Bankruptcy is discussed in detail in Chapter 32.)

Tolling of the Statute of Limitations.   The tolling of the statute of limitations does not technically discharge a party's obligations under a contract. However, once the statute of limitations has tolled, neither party can any longer sue the other for breach, so for all practical purposes the parties are no longer bound to perform.

Impossibility of Performance.   Sometimes an unforeseen event occurs that makes it physically or legally impossible for a party to carry out the terms of the contract. In such a situation, the party will be discharged on grounds of impossibility of performance. Courts distinguish between objective impossibility, meaning it is in fact not possible to lawfully carry out one's contractual obligations, and subjective impossibility, meaning it would be very difficult to carry out the contract. Objective impossibility, but not subjective impossibility, discharges the parties' obligations under the contract.

For example, if farmer Gray has a contract with the Hunts Corporation to provide it with 100 bushels of tomatoes on August 30 and a flood wipes out Gray's crop, it is not physically impossible for him to comply with the agreement. He has to go out on the market and purchase 100 bushels of tomatoes to ship to the Hunts Corporation. It may be inconvenient, and perhaps subjectively impossible, but it is not objectively impossible.

In contrast, suppose farmer Jones owns a historic farmhouse built in 1827 and he agrees to sell it to Smith, but the night before the parties are to exchange money for the title, lightning strikes the farmhouse and the building burns to the ground. It is now objectively impossible to comply with the terms of the contract, so the parties are discharged from their obligations. The historic farmhouse is not like tomatoes; the subject matter of the contract is forever destroyed and cannot be re-created.

There are three main situations in which the courts find objective impossibility. The first is *destruction of the subject matter,* as in the example of the historic farmhouse destroyed by fire. If we go back to the example of the tomatoes, note that we said the farmer still had to perform because it was still possible for him to obtain tomatoes elsewhere. To protect himself in the event that his crop was destroyed, farmer Gray could have drafted the contract to identify the subject matter as 100 bushels of tomatoes grown on the Gray family farm. In that case, if Gray's fields were flooded, it would be objectively impossible to comply with the contract because there would be no tomatoes from the Gray farm in existence.

The second situation of objective impossibility is the *death or incapacity of a party whose personal services are necessary* to fulfill the terms of the contract. For example, if a famous artist is commissioned to paint a portrait and the artist dies, the contract is discharged. The artist's style is unique, and there is no way for anyone to take over the artist's role.

The third situation is *subsequent illegality.* If the law changes after the contract is made, rendering the performance of the contract illegal, then the contract is discharged. For example, Bill orders a case of a nutritional supplement from Osco Drugs and Supplements. Before his order can be filled, the nutritional supplement is banned because of recently discovered harmful side effects. The parties are now discharged from their duties because to sell the banned substance would be to violate the law.

The opening scenario provides another example of impossibility of performance. The parties in the opening scenario do not dispute that the contract provided that "[t]he parties contemplate that the products (as hereinafter defined) shall be manufactured at CPI's Lavington facility" (the Lavington plant). When the Lavington plant was no longer available for production, it became impossible for Anchor to fulfill the terms of the contract. Ultimately, Anchor informed Encore that it considered itself discharged from the contract.

Legal Principle: A contract is objectively impossible, and therefore parties are discharged from their obligations under it, when the subject matter is destroyed, one of the parties whose personal services are required dies or becomes incapacitated, or the law changes, rendering performance of the contract illegal.

Commercial Impracticability. Commercial impracticability can be seen as a response to what some might interpret as a somewhat unfair harshness of the objective-impossibility standard. Commercial impracticability is used when performance is still objectively possible but would be extraordinarily injurious or expensive to one party. Commercial impracticability arises when, because of an unforeseeable event, one party would incur unreasonable expense, injury, or loss if that party were forced to carry out the terms of the agreement.

According to the Restatement (Second) of Contracts, Section 261 (1981), discharge by reason of impracticability requires that the party claiming discharge prove the following three elements:

1. That an event occurred whose nonoccurrence was a basic assumption of the contract.

2. That there is commercial impracticability of continued performance.

3. That the party claiming discharge did not expressly or impliedly agree to performance in spite of impracticability that would otherwise justify nonperformance.

It is sometimes difficult to know whether the potential harm to the party seeking to avoid the contract is sufficient to give rise to the use of commercial impracticability. The doctrine is most commonly used in situations in which raw materials needed for manufacturing goods under the contract become extraordinarily expensive or difficult to obtain because of an embargo, war, crop failure, or unexpected closure of a plant. Case 20-2 illustrates how the courts sometimes struggle to determine whether to apply the doctrine of commercial impracticability to discharge a contract.

CASE 20-2   THRIFTY RENT-A-CAR SYSTEM v. SOUTH FLORIDA TRANSPORT

U.S. DISTRICT COURT FOR THE NORTHERN DISTRICT OF OKLAHOMA
2005 U.S. DIST. LEXIS 38489

The plaintiffs, Thrifty Rent-A-Car System and its affiliates DTG and Rental Car Finance Corp., allowed South Florida Transport (SFT), the defendant, to establish a Thrifty franchise. In 2003, Thrifty and SFT entered into four agreements, which provided SFT the right to use Thrifty's trademark and business methods in exchange for payment to Thrifty of licensing and administrative fees. The agreements also provided that SFT would maintain a fleet of automobiles for rental.

In July 2004, SFT provided DTG with a check as payment, but the check was returned for insufficient funds. SFT continued to make delinquent payments, and by August, SFT owed Thrifty and DTG $1,134,819.40. Due to SFT's failure to make payments, Thrifty and DTG informed SFT that they were going to terminate the licensing agreements and repossess the vehicles, to which DTG had legal title. However, DTG agreed to postpone repossession due to predictions of severe weather, and allowed SFT to continue renting vehicles until repossession was completed.

When DTG repossessed the vehicles, DTG noticed that numerous cars were missing. In response, SFT notified DTG that it had sold 51 vehicles without authorization. By August 2005, SFT owed Thrifty and DTG $4,238,249.53. SFT claimed that several hurricanes rendered their business operations commercially impracticable. The plaintiffs filed a motion for summary judgment, seeking full reimbursement for the debts owed by SFT.

JUDGE EAGAN: Performance may become impracticable due to extreme and unreasonable difficulty, expense, injury, or loss to one of the parties involved. Impracticability does not equate to impracticality, however. "A mere change in the degree of difficulty or expense . . . unless well beyond the normal range does not amount to impracticability since it is this sort of risk that a fixed-price contract is intended to cover." The law also imposes an objective standard on the duty to perform for those seeking to invoke the defense of impracticability. A party to a contract is not discharged from his duty to perform merely by demonstrating that a supervening event prevented him from performing; he must also demonstrate that similarly situated parties were also deprived of the ability to perform.

The undisputed facts relevant to Greenstein's claim of impracticability are as follows: In August and September 2004, Hurricanes Charley, Frances, Ivan, and Jeanne hit the state of Florida. One of those storms, Hurricane Ivan, also affected the state of Alabama. Although some of SFT's rental car business locations incurred damage during the course of the storm, it is undisputed that the locations remained substantially intact, and the vehicles leased from DTG were not destroyed.

The hurricanes in late summer 2004 clearly constitute supervening events for the purposes of impracticability doctrine. However, the record suggests that the nonoccurrence of those hurricanes was not an assumption upon which the parties grounded their agreement. Hardy testified that he lived in Florida approximately ten years, during which time severe weather, including hurricanes, had hit the coast of Florida.

The doctrine of commercial impracticability is typically invoked in cases involving the sale of goods. Codified in section 2-615 of the Uniform Commercial Code (UCC), which has been adopted by the Oklahoma legislature, the doctrine of commercial impracticability provides a defense to a seller for a delay in delivery or nondelivery of promised goods if performance has been made impracticable by a contingency, the nonoccurrence of which is an assumption of the contract.

Commercial impracticability may excuse a party from performance of his obligations under a contract where performance has become commercially impracticable because of unforeseen supervening circumstances not within the contemplation of the parties at the time of contracting. UCC commentary provides that a party pleading commercial impracticability must demonstrate the "basic assumption" prong of the test also found in the impracticability of performance context, that is, that the nonoccurrence of the

[continued]

supervening event was a basic assumption of the parties at the time of contracting. A rise or a collapse in the market standing alone does not constitute a justification for failure to perform. A contract is deemed commercially impracticable when, due to unforeseen events, performance may only be obtained at "an excessive and unreasonable cost . . . or when all means of performance are commercially senseless." In applying the doctrine of commercial impracticability, the crucial question is "whether the cost of performance has in fact become so excessive and unreasonable that failure to excuse performance would result in grave injustice."

For many of the reasons already discussed, defendant is not entitled to the defense of commercial impracticability.

The evidence strongly suggests that the nonoccurrence of hurricanes was not a basic assumption of the parties' agreements. Moreover, defendant provides no evidence to support a suggestion that the event of the hurricanes made the cost of performance of the terms of the agreements unduly burdensome, or even remotely more expensive. Finally, the Court observes, again, that SFT was behind on its payments to Thrifty and DTG before the arrival of the hurricanes in August 2004. No genuine issue of material fact exists, and the Court holds that the defense of commercial impracticability is unavailable to defendant.

Plaintiff's motion for summary judgment granted.

CRITICAL THINKING

What are the implications of the court's decision that commercial impracticability is not constituted by the significant hurricane damages imposed on Florida in 2004? Especially given the increased rates of severe weather and natural disasters witnessed recently around the world, to what extent can parties entering into contracts reasonably be expected to plan for the effects of a rapidly changing global climate?

ETHICAL DECISION MAKING

How might ethical theories founded in deontology and in ethics of care differ in their interpretation of the behaviors examined in this case? Which interpretation do you think is more ethically defendable? Which interpretation does Judge Eagan appear to favor? Justify your response.

What purpose does this ruling appear to support? Is there a larger ethical end implied by Judge Eagan's decision? Why or why not?

BUT WHAT IF . . .
WHAT IF THE FACTS OF THE CASE OPENER WERE DIFFERENT?

Let's say that CPI left its factory to Anchor so that Anchor could still manufacture products for Encore as stated in the contract. However, manufacturing the products as CPI did would be outrageously expensive for Anchor. Does Anchor still have to remain in the contract with Encore?

Frustration of Purpose.   Closely related to impracticability is frustration of purpose. Sometimes, when a contract is entered into, both parties recognize that the contract is to fulfill a particular purpose, and the happening of that purpose is said to be a basic assumption on which the contract is made. If, due to factors beyond the control of the parties, the event does not occur, and neither party had assumed the risk of the event's nonoccurrence, the contract may be discharged.

This doctrine arose from the so-called coronation cases in England. Numerous parties had contracted for rooms along the parade route for the king's coronation, but the king became ill and the coronation was canceled. The courts held that the parties' duties under the room contracts should be discharged and that any payments made in advance should be returned as the essential purposes of the contracts could no longer be fulfilled, through no fault of any of the parties.

BUT WHAT IF . . .

WHAT IF THE FACTS OF THE CASE OPENER WERE DIFFERENT?

Let's say that Anchor and Encore had entered into the contract with the purpose of creating a certain kind of bottle that was better for the environment than normal bottles. However, the two companies tried but could not produce such a bottle. Can the contract be discharged?

This doctrine is not frequently used. For example, if you contract for an organist to play at your daughter's wedding but the groom gets cold feet at the last moment and the wedding is canceled, you cannot use frustration of purpose to discharge the contract because the groom's changing his mind was a foreseeable event, even though it was unlikely. The Case Nugget on the next page illustrates another unsuccessful attempted use of this doctrine.

Exhibit 20-3 summarizes the five methods of discharging a contract.

Exhibit 20-3

Methods of Discharging a Contract

Discharge by conditions	If precedent, concurrent, implied, and express conditions are not met or subsequent condition occurs.
Discharge by performance	If a party performs the terms of the contract or makes a tender (an offer to perform), or if the party performs to the satisfaction of the contracting party.
Discharge by material breach	If a party fails to substantially perform his obligations, thereby justifying that the nonbreaching party be discharged from the contract.
Discharge by mutual agreement	If the parties mutually agree to discharge one another, substitute a new contract, substitute a party, or substitute a different performance.
Discharge by operation of the law	If one of the following occurs: alteration of the contract, bankruptcy, tolling of the statute of limitations, impossibility, commercial impracticability, or frustration of purpose.

L02

What are the primary legal remedies available for a breach of contract?

Remedies

The fact that one party has breached a contract does not necessarily mean that the non breaching party will sue. A number of factors go into the decision of whether or not it makes sense to file suit (see Exhibit 20-4). Some of those considerations include (1) the likelihood of success, (2) the desire or need to maintain an ongoing relationship with the potential defendant, (3) the possibility of getting a better or faster resolution through some form of alternative dispute resolution, and (4) the cost of litigation or some form of ADR as compared to the value of the likely remedy.

Exhibit 20-4

Things to Consider before Filing Suit

1. The likelihood of success.

2. The desire or need to maintain an ongoing relationship with the potential defendant.

3. The possibility of getting a better or faster resolution through some form of alternative dispute resolution.

4. The cost of litigation or some form of ADR as compared to the value of the likely remedy.

AN UNFORESEEABLE EVENT?

Liggett Restaurant Group, Inc. v. City of Pontiac
260 Mich. App. 127, 676 N.W.2d 633 (Mich. App. 2003)

Elias Brothers Restaurants, Inc., had a contract with the defendant, City of Pontiac Stadium Building Authority, to provide concessions at the Silverdome until 2000. The parties renegotiated the contract in 1990, and Elias Brothers agreed to pay additional consideration for the option to extend the contract until 2005 to coordinate with the end of the Detroit Lions' sublease. The additional consideration involved paying the city a higher percentage on profits from sales. This option was exercised on December 1, 1998, and the Detroit Lions prematurely discontinued playing in the Silverdome after the 2001 football season.

The plaintiff sought to use the frustration-of-purpose doctrine to discharge its obligations under the contract extension and therefore have returned to it the additional consideration it had paid under the extension. The plaintiff argued that the contract was made on the assumption that the Lions would play in the Silverdome until their lease ran out and thus their early departure frustrated the purpose of the extension.

The court said the doctrine was inapplicable in this case. The court first set forth the conditions under which the doctrine applied: (1) The contract must be at least partially executory; (2) the frustrated party's purpose in making the contract must have been known to both parties when the contract was made; (3) this purpose must have been basically frustrated by an event not reasonably foreseeable at the time the contract was made, the occurrence of which has not been due to the fault of the frustrated party and the risk of which was not assumed by him. Then the court noted that the situation clearly did not meet the third criterion. Far from being an unforeseeable event, the Lions' leaving prematurely was expressly addressed in the original contract by a paragraph specifying a reduction in the guaranteed minimum annual payment for each year in which the Lions did not play a minimum of eight games in the stadium.

The remedies the potential plaintiff will be thinking about can generally be classified as either *legal remedies* (also known as *monetary damages*) or *equitable remedies,* some form of court-ordered action. The distinction between legal and equitable remedies can be traced back to a time in our legal system's English roots when, instead of one unitary legal system, there were two separate courts, a court of law and a court of equity. When parties were seeking money damages, they went to the court of law; but when parties needed any remedy other than money damages, they went to the High Court of Chancery, which was a court of equity. When the United States was establishing its legal system, it combined both these types of powers in a unitary system. The reasons for this joinder are not known, but it seems likely that the primary reason was that the early colonists simply did not have the resources to support two separate systems. The courts did, however, still maintain the distinction between legal and equitable remedies. However, unlike judges in the old English courts, judges in the U.S. system have the power to award both legal and equitable remedies in the same case. This section discusses these various remedies.

LEGAL REMEDIES (MONETARY DAMAGES)

Monetary damages are also referred to as *legal damages* or *legal remedies,* and they include compensatory, punitive, nominal, and liquidated damages. Whenever possible, courts award monetary damages rather than some form of equitable relief.

Compensatory Damages. The most frequently awarded damages are compensatory damages, damages designed to put the plaintiff in the position he would have been in had the contract been fully performed. These damages are said to compensate the plaintiff for his loss of the benefit of the bargain. He can recover, however, only for those provable losses that were foreseeable at the time the contract was entered into. Sometimes, the plaintiff actually may have no losses. Suppose, for example, that Dr. Wilcox hires Jeremy to work exclusively as his research assistant during the fall semester, for a salary of $2,000 per month. If Wilcox breaches the contract and terminates Jeremy for no reason with two months left on the contract, and the only job Jeremy can get as a substitute pays only $500 per month, Jeremy would be entitled to compensatory damages of $3,000. However, if Jeremy gets a new job that pays $2,500 per month, he is actually better off, so no compensatory damages would be awarded. Sometimes these damages are referred to as *expectation damages* because they compensate a person for the benefit she or he expected to gain as a result of entering into the contract.

In addition to losing the benefit of the bargain, the plaintiff may suffer other losses directly caused by the breach. These losses may be compensated for as *incidental damages*. For example, because Jeremy was unfairly terminated before his contractual term was over, he may have to spend money to find another job. His job search expenditures would be considered incidental damages.

BUT WHAT IF . . .
WHAT IF THE FACTS OF THE CASE OPENER WERE DIFFERENT?

Let's say that after Anchor and Encore stopped doing business together, Encore entered into an agreement with another company whereby it received bigger discounts than those it received from Anchor. Could Encore still sue Anchor for compensatory damages for breaching the contract?

Some kinds of contracts have special rules for determining compensatory damages, namely, contracts for the sale of goods or land and construction contracts. Each of these is discussed in a little more detail below.

Contracts for the sale of goods are governed today by the Uniform Commercial Code. If the seller breaches the contract, compensatory damages are generally calculated as the difference between the contract price and the market price on the day the goods were supposed to be delivered,[3] plus any incidental damages resulting from the breach. In other words, this measure of damages is the difference between what the buyer would have paid for the goods under the contract and what he or she is now going to have to pay to obtain the goods from another seller. Occasionally, however, the buyer may have no damages because the market price of the goods is lower than the parties had anticipated it would be at the date of delivery and so the buyer can now actually purchase the goods at a lower price than the contract price.

If the buyer breaches before accepting the goods, the seller would be able to resell the goods and recover as compensatory damages the difference between the price he sold the goods for and the contract price, plus any incidental expenses associated with the sale.[4] If the seller is unable to sell the goods to another buyer, as might be the case, for example, with shirts embroidered with a company's monogram, then the seller may be entitled to the contract price as damages. If the buyer breaches before the goods are even manufactured, the seller's damages would typically be based on the profits that would have been made from the sale.

In construction contracts, contracts whereby an owner enters into an agreement to have a building constructed, damages are calculated differently depending on who the breaching party is and what stage the construction is in when the breach occurs. If the contract is breached by the owner before the construction is begun, damages are simply lost profits, which are calculated by subtracting the projected costs of construction from the contract

---

[3] UCC §§ 2-708 and 2-713.

[4] UCC §§ 2-706 and 2-710.

price. For example, if Cameron Construction Company anticipates building a warehouse for the Johnson Corporation with a contract price of $500,000 and the cost of raw materials and labor is $420,000, Cameron could recover $80,000 in lost profits if the Johnson Corporation were to breach the contract before performance had begun.

If, however, Cameron Construction had already expended $20,000 in materials and labor on the job when the breach occurred, the company would be able to recover $100,000 in damages because the amount of damages when construction is in progress is measured by the lost profits plus any money already invested in the project. If the breach by the owner had occurred after construction was completed, the construction company would be entitled to recover the entire contract price, plus interest from the time payment for the project was due.

If the construction company or contractor breaches the contract before or during the construction, the owner's damages are generally measured by the cost of hiring another company to complete the project, plus any incidental costs associated with obtaining a new contractor, as well as any costs arising from delays in the construction project. If the contractor completes the job but finishes after the date for completion, the owner is entitled to damages for the loss of the use of the building that she would have had if the contract had been completed in a timely manner.

Consequential Damages. It should be apparent by now that contract law requires greater certainty in the proof of damages than does tort law. Damages are not recoverable for breach of contract unless they can be proved with a high degree of certainty. One type of damages in contract cases that is often especially difficult to prove is what are called consequential or special damages. Consequential damages are foreseeable damages that result from special facts and circumstances arising outside the contract itself. These damages must be within the contemplation of the parties at the time the breach occurs.

In Case 20-3, a classic case, the court distinguishes consequential damages from the damages that arise naturally from a breach of contract.

CASE 20-3 HADLEY v. BAXENDALE
COURT OF EXCHEQUER
156 ENG. REP. 145 (1854)

Plaintiffs were millers in Gloucester. On May 11, their mill was stopped when the crank shaft of the mill broke. They had to send the shaft to Greenwich to be used as a model for a new crank to be molded. The plaintiffs' servant took the shaft to the defendant, a common carrier, and told the defendant's clerk that the mill was stopped, and that the shaft must be sent immediately. The clerk said it would be delivered at Greenwich on the following day. The defendant's clerk was told that a special entry, if required, should be made to hasten the shaft's delivery. The delivery of the shaft at Greenwich was delayed by some neglect, and consequently, the plaintiffs did not receive the new shaft for several days after they would otherwise have received it. During that time the mill was shut down, and the plaintiffs thereby lost the profits they would otherwise have received had the shaft been delivered on time. They sought to recover damages for lost profits during that time. The defendant argued that the lost profits were "too

remote." The court decided for the plaintiffs and allowed the jury to consider the lost profits in awarding damages. The defendant appealed.

JUSTICE ALDERSON: We think that there ought to be a new trial in this case; but, in so doing, we deem it to be expedient and necessary to state explicitly the rule which the Judge, at the next trial, ought, in our opinion, to direct the jury to be governed by when they estimate the damages. . . .

Now we think the proper rule in such a case as the present is this: Where two parties have made a contract which one of them has broken, the damages which the other party ought to receive in respect of such breach of contract should be such as may fairly and reasonably be considered either arising naturally, i.e., according to the usual course of things, from such breach of contract itself, or such as may reasonably be supposed to have been in the contemplation of both

[continued]

parties, at the time they made the contract, as the probable result of the breach of it. Now, if the special circumstances under which the contract was actually made were communicated by the plaintiffs to the defendants, and thus known to both parties, the damages resulting from the breach of such a contract, which they would reasonably contemplate, would be the amount of injury which would ordinarily follow from a breach of contract under these special circumstances so known and communicated. But, on the other hand, if these special circumstances were wholly unknown to the party breaking the contract, he, at the most, could only be supposed to have had in his contemplation the amount of injury which would arise generally, and in the great multitude of cases not affected by any special circumstances, from such a breach of contract. For, had the special circumstances been known, the parties might have specially provided for the breach of contract by special terms as to the damages in that case; and of this advantage it would be very unjust to deprive them. . . . Now, in the present case, if we are to apply the principles above laid down, we find that the only circumstances here communicated by the plaintiffs to the defendants at the time the contract was made, were, that the article to be carried was the broken shaft of a mill, and that the plaintiffs were the millers of the mill.

But how do these circumstances show reasonably that the profits of the mill must be stopped by an unreasonable delay in the delivery of the broken shaft by the carrier to the third person? . . . But it is obvious that, in the great multitude of cases of millers sending off broken shafts to third persons by a carrier under ordinary circumstances, such consequences would not, in all probability, have occurred; and these special circumstances were here never communicated by the plaintiffs to the defendants. It follows therefore, that the loss of profits here cannot reasonably be considered such a consequence of the breach of contract as could have been fairly and reasonably contemplated by both the parties when they made this contract. For such loss would neither have flowed naturally from the breach of this contract in the great multitude of such cases occurring under ordinary circumstances, nor were the special circumstances, which, perhaps, would have made it a reasonable and natural consequence of such breach of contract, communicated to or known by the defendants.

Judgment for defendant for a new trial.

CRITICAL THINKING

What are the key terms essential to this argument? Are alternative definitions of important words or phrases possible? If so, how could the acceptability of this argument be affected by the use of these alternative meanings?

What additional information would be useful in deciding the acceptability of this argument? For instance, what do we really know about the proposed loss of profit? Does this missing information have a significant impact on the reasoning?

ETHICAL DECISION MAKING

What value preferences can be discovered in Judge Alderson's ruling? Are they properly justified? What ethical theories or guidelines might aid in their justification? Why?

Punitive Damages. Just as in tort law, punitive damages in contract law are designed to punish the defendant and deter him and others from engaging in similar behavior in the future. Because the primary objective of contract law, however, is to ensure that parties' expectations are met, punitive, or exemplary, damages are rarely awarded. Most jurisdictions award them only when the defendant has engaged in reprehensible conduct such as fraud. The primary factor in determining the amount of punitive damages is how much is necessary to "punish" the defendant; thus the amount depends on matters such as the wealth and income of the defendant.

Nominal Damages. In a case where no actual damages resulted from the breach of contract, the court may award the plaintiff nominal damages. The award is typically for $1 or $5, but it serves to signify that the plaintiff has been wronged by the defendant.

Liquidated Damages. Typically, the court determines the amount of damages to which a nonbreaching party is entitled. Sometimes, however, the parties recognize that if there is a breach of contract, it will probably be somewhat difficult for the court to determine exactly what the damages are. To prevent a difficult court battle, the parties specify in advance what the liquidated damages will be if there is a particular kind of breach. The parties specify these damages in what is called a *liquidated* or *stipulated-damage clause* in the contract. The damages may be specified as either a fixed amount or a formula for determining how much money is due. Such clauses are frequently used in construction contracts when the buyer needs to know the property is going to be available by a specific date so that she can make her plans for moving in. In such a case, the parties may estimate in advance what it will cost the buyer for storage and temporary housing if the property is not ready by the specified date. The courts generally enforce these clauses as long as they appear to bear a reasonable relationship to what the actual costs will be. If the amount specified is so unreasonable as to not seem to bear any logical relationship to foreseeable costs, the courts declare the clause a penalty clause and do not enforce it.

Mitigation of Damages.   When a contract has been breached, the nonbreaching party is often angry at the breaching party and may want to make the breaching party "pay through the nose." However, the courts do not allow a nonbreaching party to intentionally increase his damages. In fact, to recover damages in a breach-of-contract case, the plaintiff must demonstrate that he used reasonable efforts to minimize the damage resulting from the breach. This obligation is referred to as the *duty to mitigate one's damages*.

Thus, if you are the manager of a hotel and a person who had booked 10 rooms for the week calls to cancel all the reservations, you have a duty to attempt to rent the rooms to minimize the damages. The mitigation must be reasonable, however, and no one is expected to settle for something less than what was contemplated under the contract in order to mitigate the damages.

One area where interesting mitigation issues arise is cases in which an employee is wrongfully discharged and must seek new employment to mitigate her damages. If the employee does not seek alternative employment, the amount of lost wages recovered as damages will be reduced by the amount the employee reasonably could have earned in another job. If the employee does not find another job, the court must decide whether the employee could have found comparable alternative employment with reasonable effort.

EQUITABLE REMEDIES

As noted earlier, equitable remedies grew out of the English court's authority to fashion remedies when the existing laws did not provide any adequate ones. These remedies were typically unique solutions specifically crafted to the demands of the situations. Today, the most common equitable remedies include rescission and restitution, orders for specific performance, and injunctions.

As a carryover from the days of the English courts of law and equity, a party seeking equitable relief must meet five requirements. The party must prove that (1) there is no adequate legal remedy available; (2) irreparable harm to the plaintiff may result if the equitable remedy is not granted; (3) the contract is legally valid (except when seeking relief in quasi-contract); (4) the contract terms are clear and unambiguous; and (5) the plaintiff has "clean hands," that is, has not been deceitful or done anything in breach of the contract.

Rescission and Restitution.   Sometimes the parties simply want to be returned to their precontract status; they want to have the contract terminated and to have any

L03

What are the primary equitable remedies available for a breach of contract?

COMPARING THE LAW OF OTHER COUNTRIES

LIQUIDATED DAMAGES IN CHINA

Article 114 of Chapter 7, "Liability for Breach of Contracts," of the Contract Law of the People's Republic of China provides for the equivalent of the liquidated-damage clause recognized under U.S. law. The first part of the Chinese law is almost identical to our law. It provides that the parties to a contract may agree that one party shall, when violating the contract, pay breach-of-contract damages of a certain amount in light of the breach or they may agree on the calculating method of compensation for losses resulting from the breach of contract.

However, the Chinese law has an interesting twist for circumstances in which the projected damages end up being different from what the actual damages are. If the agreed breach-of-contract damages are lower than the losses caused, any party may request that the people's court or an arbitration institution increase it; if it is excessively higher than the losses caused, any party may request that the people's court or an arbitration institution make an appropriate reduction.

transferred property returned to its original owner. That is, they want rescission and restitution. Rescission is the termination of the contract, and restitution is the return of any property given up under the contract.

Restitution and rescission are most frequently awarded in situations in which there is a lack of genuine assent (discussed in Chapter 17). When a party enters into a contract because of fraud, duress, undue influence, or a bilateral mistake, the contract is voidable and the party who wants out may seek to avoid the contract or, in other words, may seek rescission and restitution.

Specific Performance. Specific performance is sometimes called *specific enforcement.* It is an order requiring that the breaching party fulfill the terms of the agreement. Courts are very reluctant to grant specific performance and will do so only when monetary damages simply are not adequate, typically because the subject matter of the contract is unique. If the subject matter is unique, then even if the nonbreaching party is given compensation, he cannot go elsewhere to buy the item from someone else, so this renders any kind of money damages inadequate.

Primarily for historical reasons, every piece of real property is considered unique. Therefore, an order for specific performance would often be the appropriate remedy for the breach of a contract for the sale of a piece of real estate.

Injunction. An injunction is an order either forcing a person to do something or prohibiting a person from doing something. Most commonly, injunctions are prohibitions against actions. Such an injunction might be used, for example, as a remedy in a contract case involving a personal service. Mandy is a lounge singer, and she has a contract to perform at JZ's Lounge every weekend night from January through June. Two months into her contract she decides to work for Bally's Lounge instead because Bally's will pay her twice as much. There is no way to adequately calculate the damages that would arise from the singer's going over to the other club to perform, so money damages would not really be an adequate remedy. Instead, the owner of JZ's may obtain an injunction prohibiting Mandy from performing in any lounge until the end of June, when her term of performance under the contract will have been completed.

Sometimes, when a party is suing another for breach of contract, one of the parties is concerned that before the court has had a chance to decide the case, the other party will do something to make it impossible for the concerned party to get the relief he would be entitled to. In such a situation, the concerned party may ask for a preliminary injunction to prohibit the other party from taking any action during the course of the lawsuit that would cause irreparable harm to any of the parties to the contract. For example, Jim agrees to sell Bob a very rare antique car for $15,000 but then says he is not going to comply with the terms of the agreement. Bob sues Jim for breach of contract, but before the case goes to trial, Bob finds out that Sara has told Jim that she would be willing to pay him $20,000 for the car. Bob may seek a preliminary injunction to prohibit Jim from selling the car to anyone else until the court decides whether Bob is entitled to an order for specific performance forcing Jim to sell the car to him. Thus, the preliminary injunction fulfills the purpose of maintaining the status quo until the case can be finally decided.

It is not always easy to predict when a court will issue a preliminary injunction, however, as Bear, Stearns & Co. recently discovered when the court refused to issue a preliminary injunction to enforce a contractual provision requiring that an employee provide 90 days' notice of termination of employment (a so-called garden-leave provision). The court's refusal was based in part on public policy concerns.[5] The company's executive director of private client services submitted his notice of resignation, effective immediately, and began working for Morgan Stanley the next day. Bear, Stearns & Co. sought to enjoin the former director from working for a competitor during the contractually specified 90-day notice period. In denying the injunction, despite a stated belief that the company would ultimately win the breach-of-contract claim, the court provided three reasons. First, the company could not establish that it would suffer irreparable harm, because its harm could be recompensed by money damages. Second, any hardship to Bear Stearns due to permitting the defendant to resume his employment with Morgan Stanley in violation of the 90-day restriction was outweighed by the risk to his "professional standing and the inability to advise his clients in times of economic turmoil." Third, the court could not order the requested relief because doing so would require the defendant to continue an at-will employment relationship against his will.[6]

Reformation.   Sometimes a written contract does not reflect the parties' actual agreement, or there are inconsistencies in the contract, such as the price being listed as "$200,000 (twenty thousand dollars)." In such a case, the written document may be rewritten to reflect what the parties had agreed on.

Recovery Based on Quasi-Contract.   When an enforceable contract does not in fact exist, the court may grant a recovery based on quasi-contract; that is, the court may impose a contractlike obligation on a party to prevent an injustice from occurring. Recovery in quasi-contract is often sought when a party thought a valid contract existed and thus gave up something of value in relying on the existence of a contract. To justify recovery under a theory of quasi-contract, sometimes referred to as *recovery in quantum meriut,* a plaintiff must prove that (1) the plaintiff conferred a benefit on the defendant; (2) the plaintiff had reasonably expected to be compensated for the benefit conferred on the defendant; and (3) the defendant would be unjustly enriched from receiving the benefit without compensating the plaintiff for it.

---

[5] "Court Declines to Issue Preliminary Injunction to Enforce Garden Leave Provision," *Labor and Employment Alert,* www.goodwinprocter.com/~/media/208D97723AA140B58BE5D0622EFEC428.ashx (accessed June 2, 2009).

[6] Ibid.

470   Part 2   Contracts

CASE OPENER WRAP-UP

Impossible Wine Bottles

Under the amended agreement between Anchor and Encore, the production of bottles was to take place at the Lavington plant. The Lavington plant was the only facility owned by CPI that was capable of producing the specific type and quality of glass container that is required by the wine industry. According to the court's ruling, when the Lavington plant was sold and the new owners did not take over CPI's obligations, the terms of the contract became impossible for Anchor to meet. As a result of the impossibility of performance, Anchor was discharged from the contract.

KEY TERMS

compensatory damages 463	consequential damages 465	monetary damages 463	restitution 468
complete performance 454	express conditions 453	nominal damages 466	special damages 465
concurrent conditions 453	implied conditions 453	novation 458	specific performance 468
condition precedent 452	injunction 468	objective impossibility 458	subjective impossibility 458
condition subsequent 452	liquidated damages 467	punitive damages 466	substantial performance 454
conditional contracts 452	material breach 455	rescission 468	tender 454

SUMMARY OF KEY TOPICS

Methods of Discharging a Contract

Contracts may be discharged in a number of different ways, including:

- The occurrence or nonoccurrence of a condition.
- Complete performance.
- Substantial performance.
- Material breach.
- Mutual agreement.
- Operation of law.

Remedies

Courts may grant parties in a breach-of-contract action legal or equitable remedies. *Legal remedies,* or money damages, include:

- *Compensatory damages:* Damages designed to put the plaintiff in the position he or she would have been in had the contract been fully performed.
- *Nominal damages:* Token damages that merely recognize that the plaintiff had been wronged.
- *Punitive damages:* Damages designed to punish the defendant.
- *Liquidated damages:* Damages specified in advance in the contract.

Equitable remedies, which are granted only when legal remedies are inadequate, include:

- *Rescission and restitution:* The termination of the contract and the return of the parties to their precontract status.
- *Specific performance:* An order requiring the defendant to perform some act.
- *Injunction:* An order prohibiting the defendant from performing some act.

POINT / COUNTERPOINT

Should Nonbreaching Parties Be Required to Mitigate Damages?	
NO	**YES**
Courts' requiring nonbreaching parties to mitigate damages is unfair. Contract law is designed to reward both parties for the agreement that they have reached. If one party is irresponsible and cannot perform as agreed, why should courts then punish the nonbreaching party by requiring him or her to mitigate damages? After all, the nonbreaching party likely made decisions subsequent to the contract on the assumption that the contract terms would be carried out, and mitigating damages introduces stress regarding those decisions. For instance, if a hotel owner entered a contract with a person who agreed to rent 50 hotel rooms and a conference room for a weekend, the hotel owner would focus his time and energy on advertising for other weekends. But to require the hotel owner, after learning that the person no longer wanted the rooms, to mitigate damages places stress on the owner that he would not have otherwise experienced. Instead of completely focusing on booking rooms for other weekends, the hotel owner must now take time away from advertising those rooms so that he can try to fill the 50 vacant rooms and conference room, even if he wants to sue for breach of contract. In addition, requiring nonbreaching parties to mitigate damages encourages irresponsible behavior on the part of contracting parties. If a party knows she can breach a contract as long as she provides enough notice, she may be able to avoid most, if not all, liability. Returning to the hotel example, if the person who contracted to rent the 50 rooms notifies the hotel owner of the breach two months before the weekend she contracted for, the hotel owner could fill the rooms and the breaching party would likely not be liable for any damages, even though the hotel owner incurred greater expense and spent additional time filling the rooms with other guests. "Mitigating damages," therefore, is just a fancy way of saying that the burden shifts back to the nonbreaching parties, rewarding the very people who should bear the costs of breaching a contract.	Courts' requiring nonbreaching parties to mitigate damages provides the most equitable solution when a contract is breached. Although a nonbreaching party could understandably be frustrated with the breaching party, such a breach does not license the nonbreaching party to force the breaching party to provide full payment for the contract, especially when many costs could have been avoided. For example, if a city contracts with a company to construct a bridge across a river and the city later learns that the roads that would connect to the bridge would disrupt a nesting bald eagle, the company should not be permitted to still build the bridge and demand full payment. The city would then have to pay for a useless bridge, even though the company could have avoided the costs of building the bridge. In this example and similar contexts, the breaching parties would have an incentive to do nothing and still demand payment, even though damages could have been reduced. For instance, if a person entered a two-year employment contract to work for a company but the company could not honor the contract, the nonbreaching party should not be entitled to sit at home for two years and still receive compensation. In other words, if nonbreaching parties were not required to mitigate damages—either by discontinuing performance, as in the bridge example, or by finding a reasonable replacement, such as a different job in the employment example—nonbreaching parties would run up the costs by completing performance under the contract or doing nothing. In the context of finding a reasonable alternative, nonbreaching parties would actually have an incentive to do nothing. Finally, mitigating damages promotes better relationships between contracting parties, making both parties more willing to contract again in the future.

QUESTIONS & PROBLEMS

1. Explain the difference between legal and equitable remedies.

2. Explain how the existence of conditions subsequent and precedent affects the discharge of a contract.

3. Explain the relationship between commercial impracticability and frustration of purpose.

4. List the conditions that must be met for a court to impose a quasi-contract.

5. The Thompsons intended to buy a pickup truck from Lithia Dodge. They signed a retail installment contract which listed the annual interest rate as 3.9 percent and which stated that the contract was not binding until financing was completed and that any disputes arising under the contract would be resolved through arbitration. The Thompsons took their new truck home and left their trade-in vehicle with Lithia Dodge. A week later, the financing manager called the Thompsons and informed them that the financing rate of 3.9 had not been accepted and they would have to come in and sign a contract at a 4.9 percent rate. The Thompsons filed suit against Lithia Dodge, which by this time had already sold their trade-in vehicle. Lithia Dodge filed a motion to dismiss, arguing that the case had to go to arbitration because of the binding arbitration clause. The district court agreed. How do you believe the appellate court ruled, and why? [*Thompson v. Lithia Chrysler Jeep Dodge of Great Falls,* 185 P.3d 332 (Sup. Ct. Mt. 2008).]

6. Turner Construction entered into a contract to provide general construction of Granby Towers. Turner then entered into a subcontract with Universal to install precast concrete floors in the Granby Towers construction project. The general construction contract was incorporated by reference into the subcontract. The contract between Turner and Universal contained a "pay-when-paid provision" that conditioned any payments to Universal on Turner's first receiving payment from Universal. Due to the economic downturn, financing for the project fell through. Universal had substantially completed all its work by that time, and it sought payment of $885,507 from Turner, which refused to pay because it had not received any payment from the owner of the project. Turner asked the court for summary judgment on Universal's breach-of-contract claim. Should the court's grant of summary judgment be upheld? Why or why not? [*Universal Concrete Products v. Turner Construction Co.,* 4th Cir. Case No. 09-1569 (2010).]

7. Mantz worked for TruGreen, a lawn care company. He, along with other TruGreen employees, signed the company's noncompete, nonsolicitation, and nondisclosure agreements. Mantz quit and went to work for Mower Brothers, a competitor. Other TruGreen employees followed Mantz to Mower Brothers. TruGreen sued Mantz and the other employees for breach of the agreements and Mower Brothers for tortuous interference with contract. What do you think the Utah high court said was the proper measure of damages in such a case? [*TruGreen Companies v. Mower Brothers, Inc.,* 2008 Utah LEXIS 193 (2008).]

8. On November 7, 2005, Briarwood signed an agreement to sell Toll Brothers a planned 66-acre, 41-lot subdivision property in the Village of Pomona, New York, for $13,325,000. The agreement expressly conditioned Toll's payment obligations on Briarwood's delivery, at its sole cost and expense, of final, unappealable subdivision approval of the property in accordance with the subdivision plan and the satisfaction by Briarwood of any conditions of the final approval, such that on posting of customary security and payment of application and inspection fees by Toll Brothers, the company would be able to file the plat and commence infrastructure improvements and apply for and obtain building permits.

The agreement stated that the conditions set forth in the approval shall be subject only to "such conditions as Toll may approve at its sole discretion, which approval shall not be unreasonably withheld with respect to those modifications which do not have a material adverse effect on the proposed development." Closing was to take place 30 days following the date on which all conditions to closing set forth in the approval have been satisfied and, "[i]f on or before the date of closing all contingencies and conditions specified herein are not or cannot be satisfied, then Toll shall have the option of . . . cancelling this Agreement."

On January 12, 2006, Briarwood obtained preliminary subdivision approval of the property from the Pomona Planning Board. Final subdivision approval of the property, however, was subject to a number of conditions. By letter dated December 22, 2006, Toll notified Briarwood that five of the conditions would have a material adverse effect on the proposed development and that it would not accept them.

Toll Brothers claimed that Briarwood's December 28, 2006, response to Toll's December 22, 2006, letter was an anticipatory repudiation of the agreement.

In response to Toll's five objections, Briarwood (1) offered to post a bond to cover the potential cost of repaving Klinger Court; (2) pointed out that the steep slope condition restated the Village Code requirement to secure a site development plan permit for each lot within a subdivision; (3) agreed to pay any cost differential resulting from use of a 4 percent rather than a 10 percent grade for the cul-de-sac; (4) proposed two alternative solutions to the drainage system problem; and (5) pointed out that the landscaping plan condition, like the steep slope condition, restated a Village Code requirement.

Toll Brothers treated the letter from Briarwood as an anticipatory repudiation of the contract and refused to complete the transaction, so Briarwood sued for breach of contract. Both parties filed motions for summary judgment.

The district found that no reasonable reader could construe Briarwood's response as a positive and unequivocal repudiation of the agreement and that it did not signal that Briarwood was unwilling to comply with paragraph 16(a)(iii) or any other provision of the agreement. The court therefore granted summary judgment to Briarwood. Toll Brothers appealed. How do you believe the court of appeals ruled, and why? [*Briarwood Farms, Inc. v. Toll Bros., Inc.,* 452 Fed. Appx. 59, 2011 WL 6415185 (C.A.2, N.Y. 2011).]

9. Two companies had an agreement in which Sunrich was providing a food product to Nutrisoya. However, Sunrich allegedly did not deliver the products covered in the contract, and Nutrisoya took the company to court for material breach of contract. The seller wanted the district court to instruct the jury on the difference between a breach of a single installment and a breach of an entire installment contract, arguing that a single-installment breach did not disregard the value of the whole contract. However, the district court did not give such an instruction and left the defendant to argue the point. How do you think the jury decided? [*Nutrisoya v. Sunrich,* 641 F.3d 282, 2011 U.S. App. LEXIS 11561.]

10. The opera company was hired to perform in the outside pavilion of the Wolf Trap Foundation. The company performed the three performances without problem. Then, right before the last performance, a severe thunderstorm moved into the area and created an electrical storm. The storm cut the power on the pavilion where the performance was to have taken place. The Wolf Trap Foundation never paid the opera company for the last performance. Thus, the company took the foundation to court, demanding payment because the performers were ready and willing to perform at the event for which the company was scheduled. The foundation argued that it was dismissed from the contract due to impossibility to perform. The first court found in favor of the opera company, and the foundation appealed. How do you think the appellate court decided? [*The Opera Company of Boston, Inc., v. the Wolf Trap Foundation for the Performing Arts,* 817 F.2d 1094 (1987).]

Looking for more review materials?

The Online Learning Center at **www.mhhe.com/kubasek3e** contains this chapter's "Assignment on the Internet" and also a list of URLs for more information, entitled "On the Internet." Find both of them in the Student Center portion of the OLC, along with quizzes and other helpful materials.

CHAPTER

Agency Formation and Duties

33

LEARNING OBJECTIVES

After reading this chapter, you will be able to answer the following questions:

1 What is agency law?

2 How is an agency relationship created?

3 What are the different types of agency?

4 What are the different types of agency relationships?

5 What are the duties of the agent and principal?

6 What are the rights and remedies of the agent and principal?

CASE OPENER

FedEx and Independent Contractors

In July 2006, the International Brotherhood of Teamsters, Local Union 25, filed two petitions and held an election for a collective bargaining representative at two FedEx locations. However, FedEx refused to bargain with the union. FedEx did not contest the vote count of the election; instead, FedEx refused to collectively bargain because it believed that its single-route drivers were not "employees" but, rather, "independent contractors," and the rules of collective bargaining in this situation apply only to employees. However, the National Labor Relations Board concluded that FedEx committed an unfair labor practice by refusing to bargain with the union certified as the collective bargaining representative of the drivers. FedEx sought judicial review of the decision of the board, and the board cross-applied for enforcement of its order requiring that the company bargain.

1. Do you agree with the National Labor Relations Board's ruling that FedEx engaged in an unfair labor practice? Why?

2. What duties and rights would the FedEx drivers have if they were considered employees? How would their duties and rights differ if the drivers were considered independent contractors of the company?

The Wrap-Up at the end of the chapter will answer these questions.

One of the most important relationships in the business world is the agency relationship, in which the employee may be an agent of the employer and have the ability to bind that employer legally. The use of agents and independent contractors allows corporations to enter into contracts and conduct business in multiple locations simultaneously. This chapter explores the nature and creation of the agency relationship, as well as the legal obligations of the parties in such a relationship.

Introduction to Agency Law

L01

What is agency law?

Agency is generally defined as a relationship between a principal and an agent. In the agency relationship, the agent is authorized to act for and on behalf of the principal, who hires the agent to represent him or her. The Restatement of Agency defines agency as "the fiduciary relationship that results from the manifestation of consent by one person to another that the other shall act in his behalf and subject to his control, and consent by the other so to act."[1] (A *fiduciary* is a person who has a duty to act primarily for another person's benefit. A lawyer, for example, is a fiduciary for his or her client. We discuss fiduciaries in greater depth later in this chapter.)

Agency law is primarily state law. Thus, it can vary somewhat from state to state. As of July 2010, 40 states had enacted statutes governing the behavior of sports agents. The specific legislation that regulates the conduct of athlete agents in these 40 states is the Uniform Athlete Agents Act (UAAA). There are also non-UAAA laws that regulate athlete agents in California, Michigan, and Ohio. The UAAA provides for criminal, civil, and/or administrative penalties based on the particular state's statute. Twenty-four states (including California and Florida) have established criminal penalties for sports agents who violate the state statute. In contrast, only five states have criminalized violations of the statute by the athletes themselves. In addition to state laws protecting athletes and agents, players associations' model contracts describe the nature of the services agents can perform on behalf of their principals and the duties the parties owe to one another. For example, the Major League Baseball Players Association's (MLBPA's) Regulations Governing Player Agents expressly state that agents act in a fiduciary capacity vis-à-vis their athlete clients.

Agency law is especially important for U.S. firms doing business globally. While foreign countries offer fresh markets and eager consumers, U.S. companies often run into legal difficulties due to language barriers or lack of knowledge about local laws. To avoid such problems, many companies hire agents familiar with local laws, customs, and customers to help them function smoothly in foreign markets.

Creation of the Agency Relationship

L02

How is an agency relationship created?

Agency relationships are consensual relationships formed by informal oral agreements or formal written contracts. There are two criteria for the creation of agency relationships. First, like contracts, they can be created only for a lawful purpose; thus, a principal could not hire an agent to kill someone on his or her behalf.[2] Second, almost anyone can act as an agent; however, an individual who does not have contractual capacity, such as a minor, cannot hire an agent to make contracts on his or her behalf. (See Exhibit 33-1.)

---

[1] Restatement (Second) of Agency, sec. 1(1). A valuable reference that summarizes agency law, the Restatement is well respected in the legal profession and frequently cited by judges as well as attorneys and scholars in making legal arguments.

[2] Restatement (Second) of Agency, sec. 19.

Exhibit 33-1

Creation of the Agency Relationship

Agency relationships can be formed if and only if:
1. They are being created for a lawful purpose.
2. The person who is to act as an agent has contractual capacity.

Agency relationships can exist as one of four types:
1. *Expressed agency,* in which parties form the agency relationship by making a written or oral agreement.
2. *Agency by implied authority,* in which the agency relationship is implied by the conduct of the parties.
3. *Apparent agency,* in which the principal falsely leads a third party to believe another individual serves as his or her agent.
4. *Agency by ratification,* in which an individual misrepresents himself as another party's agent and the principal accepts the unauthorized act.

As long as these two criteria are met, agency relationships can be created on the basis of any of the following four forms of authority:

1. By expressed agency or agency by agreement.
2. By implied authority.
3. By apparent agency, or agency by estoppel.
4. By ratification.

The following pages discuss all four forms. Agency agreements usually do not need to be in writing, with two important exceptions. First, the agreement must be in writing whenever an agent will enter into a contract that the statute of frauds requires to be in writing. Janet wants Phil to act as her agent and grants him the power to enter into contracts. The statute of frauds, or, more specifically, the equal dignities rule, mandates that the type of contracts Phil is allowed to enter into must be in writing. Therefore, Phil's agreement with Janet must also be in writing. Second, the agreement must be in writing whenever an agent is given power of attorney (discussed below).

A *gratuitous agent* is one who acts without consideration; that is, such an agent is not paid for his or her services. Gratuitous agents function much like regular agents, with a few exceptions noted later in this chapter.

Legal Principle: **Agency relationships cannot be created to conduct illegal activities.**

Types of Agency

EXPRESSED AGENCY (AGENCY BY AGREEMENT)

When parties form an agency relationship by making a written or oral agreement, the agency is known as an expressed agency, or agency by agreement. Expressed agency is the most common type of agency and gives the agent the authority to contract on behalf of the principal. While a contract is not necessary to form the agency, if there is one it must meet all the elements of a contract discussed in Chapter 13. If the principal agrees to hire no other agent for a period of time or until a particular job is done, the principal and agent have entered into an exclusive agency contract.

A *power of attorney* establishes an agency by agreement that gives an agent authority to sign legal documents on behalf of the principal. A general power of attorney grants broad authority, while a specific power of attorney gives authority only for the specific areas or purposes listed in the agreement.

L03

What are the different types of agency?

CASE NUGGET

DURABLE POWER OF ATTORNEY

Penny Garrison et al. v. The Superior Court of Los Angeles et al.
132 Cal. App. 4th 253 (2005)

On Ella Needham's request, her daughter, Penny Garrison, was designated Needham's agent through a durable power of attorney. Needham was later admitted to a residential care facility. As part of the admissions process, Garrison, acting under the durable power of attorney, executed two arbitration agreements. After Needham's death, Garrison and Needham's other daughters sought to sue the facility for a number of concerns the family had regarding the care their mother had received. The facility sought to enforce the two arbitration agreements. However, the family contended that the agreements were unenforceable because Garrison could not legally enter into them.

The durable power of attorney had given Garrison power to (1) make all health care decisions for Needham according to what she believed was in Needham's best interest and (2) make decisions relating to Needham's personal care, including but not limited to determining where she lived. Therefore, Garrison was legally in charge of picking the residential care facility, and she had the power to enter into agreements regarding Needham's care.

Nowhere in the enumerated legal powers did the durable power of attorney state that Garrison could not enter into arbitration clauses. Moreover, the arbitration clauses were optional to the original contract, and they allowed a 30-day period during which Garrison could cancel them. Because the durable power of attorney was legal and enforceable, Garrison could not cancel the agreements into which she entered.

BUT WHAT IF . . .
WHAT IF THE FACTS OF THE CASE OPENER WERE DIFFERENT?

Let's say, in the Case Opener, that all FedEx delivery drivers had written employment agreements with FedEx in which the agency agreement was clearly stated. What kind of agency would this represent?

Powers of attorney are often given for business and health care purposes. Hence, an agent can make decisions about a principal's medical care if the principal cannot. Given that a principal must have the ability to enter into contracts to create an agency relationship, a principal may not enact a power of attorney after becoming incompetent. Therefore, a principal may preemptively enact a *durable power of attorney,* a written document expressing his or her wishes for an agent's authority not to be affected by the principal's subsequent incapacity. Alternatively, a durable power of attorney might become active only after a principal becomes incapacitated in any matter. (See Exhibit 33-2 for a comparison of a power of attorney and a durable power of attorney.) The Case Nugget examines the boundaries of the durable power of attorney.

Exhibit 33-2

Comparison of Powers of Attorney

Durable power of attorney — a document that states either the power of the agent is to continue to be effective if the principal becomes incapacitated or the power of the agent is to take effect after the principal has become incapacitated.

Power of attorney — a document giving an agent authority to sign legal documents on behalf of the principal; the power can be general or specific, limiting the authority of the agent.

COMPARING THE LAW OF OTHER COUNTRIES

FORMATION OF POWER OF ATTORNEY IN LUXEMBOURG

In the United States and other common law jurisdictions, a power of attorney authorizes the agent only to "conduct a series of transactions" under instruction from the principal. This limitation makes the power of attorney in common law distinctly different from that provided by civil law, which authorizes the agent to do "everything and anything which the principal himself could do."

Under the law of the Grand Duchy of Luxembourg, the person on whose behalf the power of attorney is created is called a *donor,* instead of a principal. Under Luxembourg law, there are two types of power of attorney from which a donor must choose. The first type is a power of attorney that is valid until death, and the second type is a power of attorney that has unlimited validity even after death. The actions that are permitted to be performed under a power of attorney are completely determined by the law in Luxembourg.

The law in Luxembourg also requires that the power of attorney be authenticated by a public authority or a public notary by providing the donor's certified identification card or passport, as well as proof of residency.

The Restatement says, "[A]n agency relation exists only if there has been a manifestation by the principal to the agent that the agent may act on his account, and consent by the agent so to act."[3] Therefore, in addition to the above criteria, the principal must agree to have the person act as an agent, and the agent must agree to act for the principal. As noted below, the parties can reach this agreement in several ways.

AGENCY BY IMPLIED AUTHORITY

In some cases, an agency relationship is not created by an express agreement but is instead implied by the conduct of the parties. For example, if a homeowner asked a real estate broker to help sell her home, her words imply that an agency relationship has been formed. The circumstances determine the extent of an agent's ability to conduct business on behalf of the principal. However, implied authority cannot conflict with any express authority.

Legal Principle: **Agency by implied authority cannot conflict with any express authority.**

BUT WHAT IF . . .

WHAT IF THE FACTS OF THE CASE OPENER WERE DIFFERENT?

Let's say, in the Case Opener, that FedEx had released a television commercial that made it seem as though all FedEx drivers worked directly for FedEx. A month after the release of the commercial, FedEx refused to collectively bargain with a union rep for Jerry, a single-route driver. FedEx said that there was no written contract that proved an agency relationship existed and thus Jerry was not an agent of FedEx. Is FedEx correct in this argument? Why or why not?

APPARENT AGENCY (AGENCY BY ESTOPPEL)

Suppose a principal falsely leads a third party to believe another individual serves as his or her agent. Does an agency relationship exist? Yes, because by his or her conduct, the principal has created apparent agency or agency by estoppel. According to the principal's conduct, the agent has apparent authority to act; thus, the principal is estopped, or prevented, from denying that the individual is an agent.[4] An apparent agency can be created only on the acts of the principal—never on the basis of what the purported agent says or does. When a third party relies on the principal's conduct and makes an agreement with an

---

[3] Restatement (Second) of Agency, sec. 15.

[4] Restatement (Second) of Agency, sec. 8B.

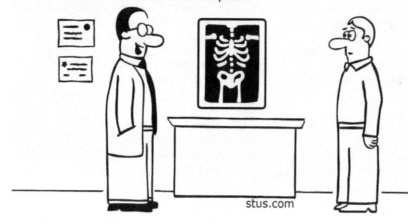

Yes, I'm a radiologist. And yes I work at the hospital. And yes I'm the only choice the hospital offers. But why would you think I work for the hospital?

stus.com

apparent agent, the principal must uphold any agreements made by the agent. If the principal attempts to deny that an agency relationship existed, the third party must demonstrate that he or she reasonably believed, on the basis of the principal's conduct, that an agency relationship existed. The court will consider the principal's conduct in determining whether an agency relationship existed.

Suppose a salesman enters the office of a third party claiming he represents a company that wants to do business. If he is really not an agent for the company and provides no evidence of a link with it, the company will not be held responsible under apparent agency because the third party had no interaction with it. The third party had no reason to believe an agency relationship existed, other than the agent's words. However, if the president of the company suggests to the third party that the salesman *is* a representative of the company, the president's conduct suggests that the salesman is an agent. Thus, the company would have to uphold any agreement the third party made with the apparent agent. In Case 33-1, pay close attention to how the court determines whether the party had apparent authority in this agency issue.

CASE 33-1   ACKERMAN v. SOBOL FAMILY PARTNERSHIP, LLP
SUPREME COURT OF CONNECTICUT
298 CONN. 495 (2010)

On May 29, 2008, the plaintiff's attorney, Glenn Coe, met the defendants for mediation. At the mediation, Coe made a detailed offer of settlement with the defendants. The defendants rejected this proposal, and afterward negotiations continued, during which Coe made an offer to settle the litigation through a series of conversations with the attorneys who represented the defendant Bank of America.

During a two-day period in June 2008, Coe expressly assured the defendants' attorneys on separate occasions, in response to direct questioning on the issue, that the settlement offer proposed by him at that time was fully authorized by his clients as well as the additional plaintiff's attorney, and that if accepted by the defendants, it would resolve the litigation.

The final settlement demand by the plaintiffs' counsel to the Bank of America was the sum of $1.1 million. The Bank of America accepted the $1.1 million settlement proposal on

July 1, 2008, prior to the 5 p.m. deadline. At this time, the global settlement offer had been accepted by all defendants. At no time prior to the acceptance of the settlement proposal were the defendants or their attorneys notified that the offer had been withdrawn, unauthorized, or otherwise ineffective.

After the proposal had been accepted by the defendants, the plaintiffs sued the defendants, claiming that the plaintiffs' lead attorney, Glenn Coe, lacked the authority to make several settlement proposals or bind them to a global settlement agreement with Bank of America and the other defendants. The defendants filed motions to enforce the settlement agreement, and the Superior Court granted the defendants' motions and rendered judgments for defendants. The plaintiffs appealed.

JUDGE ZARELLA: The principal issue in this consolidated appeal . . . is whether the plaintiffs' attorney had

[continued]

apparent authority to make settlement proposals, engage in settlement discussions and bind the plaintiffs to a global settlement agreement with the defendants. The plaintiffs claim that the trial court's enforcement of a settlement agreement between the parties, based on a finding of apparent authority on the part of the plaintiffs' attorney to bind the plaintiffs to the agreement, was clearly erroneous in the absence of conduct by the plaintiffs (1) manifesting that their attorney had authority to settle the pending litigation, and (2) leading the opposing defense attorneys reasonably to believe that the plaintiffs' attorney had full and final authority to settle the litigation, as distinguished from authority only to negotiate. The plaintiffs also claim that they were denied their right to a jury trial on issues of fact under article first, § 19, of the Connecticut constitution, as amended by article four of the amendments, when the trial court, in the midst of voir dire, made findings of fact and determined that the litigants had reached a settlement of the pending litigation. The defendants respond that the trial court's finding that the plaintiffs' counsel had apparent authority to settle the litigation was not clearly erroneous and that the plaintiffs had no right to a jury trial on their equitable motions seeking to enforce the agreement. We affirm the judgment of the trial court.

Since the case of *Tomlinson v. Board of Education,* the court's inquiry as to the doctrine of apparent authority is now refined to a two part analysis. Apparent authority exists, one, where the principal held the agent out as possessing

sufficient authority to embrace the act in question and knowingly permitted him to act as having such authority; and, two, in consequence thereof, the person dealing with the agent acting in good faith reasonably believed under all the circumstances that the agent had the necessary authority.... Based upon the court's prior findings in this matter, the court finds that [Coe] certainly did have apparent authority from his client[s]. Further . . . the court so finds, [it was] acknowledged in testimony, that the defendants' counsel reasonably believed that [Coe] was, in fact, authorized by the plaintiffs to make the settlement offer at issue, and further, that [the] defendants' counsel at all . . . relevant times were acting in good faith in their respective efforts to settle the case on the terms proposed by [Coe].

As noted earlier, [Coe] had been, in fact, engaged in settlement discussions with his client's obvious assent. [Rena Ackerman] had accompanied him to the mediation for over [one] month prior to the time the settlement was reached. [Coe] was certainly held out as being authorized to negotiate settlement on behalf of the plaintiffs and the defendants acted reasonably in believing that he had authority to do so. [Coe] acknowledged in testimony that both [Wyld] and [Schneider] acted reasonably in relying on his stated authority. Further, there was no evidence at all that [Coe's] apparent authority had been terminated at any time by [Rena] Ackerman. We affirm the judgment of the trial court.

AFFIRMED.

CRITICAL THINKING

Is any important information missing from this decision that might further clarify the nature of the issue of agency between the concerned parties? Could it change the acceptability of the judge's reasoning?

ETHICAL DECISION MAKING

Does this ruling appear to follow a coherent ethical guideline? If so, what form does it take? Who are the stakeholders in this situation? Are they awarded proper consideration under the selected ethical guideline?

AGENCY BY RATIFICATION

Francisco is driving home and sees a car with a "For Sale" sign in the window. He stops to look at it because his friend Miles wants to buy a used car. Impressed by the car's price and quality, Francisco tells the owner his friend wants to buy it. The owner claims another individual is coming to probably buy the car in an hour. To ensure that Miles gets the car, Francisco signs a contract to purchase it but notes on the contract that he is an agent of Miles. Because Francisco is not his agent, Miles is not required to uphold the contract.

However, if Miles does agree to purchase the car, he has accepted Francisco as his agent for the contract. Miles is now bound by the contract, and Francisco cannot be held liable for misrepresenting himself. This type of agency relationship is *agency by ratification.* As the example suggests, it has two requirements:

1. An individual must misrepresent himself or herself as an agent for another party.
2. The principal must accept or ratify the unauthorized act.

For ratification to be effective, two additional requirements must be met:

3. The principal must have complete knowledge of all material facts regarding the contract.
4. The principal must ratify the entirety of the agent's act. (The principal cannot accept certain parts of the agent's act and reject others.)

Agency Relationships

LO4

What are the different types of agency relationships?

Agency laws are relevant to three types of business relationships: the principal-agent relationship, the employer-employee relationship, and the employer–independent contractor relationship (see Exhibit 33-3). We discuss all three in the following sections.

PRINCIPAL-AGENT RELATIONSHIP

The *principal-agent relationship* typically exists when an employer hires an employee to enter into contracts on its behalf. This is the most basic type of agency relationship. Suppose a salesclerk at Abercrombie sells Amanda a shirt. The clerk is acting on behalf of Abercrombie's owner; consequently, any sales she makes are binding on it. Think of all the advertisements you've seen in which a professional athlete speaks on behalf of a product. The athlete usually hires an agent to find and make agreements on his or her behalf to promote products.

EMPLOYER-EMPLOYEE RELATIONSHIP

Whenever an employer hires an employee to perform some sort of physical service, the parties have created an *employer-employee relationship* in which the employee is subject to the employer's control.[5] Generally, all employees are considered agents of the employer, even those not legally authorized to enter into contracts binding their employer or to interact with third parties. However, not all agents are employees.

Legal Principle: **Employees are agents of an employer.**

EMPLOYER–INDEPENDENT CONTRACTOR RELATIONSHIP

The Restatement of Agency defines an *independent contractor* as "a person who contracts with another to do something for him but who is not controlled by the other nor subject to the other's right to control with respect to his physical conduct in the performance of the undertaking."[6] Building contractors, doctors, stockbrokers, and lawyers are types

Exhibit 33-3

Types of Agency Relationships and Their Significance

RELATIONSHIP	HOW TO IDENTIFY	SIGNIFICANT FOR WHAT ISSUES?
Principal-agent	Parties have *agreed* that agent will have power to bind principal in contract.	Contract law
Employer-employee	Employer has right to *control* conduct of employees.	Tort law, tax law, wage law, discrimination law, copyright law
Employer–independent contractor	Employer has *no control* over details of conduct of independent contractor.	Tort law, tax law, wage law, discrimination law, copyright law

[5] Restatement (Second) of Agency, sec. 2.

[6] Restatement (Second) of Agency, sec. 2.

of independent contractors. They are also agents, but not employees. However, not all independent contractors are agents. They cannot enter into contracts on behalf of the principal unless the principal authorizes them to do so.

Legal Principle: **Independent contractors cannot enter into contracts on behalf of the principal unless the contractor possesses authority from the principal.**

Employee or Independent Contractor? The question of whether a worker is an employee or an independent contractor has important implications because the employer–employee relationship is subject to the workers' compensation, workplace safety, employment discrimination, and unemployment statutes, while the employer–independent contractor relationship is not. Employers are also generally liable in tort for the actions of their employees, while they are generally not liable for the actions of independent contractors (see Chapter 34).

BUT WHAT IF . . .

WHAT IF THE FACTS OF THE CASE OPENER WERE DIFFERENT?

Let's say, in the Case Opener, that a single-route driver named Rick was an independent contractor for FedEx. He delivered a package to a woman named Sarah, but Sarah's package had been damaged at a FedEx center. Rick formed a contract for Sarah, telling her that FedEx would award her the cost of the item that was shipped. Is Rick legally correct in this scenario? Why or why not?

When courts are deciding whether a worker is an employee or an independent contractor, perhaps the most important consideration is employer control.[7] If the employer has the right to substantially control the worker's day-to-day operations, the worker is generally considered an employee. Employers will sometimes have some control over the operations of a contractor; however, this control does not always mean that the contractor is an employee. In the Case Opener, the main issue for the court to determine was whether the FedEx drivers were employees or contractors. To do so, the court relied on the standard agency principle of determining how much control the employer exerted over the agent drivers. (See Exhibit 33-4 for more criteria that distinguish employees and independent contractors.)

Exhibit 33-4 Independent Contractor or Employee?

CRITERIA	EMPLOYEE	INDEPENDENT CONTRACTOR
Does the worker engage in a distinct occupation or an independently established business?	No	Yes
Is the work done under the employer's supervision, or does a specialist without supervision complete the work?	Employer supervision	Specialist without supervision
Does the employer supply the tools?	Yes	No
What skill is required for the occupation?	No specialized skill	Great degree of skill
What is the length of time for which the worker is employed?	Long time	Varies
Is the worker a regular part of the business of the employer?	Yes	No
How is the worker paid?	Regular payments according to time	When the job is completed

[7] Restatement (Second) of Agency, sec. 2(3).

COMPARING THE LAW OF OTHER COUNTRIES

FORMATION OF AGENCY IN ITALIAN LAW

The Italian legal system has created an agency relationship that gives the agent unique powers. Although not formally recognized by the Italian Civil Code, this relationship is common in business practices and has been upheld in a number of court cases.

The agency relationship begins much like agency in the United States: The principal and agent enter into a contract under which the agent agrees to the principal's stipulations. This contract, however, also requires that the agent maintain the principal's property. Under Italian law, the agent then becomes legal owner of the property and can transfer or contract it without the principal's consent. Such autonomous powers are not granted to agents in the United States, who must maintain communication with and receive permission from principals unless otherwise specified.

The extended freedom of the agent under the Italian Civil Code results in considerably lengthy and detailed contracts between agents and principals. Both parties are looking to protect their own interests.

The IRS also must decide who is an employee and who is an independent contractor to ensure that the employer is not simply trying to lower its tax burden. The IRS has outlined 20 different criteria for its auditors to consider in determining whether someone is an independent contractor. In 1997, under advisement of the court, the IRS changed its criteria to focus on one element: how much control the employer exerts over the agent. The IRS needs to determine when people are employees and when they are independent contractors because of different tax liabilities employers face. When the IRS determines an independent contractor is really an employee, the employer becomes liable for all applicable taxes, such as Social Security and unemployment taxes.

Case 33-2 provides an illustration of the court's consideration of the criteria that establish whether a worker is an employee or an independent contractor.

CASE 33-2 CYNTHIA WALKER v. JOHN A. LAHOSKI ET AL.
COURT OF APPEALS OF OHIO, NINTH APPELLATE DISTRICT, SUMMIT COUNTY
1999 OHIO APP. LEXIS 3435 (1999)

In 1995, Cynthia Walker contracted with Genny's Home Health Care to find her employment as a home health-care worker. When Ben Lahoski contacted Genny's to obtain twenty-four-hour home health care for his wife Ann, Walker and another worker were assigned to her. Each would stay at the Lahoski's for either forty-eight or seventy-two hours, at which time the two would switch. In September 1995, while Walker was mopping the floor in the Lahoski home, the mop handle knocked a cast iron clock off the wall. Walker was hit on the head by the clock and suffered a sprain of the neck and contusions on her face, scalp, and neck. Walker filed a claim with the Ohio Bureau of Workers' Compensation, naming Ben and Ann Lahoski as her employers. The Ohio Bureau refused Walker's claim by arguing the Lahoskis were not Walker's employers.

Walker filed a claim in court against the Lahoskis for denying her workers' compensation. The trial court granted summary judgment to the Lahoskis. Walker appealed.

JUDGE BAIRD: To prevail in her workers' compensation claim, Ms. Walker would have to establish she was an employee of Ben and Ann Lahoski at the time her injury occurred. The trial court's denial of her claim is based on its finding she was not their employee, but an independent contractor.

Appellees in this matter argue Walker was an independent contractor. In support of their position they point out there was no contract between Walker and the Lahoskis, the Lahoskis did not pay Walker but paid the agency, and Walker's contract with the agency specifically stated she was an independent contractor.

Courts have distinguished an employee from an independent contractor by resolving two key questions. The first is whether the "employer" controls the "manner or means" by which the work is done or if the "employer" is interested only in the results to be achieved. In the first case, the worker would be an employee while in the second case the worker would be an independent contractor.

The second question is how the worker is paid. If the worker is paid on an hourly basis, this tends to indicate the worker was an employee, while payment by the job tends to indicate the worker was an independent contractor.

[continued]

Thus, the overriding consideration for the fact-finder in these cases is who has the right to control the manner or means of the work performed.

In the instant case, Walker signed a contract in which she acknowledged she was an independent contractor relative to Genny's and she would be an independent contractor relative to the customer, absent agreement by the customer she could be considered the customer's employee. However, such a contract provision is not necessarily controlling. The trial court must look to the substance of the relationship, not merely to a label attached to the relationship.

Appellees also assert when Walker and her coworker Peggy J. Seifert began to work for Ben Lahoski, Mr. Lahoski only briefly gave the women a tour of the house, then left it to them to perform their work as they saw fit. However, Cynthia Walker has testified otherwise, asserting Ben Lahoski was actively involved in directing her work for Mrs. Lahoski. In considering whether summary judgment was appropriate in this case, we must resolve the conflict in testimony in favor of the nonmoving party, Ms. Walker. Furthermore, the factual determination to be made in this case is who had the right to exercise control over the manner or means of the work performed.

[T]he "right to control" is agreeably the key factor in making the determination of whether an individual is an independent contractor or an employee. . . .

In the instant case, appellees merely assert "it is clear that Ben Lahoski did not reserve the right to control the manner or means of Appellant's work[.]" In point of fact, it is not clear Mr. Lahoski did not exercise such control. The statements of the two workers conflict on this point. Furthermore, even if Ben Lahoski did not exercise right to control, there is sufficient evidence to indicate he had the right to exercise that control.

The record below contains disputed facts and several indicia of employee status, such as hourly payment, control of hours worked, and control over the manner or means the work was performed. Appellees failed to meet their burden to show there was no genuine issue of material fact and reasonable minds could only decide favorably for the appellees. Thus, the trial court erred in granting summary judgment in favor of the defendants.

REVERSED.

CRITICAL THINKING

Clearly, all relevant information regarding the agreement is critical to the judge's conclusion. What missing information might be reason for the judge to form a different conclusion?

ETHICAL DECISION MAKING

The court felt that the law governing agency in this particular fact pattern was unclear enough that the lower court should not grant a summary judgment. But Walker and Seifert worked for the Lahoskis. Are there values that employers in a position like that of the Lahoskis should act on in their relationship with those who work for them? Should these values push employers beyond what they are required to do by law?

The classification as an employee or independent contractor is also important in determining who owns the output of a work project. According to the Copyright Act of 1976,[8] when an employee completes work at the request of the employer, the product is considered a "work for hire" and the employer owns the copyright. Conversely, an independent contractor normally maintains ownership of copyrights for his or her work product. Only by an agreement of both parties that a specific work is a work for hire may an employer gain copyright ownership of the work of an independent contractor.

BUT WHAT IF . . .
WHAT IF THE FACTS OF THE CASE OPENER WERE DIFFERENT?

Let's say, in the Case Opener, that single-route drivers did have agency relationships with FedEx. Although Jim, a FedEx driver, was not driving a FedEx vehicle, he had to travel to another city to perform a FedEx duty. He asked FedEx for gas money to travel, but FedEx declined. Which party is correct in this situation?

[8]17 U.S.C. §§ 101-810.

Duties of the Agent and the Principal

L05

What are the duties of the agent and principal?

An agency relationship is a fiduciary relationship of trust, confidence, and good faith. Thus, its formation creates certain duties that the principal and agent owe each other (see Exhibit 33-5). We discuss them in the following sections.

PRINCIPAL'S DUTIES TO THE AGENT

The principal owes certain duties to the agent. If these duties are not fulfilled, the principal has violated the agent's rights and the agent can sue for contract or tort remedies. The agent can also refuse to act on behalf of the principal until the failure is remedied.

> **Legal Principle:** **The principal owes specific duties to the agent. Failure to fulfill these duties provides the basis for a tort or contract action against the principal.**

Duty of Compensation.   The principal has a duty to compensate the agent for services provided, unless the parties have agreed the agent will act gratuitously. The agency contract will usually specify the type and amount of compensation as well as the time at which it will be paid. If there is no agreement on the amount, the courts suggest compensation should be calculated according to the customary fee in the situation.[9] The Case Nugget examines which individuals are responsible under the duty to compensate.

Exhibit 33-5   Duties of Principal and Agent

PRINCIPAL DUTIES	
Compensation	The principal has a duty to compensate the agent for services provided unless the parties have agreed that the agent will act gratuitously.
Reimbursement and indemnification	The principal has a duty to reimburse or indemnify the agent for any authorized expenditures or any losses the agent incurs in the course of working on behalf of the principal.
Cooperation	The principal must assist the agent in the performance of his or her duties and cannot interfere with the reasonable conduct of the agent.
Safe working conditions	The principal has a duty to ensure safe working conditions and to warn the agent if the principal is aware of any potential danger.

AGENT DUTIES	
Loyalty	The agent has a responsibility to act in the best interest of the principal; this duty is important because the agency relationship is founded on trust.
Notification	The agent must notify the principal of any relevant information in a timely manner.
Obedience	The agent must follow the lawful instruction and direction of the principal.
Accounting	The agent must keep an accurate account of the transactions made on behalf of the principal and provide the accounting information to the principal on request.
Performance	The agent must perform the duties as specified in the agency agreement with reasonable skill, care, and professionalism.

[9] Restatement (Second) of Agency, sec. 443.

DUTY TO COMPENSATE

Ralph T. Leonard et al. v. Jerry D. McMorris et al.
320 F.3d 1116 (2003)

NationsWay was one of the largest privately held trucking companies in the United States, with 3,200 employees operating in 43 different states. In 1999, NationsWay filed for Chapter 11 bankruptcy and terminated most of its employees. Ralph Leonard, and a number of the other employees who were terminated, sued Jerry McMorris and other NationsWay executives, arguing they were personally liable for unpaid wages under their duty to compensate arising from the employer-employee relationship.

The defendants argued they could not be held personally liable for agreements made between the employees and the corporation. As the case began, NationsWay was continuing its bankruptcy filings, under which the former employees were to receive approximately $3 million in unpaid wages. However, the plaintiffs wanted additional amounts covering accrued vacation pay, sick-leave pay, holiday pay, and other nonwage compensation, as well as a 50 percent penalty and attorney fees.

In deciding the case, the court addressed "[w]hether officers of a corporation are individually liable for the wages of the corporation's former employees under the Colorado Wage Claim Act." The court concluded, "[U]nder Colorado's Wage Claim Act, the officers and agents of a corporation are *not* jointly and severally liable for payment of employee wages and other compensation the corporation owes to its employees under the employment contract and the Colorado Wage Claim Act." Although there is a duty to compensate for the corporation, the executives who were the defendants were not individually liable to the former employees for the unpaid wages.

Duty of Reimbursement and Indemnification. The principal has a duty of reimbursement and indemnification to the agent. If an agent makes authorized expenditures in the course of working on behalf of the principal, the principal has a duty to reimburse the agent for that amount of money.[10] Thus, if an agent takes a trip on behalf of the principal, the principal must have authorized this trip if the agent is to be reimbursed.

Similarly, the principal has the duty to indemnify or reimburse the agent for any losses the agent incurs while working within the scope of authority on the principal's behalf.[11] Suppose an agent makes an agreement with a third party on behalf of the principal and the principal fails to uphold the agreement. The third party could sue the agent for damages, but the principal has a duty to indemnify the agent for the losses the third party regains.

Duty of Cooperation. The principal also owes a *duty of cooperation* to the agent and must therefore assist the agent in the performance of his or her duties. Furthermore, the principal can do nothing to interfere with the agent's reasonable conduct. If Suzi hires someone to sell her car for her, she must be willing to let the agent show the car to interested buyers.

Duty to Provide Safe Working Conditions. The principal has a *duty to provide safe working conditions* for the agent, including equipment and premises. A principal aware of unsafe working conditions has a duty to warn the agent and make necessary repairs. Federal and state statutes, such as the Occupational Safety and Health Act (OSHA), set specific standards for the working environment. Employers that violate these standards may be subject to fines.

AGENT'S DUTIES TO THE PRINCIPAL

Because the agent makes agreements on behalf of the principal in a fiduciary relationship of trust and confidence, he or she can also harm the principal. Suppose an agent makes

---

[10] Restatement (Second) of Agency, sec. 438.
[11] Restatement (Second) of Agency, secs. 438 and 439.

numerous contracts the principal could not possibly carry out all at once. The third parties may sue the principal for not carrying out the agreements. If the agent breaches his or her duties, the principal can sue the agent and may be entitled to a variety of contract and tort remedies beyond those stated in the contract.

> **Legal Principle:** **When an agent fails to fulfill his duties to the principal, that failure provides the basis for a contract or tort action against the agent.**

Duty of Loyalty.   Courts suggest that the duty of loyalty is the most important duty an agent owes to a principal. Because of their fiduciary relationship, the agent has a responsibility to act in the interest of the principal,[12] including avoiding conflicts of interest and protecting the principal's confidentiality.

An agent cannot represent both the principal and a third party in an agreement, because there could be a conflict of interest. The agent also has a duty to notify the principal of any offers from third parties. Suppose Tony has hired a real estate agent to make land purchases for him. A third party notifies the real estate agent that some of her property will soon be going up for sale and wants to know whether Tony would be interested in buying it. The real estate agent cannot decide to buy that property for himself or herself until (1) the real estate agent has communicated the offer to Tony and (2) Tony has considered and rejected the offer.

The duty of loyalty also requires that the agent keep confidential any information about the principal, during the course of agency as well as after the agency relationship has been terminated. The agent cannot disclose or misuse any information received during or after the agency relationship with the principal.

Duty of Notification.   The agent has to communicate not only offers from third parties but also, under the duty of notification, any information he or she thinks could be important to the principal.[13] If a third party has made an agreement with a principal through an agent and fails to meet the agreement, the agent must notify the principal in a timely manner. The law typically assumes that the principal is aware of all information revealed to the agent, regardless of whether the agent shares it with the principal.

Case 33-3 pays special attention to the duties of the agent to the principal and explains what happens when an agent violates the specific duty of loyalty.

[12] Restatement (Second) of Agency, sec. 401.

[13] Restatement (Second) of Agency, sec. 381.

CASE 33-3   INTERNATIONAL AIRPORT CENTERS v. JACOB CITRIN
COURT OF APPEALS FOR THE SEVENTH DISTRICT
440 F.3D 418 (2006)

The defendant, Mr. Citrin, was employed by the plaintiffs' real estate business, IAC. In the course of their business relationship, IAC lent Citrin a laptop to use to record work data. Eventually Mr. Citrin quit his job at IAC and started his own business, which was in breach of his employment contract. Before returning the laptop to IAC, he deleted all of the business data in the computer. Ordinarily, pressing the "delete" key on a computer merely removes the index entry and such "deleted" files are easily recoverable. But

Mr. Citrin loaded into the laptop a secure-erasure program to prevent the recovery of the files. Subsequently, IAC sued him for violating the Computer Fraud and Abuse Act and his duty of loyalty that agency law imposes on an employee. The district court dismissed the suit and IAC appealed.

JUDGE POSNER: [Mr. Citrin's] authorization to access the laptop terminated when, having already engaged in misconduct and decided to quit IAC in violation of his

[continued]

employment contract, he resolved to destroy files that incriminated himself and other files that were also the property of his employer, in violation of the duty of loyalty that agency law imposes on an employee.

Muddying the picture some, the Computer Fraud and Abuse Act distinguishes between "without authorization" and "exceeding authorized access," 18 U.S.C. § § 1030(a)(1), (2), (4), and, while making both punishable, defines the latter as "accessing a computer with authorization and . . . using such access to obtain or alter information in the computer that the accesser is not entitled so to obtain or alter." § 1030(e)(6). That might seem the more apt description of what Citrin did.

The difference between "without authorization" and "exceeding authorized access" is paper thin, but not quite invisible. In *EF Cultural Travel BV v. Explorica, Inc.,* for example, the former employee of a travel agent, in violation of his confidentiality agreement with his former employer, used confidential information that he had obtained as an employee to create a program that enabled his new travel company to obtain information from his former employer's website that he could not have obtained as efficiently without the use of that confidential information. The website was open to the public, so he was authorized to use it, but he exceeded his authorization by using confidential information to obtain better access than other members of the public.

Our case is different. Citrin's breach of his duty of loyalty terminated his agency relationship (more precisely, terminated any rights he might have claimed as IAC's agent—he could not by unilaterally terminating any duties he owed his principal gain an advantage) and with it his authority to access the laptop, because the only basis of his authority had been that relationship. "Violating the duty of loyalty, or failing to disclose adverse interests, voids the agency relationship." *(State v. DiGiulio.)* "Unless otherwise agreed, the authority of the agent terminates if, without knowledge of the principal, he acquires adverse interests or if he is otherwise guilty of a serious breach of loyalty to the principal."

Citrin points out that his employment contract authorized him to "return *or destroy*" data in the laptop when he ceased being employed by IAC. But it is unlikely, to say the least, that the provision was intended to authorize him to destroy data that he knew the company had no duplicates of and would have wanted to have—if only to nail Citrin for misconduct. The purpose of the provision may have been to avoid overloading the company with returned data of no further value, which the employee should simply have deleted. More likely the purpose was simply to remind Citrin that he was not to disseminate confidential data after he left the company's employ—the provision authorizing him to return or destroy data in the laptop was limited to "Confidential" information. There may be a dispute over whether the incriminating files that Citrin destroyed contained "confidential" data, but that issue cannot be resolved on this appeal.

REVERSED and REMANDED.

CRITICAL THINKING

Why do you think the original trial court ruled in the opposite manner? Why might you conclude that the agent in the case (Citrin) did not violate his duties to the principal (IAC)?

ETHICAL DECISION MAKING

Recall the WPH framework for ethics. A classmate argues that Citrin made the correct decision in deleting the data because he himself was a stakeholder and deleting the data bettered his own position. Do you agree? Who are the relevant stakeholders negatively affected by Citrin's decision to destroy the business data on the computer?

Duty of Performance. The *duty of performance* the agent owes the principal is twofold. First, the agent must perform the duties as specified in the agency agreement. Suppose an insurance agent contacts Bethany about purchasing a car insurance policy. Bethany agrees to purchase it, but for some reason the agent never obtains the policy for her. Bethany discovers the insurance agent's mistake when she gets into a car accident. The insurance agent did not meet the duty of performance; thus Bethany could bring a claim against the agent.

Second, the agent must perform the specified duties with the same skill, care, and professionalism as a reasonable person in the same situation would provide. An attorney who advertises he is a specialist in certain types of law will be held to the reasonable standard of care in that specialty.[14] A gratuitous agent cannot be found liable for a breach

[14] Restatement (Second) of Agency, sec. 379.

of contract for failure to perform because no contract exists between the principal and the agent. However, if a gratuitous agent begins to act as an agent and the principal affirms the relationship, a duty to perform arises insofar as the agent has begun a specific task for the principal.

Duty of Obedience.   Under the *duty of obedience,* the agent must follow the lawful instruction and direction of the principal.[15] An agent who makes an unauthorized agreement has failed to meet the duty of obedience. However, if the principal gives unlawful or unethical instructions, the agent is not required to behave in accordance with them. Let us say a principal tells an agent to sell a basketball autographed by Michael Jordan and the agent knows that the principal forged the signature. The agent is not required to obey this instruction.

Duty of Accounting.   Under the *duty of accounting,* the agent must keep an accurate account of the transactions of money and property made on behalf of the principal.[16] If the principal asks to see this accounting, the agent has a duty to provide it. The agent must also keep separate accounts for the principal's funds and the agent's funds and not allow them to mix.

Rights and Remedies

PRINCIPAL'S RIGHTS AND REMEDIES AGAINST THE AGENT

LO6

What are the rights and remedies of the agent and principal?

Because the agency relationship generally *is* a contractual relationship, a principal has available contract remedies, discussed in depth in Chapter 20, for breach of fiduciary duties. In addition, a principal may utilize tort remedies for an agent's misrepresentations, negligence, or other business failings causing damage to the principal. When an agent breaches his or her fiduciary duties, the principal has the right to terminate the agency relationship. Of numerous remedies available to the principal, the three main ones are constructive trust, avoidance, and indemnification.

Legal Principle: **When an agent breaches his or her duties to the principal, the principal can terminate the agency relationship and seek remedies.**

Constructive Trust.   Agency relationships exist primarily for the benefit of the principal. Therefore, principals are the legal owners of anything an agent may come to possess through the employment or agency relationship. Accordingly, an agent who through deceit or other means retains such profits or goods has breached his or her fiduciary duties. Joy, an agent of Sarah's selling real estate, sells a piece of property for $2,000 more than Sarah anticipated. Joy keeps the extra $2,000 and reports the sale at the price Sarah anticipated. By law the profits belong to Sarah, and Joy has breached her fiduciary duties by keeping the money.

An agent also may not use the agency relationship to obtain goods or property for himself or herself when the principal desired to obtain the same goods or property; the principal always has right of first refusal. If Joy were to buy a piece of land for herself that she knew Sarah wanted to purchase, she again would have breached her fiduciary duties to Sarah.

---

[15] Restatement (Second) of Agency, secs. 383 and 385.

[16] Restatement (Second) of Agency, sec. 382.

COMPARING THE LAW OF OTHER COUNTRIES

DUTIES OF THE AGENT IN AUSTRALIA

Agents in Australia and the United States share many of the same duties to the principal, including following the principal's instructions, exercising reasonable care and skill, and not inappropriately divulging or concealing confidential information.

Agents in Australia do have a unique duty, however. They are obligated to "act personally" on behalf of the principal. Suppose an agent is hired to sell apartments owned by the principal. If the agent hires an individual to sell the apartments for him, he cannot receive commission from the sale.

The basis for such a law is quite logical. The agent was hired to exercise personal skills, such as availability, in the absence of the principal. When no personal skill is demonstrated, the agent shall not be granted any compensation or reward. Specifying that duties must be performed personally may seem like an obvious and unnecessary stipulation, but this specificity is important in protecting the interests of the principal.

When an agent illegally benefits from the agency relationship, the principal may enact a constructive trust on the profits, goods, or property in question. A constructive trust is an equitable trust imposed on someone who wrongfully obtains or holds legal right to property he or she should not possess. The court then rules that the agent is merely holding the property or goods in trust for the principal, granting the principal legal right or possession.

Avoidance.   When an agent breaches an agency contract or his fiduciary duties, the principal may use her right of *avoidance* to nullify at her discretion any contract the agent negotiated.

Indemnification.   A third party who believes that an agent is acting with actual or apparent authority may sue the principal for any breach of contract. However, if the breach was caused by the agent's negligence, the principal has a right to *indemnification;* that is, when sued by a third party, a principal may sue his agent to recover the amount assessed to the third party. As Ricardo's agent, Mercedes enters into a contract with Christina knowing that Ricardo cannot possibly fulfill it. Christina sues Ricardo for breach of contract and recovers damages. Ricardo, under indemnification, is entitled to sue Mercedes to recover what he had to pay.

A principal can also recover if an agent fails to follow the principal's instructions. Ricardo tells Mercedes not to take any more orders for the widgets he produces. While Ricardo is out of town, Mercedes takes Christina's order for 1,000 widgets. When Christina sues Ricardo for breach of contract, he can recover damages from Mercedes because she did not follow his instructions. Courts have had difficulty determining when a principal gives limiting instructions and when she merely gives advice. Going against advice does not impose liability on an agent, but violating limiting instructions does. To avoid a potential lawsuit from a third party, the principal should notify the third party whenever a relationship with an agent ceases or limiting instructions are given.

AGENT'S RIGHTS AND REMEDIES AGAINST THE PRINCIPAL

While agency relationships are intended to benefit the principal, the agent is not without rights and remedies. Whenever a duty is imposed on the principal, a corresponding right exists for the agent. Agents have available tort and contract remedies, in addition to the right to demand an accounting.

Tort and Contract Remedies.   Tort and contract remedies available when a principal violates an agency agreement are the standard tort and contract remedies discussed in Chapters 8 and 20, respectively.

Demand for an Accounting.   An agent who feels she is not being properly compensated, especially when working on commission, may *demand an accounting* and may withhold further performance of her duties until the principal supplies appropriate accounting data. Hal is a used-car salesman working for Not a Lemon Car Dealers. When he receives his pay, he believes he has been shorted the appropriate amount he made on commission. Hal can request that Not a Lemon obtain an auditor to perform an audit and determine whether he was in fact paid the proper amount for his sales.

BUT WHAT IF . . .
WHAT IF THE FACTS OF THE CASE OPENER WERE DIFFERENT?

Let's say, in the Case Opener, that Janelle, a truck driver, was an independent contractor for FedEx. She looked at her income over the course of the prior year and was quite certain that she was not being paid her promised compensation. She demanded that FedEx hire an auditor to go over the company's records and make sure she and other independent contractors in her area had been paid fairly. Does FedEx have a duty to Janelle to do this?

Specific Performance.   When a contract exists and a principal agrees to certain conditions but fails to perform, under contract remedies the agent may seek court assistance in forcing the principal to perform the contract as stipulated. However, when the agency relationship is not contractual or the contract is for personal services, an agent does not have this right. The agent may recover for services rendered and/or future damages but may not force the principal to fulfill the specific contractual agreements or even to continue to employ the agent.

CASE OPENER WRAP-UP

FedEx and Independent Contractors

Ultimately, the court ruled in favor of FedEx and found that the board's decision was unenforceable because the drivers in question were independent contractors rather than employees. To determine whether the FedEx drivers should be classified as employees or independent contractors, the court applied traditional agency law principles. It discovered that FedEx "may not prescribe hours of work, whether or when the drivers take breaks, what routes they follow, or other details of performance"; drivers "are not subject to reprimands or other discipline"; and the owners of the FedEx stores (called *contractors*) are responsible for all the costs associated with operating and maintaining their vehicles. Therefore, FedEx does not exercise the degree of control necessary for the relationship to be considered employer-employee. Rather, in this situation, the route drivers are independent contractors who have "significant entrepreneurial opportunity for gain or loss" because they can operate multiple routes, hire additional drivers and helpers, sell routes without permission, and negotiate their price to deliver the packages. Therefore, the rights and duties of employees as agents discussed throughout the chapter do not apply to FedEx drivers.

This case illustrates the importance of understanding agency relations and whether a person is an employee or independent contractor. Although FedEx was successful in the case, this case suggests that it is essential for businesses to have knowledge of the kinds of agency relationships involved in their transactions. In the future, your knowledge about agency relationships could save you or your company large amounts of time and money that would have been spent on litigation.

KEY TERMS

agency 728	agency	constructive trust 743	duty to compensate 738
agency by	relationship 728	duty of loyalty 740	expressed agency 729
estoppel 731	apparent agency 731	duty of notification 740	

SUMMARY OF KEY TOPICS

Agency: The relationship between a principal and an agent.

Introduction to Agency Law

Agent: One authorized to act for and on behalf of a principal.

Principal: One who hires an agent to represent him or her.

Fiduciary: One with a duty to act primarily for another person's benefit.

Agency relationships can be created only for a lawful purpose, and almost anyone can serve as an agent. Agency relationships are consensual relationships formed by informal oral agreements or formal written contracts.

Creation of the Agency Relationship

Expressed agency: Agency formed by making a written or oral agreement.

Types of Agency

Power of attorney: Document giving an agent authority to sign legal documents on behalf of the principal.

Durable power of attorney: Power of attorney intended to continue to be effective or to take effect after the principal has become incapacitated.

Agency by implied authority: Agency formed by implication through the conduct of the parties.

Agency by estoppel: Agency formed when a principal leads a third party to believe that another individual serves as his or her agent but the principal had made no agreement with the so-called agent.

Agency by ratification: Agency that exists when an individual misrepresents himself or herself as an agent for another party and the principal accepts or ratifies the unauthorized act.

An *agency relationship* is a fiduciary relationship (a relationship of trust) in which an agent acts on behalf of the principal.

Agency Relationships

A *principal-agent relationship* exists when an employer hires an employee to enter into contracts on behalf of the employer.

An *employer-employee relationship* exists when an employer hires an employee to perform some sort of physical service.

An *employer–independent contractor relationship* exists when an employer hires persons, other than employees, to conduct certain tasks.

Duties of the Agent and the Principal

The duties of the principal:

- Duty of compensation
- Duty of reimbursement and indemnification
- Duty of cooperation
- Duty of safe working conditions

The duties of the agent:

- Duty of loyalty
- Duty of performance
- Duty of notification
- Duty of obedience
- Duty of accounting

Rights and Remedies

The rights and remedies of the principal:

- Constructive trust
- Avoidance
- Indemnification

The rights and remedies of the agent:

- Tort and contract remedies
- Demand for an accounting
- Specific performance

POINT / COUNTERPOINT

Should Sports Agents Be Held Personally Accountable for NCAA Violations Involving Signing College Athlete Clients?	
YES	**NO**
The Uniform Athlete Agents Act (2000) regulates the behavior of sports agents and their activities in representing athletes. Since the creation of the UAAA, 40 states have adopted the regulations listed in the act. While agents who violate the act can be penalized, it is more common for athletes to suffer the consequences of fines and game suspension. Likewise, it is rare for an agent to be charged at all. One of the most common violations occurs in the relationship between college athletes and agents looking to sign their principals to professional sports franchises. Moreover, it is unjust for a college athlete to be penalized for a lack of diligence on the part of the athlete's agent. Three reasons suggest the prudence of holding the agent responsible for these violations.　　First, in the event of a penalty, schools and students can be punished for the actions of agents. Current college	A common, yet illegal, practice of sports agents—influencing the career decisions of college athletes—has been costing universities and players their presence at important games and hundreds of thousands of dollars in civil suits. The NCAA and 40 states have passed regulations banning this practice; however, it has continued. While the outcomes may seem minor, a suspension of a player from an important game could cost the player a desirable draft position, affecting the player's salary and career prospects. While some wish to see the sports agents penalized for their involvement, three important reasons suggest against this.　　First, targeting sports agents will hinder only one part of the process. To successfully conspire to secretively direct a college athlete's professional signing decision, at least three parties must be involved: the player, the agent

sports rules forbid students from entering into contracts with professional agents; however, the NCAA only polices schools and student athletes. As a result, agents are infrequently held accountable, and students and schools are penalized. For example, University of Southern California (USC) running back Reggie Bush was found in violation of NCAA policies that prohibit students from receiving gifts from agents. As a result, USC was prohibited from entering lucrative bowl games for two years and was put on four years of probation, and Bush was forced to vacate and return his Heisman Trophy. Furthermore, no legal action has since been sought against the agent who presented Bush with the gifts or his agency. Because Bush's agent played an integral role in the act, he too should be held accountable. Therefore, agents should be liable for violating NCAA laws that affect their college clients.

Second, it is the responsibility of agents to represent their clients scrupulously. The core of the agent-principal relationship is trust that the agent is acting in the principal's best interest. However, violating regulations and incurring fines and suspensions are to the detriment of the principal. Furthermore, if there is likely to be no penalty for the unscrupulous agent, he or she has every incentive to use gifts and money to attract a potential athlete to the team with the highest offer. A higher standard of conduct should be expected from adult professional agents than from the college students they are wooing. Additionally, an agent-principal relationship cannot be used to conduct illegal activities, such as buying placement on a team through favors or gifts. Therefore, agents should be held to higher legal standards than those of the college-age athletes whom they represent.

Third, agents represent the only common point in an illegal conspiracy involving agents, teams, and players. While all three parties can be held responsible for their involvement in illegal recruiting, the agents not only are the common thread in most of the arrangements but, in many cases, are the sole facilitators of the deals. For example, one agent may be working with 50 players and 20 teams at any given time yet be the only common factor in each deal. To lessen the problem of illicit athletic dealings, penalizing agents would be the most effective method. Moreover, one cannot expect a player or a team to come forward, as the player's or team's career future is hanging in the balance. Thus, targeting agents and holding them personally liable is in the interest of achieving the greater goal of eliminating illegal college athletic dealings.

and a representative from the professional franchise. However, cases in the past have revealed the involvement of coaches and family members as well. While it is true that agents facilitate the relationship between the player and the future team, it is not inherently clear that the agent is most at fault. The conduct of agents, as regulated by the UAAA, requires only that all agents register and volunteer to be monitored by a state authority. Even if every state passed this regulation, athletes and team representatives could conspire to defraud the NCAA standards and practices. Additionally, an agent only facilitates the needs of clients. As a result, the agent is acting only on behalf of the will of the college athlete. Moreover, if the athlete doesn't want to be involved in any dirty dealings, the athlete is not obligated to abide by the agent's suggestion. It is therefore reasonable to assume that both athletes and professional team representatives are in favor of this widespread practice. Therefore, targeting agents would not successfully end the practice of improper college athlete agreements.

Second, agents represent an important role in the negotiation process, and their actions both protect the interests of their clients and create very few negative outcomes. College athletes work with sports agents because agents can assist them in signing to a professional team and furthering their careers. With possibly millions of dollars on the line, agents protect inexperienced athletes facing important career decisions. Targeting agents will affect the student athletes that they represent, as agents set out to find the best course of action for their respective principals. Conversely, the harm created by these inside dealings is extremely minimal. Though the practice is far from fair, aside from the rare prosecution, those involved get their desired outcomes without negatively impacting others. Thus, targeting agents will both harm the interests of the students they represent and have a small effect on harm reduction.

Third, holding sports agents personally accountable results in targeting the party with the least to gain in a deal. While initial contracts for professional athletes can be in the tens of millions of dollars, agents stand to gain only a percentage of this amount. A common amount ranges between 4 and 10 percent. Furthermore, fines levied against players who have already signed contracts pale in comparison to the potentially millions of dollars for their first-year contract. Likewise, colleges and professional sports teams profit considerably from successful teams and players. Of all those involved, agents stand to gain the least amount of money. In conclusion, targeting athletes, schools, or teams would be a more effective strategy for slowing the underhanded dealings between agents, players, and teams.

Source: Robert N. Davis, "Exploring the Contours of Agent Regulation: The Uniform Athlete Agents Act," *Villanova Sports & Entertainment Law Journal* 8 (2001), p. 1; and Alan Scher Zagier, "Laws on Sports Agents Rarely Enforced," *The Huffington Post,* August 17, 2010, www.huffingtonpost.com/2010/08/17/laws-on-sports-agents-rar_n_685000.html.

QUESTIONS & PROBLEMS

1. What are the similarities and differences between the types of agency relationships?

2. How is apparent agency, or agency by estoppel, different from expressed agency?

3. What are a principal's duties to an agent and an agent's duties to a principal?

4. William Roberts operated a McDonald's restaurant under a franchise agreement with McDonald's Corporation. Roberts hired 23-year-old David Mabin, who was just released from jail for robbery, drug use, and theft, as an hourly worker. Soon Roberts promoted Mabin to assistant manager on the night shift at the restaurant. A 15-year-old girl began working at the McDonald's, and she quickly became involved with Mabin, who provided her with free food, alcohol, and drugs (including ecstasy) and kissed her openly in the workplace. Just before the girl's 16th birthday, Mabin took her to a motel where they spent the night and engaged in sexual intercourse. The girl and her family later brought suit against McDonald's Corporation on the basis that McDonald's Corporation was the principal to Roberts through apparent agency. McDonald's Corporation was supposed to be a business with a wholesome reputation and safe workplace, but instead the minor was taken advantage of by her assistant manager. The girl argued for apparent agency with McDonald's as the principal because she claimed that as far as she was concerned, she worked for McDonald's Corporation, not just the franchise. She had a McDonald's logo on her uniform, her paycheck, and restaurant products. However, the application she filled out for employment stated, "I understand that my employer is an independent Owner/Operator of a McDonald's franchise and that I am not employed by McDonald's Corporation or any of its subsidiaries. The independent Owner/Operator of this restaurant is solely responsible for all terms, conditions and any other issues concerning my employment." Was there an apparent agency relationship between McDonald's Corporation and the franchise? Why or why not? [*D.L.S. et al. v. David Mabin et al.,* 130 Wn. App. 94, 121 P.3d 1210 (2005).]

5. Jack Kotlar was a realtor who leased commercial property on Pico Boulevard in Los Angeles. In early 1994, Kotlar leased a property to Meir Sharvit, doing business as Meir Produce. Under the lease Meir agreed to maintain liability insurance for the benefit of Kotlar.

Meir purchased a commercial general liability insurance policy from Hartford Fire Insurance Company and named Meir and Kotlar as insureds. Subsequently, Kotlar received a certificate of insurance informing him he was named as an additional insured on the policy. The document also contained a provision in which Hartford promised it would "endeavor" to give Kotlar 30 days' advance notice of cancellation of the policy.

The policy was to be effective from September 22, 1994, to September 22, 1995. However, at some time prior to the scheduled expiration date, Hartford canceled the policy because Meir failed to pay the premiums. Hartford sent notice of its intent to cancel the policy to Meir but not to Kotlar. The brokers who sold the policy to Meir also failed to provide notice of cancellation to Kotlar. Kotlar alleged that he was unaware the policy had been canceled and that neither Hartford nor the brokers made any effort to notify him of the cancellation before it occurred.

After the policy was purportedly canceled, one of Meir's customers slipped and fell on the property, suffering a fractured hip. This resulted in a lawsuit in which Kotlar was named as a defendant. Kotlar tendered defense of the action to Hartford, which refused to defend or indemnify Kotlar on the ground that the policy had been canceled for nonpayment of premiums prior to the accident.

Kotlar then brought an action against Hartford and the brokers, TriWest Insurance Services, USI Insurance Services Corp. Companies, and Max Behm and Associates. Kotlar's third amended complaint alleged causes of action for breach of contract against Hartford and negligence against the brokers. Was Kolter right in bringing the suit? Why or why not? [*Kotlar v. Hartford Fire Ins. Co.,* 83 Cal. App. 4th 1116 (2000).]

6. Jay Hellinger is a homeowner in Los Angeles County in California. He and his brother, Lee Hellinger, lived in the residence at the time. The Hellingers purchased a single homeowner's insurance policy from Farmers Insurance Exchange, Fire Insurance Exchange, and Mid-Century Insurance

Company. In 1992, the Hellinger brothers purchased a separate earthquake insurance policy for the home from Mid-Century Insurance Company. The earthquake policy provided: "We may not be sued unless there has been full compliance with all the terms of this policy. Suit on or arising out of this policy must be brought within one year after the loss occurs." In 1994, the Northridge earthquake occurred, damaging the house. Before the earthquake, Lee Hellinger had transferred his interest in the residence to his brother, Jay.

Within days of the earthquake, the Hellingers noticed cracks in interior and exterior walls, the driveway, the patio, the gazebo, and a block wall; a leak near the chimney; and electrical problems with various appliances. Farmers' agent Howard Hammer called the Hellingers within a week of the earthquake to ask about the status of their home. Lee Hellinger told Hammer about the damage to the home. After some discussion, Hammer told Lee Hellinger that he thought the losses would not exceed the deductible and that damages to the gazebo, retaining wall, sidewalk, Jacuzzi, and landscaping were not covered by the policy. Agent Hammer did not report the loss to Farmers, nor did he ask an adjuster to inspect the Hellinger home. In April 1994, the Hellingers hired a contractor to repair the visible damage caused by the earthquake, at a cost of $4,350. In July 1995, while gardening, Lee Hellinger noticed a large crack in the concrete foundation under the soil line. He reported this damage to Hammer and asked for an inspection.

Farmers sent a claims adjuster to inspect the damage in mid-September 1995. The Hellingers' claim was denied in writing on November 27, 1995, citing the policy clause which requires that suit be brought within one year of the loss. The Hellingers sued Farmers, Fire Insurance Exchange, and Mid-Century on August 26, 1996. In their original complaint, they alleged causes of action for breach of contract, breach of the implied covenant of good faith and fair dealing, and fraud. Do you think that Farmers should have paid for the damage? Also, what should have happened differently for the incident to be covered by Farmers? [*Hellinger v. Farmers Group Inc.,* 91 Cal. App. 4th 1049 (2001).]

7. Marsh &McLennan Companies is the largest provider of insurance brokerage services in the world. It holds itself out to its clients as a fiduciary that will act solely on clients' behalf in purchasing insurance policies for them. Starting in 1987, Emerson Electric Company hired Marsh to act as its fiduciary in procuring various insurance policies, such as excess liability, aircraft, and international. Emerson paid Marsh substantial amounts of money to recommend insurance policies that met its needs at the lowest possible price. Unknown to Emerson, Marsh embarked on a business plan in the early 1990s in violation of its fiduciary duties to Emerson: Marsh entered into agreements with insurance companies under which the insurers agreed to pay Marsh monies in consideration of Marsh's pledge to direct business to them. These agreements were referred to by various names such as *placement service agreements* or *market service agreements.* These documents were referred to as "kickbacks." At no time did Marsh's disclose the nature or extent of kickbacks that it was receiving. As a result of Marsh's breach of its fiduciary duties, Emerson paid an inflated price for its insurance policies. Additionally, Marsh directed Emerson to make its premium payments through Marsh itself, rather than directly to the insurance companies. The checks were made payable to Marsh. Unbeknownst to Emerson, Marsh did not immediately forward the premium payments to the insurers; instead, for a period of time before the insurance companies would be paid, Marsh would invest Emerson's premium payments to earn interest, which it retained as profit. In Marsh's 2003 Annual Report, it referred to this revenue item as "fiduciary interest income." Is this considered a breach of fiduciary duty? Why or why not? [*Emerson Electric Co. v. Marsh & McLennan Companies* (Mo. Ct. App 2011). Case No. 22054–00569, www.courts. mo.gov, accessed September 6, 2011.]

8. John Ray Lawrence, an employee of H.W. Campbell Construction Company, was killed when his head was crushed in the "pinch point" area of a crane. Coastal Marine Services of Texas, Inc., owned the crane, and Campbell employees were using it on Coastal's property when the accident occurred. Campbell took custody of the crane and began continued occupation of Coastal's property. Campbell was an independent contractor of Coastal, and no written contract existed between the two companies. Coastal employees were not directing or supervising Campbell's work on the project, nor were they on the job site when the accident occurred. Lawrence's surviving family and estate sued Campbell and Coastal,

alleging, among other things, negligence. During the trial Coastal asserted that the Lawrences had presented no evidence that Coastal retained the right to control Campbell's work, a prerequisite for finding Coastal liable under a premises liability theory. The trial court agreed and submitted an instruction precluding a finding of negligence based on the manner in which Coastal controlled the premises. The jury found no negligence on Coastal's part. At trial, in response to a series of hypothetical questions, Campbell employees testified that they would have complied with any instructions from Coastal about the movement of the crane if Coastal had given such instructions. On the basis of the Campbell employees' testimony, the court of appeals reversed the trial court's judgment, concluding that the testimony created a fact issue about Coastal's right to control the crane. Coastal appealed. What duties did Coastal owe Campbell as an independent contractor? How did the court rule on appeal? [*Coastal Marine Serv., Inc. v. Lawrence,* 988 S.W.2d 223 (1999).]

9. In 2000, Loretta Henry was pregnant and experiencing pain in her abdomen. After visiting a clinic, she was referred to Flagstaff Medical Hospital. Once there, she was examined and treated by Dr. Kraig Knoll, a physician with a physician's group providing a service for the hospital. Knoll advised her to have her gallbladder removed, and he performed the surgery. Although Henry read and signed two consent forms, she was never told that Knoll was not an employee of the hospital and was instead an independent contractor. Subsequently, Henry sued the hospital for negligence when after her child was born, both mother and child sustained injuries. She claimed there was an apparent agency relationship. The hospital argued that Henry could not establish an agency relationship between Flagstaff Hospital and Knoll. What duties did Flagstaff Hospital owe Knoll as an independent contractor? Did the court find enough evidence to establish an agency relationship? [*Loretta Henry/ Charles Arnold v. Flagstaff Medical,* 212 Ariz. 365, 132 P.3d 304, 2006 Ariz. App. LEXIS 53, 476 Ariz. Adv. Rep. 11.]

10. Nu-Look Design, Inc., operated as a residential home improvement company. During calendar years 1996, 1997, and 1998, Ronald A. Stark not only was Nu-Look's sole shareholder and president but also managed the company. He solicited business, performed necessary bookkeeping, otherwise handled finances, and hired and supervised workers. Rather than pay Stark a salary or wages, Nu-Look distributed its net income during 1996, 1997, and 1998 to him "as Mr. Stark's needs arose." Nu-Look reported on its tax returns in 1996, 1997, and 1998 net incomes of $10,866.14, $14,216.37, and $7,103.60, respectively. Stark, in turn, reported the very same amounts as nonpassive income on his 1996, 1997, and 1998 tax returns. On June 8, 2001, the IRS issued to Nu-Look a "Notice of Determination Concerning Worker Classification." The notice advised that the IRS had classified an individual at Nu-Look as an employee for purposes of federal employment taxes and that such taxes "could" be assessed for calendar years 1996, 1997, and 1998. Nu-Look challenged this determination by filing a petition for redetermination in the United States Tax Court, disputing the propriety of the determination that Stark was an employee, and also sought relief from that determination. The tax court found that Stark performed more than minor services for Nu-Look and had received remuneration for those services. As a result, the court held that Stark was an employee of Nu-Look and that Nu-Look was not entitled to relief. Nu-Look appealed. Does Stark meet the requirements for an employee? Should Nu-Look be liable for a tax assessed under the assumption that Stark is an employee? [*Nu-Look Design, Inc. v. Commission of Internal Revenue,* 356 F.3d 290 (2004).]

Looking for more review materials?

The Online Learning Center at **www.mhhe.com/kubasek3e** contains this chapter's "Assignment on the Internet" and also a list of URLs for more information, entitled "On the Internet." You can find both of them in the Student Center portion of the OLC, along with quizzes and other helpful materials.

Liability to Third Parties and Termination

LEARNING OBJECTIVES

After reading this chapter, you will be able to answer the following questions:

1 Under what circumstances might a principal be held liable to a third party on a contract negotiated by an agent?

2 Under what circumstances might a principal be held liable for the tortious behavior of its agent or independent contractor?

3 How can an agency relationship be terminated?

CASE OPENER

Vicarious Liability and Medical Malpractice Suits

In May 2001, Joann Abshure received a colonoscopy from Dr. Jeremiah Upshaw, after complaining of bloating and changes in bowel patterns. After the colonoscopy procedure, Abshure began experiencing significant discomfort in her abdominal region. Once her condition worsened, her husband called an ambulance, and Abshure was transported to Methodist Hospital. Abshure informed the emergency room doctor, Dr. Ogle, of her previous colonoscopy and of her extreme discomfort. Ogle ordered a series of lab work including CT scans and X-rays of Abshure's abdominal region. While waiting for the results of the lab work, Ogle administered several enemas to Abshure. She then began experiencing extraordinary pain. Eventually, Dr. Ogle performed a colostomy on Abshure and left her surgical incision open after packing the wound.

After time recovering in the intensive care unit, Abshure developed adult respiratory distress syndrome and sepsis. Jones eventually closed the surgical incision on May 30, 2001, and Abshure was discharged from Methodist Hospital on May 31, 2001.

Abshure initially filed a vicarious liability suit against her two treating physicians and the hospital. Later, she voluntarily dismissed the emergency room doctor from the suit. After the voluntary dismissal of the doctor, the defendant hospital filed a motion for dismissal of the plaintiff's vicarious liability claims against it. The trial court granted the defendant hospital's motion for dismissal, and upon appeal, the court affirmed the trial court's decision. Once more, the plaintiff appealed.

1. When may a principal be held vicariously liable for the negligent acts of its agent?
2. What must the plaintiff demonstrate to establish employer liability?

The Wrap-Up at the end of the chapter will answer these questions.

In the preceding chapter, we discussed how an agency relationship and its resulting authority could be created. We also introduced (1) expressed agency, or agency by agreement; (2) implied agency; and (3) agency by estoppel. Each of these avenues for creating agency includes a corresponding form of agent authority.

Contractual Liability of the Principal and Agent

L01

Under what circumstances might a principal be held liable to a third party on a contract negotiated by an agent?

When making decisions about an agency relationship's liability to third parties, courts must first identify the type of authority an agent has (see Chapter 33) and then determine the classification of the principal. Finally, the court must decide whether the principal authorized the actions of the agent. A special type of express agent authority is known as a power of attorney. The power of attorney is a specific form of express authority, usually in writing, granting an agent specific powers. There are two basic types of power of attorney: special and general. A special power of attorney grants the agent express authority over specifically outlined acts. In contrast, a general power of attorney allows the agent to conduct all business for the principal. While powers of attorney tend to terminate on the principal's death or incapacitation, a durable power of attorney specifies that the agent's authority is intended to continue beyond the principal's incapacitation.

Even with explicit instructions given through express authority, sometimes conflicts arise between principal-agent relationships in power of attorney.

Case 34-1 examines how a court determines the extent of power of attorney.

CASE 34-1   **IN RE ESTATE OF KURRELMEYER**
SUPREME COURT OF VERMONT
187 VT. 620, 992 A.2D 316 (2010)

After Louis H. Kurrelmeyer Sr. died in 2001, his son brought suit against the wife of Kurrelmeyer for an alleged invalid transfer of the decedent's home, into a trust. The son argued that the wife's transfer of the property into the trust was invalid because the wife did not have the authority to make the transfer under the written terms of the power of attorney. Specifically, the son asserted that the transfer was in violation of an express provision in the power of attorney prohibiting the wife from "making gifts to herself," as well as the fact that the power of attorney did not explicitly grant the wife the authority to transfer the property into the trust.

The court ruled in favor of the defendant, and the son appealed, arguing that the court erred in considering extrinsic evidence to determine the scope of the wife's authority under a power of attorney.

JUDGE REIBER: This is not the first time that this case has come to this Court on appeal. In 2006, we issued an opinion addressing challenges to wife's establishment of a trust (Kurrelmeyer I). In Kurrelmeyer I, we remanded the case to the trial court, and it is the trial court's decision on remand that is the subject of the current appeal.

On remand, the trial court held a hearing. At the hearing, the trial court allowed wife to present evidence—mainly in the form of testimony and written notes from the estate planning attorney—that the transfer of the Clearwater property carried out the intent of decedent to enhance the financial position of wife while also avoiding estate taxation through the use of trust instruments that were specifically recommended and designed by the attorney to accomplish decedent's goals. Son argues on appeal, as he argued in

[continued]

Kurrelmeyer I, that we should adopt a rule of strict construction whereby a power of attorney grants only those powers that are clearly and *explicitly delineated.* Thus, according to son, because the power of attorney did not explicitly grant wife authority to transfer the Clearwater property into the trust, wife did not have that authority. Son argues that this ends the matter and that the trial court therefore erred in considering extrinsic evidence in determining the scope of wife's authority. We disagree.

In Kurrelmeyer I, we recognized that other jurisdictions have adopted the rule of strict construction urged by son, but we rejected this approach: "we will not apply a rule of narrow construction to particular words and phrases used in the power of attorney, but will examine the express terms and the context of the instrument as a whole to give effect to the principal's intent." Although we did not explicitly state that courts could look at extrinsic evidence, such a holding was implicit in our direction to "examine the context" in which the power of attorney was created. Our remand also directed the trial court to examine "all the relevant circumstances" surrounding the creation of the trust in 2000. One of the relevant circumstances here was whether wife was acting to fulfill the intent for which decedent granted

wife the power of attorney in 1996. As we stated in Kurrelmeyer I, when interpreting a document such as a power of attorney, it is a "cardinal rule that the court determine the intention of the parties." Ideally, the intention of the parties will always be apparent from the express language of the power of attorney itself. Unfortunately, that is not always the case. Thus, in an instance such as this one, where there was significant and well-documented extrinsic evidence of the reasons for which decedent created the power of attorney, the trial court did not err in taking that evidence into consideration.

The trial court had ample support for its conclusions that "[d]ecedent's overarching goal was to provide for his surviving wife" and that decedent intended that the power of attorney would allow wife to transfer the Clearwater property into the trust that she created. As the evidence indicated and as the trial court held, decedent intended the power of attorney to allow wife to take the precise actions she took here when she transferred the Clearwater property into a trust. Wife's actions were therefore in accord with decedent's intent, and there was no improper self-dealing.

AFFIRMED.

CRITICAL THINKING

What reasoning did the court use to come to the conclusion that the power of attorney did include transfers of property into trusts? If you were a judge, would you have found that the deceased's wife was authorized to transfer the property into a trust? Why or why not?

ETHICAL DECISION MAKING

What is the purpose of creating rules surrounding the extent of power of attorney? Who are the stakeholders that are affected by the conflicts that arise between principal-agent relationships in power-of-attorney cases?

CLASSIFICATION OF THE PRINCIPAL

We classify principals from the perspective of the third party's knowledge about them. The law of agency places special weight on this viewpoint of the agency relationship.

When the third party is aware that the agent is making an agreement on behalf of a principal and also knows who the principal is, the principal is a disclosed principal. If the third party is aware of the principal's existence but not his or her identity, we classify the principal as a partially disclosed principal or an unidentified principal. Finally, if the third party does not know that an agent is acting on behalf of a principal, we have an undisclosed principal. Classification of the principal is important because it helps determine the principal's liability.[1] If a principal is partially disclosed, the agent and the principal are both considered parties to the contract and each may be liable separately from the other.

---

[1] Restatement (Second) of Agency, sec. 4.

?

BUT WHAT IF . . .
WHAT IF THE FACTS OF THE CASE OPENER WERE DIFFERENT?

Let's say, in the Case Opener, that Abshure's emergency room doctor, Dr. Ogle, was working for the defendant hospital but he was a home-visit doctor and didn't work at the hospital's campus. When Ogle treated Abshure, he did so at her home and she had no idea what hospital he worked for or whether he worked for one at all. What kind of principal would the defendant hospital qualify as? Why is this distinction important?

AUTHORIZED ACTS

An agent who acts within the scope of her authority on behalf of a disclosed or partially disclosed principal is not liable for the acts of the principal.[2] The principal is liable only if the agent has authority to act on the principal's behalf. With a disclosed principal, the agent is not liable because she is not a party to the transaction. If the principal is *partially* disclosed, the agent herself can be held liable for contractual nonperformance because the courts generally treat the agent as a party to the contract.[3] Whether disclosed or partially disclosed, apart from any liability the agent might have, the principal is liable for the agreements made with the third party.

When the agent acts within her authority on behalf of an undisclosed principal, the law will likely hold her liable for the agreement. In the eyes of the third party, the agent is the only person who could be liable. Yet, if the agent is liable to the third party, then the undisclosed principal is liable to the agent. However, in certain situations the agent is the only party liable for the contract. These situations are:

1. The contract expressly excludes the principal from the contract. If the principal was not a party to the contract, he or she has no liability to the agent.

2. The agent enters into a contract that is a negotiable instrument. The Uniform Commercial Code (UCC) governs negotiable instruments and states that other parties, that is, principals, cannot be liable for them if their name is not on the instrument or if the agent's signature does not indicate that it was made in a representative capacity.[4]

3. The third party enters into a contract with the agent such that the agent's performance is required and the third party may reject the performance of the principal. For example, if the agent is a photographer and he enters into a contract for his principal without disclosing this fact, the third party may reject the principal's attempt to fulfill the contract by taking the third party's picture.

4. The principal or agent knows a third party would not enter into a contract with the principal if the principal's identity were disclosed but the agent does so anyway. The agent will be the only party liable should the third party rescind the contract.

When the third party comes to know of the undisclosed principal's identity, a judgment for the third party against the agent releases the principal from liability.[5] A judgment against a previously undisclosed principal likewise frees the agent from liability.[6]

Exhibit 34-1 summarizes contractual liability to third parties for authorized acts of the agent.

---

[2] Restatement (Second) of Agency, sec. 320.

[3] Restatement (Second) of Agency, sec. 321.

[4] UCC § 3-402(b)(2).

[5] Restatement (Second) of Agency, sec. 210.

[6] Restatement (Second) of Agency, sec. 337.

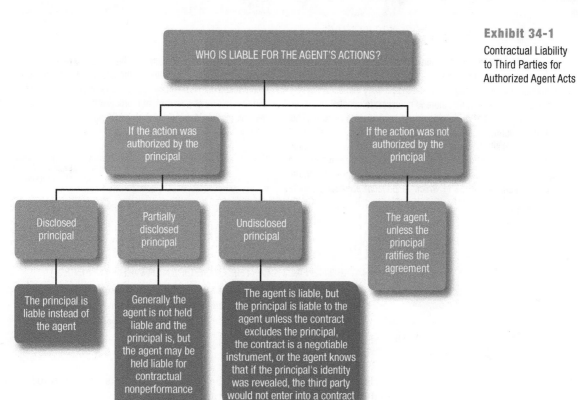

Exhibit 34-1

Contractual Liability
to Third Parties for
Authorized Agent Acts

In the Case Opener, one question the court must consider is whether the emergency room doctors are independent contractors or employees of the hospital. If they are employees, the hospital can be responsible for the conduct of the doctors through *respondeat superior.* However, if they are independent contractors, the hospital cannot be held liable.

UNAUTHORIZED ACTS

If an agent has no authority to act on behalf of a principal but still enters into a contract with a third party, the principal, regardless of the classification, is not bound to the contract unless the principal ratifies the agreement.

When the agent exceeds his authority to act on behalf of the principal, the agent will likely be personally liable to the third party. Yet, when the third party is aware that the agent does not represent the principal, the law does not hold the agent liable for the agreement. In almost all other cases in which the agent claims to have authority to contract on behalf of the principal, the law holds the agent liable to the third party. If an agent enters into a contract knowingly misrepresenting his alleged authority, the agent is liable to the third party in a tort action.

Agents who go beyond their authority when the principal is disclosed or partially disclosed are liable for a breach of implied warranty. They cannot be liable for breach of contract because they were never an intended party to the contract, even when exceeding their authority. The agent can breach the implied warranty intentionally, through a knowing misrepresentation, or unintentionally, through a good-faith mistake such as simply misjudging his or her authority. In either case, the agent is liable if the third party relied on the agent's alleged status.

COMPARING THE LAW OF OTHER COUNTRIES

RESPONDEAT SUPERIOR IN IRAQ

Unlike the United States' broad employment of the *respondeat superior* doctrine, the Iraqi Civil Code generally rejects the idea of *respondeat superior*. Iraq's Civil Code is partially influenced by classical Islamic law, in which there is no separate concept of tort and which suggests that those who cause harm should repair it. Thus, classical Islamic legal systems tend to follow a rule of strict and "specific" liability for torts. This notion of specific liability rejects the idea of vicarious liability of superiors and custodians and constrains liability to the actual wrongdoer. However, Iraqi law does contain some limited exceptions in which *respondeat superior* principles are permitted. These include the liability of owners of animals for damage caused by the animals, the liability of a parent of a minor who causes injury, the liability of owners of buildings that collapse, and the liability of government municipalities and commercial entities for injuries caused by their employees during the course of their service.

Sources: Dan E. Stiggal, "A Closer Look at Iraqi Property and Tort Law," *Louisiana Law Review* 68 (2008), p. 765; and Dan E. Stiggal, "Refugees and Legal Reform in Iraq: The Iraqi Civil Code, International Standards for the Treatment of Displaced Persons, and the Art of Attainable Solutions," *Rutgers Law Record* 34 (2009), p. 1.

? BUT WHAT IF . . .

WHAT IF THE FACTS OF THE CASE OPENER WERE DIFFERENT?

Let's say, in the Case Opener, that Dr. Ogle had deliberately exceeded the limits his hospital had set out for him in his contract of employment. In other words, his actions were not authorized by the hospital. What would Ogle be liable for in regard to his employer? Why would Ogle not be liable for breach of contract?

Legal Principle: **As a general rule, when an agent commits an unauthorized act, the principal is neither bound to the contract nor liable.**

Tort Liability and the Agency Relationship

L02

Under what circumstances might a principal be held liable for the tortious behavior of its agent or independent contractor?

An agent who commits a tort that injures a third party is personally liable for his or her actions, regardless of both the classification and the liability of the principal.[7] The principal may also be held liable for the agent's authorized or unauthorized acts. Furthermore, tortious liability of the principal can be established directly or indirectly. Finally, if an agent is an employee and the principal/employer controls the employee's behavior, the principal can be found liable. The next section introduces these methods of establishing tortious liability.

PRINCIPAL'S TORTIOUS CONDUCT

The law holds a principal directly responsible for his or her own tortious conduct on two conditions. First, a principal who directs the agent to commit a tort is authorizing the agent's unlawful behavior and thus is liable for any damages caused by the tort.[8] Similarly, the principal who ratifies an agent's tortious act knowing that the agent acted illegally is liable, even if she does not condone the agent's conduct.[9]

Second, if the principal fails to provide proper instruments or tools or gives inadequate instructions to the agent concerning the necessity to employ competent agents, the law holds the principal liable to a third party for negligent hiring of an agent. If an agent commits a tort against a customer, the customer often argues that the principal is liable because she should have taken more care in hiring the agent.

[7] Restatement (Second) of Agency, sec. 343.
[8] Restatement (Second) of Agency, sec. 212.
[9] Restatement (Second) of Agency, sec. 218.

Respondeat Superior. The doctrine of *respondeat superior* (a Latin phrase meaning "let the superior speak") applies in the context of the principal/employer–agent/employee relationship. The principal/employer holds **vicarious liability,** which is liability assigned without fault, for any harm the agent/employee causes while working for the principal. In other words, the principal/employer is liable not because he was personally at fault but because he negligently hired an agent. The rationale is that if the employer is benefiting by the work of the employee, the employer should also be responsible for the harms the employee caused.

Thus, a third party injured through the negligence of an employee can sue either the employee or the employer.[10] To establish employer liability, the third party must show that the wrongful act occurred within the scope of the employment. The courts consider the following in determining this element:[11]

1. Did the employer authorize the employee's act?
2. Did the act occur within the time and space limits of employment?
3. Was the act performed, at least in part, on behalf of the employer?
4. To what extent were the employer's interests advanced by the act?
5. To what extent were the private interests of the employee involved?
6 Did the employer provide the means (tools) by which the act occurred?
7. Did the employee use force not expected by the employer?
8. Did the employer know that the act would include the commission of a serious crime?

If a delivery driver negligently injures a third party while making deliveries on behalf of the employer, both the employee and the employer will be held liable. Suppose the driver is using the company vehicle when he stops at a drive-through to get coffee. Could the employer be liable to a third party for an accident caused by the driver? If an agent makes a substantial departure from the course of the employer's business, the employer is not liable.

Courts often refer to an employee's substantial departure as a "frolic of his own." However, if the deviation from the employer's business is *not* substantial, the employer can be held liable. In Case 34-2, the court considers the scope of the employment relationship.

Legal Principle: As a general rule, a principal is vicariously liable for the actions of his or her agent.

[10] Restatement (Second) of Agency, secs. 216 and 219.
[11] Restatement (Second) of Agency, sec. 229.

CASE 34-2   IGLESIA CRISTIANA LA CASA DEL SENOR, INC., ETC. v. L.M.
COURT OF APPEAL OF FLORIDA, THIRD DISTRICT
783 SO. 2D 353 (2001)

L.M. sued Ali Pacheco, the former pastor of Iglesia Cristiana La Casa Del Senor, Inc. (the Church), as well as the Church, alleging Pacheco had sexually assaulted her in July 1991 when she was a minor. The allegation of sexual assault formed the basis of L.M.'s claims against the Church based on respondeat superior. When the criminal act occurred, L.M. was sixteen years old.

Before the criminal act took place, Pacheco visited L.M.'s residence twice when L.M. had been left home alone. On another occasion, Pacheco visited L.M. at her school. L.M.

told her mother about Pacheco's visit, but did not advise anyone from the Church.

According to L.M., on July 8, 1991, Pacheco called her at work and invited her to lunch to discuss her parents' marital problems. L.M. accepted, and Pacheco picked her up from work. L.M. noticed a sandwich and soft drink in the car. Pacheco drove to a Marriott Hotel. L.M. testified Pacheco led her to a room he had rented, and told her not to worry because she would finally be cured. He then proceeded to sexually assault her. Pacheco testified L.M. consented to having sex.

[continued]

According to him, their meeting was prearranged. They had discussed the matter and had in fact been to the Marriot Hotel the previous day intending to have sexual relations but had decided against it. Pacheco testified he knew what he was doing was wrong but explained it was a great temptation in his life.

The jury returned a verdict in L.M.'s favor, finding the Church liable for Pacheco's criminal act on the grounds of respondeat superior. *The Church appealed.*

PER CURIAM: Under the doctrine of respondeat superior, an employer cannot be held liable for the tortious or criminal acts of an employee, unless the acts were committed during the course of the employment and to further a purpose or interest, however excessive or misguided, of the employer. An employee's conduct is within the scope of his employment, where (1) the conduct is of the kind he was employed to perform, (2) the conduct occurs substantially within the time and space limits authorized or required by the work to be performed, and (3) the conduct is activated at least in part by a purpose to serve the master. An exception may exist where the tort-feasor was assisted in accomplishing the tort by virtue of the employer/employee relationship.

In this case, the sexual assault did not occur on Church property, and the record does not support a finding Pacheco's criminal act against L.M. constituted the kind of conduct he was employed to perform, or he was in any way motivated by his desire to serve the Church. On the contrary, the record establishes Pacheco's purpose in arranging the meeting that day was to satisfy his personal interests, not to further the Church's objectives. Regardless of the stated reason for the meeting between Pacheco and L.M., it is undisputed no counseling occurred on the day of the crime. While Pacheco may have had access to L.M. because of his position as the Church pastor, whom L.M. and her family had become friends with over time, he was not engaging in authorized acts or serving the interests of the Church during the time he tried to seduce her or on the day he raped her. The sexual assault was an independent, self-serving act by Pacheco; an act he knew was wrong to commit and the Church would surely have tried to prevent had it known of his plans.

We agree with the Church that Pacheco's sexual assault of L.M. did not occur within the scope of his employment. Accordingly, we find, as a matter of law, the Church cannot be held vicariously liable for Pacheco's criminal act.

Therefore, we reverse the trial court's final judgment and remand with instructions to enter judgment in favor of Appellant.

REVERSED and REMANDED.

CRITICAL THINKING

Assume L.M.'s account of the crime is true. Examine the exception to the "scope of employment" criteria mentioned by the judge. How could the plaintiff make an argument, using that exception, that Pacheco's conduct was within the scope of his employment?

ETHICAL DECISION MAKING

The judge in this case outlines a doctrine for determining the liability of an employer for the actions of employees. What value preference is highlighted by that doctrine?

If the third party is able to establish employee negligence such that the employer is liable, the employer has the right to recover from the employee any damages he paid the third party as a result of the employee's negligence. The right to recover damages is referred to as the *right of indemnification.* However, if the employee is innocent of negligence, the employer is also free of liability.

Intentional Torts and *Respondeat Superior.* The agent is liable for any torts he or she commits. In the same way the principal is responsible for the negligent acts of the employee under the doctrine of *respondeat superior,* the principal may also be liable for any intentional torts of the employee. Furthermore, an employer may be responsible for any tortious acts of the employee if the employer knew or should have known that the employee had a tendency to commit such acts. Hence, a principal may be liable for negligent hiring who fails to do a background check to learn about the tendencies of potential employees.

The principal of an employee with a criminal background may be held liable for tortious acts committed by her hired agent even though the employee may not recognize the wrongfulness of his act. Therefore, employers will most likely purchase liability insurance in case particular employees engage in tortious activities.

AGENT MISREPRESENTATION

Unlike tort liability, which is based on whether the agent/employee was acting in the scope of employment, *misrepresentation liability* depends on whether the principal authorized the agent's act. If the principal authorizes the agent to engage in an act and the agent misrepresents herself intentionally or unintentionally, the principal is always liable in tort to someone who relied on the agent's misrepresentation.

If an agent has misrepresented herself, the third party has two options:

1. Cancel the contract with the principal and be compensated for any money lost.
2. Affirm the contract and sue the principal to recover damages.

Legal Principle: **As a general rule, if a principal authorizes an agent to misrepresent himself or herself, the principal is always liable.**

Principal's Liability and the Independent Contractor

As we discussed in the preceding chapter, an independent contractor is not an employee of the individual who hires him or her to do work. The individual doing the hiring does not control the details of the independent contractor's performance. Consequently, an individual who hires an independent contractor cannot be held liable for the independent contractor's tortious actions under the doctrine of *respondeat superior.*

Suppose that while working on the outside of the building he is renovating, an independent contractor accidentally injures an innocent bystander when he drops a pile of bricks. The owner of the building is not liable for the innocent bystander's injuries; the independent contractor is liable.[12]

If the independent contractor engages in extremely hazardous activities, such as blasting operations, for the principal, the principal will be responsible for any damages by the independent contractor. Certain activities are held strictly liable because of their inherently dangerous nature; an employer cannot escape this liability simply by hiring an independent contractor to complete them. Nor can the employer escape liability for an independent contractor's tort if the employer directs the contractor to commit the tort.

The Case Nugget on the next page demonstrates the role of tort principles in establishing liability.

BUT WHAT IF . . .
WHAT IF THE FACTS OF THE CASE OPENER WERE DIFFERENT?

Let's say, in the Case Opener, that Ogle, being an emergency room doctor, was an independent contractor to the hospital. When Abshure sues Ogle, she sues the hospital too because Ogle was working within the hospital when he caused her injury. Is the hospital liable for Ogle's actions in such a scenario?

---

[12] Restatement (Second) of Agency, sec. 250.

CASE NUGGET

LIABILITY WHEN HIRING INDEPENDENT CONTRACTORS

Larry S. Lawrence v. Bainbridge Apartments et al. Court of Appeals of Missouri, Western District 957 S.W.2d 400 (1997)

In 1989, Smart Way Janitorial offered a bid to Larry Lawrence to wash the windows of Bainbridge Apartments, two seven-story buildings and four four-story buildings. Even though Lawrence could not create a safety line for the four-story buildings, the building manager insisted he wash the windows from the outside so that the residents would not be disturbed. When Lawrence started the work, he fell from one of the shorter buildings and suffered injuries. He brought suit against Bainbridge Apartments, arguing that Bainbridge was negligent on the basis of the "inherently dangerous activity" exception to the doctrine that landowners are not vicariously liable for injuries caused by the negligence of an independent contractor or his employees.

The trial court ruled that because Lawrence had received workers' compensation benefits, the injury was not covered by the inherently dangerous activity exception. The trial court granted summary judgment to Bainbridge; however, when Lawrence appealed, the decision was reversed and remanded because the court of appeals ruled that Lawrence was not a covered employee entitled to workers' compensation benefits.

The court argued that in establishing liability in this case, it would look to which party could best avoid the harm and manage the risk of loss in the inherently dangerous activity in question. An independent contractor who knows he will not be compensated by the landowner for his injuries has a strong incentive to take additional care and avoid neglect in performing his duties. As an expert, he is in a better position to understand the risks and costs in a particular job, and he may demand sufficient remuneration and safety measures to cover what he believes the risks to be. In return for his bargained-for price, he accepts the allocation of the risk. The court held that an injured independent contractor, although uninsured, cannot recover under the inherently dangerous activity exception.

Crime and Agency Relationships

If an agent commits a crime, clearly the agent is liable for the crime. If the agent commits the crime in the scope of employment for a principal without the principal's authorization, the principal is not liable for the agent's crime. Remember, one of the elements establishing that a crime has been committed is *intent*. If a principal is unaware of or had no intent for the agent to commit a crime, there is no rationale for the principal's criminal liability. The only time the principal can be liable for the crime of an agent is when the principal has authorized the criminal act.

Legal Principle: **If an agent commits a crime in the scope of his or her employment without authorization from the principal, the principal is not liable for the crime.**

Termination of the Agency Relationship

L03

How can an agency relationship be terminated?

The parties may choose to terminate an agency relationship, or it may terminate automatically by the lapse of time, fulfillment of purpose, or operation of law. (Exhibit 34-2 lists the ways that agency relationships can be terminated.) If the relationship has ended, the agent no longer has authority to make agreements on behalf of the principal. However, the agent's apparent authority continues until the principal notifies third parties that the relationship has ended.

Notice of the termination can be actual or constructive. Actual notice must be given to third parties who have had business interactions with the agent; it directly informs them, orally or in writing, that the agency agreement has terminated.[13] When the agent's authority was granted in writing, actual notice also must be given in writing. Parties not directly related to an agency agreement may receive constructive notice, which is how the termination of an agency agreement is generally announced.[14] Constructive notice usually

---

[13] Restatement (Second) of Agency, sec. 136(2).

[14] Restatement (Second) of Agency, sec. 136(3).

TERMINATION BY ACTS OF PARTIES	TERMINATION BY OPERATION OF LAW
1. Lapse of time	1. Death
2. Fulfillment of purpose	2. Insanity
3. Occurrence of specific event	3. Bankruptcy
4. Mutual agreement by the parties	4. Changed circumstances
5. Revocation of authority	5. Change in law
6. Renunciation by the agent	6. Impossibility
7. Agency coupled with an interest	7. Disloyalty of agent
	8. War

Exhibit 34-2
Ways that an Agency Relationship Can Be Terminated

consists of publication in a generally circulating newspaper for the area where the agency agreement existed.

Parties forming a contract of agency in a foreign jurisdiction should include the conditions of termination within the contract. A U.S. manager conducting business in the European Union needs access to the intricacies of Chapter IV of the Agency Relationship Law that focuses on termination. Released agents in the EU receive compensation if they have brought the principal new customers from whom the principal continues to profit, if they are unable to otherwise recover costs incurred through the performance of the contract, or upon their death.

EU law prohibits the agent's receiving compensation if the principal has terminated the contract due to the agent's incapacity. EU law additionally blocks the compensation if the agent terminates the contract or assigns rights and duties under it to another person. Local legal counsel should be especially knowledgeable about such provisions and be able to help managers avoid unnecessary legal battles.

Case 34-3 highlights the potentially disastrous consequences of not understanding how an agency relationship is terminated.

CASE 34-3   ANGELA & RAUL RUIZ v. FORTUNE INSURANCE COMPANY
COURT OF APPEAL OF FLORIDA, THIRD DISTRICT
677 SO. 2D 1336 (1996)

In September 1990, Angela and Raul Ruiz purchased a homeowner's insurance policy for their mobile home from Fortune Insurance Company through Bates Hernandez Associates, an insurance broker. Bates secured the insurance through Fortune's agent, Biscayne Underwriting Management. Fortune terminated its agency relationship with Biscayne in November 1990 and notified its customers in July 1991; consequently, Fortune sent the Ruizes a notice their homeowner's insurance would not be renewed.

However, in August 1991, even though the Ruizes' insurance policy had expired, Bates sent them a renewal notice. The Ruizes paid Bates $450 to renew their insurance policy with Fortune. Bates sent this money to Biscayne, which accepted it.

In August 1992, the Ruizes' mobile home was damaged by a hurricane. When the Ruizes reported the loss to Fortune, they were told they had no current insurance policy with the company. They filed suit against Fortune. In a summary judgment, the trial court ruled for Fortune. The Ruizes appealed.

OPINION PER CURIAM: Although the Ruizes contended below they never received Fortune's notice of cancellation, Fortune produced below a copy of the notice of cancellation and proof it mailed the same to the Ruizes. The law is clear that an insurer's proof of mailing of a notice of cancellation to the insured prevails as a matter of law over the insured's denial as to its receipt.

[continued]

Fortune's actual notice of cancellation to the Ruizes was legally sufficient and binding, whether the Ruizes read or understood the import of such notice. Any lack of understanding of this written notice on the part of the Ruizes only placed a duty upon them to make further inquiry of their broker, agent and/or insurer.

We further reject the Ruizes' argument on appeal that Fortune is estopped from disclaiming coverage where

Biscayne accepted the Ruizes' renewal premium after Fortune's termination of its agency relationship with Biscayne. There is no evidence that Fortune engaged in any conduct or action which would reasonably lead the Ruizes to believe Biscayne had continuing actual or apparent authority to collect such premiums on behalf of Fortune.

AFFIRMED.

CRITICAL THINKING

The judge seems to think Fortune fulfilled its obligation to the Ruizes by mailing them a notice of cancellation. Why do you think the Ruizes were confused about the cancellation? How could the plaintiffs argue that they were not properly made aware that their insurance had been canceled?

ETHICAL DECISION MAKING

Explain what you think the ethical obligations were for every party in this case: Fortune, Bates Hernandez Associates, Biscayne Underwriting Management, and the Ruizes.

TERMINATION BY ACTS OF PARTIES

The agency relationship can be terminated after certain acts, as we discuss in the following sections.

Lapse of Time. If an agency agreement specifies that the relationship will exist for a certain amount of time, it will end when that time expires.[15] An agency agreement might state that the relationship will begin on September 1 and end on September 30. While the agent and principal can agree to continue their relationship through October, they will have to make a new agreement to cover it. The agent's express authority ends when the relationship ends; thus, the principal must notify third parties that the former agent can no longer act on the principal's behalf.

Fulfillment of Purpose. Suppose John, a homeowner, enters into an agreement with Claire, a real estate agent, to sell his house. Once Claire succeeds in selling the house, she no longer has the authority to act on John's behalf. She has fulfilled the purpose of the agency relationship.[16]

Occurrence of a Specific Event. Depending on its purpose, an agency relationship can be terminated on the occurrence of a specific event. John employs Claire as an agent to sell his house. Once the sale is final, the agency relationship will terminate.

Mutual Agreement by the Parties. Agency is a consensual agreement between two parties. Consequently, if John and Claire both decide they do not wish to continue in the agency relationship, they can cancel the agreement and terminate the relationship.

Revocation of Authority. A principal can revoke an agent's authority at any time.[17] However, such revocation might constitute a breach of contract with the agent, leaving

[15] Restatement (Second) of Agency, sec. 105.
[16] Restatement (Second) of Agency, sec. 106.
[17] Restatement (Second) of Agency, sec. 119.

COMPARING THE LAW OF OTHER COUNTRIES

TERMINATION IN THE UNITED ARAB EMIRATES

After a relationship of agency ends in the United Arab Emirates (UAE), an agent is entitled to claim compensation, even if the termination occurs in accordance with the terms of the agency agreement. Whether the claim for compensation will be successful is determined by the circumstances surrounding the agent's termination.

Under the UAE Commercial Transaction Law and the UAE Civil Code, *unregistered* agents are still entitled to seek compensation in the event of termination. In the UAE, when the time comes to determine the amount of compensation to be awarded, court-appointed experts are usually the entities that are responsible for determining compensation amounts.

the principal liable for damages.[18] If the agent has somehow breached the fiduciary duty to the principal, however, the principal can revoke the agent's authority without liability.

Renunciation by the Agent. An agent can terminate the agency relationship by renouncing the authority given him or her. The agent can be liable for breach of contract if the agency agreement stated a specific amount of time that the relationship is to exist.

Agency Coupled with an Interest. An agency coupled with an interest is a special kind of agency relationship created for the agent's benefit, not the principal's. The principal may not terminate this relationship, which is also called *power given as security.* Rather, it is terminated when an event occurs that discharges the principal's obligation.

TERMINATION BY OPERATION OF LAW

Automatic termination of the agency relationship can occur when the agent is unable to fulfill his task, when the principal does not desire to continue the performance, or when further pursuit of the relationship's objectives would be illegal.

Death. If the principal or the agent dies, the agency relationship is automatically terminated. Even if one party is unaware of the other party's death, the relationship no longer exists. Suppose an agent has authority to buy antiques on behalf of a principal and continues to purchase items without knowing the principal has died. Those transactions are not binding on the principal's estate, because as soon as the principal died, the agent's authority to act was gone.

Insanity. If a principal or agent becomes insane, the agency relationship is finished. Some states have modified this law so that the agency contract still exists unless the person has been adjudicated insane.

Bankruptcy. If the principal or agent files a bankruptcy petition, the agency relationship is generally no longer in existence, particularly if the agent is filing for bankruptcy and his or her credit is important to the agency relationship. Insolvency, the inability to pay debts or the condition in which liabilities outweigh assets, does not necessarily result in the termination of the agency relationship.[19]

---

[18] Restatement (Second) of Agency, sec. 118.

[19] Restatement (Second) of Agency, sec. 113.

COMPARING THE LAW OF OTHER COUNTRIES

TERMINATION IN THE NETHERLANDS

After a relationship of agency ends in the Netherlands, the agent is entitled to compensation if his or her duties are concluded within a "reasonable" time after termination or if the agent received orders for a certain action before the termination.

In the most interesting triggering event for mandatory compensation, the agent is entitled to "goodwill compensation" if (1) the agent brought the principal new customers, (2) the agent brought new agreements with clients who are still profitable to the principal, and (3) such payment is financially reasonable for the principal (the relationship is not being terminated due to bankruptcy).

The agent must file for goodwill compensation within five years of termination. It may not exceed the equivalent of the agent's average yearly salary.

Changed Circumstances. If an unusual change in circumstances leads the agent to believe that the principal's instructions do not apply, the agency relationship terminates.[20] Suppose Danielle contracts Gregory to act as her agent to sell a painting she found in her great-aunt's attic and authorizes him to sell it for $5,000. However, in the course of showing the painting to several buyers, Gregory learns that the painting is a Van Gogh original. Because the painting is worth much more than $5,000, Gregory should infer that Danielle does not want the original agency to continue.

BUT WHAT IF . . .
WHAT IF THE FACTS OF THE CASE OPENER WERE DIFFERENT?

Let's say, in the Case Opener, that the hospital that employed Ogle had filed for bankruptcy a day before he caused injury to Abshure. What would that mean for the agency agreement between Ogle and the hospital and thus for the hospital's liability? What are the three other events that come into play in agency relationships and have the same effect as bankruptcy?

Change in Law. When a new law makes the commission of an existing agency agreement illegal, the agreement is terminated. LaToya hires Ryan to paint her house green. Then the city council passes a law making it illegal to paint houses green. The new law automatically terminates the agency agreement.

Impossibility. Suppose that while Gregory is trying to sell Danielle's painting, there is a fire in her house and the painting is destroyed. Because it is impossible for Gregory to sell the painting, the agency relationship cannot continue.[21]

If the agent loses qualifications needed to perform duties for the principal, the agency relationship also ends because of impossibility. Jackson hires a lawyer to serve as his agent who has unfortunately engaged in a series of illegal actions and is then disbarred. Because the lawyer can no longer fulfill the functions Jackson authorized him to perform, the agency relationship is terminated.

Disloyalty of Agent. An agency agreement is terminated whenever the agent, unknown to the principal, acquires interest against the principal's interest. It is also terminated if the

[20] Restatement (Second) of Agency, sec. 109.
[21] Restatement (Second) of Agency, sec. 124.

E-COMMERCE AND THE LAW

ELECTRONIC CONTRACTS IN SINGAPORE

The possibility of e-mail and electronic fraud creates certain risks in the formation of electronic contracts. Singapore passed legislation in 1997 that attempts to combat those risks and specifies the consequences of such fraud.

Agency contracts made electronically will be valid and enforceable if the principal or a principal's designated agent sent the contract. To be legally allowed to assume that the electronic record is that of the principal, the third party either follows an agreed-on procedure of clarification or is assured that the message originated from an agent endorsed by the principal.

If an agent sends an electronic record *not* approved by the principal, the third party has the right to act as a result of it. If such actions result in injuries or damages to the third party, the principal is responsible under law and cannot claim he or she was unaware of the agent's actions. While the principal may indeed not have been aware, Singapore does not recognize lack of awareness as a defense.

Singapore's legislation intends to protect third parties from the poor judgment of principals by creating this direct link between them. Making the principal answerable and liable to the third party increases the pressure to employ reliable agents.

---

agent breaches the duty of loyalty he or she has to the principal.[22] Marta is an attorney representing Lola in her suit against a pharmaceutical company. If the pharmaceutical company offers Marta a job and she accepts, the agency agreement terminates because Marta has acquired an interest opposed to Lola's interests.

War. A principal has an agent in Iran authorized to conduct business dealings on the principal's behalf.[23] If the United States goes to war with Iran, this agency relationship will no longer be in existence because there is no way to enforce the rights of the parties.

[22] Restatement (Second) of Agency, sec. 112.

[23] Restatement (Second) of Agency, sec. 115.

CASE OPENER WRAP-UP

Vicarious Liability and Medical Malpractice Suits

Upon Abshure's second appeal, the supreme court of Tennessee reversed the judgment of the court of appeals, which had affirmed the trial court's dismissal of the plaintiff's vicarious liability claims against the hospital. The supreme court argued that Abshure did in fact file a proper vicarious liability claim against Methodist Hospital before the claims against Dr. Ogle were voluntarily dismissed. The court reasoned that there is *not* a limitation on the plaintiff's ability to pursue a vicarious liability claim if the plaintiff had already filed an initial vicarious liability claim against a principal before dismissing any of the principal's agents from the claim.

As previously discussed in this chapter, in cases such as this one, a principal may be held vicariously liable for the negligent acts of its agent only if the plaintiff shows that the wrongful act occurred within the scope of the agent's employment. To demonstrate this element, the court considers facts such as whether the employer's interests were advanced, whether the employer provided the means by which the act occurred, and whether the employer authorized the employee's act.

KEY TERMS

actual notice   760
agency coupled with
    an interest   763
constructive
    notice   760
disclosed principal   753

durable power of
    attorney   752
general power of
    attorney   752
partially disclosed
    principal   753

power of attorney   752
*respondeat
    superior*   757
special power of
    attorney   752
undisclosed principal   753

unidentified
    principal   753
vicarious liability   757

SUMMARY OF KEY TOPICS

Contractual Liability of the Principal and Agent

Classification of the principal: The principal must be classified as either disclosed, partially disclosed, or undisclosed.

Authorized acts: These are acts within the scope of the agent's authority.

Unauthorized acts: These acts go beyond the scope of the agent's authority.

Tort Liability and the Agency Relationship

Principal's tortious conduct: The law holds a principal directly responsible for his or her own tortious conduct under two conditions: (1) The principal directs the agent to commit a tortious act, and (2) the principal fails to provide proper instruments or tools or adequate instructions.

Agent misrepresentation: If an agent misrepresents himself or herself to a third party, the principal may be tortiously liable for the agent's misrepresentation.

Respondeat superior: The principal/employer is liable not because he or she was personally at fault but because he or she negligently hired an agent.

Principal's Liability and the Independent Contractor

An individual who hires an independent contractor cannot be held liable for the independent contractor's tortious actions under the doctrine of *respondeat superior* unless the contractor engages in hazardous activities.

Crime and Agency Relationships

If an agent commits a crime, clearly the agent is liable for the crime.

Termination of the Agency Relationship

Termination by acts of parties: Termination may occur by lapse of time, fulfillment of purpose, occurrence of a specific event, mutual agreement by the parties, revocation of authority, or renunciation by the agent.

Termination by operation of law: The agency relationship may be terminated automatically due to death, insanity, bankruptcy, changed circumstances, change in law, impossibility, disloyalty of agent, or war.

POINT / COUNTERPOINT

Should Attorneys and Other Agents Be Required to Pass Mental Fitness Assessments before Being Given Roles in Power-of-Attorney Circumstances?

YES	NO

YES

In cases involving the granting of power of attorney by a principal to a third party acting on the principal's interest, a high degree of trust and responsibility is put into the hands of the agent. With durable power of attorney, an agent is asked to act on the interest of a principal with a diminished mental or physical ability to represent himself. Therefore, it is reasonable to insist on the mental fitness of the agent. Three important reasons suggest the wisdom of requiring that attorneys and other agents in power-of-attorney cases pass regular mental health assessments.

First, to dutifully uphold the principal-agent relationship, an agent must be mentally sound. An agent is duty-bound to act in her client's best interest; however, mental illness or defect could severely limit her ability to do so. Therefore, when an agent is asked to represent a client who has diminished mental ability, it is rational to require proof of the agent's mental fitness. For example, durable power of attorney represents an extra-sensitive situation since agents cannot confer with clients about their desires, and it gives a dangerous amount of power to an agent with a diminished capacity of her own. Thus, regular mental fitness exams should be required of attorneys and other agents because of their duty to accurately represent the interests of their principals.

Second, discovery of an agent's insanity is grounds to terminate an agent-principal relationship. The relationship between an agent and a principal is intensified in a power-of-attorney situation in which clients cannot confer with their attorneys or other agents. Moreover, attorneys who suffer from schizophrenia or severe bouts of depression may not even be capable of upholding their legal duties to their clients. Lawyers suffering from mental disease may be unable to make court appearances or maintain necessary client communications. This is why insanity found on the part of the lawyer is cause to terminate a power-of-attorney agreement. The result of not relieving an insane attorney of his duties could mean numerous legal matters may need to be revisited and decisions rendered again to make up for any perceived impropriety. Therefore, to prevent future problems, lawyers should always be found to be of sound mind, and this is best proved through regular mental fitness exams.

NO

Requiring an attorney or another agent in a power-of-attorney agreement to take regular mental health exams is both an invasion of privacy and an unnecessarily difficult task. The U.S. Bureau of Labor Statistics estimates that there are 728,200 practicing attorneys in the United States. Cataloging their mental health would not only be difficult but also be an undue burden on an already hectic legal system. Three important explanations suggest that regular mental health exams on legal professionals present more problems than they would solve.

First, regular mental fitness exams and the discussion of their results represent a serious invasion of an attorney's privacy. Because an attorney's name and reputation has a commercial value, even informal disclosure of failure to pass a mental fitness test could negatively impact an attorney's career. Under the Medical Information Privacy and Security Act, every citizen has the right to limit the disclosure of personal health information to only his or her health professionals. Likewise, the Health Insurance Portability and Accountability Act also supports this type of privacy. With regular mental fitness exams, it would be difficult to protect this right. For example, after failing an annual checkup, a lawyer would be forced to terminate all client relationships. This would reveal to the judge, jury, opposing counsel, and clients the nature of the attorney's private health issues. Furthermore, mental health problems can be an insurmountable professional stigma. This would only be intensified if there were a new standard for the mental health of attorneys. Therefore, regular mental health exams of lawyers should be avoided to protect their right to medical privacy.

Second, enforcing and upholding a standard of regular mental fitness for attorneys would be too difficult. Because there are numerous mental health conditions and a wide range of severity, it would be hard to establish exactly what the mental health standard is. While some may agree that schizophrenia should be grounds for terminating an attorney's ability to practice, many will likely disagree on standards for depression or substance abuse.

Third, attorneys are a high-risk group for mental illness, and not building a system to check on their mental fitness means ignoring a widespread problem. In 1997, the Texas Lawyer's Assistance Program received around 300 calls a month from impaired attorneys or people concerned about an attorney's mental health. The organization estimates that 80 percent of attorneys suffer from alcohol or drug abuse. While state bar exams often require a mental fitness exam of attorneys entering the profession, little is done to ensure mental health throughout their careers. Furthermore, many of the issues stemming from stress or physical impairments can arise or worsen during one's career. Requiring regular exams would help curb this problem by ensuring annual checkups to prove consistent mental fitness. Also, problems that can be solved by therapy or medication could mean an attorney is on sabbatical for only a short time. Moreover, an attorney may not even be aware of mental issues prior to a checkup. Therefore, regular psychological checkups would ensure that attorneys are being helped and fulfilling their obligations to their principals.

Third, the administration of annual tests on 728,200 attorneys would entail a huge cost to the government. The current standard for dissolving a power-of-attorney arrangement on the grounds that the lawyer is found mentally unfit is a much better and cheaper system. Under the current arrangement, lawyers are required to disclose notice of mental disease.

These three explanations show that regular mental exams are too problematic because of the difficulty of the process and that the current method is less costly and easier to enforce.

Source: Jennifer Jolly-Ryan, "The Last Taboo: Breaking Law Students with Mental Illnesses and Disabilities Out of the Stigma Straitjacket," *University of Missouri–Kansas City Law Review* 79 (2010), p. 123; and Stephen L. Braun, "What You Should Know: Lawyers and Mental Health in a Nutshell," *The Houston Lawyer* 35, no. 6 (May–June 1998), p. 36.

QUESTIONS & PROBLEMS

1. Explain when a principal is or is not contractually liable for agreements made by an agent.

2. When might a principal be liable for torts committed by an agent?

3. What terminates an agency relationship?

4. Land Transport employed Oscar Gonzalez to operate a Land Transport tractor-trailer rig. One day while working, Robert Nichols and Gonzalez were driving west on Route 9 toward Brewer, Maine. Gonzalez tried several times to pass Nichols in no-passing zones. Angered by Gonzalez's driving, Nichols made an obscene gesture to Gonzalez on two occasions. Thereafter, Gonzalez began to tailgate Nichols for several miles and continued to try to pass him. The two trucks then stopped at a traffic light. Nichols saw Gonzalez get out of his cab, and Nichols did the same. On approaching Gonzalez, Nichols attacked Gonzalez with a rubber-coated chain-linked cable. Nichols then grabbed Gonzalez, and they fell to the ground. During the scuffle, Gonzalez got up, brandished a knife, and stabbed Nichols. Nichols sued Gonzalez and Land Transport for the injuries he suffered. Land Transport moved for summary judgment. Was Land Transport successful with its motion for summary judgment? Why? [*Nichols v. Land Transport Corp.,* 103 F. Supp. 2d 25 (1999).]

5. Mala is a citizen of the U.S. Virgin Islands, and in early 2005, he decided to take his power boat out for a cruise. He was running low on gas and decided to stop at a Crown Bay fueling station. He started fueling the boat and told the attendant to watch his boat as it was being filled up. When he returned, the tank was overflowing. Mala then proceeded to clean up the excess fuel and drive away. As he did so, the engine caught fire and exploded, throwing Mala into the water. He sustained several injuries and burns. The boat was a total loss. A year later, Mala proceeded to sue Crown Bay, claiming that it was negligent in training and supervising its attendant and that it failed to maintain its gas pump. Mala's

original complaint named "Crown Bay Marina Inc." as the sole defendant. But Mala soon amended his complaint by adding other defendants—including Crown Bay's dock attendant, Chubb Group Insurance Company, Crown Bay's attorney, and Marine Management Services Inc, a registered corporation licensed to conduct business in the state of Florida. It was determined that the only parties involved were Mala, Crown Bay, and Marine Management Services. Who was responsible for the damages incurred and why? [*Mala v. Crown Bay Marina, Inc.,* 704 F.3d 239 (2013).]

6. Genito, a licensed partnership (L.P.), was contracted to build a housing development in Chesterfield County, Virginia. The National Housing Corporation (NHC) was in charge of the builder's risk insurance for the project. The NHC in turn contracted with Acordia, an insurance broker, to obtain the actual policy that would cover the housing development. Genito, in the process of building the complex, chose fly ash to fill the ground that the development sat on. As a result, the project was compromised due to cracks in the foundation and overall structure of the complex. Genito filed suit against Acordia claiming that he would have been covered by the insurance policy, but that Acordia was negligent in failing to name Genito as insured under the policy. The L.P. claimed negligence and breach of contract as it sought to receive compensation for the now invalid housing development. Why do you think that Genito claimed negligence as a reason for bringing suit? [*Acordia of. Va. Ins. Agency, Inc. v. Genito Glenn, L.P.,* 263 Va. 377, 560 S.E.2d 246 (2002).]

7. Maria D., the plaintiff, alleged that she was raped by an on-duty security guard who worked for the Westec company. At approximately 2 a.m., she was driving along Pacific Coast Highway. The Westec security guard detained her by shining a spotlight from his patrol car into her moving vehicle. He asked, "How much have you been drinking tonight?" Maria D. thought the security guard was a police officer because the spotlight was shining in her face. The security guard ordered Maria D. to perform field sobriety tests and then told her to get her purse because he was going to take her to the station. Instead, Maria D. says he took her to another location where he raped her. The security guard denied that he had pulled the plaintiff over. He testified at his deposition that he saw her car on the side of the road and stopped to offer assistance and at no point did he rape her. At the time of the encounter, the security guard was on-duty, wearing a uniform and driving a Westec vehicle equipped with a spotlight, and he carried a gun and handcuffs on his belt and had a second firearm on the front passenger seat of his car. Maria D. sued Westec, claiming that the company was vicariously liable for the actions of the security guard under the doctrine of *respondeat superior.* Westec argues that the security guard was acting outside the scope of his employment when he allegedly detained and raped her. Do you think the court found that Westec should be held vicariously liable under *respondeat superior?* Why or why not? [*Maria D. v. Westec Residential Security, Inc.,* 85 Cal. App. 4th 125 (2000).]

8. Doug Hartmann Productions, L.L.C., and the Regal Riverfront Hotel, which was owned by Gateway Hotel Holdings, entered into an agreement for a professional boxing match to be held at the hotel. The contract contained a provision stating that a $5 million indemnity insurance policy was to be provided and Hartmann Productions was to provide a doctor at ringside for the match and an ambulance on stand-by at the hotel the night of the event. Maldonado was a professional boxer who participated in the match. The fight ended when Maldonado was knocked out and later lost consciousness in his dressing room. There was no ambulance on site. An ambulance was called, and Maldonado was taken to a hospital. He suffered severe brain damage as a result of his injury. The damage could have been less severe had an ambulance been on-site for the boxing match. Maldonado sued Gateway, asserting that Hartmann Productions was an independent contractor hired by Gateway to perform an inherently dangerous activity. As such, Gateway had a duty to take special precautions to prevent injury during the inherently dangerous activity. Therefore, Maldonado argued that Gateway should be held liable for the damages resulting from the boxing match. Should the boxing match be considered an inherently dangerous activity? Did the court find Gateway liable? [*Maldonado v. Gateway Holdings, L.L.C.,* 154 S.W.3d 303 (2003).]

9. In 1989, William Petrovich's employer, the Chicago Federation of Musicians, provided health care coverage to all of its employees by enrolling them all in Share Health Plan of Illinois. Share is an HMO and pays only for medical care that is obtained within its network of physicians. To qualify for

benefits, a Share member must select a primary care physician, who will provide that member's overall care and authorize referrals when necessary. Share gives its members a list of participating physicians from which to choose. Inga Petrovich, William's wife, selected Dr. Marie Kowalski from Share's list and began seeing Kowalski as her primary care physician.

In September 1990, Mrs. Petrovich saw Kowalski because she was experiencing persistent pain in her mouth, tongue, throat, and face. She also complained of a foul mucus in her mouth. Kowalski referred her to Dr. Friedman, an ear, nose, and throat specialist who had a contract with Share. When Friedman ordered that an MRI be done, Kowalski refused and instead sent a copy of an old MRI. In June 1991, after Mrs. Petrovich had made multiple visits to both doctors, Friedman found cancerous growths in Mrs. Petrovich's mouth. He performed surgery to remove the cancer later that month.

Petrovich subsequently sued Share for medical malpractice. The complaint alleges that both Kowalski and Friedman were negligent in failing to diagnose Inga Petrovich's cancer in a timely manner and that Share is vicariously liable for their negligence. Share filed a motion for summary judgment, arguing that it cannot be held liable for the negligence of Kowalski or Friedman because they were acting as independent contractors, not as Share's agents. How should the court decide? What reasons should it give? [*Petrovich v. Share Health Plan of Illinois,* 719 N.E.2d 756 (1999).]

10. Brenda Gail Langley is a resident of Tennessee, and on October 20, 1999, she took out a $50,000 life insurance policy. In this policy, she named her three biological children—Kristin Taylor, Edward Langley, and Phillip Langley—as the three beneficiaries. The policy was taken out by Langley from Tennessee Farmers Life Reassurance Company.

A clause in the policy stated that Langley reserved the right to change the beneficiaries at any time and that the beneficiaries would share the inheritance equally. In 2002, Langley created a power of attorney, naming her sister, Linda Rose, the POA. Within the document was a clause that stated: "I, Brenda Gail Langley, do hereby appoint and constitute Linda Sue Rose, my true and lawful attorney for me and in my name and on my behalf to transact all insurance business on my behalf, to apply for or continue policies, collect profits, file claims, make demands, enter into compromise and settlement agreements, file suits or actions and take any other action necessary or proper in this regard." In October 2002, Rose contacted Tennessee Farmers and changed the beneficiaries stated in the policy. Rose claims the action to change the beneficiaries was the result of Langley's frustration with her children. Then, in November of the same year, Langley executed a will, giving only $100 to her children and the rest of her assets to her sister, Rose. The following year, Langley passed away. Rose then proceeded to submit claims to collect the insurance money from the life insurance policy. Langley's children then proceeded to file their own claims. Tennessee Farmers realized there was more than one claim being made and filed suit against Rose. The original beneficiaries of the policy— the deceased's children—answered the complaint, arguing that Rose was not entitled to the proceeds because (1) the deceased's execution of the power of attorney was brought about by duress, coercion, control, and undue influence exercised by Rose or, alternatively, (2) Rose violated her fiduciary duty, as attorney in fact, by changing the beneficiary designation on the deceased's life insurance policy. Who do you think won the case and why? [*Tennessee Farmers Life Reassurance Co. v. Linda Rose et al.,* 239 S.W.3d 743 (Tenn. 2007).]

Looking for more review materials?

The Online Learning Center at **www.mhhe.com/kubasek3e** contains this chapter's "Assignment on the Internet" and also a list of URLs for more information, entitled "On the Internet." Find both of them in the Student Center portion of the OLC, along with quizzes and other helpful materials.

PART

8

Government Regulation

CHAPTER

24 Employment and
Discrimination Law

CASE OPENER

Brad Gets Fired from So Clean!

Brad has worked in the marketing department of So Clean! for the past five years. So Clean is a company that produces household cleaners. Brad is an excellent employee and was recently promoted. Shortly after his promotion, Brad decided to reveal publicly that he is homosexual. His family and most of his co-workers have been very supportive.

Soon after his promotion and announcement that he is gay, Brad began having problems with his boss, Jennifer. She began asking Brad questions about his personal life. At first it was small things, such as asking Brad whether he was a smoker (he is, although only outside the workplace). Jennifer then began asking Brad very personal questions about his sexuality and told him she did not like weak men. The final straw for Brad occurred when Jennifer announced that she would cure his homosexuality and told him to come home with her that night after work or be fired. Jennifer was careful that there were never any witnesses around when she asked Brad personal questions or propositioned him. Brad refused Jennifer's advances and was fired. He filed an administrative complaint with the Equal Employment Opportunity Commission (EEOC) alleging wrongful termination, retaliation, sexual harassment, and sexual discrimination. Jennifer's response was that she fired Brad because of creative differences about how to run the marketing department and because he is a smoker. Jennifer denied Brad's accusations about sexual discrimination and harassment.

1. May an employer discriminate against an employee because he is gay?
2. May an employer fire an employee because the employee smokes outside the workplace?
3. May a man file a claim of sexual discrimination? Sexual harassment?
4. What defenses does an employer have to a charge of discrimination?

After reading this chapter, you will be able to answer the following questions:

LO 24-1 What does it mean to be an at-will employee?

LO 24-2 What are the federal laws governing employment discrimination?

LO 24-3 What are the legal requirements for a charge of sex discrimination or sexual harassment?

LO 24-4 What categories of people are protected from discrimination?

LO 24-5 What laws protect employees' wages, benefits, health and safety standards, and rights?

LO 24-6 What are the rights of employees and obligations of employers with regard to privacy in the workplace?

LO 24-7 What are the main laws governing labor unions?

When May an Employee Be Fired?   LO 24-1

During the eighteenth and nineteenth centuries in the United States, employees had no protection in the workplace. An employee who was injured could be fired. In fact, an employer could fire a worker for no reason at all. This concept came to be known as *at-will employment*.[1] At-will employment applied in all states with no exceptions until 1959.[2]

Today, any employee who is not employed under a contract for a set duration or under a collective bargaining agreement[3] is considered an at-will employee. This means that the employee may quit at any time for any reason or no reason at all, with no required notice to the employer.[4] Similarly, an employer may fire the employee at any time, with no notice, for almost any reason. For example, your employer could decide he doesn't like the color of your shirt and fire you on the spot! The exception to the at-will rule is that an employer may not fire an employee for an illegal reason. What is an illegal reason? Broadly, any termination based on a violation of a state statute, a state constitution, a federal law, the U.S. Constitution, or a public policy is illegal. Exceptions to at-will employment have also been found through breaches of implied contracts with employees that were based on employee handbooks.[5]

Federal Employment Discrimination   LO 24-2
Laws Governing Employers

Employees are protected in the workplace by a number of both federal and state laws. Federal laws apply to everyone in the United States. Federal law may be described as a minimum level of protection for all workers. State laws may give employees more, but not less, protection than federal laws. Exhibit 24-1 is an overview of some of the most important federal employment discrimination laws.

[1] See *Toussaint v. Blue Cross & Blue Shield of Mich.*, 408 Mich. 579, 600, 292 N.W.2d 880, 885 (1980), for an extended discussion on the at-will rule.

[2] BambooWeb Dictionary, www.bambooweb.com/articles/a/t/At-Will_Employment.html. The first judicial exception to the at-will rule was created in *Peterman v. Intl. Bhd. of Teamsters, Chauffeurs, Warehousemen, and Helpers of Am., Local 396*, 174 Cal. App. 2d 184, 344 P.2d 44 (1959).

[3] Union employees are covered by collective bargaining agreements.

[4] Most employees do give an employer notice before leaving a job as a matter of professional courtesy. Such action, however, is not required under the law.

[5] "Some challenges and exceptions to at-will employment include breach of implied contracts through employee handbooks, public policy violations, reliance on an offer of employment, and intentional infliction of emotional distress" (Legal Database, www.legal-database.net/at-will.htm).

Exhibit 24-1

Federal
Discrimination Laws

FEDERAL LEGISLATION	PURPOSE
Civil Rights Act (CRA) of 1964—Title VII (as amended by the Civil Rights Act of 1991)	Protects employees against discrimination based on race, color, religion, national origin, and sex; also prohibits harassment based on the same protected categories
Pregnancy Discrimination Act (PDA) of 1987	Amends Title VII of the CRA, expanding the definition of sex discrimination to include discrimination based on pregnancy
Age Discrimination in Employment Act (ADEA) of 1967	Prohibits employers from refusing to hire, discharging, or discriminating in terms and conditions of employment on the basis of an employee or applicant being age 40 or older
Americans with Disabilities Act (ADA) of 1990 (as amended in 2008)	Prohibits discrimination against employees and job applicants with disabilities
Equal Pay Act of 1963	Prohibits an employer from paying workers of one gender less than the wages paid to employees of the opposite gender for work that requires equal skill, effort, and responsibility

Civil Rights Act—Title VII

Title VII of the Civil Rights Act (CRA) of 1964

Federal law (amended by the Civil Rights Act of 1991) that protects employees against discrimination based on race, color, religion, national origin, and sex; also prohibits harassment based on the same protected categories.

The Civil Rights Act is divided into sections, called *titles*. Title VII of the Civil Rights Act (CRA) of 1964 deals with discrimination in employment. It prohibits employers from hiring, firing, or otherwise discriminating in terms and conditions of employment, and it prohibits segregating employees in a manner that would affect their employment opportunities on the basis of their race, color, religion, sex, or national origin. There are two ways to prove discrimination under Title VII—disparate treatment and disparate impact.

Title VII of CRA applies to employers who have 15 or more employees for 20 consecutive weeks within one year and who are engaged in a business that affects commerce. The U.S. government, corporations owned by the government, agencies of the District of Columbia, Indian tribes, private clubs, unions, and employment agencies are also covered by Title VII of CRA.

DISPARATE-TREATMENT DISCRIMINATION UNDER TITLE VII

disparate treatment

A form of intentional discrimination in which an employee is hired, fired, denied a promotion, or the like, based on membership in a protected class. This is a form of intentional discrimination.

To sue for disparate treatment under Title VII, the plaintiff must be a member of a protected class as listed in CRA. In other words, the employee must have been discriminated against on the basis of race, color, national origin, religion, or sex (i.e., gender). If the employee has been refused work, fired, denied a promotion, or the like, based on membership in a protected class, this is a form of intentional discrimination and qualifies the employee to sue for disparate-treatment discrimination. Proving disparate-treatment discrimination in employment under Title VII is a three-step process:

1. Plaintiff (the employee) must demonstrate a prima facie case of discrimination.
2. Defendant (the employer) must articulate a legitimate, nondiscriminatory business reason for the action.
3. Plaintiff (the employee) must show that the reason given by the defendant (the employer) is a mere pretext.[6]

After all the evidence has been presented, the trier of fact (a jury in most cases)[7] must decide whether discrimination has occurred. The burden of proof in a civil case is preponderance of the

---

[6] *McDonnell Douglas v. Green*, 411 U.S. 792, 802 (1973).

[7] In a bench trial, the judge becomes the trier of fact because no jury is impaneled. A discrimination case could also be decided by a judge on a motion for summary judgment.

CASE NUGGET

Must an Employer Reasonably Accommodate an Employee's Religious Practices?

Kumar v. Gate Gourmet, Inc.
Supreme Court of Washington

2014 Wash. LEXIS 387 (May 22, 2014)

The plaintiffs in this action (the employees) work near SeaTac airport for the defendant, Gate Gourmet, preparing meals for service on trains and airplanes. Due to security concerns, the employees can neither bring food with them to work nor leave the premises to obtain food during their 30-minute lunch break. Instead, Gate Gourmet provides meals for employees to consume during their break. These meals ostensibly consist of one vegetarian and one meat-based main dish. The employees allege, however, that Gate Gourmet uses animal by-products in the vegetarian option. They also allege that they informed Gate Gourmet that their various religious beliefs prohibited them from eating the beef-pork meatballs the company served, that Gate Gourmet responded by temporarily switching to turkey meatballs, that the company later switched back to the beef-pork mixture without notifying the employees, and that it now refuses to alter the employee meals.

The employees brought a class action against the employer, challenging the employer's meal policy, which barred employees from bringing in their own food for lunch (for security reasons), leaving only employer-provided food for the employees to eat. The employees claimed that the meal policy constituted a failure to accommodate their religious practices reasonably, had a disparate impact on employees who adhered to certain religions, and constituted battery and negligent infliction of emotional distress. The trial court dismissed the case, holding that there was no requirement to "reasonably accommodate" the employees' religious practices under Washington state law. The decision was affirmed by the appellate court.

Upon review by the Washington Supreme Court, the lower court decision was reversed. The Washington Supreme Court stated that under state rules of statutory interpretation and persuasive federal antidiscrimination case law (Title VII), the Washington Law Against Discrimination (WLAD) implies a requirement to accommodate religious practices reasonably. Moreover, both the disparate-impact and religious-accommodation doctrines bar facially neutral employment policies that have disproportionate adverse effects on a protected class.

evidence (i.e., more likely than not). If the jury finds in favor of the plaintiff-employee, damages must be assessed. Damages under Title VII of CRA include up to two years of back pay, compensatory damages, punitive damages (limited in some cases), attorney fees, court costs, court orders (including reinstatement), and remedial seniority. If the jury finds in favor of the defendant-employer, the plaintiff-employee receives nothing.

DISPARATE-IMPACT DISCRIMINATION UNDER TITLE VII

Disparate-impact cases are sometimes called *unintentional-discrimination* cases. Although it is very difficult to prove disparate treatment, it is even more difficult to prove disparate impact. Disparate-impact cases arise when a plaintiff attempts to establish that although an employer's policy or practice appears to apply to everyone equally, its actual effect is that it disproportionately limits employment opportunities for a protected class.

The plaintiff proves a case based on disparate impact by first establishing statistically that the rule disproportionately restricts employment opportunities for a protected class. The burden of

disparate impact
A form of discrimination that arises when an employer's policy or practice appears to apply to everyone equally but its actual effect is that it disproportionately limits employment opportunities for a protected class.

Exhibit 24-2

Disparate
Treatment and
Disparate Impact
Burden Shifting

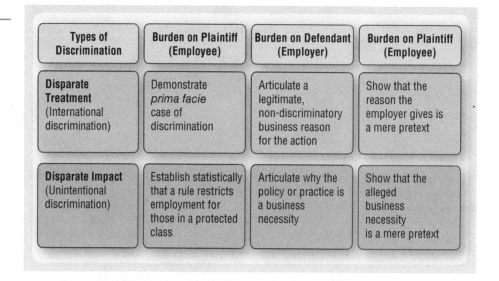

Types of Discrimination	Burden on Plaintiff (Employee)	Burden on Defendant (Employer)	Burden on Plaintiff (Employee)
Disparate Treatment (International discrimination)	Demonstrate *prima facie* case of discrimination	Articulate a legitimate, non-discriminatory business reason for the action	Show that the reason the employer gives is a mere pretext
Disparate Impact (Unintentional discrimination)	Establish statistically that a rule restricts employment for those in a protected class	Articulate why the policy or practice is a business necessity	Show that the alleged business necessity is a mere pretext

proof then shifts to the defendant, who can avoid liability by demonstrating that the practice or policy is a business necessity. The plaintiff, at this point, can still recover by proving either that the necessity was promulgated as a pretext for discrimination or that an alternative employment practice had less discriminatory effect and the employer failed to adopt such practice.

The initial steps for proving a prima facie case of disparate impact were set forth in *Griggs v. Duke Power Co.*[8] In that case, the employer-defendant required all applicants to have a high school diploma and a successful score on a professionally recognized intelligence test for all jobs except laborer. The stated purpose of these criteria was to upgrade the quality of the workforce.

The plaintiff statistically demonstrated the discriminatory impact by showing that 34 percent of the white males in the state had high school diplomas, whereas only 12 percent of the black males did, and by introducing evidence from an EEOC study showing that 58 percent of the whites, compared to 6 percent of the blacks, had passed tests similar to the one given by the defendant. Because the defendant could not demonstrate any business-related justification for either employment policy, the plaintiff was successful. Requiring a high IQ or high school or college diploma may be necessary for some jobs but not for all jobs at Duke Power.

SEXUAL HARASSMENT UNDER TITLE VII

sexual harassment
Unwelcome sexual advances, requests for sexual favors, and other verbal or physical conduct of a sexual nature that makes submission a condition of employment or a factor in employment decisions or that creates an intimidating, hostile, or offensive work environment. The two types are hostile environment and *quid pro quo.*

Harassment first developed in the context of discrimination based on sex, and it evolved to become applicable to other protected classes. The definition of sexual harassment stated in the Equal Employment Opportunity Commission (EEOC) guidelines and accepted by the U.S. Supreme Court is "unwelcome sexual advances, requests for sexual favors, and other verbal or physical conduct of a sexual nature" that implicitly or explicitly makes submission a term or condition of employment; makes employment decisions related to the individual dependent on submission to or rejection of such conduct; or has the purpose or effect of creating an intimidating, hostile, or offensive work environment. In the Case Opener, did the actions of Jennifer create a sexually hostile environment for Brad?

Two distinct forms of sexual harassment are recognized. The first, and generally easiest to prove, is *quid pro quo,* which occurs when a supervisor makes a sexual demand on someone and this demand is reasonably perceived as a term or condition of employment. The second form of sexual harassment involves the creation of a hostile work environment. Case 24-1 demonstrates the standard the U.S. Supreme Court uses to determine whether an employer's conduct has created a hostile work environment.

[8] *Griggs v. Duke Power,* 401 U.S. 424 (1971).

CASE 24-1

TERESA HARRIS v. FORKLIFT SYSTEMS, INC.
UNITED STATES SUPREME COURT
510 U.S.17, 114 S. Ct. 367 (1994)

FACTS: *During her tenure as a manager at defendant Forklift Systems, Inc., plaintiff Harris was repeatedly insulted by the defendant's president because of her gender and subjected to sexual innuendos. In front of other employees, the president frequently told Harris, "You're just a woman, what do you know?" He sometimes asked Harris and other female employees to remove coins from his pockets and made suggestive comments about their clothes. He suggested to Harris in front of others that they negotiate her salary at the Holiday Inn. When Harris complained, he said that he would stop, but he continued behaving in the same manner, so Harris quit. She then filed an action against the defendant for creating an abusive work environment on the basis of her gender. The district court found in favor of the defendant, holding that some of the comments were offensive to the plaintiff but were not so serious as to affect Harris's psychological well-being severely or interfere with her work performance. The court of appeals affirmed. Plaintiff Harris appealed to the U.S. Supreme Court.*

ISSUE: Must an employee suffer serious psychological damage to pursue damages for a claim of sexual harassment?

REASONING: In the Court's own words:

> As we made clear in *Meritor Savings Bank v. Vinson,* this language [of Title VII] "is not limited to 'economic' or 'tangible' discrimination. The phrase 'terms, conditions, or privileges of employment' evinces a congressional intent 'to strike at the entire spectrum of disparate treatment of men and women' in employment," which includes requiring people to work in a discriminatorily hostile or abusive environment. When the workplace is permeated with "discriminatory intimidation, ridicule, and insult," that is "sufficiently severe or pervasive to alter the conditions of the victim's employment and create an abusive working environment."
>
> This standard, which we reaffirm today, takes a middle path between making actionable any conduct that is merely offensive and requiring the conduct to cause a tangible psychological injury. As we pointed out in *Meritor,* "mere utterance of an . . . epithet which engenders offensive feelings in a employee," does not sufficiently affect conditions of employment to implicate Title VII. . . .

Likewise, if the victim does not subjectively perceive the environment to be abusive, the conduct has not actually altered the conditions of the victim's employment, and there is no Title VII violation.

But Title VII comes into play before the harassing conduct leads to a nervous breakdown. A discriminatorily abusive work environment, even one that does not seriously affect employees' psychological well-being, can and often will detract from employees' job performance, discourage employees from remaining on the job, or keep them from advancing in their careers. Moreover, even without regard to these tangible effects, the very fact that the discriminatory conduct was so severe or pervasive that it created a work environment abusive to employees because of their race, gender, religion, or national origin offends Title VII's broad rule of workplace equality. The appalling conduct alleged in *Meritor,* and the reference in that case to environments "so heavily polluted with discrimination as to destroy completely the emotional and psychological stability of minority group workers," merely present some especially egregious examples of harassment. They do not mark the boundary of what is actionable.

. . . Certainly Title VII bars conduct that would seriously affect a reasonable person's psychological well-being, but the statute is not limited to such conduct. So long as the environment would reasonably be perceived, and is perceived, as hostile or abusive, there is no need for it also to be psychologically injurious.

This is not, and by its nature cannot be, a mathematically precise test. But we can say that whether an environment is "hostile" or "abusive" can be determined only by looking at all the circumstances. These may include the frequency of the discriminatory conduct; its severity; whether it is physically threatening or humiliating, or a mere offensive utterance; and whether it unreasonably interferes with an employee's work performance. The effect on the employee's psychological well-being is, of course, relevant to determining whether the plaintiff actually found the environment abusive. But while psychological harm, like any other relevant factor, may be taken into account, no single factor is required.

DECISION AND REMEDY: The lower court's decision was reversed and remanded in favor of the plaintiff.

SIGNIFICANCE: In this case, the Supreme Court for the first time held that harassment in and of itself is illegal and actionable, regardless of the amount of damage to the victim.

CRITICAL THINKING

Identify the Court's reasons for its finding. Do you think these reasons were sufficient to overturn the previous ruling? Why or why not?

ETHICAL DECISION MAKING

Imagine that the judge is operating under a duty-based system of ethics. What duty is she advocating in terms of employer–employee relationships? Would this ruling serve well as a universal standard?

LO 24-3

Same-Sex Harassment—The Supreme Court Speaks   Initially, same-sex harassment was not covered under CRA. By 1997, however, the courts were split on the issue. This issue was resolved in 1998 in *Oncale v. Sundowner Offshore Services, Inc.*[9] Oncale, a male, was forcibly subjected to sex-related, humiliating actions against him by other male employees. He was physically sexually assaulted and threatened with rape. He complained, to no avail, so he filed a lawsuit alleging discrimination based on sex. The district court granted a motion for summary judgment for the defendant employer, holding that a male had no cause of action under Title VII for harassment by male co-workers. The case was appealed to the U.S. Supreme Court, which concluded that sex discrimination consisting of same-sex sexual harassment is actionable under Title VII. The Court reversed the appellate court's order and remanded the case for further proceedings.

Harassment by Nonemployees under Title VII   Employers may be held liable for harassment of their employees by nonemployees under very limited circumstances. If an employer knows that a customer repeatedly harasses an employee yet the employer does nothing to remedy the situation, the employer may be liable. For example, in *Lockhard v. Pizza Hut, Inc.*,[10] the franchise was held liable for the harassment of a waitress by two male customers because no steps had been taken to prevent the harassment.

HARASSMENT OF OTHER PROTECTED CLASSES UNDER TITLE VII

Hostile-environment issues have also been used in cases of discrimination based on religion and race. For example, in a 1986 case, *Snell v. Suffolk County,*[11] Hispanic and black corrections workers demonstrated that a hostile work environment existed by proving that they had been subjected to continuing verbal abuse and racial harassment by co-workers and that the county sheriff's department had done nothing to prevent the abuse. The white employees had continually used racial epithets and posted racially offensive materials on bulletin boards, such as a picture of a black man with a noose around his neck, cartoons favorably portraying the Ku Klux Klan, and a "black officers' study guide," consisting of children's puzzles. White officers once dressed a Hispanic inmate in a straw hat, sheet, and sign that said "spic." Such activities were found by the court to constitute a hostile work environment.

PREGNANCY DISCRIMINATION ACT OF 1987—AN AMENDMENT TO TITLE VII

In 1987, Title VII was amended by the Pregnancy Discrimination Act (PDA). This law expanded the definition of discrimination based on gender to include discrimination based on pregnancy. "Discrimination on the basis of pregnancy, childbirth or related medical conditions constitutes unlawful sex discrimination under Title VII."[12] Under the act, temporary disability caused by pregnancy must be treated the same as any other temporary disability.

DEFENSES TO CLAIMS UNDER TITLE VII

As a business owner or manager, how would you respond if one of your employees filed a lawsuit under Title VII? Are there any legal exceptions for discriminating against a protected class? The answer, surprising to many business owners and managers, is yes. The three most important defenses available to defendants in Title VII cases are the bona fide occupational qualification, merit, and seniority system defenses. These defenses are raised by the defendant after the plaintiff has established a prima facie case of discrimination based on either disparate treatment or disparate impact. They would obviously not be applicable to a claim based on harassment.

The Bona Fide Occupational Qualification Defense   The bona fide occupational qualification (BFOQ) defense allows an employer to discriminate in hiring on the basis of sex, religion, or

[9] 523 U.S. 75, 118 S. Ct. 998 (1998).
[10] 162 F.3d 1062 (10th Cir. 1998).
[11] 782 F.2d 1094 (1986).
[12] EEOC, "Facts about Pregnancy Discrimination," www.eeoc.gov/facts/fs-preg.html

national origin (but not race or color) when doing so is necessary for the performance of the job. Necessity must be based on actual qualifications, not stereotypes about one group's abilities. For example, being a male cannot be a BFOQ for a job simply because it is a dirty job, although there may be a valid requirement that an applicant be able to lift a certain amount of weight if such lifting is part of the job. Conversely, being a female may be a BFOQ for modeling female clothing. An employer would not be required or expected to hire a male for such a job. Employer arguments about inconvenience to the employer, such as having to provide two sets of restroom facilities, have not been persuasive in the courts. Nor have customer preferences to be served by a particular gender or nationality. The only exception to customer preference is sexual privacy (e.g., female restroom attendants in the women's restroom and male attendants in the men's room).[13]

The Merit Defense   The merit defense is usually raised when hiring or promotion decisions are partially based on test scores. Professionally developed ability tests that are not designed, intended, or used to discriminate may be used. Although these tests may have an adverse impact on a class, as long as they are manifestly related to job performance, they do not violate the act. Since 1978, the "Uniform Guidelines on Employee Selection Procedures" (UGESP) resource has guided government agencies charged with enforcing civil rights, and they provide guidance to employers and other interested persons about when ability tests are valid and job-related. Under these guidelines, tests must be validated in accordance with standards established by the American Psychological Association.

Three types of validation are acceptable: (1) *criterion-related validity,* which is the statistical relationship between test scores and objective criteria of job performance; (2) *content validity,* which isolates some skill used on the job and directly tests that skill; and (3) *construct validity,* wherein a psychological trait needed to perform the job is measured. A test that required a word processor to use a computer would be content-valid. A test of patience for a teacher would be construct-valid.

The Seniority System Defense   A bona fide seniority system is a legal defense under Title VII. Even though a seniority system, in which employees are given preferential treatment based on their length of service, may perpetuate past discrimination, such systems are considered bona fide and are thus not illegal if (1) the system applies equally to all persons; (2) the seniority units follow industry practices; (3) the seniority system did not have its genesis in discrimination; and (4) the system is maintained free of any illegal discriminatory purpose.

REMEDIES UNDER TITLE VII

A plaintiff may seek both equitable and legal remedies for violations of Title VII. Courts have ordered parties to engage in diverse activities ranging from publicizing their commitment to minority hiring to establishing special training programs for minorities. A successful plaintiff may recover back pay for up to two years from the time of the discriminatory act.

A plaintiff who was not hired for a job because of a Title VII violation may also receive remedial seniority dating back to the time when the plaintiff was discriminated against; compensatory damages, including those for pain and suffering; and, in some cases, punitive damages.

In cases based on discrimination other than race, however, punitive damages are capped at $300,000 for employers of more than 500 employees, $100,000 for firms with 101 to 200 employees, and $50,000 for firms with 100 or fewer employees. An employer will not be held vicariously liable for punitive damages as long as it made good-faith efforts to comply with federal law.

Attorney fees may be awarded to a successful plaintiff in Title VII cases. They are typically denied only when special circumstances would render the award unjust. If it is determined that the plaintiff's action was frivolous, unreasonable, or without foundation, the courts may award attorney fees to the prevailing defendant. For more information on Title VII, visit the EEOC website at www.eeoc.gov

---

[13] *In the Matter of the Accusation of the Department of Fair Employment and Housing v. San Luis Obispo Coastal Unified School District, Respondent; Marlene Anne Mendes, Complainant,* Case No. E95-96 L-0725-00s, 98-14 (October 7, 1998). See www.dfeh.ca.gov/PrecedentialD/1998-14.html

PROCEDURE FOR FILING A CLAIM UNDER TITLE VII

Filing a claim under Title VII is much more complicated than simply filing a lawsuit. Failure to follow the proper procedures within the strict time framework may result in the plaintiff losing his or her right to file a lawsuit under Title VII.

The first step in initiating a Title VII action is for the aggrieved party to file a charge with the state Equal Opportunity Commission or, if no such agency exists, the federal EEOC. A *charge* is a sworn statement that states the name of the charging party, the name(s) of the defendant(s), and the nature of the discriminatory act. Title VII charges must be filed with the EEOC within 180 days of the alleged discriminatory act.

Within 10 days of receiving the charge, the EEOC must notify the alleged violator of the charge. Then the EEOC investigates the matter to determine whether there is reasonable cause to believe that a violation has occurred. If the EEOC does find such reasonable cause, it attempts to eliminate the discriminatory practice through conciliation, that is, by trying to negotiate a settlement between the two parties. If unsuccessful, the EEOC *may* file suit against the alleged discriminator in federal district court. Failure to file suit does not necessarily mean that the EEOC thinks the plaintiff does not have a valid claim; the EEOC may simply feel that the claim is not the type it wishes to use its limited resources on pursuing.

If the EEOC decides not to sue, it notifies the plaintiff of his or her right to file an action and issues the plaintiff a *right-to-sue letter,* which is not intended to be anything other than a statement that the plaintiff has followed the proper initial procedures and therefore may file a lawsuit. The plaintiff must have this letter to file a private action.

Discrimination Based on Sexual Orientation—Actionable?

No federal legislation currently prohibits discrimination based on sexual orientation. However, state laws prohibiting such discrimination exist in 21 states and one district.

What do these laws mean to Brad, the employee in our Case Opener? It depends on where Brad lives. If Brad lives in Texas and is fired for being gay, he has absolutely no legal rights and cannot sue his employer. Conversely, if Brad lives in California, he may sue Jennifer and So Clean, his employer, for discrimination based on sexual orientation. In California and a handful of other states, discriminating in terms of employment (i.e., failure to hire, firing, failure to promote) based on a person's sexual orientation is prohibited.

Discrimination Based on Marriage

The federal Defense of Marriage Act (DOMA), passed by Congress in 1996,[14] defines marriage to be between one man and one woman and permits states to disregard marriages legally performed in other states. DOMA has two key provisions. Section 2 says that no state "shall be required to give effect" to same-sex marriages granted by other states. Section 3 limits the federal definition of "marriage" to be between one man and one woman. The significance of section 3 is that all federal marital rights are tied to the definition of marriage set forth in DOMA. Excluding same-sex married couples from the federal definition of marriage precluded them from receiving 1,100 federal benefits (e.g., family medical leave for a sick spouse).

In 2013, the U.S. Supreme Court struck down section 3 of DOMA as a violation of Fifth Amendment's guarantee of equal protection under the laws as applied to persons of the same sex who are legally married in their state.[15] As a result, legally married same-sex spouses are now entitled to marriage based federal benefits such as family medical leave under the Family and

---

[14] 1 U.S.C. § 7; 28 U.S.C. § 1738C (2006).

[15] *United States v. Windsor,* 570 U.S. 12 (2013).

Medical Leave Act (FMLA), Consolidated Omnibus Budget Reconcillation Act (COBRA),[16] and all other federal benefits available to opposite sex-spouses.

Section 2 of DOMA remains in effect. This means that individual states may decide whether to permit same-sex marriage in their state. Currently, 31 states ban same-sex marriage. Nineteen states plus the District of Columbia now issue marriage licenses to same-sex couples: Massachusetts (2004), Connecticut (2008), Iowa (2009), Vermont (2009), New Hampshire (2010), District of Columbia (2010), New York (2011), Washington (2012), Rhode Island (2013), Delaware (2013), Minnesota (2013), Maryland (2013), California (2013), New Jersey (2013), New Mexico (2013), Hawaii (2013), Rhode Island (2013), Illinois (2014), and Pennsylvania (2014).[17]

Age Discrimination in Employment Act of 1967

LO 24-4

The Age Discrimination in Employment Act (ADEA) of 1967 was enacted to prohibit employers from refusing to hire, discharging, or discriminating in terms and conditions of employment against employees or applicants age 40 or older. The language describing the prohibited conduct is virtually the same as that of Title VII, except that age is the prohibited basis for discrimination. ADEA applies to employers having 20 or more employees.

Age Discrimination in Employment Act (ADEA) of 1967
Federal law that prohibits employers from refusing to hire, discharging, or discriminating in terms and conditions of employment on the basis of an employee or applicant being age 40 or older.

Americans with Disabilities Act

The goal of the Americans with Disabilities Act (ADA) is preventing employers from discriminating against employees and applicants with disabilities. ADA attempts to attain this objective by requiring employers to make reasonable accommodations to the known physical or mental disabilities of an otherwise qualified person with a disability unless the necessary accommodation would impose an undue burden on the employer's business.

Americans with Disabilities Act (ADA)
Federal law that prohibits discrimination against employees and job applicants with disabilities.

> When the ADA was before Congress, some members predicted a flood of lawsuits that would bankrupt or at least overburden business. . . . Studies have shown, however, that businesses have adapted to the ADA much more easily—and inexpensively—than the doomsayers predicted. . . . Law Professor Peter Blanck of the University of Iowa has studied business compliance with the ADA, including Sears Roebuck and many other large businesses, and found that compliance was often as easy as raising or lowering a desk, installing a ramp, or modifying a dress code. Another survey found that three-quarters of all changes cost less than $100. Moreover, the predicted flood of lawsuits proved to be imaginary. Almost 90 percent of the cases brought before the Equal Employment Opportunity Commission are thrown out. And only about 650 lawsuits were filed in the ADA's first five years—a small number compared to 6 million businesses, 666,000 public and private employers, and 80,000 units of state and local governments that must comply. The American Bar Association recently conducted a survey and learned that, of the cases that actually go to court, 98 percent are decided in favor of the defendants, usually businesses.[18]

ADA is enforced by the EEOC in the same way that Title VII is enforced. To bring a successful claim under ADA, the plaintiff must show that he or she meets all of the following:

- Had a disability.
- Was otherwise qualified for the job.
- Suffered an adverse employment decision because of that disability.

Remedies for ADA violations are similar to those available under Title VII. A successful plaintiff may recover reinstatement, back pay, and injunctive relief. In cases of intentional discrimination, limited compensatory and punitive damages are also available. An employer who has repeatedly violated the act may be subject to fines of up to $100,000.

---

[16] See second half of Chapter 24 for a discussion of COBRA and other federal benefits.

[17] ProCon.org, *Gay Marriage*, http://gaymarriage.procon.org/view.resource.php?resourceID=004857

[18] Center for an Accessible Society, "Disability Issues Information for Journalists," www.accessiblesociety.org/topics/ada

May an Employer Discriminate against a Smoker?

In the Case Opener, Jennifer discovered that Brad was a smoker. Later, she fired him. One of Jennifer's given reasons for terminating Brad's employment was that he was a smoker. May Jennifer and So Clean legally fire an employee for smoking outside the workplace? The answer is, "It depends!"

A recent trend has been for employers to consider a potential employee's lifestyle when deciding whether to hire that person. Employers argue that smokers have higher health care costs and miss more work, lowering productivity.

> The Centers for Disease Control and Prevention estimated that $75 billion is spent annually on medical expenses attributed to smoking. Businesses lose $82 billion in lost productivity from smokers. And smokers take about 6.5 more sick days a year than nonsmokers. About one in five Americans—or 46 million people—smoke.[19]

As a result, some companies either won't hire smokers or are threatening to fire current employees who will not or are unable to quit smoking. In 2005, Michigan-based Weyco, Inc., announced that it would terminate all workers who did not stop smoking.[20] Many states have passed laws preventing companies from engaging in such action.

> Michigan, with 1.9 million smokers and one of the highest cigarette taxes in the nation, has no "smoker's rights law" found in 29 other states, so there isn't much that employees can do. Weyco terminated four of its employees after they refused to submit to a smoking breath test in light of the company's new policy that bans tobacco use among its 200 employees during work and even when they are off the clock. "We are saying people can smoke if they choose to smoke. That's their choice," said Gary Climes, Weyco's chief financial officer. "But they just can't work for us."[21]

If Brad works in Michigan, Jennifer and So Clean may legally terminate him for smoking outside the workplace. Conversely, if Brad works in the District of Columbia or any of the 29 states with smoker's rights laws, he could not be legally terminated for smoking outside the workplace.[22] Finally, employers should be aware that giving breaks on health care plans to employees who are nonsmokers could be in violation of a smoker's rights law.

Equal Pay Act of 1963

Equal Pay Act (EPA) of 1963

Federal law that prohibits an employer from paying workers of one gender less than the wages paid to employees of the opposite gender for work that requires equal skill, effort, and responsibility.

Although we generally think of Title VII as the primary means of protecting women from discrimination, an earlier law actually was designed specifically to protect women from wage discrimination: the Equal Pay Act (EPA) of 1963. When EPA was passed, the average wages of women were less than 60 percent of those of men. The primary purpose of the law was to eliminate situations in which women, working alongside men or replacing men, would be paid lower wages for doing substantially the same job. EPA prohibits any employer from discriminating within any "establishment . . . between employees on the basis of sex by paying wages to employees in such establishment at a rate less than the rate at which he pays wages to employees of the opposite sex . . . for equal work on jobs the performance of which requires equal skill, effort, and responsibility, and which are performed under similar working conditions, except where payment is made pursuant to (i) a seniority system; (ii) a merit system; (iii) a system which measures earnings by quantity or quality of production; or (iv) differential based on any factor other than sex."[23]

---

[19] "Workers Fume as Firms Ban Smoking at Home," www.detnews.com/2005/business/0501/27/A01-71823.htm

[20] Ibid.

[21] Ibid.

[22] Twenty-nine states plus the District of Columbia have laws in effect elevating smokers to a protected class. American Lung Association, http://www.lungusa2.org/slati/appendixf.php

[23] 29 U.S.C. § 206(d)1.

Exhibit 24-3

Significant Laws
Governing the
Employment
Relationship

LAW	IMPACT
Wage and hour laws	Federal and state laws that impose minimum-wage and hour requirements for employees.
Family and Medical Leave Act (FMLA)	Federal act requiring certain employers to establish a policy that provides all eligible employees with up to 12 weeks of unpaid leave during any 12-month period for several family-related occurrences (e.g., birth of a child, care of a sick spouse).
Unemployment compensation	State system, created by the Federal Unemployment Tax Act (FUTA), that provides unemployment compensation to qualified employees who lose their jobs.
Consolidated Omnibus Budget Reconciliation Act (COBRA)	Federal law that ensures that when employees lose their jobs or have their hours reduced to a level at which they would not be eligible to receive medical, dental, or optical benefits from their employer, the employees will be able to continue receiving benefits under the employer's policy for up to 18 months by paying the premiums for the policy.
Employee Retirement Income Security Act (ERISA)	Federal law that sets minimum standards for most voluntarily established pension and health plans in private industry to provide protection for individuals in these plans. HIPAA and COBRA are amendments to ERISA.
Occupational Safety and Health Act (OSHA) of 1970	Federal law that established the Occupational Safety and Health Administration, the agency responsible for setting safety standards under the act, as well as enforcing the act through inspections and levying fines against violators.

Additional Laws Governing the Employment Relationship

LO 24-5

Several major categories of state and federal laws cover employee rights with regard to wages, benefits, and health and safety standards. Exhibit 24-3 lists significant state and federal legislation protecting employees.

FAIR LABOR STANDARDS ACT

The Fair Labor Standards Act (FLSA) requires a minimum wage of a specified amount to be paid to all employees in covered industries. Congress raises the specified amount periodically to compensate for increases in the cost of living caused by inflation. In the summer of 2009, the federal minimum wage was raised to $7.25. This was the first increase in almost 10 years.

In 2014, President Obama called for an increase in the federal minimum wage to $10.10.[24] Though Congress has yet to pass any such legislation, President Obama did sign an Executive Order increasing the minimum wage to $10.10 for individuals working on new federal contracts.

FLSA mandates employees who work more than 40 hours in a week to be paid no less than one and one-half times their regular wage for all the hours beyond 40 that they work during a given week. Four categories of employees are excluded:

- Executives
- Administrative employees
- Professional employees
- Outside salespersons

Fair Labor Standards Act (FLSA)
Federal law requiring a minimum wage of a specified amount be paid to all employees in covered industries; also mandates that employees who work more than 40 hours in a week be paid no less than 1½ times their regular wage for all hours beyond 40 worked in a given week.

[24] Raise the Wage: White House, http://www.whitehouse.gov/raise-the-wage

FAMILY AND MEDICAL LEAVE ACT

Family and Medical Leave Act (FMLA)

Federal act requiring employers to provide all eligible employees with up to 12 weeks of leave during any 12-month period for several family-related occurrences (e.g., birth of a child, care of a sick spouse).

When the Family and Medical Leave Act (FMLA) went into effect in 1993, it was hailed by its supporters as a breakthrough in American law and feared by its opponents as an unwieldy encumbrance on business. FMLA covers all public employers and private employers with 50 or more employees. It guarantees all eligible employees (those who have worked at least 25 hours a week for each of 12 months prior to the leave) up to 12 weeks of *unpaid* leave during any 12-month period for any of the following family-related occurrences:

- The birth of a child.
- The adoption of a child.
- The placement of a foster child in the employee's care.
- The care of a seriously ill spouse, parent, or child.
- A serious health condition that renders the employee unable to perform any of the essential functions of his or her job.

UNEMPLOYMENT COMPENSATION

unemployment compensation

A state system, created by the Federal Unemployment Tax Act (FUTA), that provides unemployment compensation to qualified employees who lose their jobs.

Although FMLA in some cases helps employees retain their jobs, what happens if they lose their jobs? The Federal Unemployment Tax Act (FUTA),[25] passed in 1935, created a state system to provide unemployment compensation to qualified employees who lose their jobs. Under this law, employers pay taxes to the states, which deposit the money into the federal government's Unemployment Insurance Fund. Each state has an account from which it can access the money in the fund in accordance with the rules the state establishes for eligibility. States have different minimum standards for qualifying for unemployment compensation, although almost all states require that the applicant did not voluntarily quit or get fired for cause.

WORKERS' COMPENSATION LAWS

workers' compensation laws

State laws that provide for financial compensation to employees or their dependents when a covered employee is injured on the job.

Unlike many other laws affecting the employment relationship, workers' compensation legislation is purely state law. Our coverage of this topic must therefore be rather generalized. Prudent businesspeople will familiarize themselves with the workers' compensation statutes of the states within which their companies operate.

Workers' compensation laws ensure that covered workers who are injured on the job can receive financial compensation through an administrative procedure rather than having to sue their employer. For administrative convenience, most states exclude certain types of businesses and small firms from coverage. Some states also allow businesses that have sufficient resources to be self-insured rather than participate in the state program.

CONSOLIDATED OMNIBUS BUDGET RECONCILIATION ACT OF 1985

Consolidated Omnibus Budget Reconciliation Act (COBRA)

Federal law that ensures that when employees lose their jobs or have their hours reduced to a level at which they would not be eligible to receive medical, dental, or optical benefits from their employer, the employees will be able to continue receiving benefits under the employer's policy for up to 18 months by paying the premiums for the policy.

The Consolidated Omnibus Budget Reconciliation Act (COBRA) ensures that employees who lose their jobs or have their hours reduced to a level at which they are no longer eligible to receive medical, dental, or optical benefits can pay to continue receiving benefits for themselves and their dependents under the employer's policy. The employee must pay the premiums for the policy, plus up to a 2 percent administration fee, to maintain the coverage for up to 18 months, or 29 months for a disabled worker. This is often quite expensive. An employee has 60 days after coverage would ordinarily terminate to decide whether to maintain the coverage.

This obligation does *not* arise under either of two conditions:

1. The employee is fired for gross misconduct.
2. The employer decides to eliminate benefits for all current employees.

[25] 26 U.S.C. §§ 3301–3310.

GLOBAL Context

Legal Discrimination against Women in Saudi Arabia

In Saudi Arabia, not only are women not entitled to pay equal to that of men, but there are actual legal statutes sanctioning discrimination against women in both public and private situations. Women, who are not even allowed to drive, constitute only 5 percent of Saudi Arabia's work-force. This number may not be surprising considering the limited labor opportunities for women. The law severely limits the industries in which women can be employed. Women are forbidden to receive business licenses if they may have to interact with males or government officials. If a woman is fortunate enough to find a job, it will prob-ably be in education or health care. Some women can be

found in various retail businesses or the banking industry. Despite its difficulties, finding a job may be easy in com-parison to the discrimination Saudi Arabian women will face at work. For instance, all places of employment are segregated by sex. The only way women can be in contact with a man is by telephone or electronic exchange. Many women complain of sexual and physical abuse while on the job. These complaints come from women at all levels in the workforce, from sweatshops to hospitals, and their situation is made worse because they have basically no legal redress. The courts have unreasonably strict eviden-tiary rules for harassment and discrimination cases. These rules, as well as the social shame that would arise from try-ing to challenge a man in public, deter women from seeking a legal solution to discriminatory treatment.

EMPLOYEE RETIREMENT INCOME SECURITY ACT OF 1974

The Employee Retirement Income Security Act (ERISA) is "a federal law that sets minimum standards for most voluntarily established pension and health plans in private industry to provide protection for individuals in these plans."[26] Under ERISA, employers must provide participants with all the following:

1. Plan information (i.e., features and funding).
2. Assurances of the fiduciary responsibility of those in charge of managing and controlling the plan assets.
3. A grievance and appeals process for participants to get benefits from their plans.
4. The right to sue for benefits and breaches of fiduciary duty.[27]

Employers are required to provide to employees, free of charge, a *summary plan description (SPD)*, which provides information on how the plan operates, the benefits under the plan, how to apply for such benefits, when such benefits vest, and when benefits may be paid out.

> **Employee Retirement Income Security Act (ERISA)**
> Federal law that sets minimum standards for most voluntarily established pension and health plans in private industry to provide pro-tection for individuals in these plans.

OCCUPATIONAL SAFETY AND HEALTH ACT OF 1970

The federal government regulates workplace safety primarily through the Occupational Safety and Health Act (OSHA) of 1970, which requires every employer to "furnish to each of his employees . . . employment . . . free from recognized hazards that are likely to cause death or serious physical harm." The Occupational Safety and Health Administration (abbreviated OSHA, the same as the act) is the agency that is responsible for promulgating workplace safety standards, inspecting facili-ties to ensure compliance with the standards, and bringing enforcement actions against violators. In addition, OSHA undertakes educational programs for employers and employees.

> **Occupational Safety and Health Act (OSHA) of 1970**
> Federal law that estab-lished the Occupational Safety and Health Administration, the agency responsible for setting safety stan-dards under the act and enforcing the act through inspections and the levying of fines against violators.

Employee Privacy in the Workplace   LO 24-6

With the rapid expansion of technology, new issues related to workplace privacy have evolved. Technology has stimulated the growth of such issues in a number of ways. On the one hand, technology has given employers new ways to gather information about employees. On the other hand, new technologies have provided more temptations for employees to be off the job at work,

---

[26] Department of Labor, Employee Retirement Income Security Act, www.dol.gov/dol/topic/health-plans/erisa.htm.
[27] Ibid.

thus creating a stimulus for more employer monitoring. For example, surveys have shown that 90 percent of employees with Internet access at work look at non-work-related websites at least once a day,[28] 90 percent receive non–work related e-mail,[29] and 84 percent send non–work related e-mail.[30] Given such statistics, it is understandable that employers would want to monitor what employees are doing when they are supposed to be on the job.

ELECTRONIC MONITORING AND COMMUNICATION

Business owners need to understand the extent to which they can monitor employees' telephone conversations, read their e-mail, and listen to their voice mail. Questions related to such monitoring primarily involve the common law tort of invasion of privacy and two federal statutes: the Omnibus Crime Control and Safe Streets Act of 1968,[31] as amended by the Electronic Communications Privacy Act of 1986.[32]

> **Omnibus Crime Control and Safe Streets Act of 1968**
> Federal statute banning employers from listening to the private telephone conversations of employees or disclosing the contents of these conversations. Employers may ban personal calls and monitor calls for compliance as long as they discontinue listening to any conversation once they determine it is personal.

Under the Omnibus Crime Control and Safe Streets Act of 1968, employers cannot listen to the private telephone conversations of employees or disclose the contents of these conversations. They may, however, ban personal calls and monitor calls for compliance as long as they discontinue listening to any conversation once they determine it is personal. Violators may be subject to fines of up to $10,000. Under the Electronic Communications Privacy Act (ECPA) of 1986, employees' privacy rights were extended to electronic forms of communication, including e-mail and cellular phones. ECPA outlaws the intentional interception of electronic communications and the intentional disclosure or use of the information obtained through such interception.

> **Electronic Communications Privacy Act (ECPA) of 1986**
> Federal law that extended employees' privacy rights to electronic forms of communication, including e-mail and cellular phones; outlaws the intentional interception of electronic communications and the intentional disclosure or use of the information obtained through such interception.

In recognition of the fact that employers may sometimes need to monitor employee conversations for the purpose of improving employee performance or protecting employees from harassing calls, ECPA includes a business-extension exemption that allows employers to monitor employee telephone conversations in the ordinary course of their employment. This exception is subject to the constraint preventing the employer from continuing to listen to conversations after it becomes apparent that they are personal. Also, monitoring is allowed when employees give their prior consent.

The key question in cases involving employer monitoring and interception of employee communications via e-mail, telephone, or voice mail is whether the employee had a *reasonable expectation of privacy* with respect to the communication in question. Employers are in the strongest position if they have a clear policy establishing that there is no reasonable expectation of privacy. Employment law experts advise that having a clear employee privacy policy that employees sign will minimize the likelihood of being sued by employees for invasion of privacy. These policies should be spelled out in the employee handbook and explained to employees. At a minimum, employer privacy policies should cover the following issues:

1. Employer monitoring of telephone conversations.
2. Employer surveillance policies.
3. Employee access to medical and personnel records.
4. Drug testing policies.
5. Lie detector policies.
6. Ownership of computers and all issues unique to the electronic workplace.

LO 24-7   Labor Laws and Unions

Many people would argue that the laws that improved workers' conditions most significantly were not any of those previously discussed but, rather, were the laws that gave employees the right to organize and bargain collectively over wages and terms and conditions of employment. During the Great Depression, workers were first given the right to organize, and since that time

---

[28] Dyland Loeb McClain, "I'll Be Right with You, Boss, as Soon as I Finish My Shopping," *New York Times,* January 10, 2001, p. G1.
[29] Ibid.
[30] Ibid.
[31] 18 U.S.C. § 2210 et seq.
[32] 18 U.S.C. §§ 2510–2521.

CASE Nugget

When Can Employees Be Forced to Take a Lie Detector Test?

Polkey v. Transtrecs Corp.
U.S. Court of Appeals for the Eleventh Circuit

404 F.3d 1264 (11th Cir. 2005)

Polkey was a supervisor in the mailroom at Pensacola Naval Air Station. The mailroom was run by a company called Transtrecs. After discovering that some mail had been tampered with, Polkey reported it to her supervisor. Transtrecs asked all six employees, including Polkey, to take a lie detector (i.e., polygraph) test. The employee most suspected was tested first, and the lie detector test indicated that he might have been the one who tampered with the mail. Polkey and the remaining employees then refused to take the lie detector test. Transtrecs fired Polkey. She sued for violation of the Employee Polygraph Protection Act (EPPA). The district court granted summary judgment for Polkey. Transtrecs appealed.

On appeal, the district court's judgment was affirmed. The court held that Transtrecs violated EPPA by requesting and even suggesting that the employees take a polygraph test. Transtrecs argued that it was exempt because of national security, but the appellate court said that this applies only to the government. Transtrecs was merely a contractor for the government. Transtrecs also argued that it was exempt because the polygraph was part of an ongoing investigation of Polkey and that she was under suspicion. For this exemption to apply, an employer must have an articulable basis in fact to indicate that the employee was involved in or responsible for an economic loss. Transtrecs could make no such showing. Polkey prevailed.

unionization rates have varied significantly. During the post–World War II period, more than one-third of American workers were organized. In 2013, the percentage of workers belonging to a union in the United States was 11.3 percent.[33]

Not all occupations are equally organized. The union membership rate for public-sector workers (35.3%) was substantially higher than the rate for private-sector workers (6.7%). Within the public sector, the union membership rate was highest for local government (40.8%), which includes employees in heavily unionized occupations, such as teachers, police officers, and firefighters. In the private sector, industries with high unionization rates included utilities (25.6%), transportation and warehousing (19.6%), telecommunications (14.4%), and construction (14.1%).[34]

Labor-management relations in the United States today are governed by three major pieces of legislation:

1. The Wagner Act of 1935.
2. The Taft-Hartley Act of 1947.
3. The Landrum-Griffin Act of 1959.

The Taft-Hartley Act amended the Wagner Act, and they are jointly referred to as the *National Labor Relations Act (NLRA)*.

THE WAGNER ACT OF 1935

The first major piece of federal legislation adopted explicitly to encourage the formation of labor unions and provide for collective bargaining between employers and unions as a means of obtaining the peaceful settlement of labor disputes was the Wagner Act. Collective bargaining "consists of negotiations between an employer and a group of employees so as to determine the conditions of employment."[35]

collective bargaining
The process whereby workers organize collectively and bargain with employers regarding the workplace.

Wagner Act
The first major piece of federal legislation adopted explicitly to encourage the formation of labor unions and provide for collective bargaining between employers and unions as a means of obtaining the peaceful settlement of labor disputes.

[33] Bureau of Labor Statistics (January 24, 2014), http://www.bls.gov/news.release/union2.nr0.htm
[34] Ibid.
[35] Legal Information Institute, www.law.cornell.edu/topics/collective_bargaining.html

CASE Nugget

May an Employee Be Fired for Trashing Her Employer on Facebook?

Fair Labor Standards Board [on behalf of Dawnmarie Souza] v. American Medical Response of Connecticut Unpublished

Case settled by unpublished agreement between parties, February 2011

Dawnmarie Souza was employed by American Medical Response (AMR) of Connecticut. A customer complained about her work, and she was required to prepare a response. Her supervisor refused to permit a representative of the Teamsters, the union representing the company's workers, to help prepare her response. Souza then mocked her supervisor on Facebook, reportedly using several vulgarities to ridicule him. According to copies of Souza's Facebook posts obtained by CNET, she called her supervisor a "dick" in one and "a scumbag" in another. The Connecticut ambulance company fired Souza on December 1, 2009. The National Labor Relations Board (NLRB) sued AMR of Connecticut on October 27, 2010, claiming the employee, Dawnmarie Souza, was illegally fired and denied union representation.

The closely watched case touched on whether employers have the right to discipline employees for comments they make on social-networking sites. The NLRB complaint said that Souza "engaged in concerted activities with other employees by criticizing respondent's supervisor . . . on her Facebook page" on November 8, 2009. In response to the NLRB complaint, AMR claimed Souza's comments were not protected activity. However, the NLRB contended that AMR's termination of Souza's employment violated the National Labor Relations Act, which allows employees to discuss the terms and conditions of their employment with co-workers and others.

In February 2011, the case was settled. Under the terms of the settlement, AMR agreed to revise "overly broad rules" in the employee handbook regarding how employees can communicate on the Internet and with co-workers regarding their work conditions. According to the Fair Labor Standards Board (FLSB), the company also agreed not to discipline employees for requesting union representation. The allegations regarding Souza's discharge were resolved in a separate, private agreement between Souza and AMR. Financial terms were not revealed.

Sources: Steven Musil, "Company Settles Facebook Firing Case," February 7, 2011, http://news.cnet.com/8301-1023_3-20030955-93.html; see also Erline Aguiluz, "AMR Settles Dawnmarie Souza's Wrongful Termination Lawsuit," February 11, 2011, http://philadelphiaemploymentlawnews.com/2011/02/amr-settles-dawnmarie-souzas-wrongful-termination-lawsuit.html

Taft-Hartley Act
Federal legislation designed to curtail some of the powers that unions had acquired under the Wagner Act; designates certain union actions as unfair. Also called *Labor-Management Relations Act*.

The Wagner Act also created an administrative agency, the *National Labor Relations Board (NLRB),* to interpret and enforce the NLRA. Finally, the act provides for judicial review in designated federal courts of appeal.

THE TAFT-HARTLEY ACT OF 1947

The 12 years between passage of the Wagner Act and that of the Taft-Hartley Act saw a huge growth in unionization, which resulted in an increase in workers' power. Public perception of this trend led to the passage of the Taft-Hartley Act, also known as the Labor-Management Relations Act, which was designed to curtail some of the powers the unions had acquired under the Wagner Act.

Landrum-Griffin Act
Federal legislation that primarily governs the internal operations of labor unions. It requires financial disclosures by unions, establishes penalties for financial abuses by union officials, and includes "Labor's Bill of Rights" to protect employees from their own unions.

THE LANDRUM-GRIFFIN ACT OF 1959

The Landrum-Griffin Act primarily governs the internal operations of labor unions. This act, which was a response to evidence of certain undesirable internal labor union practices, requires certain financial disclosures by unions and establishes civil and criminal penalties for financial abuses by union officials. "Labor's Bill of Rights," contained in the act, protects employees from their own unions.

THE NATIONAL LABOR RELATIONS BOARD

The National Labor Relations Board (NLRB) is the administrative agency that interprets and enforces the *National Labor Relations Act (NLRA)*. The NLRB's three primary functions are to:

1. Monitor the conduct of the employer and the union during an election to determine whether workers want to be represented by a union.

2. Prevent and remedy unfair labor practices by employers or unions.

3. Establish rules interpreting the NLRA.

The NLRB has jurisdiction over all employees *except* those who work in federal, state, and local government and those covered by the Railway Labor Act (employees in the transportation industry); independent contractors; agricultural workers; household domestics; persons employed by a spouse or parent; and supervisors, managerial employees, and confidential employees. In the preceding Case Nugget, the NLRB brought a lawsuit against a company after the company fired an employee for posting negative comments about a supervisor on Facebook.

THE COLLECTIVE BARGAINING PROCESS

Once the union has been certified, union and management must begin to bargain in good faith about wages, hours, and other terms and conditions of work. Note that the NLRB can order only the parties to bargain in good faith; it cannot order them to reach an agreement with respect to any contract term.

The NLRA requires both the employer and the bargaining-unit representative to bargain collectively in good faith with respect to wages, hours, and other terms and conditions of employment.

National Labor Relations Board (NLRB)
An administrative agency created by the Wagner Act to interpret and enforce the National Labor Relations Act.

SUMMARY

When May an Employee Be Fired?	*At-will employment* means that any employee who is not employed under a contract or a collective bargaining agreement may quit at any time for any reason or no reason at all, with no required notice to the employer. Moreover, the employer may fire the employee at any time, with no notice, for almost any reason.
Federal Employment Discrimination Laws Governing Employers	Federal law may be described as a minimum level of protection for all workers. State laws may give employees more, but not less, protection than federal laws. Some of the most important federal employment discrimination laws are the Civil Rights Act (CRA) of 1964— Title VII (as amended by the Civil Rights Act of 1991); Pregnancy Discrimination Act (PDA) of 1987; Age Discrimination in Employment Act (ADEA) of 1967; Americans with Disabilities Act; and Equal Pay Act of 1963.
Civil Rights Act— Title VII	Title VII of CRA (1964, as amended by the Civil Rights Act of 1991) protects employees against discrimination based on race, color, religion, national origin, and sex. It also prohibits harassment based on the same protected categories. Defenses to a charge of discrimination under Title VII include *merit, seniority system,* and *bona fide occupational qualification (BFOQ).*

- *Disparate treatment:* If the employee has been hired, fired, denied a promotion, and so on, based on membership in a protected class under Title VII, this is a form of intentional discrimination and qualifies the employee to sue for disparate-treatment discrimination.

- *Disparate impact: Disparate-impact cases arise when a plaintiff attempts to establish that although an employer's policy or practice appears to apply to everyone equally, its actual effect is that it disproportionately limits employment opportunities for a protected class.*

- *Sexual harassment:* Sexual harassment includes unwelcome sexual advances, requests for sexual favors, and other verbal or physical conduct of a sexual nature that implicitly or explicitly makes submission a term or condition of employment; makes employment decisions related to the individual dependent on submission to or rejection of such conduct; or has the purpose or effect of creating an intimidating, hostile, or offensive work environment. Two recognized forms are *hostile environment* and *quid pro quo harassment.*

Pregnancy Discrimination Act of 1987: PDA amended Title VII of CRA, expanding the definition of sex discrimination to include discrimination based on pregnancy.

Equal Employment Opportunity Commission: The EEOC is the federal agency charged with overseeing Title VII of the Civil Rights Act. Administrative complaints must be filed with the EEOC (or an equivalent state agency) prior to filing a lawsuit for discrimination or harassment.

Discrimination Based on Sexual Orientation— Actionable?	No federal legislation currently prohibits discrimination based on sexual orientation. What does exist are individual state laws that prohibit such discrimination. State laws prohibiting discrimination based on sexual orientation exist in 17 states.
Discrimination Based on Marriage	Section 2 of DOMA says that no state "shall be required to give effect" to same-sex marriages granted by other states. Section 3 of DOMA, which denied federal benefits to legally married same-sex couples, was struck down by the U.S. Supreme Court in 2013.
Age Discrimination in Employment Act of 1967	ADEA prohibits employers from refusing to hire, discharging, or discriminating in terms and conditions of employment on the basis of an employee or applicant being age 40 or older.
Americans with Disabilities Act	ADA prohibits discrimination against employees and job applicants with disabilities.
May an Employer Discriminate against a Smoker?	Some companies either won't hire smokers or are threatening to fire current employees who will not or are unable to quit smoking. Many states have passed laws preventing companies from engaging in such action.
Equal Pay Act of 1963	EPA prohibits an employer from paying workers of one gender less than the wages paid to employees of the opposite gender for work that requires equal skill, effort, and responsibility.
Additional Laws Governing the Employment Relationship	*Fair Labor Standards Act:* Employers must follow federal minimum-wage and hour laws. FLSA covers all employers engaged in interstate commerce or the production of goods for interstate commerce and requires a minimum wage of a specified amount to be paid to all employees in covered industries. Congress periodically raises the specified amount to compensate for increases in the cost of living caused by inflation. The current minimum wage is $7.25.

Family and Medical Leave Act: The FMLA covers all public employers as well as private employers with 50 or more employees. It guarantees all eligible employees (those who have worked at least 25 hours a week for each of 12 months prior to the leave) up to 12 weeks of unpaid leave during any 12-month period for any of the following family-related occurrences: the birth of a child; the adoption of a child; the placement of a foster child in the employee's care; the care of a seriously ill spouse, parent, or child; or a serious health condition that renders the employee unable to perform any of the essential functions of his or her job.

Unemployment compensation: The Federal Unemployment Tax Act (FUTA) created a state system that provides unemployment compensation to qualified employees who lose their jobs.

Workers' compensation laws: State laws provide for financial compensation to employees or their dependents when a covered employee is injured on the job.

Consolidated Omnibus Budget Reconciliation Act: COBRA ensures that when employees lose their jobs or have their hours reduced to a level at which they would not be eligible to receive medical, dental, or optical benefits from their employer, the employees will be able to continue receiving benefits under the employer's policy for up to 18 months by paying the premiums for the policy.

Employee Retirement Income Security Act: ERISA sets minimum standards for most voluntarily established pension and health plans in private industry to provide protection for individuals in these plans.

Occupational Safety and Health Act of 1970: The Occupational Safety and Health Administration is responsible for setting safety standards under OSHA and enforcing the act through inspections and levying fines against violators.

Employee Privacy in the Workplace

Privacy issues are of increasing importance in the workplace. Privacy policies should cover matters such as employer surveillance policies, control of and access to medical and personnel records, drug testing, and e-mail policies.

Omnibus Crime Control and Safe Streets Act of 1968: Employers cannot listen to the private telephone conversations of employees or disclose the contents of these conversations. They may, however, ban personal calls and monitor calls for compliance as long as they discontinue listening to any conversation once they determine it is personal. Violators may be subject to fines of up to $10,000.

Electronic Communications Privacy Act of 1986: Under ECPA, employees' privacy rights were extended to electronic forms of communication, including e-mail and cellular phones. ECPA outlaws the intentional interception of electronic communications and the intentional disclosure or use of the information obtained through such interception.

Labor Laws and Unions

Wagner Act of 1935: The Wagner Act was the first major piece of federal legislation adopted explicitly to encourage the formation of labor unions and provide for collective bargaining between employers and unions as a means of obtaining the peaceful settlement of labor disputes.

Collective bargaining: Collective bargaining consists of negotiations between an employer and a group of employees to determine the conditions of employment.

National Labor Relations Board: The Wagner Act created the NLRB, an administrative agency, to interpret and enforce the National Labor Relations Act (NLRA) and to provide for judicial review in designated federal courts of appeal.

Taft-Hartley Act of 1947: Also known as the Labor-Management Relations Act, the Taft-Hartley Act was designed to curtail some of the powers the unions had acquired under the Wagner Act. Just as the Wagner Act designated certain employer actions as unfair, the Taft-Hartley Act designated certain union actions as unfair.

Landrum-Griffin Act of 1959: The Landrum-Griffin Act primarily governs the internal operations of labor unions. It requires certain financial disclosures by unions and establishes civil and criminal penalties for financial abuses by union officials. "Labor's Bill of Rights," contained in the act, protects employees from their own unions.

Point/Counterpoint

Should Employers Be Permitted to Fire Employees for Activities, Such as Smoking, That They Do Outside Working Hours?	
YES	**NO**
The Centers for Disease Control and Prevention estimated that $75 billion is spent annually on medical expenses attributed to smoking. Businesses lose $82 billion in lost productivity from smokers. Smokers take about 6.5 more sick days a year than nonsmokers.	Employers should have no say in what employees do outside the workplace. Forcing employees to take tests to reveal whether they are smokers is an invasion of the employees' privacy. Many employees are addicted to cigarettes and would unfairly lose badly needed employment if unable to quit smoking.

Questions & Problems

1. Name five statutes that prohibit discrimination in employment.

2. Does Title VII apply to same-sex harassment?

3. What is the current amount of the federal minimum wage? When was the last time the federal minimum wage was increased?

4. What is required for an employee to be eligible for benefits under the Family and Medical Leave Act?

5. Whom does the Age Discrimination in Employment Act protect?

6. List the protected classes under the Civil Rights Act of 1964 (as amended in 1991).

7. Vania Santiero (plaintiff) was hired as a server at a Denny's Restaurant on August 29, 2009, and she was employed there until she voluntarily left her position on December 9, 2009. Defendant Den-Forest LLP (Den-Forest) owns the store, and Assad A. Shorrosh is the managing member of Den-Forest. Plaintiff alleges that her supervisor, Shadi Hadi, began harassing her the moment she began working by grabbing her bottom on August 29, 2009. The following day, Hadi demanded that Santiero expose herself to him to be placed on the work schedule. She complied by lifting her shirt, but then Hadi allegedly assaulted Santiero by following her into a restroom where he pulled her shirt up and fondled her without her consent. Plaintiff did not report Hadi's actions until she called Assad Shorrosh on September 15, 2009. Hadi was suspended by Den-Forest on September 17, 2009, and Hadi's employment was terminated on September 21, 2009. Plaintiff worked for Den-Forest without further incident until her voluntary resignation almost three months later. She then sued for *quid pro quo* sexual harassment and a hostile work environment arising under Title VII of the Civil Rights Act of 1964 (Title VII). Does the plaintiff have a case for *quid pro quo* harassment? Why or why not? Does the plaintiff have a case for hostile environment sexual harassment? Explain your reasoning. [*Santiero v. Denny's Rest. Store,* 786 F. Supp. 2d 1228 (2011)].

8. Cheryl Hall maintains that she was fired by Nalco Company for taking time off from work to undergo in vitro fertilization after being diagnosed with infertility. She filed suit under Title VII of the Civil Rights Act of 1964, as amended by the Pregnancy Discrimination Act (PDA), alleging her termination constituted discrimination on the basis of sex. The district court concluded that Hall's allegations did not state a Title VII claim because infertility is a gender-neutral condition entitled to no protection under the language of the PDA. The case went up on appeal. Do you agree with the district court that infertility is a gender-neutral condition? Or should the appellate court reverse the district court and hold that Hall was discriminated against on the basis of sex? Explain your reasoning. [*Cheryl Hall v. Nalco Company,* 534 F.3d 644 (2008).]

9. Exxon maintained a corporate policy that prohibited its pilots from flying corporate aircraft after they reached the age of 60 and forced such pilots to retire involuntarily at age 60. This rule mirrored a rule the Federal Aviation Administration applied to pilots flying for commercial airlines. Based on the age 60 rule, Exxon forced at least three pilots to retire in 2006 and 2007. The EEOC brought suit on behalf of these pilots and others alleging age discrimination. Exxon argued that the requirement for pilots to be under age 60 is a *bona fide occupational qualification.* Do you agree? Why or why not? [*EEOC v. Exxon Mobil Corp.,* 2012 U.S. Dist. LEXIS 183101].

10. Baxter Pharmacy paid its pharmacists a salary but no overtime pay. Under the Fair Labor Standards Act (FLSA), employers must pay employees overtime for hours worked in excess of 40 hours per week. Baxter Pharmacy believes that the pharmacists are exempt under FLSA because they are professionals. The pharmacists disagree. Is being a professional an exemption from the requirement to pay overtime under FLSA? Are pharmacists professionals? How do you think the court ruled? [*De Jesus-Rentas v. Baxter Pharmacy Services Corp.,* 400 F.3d 72 (1st Cir. 2005).]

11. Lisa Harrison (Harrison) was hired by Defendant at Family House of Louisiana (Family House), a long-term residential treatment facility for chemically dependent women and their children, on November 23, 1999. She was hired as a Prevention/Intervention Specialist, and her job included overseeing a day care program for the children of mothers staying at Family House. At the time she was hired, Harrison weighed more than 400 pounds. On September 6, 2007, Harrison was terminated from her position at Family House. At the time of her termination, she weighed 527 pounds. On October 17, 2007, Harrison filed a charge of discrimination with the Equal Employment Opportunity Commission (EEOC), alleging that she had been terminated because Defendant regarded her as disabled due to her obesity. Is obesity a disability under the Americans with Disabilities Act? [*EEOC v. Res. for Human Dev., Inc.,* 25 Am. Disabilities Cas. (BNA) 964 (2012)].

12. Cynthia Anderson worked for the city of Columbus, Georgia, answering telephone calls from citizens. Anderson knew that calls from citizens were recorded, but she was unaware that due to a glitch, the telephone system continued to record her statements through her headset after a call was terminated. Anderson made disparaging remarks about the city manager's office, and her employment was terminated. Anderson sued the city, alleging that it had no right to record her private conversations with co-workers, which were unrelated to city business. Who should prevail? Why? [*Anderson v. City of Columbus, Georgia,* 2005 U.S. Dist. LEXIS 12612.]

13. Meadows worked as an assistant manager at a Dollar General store. While she was ringing up an order for a customer, he became verbally abusive. After she finished ringing up the sale, the customer threw the bag, containing a can of motor oil, at Meadows, hitting her in the eye. Meadows suffered a detached retina. The trial court awarded Meadows permanent partial disability under workers' compensation for her injury. Dollar General appealed the decision, arguing that the injury did not occur in the course of employment. Do you believe that Meadows's injury occurred during the course of her employment? Why or why not? Was the trial court correct in granting her permanent partial disability, or did the appeals court overturn that decision? [*Dollar General Corp. v. Meadows,* 63 P.3d 548 (2002 WL 31991909, Okla. Ct. Civ. App. 2002).]

14. Occupational exposure to lead entails health risks, including the risk of harm to any fetus carried by a woman subjected to such exposure. Eight employees of an employer, in whose battery manufacturing process lead was a primary ingredient, became pregnant while maintaining blood-lead levels in excess of the level that appeared to be the critical level the Occupational Safety and Health Administration (OSHA) noted for a woman who was planning to have a family. Afterward, the employer announced a policy barring all women, except those whose inability to bear children was medically documented, from jobs involving exposure or potential exposure to lead at a level exceeding OSHA standards. A group of employees who had been affected by the employer's fetal-protection policy filed, in the U.S. District Court for the Eastern District of Wisconsin, a class action challenging the policy as sex discrimination that violated Title VII of the Civil Rights Act of 1964, as amended, which prohibits sex-based classifications in terms and conditions of employment, in hiring and discharge decisions, and in other employment decisions. May the employer defend by arguing that being male is a bona fide occupational qualification for the job of manufacturing batteries? Or does the employer's action violate Title VII? Explain your reasoning. [*International Union, United Automobile, Aerospace & Agricultural Implement Workers of America, UAW et al., Petitioners v. Johnson Controls, Inc.,* 499 U.S. 187 (1991).]

15. Anthony Romeo was an openly gay student at Seton Hall, a Catholic university. He claimed that he elected to attend Seton Hall in part because of its published antidiscrimination policy. In 2003, he applied to the Seton Hall University Department of Student Affairs for provisional recognition of a gay and lesbian student organization. Dr. Laura Wankel, vice president of student affairs at Seton Hall, responded to Romeo's application in a letter, stating in pertinent part: "I am informing you that your application for provisional recognition has been denied. No organization based solely upon sexual orientation may receive formal University recognition." Wankel went on to say that "the Division of Student Affairs remains prepared to work with gay and lesbian students to meet their needs. I am committed to working collaboratively with you and other students in fostering a positive, safe and caring community." Wankel then made a modest proposal giving the group some rights. The proposal, however, was not satisfactory to the students, and Romeo filed his complaint alleging violations of New Jersey's Law against Discrimination. He also cited Seton Hall's nondiscrimination policy: "No person may be denied employment or related benefits or admission to the University or to any of its programs or activities, either academic or nonacademic, curricular or extracurricular, because of race, color, religion, age, national origin, gender, sexual orientation, handicap and disability, or veteran's status." How should the court rule? May a Catholic university prevent recognition of a gay and lesbian student organization? Does the university's nondiscrimination policy make a difference? Why or why not? [*Romeo v. Seton Hall University,* 2005 N.J. Super. LEXIS 197.]

Business Organizations

Forms of Business Organization

CASE OPENER

The Dunkin' Donuts Franchise Agreement

Dunkin' Donuts Corporation operates numerous restaurants worldwide, organizing many of them as franchises. Dunkin' Donuts has the exclusive license to use and to license others to use its trademarks, service marks, and trade name. These marks and trade name have been used continuously since 1960 to identify Dunkin's doughnut shops as well as the doughnuts, pastries, coffee, and other products associated with those shops. Dipak N. Bhayani operated two Dunkin' Donuts franchises in Illinois for many years. Dunkin' Donuts later notified Bhayani that his two franchises had been violating parts of the franchise license agreement. After repeated incidents and failure to cure the violations over a substantial period of time, Dunkin' Donuts (the franchisor) demanded termination of both of Bhayani's franchises.

1. Did Dunkin' Donuts lawfully revoke Bhayani's franchises?
2. What are some potential problems that a franchisor and a franchisee might experience in their relationship?

LEARNING OBJECTIVES

After reading this chapter, you will be able to answer the following questions:

LO 21-1   What are the major forms of business organization?

LO 21-2   What are the advantages of each alternative form of business organization?

LO 21-3   What is the special significance of the operating agreement in a limited liability company?

LO 21-4   What are the differences among the different forms of business organization?

LO 21-5   What are the specialized forms of business organization?

E-COMMERCE and the Law

Exploring Forms of Business Organization on the Internet

If you are considering starting a business, the Internet can provide much information to help you decide which form of business you should create. This format for acquiring information about which form of business is optimal should improve the quality of decisions about this crucial step in operating a business. For example, at Business Tools (http://smallbiz.findlaw.com/book), you can read

more about sole proprietorships, partnerships, and corporations. Furthermore, using the Internet, you can learn about the laws that affect the forms of business within your specific state. For example, at Texas Business Forms (www. sos.state.tx.us/corp/forms.shtml), you can read about and actually retrieve the forms required to create various business types in Texas. Thus, the Internet can ease the difficulties associated with creating a business by increasing the information available to you about forms of business organization.

Suppose that you get an idea to produce a novel product. You think that production of this new product could lead to enormous profits. But what is the best way to produce this product? Should you produce it yourself by creating your own business? Do you have enough money to create your own business? What are the legal ramifications for you if your business is not successful? What legal responsibilities do you have with respect to your business?

Maybe you share your idea for this new product with your best friend, who suggests that the two of you become partners in the production and sale of this product. What are the benefits associated with forming a partnership? What are the disadvantages? Are there other forms of businesses that you should consider?

Deciding what form of business to create is one of the most important decisions a business makes. The extent of liability, as well as the extent of the control the owner will have over the business, depends on the form of the business. However, the business world is not static, and businesses can, and do, change form over time. Accordingly, this chapter is relevant not only to new businesses but also to existing businesses. The first section in this chapter introduces the major types of business organization, describing how these forms are both created and ended. The second section considers several types of business organization that are less well known but important nevertheless.

LO 21-1   Major Forms of Business Organization

SOLE PROPRIETORSHIP

sole proprietorship
A business in which one person (sole proprietor) is in control of the management and profits.

sole proprietor
The single person at the head of a sole proprietorship.

If you decide to go into business on your own, you are creating a sole proprietorship, a business organization in which you, as the sole proprietor, are in sole control of the management and the profits. Thus, if you wanted to open a lawn-mowing business or a sewing shop, you would likely be creating a sole proprietorship. It is a naturally occurring form of business organization in the sense that if you started doing business without thinking about the form, you would be a sole proprietor.

Why might an entrepreneur choose to create a sole proprietorship over other business organizations? First, a sole proprietorship requires very few legal formalities. Thus, one advantage of the sole proprietorship is the ease of creating such a business. Second, a sole proprietor has complete control of the management of the business. Consequently, the sole proprietor has great freedom to hire employees, determine business hours, and expand or change the nature of the business. Finally, the sole proprietor keeps all the profits from the business. These profits are taxed as the personal income of the sole proprietor.

However, sole proprietorships have disadvantages too. Suppose you are the sole proprietor of a restaurant in which someone is injured. This customer sues your business. You are personally liable for any losses or any obligations associated with the business. Consequently, if you accrue

ADVANTAGES	DISADVANTAGES
1. Creation is easy.	1. Proprietor has personal liability for all losses.
2. Proprietor is in total control of management.	2. Funding is limited to personal funds and loans.
3. Proprietor keeps all profits.	

Exhibit 21-1

Advantages and Disadvantages of the Sole Proprietorship

large debts because of your business, you might have to sell your home to cover those debts. Moreover, because the sole proprietorship is not considered a separate legal entity, you, as the owner and sole proprietor, can be personally sued. Sole proprietorships are terminated, however, when the sole proprietor dies.

Not only are you personally liable for any debts of the business, but the funding for your business is limited to your personal funds as well as loans you might be able to obtain. Thus, sole proprietorships often struggle in the initial stages of business because of large start-up costs in relation to the profits they make.

Sole proprietorships are by far the most popular form of business organization in the United States. Exhibit 21-1 summarizes their advantages and disadvantages.

An alternative form of business organization that retains many of the advantages of the sole proprietorship but that addresses the funding drawback in part is the partnership.

PARTNERSHIP

Suppose you and your best friend from college decide to create a business in which you plan to buy and sell used books and DVDs through the Internet. You both agree that you will share control of the Internet business and will split the profits equally. According to the Uniform Partnership Act (UPA), you have created a **partnership**, a voluntary association between two or more persons who co-own a business for profit. Except in a few cases, a partnership is not considered a separate legal entity and is dissolved when a partner dies. The UPA governs partnerships in most states in the absence of an express agreement.

What are the advantages associated with creating a partnership? First, the creation of a partnership is easy. The partners, each of whom is considered an agent of the partnership, are generally not required to create an official or even written agreement to create the partnership. Second, because the partnership is in most cases not considered a separate legal entity, the income from the business is taxed as individual income for each partner. Because the income is taxed as personal income, the partners can deduct the business losses.

Although there are certain advantages to creating a partnership, there are also disadvantages associated with partnerships. Most important, the partners are personally liable for the debts of the partnership. For instance, suppose you are in a partnership with your best friend, who embezzles $50,000 through your partnership. Because of the partnership, you would likely be held personally liable for the debts of the partnership. In other words, you would likely be responsible for the $50,000. Exhibit 21-2 summarizes the advantages and disadvantages of partnerships.

Although it is not listed in Exhibit 21-2, one advantage of a partnership is the ability to choose the people with whom you want to be partners. As the Case Nugget demonstrates, the courts recognize the right to choose one's partners as a basis for partnership law.

partnership
A voluntary association between two or more people who co-own a business for profit.

ADVANTAGES	DISADVANTAGES
1. Creation is easy.	1. Each partner has personal liability for all losses, including those of another partner (in most cases).
2. Income of business is personal income.	
3. Business losses can be deducted from taxes.	

Exhibit 21-2

Advantages and Disadvantages of Partnerships

CASE Nugget

Do Partners Have a Duty to Remain Partners?

Colette Bohatch v. Butler & Binion
Supreme Court of Texas

977 S.W.2d 543

Colette Bohatch became an associate in the Washington, D.C., office of Butler & Binion in 1986. John McDonald and Richard Powers, both partners, were the only other attorneys in the office. After Bohatch was made a partner in February 1990, she became concerned that McDonald was overbilling Pennzoil, the main client of the office. Bohatch met with the law firm's managing partner, Louis Paine, to report her concern regarding McDonald's overbilling. In July 1990, McDonald met with Bohatch to report that Pennzoil was dissatisfied with her work.

The next day, Bohatch relayed her concern to Paine as well as to two other members of the law firm's management committee. Paine led an investigation of Bohatch's complaint and discussed the billed hours with the in-house counsel at Pennzoil, who concluded that the bills were reasonable. In August 1990, Paine met with Bohatch, telling her that there was no basis for her claims against McDonald and that she should look for work elsewhere. The firm refused Bohatch a year-end partnership distribution for 1990. Finally, in August 1991, Bohatch was given until November to vacate her office. She filed suit in October 1991, and the firm voted to expel her from the partnership three days later.

At trial, the jury ruled that the firm breached the partnership agreement and its fiduciary duty and awarded Bohatch $57,000 for past lost wages, $250,000 for past mental anguish, $4,000,000 total in punitive damages (this amount was apportioned against several defendants), and attorney fees. Later, the trial court reduced the punitive damages to around $237,000. The court of appeals ruled that the firm's only duty to Bohatch was to avoid expelling her in bad faith. When the court found no evidence that the firm fired Bohatch for self-gain, it ruled that Bohatch could not recover for breach of fiduciary duty. The case was appealed to the state supreme court.

The supreme court ruled that the firm did not owe Bohatch a duty to remain partners. Although Bohatch presented a compelling argument that firms should not be permitted to expel partners who whistle-blow in good faith, the court could not ignore one basis of partnership law: a belief that partners should be allowed to choose their partners. The court found that forcing firms to keep whistle-blowing partners would cause partners to engage in business with people they could no longer trust, thereby undermining the viability of the partnership. Therefore, the supreme court affirmed the ruling of the court of appeals.

Duties of Partners to One Another   Most of the duties that partners hold to one another involve a duty to be loyal. They include the fiduciary duty to the other partners, the duty of obedience, and the duty of care.

Perhaps the most important duty of the partners is their fiduciary duty. They must, in good faith, work for the benefit of the partnership and refrain from taking any kind of action that will undermine the partnership. Consequently, the partners must not engage in any business that competes with the partnership.

Partners must disclose any material facts affecting the business. If a partner derives some kind of benefit from the partnership without the consent of the other partners, he or she must notify the partners of this benefit.

The second duty that the partners have to each other is the duty of obedience, to obey the partnership agreement. If they do not obey the agreement, they can be held liable for any losses that the partnership incurs.

The third duty the partners have is a duty of care to the other partners. Each partner must perform her management functions to the best of her abilities. If a partner makes an honest mistake in fulfilling her responsibilities to the partnership, she will not be held liable for the mistake.

Formation of the Partnership   Although an explicit written agreement is not required to create a partnership, the partners are advised to create one. The written agreement ensures that the terms of the partnership will be upheld. For example, suppose that you and your partner orally agree that you will receive three-fourths of the profits because you are doing significantly more management tasks. However, when you distribute the funds, your partner sues you because you give him only one-fourth of the profits. Without a written partnership agreement, the courts will have a difficult time ruling in your favor. A written agreement that creates a partnership is called the articles of partnership.

articles of partnership
the written agreement that creates the partnership

What kind of information do the articles of partnership usually include? First, the partners' names, as well as the name of the partnership, should be listed on the document. Second, the agreement should address the duration of the partnership. The agreement could include the date or event on which the partnership agreement would expire. Alternatively, the agreement could specify that the term of the partnership is indefinite. Third, the agreement should state the division of profits and losses. Fourth, the articles of partnership should establish the division of management duties. Fifth, the agreement should state exactly what capital contributions will be made by each partner. Creating articles of partnership can prevent legal problems by explicitly establishing the terms of the partnership agreement.

In some cases, parties who are not named in partnership agreements can be considered partners. How? Suppose you create a partnership agreement with your best friend. When you interact with your first potential customer, you tell this customer that your parents are also partners in this business. On the basis of your parents' participation in the partnership, the customer decides to place an order to purchase certain goods from you. Your parents discover that you have reported that they are your partners, but they do not contact the customer to tell her that they are not your partners. When your business cannot afford to purchase these goods to sell them to the customer, the customer sues you as well as your parents. Because your parents were aware of the misrepresentation but did not correct it, they will be *estopped* from denying they are your partners. Although they will not be able to claim the rights associated with being a partner (e.g., sharing the profits), in many states they could be held liable for the costs of the damages to the customer.

Most states recognize two situations in which a *partnership by estoppel* exists. First, as in the preceding example, if a third party is aware of a misrepresentation of partnership and consents to the misrepresentation, a partnership by estoppel is present. Second, if a nonpartner has represented himself or herself as a partner, and a third party *reasonably relies* on this information to his or her detriment, the nonpartner can be held liable for the third party's damages.

Termination of the Partnership   Before the termination of any partnership can be considered complete, a partnership must experience what are referred to as the *dissolution stage* and the *winding-up stage*. The first of these stages, dissolution, is considered complete when any partner stops fulfilling the role of a partner to the business (by choice or default). Section 29 of UPA defines dissolution as "the change in the relation of the partners caused by any partner's ceasing to be associated with the carrying on, as distinguished from the winding up"—the activity of completing unfinished partnership business, collecting and paying debts, collecting partnership assets, and taking inventory—"of the business."

dissolution
the first stage in the termination of a partnership

Depending on the reason for the dissolution, the dissolution will be considered rightful or wrongful. Exhibit 21-3 lists reasons that may be given to dissolve a partnership rightfully.

Once a partnership is liquidated, the partners begin the process of winding up, the activity of completing unfinished partnership business, collecting and paying debts, collecting partnership

winding up
the second stage in the termination of a partnership.

Exhibit 21-3

Reasons for
Rightful Dissolution
of a Partnership

1. The term established in the partnership agreement expires.
2. The partnership meets its established objective.
3. A partner withdraws from the partnership at will.
4. A partner withdraws in accordance with the partnership agreement.
5. A partner is expelled from the partnership in accordance with the partnership agreement.
6. A partner dies.
7. A partner is adjudicated bankrupt.
8. The business of the partnership becomes illegal.
9. A partner is adjudicated insane.
10. A partner becomes incapable of performing the duties as established by the partnership agreement.
11. The business of the partnership can be carried on only at a loss of profits.
12. A disagreement between the partners is such that it undermines the nature of the partnership.
13. Other circumstances of the partnership necessitate the dissolution.

assets, and taking inventory. During the winding up, the partners must still fulfill their fiduciary duty to one another, in the sense that they must disclose all information about the partnership assets. However, during the winding-up process, the partners can now engage in business that competes with the partnership business.

Who can demand that the winding-up process begin? If a partnership has been rightfully dissolved, any partner can demand the winding-up stage to begin. However, if a partner wrongfully dissolves a partnership, that partner has no right to demand a winding up.

CASE Nugget

When Does a Partnership Dissolve?

In re Leah Beth Woskob, Debtor; Alex Woskob;
Helen Woskob; the Estate of Victor Woskob v. Leah
Beth Woskob, Appellant U.S. Court of Appeals for the Third Circuit

305 F.3d 177 (2002)

In 1996, Leah Beth Woskob and Victor Woskob formed a partnership, the Legends Partnership, to construct, own, and operate the Legends, an apartment building. They were married at the time that the partnership was formed; however, they separated and filed for divorce the following year. During the divorce proceedings, Victor prevented Leah from receiving any of the partnership proceeds. Leah was granted a petition for special relief and awarded the exclusive right to manage and derive income from the partnership. Shortly thereafter, Victor filed for bankruptcy. Leah continued to file tax returns on behalf of the partnership, each of which listed Victor as a general partner. When Victor died in a car accident in 1999, Leah gave his estate notice that she was exercising her right to buy out Victor's interest in the partnership. Victor's estate sued, claiming that the partnership had been dissolved previously and requesting that someone be appointed to oversee the winding up of the partnership and a full accounting of the company's assets. When Leah filed for bankruptcy, the suits were moved to the bankruptcy court. The bankruptcy court ruled in favor of Leah, finding that the partnership had dissolved on Victor's death. Victor's estate appealed to the district court, which found that the partnership had dissolved two years before Victor's death, making Leah's attempt to buy out Victor's interest untimely. Leah appealed.

The task before the appeals court was to determine the timeliness of Leah's attempt to buy out Victor's interest in the partnership, which depended entirely on the date of the dissolution of the partnership. The court looked to the Uniform Partnership Act (UPA), which defined the dissolution of a partnership as "the change in the relation of the partners caused by any partner ceasing to be associated in the carrying on, as distinguished from the winding up, of the business." Victor's estate claimed that the dissolution of the partnership occurred at any one of three points, each at least 18 months prior to Victor's death. First, Victor excluded Leah from the partnership after they separated; second, Leah excluded Victor from the partnership after seeking special relief from the Court of Common Pleas; third, Victor filed for bankruptcy. The appeals court found that the exclusions of Leah and Victor from the partnership were not, in and of themselves, grounds for automatic dissolution of the partnership. Rather, the exclusions could have provided a basis for dissolution, had either Leah or Victor sought judicial decree of the dissolution after the exclusions. In addition, bankruptcy in and of itself is not grounds for automatic dissolution of the partnership. If the nondebtor partner does not consent to continue the partnership with the debtor, bankruptcy may be grounds for dissolution. However, Leah continued to list Victor as a general partner on the tax returns she filed for the partnership, even after he filed for bankruptcy. Thus, the appeals court found that the partnership had not dissolved prior to Victor's death in 1999 and that Leah's attempt to buy out Victor's interest in the partnership was therefore timely.

DIFFERENT TYPES OF PARTNERSHIPS

There are several types of partnerships: general partnerships, limited partnerships, and limited liability partnerships. A general partnership consists of an agreement that the partners will divide the profits (usually equally) and management responsibilities and share unlimited personal liability for the partnership's debts. Thus, in our Internet business example, you and your best friend would form a general partnership by agreeing to share the management responsibilities and profits as well as assuming unlimited personal liability.

Now imagine that your parents want to invest in your Internet business. Suppose that they want to share in the profits associated with the business, but they do not want to share in the management responsibilities or assume personal liability for the debts of the partnership. Your parents can join your business as limited partners, and your partnership would become a limited partnership. A limited partnership (LP) is an agreement between at least one general partner and at least one limited partner. The *general* partners, you and your best friend, assume unlimited personal liability for the debts of the partnership. However, your parents, the *limited* partners, assume no liability for the partnership beyond the capital they have invested in the business. Moreover, the limited partners do not have any part in the management of the company. However, limited partners pay taxes on their share of the business profit.

If a limited partner dies, the limited partnership is usually unaffected. If a general partner dies, however, the limited partnership is usually dissolved.

The limited partnership must meet certain requirements that are not expected of general partnerships. First, the limited partnership must use the word *limited* in its title. Second, to create a limited partnership, the parties must file a certificate of partnership with a state office. If the certificate of partnership is incorrectly filed, or simply not filed at all, the courts will rule that a general partnership exists. Consequently, all parties will be held personally liable for all the debts of the partnership.

Now suppose that you are an attorney and a partner in a law firm with 30 other partners. Suppose further that one of your partners is sued because he was negligent in his duties as an attorney. This partner has unlimited liability because of professional malpractice. But will you and the other partners at the firm be held liable for this partner's malpractice?

If you and your fellow partners have created a limited liability partnership (LLP), a different form of partnership than the LP, all the partners assume liability for any partner's professional malpractice to the extent of the partnership's assets. In other words, the limited liability partnership is different from other forms of partnership because the partners' liability for professional

general partnership
A partnership in which the partners divide profits and management responsibility and share unlimited personal liability for the partnership's debts.

limited partnership (LP)
A partnership consisting of at least one general partner and at least one limited partner in which the general partners assume all liability for the partnership's debts, and the limited partners assume no liability beyond their originally invested capital.

limited liability partnership (LLP)
A partnership in which all the partners assume liability for any partner's professional malpractice to the extent of the partnership's assets.

malpractice is limited to the partnership. If one partner in an LLP is guilty of malpractice, the other partners' personal assets cannot be taken. Therefore, professionals who do business together commonly use the LLP. It is the extra protection awarded partners in an LLP that makes the LLP a *separate* form of partnership from a limited partnership. Limited partnerships are not the same as limited liability partnerships.

BUT WHAT IF . . .

WHAT IF THE FACTS OF THE CASE OPENER WERE DIFFERENT?

Let's say that in the Case Opener two women, Sara and Melissa, owned Dunkin, Donuts as a partnership. Let's say that Melissa was embezzling funds from the business that made the company incur $50,000 in debt. Sara had all of the documentation to prove that Melissa had embezzled the funds from the business, and she wanted only Melissa to be liable for the debt. How would the court decide in this case?

Limited liability partnerships are fairly new; in 1991, Texas was the first state to enact a statute permitting the creation of LLPs. Almost all states now have similar statutes. Like the limited partnership, the LLP has several special requirements. First, the business name must include the phrase *Limited Liability Partnership* or the abbreviation *LLP.* Second, the parties must file a form with the secretary of the state to create the LLP.

The LLP is not considered a separate legal entity. Each partner pays taxes on his or her share of the income of the business.

An alternative form of business organization, the corporation, separates business ownership from business control.

CORPORATION

corporation

A legal entity formed by issuing stock to investors, who are the owners of the corporation.

When you hear the word *business,* you probably think about businesses such as Walmart, Kmart, McDonald's, and Nike. Perhaps the most dominant form of business organization is the corporation, a legal entity formed by issuing stock to investors, who are the owners of the corporation. The investor-owners are called shareholders. These shareholders elect a board of directors, which is responsible for managing the business. The board of directors, in turn, hires officers to run the day-to-day business.

shareholders

Investors in a corporation, who own the corporation.

The corporation is considered a separate legal entity; thus, the corporation can be sued. None of the other forms of business we have discussed are considered separate legal entities. How does a corporation become a separate legal entity? It must be created according to state law.

What are the consequences of a corporation's status as a separate legal entity? First, although the corporation can be held liable, shareholders cannot be held personally liable for the debts of the corporation. Their liability is usually limited to the amount they have invested. Second, the corporation is not dissolved when the shareholders die. Third, the corporation must pay taxes on its profits. In addition, the shareholders must pay taxes on the dividends they receive from the corporation.

S corporation

A corporation that enjoys the tax status of a partnership.

One way that a corporation can avoid this double taxation is by forming an S corporation, a business organization formed under federal tax law that is considered a corporation yet is taxed like a partnership as long as it follows certain regulations. For example, the S corporation cannot have more than 100 shareholders. Any income of the corporation is taxed when it is distributed to the shareholders, who must report the income on their personal income tax forms. S corporations are always formed under federal law. S corporations cannot be formed under state law, whereas other forms of corporations are created under state law.

Exhibit 21-4 summarizes the advantages and disadvantages of the corporate form of business.

Exhibit 21-4

Advantages and
Disadvantages of
Corporations

ADVANTAGES	DISADVANTAGES
1. Limited liability for shareholders 2. Ease of raising capital by issuing stock 3. Profits taxed as income to the shareholders, not the partners	1. Corporate income taxed twice 2. Formalities required in establishing and maintaining corporate form

LIMITED LIABILITY COMPANY

One of the newest forms of business organization in the United States is the limited liability company (LLC), an unincorporated form of business organization that many people see as combining the most advantageous features of partnerships and corporations. It combines the tax advantages and management flexibility of a partnership with the limited liability of a corporation.

This form of business organization was first recognized in the United States in 1977 in Wyoming and is now recognized in every state, although the rules regarding this new form did not evolve uniformly. As with other areas of law, the National Conference of Commissioners on Uniform State Laws recognized the desirability of bringing some uniformity to this area of law and drafted the Uniform Limited Liability Company Act (ULLCA) in 1995. In 2006, the commissioners revised the ULLCA. This act provides a model for states to follow, but it has not been uniformly adopted, so it is always necessary when establishing an LLC to check the exact requirement of the law for LLCs in the state in which you wish to create your company.

limited liability company (LLC)
An unincorporated business that is taxed like a partnership, with the members paying personal income taxes, and has the limited liability of a corporation.

Key Reasons for the Rapid Acceptance of LLCs   As previously mentioned, the LLC form offers its members the same limited liability for business debts as that offered by the corporate form. However, unlike the corporate form, it does not require profits and losses to be allocated in proportion to ownership interests. Also unlike corporations, LLCs are not required to hold an annual meeting and draft meeting minutes, so record keeping is simpler and more flexible. Unlike the case in limited partnerships, to obtain limited liability, the owner (referred to as a *member*) does not have to give up his or her right to participate in management of the LLC. In fact, an additional advantage of the LLC form is the flexibility it offers members in terms of alternative ways to structure its management.

LO 21-2

The most frequently cited advantage of the LLC is that the IRS generally treats it like a partnership or sole proprietorship, with members reporting their share of the profits and losses of the LLC on their personal tax returns, and no separate tax is assessed on the company itself, thereby allowing its members to avoid the double taxation that owners of a corporation pay. However, if an LLC's members prefer, they may elect to have the entity taxed like a corporation. In a situation in which most of the profits will be reinvested in the business, this option allows the profits to be taxed at the lower corporate rate. So, although we think of the opportunity to avoid double taxation as a key benefit of the LLC, more important perhaps is the fact that the members have the choice of how they want to be taxed.

In our global environment, an increasingly important advantage of LLCs is that members need not be citizens or permanent residents of the United States. Other organizational forms, such as the subchapter S corporation, are available only when all the owners are U.S. citizens. Finally, as with a corporation, ordinary business expenses, such as salaries paid to owners, can be deducted from the profits of an LLC before the LLC's income is allocated to its owners for tax purposes.

Formation and Management of LLCs   A limited liability company is formed by filing articles of organization in the state in which members want to establish their LLC. Although precise requirements vary by state, typically the articles include the name of the business, which must include the words *Limited Liability Company* or the initials *LLC,* its principal business address, the name and address of a registered agent for service, the names of the owners, and information about how the company's management will be structured.

LO 21-3

LLCs typically want to do business in states other than the state in which they are formed, and they usually need to register in every additional state in which they want to operate, a process typically referred to as *qualification.* Qualification simply entails filing a certificate of authority or a similar document and getting a business license in each additional state in which the business plans to operate. The LLC will usually be referred to as a *foreign company* in the additional states, and under most state statutes, the LLC will be governed by the LLC rules of the state in which it was created, regardless of where it is transacting business.

For purposes of jurisdiction, however, an LLC is considered a citizen of every state in which its members reside. Remember that a party can be sued in federal court over a matter involving more than $75,000 when diversity of citizenship exists, that is, when no plaintiff and defendant are residents of the same state. For determining whether diversity exists, a corporation is considered a resident of both the state in which it is incorporated and the state in which it has its primary place of business. However, this rule does not apply to LLCs because their citizenship is determined by the residences of their members. Consequently, if parties want the flexibility to avail themselves of the federal courts, they may want to limit their membership to individuals of only one or a few states or use a different form of business organization.

When members form an LLC, they typically draft an operating agreement, which is the foundational contract among the entity's owners. It spells out such matters as how the company is to be managed, how the profits and losses will be allocated, how interests may be transferred, and how and when the LLC may be dissolved. Any matter not covered in the operating agreement will be resolved in accordance with the state LLC statute; if a matter is not covered by the relevant statute, the principles of partnership law are generally followed.

Although an LLC is not required to have a detailed, written operating agreement, to ensure the smooth functioning of the company, it is a good idea to have such an agreement. Failure to have a detailed, written agreement may result in a court imposing standards on the company that may be very different from what the members had in mind when forming the company.

It is very important, however, to make sure that everyone understands the terms of the operating agreement, because once the parties enter into such an agreement, the courts will enforce it.

One of the key issues to be determined in the operating agreement is how the company is to be managed. There are two options: member-managed and manager-managed. Under the ULLCA, unless the operating agreement specifies otherwise, LCCs are member-managed. In a *member-managed LLC,* all members participate in management, with decisions in the ordinary course of business activities made by a majority vote. The consent of all members, however, is required to sell, lease, exchange, or otherwise dispose of all, or substantially all, of the company's property; approve a merger or conversion to a different form; undertake any other act outside the ordinary course of the company's activities; and amend the operating agreement. The members in such an LLC all have the apparent and actual authority to enter into contracts on behalf of the LLC.

In a *manager-managed LLC,* the members select a group of managers to manage the affairs of the company. The managers may be selected from the members or may be nonmembers. The managers have the apparent and actual authority to enter into contracts on behalf of the LLC, whereas the members who are not managers do not have such authority. The managers owe the LLC and its members the same fiduciary duties as the officers and directors of a corporation owe to the corporation and its shareholders.

BUT WHAT IF . . .

WHAT IF THE FACTS OF THE CASE OPENER WERE DIFFERENT?

Let's say in the Case Opener that two donut shops, Dunkin, Donuts and Harry's Bagels, joined to produce one kind of donut that turned out to be a big hit. The two companies decided to form a partnership in producing this donut together. What kind of company would this be called?

Exhibit 21-5

Comparison of Alternative Forms of Business Organization

	SOLE PROPRIETORSHIP	GENERAL PARTNERSHIP	LIMITED PARTNERSHIP	CORPORATION	LIMITED LIABILITY COMPANY
Legal Position	Not a separate legal entity.	Not a separate legal entity in most states.	A separate legal entity.	A separate legal entity.	A separate legal entity for purposes of liability but not always for taxes.
Control Considerations	Sole proprietor has total control.	Each partner is entitled to equal control.	Each partner is entitled to equal control.	Separation of ownership and control.	Members control allocation of control.
Liability	Sole proprietor has unlimited personal liability.	Each partner has unlimited personal liability for partnership debts.	Each partner has liability limited up to his or her capital contribution.	Liability is limited to loss of capital contribution.	Liability is limited to loss of capital contribution.
Lifetime	Limited to life of proprietor.	Limited by life of partners.	Limited to life of general partners.	Can have unlimited life.	Operating agreement spells out the lifetime.
Taxation	Profits are taxed directly as income to the sole proprietor.	Profits are taxed as income for partners.	Profits are taxed as income for partners.	Profits are taxed as income to corporation and as income to partners in the form of dividends.	Operating agreement spells out whether profits will be taxed as a corporation or partnership.
Transferability of Ownership Interest	Nontransferable.	Nontransferable.	Nontransferable.	Generally unlimited transfer.	Operating agreement spells out the transferability.

Dissolution of LLCs   Under the ULLCA, an LLC dissolves on the happening of any event that the operating agreement specifies will cause dissolution, the consent of all the members, the passage of 90 consecutive days during which the company has no members, or the issuance of a court order for dissolution. Under the ULLCA and most state LLC statutes, a member's voluntary withdrawal from the LLC, referred to as *dissociation,* does not terminate the LLC.

Exhibit 21-5 provides a comparison of the alternative forms of business organization.

LO 21-4

Specialized Forms of Business Organization

LO 21-5

In addition to the more traditional forms of business organization mentioned, the following specialized forms of business organization have become increasingly important: cooperatives, joint stock companies, business trusts, syndicates, joint ventures, and franchises.

COOPERATIVE

A cooperative is an organization formed by individuals to market products. The cooperative is a business organization in which the members usually pool their resources to gain some kind of advantage in the market. For instance, farmers might pool certain crops to ensure that they get a high market price for their crops. Usually, members of the cooperative receive dividends in proportion to how many times a year they engage in business with the cooperative.

cooperative
An organization formed by individuals to market new products. Individuals in a cooperative pool their resources to gain an advantage in the market.

GLOBAL Context

Limited Liability Partnerships in Japan

The limited liability partnership was not introduced in Japan until 2005. Japan's LLP limits the liability of its members to their capital contribution. Regarding profits, the LLP requires the members to manage the business and negotiate among each other to determine how profits and losses should be distributed among individual members. When establishing the rules of the LLP, Japan requires either the agreement of all members or a majority of at least two thirds of the members.

Japan also establishes additional limitations and regulations to ensure the preservation of assets of the LLPs. In Japan, the Limited Liability Partnership Law requires members to work to preserve the assets of limited liability partnerships by putting restrictions on which types of capital contribution are permitted and on the distribution of partnership assets.

Cooperatives may be incorporated or unincorporated. Unincorporated cooperatives are treated like partnerships, meaning that the members share joint liability for the cooperative's actions. Members of incorporated cooperatives, on the other hand, enjoy limited liability just as do the shareholders of a corporation.

JOINT STOCK COMPANY

joint stock company
A partnership agreement in which company members hold transferable shares whereas all the goods of the company are held in the names of the partners.

A joint stock company is a partnership agreement in which company members hold transferable shares whereas all the goods of the company are held in the names of the partners. Thus, the joint stock company is a mixture of a corporation and a partnership. As with the corporation, the members who hold shares of stock own the joint stock company. As with the partnership, the shareholders have personal liability, and in most cases the company is not a separate legal entity. The joint stock company is formed by agreement rather than by statute.

BUSINESS TRUST

business trust
A business organization governed by a group of trustees, who operate the trust for beneficiaries.

A business trust is a business organization governed by a group of trustees, who operate the trust for the beneficiaries. A written trust agreement establishes the duties and powers of the trustees and the interests of the beneficiaries.

As with a corporation, the trustees and beneficiaries enjoy limited liability, and in most states business trusts are taxed like corporations.

trustee
A person who operates a trust for beneficiaries in a business trust.

SYNDICATE

beneficiary
A person who can expect to benefit from a relationship.

An investment group that comes together for the explicit purpose of financing a specific large project is a syndicate. Syndicates are often used in the purchase of professional sports teams. The syndicate is quite useful in the sense that it can raise large amounts of money in a small amount of time. Syndicates are usually considered a type of joint venture; thus, they are almost always governed by partnership law.

syndicate
An investment group that comes together for the explicit purpose of financing a specific large project.

JOINT VENTURE

A joint venture is a relationship between two or more persons or corporations created for a specific business undertaking. This relationship may entail financing, producing, and selling goods, securities, and commodities. Participants in the joint venture usually share the profits and losses of the joint venture equally.

joint venture
An association between two or more parties wherein the parties share profits and management responsibilities with respect to a specific project.

Joint ventures can be agreements between small businesses as well as agreements between very large businesses. For example, Nestlé and Häagen-Dazs entered into a joint venture to create Ice Cream Partners, USA. Generally, joint ventures are taxed like partnerships. In fact, from a legal standpoint, partnerships and joint ventures are virtually the same. Thus, courts frequently apply partnership law to joint ventures. Joint ventures differ from partnerships, however, because a joint venture is usually created for making and selling a single product whereas a partnership creates an ongoing full business. Once all the single products are sold, the joint venture is usually terminated. The members, however, can determine when the joint venture will end.

Despite the similarities, there are several minor differences between partnerships and joint ventures in the eyes of the law. First, if one of the members of a joint venture dies, the joint venture is not automatically terminated. Second, the members of a joint venture have less authority than general partners because members of a joint venture are not agents of the other members.

The parties who comprise a joint venture usually share equal management of the task for which they have come together. They, however, can make an agreement to give one party greater management responsibilities. Furthermore, all the parties usually assume liability for the project. Each party can be held responsible for the liability of another party in the joint venture.

Like a partnership, a joint venture may be formed without drawing up a formal agreement. Case 21-1 provides a judicial discussion of the elements necessary for the establishment of a joint venture.

CASE 21-1

MEYER v. CHRISTIE
U.S. COURT OF APPEALS FOR THE TENTH CIRCUIT
634 F. 3D 1152 (2011)

FACTS: *In March of 2005, David Christie and Alexander Glen met with Alan Meyer and John Pratt and allegedly entered into an oral joint venture agreement to purchase and manage an area for residential housing. The four agreed that they would call the joint venture Junction City Partners, that Mr. Christie and Mr. Glen would be fifty/fifty partners with Mr. Meyer and Mr. Pratt, and that they would hire a contractor from Dovetail Builders. However, a few weeks later, Mr. Christie and Mr. Glen terminated their relationship with Mr. Meyer and Mr. Pratt and formed a corporation, The Bluffs, LLC. Christie and Glen then gave fifty percent partnership interest in the The Bluffs, LLC, to two outside individuals.*

At this time, plaintiffs Meyer and Pratt, joined by Dovetail Builders, filed a claim of breach of the joint venture agreement and claims of breach of fiduciary duty and wrongful dissociation against the defendants, Christie and Glen. The jury found in favor of the plaintiffs on all of these claims and found more than $9 million in damages. The defendants appealed, asserting the lack of existence and enforceability of the alleged joint venture agreement.

ISSUE: Did the defendants breach the joint venture agreement by terminating their contract with the plaintiffs?

REASONING: The defendants argue that a joint venture does not exist because the fourth factor of the following

five have not fully been met, and a party must prove these factors to prove that a joint venture exists according to *Terra Venture, Inc. v. JDN Real-Estate Overland Park, L.P.* The five factors for determining whether a joint venture exists are: (1) the joint ownership and control of property; (2) the sharing of expenses, profits, and losses and having and exercising some voice in determining the division of net earnings; (3) a community of control over and active participation in the management and direction of the business enterprise; (4) the intention of the parties, express or implied; and (5) the fixing of salaries by joint agreement.

The court was not persuaded by the defendants' argument. The court reasoned that the evidence presented in this case to prove that a joint venture existed was much stronger than the evidence available in *Terra Venture:*

> In *Terra Venture*, the only evidence suggesting the parties intended to form a joint venture was their agreement that they would refer to their project as a joint venture in press releases. In this case, by contrast, the evidence was that the parties agreed they would in fact form a joint venture, not just that they would refer to their project as such. The evidence also indicated that Plaintiffs and Defendants informed not just the public but also their employees and attorneys that they were jointly working on the project. Furthermore, although it is undisputed the parties did not actually share expenses, profits, and losses, the evidence introduced at trial was that they agreed they would share future profits and losses and would true-up expenses when the corporation paperwork had been completed.

(continued)

DECISION AND REMEDY: Mr. Meyers and Mr. Pratt's claims against defendants were affirmed.

SIGNIFICANCE: This case discusses the elements that are required to prove that a joint venture exists. The case also provides an illustration of how a judge weighs the strengths and weaknesses of various pieces of evidence to determine that a joint venture exists.

CRITICAL THINKING

The process of critical thinking requires us to ask critical questions to evaluate whatever reasoning we encounter, even if, as in this case, the reasoning appears very convincing. Of the five criteria Judge McKay uses to determine whether a joint venture exists, which criterion do you think he provides the least justification for?

ETHICAL DECISION MAKING

Essentially, the court ruled in favor of the plaintiffs and determined that the defendants did in fact breach a joint venture agreement. What theory or theories of ethical decision making might lead a judge to rule in favor of the defendants instead? Who in the business community would be affected if this theory of ethical decision making was employed? Explain.

---

franchise

A business arrangement between an owner of a trade name or trademark and a person who sells goods or services under the trade name or trademark.

franchisor

The owner of the trade name or trademark in a franchise.

franchisee

The seller of goods or services under a trade name or trademark in a franchise.

FRANCHISE

When you go into McDonald's to eat lunch, what type of business are you patronizing? You are likely eating at a **franchise**, a business that exists because of an arrangement between the **franchisor**, an owner of a trade name or trademark, and the **franchisee**, a person who sells goods or services under the trade name or trademark.

What are the advantages and disadvantages for the franchisor and the franchisee? Exhibits 21-6 and 21-7 summarize these advantages and disadvantages. First, the franchisee enjoys the franchisor's help in opening the franchise. Second, think about how many times you have driven through a strange town and felt relieved when you saw a Burger King. Even though you may have never been to that town before and did not know who controlled that particular business, you know Burger King. Before you walk into the restaurant, you know almost exactly what will be on the menu. Thus, on the one hand, the franchisee benefits from the franchisor's strong trade name or trademark. Moreover, the franchisee benefits from the franchisor's worldwide advertising of the trade name or trademark. The franchisor, on the other hand, does not take a large risk in creating the franchise, yet it can greatly benefit from the income it receives from the franchisee.

Exhibit 21-6

Advantages and Disadvantages to the Franchisee of Starting a Franchise

ADVANTAGES	DISADVANTAGES
1. Help from the franchisor in starting the franchise	1. Must meet the franchisor's standards or risk losing the franchise
2. Instant recognition due to the franchisor's strong trademark or trade name	2. Has little to no creative control over the business
3. Benefits from the franchisor's worldwide advertising	

ADVANTAGES	DISADVANTAGES
1. Low risk in starting a franchise	1. Has little control over the franchise
2. Increased income from franchises	2. Can become liable for the franchise if it exerts too much control

Exhibit 21-7

Advantages and Disadvantages to the Franchisor of Starting a Franchise

Exhibit 21-8

Types of Franchises

FRANCHISE TYPE	DESCRIPTION
Chain-style business operation	Franchisor helps franchisee set up a business run under the franchisor's business name according to the franchisor's usual methods and standards.
Distributorship	Franchisor licenses franchisee to sell the franchisor's product in a specific area.
Manufacturing arrangement	Franchisor provides the franchisee with the technical knowledge needed to manufacture the franchisor's product.

Exhibit 21-9

The Top 10 Global Franchises, 2013

1. 7-Eleven, Inc.
2. Subway
3. Hampton Hotels
4. Kumon Math & Reading Centers
5. McDonald's
6. KFC Corp.
7. Jiffy Lube International, Inc.
8. Pizza Hut, Inc.
9. Baskin-Robbins
10. Anytime Fitness

Source: Ranked by *Entrepreneur Magazine* on the basis of financial strength and stability, growth rate, and size of the system, www.entrepreneur.com/franchises/rankings/topglobal-115388/2013,-1.html

Generally, franchises fall into one of three categories. McDonald's and Burger King are examples of chain-style business operations. In a chain-style business operation, the franchise operates under the franchisor's business name and is required to follow the franchisor's standards and methods of business operation.

The second category of franchises is the distributorship. Distributorships are franchises in which the franchisor manufactures a product and licenses a dealer to sell the product in an exclusive territory. A car dealership is an example of a distributorship.

Finally, the third category of franchises is the manufacturing arrangement. In a manufacturing arrangement, the franchisor provides the franchisee with a formula or necessary ingredient to manufacture a product. The franchisee then manufactures the product and sells it according to the franchisor's standards.

Exhibit 21-8 describes the various types of franchises. Exhibit 21-9 provides a sense of just how important franchises are for the market economy.

Look at Case 21-2 to see how the supreme court of Arkansas determined whether a franchise agreement existed between Mary Kay Cosmetics and Janet Isbell.

Franchise Law   Because franchisors are usually larger than franchisees and have more resources, they often have the upper hand in franchise relationships. Federal and state laws, however, have been established to protect the franchisee in the franchise relationship.

A franchise is a contractual relationship between the franchisor and the franchisee. Thus, contract law, and the Uniform Commercial Code in particular, applies to the franchise relationship. If the terms of the contract are not met, either side can sue for breach of contract. For example, in *Ford Motor Co. v. Lyons,*[1] Lyons sued Ford for breach of its dealer franchise obligations. In the franchise agreement, Ford had agreed to send factory representatives to the dealership and offer Lyons assistance with his business. However, Ford failed to perform its duties. Lyons sued,

chain-style business operation

A type of franchise in which the franchise operates under the franchisor's business name and is required to follow the franchisor's standards and methods of business operation.

distributorship

A type of franchise in which the franchisor manufactures a product and licenses a dealer to sell the product in an exclusive territory.

manufacturing arrangement

A type of franchise in which the franchisor provides the franchisee with a formula or necessary ingredient to manufacture a product.

[1] 405 N.W.2d 354 (Wis. Ct. App. 1987).

CASE 21-2

MARY KAY, INC., A/K/A MARY KAY COSMETICS, INC. v. JANET ISBELL
SUPREME COURT OF ARKANSAS
338 Ark. 556; 999 S.W.2d 669; 1999 Ark. LEXIS 443

FACTS: *In 1980, Janet Isbell signed an agreement to become a beauty consultant for Mary Kay. This agreement established that she would sell products to customers at home demonstration parties, but she was prohibited from selling the products in retail establishments. In 1981 and 1991, Isbell signed agreements to become a unit sales director. In addition to serving as a beauty consultant, Isbell recruited beauty consultants. In 1994, she rented a space in a shopping mall to serve as a training center. In April 1994, Mary Kay's legal coordinator contacted Isbell, stating that the store space was not to be used to sell Mary Kay products. According to the agreement, Isbell's office could not look like a Mary Kay store. In September 1995, the vice president of sales development notified Isbell that Mary Kay was terminating its agreements with Isbell. Isbell filed suit against Mary Kay, claiming that she was a franchise under the Arkansas Franchise Practices Act. She argued that Mary Kay violated the Franchise Practices Act by refusing to comply with the FPA provisions for termination of a franchise. The trial court granted summary judgment to Isbell, but it did not explain why Isbell's relationship with Mary Kay could be considered a franchise. The trial court ruled as a matter of law that Mary Kay's termination of Isbell had violated the act, and a jury awarded Isbell $110,583.33. Mary Kay appealed.*

ISSUE: Was Janet Isbell a franchisee of Mary Kay?

REASONING: Sections 4-72-203 and 4-72-202 (6) of the Arkansas Franchise Practices Act establish that the act applies only to a franchise that contemplates or requires the franchise to establish or maintain a place of business in the state. A place of business is defined as "a fixed geographical location at which the franchisee [1] displays for sale and sells the franchisor's goods or [2] offers for sale and sells the franchisor's services." In this case, there was no evidence that Isbell sold Mary Kay products from a fixed geographic location. Isbell was, in fact, prohibited from selling products from her office or center. Isbell was to sell products in customers' homes. In addition, the agreements Isbell signed make no mention of a fixed geographic location as a place of business. There was no evidence that Mary Kay contemplated that Isbell would maintain a place of a business in Arkansas.

DECISION AND REMEDY: The Arkansas Franchise Practices Act did not apply to Isbell because Isbell did not meet the definition of a franchise. The trial court's ruling was reversed, and the case was dismissed.

SIGNIFICANCE OF THE CASE: This case raises questions about legal protections for people like Janet Isbell who sell products for companies that, like Mary Kay, don't require the sellers to maintain a fixed place of business. If those sellers are not franchisees, what is their role? Independent contractors? Agents? Employees? What legal protections are offered to the sellers?

CRITICAL THINKING

What missing information would you call for when considering the facts of this case?

Would you interpret the Arkansas Franchise Practices Act and how it applies to the facts of the case differently than the judge did? Why or why not?

ETHICAL DECISION MAKING

Consider the WH framework. What values was Isbell promoting? What values were in conflict? Was the court fair in assessing her actions in light of these values?

bringing forth evidence showing that Ford had intentionally failed to perform its contractual duties because one of the other dealership franchises was jealous of the dealership territory Ford had given to Lyons as part of the franchise agreement.

In addition, several laws that are more specific have been established to govern the franchise relationship. For example, the Federal Trade Commission has a franchise rule requiring franchisors to present prospective franchisees with the material facts necessary for the franchisee to make an informed decision about entering a franchise relationship. Moreover, the Automobile Dealers' Franchise Act of 1965 prohibits car dealership franchisors from terminating franchise relationships in bad faith. Thus, for example, DaimlerChrysler could not terminate its franchise relationship with a dealer because the dealer failed to meet impossible standards. Finally, the Petroleum Marketing Practices Act of 1979 outlines the reasons for which a franchisor may terminate a gas station franchise. Franchises must also be aware of federal antitrust laws. Antitrust laws prohibit specific forms of anticompetitive behavior and might be applicable to franchises.

Many states have adopted additional laws to protect franchisees. Fifteen states, for example, require franchisors to provide prospective franchisees with a host of information about the franchise relationship before the agreement can be signed. What ethical standards do you think these 15 states are promoting in their decision to mandate franchise protections?

Creation of the Franchise   In the franchise relationship, the parties make a franchise agreement regarding various factors: the payment to the franchisor, the location of the franchise, the restrictions the franchisee must follow, and the method of termination of the franchise.

> **franchise agreement**
> A contract whereby a company (the franchisor) grants permission (a license) to another entity (the franchisee) to use the franchisor's name, trademark, or copyright in the operation of a business and associated sale of goods in return for payment.

First, the franchise agreement usually states that the franchisee is to pay a large sum to the franchisor for use of the trade name or trademark. Moreover, the agreement determines what percentage of the income from the sales of the goods will go to the franchisor.

Second, the agreement usually determines where the franchise will be located. If the franchise requires a building, the agreement specifies who will pay for buying or renting the building. Similarly, if the building must be constructed, the agreement states who is responsible for the costs of the construction of the building.

Third, the franchisor usually includes in the agreement certain business practices that are forbidden and other business standards that must be met. For example, the franchisor might require the business to meet specific levels of cleanliness. Moreover, the franchisor can set certain sales quotas as well as requirements for record keeping by the franchisee. The franchisor can require the franchisee to purchase certain supplies from the franchisor at a set price, but the franchisor cannot attempt to establish the price at which the franchisee must sell the goods.

The disagreement in the opening scenario for this chapter arose because of the third factor in franchise agreements. Because many Dunkin' Donuts restaurants are owned by franchisees, Dunkin' Donuts established guidelines and policies that promote business practices that enhance the quality of food and services at each restaurant. Dunkin' Donuts also has quality, safety, and cleanliness standards for each of its franchises. The franchise agreement stipulated that Dunkin' Donuts could inspect Bhayani's restaurant at any reasonable time.

Although the franchisor has the legal authority to ensure that the franchisee maintains the quality of goods and services associated with the franchise, the franchisor must be cautious. If it exercises too much authority in the day-to-day affairs of the business, the franchisor could be held liable for the torts of the franchisee's employees.

Termination of the Franchise   The franchise agreement establishes how the franchise will be terminated. The franchise is usually established for a trial period, such as a year. If the franchisee does not meet the requirements established in the franchise agreement, the franchisor can terminate the franchise agreement, but the franchisor must give the franchisee sufficient notice of the termination. Furthermore, the termination usually must have cause. Much of the litigation associated with franchises regards wrongful termination of a franchise. The typical agreement gives the franchisor broad authority to terminate a franchise. In recent years, however, many states have been giving the franchisee greater termination protection.

The courts usually rely heavily on the written franchise agreement when determining whether a franchise was wrongfully terminated. Look at Case 20-3, which illustrates the importance of the written franchise agreement.

CASE 21-3

COUSINS SUBS SYSTEMS, INC. v. MICHAEL R. MCKINNEY
U.S. DISTRICT COURT FOR THE EASTERN DISTRICT OF WISCONSIN
59 F. Supp. 2d 816 (1999)

FACTS: *Cousins Subs Systems entered into an agreement with Michael McKinney, a Minnesota businessman who owned a company that operated a chain of gas stations, for McKinney to operate several Cousins submarine sandwich shops. The sub shops were to be placed in the gas stations. In April 1998, McKinney became disillusioned with the agreement and terminated the agreement. McKinney claimed that Cousins guaranteed him annual sales at each of his franchises ranging from $250,000 to $500,000. Furthermore, McKinney argued that Cousins promised to provide advertising for the franchises. McKinney also claimed that Cousins guaranteed it would provide assistance in recruiting other franchises. McKinney alleges that he terminated the agreement because Cousins failed to uphold these promises. In June 1998, Cousins filed suit against McKinney for wrongfully terminating the agreement with Cousins. Later in 1998, McKinney filed a counterclaim against Cousins. Cousins filed a motion to dismiss the counterclaim.*

ISSUE: Did Cousins Subs Systems make misleading statements of material facts?

REASONING: McKinney alleges that Cousins violated the Minnesota statute prohibiting businesses from using false statements of material facts (or omissions of material facts) to sell franchises. McKinney claims that Cousins made false verbal statements of material facts; however, when an alleged verbal statement contradicts a written contract, the written contract carries more weight. In this case, the written contracts, signed by McKinney and Cousins and later entered as exhibits, contradict the verbal statements McKinney claims Cousins made. The contracts state that no promises were made regarding the profit McKinney would earn, that advertising was McKinney's responsibility, and that the contracts contained all terms, conditions, and promises made by Cousins.

DECISION AND REMEDY: As demonstrated by the contracts McKinney signed, Cousins did not make any misleading statements of material facts. The counterclaim was dismissed.

SIGNIFICANCE: It is unclear whether Cousins made the verbal promises alleged by McKinney. Regardless, McKinney did sign contracts that contradicted the alleged verbal promises. This case demonstrates how important it is for businesspeople to read contracts thoroughly and to ensure that all terms, conditions, and promises are contained in those contracts.

CRITICAL THINKING

What are the primary facts of this case? How would you word the issue of the case in your own words?

The judge stated that the written terms of the contracts between Cousins and McKinney were inconsistent with any alleged oral agreements that they made. Do you agree that written contracts should overrule oral agreements in most instances? Why or why not?

ETHICAL DECISION MAKING

The court ruled in favor of Cousins. Who are the primary stakeholders affected by the court's ruling for Cousins?

The decisions of a court have implications for business ethics. Although Chapter 2 distinguishes between what the law requires of a manager and what ethics requires, the relationship between the law and ethics is reciprocal. Ethical judgments lie behind various laws, but the law also has impacts on business ethics. For example, in Case 21-3, the court's decision is reminding us that business ethics must pay attention to the various stakeholders who feel the impacts of any business agreement.

SUMMARY

Major Forms of Business Organization	*Sole proprietorship:* The owner has total control and unlimited personal liability, and profits are taxed directly as income to the sole proprietor.
	General partnership: For most purposes, the partnership is not a legal entity, and each partner has equal control and unlimited liability, with profits that are taxed as income for partners.
	Limited partnership: Limited partnerships are similar to general partnerships, except that limited partners' liability is limited to the extent of their capital contributions.
	Corporation: A corporation is a separate legal entity wherein the owners' liability is limited to the amount of their contributions, and the profits are taxed as income to the corporation.
	Limited liability company: A limited liability company combines the best tax and liability features of partnerships and corporations. In an LLC, all members may participate in management of the business entity while enjoying a shield of limited liability for their personal assets.
Specialized Forms of Business Organization	The specialized forms are cooperatives, joint stock companies, syndicates, business trusts, joint ventures, and franchises.
	A *franchise* is a contractual relationship between the franchisor and the franchisee. Thus, contract law, and the Uniform Commercial Code in particular, applies to the franchise relationship. If the terms of the contract are not met, either side can sue for breach of contract.

Point/Counterpoint

Should a New Restaurateur Open a New Location of a Restaurant Franchise Rather Than Become a Sole Proprietor?	
YES	**NO**
A businessperson new to the restaurant business should open a restaurant as part of an existing franchise rather than begin an individual restaurant as a sole proprietor. A new restaurateur encounters substantial risks when opening a business as a sole proprietor. Sole proprietors have unlimited personal liability, meaning they are held solely accountable for the finances in their businesses. For example, a sole proprietor often needs to provide her house as collateral to obtain a small business loan. Additionally, a restaurant sole proprietor can be held personally liable for injury in her restaurant. This	A new restaurateur should open a new restaurant as a sole proprietor rather than as a franchisee. A businessperson new to the restaurant business has greater potential for long-term success as a sole proprietor than as a franchisee. The main appeal of a franchise is less personal risk and liability at the start of the business. However, with careful research and expert advice, sole proprietors can obtain low-risk, longer-term loans that are unlikely to jeopardize their personal assets. Furthermore, sole proprietors always hold the option of later adding a full business partner or a limited partner. Franchisees, however, usually do not retain that right after entering

personal liability means the restaurant owner could be personally sued for employee or customer injury. One main advantage of becoming a franchisee is that the franchisee usually is not held solely liable for an injury.

One primary concern should be that the businessperson is *new* to the restaurant business. The franchisee encounters limited financial risk. Additionally, a franchisor can fulfill the vital role of supervision and provide crucial guidance to a new businessperson. Because restaurant franchises are already successful, the new franchisee has a clear idea of business practices that have been proved successful by the franchisor.

Further, most franchisors offer new franchisees a clear outline of forbidden practices that would endanger the new franchise and minimum standards (cleanliness, service) that will assist the new franchise. Sole proprietors must experience a trial-and-error time period as they learn which business practices should be implemented. The franchisor's assistance eliminates the trial-and-error period because the franchisee is informed of and warned not to repeat past errors.

business with the franchisor. To decrease liability, sole proprietors can implement additional safety measures.

One major disadvantage of opening a new franchise is that the new franchise must pay the franchisor a percentage of profits as long as the new franchise exists. For a sole proprietor, after debts are repaid, all profits are kept in the business for improvements and personal income.

Franchises are extremely restrictive in creativity. A sole proprietor is truly her own boss. A sole proprietor can change the look of her restaurant at any time.

Sole proprietors can determine how many and which hours they would like to be in operation. Sole proprietors can also decide whether to hire a manager or manage their restaurants directly. In addition, sole proprietors can decide how many and what kind of individuals they would like to employ at their restaurants. Franchisees often face restrictions and limitations regarding size, hours, management, and employment practices.

Perhaps most important, a sole proprietor retains flexibility if the economy changes, which it frequently does. If need be, a sole proprietor can simply uproot the restaurant and move to a different location. Further, a sole proprietor can change her restaurant's menu and appearance if the customer constituency in her area changes.

Questions & Problems

1. What is the distinction between a general partnership and a limited partnership?

2. Explain why a cooperative could not claim to be a syndicate.

3. Suppose you were asked to review and assess a franchise agreement. What responsibilities would you expect to be included in that agreement?

4. Tracy Allen rented a home in which she had been residing since the summer of 1998. The landlord-owner of the house later failed to pay taxes on the property, and on March 16, 2000, Hard Assets LLC acquired the property from the owner in lieu of foreclosure. When Hard Assets obtained title, it did not intend to lease the property, nor were its members aware that Allen was living at the property. Once Hard Assets became aware that Allen was residing at the property, Hard Assets advised her and her family that they were not supposed to be there and that they had 30 days to vacate the premises. After 30 days, Allen had not vacated the property. While residing at the property, the children living with Allen suffered elevated blood-lead levels and were allegedly injured

from lead paint exposure. As a result, the children's mother filed a suit against one of the members of the LLC for violations of the city's housing code and negligence. Should the member of the LLC be held personally liable for the alleged injuries of the children who lived at Allen's home? Why or why not? [*Allen v. Dackman*, 964 A.2d 210 (2009).]

5. The Meehans entered into a franchise agreement with Consumers Club. However, the Meehans' franchise failed. The Meehans alleged that, just before they entered into the franchise agreement, Consumers Club made false statements and misleading representations to them about (1) earnings, (2) success rates, (3) pricing, and (4) warranties, support, and service. The district court dismissed both counts, determining that the express disclaimers contained in the franchise agreement precluded the Meehans from proving justifiable reliance, if any misrepresentations were made. Meehan contended the disclaimers do not defeat the misrepresentation claim because they do not contain evidence of whether actual representations were made and relied on. How do you think the court ruled

regarding the alleged false and misleading representations made regarding the Meehans' franchise? (*Hint:* Review the discussion on Case 20-3 and the power of written franchise agreements.) [*Meehan v. United Consumers Club Franchising Corp.,* 312 F.3d 909 (2002).]

6. Mike Karimi has been in the hotel management business since the 1980s. The name of Karimi's company is MAK, LLC, which manages and operates several hotels in the United States. In 2004, two brothers, the Khatris, who were friends of Karimi's, wanted him to take over the operation of one of their hotels. The problem with the hotel was that only 40 out of the 186 hotel rooms were suitable for guests to inhabit. This concerned Karimi, who nevertheless agreed to take over the hotel. Karimi received the rights to the hotel from the previous leasers. The hotel, Red Lion, wrote up a franchise agreement with Karimi. In the agreement, it states: "An 'Event of Default' will occur if you fail to satisfy or comply with any of the obligations, requirements, conditions, or terms set forth in this Agreement, the Manual, or any attachment to this Agreement. An 'Event of Default' will also occur if you make any misrepresentations to us, whether in entering into this Agreement, or in the performance of your obligations to us." After the renovations were underway, a representative of Red Lion Hotels decided to tour the hotel to check on the renovations. This representative decided that the hotel looked "old and tired." In early 2008, Red Lion sent Karimi a "notice of default and termination." Did Red Lion have the right to send this notice to Karimi? [*Red Lion Hotels Franchising Inc. v. MAK, LLC,* 663 F.3d 1080 (2011).]

7. Brothers Aurelio and Hugo V. Garcia founded a trash removal business called Garcia's, Inc., in the early 2000s. Hugo served as president and director. Garcia's decided to lease trucks and equipment to United Leasing. However, United required, as a part of the agreement, that the stock of Garcia's would be collateral and that United could vote Garcia's share in the company if Garcia's defaulted. Suddenly, United claimed that Garcia's had defaulted, and United liquidated the company's assets and took control. James C. Lehner, a former employee of United, formed the Lehner Family Business Trust in 2005, and shortly thereafter Lehner offered Hugo $50,000 to assign all claims against United to the trust. Hugo executed the requested assignment, which assigned all of the legal claims, rights, and causes of action that Garcia's, "a Virginia corporation in dissolution," and Hugo, "individually and as trustee in liquidation for Garcia's, Inc.," had under the equipment leases with United and otherwise. The Lehner Trust sued United Leasing

for breach of contract, claiming that "[b]y assignment, the Trust acquired all of Garcia's claims, causes of action, choses in action, rights of action, rights and interests against [United Leasing] and all claims and rights, etc., relating to the Garcia's Leases." Also, the trust claimed that United had been secretly holding over $1 million from Garcia's, which rightfully deserved it. Was the Trust right in suing United Leasing? [*United Leasing Corp. v. Lehner Family Business Trust,* 279 Va. 510 (2010).]

8. Milburn Pierce was the sole proprietor of the Pierce Painting Company, a painting contracting company with two employees in addition to Pierce. Pierce bought workers' compensation insurance for his business through the Louisiana Workers' Compensation Corporation, but in the written agreement, he chose to exclude himself from the policy's coverage. In August 2002, Pierce was working on a job for Tom Fullilove Construction Company when he fell off a roof. Pierce broke his left wrist and left femur and incurred more than $30,000 in medical bills for his treatment and therapy. Pierce filed a compensation claim in September 2002, and Fullilove paid his medical bills. In October 2002, Fullilove sued Pierce for reimbursement of the compensation payments. The Office of Workers' Compensation found for Fullilove. Pierce appealed, arguing that a Louisiana statute provided that a "sole proprietor with respect to such sole proprietorship may by written agreement elect not to be covered" under workers' compensation insurance. Thus, Pierce argued, he had elected not to be covered with respect to his sole proprietorship, a separate legal entity. But with respect to Tom Fullilove Construction Company, Pierce argued that he never elected not to be covered. How do you think the appellate court ruled? Why? [*Pierce v. Tom Fullilove Constr. Co.,* 892 So. 2d 757 (2005).]

9. 1-800-Got Junk? is a junk removal franchise business headquartered in Vancouver, British Columbia, Canada. In late 2003, Got Junk entered a franchise agreement with Millenium Asset Recovery, Inc. The agreement stated that the franchisee, Millennium, would pay a percentage of its gross revenue to Got Junk on every junk removal job it performs. In 2007, Got Junk terminated Millennium's franchise on the grounds that Millennium deliberately had not reported certain jobs and the gross revenue derived from such jobs. Was Got Junk right in terminating the agreement? Why or why not? [*1-800-Got Junk? LLC v. Superior Court (Millennium Asset Recovery, Inc.),* Cal.App.4th, Second Dist., Div. Three. (2010).]

10. Chic Miller operated a General Motors (GM) franchise car dealership. His written franchise agreement with GM stipulated that Miller had to maintain

a floor-plan financing agreement with a lender to enable him to buy new cars from GM. Initially, Miller maintained a line of credit with a GM affiliate (GMAC), but he terminated the agreement because he felt that GMAC charged him an exorbitant interest rate. Miller was able to find another line of credit from Chase Manhattan Bank, but Chase withdrew its financing agreement with Miller after one year. Miller attempted to resume the agreement with GMAC, but GMAC refused. Miller alleged *ipse dixit* (an assertion without evidence) that GMAC discouraged other lenders from providing a line of credit to Miller. GM then notified Miller that it was terminating its franchise relationship with him because he failed to satisfy the financing stipulation of the written franchise agreement. Two months after receiving this notice from GM, Miller attempted to sell his franchise to Kenneth Crowley, the owner of another car dealership. GM rejected this sale, alleging that Miller no longer had a franchise to sell because GM had terminated the franchise agreement two months earlier. Miller sued GM for failing to help his franchise obtain floor-plan financing and for rejecting the sale of his franchise to Crowley. How do you think the court ruled in this case? What requirements must GM meet to terminate a franchise lawfully? Did GM meet those requirements? [*Chic Miller's Chevrolet, Inc. v. GMC,* 352 F. Supp. 2d 251 (2005).]

11. Margaret Miller operated an H&R Block tax-preparation franchise for 15 years. She hired William Hehlen as an income tax return preparer for five years, from 1997 to 2001. Each year, Miller and Hehlen signed an employment agreement drawn up by H&R Block. The 2001 agreement was between Hehlen and "Margaret Miller, doing business as H&R Block," and included stipulations prohibiting Hehlen from reproducing confidential business information and from soliciting clients away from Miller's business. Hehlen maintained on his home computer a spreadsheet of customer names that he obtained from Miller. In April 2001, H&R Block terminated its franchise agreement with Miller, and Miller subsequently operated her business as a sole proprietorship under the name of MJM & Associates. Hehlen's employment with Miller ended after the 2001 tax season. In December 2001, Miller sent advertising postcards to clients referring to Hehlen as one of her associates. When Hehlen, who went to work for another H&R Block office, learned of the postcards, he began telephoning the customers whose names he had obtained from Miller. Miller learned of the calls in February 2002 and filed a cease-and-desist action against Hehlen, arguing that Hehlen was violating his employment contract with Miller. Hehlen argued that his employment contract was with Miller's H&R Block franchise, which ceased to exist after April 2001. Do you think Hehlen's employment contract was signed with Miller's franchise or with Miller's sole proprietorship? If you think Hehlen's contract was with Miller's franchise, should Miller have the right to enforce the contract provisions after H&R Block terminated her franchise agreement? Why or why not? [*Miller v. Hehlen,* 104 P.3d 193 (2005).]

12. Harvey Pierce was a work-release inmate from the local county jail who worked at an Arby's franchise restaurant owned by Dennis Rasmussen, Inc. (DRI). One day in June 1999, Pierce walked off the job without permission and crossed the street to wait for his former girlfriend, Robin Kerl, and her fiancé, David Jones, in the parking lot of the Walmart store where both Kerl and Jones worked. When Kerl and Jones exited the store, Pierce shot both of them in the head, killing Jones and seriously injuring and permanently disabling Kerl. Pierce then shot himself and died immediately. Kerl and Jones's estate sued Arby's and DRI for negligent supervision, hiring, and retention, arguing that Arby's, the franchisor, was vicariously liable for the negligence of DRI, the franchisee. Do you think Arby's should be vicariously liable for the negligence of its franchisee? Why or why not? [*Kerl v. DRI and Arby's, Inc.,* 682 N.W.2d 328 (2004).]

Business Organizations

CHAPTER 22

Corporations: Formation and Organization

CASE OPENER

The Formation of the Facebook Corporation

On October 28, 2003, Mark Zuckerberg was a sophomore at Harvard University when he created a website called Facemash that was similar to an existing web service called Hot or Not. However, the following semester, in 2004, Zuckerberg began working on a new code for a new website to be called Facebook. His friends Eduardo Saverin, Dustin Moskovitz, Andrew McCollum, and Chris Hughes joined Zuckerberg to promote the new social networking site. Membership on the site quickly grew from only students at Harvard College to students at most universities in the United States. In the summer of 2004, Facebook was incorporated. As a corporation, Facebook is an artificial person, a status with legal ramifications for both the corporate entity and its owners.

1. What are the legal implications of Facebook's status as a corporation?
2. How are corporations formed? What factors should a businessperson consider in forming a corporation?

LEARNING OBJECTIVES

After reading this chapter, you will be able to answer the following questions:

LO 22-1 What are the powers granted to corporations by the states?

LO 22-2 How are corporations formed?

LO 22-3 What is the role of a director, an officer, and a shareholder?

LO 22-4 What are the duties of directors, officers, and shareholders?

LO 22-5 In what ways can a director, officer, and shareholder be held liable?

LO 22-6 What are the rights of directors, officers, and shareholders?

LO 22-7 What are mergers and consolidations?

This chapter explains the steps necessary to establish a corporate entity. Although state law generally governs corporations and each state has its own corporate regulatory statutes, the Revised Model Business Corporation Act (RMBCA) is the basis of most state statutes. More than 25 states have adopted at least part of RMBCA.

In addition, the chapter describes the legal relationships among the many groups of individuals with various priorities and agendas within a corporation. Not surprisingly, these priorities and agendas often come into conflict. To ensure that individuals, corporations, and the public achieve fair outcomes to conflicts within corporations, statutory laws have been designed to delegate particular roles, duties, and rights to each group of individuals within corporations.

Characteristics of Corporations

How are corporations different from other forms of business organization?

LEGAL ENTITY

In U.S. law, corporations are legal entities. In other words, corporations exist separately from their shareholders. Thus, corporations can sue or be sued by others.

RIGHTS AS A PERSON AND A CITIZEN

Courts consider corporations to be legal persons. Thus, in most cases, corporations, like natural persons, have certain rights according to the Bill of Rights. Specifically, the Fifth and Fourteenth Amendments state that government cannot deprive any person of life, liberty, or property without due process. Courts have held that corporations are persons in this case and thus have a right to due process.

Furthermore, courts consider corporations to be persons with respect to the Fourth Amendment. Hence, the Fourth Amendment protects corporations from unreasonable searches and seizures. Finally, courts consider corporations to be persons that have free-speech rights protected by the First Amendment.

CREATURE OF THE STATE

State incorporation statutes establish the requirements for corporate formation. Each individual corporation's charter creates a contract between that corporation and the state.

LIMITED LIABILITY

Because corporations are legal entities distinct from their shareholders, corporations are liable for corporate actions. Shareholders' liability, therefore, is limited to their investment in the corporation. For example, in 1977 Big O Tire Dealers sued Goodyear Tire & Rubber Company. Big O Tire accused Goodyear of copying its BIGFOOT trademark on new tires. The court agreed and awarded Big O Tire several million dollars in damages. The Goodyear corporation, and not individual Goodyear shareholders, paid the damages. Although payment of damages to Big O Tire may have reduced the dividends shareholders received, the court did not hold the shareholders individually liable for any portion of the award.

FREE TRANSFERABILITY OF CORPORATE SHARES

Generally, shareholders can freely transfer their corporate shares. For example, shareholders can sell their shares or give them to charity.

PERPETUAL EXISTENCE

The life of a corporation does not end when the lives of its owners end. If shareholders die, corporations do not dissolve. Similarly, if corporate directors or officers withdraw or die, the corporation continues to exist. In some cases, the *articles of incorporation,* a document a corporation files with the state explaining its organization, may include a restriction on the duration of the corporation. Otherwise, in most states, corporations continue to exist indefinitely.

A small number of states, however, set a maximum length of existence for corporations. After the maximum duration expires, corporations must formally renew their corporate existence.

CENTRALIZED MANAGEMENT

Unless the articles of incorporation specify otherwise, shareholders do not participate in corporate management. Instead, shareholders elect a board of directors. The board, in turn, selects officers to manage the day-to-day business of the corporation.

CORPORATE TAXATION

Because corporations are separate legal entities, government taxes their income directly. (S corporations are an exception; this chapter discusses them, and their tax advantages, in detail later.) Corporations must pay federal and state taxes on their income.

Corporations, however, have control over their income. Corporations can distribute their income to shareholders in the form of dividends, although they do not receive tax deductions for distributing these dividends. When corporations distribute income to shareholders, the shareholders pay taxes on that income. Because the corporation pays income taxes and the shareholders are also paying taxes on their dividends, the dividends are subjected to double taxation, thus creating a disadvantage for corporations. Alternatively, corporations can keep profits, or retained earnings, to reinvest. Corporations' investment of retained earnings can lead to higher stock prices, thus benefiting shareholders when they sell their stock.

dividend
A distribution of corporate profits or income ordered by the directors and paid to the shareholders.

retained earnings
Profits that a corporation keeps.

BUT WHAT IF . . .

WHAT IF THE FACTS OF THE CASE OPENER WERE DIFFERENT?

Let's say in the Case Opener that after Zuckerberg had Facebook incorporated, he and the other corporate shareholders were on a private jet when it crashed, killing all the travelers. Without any of the shareholders, what would happen to Facebook? Does state or federal government put a limit on how long a corporation can exist?

LIABILITY FOR OFFICERS AND EMPLOYEES

Because the relationship between corporations and their directors, officers, and employees is an agency relationship, corporations are liable for torts and crimes committed by their agents during the scope of their employment. Courts refer to this liability as the doctrine of *respondeat superior* (Latin for "let the master answer"). Although in the past courts were reluctant to impose criminal liability on corporations, prosecutions today are much more common.

Exhibit 22-1 presents a summary of nine characteristics of corporations.

LO 22-1

Exhibit 22-1

Characteristics of Corporations

1. Separate legal entity
2. Status as "legal person" and "citizen"
3. Creature of the state
4. Limited liability of shareholders
5. Free transferability of corporate shares
6. Perpetual existence
7. Centralized management separate from owners
8. Unique taxation method
9. Corporate liability for torts and crimes of agents

Corporate Powers

Because corporations are creatures of the state, they have only those powers states grant them. States give powers to corporations through state incorporation statutes and through each corporation's articles of incorporation.

EXPRESS AND IMPLIED POWERS

State incorporation statutes typically grant the following express powers to corporations: the power to have perpetual existence, the power to sue and be sued in the corporation's name, the power to acquire property, the power to make contracts and borrow money, the power to lend money, the power to make charitable donations, and the power to establish rules for managing the corporation. In addition, corporations may take whatever actions are necessary to execute these express powers. Thus, corporations have implied powers. Generally, the statement of corporate purpose in each corporation's articles of incorporation gives each corporation its implied powers.

ULTRA VIRES ACT

If corporations act beyond their express and implied powers, the act is called an *ultra vires* (Latin for "beyond powers") act. Corporations commit *ultra vires* acts most frequently when they create contracts outside the scope of their powers.

Today, most state incorporation statutes permit businesses to incorporate for any lawful purpose; thus, most articles of corporation do not limit corporate powers. Hence, the doctrine of *ultra vires* is much less significant today than it was in the past because very few corporate acts qualify as *ultra vires*.

Historically, courts have ruled that *ultra vires* acts are null and void. More recently, however, courts have permitted corporations to use the *ultra vires* defense if neither party to the contract has performed the terms of the contract. Yet courts uphold *ultra vires* contracts if one of the parties has executed her or his part of the contract.

For example, suppose a timber corporation's articles of incorporation specified that the corporation's purpose was to harvest and sell timber. Suppose further that the directors of the corporation entered into an *ultra vires* contract with a machinery company to purchase machines to mine coal on the corporation's cleared land. As long as the machinery company has not delivered the machinery to the timber corporation, courts will hold the contract null and void. If, however, the machinery company has delivered the machinery to the timber corporation, courts will uphold the *ultra vires* contract and require the timber corporation to fulfill the terms of the contract. Can you see which party the court is trying to protect by upholding the *ultra vires* contract in this situation?

If a corporation commits an *ultra vires* act, RMBCA provides several remedies:

1. Shareholders may sue to prohibit the corporation from fulfilling the *ultra vires* contract.
2. The corporation or shareholders may sue corporate directors or officers for the damages caused by the *ultra vires* act.
3. The state attorney general can have the corporation dissolved or prevent the corporation from fulfilling the *ultra vires* contract.

Classification of Corporations

Corporations can be classified as public or private; profit or nonprofit; domestic, foreign, or alien; publicly or closely held; S corporations; or professional corporations.

PUBLIC OR PRIVATE

public corporation
A corporation that is created by government to help administer law.

private corporation
A corporation that is created by private persons and does not have government duties.

A public corporation is a corporation created by government to help administer law. Thus, public corporations often have specific government duties to fulfill. The Federal Deposit Insurance Corporation (FDIC) is an example of a public corporation. In contrast, private persons create private corporations for private purposes. Private corporations do not have government duties.

PROFIT OR NONPROFIT

for-profit corporation
A corporation whose objective is to make a profit.

Most corporations are for-profit corporations. Thus, their objective is to operate for profit. Shareholders seeking to make a profit purchase the stock these corporations issue. This profit can take two forms. First, shareholders receive dividends from the corporation. Second, the market price of the stock can increase. Shareholders can then sell their stock at a higher price than the purchase price of the stock.

Nonprofit corporations may earn profits, but they do not distribute these profits to shareholders. In fact, nonprofit corporations do not have shareholders. More important, nonprofit corporations' objective is not to earn profit. They do not issue stock. Instead, nonprofit corporations provide services to their members (not shareholders). These corporations reinvest most of their profits in the business. Churches and charitable organizations are examples of nonprofit corporations.

DOMESTIC, FOREIGN, AND ALIEN CORPORATIONS

Every corporation is incorporated in a particular state. A corporation is a domestic corporation in the state in which it is incorporated. Many corporations, however, do business in more than one state. A corporation that does business in states other than the state in which it is incorporated must obtain a certificate of authority in each state in which it does business. A corporation is a foreign corporation in states in which it conducts business but is not incorporated. For example, the McDonald's Corporation is incorporated in Delaware but does business in all 50 states. Thus, McDonald's is a domestic corporation in Delaware and a foreign corporation in the other 49 states.

An alien corporation is a business incorporated in another country. Thus, if a U.S. corporation wants to do business in Canada or Mexico, it is an alien corporation in those countries.

PUBLICLY HELD OR CLOSELY HELD

The stock of publicly held corporations is available to the public. Thus, if you want to invest in a corporation, you could purchase stock in a publicly held corporation. Most publicly held corporations have many shareholders, and managers of these corporations usually do not own large percentages of the corporation's stock. Shareholders wishing to sell their shares do not face many transfer restrictions.

In contrast, closely held corporations (also called *close, family,* or *privately held corporations*) generally do not offer stock to the general public. Shareholders are usually family members and friends who are often active in the business. Controlling shareholders typically manage closely held corporations. Because closely held corporations are often family businesses, they often maintain restrictions on the transfer of shares to prevent outsiders from obtaining control of the business. Although they account for only a small fraction of corporate assets and revenues, most U.S. corporations are closely held corporations.

SUBCHAPTER S CORPORATION

S corporations are named after the subchapter of the Internal Revenue Code that provides for them. They are a particular type of closely held corporation. Government taxes S corporations differently from other corporations. Government taxes most corporations twice on their income: Corporations must pay income tax, and shareholders must pay taxes on dividends they receive. S corporations, however, enjoy the tax status of partnerships. Thus, shareholders of S corporations report their income from the corporation as personal income.

In addition to the avoidance of double taxation, S corporations offer two more important tax advantages. First, shareholders in an S corporation are allowed to deduct corporate losses from their personal income, ultimately lowering how much the shareholders have to pay in taxes. Second, depending on a shareholder's income, choosing to be an S corporation can result in the corporation paying lower taxes.

To be classified as an S corporation, a corporation must meet certain requirements. First, it cannot have more than 100 shareholders. Second, only individuals, trusts, and (in certain circumstances) corporations can be shareholders (partnerships cannot be shareholders). Third, S corporations can issue only one class of shares, although not all shares must have identical voting rights. Fourth, all S corporations must be domestic corporations. Fifth, no shareholder of an S corporation can be a nonresident alien.

nonprofit corporation
A corporation that operates for educational, charitable, social, religious, civic, or humanitarian purposes rather than to earn a profit.

domestic corporation
A corporation in the state in which it is incorporated.

foreign corporation
A corporation in a state in which it conducts business but is not incorporated.

alien corporation
A business that is incorporated in a foreign country.

publicly held corporation
A corporation whose stock is available to the public.

closely held corporation
A corporation that does not sell stock to the general public.

S corporation
A corporation that enjoys the tax status of a partnership.

PROFESSIONAL CORPORATION

If a group of dentists, doctors, or other professionals wants to practice as a corporation, all 50 states permit them to incorporate. Because of the nature of professional work, however, courts sometimes alter the liability associated with such corporations. For example, courts often impose personal liability on doctors in professional corporations for medical malpractice performed under their oversight.

LO 22-2

Formation of the Corporation

The creation of a corporation involves two parts: general organizational activities and legal activities necessary for incorporation.

ORGANIZING AND PROMOTING THE CORPORATION

Two groups of important players are responsible for the organization of the corporation: promoters and subscribers.

promoter
A person who begins the corporate creation and organization process.

subscription agreement
An agreement between promoters (persons raising capital for a new corporation) and subscribers (investors), in which the subscribers agree to purchase stock in the new corporation.

subscriber
An investor who agrees to purchase stock in a new corporation.

Promoters Promoters begin the corporate creation and organization process by arranging for necessary capital, financing, and licenses. Promoters raise capital for the infant corporation by making subscription agreements with subscribers (investors) in which the subscribers agree to purchase stock in the new corporation.

Promoters have other organizational responsibilities besides making subscription agreements. For example, promoters prepare the corporation's incorporation papers. Promoters can also enter into contracts as needed to establish the new corporation. For example, promoters can purchase or lease buildings for the corporation. Frank Seiberling was the promoter who founded the Goodyear Tire & Rubber Company. In 1898, Seiberling purchased Goodyear's first plant in Akron, Ohio, with $3,500 borrowed from his brother-in-law. Seiberling also established Goodyear workers' hourly wages between 13 and 25 cents.

When problems with preincorporation contracts arise, courts generally hold promoters liable and rule that these contracts do not bind infant corporations. Courts usually hold that promoters are not agents of the infant corporation because promoters cannot serve as agents for a principal (the new corporation) that does not yet exist.

Once incorporated, however, corporations can accept or reject preincorporation agreements. However, even if a corporation accepts a preincorporation agreement, courts usually still hold promoters liable for the contract.

Subscribers Subscribers make offers to purchase stock in a corporation in the incorporation process. A subscriber becomes a shareholder once the corporation incorporates or accepts her purchase offer, whichever occurs first.

SELECTING A STATE FOR INCORPORATION

Next, an infant corporation must select a state in which to incorporate. Each state has different laws governing the incorporation process and different corporate tax rates. Other factors corporations consider when selecting a state for incorporation include the following:

- How much flexibility does the state grant to corporate management?
- What rights do state statutes give to shareholders?
- What restrictions does the state place on the distribution of dividends?
- Does the state offer any kind of protection against takeovers?

Although most corporations incorporate in the state in which they are located and do most of their business, more than half of all publicly held corporations, including more than half of the Fortune 500 companies, are incorporated in Delaware. Decades ago, Delaware law offered extremely low corporate tax rates and granted more extensive rights to management in the event of a takeover than did other states. Thus, in the 1940s and 1950s, many corporations changed their state of incorporation to Delaware. Since then, other states have made their corporate laws more attractive to corporations. Many corporations remain incorporated in Delaware, however, because Delaware courts are highly experienced in issues involving corporate law.

Closely held corporations and professional corporations, however, almost always incorporate in the state in which most of their stockholders live.

Although a corporation can incorporate in only one state, it can file a certificate of authority to do business in other states. Some states fine corporations that fail to obtain a certificate of authority before conducting business in the state. Other states fine directors and officers of these corporations directly and hold them personally liable for contracts made in the state.

Once a corporation chooses a state for incorporation, it can begin the formal legal process of incorporation.

Legal Process of Incorporation

SELECTION OF CORPORATE NAME

All state incorporation statutes require corporations to indicate in the name of the corporation that the business is incorporated. Every corporation must attach *Corporation, Company, Limited,* or *Incorporated,* or an abbreviation of one of these terms, to the end of its business name. In addition, every corporation must distinguish its name from the names of all other domestic or foreign corporations licensed to do business within the state. This requirement protects third parties from confusion about similar names. Once the corporation has chosen a name, this name is subject to the approval of the state.

INCORPORATORS

An incorporator is an individual who applies to the state for incorporation on behalf of a corporation. RMBCA requires only one incorporator to incorporate a business, although it permits more. Generally, the incorporators' only duty is to sign the articles of incorporation.

incorporator
An individual who applies for incorporation on behalf of a corporation.

ARTICLES OF INCORPORATION

One of the most important elements of the corporate formation process is the articles of incorporation, a document providing basic information about the corporation. According to RMBCA, a corporation's articles of incorporation must include (1) the name of the corporation, (2) the address of the registered office, (3) the name of the registered agent (i.e., the specific person who receives legal documents on behalf of the corporation), and (4) the names and addresses of the incorporators.

articles of incorporation
A document that contains basic information about a corporation and is filed with the state.

The incorporators must execute and sign the articles of incorporation and file the document with the secretary of state, including the required filing fee, to legally form the corporation. Once the incorporators file the document, it governs the corporation. Next, the secretary of state usually issues a certificate of incorporation, a document certifying that the corporation is incorporated in the state and is authorized to conduct business.

certificate of incorporation
A document certifying that a corporation is incorporated in the state and is authorized to conduct business.

FIRST ORGANIZATIONAL MEETING

After the secretary of state issues the certificate of incorporation, the shareholders meet to elect the corporate board of directors, pass corporate bylaws, and carry out other corporate business. In some cases, however, shareholders name the board of directors before the first organizational meeting and list the board members in the articles of incorporation. In these situations, the directors usually run the meeting.

bylaws
Rules and regulations that govern a corporation's internal management.

At the first organizational meeting, shareholders adopt a set of corporate bylaws, or rules and regulations that govern the corporation's internal management. The articles of incorporation determine who has the power to amend the corporate bylaws after the first organizational meeting: shareholders, directors, or both.

Potential Problems with Formation of the Corporation

Most businesses incorporate to enjoy limited liability or the perpetual existence of the corporation. Shareholders enjoy these benefits, however, only if the promoters and incorporator formally and correctly incorporate the business. If the incorporator or promoters make an error or omission during the incorporation process, courts may rule that the organization is not a corporation. In this case, the organization is a defective corporation. Shareholders may be personally liable for a defective corporation's actions.

defective corporation
A corporation about which an error or omission was made during its incorporation process.

RESPONSES TO DEFECTIVE INCORPORATION

Suppose an incorporator incorrectly indicates the address of the corporate office in the articles of incorporation. Does the corporation still exist? Depending on the seriousness of the error, courts may disregard an error in the articles of incorporation by recognizing the corporation as a *de jure* or *de facto* corporation.

de jure corporation
Latin for "lawful corporation"; a corporation that has met the mandatory statutory provisions and thus received its certificate of incorporation.

De Jure Corporations   A *de jure* corporation (literally, a "lawful corporation") has met the substantial elements of the incorporation process. A corporation that has received its certificate of incorporation has met the mandatory statutory provisions and is thus a *de jure* corporation. Courts usually hold that corporations that make minor errors in the incorporation process still enjoy *de jure* corporate status. Figure 22-1 illustrates the process for creating a *de jure* corporation.

Thus, even if the incorporator wrote the incorrect address of the corporate office in the articles of incorporation, courts would not revoke the corporation's limited liability. No party can question a *de jure* corporation's status as a corporate entity in court.

de facto corporation
Latin for "corporation in fact"; a corporation that has not substantially met the requirements of the state incorporation statutes.

De Facto Corporation   Suppose, however, that the incorporator makes a more serious mistake or omission. For example, suppose the incorporator did not file the articles of incorporation with the secretary of state. In this case, courts may recognize the corporation as a *de facto* corporation (literally, a "corporation in fact"). A *de facto* corporation has not substantially met the requirements of the state incorporation statute, but courts recognize it as a corporation for most purposes to avoid unfairness to third parties who believed it was properly incorporated. *De facto*

Figure 22-1

De Jure Corporation Formation

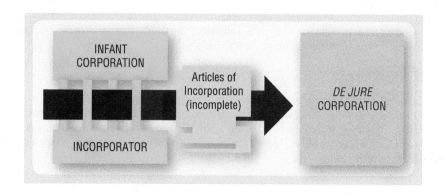

GLOBAL Context

Corporate Structure in China

As you may expect, corporate governance varies among countries. Specifically, there are countries that have a one-tier board system (as in the United States), and there are others that have a two-tier board system. In a one-tier board all directors (both executive directors and nonexecutive directors) form one board. A two-tier board consists of a management board (all executive directors) and a separate supervisory board (all nonexecutive directors). German corporation law, for example, requires all corporations to have two boards.

In recent years, China has followed the German model and adopted a two-tier board structure, with both a board of directors and a supervisory board. Corporations following this model are required to provide in their annual reports a supervisory board report (SBR). In China, the supervisory

board has significant power to supervise directors, examine financial documents, and convene shareholder meetings. In these respects, supervisors exercise substantial control over corporate managers.

Although corporations in China are not required to have a supervisory board (unlike the case in Germany), there is usually a supervisory board that consists of shareholder representatives and an employee representative. However, the supervisory board does not always function at the level that many envisioned it would. In practice, supervisory boards in China have not functioned effectively because they do not have genuine power to select or discipline directors and managers. Furthermore, some critics argue that there is some overlap between the function of the supervisory board and that of the board of directors. What do you think are the advantages and disadvantages of the two-tier board system?

corporations, regardless of whether the state has a general corporation statute, must meet the following requirements:

- The promoters, subscribers, and incorporator made a good-faith attempt to comply with the incorporation statute.
- The organization has already conducted business as a corporation.

The process for recognizing a corporation as a *de facto* corporation is depicted in Figure 22-2. Only the state can challenge a *de facto* corporation's existence as a corporate entity.

Corporation by Estoppel   Defective corporations cannot escape corporate entity status due to mistakes or omissions in their incorporation procedures. For example, suppose a corporation's

Figure 22-2

De Facto Corporation Recognition Process

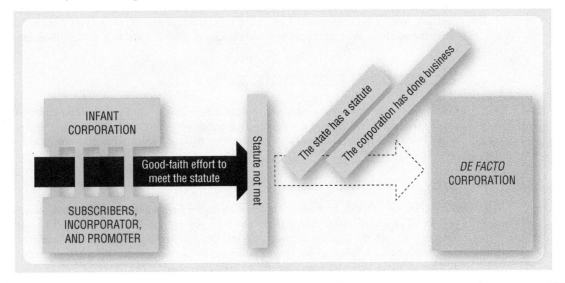

articles of incorporation do not include the name of its registered agent. Suppose further that the corporation's directors, managers, and shareholders are unaware of the mistake. If the corporation conducts business with a third party who later sues for breach of contract, the corporation cannot claim that it is not a corporate entity to escape liability.

In such cases, courts hold that the corporation is a corporation by estoppel; thus, courts *estop* (prevent) the corporation from denying its corporate status. Although a court ruling of corporation by estoppel prevents the business from denying corporate status, it does not remedy the error or grant the organization corporate status for conducting future business.

If a corporation makes a significant error in the incorporation process and is not a *de jure* or *de facto* corporation, and corporation by estoppel does not apply to the situation, courts usually deny the organization corporate entity status. Thus, the organization does not enjoy limited shareholder liability.

corporation by estoppel
A defective corporation that has conducted business with a third party and therefore cannot deny its status as a corporation to escape liability.

BUT WHAT IF. . .

WHAT IF THE FACTS OF THE CASE OPENER WERE DIFFERENT?

Let's say in the Case Opener that when filling out documents for the incorporation of Facebook, Zuckerberg's attorney became confused and wrote the wrong address for company on the documents. Later, long after Facebook was incorporated, Zuckerberg saw the incorrect company address on the documents. Should Zuckerberg worry about the clerical error? What could be the effects of having the wrong company information on such documents?

Piercing the Corporate Veil   In some cases, courts will deny limited liability to a corporation that would normally have *de jure* or *de facto* status because shareholders have used the corporation to engage in illegal or wrongful acts. Shareholders attempt to hide behind the corporate veil of limited liability to protect themselves from personal liability. In these cases, courts *pierce the corporate veil,* or impose personal liability on shareholders. Courts are likely to pierce the corporate veil when:

- A corporation lacked adequate capital when it initially formed.
- A corporation did not follow statutory mandates regarding corporate business.
- Shareholders' personal interests and corporate interests are commingled such that the corporation has no separate identity.
- Shareholders attempt to commit fraud through a corporation.

For example, corporations must keep corporate funds and records separate from shareholder funds and records. If a corporation does not carefully maintain these separate records, courts may pierce the corporate veil and impose personal liability on shareholders, as Case 22-1 illustrates.

Corporate Financing

Corporations, like other businesses, need a source of funding. Corporations most commonly obtain financing by issuing and selling corporate securities: debt securities (bonds), which represent loans to a corporation, and equity securities (stocks), which represent ownership in a corporation.

DEBT SECURITIES

debt securities
Securities that represent loans to a corporation.

equity securities
Securities that represent ownership in a corporation.

Debt securities, or bonds, represent loans to a corporation from another party. Bonds are usually long-term loans on which the corporation promises to pay interest. Bonds frequently list a maturity date on which the corporation must repay the face amount of the loan. Before the maturity date, however, corporations usually pay bondholders fixed-dollar interest payments on a scheduled basis. Hence, bonds are sometimes called *fixed-income securities.*

CASE 22-1

J-MART JEWELRY OUTLETS, INC. v. STANDARD DESIGN
COURT OF APPEALS OF GEORGIA
218 Ga. App. 459 (1995)

FACTS: *Jim Halter, the major shareholder of J-Mart Jewelry Outlets, Inc., and several other corporations, was aware that J-Mart was in financial trouble. Before J-Mart went out of business, Halter paid off his personal credit cards using corporate funds. Halter also paid the corporation $1 for a corporate car purchased with corporation funding. Four of J-Mart's creditors brought suit against Halter in an attempt to recover corporate funds. The trial court jury pierced the corporate veil to hold Halter personally responsible for the debts. Halter appealed the court's denial of his request for a directed verdict.*

ISSUE: Has the appellant used his position as the major shareholder of a corporation to disregard the legal separation between a shareholder and the corporation, thereby permitting a piercing of the corporate veil?

REASONING: The judge argued that for the veil to be pierced,

> [t]here must be evidence of abuse of the corporate form. Plaintiff must show that the defendant disregarded the separateness of legal entities by commingling on an interchangeable or joint basis or confusing the otherwise separate properties, records or control. . . .

Halter knew as early as late April but not later than June 1991 that J-Mart would have to cease operations as a result of its financial difficulties. There was direct evidence

that the $6,902.87 balance on Halter's American Express personal account was paid by J-Mart on December 23, 1991, eight days before it ceased doing business. The check was marked "PAYMENT IN FULL: JIM'S PERSONAL[,]" indicating that a material question of fact existed of whether Halter used corporate funds to pay a personal debt. The evidence also established that J-Mart, with knowledge that it would soon cease doing business, purchased a new Cadillac for Halter's use. It thereafter made three payments on the vehicle before transferring it to Halter for $1 and allowing him to assume the remaining payments, indicating the presence of further questions of material fact relative to a *de facto* unauthorized payment for Halter's personal benefit.

DECISION AND REMEDY: The court determined that "[i]n light of the evidence presented, the trial court properly denied the motion for a directed verdict upon the claim of Halter's personal liability for violation of the corporate form. . . . On appeal, we construe all the evidence most strongly in support of the verdict. . . . [T]he jury's verdict was proper and must stand."

SIGNIFICANCE OF THE CASE: This case illustrates the requirements that a plaintiff must meet to establish a basis for piercing the corporate veil and affirms the jury's role in judging material questions of fact in these cases.

CRITICAL THINKING

Given what you know of the facts of the case, could Halter have provided any information would lead you to believe that he was not responsible for the debts? What would this information be?

ETHICAL DECISION MAKING

Describe the ethical conflict Halter was facing. For what purpose, or value, was he acting? If Halter had followed the Golden Rule, would he have chosen to act in the way he did? Given this information, what could have been done to convince Halter to refrain from using corporate funds to pay off his personal credit cards?

EQUITY SECURITIES

Stocks and bonds are not identical. Whereas bond owners have loaned money to a corporation, stock owners actually own part of a corporation. Thus, bond owners have no voice in corporate management; stockholders have a voice in control of the corporation. Not all corporations issue bonds, but all for-profit issue stock. Common stock and preferred stock are the two major types of stock.

preferred stock
Stock that conveys preferences to its holders with respect to assets and dividends.

Preferred Stock   Owners of preferred stock, or *preferred shares,* enjoy preferences with respect to assets and dividends. Corporations often have several classes of preferred shares. Preferred stock shares many characteristics with bonds. For example, preferred stock owners usually receive a percentage of dividends associated with the face value of their preferred stock. Furthermore, corporations pay dividends to owners of preferred stock before they pay owners of common stock. Some corporations limit preferred stock owners' voting rights.

common stock
Corporate stock that does not convey any preferences to its holders.

Common Stock   Owners of common stock, or *common shares,* own a portion of a corporation but do not enjoy any preferences. A common stock owner is entitled to a portion of the corporation's dividends in proportion to the number of shares of common stock she owns. Common stock owners also have the right to vote in corporate elections. Each share is usually worth one vote in corporate elections. Thus, if you own 20,000 common shares of a corporation, you have 20,000 votes. In some cases, however, most notably the election of the board of directors, corporations use a method called *cumulative voting* to increase the influence of shareholders who own a small number of shares.

Common stock owners have the lowest priority when a corporation distributes dividends. Creditors and preferred stock owners receive dividends first. Once a corporation pays these groups, however, common stock owners have a claim to the remainder of the corporate earnings.

Importance of Regulating Interactions among Directors, Officers, and Shareholders within a Corporation

The three major groups of individuals within a corporation are *directors, officers,* and *shareholders.* All three groups have different interests, and in many situations the interests of one group conflict with the interests of another. Statutory law provides rules to ensure that the directors, officers, and shareholders within a corporation work together to the benefit of all involved.

Although directors and officers play different roles within the corporation, they share the same goal. Both directors and officers attempt to ensure that their institution survives and that they keep their jobs. Shareholders, on the other hand, have a different agenda. Their goal is to raise the value of the company's stock.

These different agendas can lead to conflict within corporations. If a corporation has an opportunity to make a decision that will raise the value of its stock quickly, shareholders will push the directors and officers to make this decision. However, if the directors and officers believe that the decision might jeopardize their jobs, they will resist the pressure of the shareholders. To resolve these conflicts, the law gives legal duties and rights to different groups within the corporation.

LO 22-3   Roles of Directors, Officers, and Shareholders

Before discussing the duties and rights of each position within the corporation, it is important to understand the specific roles that directors, officers, and shareholders play. The rights and duties of each group of individuals depend on these roles.

DIRECTORS' ROLES

Directors play a vital role within every corporation. When a corporation faces important decisions, the board of directors meets to decide what course of action the corporation will take.

Elections Typically, shareholders use a majority vote to elect directors. The only exception occurs during incorporation. Because there are no shareholders in the beginning, either the incorporators appoint board members or the corporate articles name the board members. This first board then serves until the first shareholder meeting, at which the shareholders elect a new board. The corporate articles or bylaws specify the number of corporate directors.

In the past, the minimum number of directors required was three, but today many states allow fewer. In fact, if a corporation has fewer than 50 shareholders, Section 7.32 of RMBCA allows companies to eliminate the board of directors altogether.

Interestingly, almost anyone can become a director. The legal requirements for director qualification are incredibly lax. In most states, directors are not even required to own stock in the corporation. In some cases, however, statutory law and corporate bylaws require not only ownership but also a minimum age.

Directors typically serve for one year, but most state statutes allow for longer terms if the terms of the various directors are staggered. These terms can be terminated and the directors can be removed from their positions *for cause*—for failing to perform a required duty. Directors who are removed for cause, however, can ask the courts to review the legality of the removal.

Meetings and Voting A minimum number of directors, or a quorum, must be present at each meeting of the board of directors for decisions made at the meeting to be valid. Quorum requirements are different in each state, but most states leave the decision up to the corporation itself. Because a quorum is required at each meeting, directors are notified whenever special meetings are called. Directors vote in person, and each director has one vote. Although ordinary decisions require a majority vote, more important decisions sometimes require a two-thirds vote.

Directors as Managers Although directors meet to vote on major decisions about the corporation, they are also responsible for many day-to-day managerial activities of the company. The directors appoint, supervise, and remove corporate officers as they see fit, and they declare and pay corporate dividends to shareholders. They are also responsible for making financial decisions and authorizing corporate policy decisions. Some directors are also officers or employees of the corporation; these directors are known as *inside directors*. Directors who are not officers or employees of the corporation are called *outside directors*. Outside directors are further divided into two groups: *affiliated directors* and *unaffiliated directors*. Affiliated directors have business contacts with the corporation; unaffiliated directors do not.

Because the day-to-day tasks of a corporation can be overwhelming for a small board of directors that has larger issues to address, directors often appoint an executive committee to handle day-to-day responsibilities.

OFFICERS' ROLES

Officers are executive managers whom the board of directors hires to run the organization. Although directors are in charge of major policy decisions, officers run the day-to-day business of the corporation. Officers act as agents of the corporation; thus, the rules of agency apply to their work.

Qualifications required of officers are set forth in the corporate articles and bylaws of each corporation, but in most cases an individual may serve as both a director and an officer. Many corporations find it beneficial to include an officer on their board of directors so that the board can stay in touch with the day-to-day operations of the company.

SHAREHOLDERS' ROLES

Shareholders own the firm. As soon as an individual purchases the stock of a particular corporation, she becomes an owner of the corporation. Although she is not legally recognized as an owner of corporate property, she has an *equitable,* or ownership, interest in the company. Shareholders are not directly responsible for the daily management of the corporation, but they elect the directors who are responsible for that management.

Power of Shareholders   The articles of incorporation established within each corporation and general incorporation law in each state grant shareholders certain powers within the institution. Because shareholders must approve major corporate decisions, they are in a sense empowered to make major decisions for the corporation.

Their most influential power, however, is the power to elect and remove members of the board of directors. The board of directors is responsible for making crucial policy decisions for the corporation, and the shareholders have the power to decide who the directors will be.

Shareholders also have the power to propose ideas for the corporation. If a shareholder feels that he has a worthwhile idea for the company, he can include his proposal in the *proxy materials* sent out to the shareholders before their annual meeting. The Securities and Exchange Commission (SEC) has established that any shareholder who owns more than $1,000 worth of stock in the corporation can submit proposals to be included in proxy materials.

Meetings   Typically, shareholders meet once a year, but in emergencies they can meet more often. The board of directors, shareholders who own at least 10 percent of the corporation's outstanding shares, and others authorized in the articles of incorporation may call a special shareholder meeting. Before each meeting, each shareholder receives notice of the time and place of the meeting. If the meeting is a special meeting, the purpose of the meeting is also included in the notice.

Like directors' meetings, shareholder meetings require a quorum. Generally, a quorum of shareholders exists when shareholders holding more than 50 percent of the outstanding shares are present. Once a quorum is present, a majority vote of the shares represented at the meeting is required to pass resolutions. Occasionally, however, articles of incorporation include supermajority provisions, which state that more than a majority is needed to pass major corporate proposals, such as corporate merger or dissolution.

Voting   Like directors, each shareholder is entitled to one vote per share in most instances. Corporations practice unique voting processes, however, that alter the influence of each shareholder's votes. These voting processes are especially important for minority shareholders within a corporation. One voting process required in most states, called *cumulative voting,* ensures that minority shareholders have a voice in electing the board of directors.

The cumulative-voting process divides shareholders into majority and minority shareholders, and each group has a certain number of votes to cast in the election. The number of votes is determined by multiplying the number of shares the group owns by the number of open director positions. If a company is electing eight directors and the minority shareholders own 2,000 shares, the minority shareholders get 16,000 votes to cast in the election. If the majority shareholders in the same corporation own 8,000 shares, they get 64,000 votes.

Although it may seem that the minority shareholders have little influence in the election, the cumulative-voting process permits them to vote at least one director onto the board because they can cast all of their votes for one candidate. If the majority shareholders wish to elect all eight directors from their nominees, each nominee must receive more than 16,000 votes to beat the 16,000 votes of the minority nominee. However, because the majority shareholders have only 64,000 votes to cast in the election, they cannot cast more than 16,000 votes for eight candidates ($16,000 \times 8 = 128,000$). Thus, if the minority shareholders cast all of their 16,000 votes for one candidate, they guarantee that candidate's election.

Cumulative voting is more egalitarian than simple majority voting because it ensures that every voice within the corporation is heard. Cumulative voting, however, occurs only when the corporation's articles of incorporation provide for it.

Exhibit 22-2 summarizes the respective roles of directors, officers, and shareholders.

Shareholders
Role: the Owners
The shareholders own the stock of the company.
Goal: to increase the value of the company's stock

Directors
Role: the Decision Makers
The directors share in the power of deciding the course of action for the corporation.
Directors also appoint and supervise officers and declare and pay corporate dividends.
Goal: to ensure that the institution survives and that they keep their jobs

Officers
Role: the Managers
The officers manage the day-to-day activities of running the business,
including acting as agents for the corporation.
Goal: to ensure that the institution survives and that they keep their jobs

Duties of Directors, Officers, and Shareholders

LO 22-4

Because all individuals within a corporation depend on one another, the law requires directors, officers, and shareholders to perform certain duties within the business. In other words, individuals within the corporation have legal responsibilities to the corporation. These duties to the corporation are called *fiduciary duties.* Because individuals play different roles within the corporation, the fiduciary duties of individuals depend on whether they are directors, officers, or shareholders.

DUTIES OF DIRECTORS AND OFFICERS

Because the owners of the corporation, the shareholders, have little input in the day-to-day operations of the corporation, they trust the directors and officers to run the company to the best of their ability. Thus, directors and officers have duties to the shareholders and to the corporation. The two primary fiduciary duties of directors and officers are the duty of care and the duty of loyalty.

Duty of Care   Directors and officers have a fiduciary *duty of care,* meaning that they must exercise *due care* when making decisions for the corporation. The phrase *due care* is ambiguous, and various courts have interpreted it differently over time. In general, however, acting with due care requires one to exercise the care that an ordinary prudent person would exercise in the management of her own assets.

Because directors and officers have a duty to act in the best interest of the company, they must supervise, to a reasonable extent, employees who work for the corporation. They also have a duty to attend director and corporate business meetings. Most important, however, directors and officers have a fiduciary duty to make informed and reasonable business decisions.

The directors and officers of Enron failed in their duty of care with regard to their shareholders by not acting in the best interest of the company. The directors and officers continued to urge

E-COMMERCE and the Law

When a B2B Company Cooks the Books

When a business student thinks about companies that cook the books, it is not surprising that companies such as Enron, Tyco, and Adelphia come to mind. Issues related to the duty of care of officers and directors are expressed in questions such as, "Why did the officers and directors of the company fail to realize accountants were cooking company books? Were any officers or directors involved in the fraud?"

Students may have to revise their images of corrupt companies by adding business-to-business (B2B) e-commerce companies to their Enron-Tyco-Adelphia list. They may have to ask, "Why did the officers and directors of an *e-commerce business* fail to realize accountants were cooking company books? Were any officers or directors involved in the fraud?"

PurchasePro is one example of an e-commerce company that allegedly engaged in "overstating revenues, engaging in aggressive accounting practices and mismanaging corporate assets." Basically, the company manipulated its financial records to make it look far more successful than it really was. PurchasePro, which provided a business-to-business software application that gave companies access to an online marketplace, went bankrupt in September 2002.

Federal prosecutors charged company officers and directors with conspiracy, securities fraud, and obstruction of justice. Two senior officers, Jeffrey R. Anderson and Scott H. Miller, pleaded guilty to federal crimes in 2003. Their behavior was similar to that of officers of other, more well-known companies that have cooked the books—they had secret side deals with purchasers that gave the appearance of sales, but the sales did not exist; they misrepresented the company's financial health, so investors could not make informed decisions; and, when news of alleged fraud surfaced, the officers used their energy to shred incriminating documents.

---

employees to invest in the employee stock-sharing options, even though it appears that the directors and officers knew the stock was drastically overpriced. Furthermore, the directors and officers failed in their duty of care regarding oversight. They either did not pay enough attention to see the collapse of the company's stock coming or purposely kept the information secret. Either way, the directors and officers at Enron breached their fiduciary duty of care and therefore are liable to their shareholders, many of whom were employees of Enron.

Directors and officers are expected to stay abreast of all important corporate matters. In other words, they must obtain information about business transactions, review contracts, read reports, and attend presentations. Because some directors are too busy to stay informed on every subject, RMBCA allows directors to make decisions on the basis of information gathered by other employees.

The decisions that corporate directors and officers make must not only be informed, however, but also be reasonable. If a director or officer is taken to court for breaching his duty of care by making an unreasonable decision, the court typically inquires whether the decision had any rational business purpose. In other words, the courts ask whether there was good reason to think that the decision *could* have helped the company.

Part of the duty of care a director or officer owes a corporation, as was previously stated, is to act in the corporation's best interest. Therefore, when the corporation is doing something the director or officer does not think is in its best interest, it is up to her to voice her dissent.

Duty of Loyalty   Because directors and officers have great decision-making freedom, they have the power to make business decisions that will benefit themselves while harming the company. Thus, to protect shareholders, directors and officers have a fiduciary *duty of loyalty*. In other words, they have a fiduciary duty to put the corporation's interest above their own when making business decisions.

self-dealing

Any instance in which directors or officers make decisions that violate their corporate duty of loyalty.

When directors or officers violate their duty of loyalty, they are self-dealing. There are two types of self-dealing in which a director or officer can engage. The first form of self-dealing, called *business self-dealing*, occurs when a director or officer makes decisions that benefit other companies with which he has a relationship. The second form of self-dealing, called *personal self-dealing*, occurs when a director or officer makes business decisions that benefit her personally. When Enron directors and officers advocated employees buying more Enron stock so that the directors and officers would make more money, they engaged in self-dealing in breach of their fiduciary duty of loyalty.

CASE Nugget

How Should Directors Handle Personal Interests That Conflict with Corporate Interests?

Patrick v. Allen
United States District Court, S.D. New York

355 F. Supp. 2d 704 (2005)

RPO, a privately traded corporation, rented land to a private golf course of which several of RPO's directors were members. The directors charged the golf course enough rent to cover only the property taxes on the land. Patrick, a shareholder of RPO, brought a suit against the directors of RPO, alleging that RPO's directors breached their fiduciary duty of loyalty to the corporation by failing to maximize the value of the corporation for shareholders. The directors argued that they were exempt from liability under the business judgment rule. (The business judgment rule is covered in the section entitled "Liabilities of Directors, Officers, and Shareholders," which follows shortly.)

The U.S. District Court for the Southern District of New York ruled against the RPO's directors, holding:

> The business judgment rule will not protect a decision that was the product of fraud, self-dealing, or bad faith. Directors may benefit from the rule only if they possess a disinterested independence and do not stand in a dual relation which prevents a nonprejudicial exercise of judgment. It is black-letter, settled law that when a corporate director or officer has an interest in a decision, the business judgment rule does not apply. . . . A director is considered interested in a transaction if the director stands to receive a direct financial benefit from the transaction which is different from the benefit to shareholders generally. . . . The duty of loyalty requires a director to subordinate his own personal interests to the interest of the corporation.

In many situations, when a director or officer is self-dealing, he forces the corporation into unfair business deals. Directors and officers can also breach their fiduciary duty of loyalty, however, by *preventing* corporate opportunity. This breach usually happens when directors or officers own other companies that compete with their corporation without the consent of the board of directors or the shareholders. If a director or officer uses corporate assets to start another business, goes into the same line of business, or uses her position in the company to develop a new business that the company might have pursued, she is preventing corporate opportunity and can be held liable for violating her fiduciary duty of loyalty.

A director or officer convicted of breaching his duty of loyalty is required to cede to the corporation all the profits he earned as a result of the breach. The goal of this rule is to create incentives that discourage breaches of the duty of loyalty by taking from the director or officer all the profits that he made.

The fiduciary duties of care and loyalty are rooted in ethics. Without these legal duties, directors and officers could pursue their own interests at the expense of others. Through these fiduciary duties, however, the law requires directors and officers to consider the interests of others. Think back to Chapter 1 and the different ethical guidelines used to make ethical decisions. Which ethical guideline is the legal system using when it delegates fiduciary duties?

Duty to Disclose Conflict of Interest   Because there are many times when individual directors and officers may personally benefit from decisions made by the board of directors, the directors and officers have a fiduciary duty to disclose conflicts of interest fully that arise in corporate transactions. Moreover, if the board of directors addresses an issue that might personally benefit a particular director, the director is required not only to disclose the self-interest but also to abstain from voting on that issue. Note that a decision can be made that will personally benefit one director or officer as long as (1) there is full disclosure of the interest and (2) the disinterested board members and/or disinterested shareholders approve the decision.

DUTIES OF SHAREHOLDERS

Although shareholders typically have few legal duties, in rare instances majority shareholders have fiduciary duties to the corporation and to minority shareholders. In some corporations, the majority shareholder owns such a significant portion of the corporation's stock that she essentially controls the firm. When the majority shareholder sells her shares, control of the company shifts to another individual. Thus, the majority shareholder in this situation has a fiduciary duty to act with care and loyalty when selling her shares.

As noted earlier, more than half of all U.S. publicly traded corporations are incorporated in Delaware. Thus, when Delaware courts rule on the duties of majority shareholders to minority shareholders, for example, the courts' rulings have a far-reaching impact. In Case 22-2, a minority shareholder sued the majority shareholder of a corporation for violating its fiduciary duties.

CASE 22-2

MCCANN v. MCCANN SUPREME COURT OF IDAHO
275 P. 3D 824 (2012)

FACTS: *McCann Ranch & Livestock Company, Inc., was a closely held corporation created by William McCann, Sr. In the 1970s, Ron and Bill McCann, the creator's sons, were each given 36.7 percent of the shares of the corporation. The remaining shares were held by the creator, William, until those shares were transferred to a trust to benefit his wife, Gertrude. The trustee, Gary Meisner, was given the power and discretion to vote and sell Gertrude's shares under certain circumstances. Upon the death of the corporation's creator, William, Bill became the President and CEO of the corporation. Then, upon the death of Gertrude, Bill received her remaining shares.*

In June 2008, Ron, a minority shareholder, filed an initial complaint, alleging that the corporation breached its fiduciary duty owed to him as a shareholder by engaging in a squeeze-out and that such injury is grounds for a direct action. Ron's claim mentioned his treatment by the corporation as well as financial transactions of the corporation. The district court granted summary judgment in favor of the respondent, Bill. Ron appealed.

ISSUE: May a minority shareholder bring suit against the majority shareholder for breach of fiduciary duty?

REASONING: Squeeze-outs are actions taken by controlling shareholders to deprive a minority shareholder of his or her interest in a business or a fair return on an investment. Courts have analyzed the legality of squeeze-outs by referring to the conduct of the majority shareholders and how such conduct affects the minority shareholders. In other words, the law recognizes that directors owe a fiduciary duty to minority shareholders.

In this case, the court reasoned that the conduct of the corporation could not be excused under the business judgement rule. Specifically, the corporation had not paid dividends despite sufficient cash flow, not provided board membership to Ron, authorized phony transactions to Gertrude to avoid any benefit to Ron, and had made management decisions that benefited Bill and Gertrude at the expense of Ron. The court inferred from these observations, along with the fact that Ron was specifically hurt from the payments that the corporation made to Gertrude, that a material question existed with regard to the corporation engaging in a squeeze-out.

DECISION AND REMEDY: The court reversed in favor of Ron and remanded to address the questions of whether the alleged squeeze-out constituted a violation of fiduciary duties.

(continued)

SIGNIFICANCE: This case highlights the legal obligations of majority stakeholders to minority stakeholders because of the overwhelming power majority stakeholders have over the operation of the corporation.

CRITICAL THINKING

What reasons does the court give for its conclusion? Are you persuaded by those reasons?

ETHICAL DECISION MAKING

Clearly, the court emphasizes particular values in its ruling. What are these values? Which shareholders in the business community are affected by focusing on these values when assessing a corporation's fiduciary duties?

Liabilities of Directors, Officers, and Shareholders

LO 22-5

Because almost all individuals within a corporation have legal fiduciary duties to the corporation, almost all individuals within the firm can be held liable for harming the business by violating these duties. There are, however, certain instances in which directors, officers, and shareholders cannot be held liable for harming the business.

LIABILITY OF DIRECTORS AND OFFICERS

Directors and officers are held liable for many of the same actions because they have nearly identical fiduciary duties to the corporation. A shareholder can sue them if the shareholder feels that they have caused harm to the business by violating their fiduciary duties. Directors and officers can be held liable for the torts and crimes of their employees.

Liability for Torts and Crimes   Although the corporations themselves are liable for the torts and crimes of their directors and officers, directors and officers can also be held personally responsible for their own torts and crimes. They can even be held personally responsible for the torts and crimes of other employees within the organization when they have failed to supervise the employees' behavior adequately.

According to the *responsible person doctrine,* a court may find a corporate officer criminally liable regardless of the extent to which the officer took part in the criminal activity. Even if the officer knew nothing about the criminal activity, the officer can still be held criminally liable if the court determines that a responsible person would have known about and could have prevented the illegal activity.

Corporate directors and officers may also be held liable for wrongful personal transactions involving company stock. Directors and officers who use inside information to trade the corporation's stock for a profit can be held liable for breaching their fiduciary duty to the shareholders from whom they purchase or to whom they sell the stock.

Business Judgment Rule   Although directors and officers are expected to make decisions that are in the best interest of the corporation, they are not expected to make perfect decisions all the time. Many directors and officers make decisions that inadvertently harm the corporation. Although shareholders may want to hold their directors and officers liable for these decisions, the *business judgment rule* does not allow them to do so.

Under this rule, directors and officers are not liable for decisions that harm the corporation if they were acting in good faith at the time of the decision. In other words, if there was reason to believe that the decision was a good decision at the time, the directors and officers are not liable for the resulting harm.

Although the business judgment rule is not a statute, it is common law recognized by almost every court in the country. The rule is practical because it grants directors the freedom to work without constant fear of personal liability. The business judgment rule also encourages individuals to serve as directors by removing the threat of personal liability for inadvertent mistakes.

CASE Nugget

The Business Judgment Rule

Auerbach v. Bennett
N.Y. Court of Appeals

393 N.E.2d 994 (1979)

An internal audit of the GTE Corporation suggested that the corporation's management had paid more than $11 million in bribes and kickbacks both in the United States and abroad over a four-year period. Auerbach, a GTE shareholder, immediately initiated a shareholder derivative action (discussed below) against GTE's directors. The Court of Appeals of New York, however, held that the business judgment rule exempted the GTE directors from liability for their poor business decisions. The court stated: [The business judgment doctrine] bars judicial inquiry into actions of corporation directors taken in good faith and in the exercise of honest judgment in the lawful and legitimate furtherance of corporate purposes. Questions of policy of management, expediency of contracts or action, adequacy of consideration, lawful appropriation of corporate funds to advance corporate interests, are left solely to their honest and unselfish decision, for their powers therein are without limitation and free from restraint, and the exercise of them for the common and general interests of the corporation may not be questioned, although the results show that what they did was unwise or inexpedient.

LIABILITY OF SHAREHOLDERS

The main liability that shareholders face is liability for the debts of the corporation. Because shareholders are the owners of the corporation, they are liable to the extent of their investment when the company loses money. There are rare instances, however, in which shareholders are personally liable.

par-value shares
Stock shares that have a fixed face value noted on the stock certificate.

no-par shares
Stock shares that do not have a par value.

watered stock
Stock that is issued to individuals below its fair market value.

For instance, in some cases, individuals sign stock subscription agreements before incorporation. Once an individual signs a stock subscription agreement, she is contractually obligated to purchase shares in the corporation. For par-value shares, or shares that have a fixed face value noted on the stock certificate, the shareholder must pay the corporation at least the par value of the stock. For no-par shares, or shares without a par value, the shareholder must pay the corporation the fair market value of the shares. The shareholder is personally liable for breach of contract if she does not buy shares.

Alternatively, a shareholder can be held personally responsible if he receives watered stock. Watered stock is stock issued to individuals below its fair market value. When watered stock is issued to a shareholder, the shareholder is individually liable for paying the difference between the price he paid for the shares and the stated corporate value of the shares.

Rights of Directors, Officers, and Shareholders

Along with their specific roles and duties, directors, officers, and shareholders have specific rights within the corporation. Because shareholders are in a position of limited decision-making power, they have rights that allow them to participate within the corporation. Directors and officers also have specific rights that allow them to perform their duties within the corporation to the best of their abilities.

DIRECTORS' RIGHTS

The unique responsibilities of corporate directors call for unique rights. Directors have four major rights within a corporation: rights of compensation, participation, inspection, and indemnification.

All corporate directors have a *right to compensation* for their work, and different corporations grant compensation in different ways. Most directors hold other managerial positions within their companies and receive their compensation through those positions. Another common avenue for compensating directors is paying them nominal sums as honorariums for their contributions to the company.

Because directors are required to make informed business decisions, they have the *rights of participation and inspection.* In other words, they have the right to get involved in and understand every aspect of the business. A corporate director has the right to be notified of all meetings and has access to all books and records.

Finally, because directors are in positions of great legal vulnerability, they have the *right to indemnification.* That is, they have the right to reimbursement for any legal fees incurred in lawsuits against them.

OFFICERS' RIGHTS

Because corporate officers are technically employees of the corporation, their rights are defined by employment contracts drawn up by the board of directors or the incorporators. They are in a contractual relationship with the corporation, and if they are removed from their positions in violation of the terms of the contract, the corporation may be liable for breach of contract.

SHAREHOLDERS' RIGHTS

Although shareholders' most powerful right is the right to vote at shareholders' meetings, they also possess many other rights.

Stock Certificates   Some corporations issue stock certificates to shareholders as proof of ownership in the corporation. Each certificate includes the corporation's name and the number of shares represented by the certificate. An example of a stock certificate is shown in Figure 22-3. A shareholder's ownership in the corporation, however, does not depend on his possession of the physical stock certificate. For example, if the certificate is destroyed in a fire, the shareholder's ownership in the corporation is not destroyed.

stock certificate
A document that serves as a stockholder's proof of ownership in a corporation.

Preemptive Rights   Under common law, shareholders have *preemptive rights.* Preemptive rights give preference to shareholders to purchase shares of a new issue of stock. Each shareholder receives preference in proportion to the percentage of stock she already owns.

For example, suppose that a shareholder owns 1,500 shares in a corporation with 5,000 outstanding shares. She owns 30 percent of the corporation's outstanding stock. Now suppose that the corporation decides to issue an additional 10,000 shares. If the corporation does not grant preemptive rights, her relative control of the corporation will fall because she now owns only

GLOBAL Context

Criminal Liability in France

The French Penal Code does not adhere to a detailed or large list of corporate offenses but, instead, adopts what is called the specialty principal, which requires corporate criminal liability to be applicable only when an "express mention in the law or in a French regulation exists."

The French system of corporate criminal liability sharply contrasts with that of the United States in that it has often been described as scientific. This is because the French system requires heavy statistics outlining the frequency of a corporate officer's involvement in a crime before any criminal liability may be enforced. This approach differs from the approach here in the United States because our responsible-person doctrine may require a corporate officer to be held criminally liable regardless of the extent of participation in a crime.

1,500 of the corporation's 15,000 outstanding shares, or 10 percent of its stock. In contrast, if the corporation does reserve preemptive rights, and the shareholder elects to purchase 3,000 shares of the newly issued stock, then she owns 4,500 shares of the corporation's 15,000 outstanding shares (30 percent). Thus, with preemptive rights, she can maintain her proportionate control of the corporation.

In most states, a corporation's bylaws can negate preemptive rights, so the corporation determines whether to grant preemptive rights. Preemptive rights are especially important for individuals who own stock in closely held corporations due to the relatively small number of issued shares. If a closely held corporation issues additional shares, an individual shareholder may lose proportional control over the firm if he does not buy newly issued shares. However, if preemptive rights exist within the corporation, all shareholders receive stock warrants, which they can redeem for a certain number of shares at a specified price within a given time period.

stock warrant

A type of security issued by a corporation (usually together with a bond or preferred stock) that gives the holder the right to purchase a certain amount of common stock at a stated price.

Dividends   If directors fail to declare and distribute dividends, shareholders have the right to take legal action to force the directors to declare the dividends. In many cases, however, directors have good reason to hold dividends for a limited amount of time to finance major undertakings such as research or expansion. Thus, shareholders must show that the directors are acting unreasonably and abusing their discretion in withholding the dividend.

Inspection Rights   All shareholders have the right to inspection under both statutory and common law. A shareholder can, moreover, appoint an agent to conduct the inspection on her behalf.

Figure 22-3

Example of a Stock Certificate

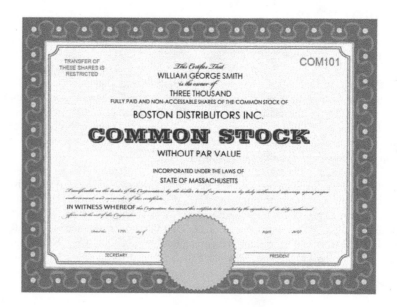

To prevent abuse, however, this right has many limitations. Shareholders can inspect records and books only if they ask in advance and have a *proper purpose.* Many states have other statutory limitations to this right. For example, some states allow only shareholders with a minimum number of shares to inspect. Other states require the shareholder to own stock for a minimum amount of time before inspection. Additionally, corporations can deny shareholders' right to inspect confidential corporate information, such as trade secrets.

Share Transfer   The law generally permits property owners to transfer their property to another person, and, in most cases, stock is considered transferable property. In closely held corporations, however, the transfer of stock is usually restricted so that shareholders can choose the corporation's other shareholders.

One method of restricting stock transferability is called the right of first refusal. If a corporation establishes this right in its bylaws, the corporation or its shareholders have the right to purchase any shares of stock offered for resale by a shareholder within a specified period of time.

right of first refusal
A method of restricting stock transferability whereby a corporation or its shareholders have the right to purchase any shares of stock offered for resale by a shareholder within a specified time frame.

Corporate Dissolution   Shareholders have the right to petition the court to dissolve their corporation if they feel the company cannot continue to operate profitably. According to Section 14.30 of RMBCA, if a corporation engages in any of the following behaviors, shareholders have a legal right to initiate dissolution.

1. Directors are deadlocked in managerial decisions and harming the corporation.
2. Directors are acting in illegal, oppressive, or fraudulent ways.
3. Assets are being wasted or used improperly.
4. Shareholders are deadlocked and cannot elect directors.

Once dissolution has taken place and the corporation has settled its debts with its creditors, shareholders have a right to receive the remaining assets of the company in proportion to the number of shares they own.

Shareholder's Derivative Suit   One of the shareholder's most important rights is the right to a derivative suit. If corporate directors fail to sue when the corporation has been harmed by an individual, another corporation, or a director, individual shareholders can file a shareholder's derivative suit on behalf of the corporation. In most jurisdictions, to be able to file a shareholder's derivative suit, a shareholder must have held stock at the time of the alleged wrongdoing. Before filing the suit, the shareholder must file a complaint with the board of directors. If nothing is done in response to the complaint, the shareholder can proceed with the suit. Enron shareholders brought shareholder's derivative suits against various directors and officers of Enron.

shareholder's derivative suit
A lawsuit filed by a shareholder on behalf of the corporation.

Derivative suits are important when shareholders believe that directors of the corporation are harming the corporation. It seems highly unlikely that directors will sue themselves for damages they cause in such cases. Thus, the shareholder's derivative suit is important for holding the directors accountable for their behavior. Because the shareholder files this suit on behalf of the corporation, all damages recovered are given to the corporation, not the individual shareholder.

Shareholder's Direct Suit   In addition to their right to bring suit on behalf of the corporation, shareholders can also bring a direct suit against the corporation. In a shareholder's direct suit, the shareholder alleges that she has suffered damages caused by the corporation. For example, shareholders can bring a direct suit if the board of directors is improperly withholding dividends or if a shareholder is wrongly denied his right to inspect corporate records. If a court awards damages as a result of a shareholder's direct suit, the damages go to the shareholder personally.

shareholder's direct suit
A lawsuit filed by a shareholder against the corporation.

Exhibit 22-3 summarizes the respective rights of directors, officers, and shareholders.

Exhibit 22-3

Rights of
Directors, Officers,
and Shareholders

POSITION	RIGHT
Directors	Right to compensation
	Right to participation
	Right to inspection
	Right to indemnification
Officers	Rights determined in employment contract
Shareholders	Right to have stock certificates
	Preemptive rights
	Right to dividends
	Right to transfer shares
	Inspection rights
	Right to corporate dissolution
	Right to file a derivative suit
	Right to file a direct suit

LO 22-7

Introduction to Mergers and Consolidations

Although many people believe that *mergers* and *consolidations* are synonymous, they are in fact legally distinct procedures. Nevertheless, in both mergers and consolidations, corporations, shareholders, and creditors have the same rights and liabilities.

MERGERS

merger
A combination of two or more corporations in which only one of the corporations continues to exist.

A merger occurs when a legal contract combines two or more corporations and only one of the corporations continues to exist. A useful way to understand a merger is to think of one corporation absorbing another corporation (called an *absorbed corporation* or a *disappearing corporation*), yielding a single surviving corporation.

The surviving firm remains a single corporation, but it changes in several ways after the merger. First, its shareholders must amend its articles of incorporation according to the specific conditions of the merger. Second, the surviving corporation becomes liable for all debts and obligations of the absorbed corporation.

The surviving corporation also grows from the merger because it obtains the absorbed corporation's property and assets. In addition, it acquires the absorbed corporation's rights, powers, and privileges.

CONSOLIDATIONS

consolidation
A combination of two or more corporations in which the combining corporations cease to exist and a new corporation is formed.

Like mergers, consolidations legally combine two or more corporations. In a consolidation, however, neither of the original corporations continues to exist legally. Rather, they form an entirely new corporation with its own legal status.

Because the new corporation has independent legal status, the articles of incorporation of the original companies are void. The shareholders of the new corporation create new articles of incorporation, called *articles of consolidation,* according to the details of the consolidation.

The consolidated firm assumes the liabilities, debts, and obligations of the original corporations. The new corporation also acquires the original corporations' property and assets. Finally, the consolidated corporation takes on the rights, privileges, and powers of the original companies.

Today, consolidations are very rare. As Section 11.01 of RMBCA reads, "In modern corporate practice consolidation transactions are obsolete since it is nearly always advantageous for one of the parties in the transaction to be the surviving corporation."

GLOBAL Context

Merger Control in South Africa

South Africa, like many other countries, takes measures to secure a competitive but fair environment for mergers. Specifically, the Companies Act and the rules of the Johannesburg Stock Exchange control mergers. The Companies Act provides protection for minority shareholders. For instance, shareholders cannot approve a merger unless 90 percent of all shareholders vote to accept the offer. In addition, minority shareholders have access to South African courts and may employ them when disputes arise. The Companies Act also establishes a panel to inquire about mergers or takeovers.

The Johannesburg Stock Exchange has established rules that govern the treatment of shareholders in mergers and takeovers. For example, if a change of corporate control takes place outside the stock exchange, the initiator of the merger must extend the offer to the shareholders and disclose all pertinent information to them within a reasonable amount of time.

THE RIGHTS OF SHAREHOLDERS

When shareholders invest in corporations, they expect the board of directors to handle daily business issues. They also expect, however, to vote on exceptional matters, including mergers, consolidations, changes in partners, sales or leases of the corporation, and exchanges of assets. Because shareholders have a vested interest in the survival and prosperity of the corporation, these matters are of great significance to them. Thus, the merger and consolidation procedures require shareholder approval.

APPRAISAL RIGHTS

The law protects shareholders as a group from corporations, but it also protects individual shareholders from one another. Suppose that although an overwhelming majority of shareholders vote to approve a merger, a single shareholder dissents. In this situation, the law does not force the dissenting shareholder to become a shareholder in a corporation different from the one in which she originally invested. Thus, the law permits dissenting shareholders to exercise their appraisal rights. An appraisal right is a dissenting shareholder's right to have her shares appraised and to receive monetary compensation from the corporation for their value.

Strict procedures govern appraisal rights. Before a shareholder vote, dissenting shareholders must submit a notification of dissent. By conveying their disapproval before the vote, the dissenting shareholders may sway other shareholders to reconsider their decision. If, however, the shareholder vote approves the transaction, the dissenting shareholders must issue another statement demanding adequate compensation for their shares.

The corporation must then present the dissenting shareholders with a document stating the value of their shares. Shareholders and corporations often clash when determining the value of these shares. Generally, however, they use the value of the shares on the day before the shareholder vote. The language of the law is of little help; it ambiguously calls for the "fair value of shares" (RMBCA 13.01). If the dissenting shareholders and the corporation cannot reach an agreement, courts intervene to establish the shares' value.

Exhibit 22-4 summarizes the core concepts of corporation consolidations and mergers.

appraisal right
A dissenting shareholder's right to have his or her shares appraised and to receive monetary compensation from the corporation for their value.

- A merger occurs when a legal contract combines two or more corporations and only one corporation continues to exist.
- A consolidation occurs when a legal contract combines two or more corporations and an entirely new corporation results.
- An appraisal right is a dissenting shareholder's right to have her or his shares appraised and to receive monetary compensation from the corporation for that value.

Exhibit 22-4

Review of Mergers and Consolidations

Purchase of Stock

takeover

The purchase of one corporation's stock by another corporation as a means of gaining control of the selling corporation.

Besides engaging in mergers and consolidations, corporations can extend their operations by purchasing another corporation's stock. An acquiring corporation, or *aggressor,* can buy any or all of another corporation's voting shares. Through such a stock purchase, the purchasing corporation gains control of the selling corporation in a corporate takeover.

The Nature of Takeovers

During the 1980s, not only did the number of corporate takeovers increase, but so too did the number of hostile takeovers. Hostile takeovers are takeovers to which the management of the target corporation objects. When a hostile takeover succeeds, the target corporation's management frequently compares the transition to a full-scale invasion characterized by layoffs and dramatic changes in company policy.

hostile takeover

A takeover to which the management of the target corporation objects.

TYPES OF TAKEOVERS

tender offer

A type of takeover in which the aggressor corporation offers the target shareholders a price above their stock's current market value.

To initiate a stock purchase, the aggressor must appeal directly to the shareholders of the corporation it hopes to buy, known as the *target corporation.* The aggressor can offer several types of deals to the target shareholders. It can make a tender offer, in which it offers target shareholders a price above the current market value of the stock. Aggressors, however, often require them to receive a certain number of shares within a certain time frame.

exchange tender offer

A type of takeover in which the aggressor corporation offers to exchange the target shareholders' current stock for stock in the aggressor's corporation.

Alternatively, the aggressor may make an exchange tender offer. In an exchange tender offer, the aggressor offers to exchange target shareholders' current stock for stock in the aggressor's corporation. The aggressor may also make a cash tender offer to the target shareholders in which it pays them cash for their stock.

After acquiring a substantial number of the target corporation's shares, the aggressor initiates a proxy fight by fighting for control over target shareholders' proxies. Before an aggressor can gain control of the target corporation through proxies, it needs a key piece of information: a list of target shareholders. Although resistant target corporations often want to conceal this information, federal securities law requires target corporations to assist aggressors in some ways. Thus, to avoid lengthy and expensive lawsuits, target corporations often provide a list of shareholders voluntarily.

cash tender offer

A type of takeover in which the aggressor corporation offers to pay the target shareholders cash for their stock.

Those seeking to acquire corporations have developed tactics to overcome the law's rules encouraging cooperation from target corporations. Because contacting each individual target shareholder is expensive, aggressors often try to win the favor of a few institutional investors that own a large block of shares. If an aggressor can obtain the proxies of these investors, it can win control of the target corporation.

RESPONSE TO TAKEOVERS

self-tender offer

A takeover-resistance strategy in which the target corporation offers to buy its shareholders' stock.

Once an aggressor has presented its offer to the target corporation's shareholders, the target corporation's board of directors must inform shareholders of all facts pertinent to shareholders' votes. After reviewing these material facts, the directors vote to accept or reject the offer and advise shareholders accordingly.

If the directors conclude that a takeover is not in the company's best interest, the company may employ many methods of resistance. One common method is a self-tender offer, in which the target corporation offers to buy its shareholders' stock. If the shareholders accept the offer, the target corporation maintains control of the business.

leveraged buyout (LBO)

A takeover-resistance strategy in which a group within the target corporation buys all the corporate stock held by the public, thereby turning the company into a privately held corporation.

Alternatively, target corporations may defend themselves using leveraged buyouts. A leveraged buyout (LBO) occurs when a group within a corporation (usually management) buys all the outstanding corporate stock held by the public. Thus, the group gains control over corporate operations by going private, or becoming a privately held corporation.

LBOs are usually high-risk endeavors, however, because the target corporation must borrow money to purchase the outstanding stock. It may have to borrow money from an investment bank or issue corporate bonds.

In Case 22-3, the U.S. Court of Appeals for the Sixth Circuit considered the legality of a golden parachute, a clause in an executive's contract specifying that he or she will receive large benefits if the executive's employment is terminated. Management of the target firm in this case made an agreement with its top managers to win their cooperation in resisting a takeover.

CASE 22-3

CAMPBELL, KESSER, AND WILLIAMS v. POTHAS CORPORATION
U.S. COURT OF APPEALS FOR THE SIXTH CIRCUIT
238 F.3d 792 (2001)

FACTS: *PCS, a Saskatchewan fertilizer corporation, approached Arcadian, a Tennessee fertilizer corporation, about a possible merger. They decided to merge, and Arcadian and PCS negotiated the terms of the merger and the severance agreements. The Arcadian board approved employment agreements for nine senior executives that included so-called golden parachutes. The "golden parachute" portion of the severance package provided a formula to compensate senior executives in case of a change in corporate control accompanied by a material change in the executive's position at the new company. In such a circumstance, the executive could leave the company and receive an aggregate payment in one lump sum. Three of the executives elected to take the severance package but were not compensated accordingly. Campbell (the former president and CEO), Kesser (the former vice president and general counsel), and Williams (the former vice president and CFO) sued PCS for breach of contract because PCS refused to make those severance payments to the executives. In response, PCS argued that the golden parachute agreements were not enforceable because they violated public policy.*

ISSUE: Are the golden parachutes offered to the three executives enforceable, or do they violate public policy?

REASONING: PCS argued that the golden parachutes violated public policy and therefore that the assumption agreement promising them is void. However, PCS offered golden parachutes to its own top managers. Hypocrisy aside, PCS cited no circuit case law supporting this proposition. Although the court has frowned on golden parachutes in past dicta, the court has never held that such severance packages were per se unlawful. Furthermore, PCS did not provide much reason to equate this type of executive compensation with contracts prohibited by public policy, such as ones to perform illegal acts. Although PCS cited a congressional committee report saying that golden parachutes should be discouraged, Congress decided to tax golden parachutes and not prohibit them. Therefore, PCS did not cite compelling evidence that the contracts were prohibited by public policy.

DECISION AND REMEDY: The court ruled that the golden parachutes did not violate public policy, and it subsequently ordered enforcement of the severance agreements. PCS already received the benefit of the bargain it struck concerning golden parachutes in having an orderly change in corporate control, and it cannot refuse payment in return.

SIGNIFICANCE OF THE CASE: This case illustrates the trouble firms can get into when they engage in mergers and severance packages. PCS made an agreement to secure the loyalty of its top management, but when the time came to fulfill its part of the bargain, the company tried to argue that enforcement of such a contract would be unfair and unenforceable.

CRITICAL THINKING

Is there any missing information you would ask for when considering the facts of this case? If you were to argue to reverse the trial court's decision, what reasons would you offer?

ETHICAL DECISION MAKING

Think about the WH process of ethical decision making. What is the purpose of the court's decision? In other words, which value is upheld? What value is in conflict with the reasoning of the court?

E-COMMERCE and the Law

Hostile Takeovers Online

In the world of business, physical corporations are not the only ones who fear hostile takeovers. Companies such as Yahoo!, the Internet web browser and e-mail hub, have recently fallen on hard times. Advertising companies have many more outlets now in which to fund advertising, which means that advertising business is being spread thin over the online realm. This market slowdown presents a problem for Yahoo because 90 percent of Yahoo's profits come from selling advertising space. Because Yahoo's stock prices have dropped dramatically, the company is worried about hostile takeover. To help prevent this from happening, Yahoo has created a poison pill. This measure means that if another company, such as AOL Time Warner, owns a majority of Yahoo's stock, other stockholders holding shares of Yahoo may purchase more Yahoo stock at a significantly lower price. This bargain drastically increases the price the (would be) takeover company would have to pay to complete the takeover. Yahoo may then feel a little more secure about its continued independence.

Sources: http://www.forbes.com/2001/03/02/0302ecommerce.html; http://business.yourdictionary.com/poison-pill

Response to Termination

The death of a corporation occurs in two phases: *dissolution,* the legal termination of the corporation, and *liquidation,* the process by which the board of directors converts the corporation's assets into cash and distributes them among the corporation's creditors and shareholders.

DISSOLUTION

Dissolution may be voluntary or involuntary, depending on who initiates and compels the dissolution. *Voluntary dissolution* occurs when the directors or shareholders trigger the dissolution procedures. The directors can initiate the proposal and submit it to the shareholders for a vote, or the shareholders can begin dissolution procedures. *Involuntary dissolution* results when government or private parties successfully get a court order dissolving the corporation. Either way, for dissolution to be successful, shareholders must unanimously vote for the proposal.

Regardless of whether the directors or shareholders initiate dissolution, the corporation must follow specific procedures. First, the directors must file articles of dissolution with the secretary of state. These articles must include the company name, the date of dissolution, and the method of authorization of dissolution. Next, the directors must notify the shareholders. If shareholders or creditors have claims against the corporation, they must make them known within a stipulated time frame. Although the corporation establishes the time frame, the period must extend at least 120 days after the date of dissolution.

SUMMARY

Characteristics of Corporations	• Legal entity. • Rights as person and citizen. • Creature of the state. • Limited liability of shareholders. • Unrestricted transferability of corporate shares. • Perpetual existence. • Centralized management. • Corporate taxation. • Liability for corporate agents.
Corporate Powers	Corporations have both express and implied powers.
	An *ultra vires* act is a corporate action that is beyond the scope of the corporation's authority.

Classification of Corporations	<ul><li>Public or private.</li><li>For profit or nonprofit.</li><li>Domestic, foreign, or alien.</li><li>Publicly held or closely held.</li><li>S corporations.</li><li>Professional corporations.</li></ul>
Formation of the Corporation	To create a corporation:<ul><li>Promoters organize corporate formation.</li><li>Subscribers offer to purchase stock in the corporation during the formation process.</li><li>A state is selected for incorporation.</li></ul>
Legal Process of Incorporation	The legal requirements are:<ul><li>Selecting the corporate name.</li><li>Drafting and filing the articles of incorporation.</li><li>Holding the first organizational meeting.</li></ul>
Potential Problems with Formation of the Corporation	Remedies for defective incorporation include:<ul><li>*De jure* corporations.</li><li>*De facto* corporations.</li><li>Corporations by estoppel.</li><li>Piercing the corporate veil.</li></ul>
Corporate Financing	<ul><li>Debt securities (bonds).</li><li>Equity securities (preferred stock and common stock).</li></ul>
Roles of Directors, Officers, and Shareholders	Directors:<ul><li>A minimum number must attend board of directors meetings.</li><li>They are legally responsible for day-to-day managerial activities.</li></ul>Officers:<ul><li>Run the day-to-day business of the organization.</li><li>Act as agent of the corporation.</li></ul>Shareholders:<ul><li>Approve major corporate decisions.</li><li>Elect and remove members of the board of directors.</li></ul>
Duties of Directors, Officers, and Shareholders	Directors and officers:<ul><li>Duty of care.</li><li>Duty of loyalty.</li><li>Duty to disclose conflicts of interest.</li></ul>Majority shareholder:<ul><li>Duty of care and loyalty when selling shares.</li></ul>
Liabilities of Directors, Officers, and Shareholders	Directors and officers:<ul><li>Personally liable for their own torts and crimes.</li><li>Liable for torts and crimes of others when there was inadequate supervision.</li></ul>Shareholders:<ul><li>Liable for debts of the corporation to the extent of their investment.</li></ul>

490   Part VII   Business Organizations

Rights of Directors, Officers, and Shareholders

Directors:

- Compensation.
- Participation.
- Inspection.
- Indemnification.

Officers' rights are spelled out in their employment contract.
Shareholders:

- Right to vote at the shareholders' meeting.
- Preemption.
- Inspection.
- Share transfer.
- Petition for dissolution.
- Direct and derivative suits against the corporation.

Introduction to Mergers and Consolidations

Merger: A legal contract whereby two or more corporations combine and only one of the corporations continues to exist.

Consolidation: A legal contract whereby two or more corporations combine and an entirely new corporation results.

Rights of shareholders: Shareholders vote only on exceptional matters regarding the corporation.

Appraisal right: An appraisal right is the shareholder's right to have her or his shares appraised and to receive monetary compensation for their value.

Purchase of Stock

An acquiring corporation can take control of another corporation by purchasing a substantial amount of its voting stock.

The Nature of Takeovers

A corporation can expand its size and operations by purchasing the stock of another firm.

A *hostile takeover* is a takeover to which the management of the target corporation objects.

Types of takeovers:

- Tender offers.
- Exchange offers.
- Cash tender offers.

Response to Termination

Response to takeovers: Directors declare whether they accept or reject the offer. If they object to the offer, they can engage in methods of resistance.

Dissolution is the legal death of a corporation.

Point/Counterpoint

Should Corporations Be Allowed the Status of Legal Personhood and Be Given Full Protection under the Bill of Rights as Persons?	
YES	NO
On May 10, 1886, in the case of *Santa Clara County v. The Southern Pacific Railroad Company,* the Supreme Court clearly decided that "other corporations" deserved	The Bill of Rights, including the Fourteenth Amendment, was created at a time when corporations clearly existed in the United States. However, a stipulation

"equal protection of the laws," specifically the Fourteenth Amendment.

Several reasons support the position that corporations should be considered legal persons. A corporation is created by and is composed of natural persons. Actions of the corporation directly affect the natural persons associated with the corporation. The rights of the creators and shareholders cannot be violated, and violating the rights of the corporation indirectly violates the rights of the persons who created and are part of the corporation. Further, additional limitations should not be placed on a group of people simply because they have combined their efforts and formed a corporation.

Logical limitations are in place to restrict corporations' existence as persons. Corporations cannot become official citizens and cannot vote. Even though the political system affects the corporation, the natural citizens involved with the corporation are expected to vote with the corporation's best interest in mind.

Finally, corporations deserve the same rights as natural persons because a corporation fulfills the same obligations as natural persons as an entity separate from the natural persons associated with the corporation. For example, corporations pay government taxes on profits; the shareholders also pay taxes.

to include corporations *as a separate entity* was not included in the Bill of Rights. Clearly, the creators of the Bill of Rights were aware that corporations existed at the time. The corporations were not mentioned as having rights *independent of the natural persons associated with the corporations,* so the Bill of Rights was not designed to protect corporations as legal persons.

Further, classifying corporations as legal persons and allowing them protection under the Bill of Rights, although advantageous for corporate interests, is harmful to human interests. For example, corporate money speaks much louder than one person's letter as a means of influencing politicians.

If corporations are given rights as a natural person, the individuals making decisions behind the corporation are not held accountable to the larger world community. The corporation is punished for a poor decision rather than the individual who used poor judgment. When the corporation is punished rather than the individual who made the decision, the individual may not feel much, if any, of the consequences of his or her action.

Corporations should not be considered legal persons and protected as such because corporations do not face the same restrictions as a natural person. A natural person's life must end; however, a corporation is allowed perpetual existence.

Also, corporations do not face the same potential consequences as natural persons. A corporation cannot be sent to jail for its actions. A corporation cannot be rehabilitated and changed to become a profitable member of society if it breaks the law.

Questions & Problems

1. Name at least three characteristics that distinguish corporations from other forms of business organization.

2. How is an *ultra vires* act related to a corporation's powers?

3. Compare and contrast common stock and preferred stock.

4. Explain the primary duties of officers and directors.

5. What is the business judgment rule?

6. The Greek shipping company Ionia Management managed a 600-foot oil tanker that delivered oil to ports along the eastern seaboard of the United States. During these deliveries, Ionia's engine room crew, at the direction of their ship supervisors, regularly dumped oily waste into the ocean. To conceal the wrongdoing, the ship's crew falsified entries in its oil record book and lied to Coast Guard officials regarding the waste. The top executives and officials

at Ionia did not know that employees were violating company policy and falsifying ship records to cover up their wrongdoing. A jury convicted Ionia of conspiracy, pollution, and obstruction of justice, and the company was fined $4.9 million in addition to probation and assessments. The corporation appealed. Should the corporation be found criminally liable for the illegal actions of its lower-level employees under the doctrine of *respondeat superior?* Why or why not? [*United States v. Ionia Mgmt,* 555 F.3d 303 (2009).]

7. Peter Smejkal was a corporate officer and director of J.A. Morrissey, Inc. (JAM), a construction company. While employed at JAM, Smejkal had his own excavation business and secretly performed excavation work on JAM projects on his own behalf. On one occasion he also used JAM employees for construction activities that were unrelated to JAM's projects. Additionally, Smejkal abused his position

at the company and poisoned the relationship with three JAM clients while still an officer at JAM and then succeeded in obtaining those clients' projects for his own company after his termination from JAM. Did Smejkal owe duties of good faith and loyalty to JAM? If so, do you think Smejkal breached his duties of good faith and loyalty to the corporation? Why or why not? [*J.A. Morrissey, Inc. v. Smejkal,* 6 A.3d 701 (Vt. 2010).]

8. Richard Schoon was elected to the board of directors at the Troy Corporation, a private corporation in Delaware. There are three stock series of stock options. A series A share allows someone to elect four of five directors on the corporation's board. A series B share allows a stockholder to elect the fifth member of the board. Anyone who has a series C share has no voting rights. The CEO of Troy, Daryl Smith, owns the majority of the A shares; thus, he elected four directors of the board. Schoon was elected as the fifth director, although he owned no shares. Schoon claimed that Smith dominated the board because he elected the other four directors and they were compliant to his wishes. Schoon believed that in several instances, Smith took actions that benefited him personally yet harmed the corporation's finances. In 2008, Schoon filed a derivative suit that shareholders typically file. However, Schoon was not a shareholder and owned no stock in the company. Do you think the court accepted his suit? Why or why not? [*Schoon v . Smith,* Del. Supr. (2008).]

9. Emory B. Perry, who represents numerous shareholders, owned stock of The RAMP Corporation, a now-defunct company that developed communications technologies for the health care industry. Darryl R. Cohen and Andrew M. Brown are former directors of RAMP. Perry filed suit against Cohen and Brown in December 2004, alleging negligence, common law fraud, statutory fraud, and conspiracy. Perry claimed that Cohen and Brown made numerous misrepresentations in their original petition and that he received false information as a result. Perry argued that both men's misrepresentations induced the stockholders to hold and refrain from selling their RAMP stock. Is this an example of a direct suit or a derivative suit? Why? [*Perry v. Cohen,* 272 S.W.3d 661 (Tex. Ct. App. 2007).]

10. The Ray Griffith Company, Inc. (RGC) began in the 1950s in Columbia, Mississippi, when Ray Griffith purchased the rights to a patent to manufacture a pecan picker. In 1992, RGC was devised to Ray's two sons, Tom and Harry Griffith. Tom was given direct ownership of three shares of the company, and Harry was given direct ownership of two shares of the company. Additionally, a trust was set up in each son's name, with each trust holding 87½ shares. Over the years that followed, the dividends of the corporation decreased, until Tom discovered that the reason the corporation's expenses were increasing was that Harry was charging personal expenses to the corporation and charging expenses of his two other businesses to the corporation. Tom sued Harry for conversion and breach of fiduciary duty. However, Harry maintained that out of those personal expenses, his cell phone bill, car repairs, gas, and health insurance were necessary business expenses. Tom disputed this assertion. Do you think Harry breached his fiduciary duty in his capacity as the president of the corporation? Why or why not? *Griffith v. Griffith,* 997 So. 2d 218 (2008).]

11. H&R Block is one of the largest providers of income-tax preparations and the second largest of online do-it-yourself software in the United States. In 2010, the tax preparer sought to buy out its rival, 2SS Holdings, who produced TaxAct software products to consumers. TaxAct is the nation's third largest provider of tax preparation software, which caused concern for the Justice Department. According to its investigation, the merger would result in fewer free tax assistance software products and higher prices for the products that those companies charge for. H&R Block challenged by saying the merger would only give it 28 percent of the do-it-yourself tax preparation market. However, it was ultimately decided that the merger would result in an anticompetitive market; thus, the merger was denied. What aspects of merger law are included in this case? [*United States v. H&R Block,* 833 F. Supp. 2d 36; 2011 U.S. Dist. LEXIS 130219.]

Glossary

A

abandonment   Behavior in which a tenant moves out of a leased premises before the end of the term and discontinues making rent payments.

absolute privilege   A special right, immunity, permission, or benefit given to certain individuals that allows them to make any statements about someone without being held liable for defamation for any false statement made, regardless of intent or knowledge of the falsity of the claim.

absolutism   A theory of ethics which requires that individuals defer to a set of rules to guide them in the ethical decision-making process. Whether an action is moral depends on whether it conforms to the given set of ethical rules.

abuse of process   The malicious and deliberate misuse or perversion of a legal procedure.

acceptance   A key factor in the agreement element of a contract; consists of the agreement of one party, the offeree, to the terms of the offer in the contract made by the other party, the offeror.

acceptor   A person (drawee) who accepts and signs a draft to agree to pay the draft when it is presented.

accommodation party   A party who signs an instrument to provide credit for another party who has also signed the instrument.

accord and satisfaction   An arrangement between contracting parties whereby one of the parties substitutes a different performance for his or her original duty under the contract. The promise to perform the new duty is the *accord,* and the actual performance of that new duty is the *satisfaction.*

accountant-client privilege   The right of an accountant to not reveal any information given in confidence by a client. The privilege is not granted by every state or by the federal government.

accounting   A review and listing of all partnership assets and/or profit.

accredited investor   A private investor who is allowed to accept private securities offerings under certain specific guidelines set by the SEC.

act utilitarianism   A theory of ethics which requires that individuals examine all the potential actions in each situation and choose the action that yields the greatest amount of pleasure over pain for all involved.

actual cause   The determination that the defendant's breach of duty resulted directly in the plaintiff's injury.

actual eviction   An eviction in which a landlord physically prevents the lessee from entering the leased premises.

actual malice   In defamation, either a person's knowledge that his or her statement or published material is false or the person's reckless disregard for whether it was false.

actual notice   Notice of agency termination that is given by directly informing third parties, either orally or in writing.

actus reus   Latin for "guilty act"; a wrongful behavior that is associated with the physical act of a declared crime.

ad substantiation   An FTC standard requiring that advertisers have a reasonable basis for the claims made in their ads.

adhesion contract   A contract created by a party to an agreement that is presented to the other party on a take-it-or-leave-it basis. Such contracts are legal but are sometimes rescinded on the grounds of unconscionability and the absence of one party's free will to enter a contract.

administrative agency   Any government body created by the legislative branch (e.g., Congress, a state legislature, or a city council) to carry out specific duties.

administrative law   The collection of rules and decisions made by administrative agencies to fill in particular details missing from constitutions and statutes.

administrative law judge (ALJ)   A judge who presides over an administrative hearing; may attempt to get the parties to settle but has the power to issue a binding decision.

Administrative Procedures Act (APA)   Federal legislation that places limitations on how agencies are run and contains very specific guidelines on rule making by agencies.

admission   A statement made in court, under oath, or at some stage during a legal proceeding, in which a party against whom charges have been brought admits that an oral contract existed, even though the contract was required to be in writing.

advance directive   A legal instrument in which a person expresses his wishes about efforts to prolong his life.

adversarial negotiation   Negotiation in which each party seeks to maximize its own gain.

adverse possession   An involuntary property transfer in which a person acquires ownership of property by treating a piece of real property as his or her own, without protest or permission from the owner.

affiliate   A business enterprise located in one state that is directly or indirectly owned and controlled by a company located in another state. Also called *foreign subsidiary.*

affirm   An appellate court decision that accepts a lower court's judgment in a case that has been appealed.

affirmative defense   A defendant's response to a plaintiff's claim in which the defendant attacks the plaintiff's legal right to bring the action rather than attacking the fact of the claim or making excuses for unlawful behavior. Common affirmative defenses are expiration of the statute of limitations, mistake of fact, intoxication, insanity, duress, and entrapment.

after-acquired property   Property acquired by a debtor after the security arrangement is made.

Age Discrimination in Employment Act (ADEA) of 1967   Federal law that prohibits employers from refusing to hire, discharging, or discriminating in terms and conditions of employment on the basis of an employee's or applicant's being age 40 or older.

agency   The fiduciary relationship that arises when one person consents to have another act on his behalf and subject to his control and the other consents to do so.

agency by estoppel   See **apparent agency.**

agency coupled with an interest   An agency relationship that is created for the benefit of the agent, not the principal.

agency relationship   The association between one party and an agent who acts on behalf of that party.

agent   A party who has the authority to act on behalf of and bind another party.

agreement   One of the four elements necessary for a contract; consists of an offer made by one party, the offeror, and the acceptance of the offer by another party, the offeree.

alien corporation   A business that is incorporated in a foreign country.

allonge   Accompanying a negotiable instrument, a piece of paper that provides room for an endorsement if no room is available on the negotiable instrument itself.

alteration   (1) An unauthorized change to an instrument that modifies the obligation of a party to the instrument. (2) A change that affects the condition of the premises.

alternative dispute resolution (ADR)   The resolution of legal problems through methods other than litigation.

ambulatory   A term pertaining to the ability of a will to be changed by a testator.

Americans with Disabilities Act (ADA)   Federal law that prohibits discrimination against employees and job applicants with disabilities.

anatomical gift   All or part of an individual's body that the individual wishes to donate to a hospital, university, organ bank, etc.

answer   The response of the defendant to the plaintiff's complaint.

antidumping duties   Special tariffs that are imposed on imported goods in order to offset illegal dumping.

antilapse clause   In an insurance policy, a clause which states that the insured has a grace period in which to make an overdue payment.

apparent agency   An agency relationship created by operation of law when one party, by her actions, causes a third party to believe someone is her agent even though that person actually has no authority to act as her agent. Also called *agency by estoppel.*

appeal   The act or fact of challenging the decision of a trial court after final judgment or some other legal ruling by taking the matter to the appropriate appellate court, and in some cases to the U.S. Supreme Court, in an attempt to reverse the decision.

appellate court   A higher court, usually consisting of more than one judge, that reviews the decision and results of a lower court (either a trial court or a lower-level appellate court) when a losing party files for an appeal. Appellate courts do not hold trials but may request additional oral and written arguments from each party; they issue written decisions, which collectively constitute case law or the common law. Also called *court of appellate jurisdiction.*

appraisal clause   A part of an insurance contract that calls for an assessment when parties disagree about the value and loss of a specific item.

appraisal right   A dissenting shareholder's right to have his or her shares appraised and to receive monetary compensation from the corporation for their value.

appropriation for commercial gain   A privacy tort that occurs when someone uses a person's name, likeness, voice, identity, or other identifying characteristics for commercial gain without that person's permission.

arbitration   A type of alternative dispute resolution wherein disputes are submitted for resolution to private non-official persons selected in a manner provided by law or the agreement of the parties.

arbitration clause   A part of an insurance contract that calls for a dispute to be settled by an arbitrator, a neutral third party.

arraignment   The first appearance in court by the defendant, at which the defendant is advised of the pending charges, the right to counsel, and the right to trial by jury and he or she enters a plea to the charge.

arrest   The action in which the police, or a person acting under the law, seize, hold, or take an individual into custody.

arson   The crime of intentionally setting fire to another's property.

articles of incorporation   A document that contains basic information about a corporation and is filed with the state.

articles of partnership   The written agreement that creates a partnership.

artisan's lien   A claim placed on personal property to satisfy a person's debt related to the property.

assault   A civil wrong that occurs when one person intentionally and voluntarily places another in fear or apprehension of an immediate, offensive physical harm. Assault does not require actual contact.

assignee   In a contract, the party who receives the rights of another party (an assignor) to collect what was contractually agreed on in the original contract.

assignment   (1) A contracting party's (an assignor's) transfer of his or her rights to the contract to a third party (an assignee). (2) A transfer of a tenant's entire interest in a leased property.

assignor   In a contract, the party who transfers his or her rights to a contract to a third party (an assignee), giving the assignee the right to collect what was contractually agreed on in the original contract.

assumption of the risk   A defense whereby the defendant must prove that the plaintiff voluntarily assumed the risk that the defendant caused.

attachment   (1) The point at which a creditor becomes the secured party who has a security interest in the collateral. (2) A court order permitting a local court officer to seize a debtor's property.

attempt to monopolize   The use of certain business practices with the intent to gain market share by excluding competitors and thereby gain monopoly power.

automated teller machine (ATM)   A machine connected to banking computers that enables customers to conduct transactions without having to enter their bank.

automatic stay   After bankruptcy has been filed, a moratorium during which creditors cannot bring or continue action against the debtor or his or her property.

B

bail   A thing of value, such as a money bail bond or any other form of property, that is given to the court to temporarily allow a person's release from jail and to ensure his or her appearance in court.

bailment (of personal property)   A relationship that arises when one party (the bailer) gives possession of personal property to another (the bailee) with an advance agreement on the time period, the compensation, if any, and the bailee's treatment of the property.

bait-and-switch advertising   A deceptive practice in which a seller advertises a low-priced item, generally unavailable to the consumer, and then pushes the consumer to buy a more expensive item.

Bankruptcy Abuse Prevention and Consumer Protection Act (BAPCPA) of 2005   Federal law that renovated the bankruptcy system by addressing the increased number of bankruptcy filings, significant losses associated with bankruptcy filings, loopholes and incentives that allowed for abuse, and the financial ability of debtors.

bankruptcy estate   The assets that are collected from a debtor who files for bankruptcy.

battery   A civil wrong that occurs when one person intentionally and voluntarily brings about a nonconsented harmful or offensive contact with a person or something closely associated with him or her. Battery requires an actual contact.

beachhead acquisition   A takeover in which an aggressor gradually accumulates the target company's shares.

bearer instrument   An instrument payable to cash or to whoever is in possession of the instrument.

bench trial   A trial before a judge, with the judgment decided by the judge rather than a jury; occurs when the defendant has waived his or her right to a jury trial.

beneficiary   (1) A person who can expect to benefit from a relationship. (2) A person who receives, or will receive, the proceeds from an insurance policy or a will.

bid rigging   An agreement among firms to not bid against one another or to submit a certain level of bid.

bilateral contract   A promise exchanged for a promise.

bilateral free trade agreement   An international agreement between two nations that relates to trade between them.

bill of lading   A document issued by a person engaged in the business of transporting goods that verifies receipt of the goods for shipment.

binder   An agreement that gives temporary insurance until the company decides to accept or reject the insurance application.

binding arbitration clause   A contract provision mandating that all disputes arising under the contract must be settled by arbitration.

blank endorsement   A payee's or last endorsee's signature on a negotiable instrument.

blank qualified endorsement   A blank endorsement containing words that limit the enforceability of the check, such as the term *without recourse* (which means the endorser will not be liable).

blue-sky law   A law that regulates the offering and sale of purely intrastate securities.

bond   See **debt security.**

booking   After an individual is arrested, the procedure of recording the name of the defendant and the alleged crime in the investigating agency's or police department's records.

bounty payment   A government reward for an act that is beneficial to the public.

boycott   A refusal to deal with, purchase goods from, or work for a business.

bribery   A corrupt and illegal activity in which a person offers, gives, solicits, or receives money, services, or anything of value in order to gain an illicit advantage.

brief   A written legal argument, which a party presents to a court, that explains why that party to the case should prevail. Also called *factum.*

burden of proof   To convict a defendant, the duty of the plaintiff or prosecution to establish a claim or allegation by admissible evidence and to prove to the jury or court, beyond any reasonable doubt, that the defendant committed all the essential elements of the crime.

burglary A crime in which someone unlawfully enters a building with intent to commit a felony or theft.

business ethics The use of ethics and ethical principles to solve business dilemmas.

business law The enforceable rules of conduct that govern the actions of buyers and sellers in market exchanges.

business trust A business organization governed by a group of trustees who operate the trust for beneficiaries.

buyer in the ordinary course of business A person who routinely buys goods in good faith from a person who routinely sells those goods.

bylaws Rules and regulations that govern a corporation's internal management.

C

capacity The legal ability to enter into a binding contract.

case law The collection of legal interpretations made by judges. They are considered to be law unless otherwise revoked by a statutory law. Also known as *common law*.

case or controversy A term used in the U.S. Constitution to describe the structure and requirements of conflicting claims of individuals that can be brought before a federal court for resolution. A case or controversy requires an actual dispute between parties over their legal rights that remains in conflict at the time the case is presented and that is a proper matter for judicial determination. Also referred to as *justifiable controversy.*

cash tender offer A type of takeover in which the aggressor corporation offers to pay the target shareholders cash for their stock.

cashier's check A check for which both drawer and drawee are the same bank.

casualty insurance Insurance that protects a party from accidental injury.

categorical imperative The principle that an act is ethical if we want all people to act according to its dictates.

cease-and-desist order An FTC order requiring that a company stop its illegal behavior.

certificate of deposit (CD) A document whereby a bank promises to pay a payee a certain amount of money at a future time.

certificate of incorporation A document certifying that a corporation is incorporated in the state and is authorized to conduct business.

certificate of limited partnership A document signed on the formation of a limited partnership and filed with the secretary of state.

certified check Any check that is accepted by the bank from which the funds are drawn.

chain-style business operation A type of franchise in which the franchise operates under the franchisor's business name and is required to follow the franchisor's standards and methods of business operation.

charging order An order that entitles a creditor to collect a partner's profits.

chattel paper A writing that indicates both a monetary obligation and a security interest in specific goods.

check A special draft that orders a bank (the drawee) to pay a specified sum of money to the payee from the drawer's account.

choice-of-law clause A contractual clause in which the parties specify which state's law will apply to the interpretation of the contract in the event of a dispute.

chose in action After an acquisition, the surviving corporation's right to sue for debt and damages on behalf of the absorbed corporation.

circuit court of appeal A court that hears appeals from the district courts located within its circuit, as well as appeals from decisions of federal administrative agencies. Also called *federal district court of appeal.*

civil law The body of laws that govern the rights and responsibilities either between persons or between persons and their government.

Civil Rights Act (CRA) of 1964—Title VII Federal law (as amended by the Civil Rights Act of 1991) that protects employees against discrimination based on race, color, religion, national origin, and sex; also prohibits harassment based on the same protected categories.

closely held corporation A corporation that does not sell stock to the general public.

closing The meeting at which a transfer of title takes place: The seller signs over the deed, and the buyer gives the seller a check for the amount due.

codicil The document by which a testator changes his or her will.

collateral The property that is subject to a secured interest.

collecting bank Any bank, with the exception of the payor bank, that handles a check during the check collection process.

collective bargaining The process whereby workers organize collectively and bargain with employers regarding the conditions of employment.

commerce clause Clause 3 of Article I, Section 8, of the U.S. Constitution, which authorizes and empowers Congress "[t]o regulate Commerce with foreign Nations, and among the several States, and with the Indian Tribes."

commercial general liability policy A policy that generally provides protection for the insured for bodily injury, as well as for third parties for property injury.

commercial insurance Insurance that covers some type of business risk.

commercial reasonableness   Reasonable commercial standards of fair dealing, required of merchants in addition to honesty in fact.

commercial speech   Speech made by businesses about commercial matters, such as the sale of goods and services. It is protected by the First Amendment.

common areas   Areas that are used by all tenants.

common carrier   A carrier that is licensed to provide transportation services to the public.

common-carrier delivery contract   A type of contract in which purchased goods are delivered to the buyer via an independent contractor, such as a trucking line.

common law   See **case law.**

common stock   Corporate stock that does not convey any preference to its holders.

communication   In a contract, an offer made to the offeree or the offeree's agent.

comparative law   The study of the legal systems of different states.

compensatory damages   Money awarded to a plaintiff as reimbursement for her or his losses; based on the amount of actual damage or harm to property, lost wages or profits, pain and suffering, medical expenses, disability, etc.

complaint   A formal written document that begins a civil lawsuit; contains the plaintiff's list of allegations against the defendant, along with the damages the plaintiff seeks.

complete performance   Contract performance that occurs when all aspects of the parties' duties under the contract are carried out perfectly.

computer crime   Crime that is committed using a computer.

concealment   The active hiding of the truth about a material fact.

concurrent authority   Both the state and federal court systems have the power to render a binding verdict for this type of case.

concurrent conditions   In a contract, terms under which each party's performance is conditioned on the performance of the other; occur only when the parties are required to perform for each other simultaneously.

condemnation   The legal process by which a transfer of property is made against the protest of the property owner.

condition precedent   In a contract, an event that must occur in order for a party's duty to arise.

condition subsequent   In a contract, a future event that terminates the obligations of the parties when it occurs.

conditional contract   A contract that becomes enforceable only on the happening or termination of a specified condition.

conditional endorsement   An endorsement whereby payment can be made only on the fulfillment of a predecided condition, such as painting one's house.

conditional estate   An ownership interest in which the holder has the same interest as that in a fee simple absolute except that this interest is subject to a condition.

conditional privilege   A special right, immunity, permission, or benefit given to certain individuals that allows them to make any statements about someone without being held liable for defamation for any false statements made without actual malice.

conditional sales contract   A type of contract in which the sale itself is contingent on approval; can be either a sale-on-approval contract or a sale-or-return contract.

conforming goods   Goods that conform to contract specifications.

conglomerate merger   A merger in which a company merges with another company that is not a competitor or a buyer or seller to the company.

consent decree   An agreement that binds the violating party to cease his or her illegal behavior.

consent order   A statement in which a company agrees to stop disputed behavior but does not admit that it broke the law.

consequential damages   In a contract, foreseeable damages that result from special facts and circumstances arising outside the contract itself. The damages must be within the contemplation of the parties at the time the breach occurs. Also called *special damages.*

consequentialism   A general approach to ethical dilemmas which requires that we consider the consequences our actions will have on relevant people.

consideration   The bargained-for exchange; what each party gets in exchange for his or her promise under a contract.

Consolidated Omnibus Budget Reconciliation Act (COBRA)   Federal law which ensures that when employees lose their jobs or have their hours reduced to a level at which they would not be eligible to receive medical, dental, or optical benefits from their employer, the employees will be able to continue receiving benefits under the employer's policy for up to 18 months by paying the premiums for the policy.

consolidations   Combinations of two or more corporations where none of the original corporations continue to exist as a legal entity.

constitutional law   The general limits and powers of a government as interpreted from its written constitution.

constructive eviction   An eviction that occurs when a property has become unsuitable for use due to the unlivable quality of the property.

constructive notice   Notice of agency termination that is usually given by publishing an announcement in a newspaper.

constructive trust   (1) An implied trust in which a party is named to hold the trust for its rightful owner. (2) An equitable trust imposed on someone who wrongfully obtains or holds legal right to property he or she should not possess.

consumer good   A good used or bought for use primarily for personal, family, or household purposes.

consumer lease   A lease that has a value of $25,000 or less and exists between a lessor who is regularly engaged in the business of leasing or selling and a lessee who leases the goods primarily for a personal, family, or household purpose.

contract   A promise or set of promises for the breach of which the law gives a remedy or the performance of which the law in some way recognizes a duty.

contract clause   The clause in the U.S. Constitution that prohibits the government from unreasonably interfering with an existing contract.

contract under seal   Contracts simply identified with the word *seal* or the letters *L.S.* (an abbreviation for *locus sigilli,* which means "the place for the seal") at the end.

contractual capacity   The legal ability to enter into a binding agreement.

contributory negligence   A defense to negligence whereby the defendant can escape all liability by proving that the plaintiff failed to act in a way that would have protected him or her from an unreasonable risk of harm and that the plaintiff's negligent behavior contributed in some way to the plaintiff's accident.

Convention on the International Sale of Goods (CISG)   An international agreement applicable to transactions involving the commercial sale of goods.

conversion   Permanent interference with another's use and enjoyment of his or her personal property.

cooperative   An organization formed by individuals to market new products. Individuals in a cooperative pool their resources together to gain an advantage in the market.

co-ownership   A type of ownership in which multiple individuals possess ownership interests in a property.

copyright   The protection of the expression of a creative work; i.e., protection of the fixed form that expresses the ideas.

corporation   A legal entity formed by issuing stock to investors, who are the owners of the corporation.

corporation by estoppel   A defective corporation that has conducted business with a third party and therefore cannot deny its status as a corporation to escape liability.

corrective advertising   Advertising in which a company explicitly states that formerly advertised claims were untrue. Also called *counteradvertising.*

cost-benefit analysis   An economic school of jurisprudence in which all costs and benefits of a law are given monetary values. Those laws with the highest ratios of benefits to costs are then preferable to those with lower ratios.

counterclaim   A claim made by the defendant against the plaintiff that is filed along with the defendant's answer.

counteroffer   An offer made by an offeree to the offeror that relates to the same matter as the original offer but proposes a substituted bargain that differs from the one proposed in the original offer.

countervailing duties   Special tariffs imposed on subsidized goods to offset the beneficial effect of an illegal subsidy.

course of dealing   A history of previous commercial transactions between the same parties.

course of performance   The history of dealings between the parties in the particular contract at issue.

court of appellate jurisdiction   See **appellate court.**

court of original jurisdiction   See **trial court.**

covenant not to compete   An agreement not to compete against a party for a set period of time within a designated geographic area.

covenant of quiet enjoyment   A promise that a tenant has the right to quietly enjoy the land.

cover   A buyer's right to substitute goods for those due under a sales or lease agreement when the seller provides nonconforming goods.

creditor   An entity to which a debtor owes money.

creditor beneficiary   A third party who benefits from a contract in which the promisor agrees to pay the promisee's debt.

creditors' meeting   A meeting of all the creditors listed in the Chapter 7 required schedule for liquidation.

criminal fraud   Any crime or offense in which an individual intentionally uses some sort of misrepresentation to gain an advantage over another person.

criminal law   A classification of law involving the rights and responsibilities an individual has with respect to the public as a whole.

criteria pollutant   Any of the six air pollutants that are subject to the National Ambient Air Quality Standards under the Clean Air Act.

critical-thinking skills   The ability to understand the structure and worth of an argument by evaluating the facts, issue, reasons, and conclusion of the argument.

cross-licensing   An illegal contractual arrangement in which two or more parties license each other to use their specified intellectual property *only* on the condition that neither licenses anyone else to use the property without the other's consent.

cure   A breaching party's right to provide conforming goods when nonconforming goods were initially delivered; subject to a reasonable time test.

customary international law   A general and consistent practice by nations that is accepted as binding law.

customs union   A free trade area with the additional feature of a common external tariff on products originating outside the union.

cyber terrorist   A hacker whose intention is the exploitation of a target computer or network to create a serious impact, such as the crippling of a communications network or the sabotage of a business or organization, which may have an impact on millions of citizens if the terrorist's attack is successful.

cyberlaw   A classification of law regulating business activities that are conducted online.

D

de facto **corporation**   Latin for "corporation in fact"; a corporation that has not substantially met the requirements of the state incorporation statutes.

de jure **corporation**   Latin for "lawful corporation"; a corporation that has met the mandatory statutory provisions and thus received its certificate of incorporation.

debt security   A security that represents a loan to a corporation. Also called *bond*.

debtor   A party that owes money to another party.

deceptive advertising   The practice of advertising with claims that mislead or could mislead a reasonable consumer.

defamation   A false statement or an action that harms the reputation or character of an individual, business, product, group, government, or nation.

default   Failure to make payments on a loan.

default judgment   Judgment for the plaintiff that occurs when the defendant fails to respond to the complaint.

defaulted   see **default**.

defective corporation   A corporation whose incorporation process included an error or omission.

defendant   The person, party, or entity against whom a civil or criminal lawsuit is filed in a court of law.

definite and certain (terms)   The requirement, under common law, that a contract must include and clearly define all material terms.

definite-term lease   A type of lease that expires at the end of a specified term.

delegatee   A third party who is not part of the original contract but to whom duties to perform are transferred by one of the contracting parties (a delegator).

delegation   A contracting party's (a delegator's) transfer of his or her duty to perform to a third party who is not part of the original contract (a delegatee).

delegator   A party in a contract who transfers his or her duties to perform to a third party who is not a part of the original contract (a delegatee).

demand instrument   A type of draft that allows the payee to demand payment at any time from a holder.

deontology   The ethical theory which states that an action can be determined as ethical on the basis of right and wrong, regardless of its consequences.

depositary bank   The first bank that receives a check for payment.

deposition   A pretrial sworn and recorded testimony of a witness that is acquired out of court with no judge present.

design defect   A defect that is found in all products of a particular design and renders them dangerous.

digital cash   Money stored electronically and used in place of physical currency.

direct deposit   An electronic process, preauthorized by a customer, that allows funds to be deposited directly into the customer's bank account.

directed verdict   A ruling by the judge, after the plaintiff has presented her case but before any evidence is put forward by the defendant, in favor of the defendant because the plaintiff has failed to present the minimum amount of evidence necessary to establish his claim.

discharge   A written federal court order signed by a bankruptcy judge which states that the debtor is immune from creditor actions to collect debt; i.e., a release from liability.

discharged   Released from liability; term applied to negotiable instrument liability that has terminated.

disclosed principal   A principal whose identity is known to a third party. The third party is aware that the agent is making an agreement on behalf of the principal.

discovery   The pretrial phase in a lawsuit during which each party requests relevant documents and other evidence from the other side in an attempt to "discover" pertinent facts and to avoid any surprises in the courtroom during the trial. Discovery tools include requests for admissions, interrogatories, depositions, requests for inspection, and document production requests.

dishonored   Refused; specifically, a payment that has been refused despite a holder's presenting an instrument in a timely and proper manner.

dishonored instrument   An instrument that a party has refused to pay.

disparagement   A business tort that occurs when a statement is intentionally used to defame a business product or service.

disparate impact   A form of discrimination that arises when an employer's policy or practice appears to apply to everyone equally but its actual effect is that it disproportionately limits employment opportunities for a protected class.

disparate treatment   A form of intentional discrimination in which an employee is hired, fired, denied a promotion, or the like, on the basis of membership in a protected class.

Dispute Settlement Understanding   An agreement that is part of the WTO system whereby recognized governments of WTO member states may bring an action alleging a violation of GATT by other member states.

dissolution   The change in the relation of partners caused by any partner's ceasing to be associated with the carrying on of the partnership's business.

distributor   A merchant who purchases goods from a seller for resale in a foreign market.

distributorship   A type of franchise in which the franchisor manufactures a product and licenses a dealer to sell the product in an exclusive territory.

district court   A trial court in the federal system.

dividend   A distribution of corporate profits or income that is ordered by the directors and paid to the shareholders.

document of title   A transport document that, when appropriately made out, entitles the bearer to claim the goods from the carrier.

domestic corporation   A corporation located in the state in which it is incorporated.

donee beneficiary   A third party who benefits from a contract in which a promisor agrees to give a gift to the third party.

dormant commerce clause   A restriction on states' authority that is implied in the commerce clause of the U.S. Constitution: The power given to Congress to enact legislation that affects interstate commerce in effect prohibits a state from passing legislation that improperly burdens interstate commerce.

draft   An instrument validating an order by a drawer to a drawee to pay a payee.

dram shop act   A regulation under which bartenders can be held liable for injuries caused by individuals who become intoxicated in their bars.

drawee   The party that must obey an order. In the context of banking, the drawee is the bank that must pay the funds ordered by a customer's check.

drawer   The party that writes an order, or the person who writes a check.

due diligence defense   A defense in which the defendant argues that he or she applied the appropriate degree of attention, care, and research expected of a party in a given situation and had reasonable grounds to believe that certain facts and statements were accurate and had no omission of material facts.

due process clause   A clause in the Fifth Amendment of the U.S. Constitution which provides that the government cannot deprive an individual of life, liberty, or property without a fair and just hearing.

dumping   The practice wherein an exporter sells products in a foreign state for less than the price charged for the same or comparable goods in the exporter's home market.

durable power of attorney   A document which specifies that an agent's authority is intended to continue beyond the principal's incapacitation.

duress   Any unlawful act or threat exercised on a person whereby the person is forced to enter into an agreement or to perform some other act against his or her will.

duty   The standard of care a defendant must meet in order to not subject a person in the position of the plaintiff to an unreasonable risk of harm.

duty of loyalty   An agent's obligation to act in the interest of the principal.

duty of notification   An agent's obligation to inform the principal of the agent's actions on the principal's behalf and of all relevant information.

duty to compensate   A principal's obligation to pay an agent for his or her services.

E

easement   An irrevocable right to use some part of another's land for a specific purpose, without taking anything from it.

easement by prescription   An easement created by state law when certain conditions are met, most frequently by openly using a portion of another's property for a statutory period of time (usually 25 years).

effective date   The date on which insurance takes effect.

efficiency   The economic principle of getting the most output from the least input.

Electronic Communications Privacy Act (ECPA) of 1986   Federal law that extended employees' privacy rights to electronic forms of communication including e-mail and cell phones; outlaws the intentional interception of electronic communications and the intentional disclosure or use of the information obtained through such interception.

electronic fund transfer (EFT)   The transfer of funds by an electronic terminal, telephone, or computer.

embezzlement   A wrongful conversion of another's funds or property by one who is lawfully in possession of those funds or that property.

e-money   Any electronic, nonphysical form of currency.

Employee Retirement Income Security Act (ERISA)   Federal law that sets minimum standards for most voluntarily established pension and health plans in private industry to provide protection for individuals in these plans.

employment-at-will doctrine   The doctrine which provides that either the employer or the employee can terminate the employment relationship at any time.

enabling legislation   A statute that specifies the name, functions, and specific powers of an administrative agency and grants the agency broad powers for the purpose of serving the "public interest, convenience, and necessity."

endorsee   One who receives an endorsement.

endorsement for deposit or collection only   The most common type of endorsement, which provides that the instrument can only be deposited into an account.

endorsement to prohibit further endorsement   An endorsement that provides increased protection to the endorsee.

endorser   One who issues an endorsement.

English rule   A rule which states that the first assignee to give notice of assignment to the obligor is the party with rights to the contract.

entrapment   A relatively common defense under which the defendant claims that he would not have committed the crime or broken the law if he had not been induced or tricked into doing so by law enforcement officials.

entrustment   The transfer of goods to a merchant who ordinarily deals in that type of goods. If the merchant subsequently sells them to a good-faith third-party purchaser, the buyer acquires good title to the goods.

environmental impact statement (EIS)   A document that must be filed whenever there is a major federal activity that might have a significant impact on the environment. It details the environmental impact of the proposed action, any adverse environmental effects of implementing the action, and other environmental considerations.

equal dignity rule   A rule requiring that contracts that would normally fall under the statute of frauds and need a writing if negotiated by the principal must be in writing even if negotiated by an agent.

Equal Pay Act (EPA) of 1963   Federal law that prohibits an employer from paying workers of one gender less than the wages paid to employees of the opposite gender for work that requires equal skill, effort, and responsibility.

equal protection clause   A clause in the Fourteenth Amendment of the U.S. Constitution that prevents states from denying "the equal protection of the laws" to any citizen. This clause implies that all citizens are created equal.

equity security   A security that represents ownership in a corporation.

establishment clause   One of two provisions in the First Amendment of the U.S. Constitution that protect citizens' freedom of religion. It prohibits (1) the establishment of a national religion by Congress and (2) the preference of one religion over another or of religion over nonreligious philosophies in general.

estate planning   The process whereby an individual decides what to do with his or her real and personal property during and after life.

ethical dilemma   A question about how a person should behave that requires the person to reflect about the advantages and disadvantages of the optional choices for various stakeholders.

ethical guideline   A simple tool to help determine whether an action is moral.

ethical relativism   The ethical theory that denies the existence of an ultimate ethical system, holding instead that a decision must be determined as ethical on the basis of its own context.

ethics   The study and practice of decisions about what is good or right.

ethics of care   The ethical theory that emphasizes human interaction, holding that what makes a decision ethical is how well it builds and promotes human relationships.

European Union   A customs union that consists of an association of states, has a basis in international law, and was formed for the purpose of forging closer ties among the peoples of Europe.

exchange tender offer   A type of takeover in which the aggressor corporation offers to exchange the target shareholders' current stock for its own stock.

exclusive-dealing contract   An agreement in which a seller requires that a buyer buy products supplied only by that seller.

exculpatory clause   A clause in a contract that basically frees one party (usually the drafter of the agreement) from all liability arising out of performance of the contract; generally based on factors such as consumer ignorance or a great deal of unexplained fine print that serve to deprive the less powerful party of a meaningful choice.

executed   A term applied to a contract whose terms have all been fully performed.

executive agency   An agency that is typically located within the executive branch, under one of the cabinet-level departments. The agency head is appointed by the president with the advice and consent of the Senate and may be discharged by the president at any time, for any reason. Also called *cabinet-level agency.*

executive order   A directive that has the force of law but is issued by a governor or the president.

executory   A term applied to a contract whose terms have not all been fully performed.

exemplary damages   See **punitive damages.**

exempted rule making   An APA exemption from rule making that allows an agency to decide whether public participation will be allowed. Exemptions include rule-making proceedings with regard to military or foreign affairs, agency management or personnel, and public property, loans, grants, benefits or contracts of an agency.

express condition   A condition specifically and explicitly stated in a contract and usually preceded by words such as *conditioned on, if, provided that,* or *when.*

express contract   A contract in which all the terms are clearly set forth in either written or spoken words.

express trust   A trust created either while the settlor is alive or by will.

express warranty   Any description of a good's physical nature or its use, either in general or specific circumstances, that becomes part of a contract.

expressed agency   An agency created in a written or oral agreement. Also called *agency by agreement.*

extortion   A criminal offense in which a person obtains money, property, and/or services from another by wrongfully threatening or inflicting harm to his or her person, property, or reputation. Also called *blackmail.*

F

failure to provide adequate warnings A defect that arises when a potentially dangerous product is not labeled to indicate that it can be dangerous.

Fair Labor Standards Act (FLSA) Federal law which requires that a minimum wage of a specified amount be paid to all employees in covered industries; also mandates that employees who work more than 40 hours in a week be paid no less than 1½ times their regular wage for all hours beyond 40 worked in a given week.

fair-use doctrine The doctrine which provides for the lawful use of a limited portion of another's work for purposes of criticism, comment, news reporting, teaching, scholarship, or research.

False Claims Act An act that allows employees to sue employers on behalf of the federal government for fraud against the government. The employee retains a share of the recovery as a reward for his or her efforts.

false imprisonment The unlawful restraint of another against the person's will.

false light A privacy tort that occurs when highly offensive information is published about an individual that is not valid or places the person in a false light.

false pretense A materially false representation of an existing fact, with knowledge of the falsity of the representation and with the intent to defraud.

Family and Medical Leave Act (FMLA) Federal act requiring that employers provide all eligible employees with up to 12 weeks of leave during any 12-month period for several family-related occurrences (e.g., birth of a child, care of a sick spouse).

family incentive trust A trust designed to take effect on the completion of a specified behavior.

federal preemption A principle asserting the supremacy of federal legislation over state legislation when both pertain to the same subject matter. Also called *field preemption*.

Federal Register The government publication in which an agency publishes each proposed rule, along with an explanation of the legal authority for issuing the rule and a description of how the public can participate in the rule-making process, and later publishes the final rule.

Federal Unemployment Tax Act (FUTA) Federal law passed in 1935 that created a state system to provide unemployment compensation to qualified employees who lose their jobs.

federalism A system of government in which power is divided between a central authority and constituent political units.

fee simple absolute An ownership interest in which the holder has exclusive rights to ownership and possession of the land to the holder; the most comprehensive type of estate.

felony A serious crime, such as murder, rape, or robbery, that is punishable by imprisonment for more than one year or death.

fictitious payee Someone having no right to payment. Under the UCC fictitious-payee rule, any check made out to a fictitious payee and endorsed must be honored and is not considered a forgery.

finance lease A type of lease in which the lessor does not select, manufacture, or supply the goods but acquires title to the goods or the right to their possession and use in connection with the terms of the lease.

financing statement A document that lists the names and addresses of all the parties involved in the transaction, a description of the collateral, and the signature of the debtor.

fire insurance Insurance that protects against property losses incurred by damage from fire.

firm offer An offer made in writing and containing assurances that it will be irrevocable for a period of time not longer than three months despite a lack of consideration for the irrevocability.

first appearance The initial appearance of an arrested individual before a judge, who determines whether there was probable cause for the arrest. If the judge ascertains that probable cause did not exist, the individual is freed.

first-assignment-in-time rule A rule which states that the first party granted an assignment is the party correctly entitled to the contractual right.

fixture An item that was originally a piece of personal property but becomes part of realty after it is permanently attached to the real property in question.

food disparagement A tort that provides ranchers and farmers with a cause of action when someone spreads false information about the safety of a food product.

for-profit corporation A corporation whose objective is to make a profit.

foreign corporation A corporation that conducts business in a state in which it is not incorporated.

Foreign Corrupt Practices Act (FCPA) Federal law prohibiting U.S. companies from offering or paying bribes to foreign government officials, political parties, and candidates for office for the purpose of obtaining or retaining business.

foreign sales representative An agent who distributes, represents, or sells goods on behalf of a foreign seller, usually in return for the payment of a commission.

foreign subsidiary See **affiliate.**

forfeiture A party's forfeiting of his or her interest in the premises.

forgery The fraudulent making or altering of a writing in a way that changes the legal rights and liabilities of another and with the intent to deceive or defraud.

formal contract A contract that must have a special form or must be created in a specific manner.

formal rule making A type of rule making that is used when legislation requires a formal hearing process with a complete transcript; consists of publication of the proposed rule in the *Federal Register,* a public hearing, publication of formal findings, and publication of the final rule if adopted.

forum selection agreement   A contractual clause in which the parties choose the location where disputes between them will be resolved.

franchise   A business arrangement between an owner of a trade name or trademark and a person who sells goods or services under the trade name or trademark.

franchise agreement   A contract whereby a company (the franchisor) grants permission (a license) to another entity (the franchisee) to use the franchisor's name, trademark, or copyright in the operation of a business and associated sale of goods in return for payment.

franchisee   The seller of goods or services under a trade name or trademark in a franchise.

franchisor   The owner of the trade name or trademark in a franchise.

fraud   (1) An intentional deception that causes harm to another. (2) A basis for contesting a will if the testator relied on false statements when he or she made the will.

fraud in the factum   A liability defense available to a party who signs a negotiable instrument without knowing that it is a negotiable instrument.

fraudulent misrepresentation   (1) The tort that occurs when a misrepresentation is made with intent to facilitate personal gain and with the knowledge that it is false. (2) In contracts, a false representation of a material fact that is consciously false and is intended to mislead the other party. Also called *intentional misrepresentation.*

fraudulent transfer   A transfer of property that is made with intent to defraud creditors or for an amount significantly lower than the property's fair market value and that occurs within two years of filing for bankruptcy.

free-exercise clause   A clause in the First Amendment of the U.S. Constitution. which states that government (state and federal) cannot make a law "prohibiting the free exercise" of religion; has been interpreted as including absolute freedom to believe and freedom to act, which may face state restriction.

free trade agreement   An international agreement between two or more nations whereby tariffs and other trade barriers are reduced and gradually eliminated.

Freedom of Information Act (FOIA)   Federal law passed in 1966 that mandates and facilitates public access to government information and records, including records about oneself. Sensitive information (e.g., on national security) is excluded.

full eviction   An eviction in which a landlord physically prevents the lessee from entering the leased premises.

full faith and credit clause   A clause in the U.S. Constitution (Article IV, Section 1) mandating that each state must recognize, respect, and enforce the public records, legislative acts, and judicial decisions of the other states.

future interest   A person's present right to property ownership and possession in the future.

G

gambling   Agreements in which parties pay consideration (money placed during bets) for the chance, or opportunity, to obtain an amount of money or property.

garnishment   An order that satisfies a debt by seizing a debtor's property that is being held by a third party.

General Agreement on Tariffs and Trade (GATT)   A comprehensive multilateral trading system designed to achieve distortion-free international trade through the minimization of tariffs and removal of artificial barriers.

general partnership   A partnership in which the partners divide profits and management responsibility and share unlimited personal liability for the partnership's debts.

general personal jurisdiction   A doctrine permitting adjudication of any claims against a defendant regardless of whether the claim has anything to do with the forum.

general power of attorney   A type of express authority that allows an agent to conduct all business for the principal.

general warranty deed   A deed containing a covenant in which the seller agrees to protect the buyer against being dispossessed because of any adverse claim against the land.

geographic market   An area in which a company competes with others in the relevant product market.

gift *causa mortis*   A gift that is made in contemplation of one's immediate death.

Golden Rule   The idea that we should act in the way that we would like others to act toward us.

good faith   Honesty in fact.

Good Samaritan statute   A statute that exempts from liability a person, such as a physician passerby, who voluntarily renders aid to an injured person but negligently, but not unreasonably negligently, causes injury while rendering the aid.

good title   Title acquired from someone who already owns the goods free and clear.

goods   All physically existing things that are movable at the time of identification in the contract for sale.

goods in bailment   Purchased goods that are in some kind of storage under the control of a third party, such as a warehouseman.

Government in Sunshine Act   Federal law which requires that agency business meetings be open to the public if the agency is headed by a collegiate body (i.e., two or more persons, the majority of whom are appointed by the president with the advice and consent of the Senate); also requires that agencies keep records of closed meetings.

green taxes   Taxes imposed on environmentally harmful activities.

gross negligence   An act committed with extreme reckless disregard for the property or life of another person.

group boycott   A boycott in which two or more competitors agree to refuse to deal with a certain person or company. Also called *refusal to deal.*

group insurance   Insurance that is purchased by neither the insured party nor the insurer.

guaranty   A type of contract which ensures that a third party is secondarily liable for the debt to be paid; similar to a suretyship.

H

hacker   A person who illegally accesses, or enters, another person's or company's computer system to obtain information or steal money.

Hague Evidence Convention   A multilateral convention establishing procedures for transnational discovery between private persons in different states.

half-truth   Information that is true but is not complete.

health care proxy   A document that empowers an agent to make medical decisions for a principal who is unable to make those decisions for himself or herself.

historical school   A school of jurisprudence that uses traditions as the model for future laws and behavior. Also called *tradition* or *custom.*

holder   A party in possession of a negotiable instrument.

holder in due course (HDC)   An individual who acquires a negotiable instrument in good faith.

homestead exemption   An exemption that allows a debtor to retain all or a portion of the family home so that the family will retain some form of shelter.

horizontal division of market   An agreement between two or more competitors to divide markets among themselves by geography, customers, or products.

horizontal merger   A merger between two or more competitors producing the same or similar products.

horizontal restraint of trade   An agreement between two competitors in the same market to engage in a practice that restrains trade.

hostile takeover   A takeover to which the management of the target corporation objects.

hybrid agency   An agency that has characteristics of both executive and independent agencies.

hybrid rule making   A type of rule making that combines features of both formal and informal rule making; consists of publication in the *Federal Register,* a written-comment period, and an informal public hearing with restricted cross-examination.

I

identification with the vulnerable   The school of jurisprudence of pursuing change on the grounds that some higher law or body of moral principles connects all of us in the human community.

illusory promise   A situation in which a party appears to commit to something but really has not committed to anything. It is not a promise and thus not consideration.

implied authority   The authority of an agent that arises by inference from the words and actions of the principal.

implied condition   A condition that is not specifically and explicitly stated but is inferred from the nature and language of the contract.

implied contract   A contract that arises not from words of agreement but from the conduct of the parties.

implied-contract exception   An exception to the employment at-will doctrine which provides that an implied employment contract may arise from statements the employer makes in an employment handbook or materials advertising the position.

implied covenant of good faith and fair dealing exception   An exception to the employment at-will doctrine that imposes a duty on the employer to treat employees fairly with respect to termination.

implied trust   A trust created by a court when (1) an express trust fails and the court can imply the existence of a trust from certain behavior or (2) the law steps in to protect someone from fraud or other wrongdoing.

implied warranty of fitness for a particular purpose   An assurance, inferred in any UCC sale, that when a seller/lessor knows or has reason to know (1) why the buyer/lessee is purchasing/leasing the goods and (2) that the buyer/lessee is relying on him or her to make the selection, the buyer/lessee has an enforceable warranty if such assurance is false.

implied warranty of habitability   A requirement that the premises be fit for ordinary residential purposes.

implied warranty of merchantability   An assurance, inferred in every sale unless clearly disclaimed, that merchantable goods will conform to a reasonable performance expectation. The purchaser must have purchased or leased the good from a merchant.

implied warranty of trade usage   An assurance, inferred in the context of certain UCC sales, depending on the circumstances, that can be created through a well-accepted course of dealing or trade usage.

imposter rule   A rule which holds that if one party obtains a negotiable instrument by impersonating another party and endorses it with the impersonated party's signature, the loss falls on the drawer of the instrument.

in pari delicto   In equal fault.

in personam **jurisdiction** The power of a court to require that a party (usually the defendant) or a witness come before the court; extends to the state's borders in the state court system and across the court's geographic district in the federal system. Also called *personal jurisdiction* and *jurisdiction in personam.*

in rem **jurisdiction** The power of a court over the property or status of an out-of-state defendant located within the court's jurisdiction area.

incidental beneficiary One who unintentionally gains a benefit from a contract between other parties.

income beneficiary The recipient of the interest or appreciation generated by a trust.

incontestability clause A part of an insurance contract that precludes an insurance company from challenging statements in an insurance application after a certain period of time.

incorporator An individual who applies for incorporation on behalf of a corporation.

independent agency An agency that is typically not located within a government department. It is governed by a board of commissioners appointed by the president with the advice and consent of the Senate.

indictment A finding by the grand jury that there is evidence to charge the defendant and bring him or her to trial.

individual insurance Insurance in which the insured party is an individual.

indivisible contract A contract that cannot be divided and must be performed in its entirety.

industry guides Interpretations of consumer laws created by the FTC to encourage businesses to stop unlawful behavior.

infant A person who is not legally an adult (in most U.S. localities, a person under 18) and thus is considered to lack the mental capabilities of an adult. Infancy can be used as a partial defense to defuse the guilty-mind requirement of a crime.

informal contract A contract that requires no formalities. Also called *simple contract.*

informal rule making A type of rule making in which an agency publishes a proposed rule in the *Federal Register,* considers public comments, and then publishes the final rule. Also called *notice-and-comment rule making.*

information A finding by a magistrate that there is enough evidence to charge the defendant and bring her or him to trial.

informational picketing Picketing designed to truthfully inform the public of a labor dispute between an employer and the employees.

injunction A court order either forcing a party to do something or prohibiting a party from doing something.

innkeepers Entities that are regularly in the business of making lodging available to the public.

innocent misrepresentation A false statement made about a material fact by a person who believed the statement was true.

insanity An affirmative defense which claims that the defendant had a severe mental illness when the crime was committed that substantially impaired his or her capacity to understand and appreciate the moral wrongfulness of the act.

insider trading Illegal buying or selling of a corporation's securities by corporate insiders, such as officers and directors, on the basis of material, nonpublic information and in breach of a fiduciary duty or some other relationship of trust and confidence.

insolvent debtor A debtor who cannot pay debts in a timely fashion.

instrument Any writing that serves as evidence of the right to payment of money.

insurable interest A party who has an interest in property or life.

insurance A contract in which the insured party makes payments to the insurer in exchange for the insurer's promise to make payment or transfer goods to another party in the event of injury or destruction to the insured party's property or life.

insured party The party who makes a payment in exchange for payment in the event of damage or injury to property or person.

insurer The party who receives payments from the insured party and makes the payment to the beneficiary.

integrated contract A written contract intended to be the complete and final representation of the parties' agreement.

intellectual property Intangible property that is the product of one's mind and not one's hands.

intended beneficiary A third party to a contract whom the contracting parties intended to benefit directly from their contact.

intent The intended purpose or goal of an action, especially in a contract.

intentional infliction of emotional distress The tort that occurs when someone intentionally engages in outrageous conduct that is likely to cause extreme emotional distress to another person.

intentional interference with contract The tort that occurs when someone intentionally takes an action that will cause a person to breach a contract that he or she has with another.

intentional misrepresentation See **fraudulent misrepresentation.**

intentional tort A civil wrong resulting from an intentional act committed on the person, property, or economic interest of another. Intentional torts include assault, battery, conversion, false imprisonment, intentional infliction of emotional distress, trespass to land, and trespass to chattels.

inter vivos **gift**   A gift that is made by a person during his or her lifetime.

intermediary bank   Any bank, other than a payor or depositary bank, that transfers a check during the check collection process.

intermediate scrutiny   A standard of review under which a law must be necessary to achieve a substantial, or important, government interest and must be narrowly tailored to that interest.

international agreement   A written agreement between two or more nations that is governed by international law and relates to international subject matter.

International Labor Organization   An international organization operating under the principle that "labor should not be regarded merely as a commodity or article of commerce"; develops labor rights norms that serve as the basis for many international standards.

international law   The body of law that governs the conduct of nations and international organizations and their relations with one another and with natural and juridical persons.

interpretive rule   A rule that does not create any new rights or duties but is merely a detailed statement of an agency's interpretation of an existing law, including the actions a party must take to be in compliance with the law.

interrogatory   A formal set of written questions that one party to a lawsuit asks the opposing party during the pretrial discovery process to clarify matters of evidence and help determine what facts will be presented at a trial in the case. The questions must be answered in writing under oath or under penalty of perjury within a specified time. Also called *request for further information.*

Interstate Commerce Commission (ICC)   The first federal administrative agency; created to regulate the anticompetitive conduct of railroads.

intestacy statute   A statute that outlines how a person's property will be handled if that person dies without a will.

intestate   The state of dying without a will.

intrusion on an individual's affairs or seclusion   A physical, electronic, or mechanical intrusion that invades someone's solitude, seclusion, or personal affairs when he or she has the right to expect privacy. The tort occurs at the time of the intrusion; no publication is necessary.

involuntary intoxication   An affirmative defense in which the defendant claims that she took the intoxicant without awareness of its likely effect, mistook its identity, or was forced to ingest it and that it left her unable to understand that the act committed was wrong.

Islamic law   A legal system based on the fundamental tenet that law is derived from and interpreted in harmony with Shari'a (God's law) and the Koran.

J

joint and several liability   A type of liability in which a third party can choose to sue the partners separately or to sue all partners jointly in one action.

joint stock company   A partnership agreement in which company members hold transferable shares while all the goods of the company are held in the names of the partners.

joint tenancy   A type of co-ownership in which the joint tenants own equal shares of the property and, upon the death of one tenant, the property is divided equally among the surviving joint owners. The tenants may sell their shares without the consent of the other owners, and their interest can be attached by creditors.

joint tenants   Parties who hold property in joint tenancy.

joint venture   An association between two or more parties wherein the parties share profits and management responsibilities with respect to a specific project.

jointly liable   A term applied to partners who share liability for the partnership's debts.

judicial lien   A court order that allows a creditor to satisfy a debt by seizing the property of the debtor.

judicial review   The power of a court to review legislative and executive actions, such as a law or an official act of a government employee or agent, to determine whether they are constitutional.

jurisdiction   The power of a court to hear cases and resolve disputes.

justifiable use of force   The use of force that is necessary to prevent imminent death or great bodily harm to oneself or another or to prevent the imminent commission of a forcible felony.

L

lack of genuine assent   A defense to the agreement of a contract in which the offeree claims that the offeror secured the agreement through improper means, such as duress, fraud, undue influence, or misrepresentation.

landlord   The owner of a property being leased. Also called *lessor.*

landlord's lien   A court order that allows a landlord, through a sheriff, to seize a tenant's personal property as security for unpaid rent.

Landrum-Griffin Act   Federal law that primarily governs the internal operations of labor unions. It requires financial disclosures by unions, establishes penalties for financial abuses by union officials, and includes "Labor's Bill of Rights" to protect employees from their own unions.

larceny   The unlawful taking, attempting to take, carrying, leading, or riding away of another person's property with intent to permanently deprive the rightful owner of the property.

last-clear-chance doctrine   A doctrine used by a plaintiff when the defendant establishes contributory negligence. If the plaintiff can establish that the defendant had the last opportunity to avoid the accident, the plaintiff may still recover, despite being contributorily negligent.

lease   (1) A transfer of the right to possess and use goods for a period of time in return for consideration. (2) The agreement between a landlord and a tenant that specifies the terms of a property rental.

leasehold   A possessory interest, but not an ownership interest, transferred by contract (lease).

leasehold estate   The leased property.

legal assent   A promise to buy or sell that the courts will require that the parties obey.

legal object   The requirement that, to be enforceable, a contract cannot be either illegal or against public policy.

legal positivism   The school of jurisprudence which holds that because society requires authority, a legal and authoritarian hierarchy should exist. When a law is made, therefore, obedience is expected because authority created it.

legal realism   The school of jurisprudence which dictates that context must be considered as well as law. Context includes factors such as economic conditions and social conditions.

lessee   (1) A person who acquires the right to possession and use of goods under a lease. (2) The party who assumes temporary ownership of a rental property. Also called *tenant*.

lessor   (1) A person who transfers the right to possession and use of goods under a lease. (2) The owner of a rental property. Also called *landlord*.

letter of credit   A binding document that a buyer obtains from his or her bank to guarantee that payment for goods will be made to the seller.

leveraged buyout (LBO)   A takeover-resistance strategy in which a group within the target corporation buys all the corporate stock held by the public, thereby turning the company into a privately held corporation.

lex mercatoria   The "law of merchants" as defined by customs or trade usages developed by merchants to facilitate business transactions.

liability insurance   Insurance that protects a business from tort liability to third parties.

liability without fault   See **strict liability.**

license   A revocable right to temporarily use another's property.

licensing agreement   A contract in which one company (the licensor) grants permission to another company (the licensee) to use the licensor's intellectual property in return for payment.

lien   A claim to property.

life estate   An ownership interest in which the holder has the right to possess the property until his or her death.

life insurance   A contract between a policy owner and an insurance company that requires the insurance company to pay a designated beneficiary a sum of money upon the occurrence of the insured's death.

limited liability company (LLC)   An unincorporated business that is taxed like a partnership, with the members paying personal income taxes, but has the limited liability of a corporation.

limited liability partnership (LLP)   A partnership in which all the partners assume liability for any partner's professional malpractice to the extent of the partnership's assets.

limited partnership (LP)   A partnership consisting of at least one general partner and at least one limited partner in which the general partners assume all liability for the partnership's debts and the limited partners assume no responsibility beyond their originally invested capital.

liquidated damages   Damages specified as a term of the contract before a breach of contract occurs.

liquidated debt   Debt for which there is no dispute between the parties about the fact that money is owed and the amount of money owed.

liquidation   The process in which a debtor turns over all assets to a trustee.

living trust   A trust created by a trustor and administered by another party while the trustor is still alive.

living will   A document in which a person expresses his or her advance directives.

long-arm statute   A statute that enables a court to obtain jurisdiction against an out-of-state defendant as long as the defendant has sufficient minimum contacts within the state, such as committing a tort or doing business in the state.

M

mailbox rule   A rule which holds that an acceptance is valid when it is placed in the mailbox, whereas a revocation is effective only when received by the offeree. In some jurisdictions the mailbox rule has been expanded to faxes.

maker   A person who promises to pay a set sum to the holder of a promissory note or certificate of deposit.

malicious prosecution   A tort in which one person wrongfully subjects another to criminal or civil litigation for the sole purpose of causing problems for that other person, often in retaliation for previous litigation between the two.

malpractice action   A legal action filed against a professional person for failure to act in accordance with prevailing professional standards.

manifest   A document that records possession of hazardous waste from inception to disposal.

manufacturing arrangement   A type of franchise in which the franchisor provides the franchisee with a formula or ingredient that is necessary to manufacture a product.

manufacturing defect   A defect in an individual product that makes the product more dangerous than other, identical products.

marine insurance   Insurance that protects against loss of ships and cargo from the "perils of the sea."

market power   See **monopoly power.**

market share   A firm's fractional share of the relevant market.

market share theory   Product liability theory which holds that when it is impossible to identify the manufacturer of a particular product that caused harm, the plaintiff may sue all manufacturers of the product, with liability apportioned among them on the basis of each one's market share.

marketable title   Title for property to which the seller has legal title and against which there are no liens or restrictions of which the buyer is not aware.

material breach   A substantial breach of a significant term or terms of a contract that excuses the nonbreaching party from further performance under the contract and gives the nonbreaching party the right to recover damages.

material terms   In a contract, the terms that allow a court to determine what the damages are in the event that one of the parties breaches the contract; include the subject matter, quantity, price, quality, and parties.

mechanic's lien   A claim placed on real property to satisfy the debt a person incurred to have improvements made to that property.

med-arb   A type of dispute resolution process in which both parties agree to start out in mediation and, if unsuccessful, to move on to arbitration.

mediation   A type of intensive negotiation in which disputing parties select a neutral party to help facilitate communication and suggest ways for the parties to solve their dispute.

meeting-the-competition defense   A defense to the Clayton Act in which a firm engages in price discrimination to compete in good faith with another seller's low price.

members   Owners of a limited liability company.

mens rea   Latin for "guilty mind"; the mental state accompanying a wrongful behavior.

merchant   A person who deals in goods of the kind or by his occupation holds himself out as having knowledge or skill peculiar to the practices or goods involved in the transaction, or a person who employs an intermediary who, by her occupation, holds herself out as having such knowledge or skill.

merger   A combination of two or more corporations in which only one of the corporations continues to exist.

merger clause   A clause in a written agreement within the statute of frauds which states that the written agreement accurately reflects the final, complete version of the agreement.

minitrial   A type of conflict resolution in which lawyers for each side present their arguments to a neutral adviser, who then offers an opinion on what the verdict will be if the case goes to trial. This decision is not binding.

minor   A person who has not yet reached the age of 18.

Miranda rights   The rights that are read to an arrested individual by a law enforcement agent before the individual is questioned about the commission of the crime.

mirror-image rule   A principle which holds that the terms of an acceptance must mirror the terms of the offer. If the terms of the acceptance do not mirror the terms of the offer, no contract is formed and the attempted acceptance is a counteroffer.

misappropriation theory   A theory of insider trading which holds that if an individual wrongfully acquires (misappropriates) and uses inside information for trading for his or her personal gain, that person is liable for insider trading.

misdemeanor   A crime that is less serious than a felony and is punishable by a fine and/or imprisonment for less than one year.

misrepresentation   An untruthful assertion by one of the parties about a material fact.

mistake   An erroneous belief about the facts of a contract at the time the contract is concluded. When a mistake occurs, legal assent is absent.

mistake of fact   (1) A mistake that is not caused by the neglect of a legal duty by the person committing the mistake but, rather, consists of unconscious ignorance of a past or present material event or circumstance. (2) An affirmative defense in which the defendant tries to prove that she or he made an honest and reasonable mistake that negates the guilty-mind element of a crime.

mixed sale   A contract that combines one or more goods with one or more services.

mock trial   A contrived or imitation trial, recruited by a jury selection firm, that attorneys sometimes use in preparing for a real trial in order to test theories, experiment with arguments, and try to predict the outcome of the real trial.

model law   See **uniform law.**

modified comparative negligence   In some states, a defense whereby the defendant is not liable for the percentage of harm that he or she proves can be attributed to the plaintiff's own negligence if the plaintiff's negligence is responsible for less than 50 percent of the harm. If the defendant establishes that the plaintiff's negligence caused more than 50 percent of the harm, the defendant has no liability.

modify   An appellate court decision that grants an alternative remedy in a case; granted when the court finds that the decision of the lower court was correct but the remedy was not.

monetary damages   Money claimed by or ordered paid to a party to compensate for injury or loss caused by the wrong of the opposite party.

money order   A signed document indicating that funds are to be paid from the drawee to the drawer.

monopoly power   The ability to control price and drive competitors out of the market.

moral hazard   The possibility that individuals who are insulated from risk sometimes behave differently than they would if not insulated.

most-favored-nation relations   See **normal trade relations**.

motion   In a civil case, a request made by either party that asks a judge or a court to issue an order in that party's favor.

motion for judgment on the pleadings   In a civil case, a request made by either party, after pleadings have been entered, that asks a judge or a court, to issue a judgment.

motion for summary judgment   In a civil case, a request made by either party that asks a judge or a court to promptly and expeditiously dispose of the case without a trial. Any evidence or information that would be admissible at trial may be considered on a motion for summary judgment. The court may hold oral arguments or decide the motion on the basis of the parties' briefs and supporting documentation alone.

motion to dismiss   In a civil case, a request by the defendant that asks a judge or a court to dismiss the case because even if all the allegations are true, the plaintiff is not entitled to any legal relief. Also called *demurrer*.

movability   The quality of a negotiable instrument that ensures it is mobile and available.

multilateral trade agreement   An international agreement between three or more nations that relates to trade between them.

multiple-product order   A form of cease-and-desist order issued by the FTC that applies not only to a specified product but also to other products produced by the same firm.

mutual (mistake)   The result of an error by both parties about a material fact, i.e., one that is important in the context of a particular contract.

N

National Labor Relations Act   Federal labor legislation consisting of the Wagner and Taft-Hartley acts.

National Labor Relations Board (NLRB)   An administrative agency created by the Wagner Act to interpret and enforce the National Labor Relations Act (NLRA).

national treatment   A GATT principle of trade law that prohibits WTO member states from regulating, taxing, or otherwise treating imported products any differently from domestically produced products.

natural law   A school of jurisprudence that recognizes the existence of higher law, or law that is morally superior to human laws.

necessary   A basic necessity of life, generally including food, clothing, shelter, and basic medical services.

necessity   An affirmative defense in which the defendant tries to prove that he or she was acting to prevent imminent harm and that there was no legal alternative to the action the defendant took.

negligence   Behavior that creates an unreasonable risk of harm to others.

negligence per se   A doctrine that allows a judge or jury to infer duty and breach of duty from the fact that a defendant violated a statute that was designed to prevent the type of harm that the plaintiff incurred.

negligent misrepresentation   A false statement of material fact made by a person who thinks it is true but who would have known the truth about the fact had he or she used reasonable care to discover or reveal it.

negligent tort   A civil wrong that occurs when the defendant acts in a way that subjects other people to an unreasonable risk of harm (i.e., the defendant is careless, to someone else's detriment). Negligence claims are usually used to achieve compensation for accidents and injuries.

negotiable instrument   A written document signed by a person who makes an unconditional promise to pay a specific sum of money on demand or at a certain time to the holder of the instrument; an acceptable medium for exchanging value from one person to another.

negotiation   (1) A bargaining process in which disputing parties interact informally to attempt to resolve their dispute. (2) The transfer of the rights to a negotiable instrument from one party to another.

New York Convention   An international agreement governing the use of arbitration as a method of resolving private international disputes.

no-par share   A stock share that does not have a par value.

nolo contendere   A plea in which the defendant does not admit guilt but agrees not to contest the charges.

nominal damages   Monetary damages awarded to a plaintiff in a very small amount, typically $1 to $5, to signify that the plaintiff has been wronged by the defendant even though the plaintiff suffered no compensable harm.

nondisclosure   The failure to provide pertinent information about a projected contract.

nonprobate property   Property that is not part of a probate estate.

nonprofit corporation   A corporation that operates for educational, charitable, social, religious, civic, or humanitarian purposes, rather than to earn a profit.

nontariff barrier   Any impediment to international trade other than tariffs.

normal trade relations   A GATT principle of trade law which requires that WTO member states treat like goods coming from other member states on an equal basis.

North American Free Trade Agreement (NAFTA)   An international agreement between the United States, Canada, and Mexico whereby tariffs and other trade barriers will be reduced and gradually eliminated.

note   A promise by the maker of the note to pay the payee of the note.

notice-and-comment rule making   See **informal rule making.**

novation   In a contract, the substitution of a third party for one of the original parties. The duties remain the same under the contract, but one original party is discharged and the third party takes that original party's place.

nuisance   A person's use of her property in a manner that unreasonably interferes with another's use and enjoyment of his land.

O

objective impossibility (of performance)   In a contract, a situation in which it is in fact not possible to lawfully carry out one's contractual obligations.

obligee   A contractual party who agrees to receive something from the other party.

obligor   A contractual party who agrees to do something for the other party.

Occupational Safety and Health Act (OSHA) of 1970   Federal law that established the Occupational Safety and Health Administration, the agency responsible for setting safety standards under the act and for enforcing the act through inspections and the levying of fines against violators.

offer   A key factor in the agreement element of a contract; consists of the terms and conditions set by one party, the offeror, and presented to another party, the offeree.

Omnibus Crime Control and Safe Streets Act of 1968   Federal statute that prohibits employers from listening to the private telephone conversations of employees or disclosing the contents of these conversations. Employers may ban personal calls and monitor calls for compliance as long as they discontinue listening to any conversation once they determine it is personal.

option contract   An agreement whereby the offeree gives the offeror a piece of consideration in exchange for the offeror's agreement to hold the offer open for a specified period of time.

order   (1) An order to appear and bring specified documents. (2) A binding decision issued by an ALJ after a hearing.

order instrument   An instrument payable to a specific, named payee.

order of relief   An order stating that bankruptcy proceedings can continue.

organ donor card   A document that expresses a person's desire to donate organs or tissue.

overdraft   A bank's action to pay an amount specified on a check, without there being sufficient funds in its customer's account.

P

par-value share   A stock share that has a fixed face value noted on the stock certificate.

parent-subsidiary merger   See **short-form merger.**

parol evidence rule   A common law rule which states that oral evidence of an agreement made prior to or contemporaneously with a written agreement is inadmissible when the parties intend to have the written agreement be the complete and final version of their agreement.

partial eviction   An eviction in which a landlord prevents the tenant from entering part of the leased premises.

partial performance   An exception to the statute of frauds in which the performance of portions of an unwritten agreement by one or both parties can constitute proof that an oral contract exists between the parties.

partially disclosed principal   A principal whose identity is not known by a third party, although the third party is aware that the agent is making an agreement on behalf of a principal. Also called *unidentified principal.*

partnership   A voluntary association between two or more people who co-own a business for profit.

past consideration   Something given or done in the past by one party that later prompts a promise by another party. As such, nothing has been given in exchange, and the court will not enforce the promise.

patent   Protection that grants the holder the exclusive right to produce, sell, and use the patented object for 20 years; can be obtained for a product, process, invention, or machine or a plant produced by asexual reproduction.

payee   The party that receives the benefit of an order (check, etc.).

payor bank   The bank responsible for disbursing the funds indicated on a check.

per se violation   An action that by its very existence carries with it liability, as opposed to an action that violates a rule of reason.

peremptory challenge   In a jury trial, the right of the plaintiff and the defendant in jury selection to reject, without stating a reason, a certain number of potential jurors who appear to have an unfavorable bias.

perfect tender rule   The requirement that a seller deliver goods in conformity with the contract, down to the last detail.

perfection   The series of legal steps a secured party takes to protect its right in collateral from other creditors that want to have their debts returned through the same collateral.

periodic-tenancy lease   A lease created for a recurring term.

personal defense A liability defense that is not applicable to holders in due course.

personal insurance Insurance that covers an individual's health or life.

personal jurisdiction See *in personam* **jurisdiction.**

personal property Any property that is not land or permanently affixed to the land.

personal representative The person designated by a testator to collect the testator's property after he or she dies, pay the debts and taxes, and make sure the remainder of the estate gets distributed.

personal service The process in which an officer of the court hands legal documents, such as a summons or complaint, to the defendant.

petit jury A group of 6 to 12 citizens who are summoned to court and sworn in by the court to hear evidence presented by both sides and render a verdict in a trial.

petty offense A minor crime that is punishable by a small fine and/or imprisonment for less than six months in a jail.

picketing A labor activity in which individuals place themselves outside an employer's place of business for the purpose of informing passersby of the facts of a labor dispute.

plain-meaning rule A rule of interpretation which states that words in a contract should be given their ordinary meaning.

plaintiff The person or party who initiates a lawsuit (an action) before a court by filing a complaint with the clerk of the court against the defendant(s). Also known as *claimant* or *complainant.*

plea bargain An agreement in which the prosecutor agrees to reduce charges, drop charges, or recommend a certain sentence if the defendant pleads guilty.

pledge The transfer of collateral to a secured party.

point-of-sale system An EFT system that enables consumers to directly transfer funds from a bank account to a merchant.

police power The power retained by each state to pass laws that protect the health, safety, and welfare of its citizens.

policy The insurance document signed by the insured party and the insurer.

policy statement A general statement about the directions in which any agency intends to proceed with respect to its rule-making or enforcement activities; has no binding impact on anyone.

political speech Speech that is used to support political candidates or referenda. Compared to other types of speech, it is given a high level of protection by the First Amendment.

posteffective period In securities registration, the period that begins when the SEC declares the registration statement effective and ends when the issuer sells all the securities offered or withdraws them from sale.

posttrial motion A request filed after a trial is over, by either party, to the trial court. Types include a motion for a new trial, a motion for judgment notwithstanding the verdict (JNOV), and a motion to amend or nullify the judgment.

power of attorney A specific type of express authority that grants an agent specific powers.

precedent A tool used by judges to make rulings on cases on the basis of key similarities to previous cases.

predatory pricing The practice in which a company prices one product below normal cost until competitors are eliminated and then it sharply increases the price.

preexisting duty A promise to do something that one is already obligated to do. It is not considered valid consideration.

preferential payment A payment made by an insolvent debtor that gives preferential treatment to one creditor over another.

preferred stock Stock that conveys preferences to its holder with respect to assets and dividends.

prefiling period In securities registration, the period that begins when an issuer starts to think about issuing securities and ends when the issuer files the registration statement and prospectus with the SEC.

Pregnancy Discrimination Act (PDA) of 1987 Federal law that amended Title VII of the Civil Rights Act of 1964 by expanding the definition of sex discrimination to include discrimination based on pregnancy.

prejudicial error of law An error of law that is so significant that it affects the outcome of the case.

premium An insurance payment.

prenuptial agreement An agreement two parties enter into before marriage that clearly states the ownership rights each party enjoys in the other party's property. To be enforceable, it must be in writing.

presentment The act of making a demand for the drawee to pay.

presentment warranty A warranty covering the parties accepting an instrument for payment; created to ensure that the accepting or paying party is paying the proper party.

pretrial An event that includes consultation with attorneys, pleadings, the discovery process, and the pretrial conference.

pretrial conference A meeting of the judge and the attorneys for both sides to narrow the issues for trial and identify witnesses for trial.

price discrimination The practice of selling the same goods to different buyers at different prices.

price fixing A restraint of trade in which two or more competitors agree to set prices for a product or service.

prima facie Latin for "at first view"; term applied to evidence that is sufficient to raise a presumption that a wrong occurred.

primarily liable   Liable for paying the amount designated on an instrument when it is presented for payment.

primary boycott   A boycott against an employer with whom the union is directly engaged in a labor dispute.

primary-line injury   Under the Robinson-Patman Act, an injury that occurs when preferential treatment is given to a competitor.

principal   The party that an agent's authority can bind or act on behalf of.

principle of rights   The principle that judges the morality of a decision on the basis of how it affects the rights of all those involved.

Privacy Act   Federal law that mandates that a federal agency may not disclose information about an individual to other agencies or organizations without that individual's written consent.

privacy tort   A wrongful act in which invasion of privacy causes damage to an individual and for which a civil action can be brought. The four privacy torts are false light, public disclosure of private facts, appropriation for commercial gain, and intrusion on an individual's affairs or seclusion.

private corporation   A corporation that is created by private persons and does not have government duties.

private law   Law that involves suits between private individuals or groups.

private nuisance   A nuisance that affects only a single individual or a very limited number of individuals.

private placement exemption   An exemption from the SEC's securities registration process because the offerings are being made to private accredited investors and will not be advertised to the general public.

private trial   An ADR method in which a referee is selected and paid by the disputing parties to offer a legally binding judgment in a dispute.

privileges and immunities clause   The clause in the U.S. Constitution which requires that each state grant citizens of other states the same legal benefits that it grants its own citizens.

privity of contract   The relationship that exists between parties to a contract.

probable cause   Any essential element and/or standard by which a lawful officer may make a valid arrest, conduct a personal or property search, or obtain a warrant.

probate   The process of settling an estate.

problem-solving negotiation   Negotiation in which the parties seek to achieve joint gain.

procedural due process   The requirement that a government must use fair procedures before depriving a person of his or her life, liberty, or property.

procedural unconscionability   Unconscionability that derives from the process of making a contract.

proceeds   Something that is exchanged for a debtor's sold collateral.

product liability insurance   Insurance that protects a company from liability in the event that its customers suffer injury.

product market   A market in which all products identical to or substitutes for a company's product are sold.

professional insurance   Insurance that protects professionals from suits by third parties who claim negligent job performance.

profit   The right to go onto someone's land and take part of the land or a product of it away from the land.

promisee   In a third-party beneficiary contract, the party to the contract who owes something to the promisor in exchange for the promise made to the third-party beneficiary.

promisor   In a third-party beneficiary contract, the party to the contract who made the promise that benefits the third party.

promissory estoppel   The legal enforcement of an otherwise unenforceable contract due to a party's detrimental reliance on the contract.

promoter   A person who begins the corporate creation and organization process.

property insurance   Insurance that protects property from loss or damages.

prospectus   A written document filed with the SEC that contains a description of a security and other financial information regarding the company offering the security; also distributed as an advertising tool to potential investors.

proximate cause   The extent to which, as a matter of policy, a defendant may be held liable for the consequences of his or her actions. In the majority of states, proximate cause requires that the plaintiff and the type of injury suffered by the plaintiff were foreseeable at the time of the accident. In the minority of states, proximate cause exists if the defendant's actions led to the plaintiff's harm.

proxy   A writing signed by a shareholder that authorizes the individual named in the writing to exercise the shareholder's votes (corresponding to his or her shares of stock) at a shareholders' meeting.

proxy solicitation   The process of obtaining authority to vote on behalf of shareholders.

public corporation   A corporation that is created by government to help administer law.

public disclosure of private facts   A privacy tort that occurs when a person publishes a highly offensive private fact, such as information about one's sex life or failure to pay debts, about someone who did not waive his or her right to privacy.

public disclosure test   The ethical guideline that urges us to consider how others may view our actions when making a decision.

public figure privilege   A special right, immunity, or permission that allows people to make any statement about public figures, typically politicians and entertainers, without being held liable for defamation as long as false statements were not made with malice.

public law   Law that involves suits between private individuals or groups and their governments.

public policy exception   An exception to the employment-at-will doctrine that prohibits employers from firing employees for doing something that is consistent with furthering public policy.

publicly held corporation   A corporation whose stock is available to the public.

puffing   The use of generalities and clear exaggerations.

punitive damages   Compensation awarded to a plaintiff that goes beyond reimbursement for actual losses and is imposed to punish the defendant and deter such conduct in the future. Also called *exemplary damages.*

purchase-money security interest (PMSI)   A security interest formed when a debtor uses borrowed money from the secured party to buy the collateral.

pure comparative negligence   A defense accepted in some states whereby the defendant is not liable for the percentage of harm that he or she can prove can be attributed to the plaintiff's own negligence.

Q

qualified endorsement   An endorsement that does not bind the endorser to the negotiable instrument in the event that the creator does not honor that instrument.

quantitative restriction   A limit on the importation of certain goods that is imposed on the basis of number of units, weight, or value for national economic reason, or for the protection of domestic industry; prohibited by GATT.

quasi-contract   A court-imposed contractual obligation to prevent unjust enrichment.

quasi *in rem* jurisdiction   A type of jurisdiction exercised by a court over an out-of-state defendant's property that is within the jurisdictional boundaries of the court; applies to personal suits against a defendant in which the property is not the source of the conflict but is sought as compensation by the plaintiff. Also called *attachment jurisdiction.*

quick-look standard   In a restraint of trade case, the standard that allows a defendant to offer justification for his or her per se violation.

quitclaim deed   A deed that carries no warranties. The grantor simply conveys whatever interests he or she holds.

R

Racketeer Influenced and Corrupt Organizations (RICO) Act   Federal law that provides extended penalties for criminal acts performed as part of an ongoing criminal organization.

ratify   To approve an unauthorized agent's signature on an instrument.

rational-basis test   The lowest standard of review; requires that a law be designed to protect a legitimate state interest and be rationally related to that interest.

reaffirmation agreement   An agreement in which a debtor agrees to pay a debt even though it could have been discharged in bankruptcy.

real defense   A liability defense that applies universally to all parties.

real property   Land and everything permanently attached to it.

resonable expectation of privacy   Under the ECPA, the protection afforded to individuals' communications against unauthorized surveillance or access; applies only minimally to communications via an employer's equipment.

reasonable person standard   A measurement of the way members of society expect an individual to act in a given situation.

recognizance   An obligation in which a party acknowledges in court that he or she will perform some specified act and/or pay a price on failure to do so.

recording   Filing a deed, with any other related documents such as mortgages, with the appropriate county office, thereby giving official notice of the transfer to all interested parties.

red-herring prospectus   A prospectus with a warning written in red print at the top of the page telling investors that the registration has been filed with the SEC but not yet approved.

refusal to deal   See **group boycott.**

reg-neg   A type of rule making in which representatives of concerned interest groups and of the involved government agency participate in mediated bargaining sessions to reach an agreement, which is forwarded to the agency.

registration statement   A description, filed with the SEC, of securities being offered for sale; includes an explanation of how proceeds from the sale will be used, information on the registrant's business and properties, and certified financial statements.

rejection   Termination of a contract that occurs when an offeree does not accept the offer or terms of the contract.

relative permanence   The quality of a negotiable instrument that ensures its longevity.

remainderman   The recipient of the trust corpus, the property held in trust, when the trust is terminated.

remand   An appellate court decision that returns a case to the trial court for a new trial or for a limited hearing on a specified subject matter; rendered when the court decides that an error was committed that may have affected the outcome of the case.

rent   The compensation paid to a landlord for the tenant's right to possession and exclusive use of the premises.

rent escalation clause   In a lease, a clause that permits the landlord to increase the rent in association with increases in costs of living, property taxes, or the tenant's commercial business.

reply   A response by the plaintiff to the defendant's counterclaim.

request to produce documents   In a lawsuit, a discovery tool that forces the opposing party to produce certain information unless it is privileged or irrelevant to the case.

res ipsa loquitur   A doctrine that allows a judge or jury to infer that, more likely than not, the defendant's negligence was the cause of the plaintiff's harm even though there is no direct evidence of the defendant's lack of due care.

rescind   To cancel a contract.

rescission   The termination of a contract.

respondeat superior   Latin for "let the superior speak"; the principle by which liability for harm caused by an agent/employee is held by the principal/employer.

Restatements of the Law   Summaries of common law rules in a particular area of the law. Restatements do not carry the weight of law but can be used to guide interpretations of particular cases.

restitution   The return of any property given up under a contract.

restricted security   A security that has limited transferability and is usually issued in a private placement.

restrictive covenant   A promise to use or not to use one's land in particular ways.

restrictive endorsement   An endorsement that limits the transferability of an instrument or controls the manner of payment under an instrument.

retained earnings   Profits that a corporation keeps.

reverse   An appellate court decision that overturns the judgment of a lower court, concluding that the lower court was incorrect and its verdict cannot be allowed to stand.

revocation   Termination of a contract that occurs when an offeror takes back the initial offer and annuls the opportunity for the offeree to accept the offer.

RICO Act   See **Racketeer Influenced and Corrupt Organizations (RICO) Act.**

right of first refusal   A method of restricting stock transferability whereby a corporation or its shareholders have the right to purchase any shares of stock offered for resale by a shareholder within a specified time frame.

right of survivorship   The right that specific partnership property will pass on to the surviving partner(s).

right to die   A person's right to place limits on other people's efforts to prolong her or his life.

rightfully dissolved   A term applied to the dissolution of a partnership in a way that does not violate the partnership agreement.

ripeness   A measure of the readiness of a case for a decision to be made; designed to prevent premature litigation for a dispute that is insufficiently developed. A claim is not ripe for litigation if it rests on contingent future events that may not occur as anticipated or may not occur at all.

risk   A potential loss.

risk management   The transfer and distribution of risk.

robbery   The unlawful taking or attempted taking of personal property by force or threat of force and/or by putting the victim in fear.

rule-of-reason analysis   An inquiry into the competitive effects of a company's anticompetitive behavior to determine whether the benefits of the behavior outweigh the harm.

rule utilitarianism   A subset of utilitarianism which holds that general rules that *on balance* produce the greatest amount of pleasure for all involved should be established and followed in each situation.

S

S corporation   A corporation that enjoys the tax status of a partnership.

Sabbath law   A law that prohibits the performance of certain activities on Sundays.

sale   The passing of title from a seller to a buyer for a price.

sale-on-approval contract   A contract in which the seller allows the buyer to take possession of the goods before deciding whether to complete the contract by making the purchase.

sale-or-return contract   A contract in which the buyer and seller agree that the buyer may return the goods at a later time.

Sarbanes-Oxley Act   Federal law that criminalizes specific nonaudit services when they are provided by a registered accounting firm to an audit client; also increases the punishment for a number of white-collar offenses. Also known as the *Public Company Accounting Reform and Investor Protection Act of 2002.*

scienter   Deliberately or knowingly.

search warrant   A court order that authorizes law enforcement agents to search for or seize items specifically described in the warrant.

secondarily liable   Liable for paying the amount designated on an instrument should the primarily liable party default.

secondary boycott   An illegal labor action in which unionized employees who have a labor dispute with their employer boycott another company to force it to cease doing business with their employer.

secondary-line injury   Under the Robinson-Patman Act, an injury that is created when preferential treatment is granted to specific buyers.

secured interest   An interest in personal property or fixtures that secures payment or performance to a creditor.

secured party   The party that holds an interest in a secured property.

secured transaction   A transaction in which the payment of a debt is guaranteed by personal property owned by the debtor.

security A financial instrument designated as a note, stock, or bond or any other instrument named in the Securities Act of 1933.

security agreement An agreement in which a debtor gives a secured interest to a secured party.

self-dealing Any instance in which directors or officers make decisions that violate their corporate duty of loyalty.

self-tender offer A takeover-resistance strategy in which a target corporation offers to buy its shareholders' stock.

service of process The procedure by which a court delivers a copy of the statement of claim or other legal documents, such as a summons, complaint, or subpoena, to a defendant.

settlor A person who creates a trust.

severable contract A contract whose terms can be divided.

sexual harassment Unwelcome sexual advances, requests for sexual favors, and other verbal or physical conduct of a sexual nature that makes submission a condition of employment or a factor in employment decisions or that creates an intimidating, hostile, or offensive work environment. The two types are hostile environment and quid pro quo.

shadow jury An unofficial jury, hired by a party in a legal case, that watches the actual trial and deliberates at the end of each day to give the attorney an idea of how the real jurors are reacting to the case.

shareholder An investor who holds stock in a corporation, and thus is an owner of the corporation.

shareholder's derivative suit A lawsuit filed by a shareholder on behalf of the corporation.

shelter principle The principle which holds that when an item is transferred, the transferee acquires all the rights the transferor had to the item.

short-form merger A merger in which a parent corporation absorbs a subsidiary corporation. Also called *parent-subsidiary merger.*

short-swing profits Profits made from the sale of company stock within any six-month period by a statutory insider.

signal picketing An unprotected form of picketing in which services and/or deliveries to the employer are cut off.

signature liability Liability that is attributed because of a party's signature on an instrument.

simple contract A contract that is not a formal contract. Also called an *informal contract.*

simple delivery contract A type of contract in which purchased goods are transferred to a buyer from a seller either at the time of the sale or sometime later by the seller's delivery.

situational ethics An ethical theory which holds that to evaluate the morality of an action, we must imagine ourselves in the position of the person facing the ethical dilemma and then, on that basis, determine whether that person's action was ethical.

slander of quality A business tort that occurs when false spoken statements criticize a business product or service and result in a loss of sales.

slander of title A business tort that occurs when false published statements are related to the ownership of the business property.

smart card A plastic card, similar to an ATM card, that contains a microchip for storing data; used to electronically transfer funds.

social responsibility of business The responsibility of firms doing business within a community to meet the expectations that the community imposes on them.

socialist law A legal system based on the premise that the rights of society as a whole outweigh the rights of the individual.

sole proprietor The single person at the head of a sole proprietorship.

sole proprietorship A business in which one person (sole proprietor) controls the management and profits.

special damages See **consequential damages.**

special endorsement An endorser's signature accompanying the name of the endorsee.

special power of attorney A type of express authority that allows an agent to act on behalf of the principal only in regard to specifically outlined acts.

special qualified endorsement A special endorsement containing words that limit the enforceability of the check, such as the term *without recourse* (which means the endorser will not be liable).

special warranty deed A deed which promises only that the seller has not done anything to lessen the value of the estate.

specific performance An order of the court requiring that a nonbreaching party fulfill the terms of the contract.

specific personal jurisdiction A doctrine permitting adjudication of a claim against a defendant only if the defendant purposefully availed himself or herself of the protections of the forum and if the selected forum is reasonable.

stakeholders The groups of people affected by a firm's decisions.

stale check A check that is not presented to a bank within six months of its date.

standing The legal right of a party to bring a lawsuit by demonstrating to the court sufficient connection to and harm from the law or action challenged (i.e., the plaintiff must demonstrate that he or she is harmed or will be harmed). Otherwise, the court will dismiss the case, ruling that the plaintiff "lacks standing" to bring the suit.

stare decisis Latin for "standing by the decision"; a principle stating that rulings made in higher courts are binding precedent for lower courts.

statute of frauds State-level legislation that addresses the enforceability of contracts that fail to meet the requirements set forth in the statute; serves to protect promisors from poorly considered oral contracts by requiring that certain contracts be in writing.

statutory insiders Certain large stockholders, executive officers, and directors who are deemed insiders by the Securities Exchange Act of 1934.

statutory law The assortment of rules and regulations put forth by legislatures.

stock certificate A document that serves as a stockholder's proof of ownership in a corporation.

stock warrant A type of security issued by a corporation (usually together with a bond or preferred stock) that gives the holder the right to purchase a certain amount of common stock at a stated price.

stop-payment order An order by a drawer that instructs the drawee bank not to pay an issued check.

stored-value card A plastic card that contains data regarding the value of the card, thereby allowing EFTs to be made.

strict liability Liability in which responsibility for damages is imposed regardless of the existence of negligence. Also called *liability without fault*.

strict-liability offense An offense for which no *mens rea* is required.

strict-liability tort A civil wrong that occurs when a defendant takes an action that is inherently dangerous and cannot ever be undertaken safely, no matter what precautions the defendant takes. The defendant is liable for the plaintiff's damages without any requirement that the plaintiff prove that the defendant was negligent.

strict product liability Liability under which, courts may hold the manufacturer, distributor, or retailer liable for any reasonably foreseeable injured party.

strict scrutiny The most exacting standard of review used by the courts in determining the constitutionality of a statute; requires a compelling government interest and the least restrictive means of attaining that objective.

strike A temporary, concerted withdrawal of labor.

subject-matter jurisdiction The power of a court over the type of case presented to it.

subjective impossibility (of performance) In a contract, a situation in which it would be very difficult for a party to carry out his or her contractual obligations.

sublease A transfer of less than all of a tenant's interest in a leased property.

submission agreement A contract which provides that a specific dispute will be resolved in arbitration.

subpoena An order to appear at a particular time and place and provide testimony.

subpoena *duces tecum* An order to appear and bring specified documents.

subscriber An investor who agrees to purchase stock in a new corporation.

subscription agreement An agreement between promoters (persons raising capital for a new corporation) and subscribers (investors) in which the subscribers agree to purchase stock in the new corporation.

subsidy A financial contribution by a government that confers a benefit on a specific industry or enterprise.

substantial evidence The type of evidence required by a court to support an agency's fact finding.

substantial impairment A concept, used to modify the perfect tender rule, whereby a buyer can revoke acceptance of goods or a buyer/lessee can reject an installment of a particular item only if the defects substantially impair the value of the goods.

substantial performance Contract performance that occurs when nearly all the terms of the agreement have been met, there has been an honest effort to complete all the terms, and there has been no willful departure from the terms of the agreement.

substantive due process The requirement that laws depriving an individual of life, liberty, or property be fair and not arbitrary.

substantive unconscionability Unconscionability that derives from contract terms that are so one-sided, unjust, or overly harsh that the contract should not be enforced.

summary jury trial An abbreviated trial that leads to a nonbinding jury verdict.

summons A legal document issued by a court and addressed to a defendant that notifies him or her of a lawsuit and specifies how and when to respond to the complaint. A summons may be used in both civil and criminal proceedings.

supremacy clause Article VI, Paragraph 2, of the U.S. Constitution, which states that the Constitution and all laws and treaties of the United States constitute the supreme law of the land. Thus, any state or local law that directly conflicts with the U.S. Constitution or federal laws or treaties is void.

suretyship A contract between a creditor and a third party who agrees to pay another person's debt.

surrender A mutual agreement between a landlord and a tenant in which the lessee returns his or her interest in the premises to the landlord.

syndicate An investment group that comes together for the explicit purpose of financing a specific large project.

T

Taft-Hartley Act Federal legislation designed to curtail some of the powers that unions had acquired under the Wagner Act; designates certain union actions as unfair. Also called *Labor-Management Relations Act*.

takings clause A clause in the Fifth Amendment of the U.S. Constitution requiring that when government uses its power to take private property for public use, it must pay the owner just compensation, or fair market value, for the property. Also called *just-compensation clause*.

tariff A tax levied on imported goods.

teller's check A check for which the drawer and drawee are separate banks.

tenancy-at-sufferance lease A lease that is created when a tenant who was lawfully in possession of a leased property remains in possession of that property unlawfully after the lease ends because the person with the power to evict him failed to do so.

tenancy-at-will lease A lease that may be terminated by the parties at any time.

tenancy by the entirety A type of co-ownership that is available only to married couples. The spouses' shares are equal, and if one owner dies, the surviving spouse assumes full ownership.

tenancy in common A type of co-ownership in which each owner has the right to sell his or her interest without the consent of the other owners, may own an unequal share of the property, and may have a creditor attach his or her interest.

tenant A person who assumes the temporary legal right to possess property. Also called *lessee.*

tender An offer by a contracting party to perform, along with being ready, willing, and able to perform, a duty outlined in the contract.

tender of delivery A requirement that a seller/lessor have and hold conforming goods at the disposal of the buyer/lessee and give the buyer/lessee reasonable notification to enable him or her to take delivery.

tender offer A type of takeover in which an aggressor corporation offers the target shareholders a price above their stock's current market value.

term-life insurance Life insurance that provides coverage for a specified term.

termination In a contract, the point at which an offer can no longer be accepted as part of a binding agreement or an offeree no longer has the power to form a legally binding contract by accepting the offer; can occur through revocation by the offeror, rejection by the offeree, death or incapacity of the offeror, destruction or subsequent illegality of the subject matter of the offer, or lapse of time or failure of another condition stated in the offer.

termination statement An amendment to a financing statement which states that the debtor has no obligation to the secured party.

tertiary-line injury Under the Robinson-Patman Act, an injury that occurs when someone who is given an illegally low price passes his savings on to his customers.

testamentary capacity The minimum age required to write a legal will and be of sound mind.

testamentary trust An express trust created by a will.

testator A person who writes a will.

third-party beneficiary A recipient of contractual benefits who is not one of the contracting parties; created when two parties enter into a contract with the intended purpose of benefiting a third party.

time instrument A type of draft that allows the payee to collect payment only at a specific time in the future.

tippee An individual who receives confidential information from an insider.

tipper An insider who gives inside information to someone.

tipper/tippee theory A theory of insider trading which holds that any individual (tippee) who acquires material inside information as a result of an insider's (tipper's) breach of duty has engaged in insider trading.

Title VII See **Civil Rights Act (CRA) of 1964—Title VII.**

tombstone advertisement A print advertisement that announces a forthcoming sale of securities in a format similar to that of a tombstone.

tort A violation of another person's rights or a civil wrongdoing that does not arise out of a contract or statute; primary types are intentional, negligent, and strict-liability torts.

tortfeasor A person who commits an intentional or through-negligence tort that causes a harm or loss for which a civil remedy may be sought.

trade dress The overall appearance and image of a product.

trade libel A business tort that occurs when false printed statements criticize a business product or service and result in a loss of sales.

trade secret A process, product, method of operation, or compilation of information that gives a businessperson an advantage over his or her competitors.

trademark A distinctive mark, word, design, picture, or arrangement that is used by a producer in conjunction with a product and tends to cause consumers to identify the product with the producer.

trademark dilution The use of a distinctive or famous trademark, such as "McDonald's," in a manner that diminishes the value of the mark.

transfer warranty A warranty regarding a negotiable instrument and its transfer; created by the party who transfers the instrument.

traveler's check An order that is payable on demand, is drawn on or through a bank, is designated by the phrase *traveler's check,* and requires a countersignature by the person whose signature appears on the check.

treaty A binding agreement between two nations or international organizations.

trespass to personalty The temporary interference with a person's use or enjoyment of his or her personal property.

trespass to realty A tort that occurs when someone goes on another's property without permission or places something on another's property without permission.

trial An event in which parties to a dispute present evidence in court, before a judge or a jury, in order to achieve a resolution to their dispute.

trial court A court in which most civil or criminal cases start when they first enter the legal system. The parties present evidence and call witnesses to testify. Trial courts are referred to as *courts of common pleas* or *county courts* in state court systems and *district courts* in the federal system. Also called *court of original jurisdiction* and *court of first instance.*

trust   (1) A business arrangement in which stock owners appoint beneficiaries and place their securities with a trustee, who manages the company and pays a share of the earnings to the stockholders. (2) An estate-planning arrangement whereby a person transfers property to another person and the property is used for the benefit of a third person.

trust endorsement   An endorsement that is used when the instrument is being transferred to an agent or trustee for the benefit of either the endorser or a third party; gives the endorser the rights of a holder.

trustee   (1) In bankruptcy proceeding, an individual who takes over administration of a debtor's estate. (2) A person who operates a business trust for beneficiaries.

tying arrangement   Illegal agreement in which the sale of one product is tied to the sale of another.

U

unconscionability   Ground for rescinding an unconscionable contract.

unconscionable   A term applied to a contract in which one party has so much more bargaining power than the other party that the powerful party dictates the terms of the agreement and eliminates the other party's free will.

underwriter   A party who receives payments from an insured party and makes the payment to the beneficiary.

undisclosed principal   A principal whose existence is not known by a third party. That is, the third party does not know that an agent is acting on behalf of a principal.

undue influence   The situation in which one person takes advantage of his or her dominant position in a relationship to unfairly persuade the other person and interfere with that person's ability to make his or her own decision.

unemployment compensation   The state system, created by the Federal Unemployment Tax Act, that provides unemployment compensation to qualified employees who lose their jobs.

unenforceable   A term applied to a contract that, because of a law, cannot be enforced by the courts.

unfair competition   The act of competing with another not to make a profit but for the sole purpose of driving that other out of business.

unfortunate accident   An incident that simply could not be avoided, even with reasonable care.

unidentified principal   See **partially disclosed principal**.

Uniform Commercial Code (UCC)   A statutory source of contract law in the United States that is applicable to transactions involving the sale of goods. The UCC was created in 1952 and adopted by all 50 states, the District of Columbia, and the Virgin Islands; it may be modified by each state to reflect the wishes of the state legislature.

uniform law   A law created to account for the variability of laws among states; serves to standardize the otherwise different interstate laws. Also called *model law*.

Uniform Probate Code   A statute that clarifies laws that govern transfers accomplished through wills and trusts.

unilateral   A mistake that is the result of an error by one party about a material fact, that is, a fact that is important in the context of the particular contract.

unilateral contract   A promise exchanged for an act.

unilateral mistake   The result of an error by one party about a material fact, i.e., a fact that is important in the context of a particular contract.

United Nations Convention on Contracts for the International Sale of Goods (CISG)   The legal structure for international sales, including business-to-business sales contracts.

universalization test   The ethical guideline that urges us to consider, before we act, what the world would be like if everyone acted in that way.

unliquidated debt   A debt for which the parties either dispute the fact that any money is owed or agree that some money is owed but dispute the amount.

unprotected speech   Speech that is not protected by the First Amendment; includes hate speech, insulting or fighting words, obscenity, and defamation.

unqualified opinion letter   A letter issued by an auditor when the financial statements presented are free of material misstatements and are in accordance with GAAP.

usage of trade   Any practice that members of an industry expect to be part of their dealings.

usury   The lending of money at an exorbitant or unlawful rate of interest.

utilitarianism   The ethical principle that urges individuals to act in a way that creates the most happiness for the largest number of people.

V

valid   A term applied to a contract that includes all four elements of a contract—agreement (offer and acceptance), consideration, contractual capacity, and legal object—and thus is enforceable.

values   Positive abstractions that capture our sense of what is good and desirable.

venue   The court with subject-matter and personal jurisdiction that is the most appropriate geographic location for the resolution of a dispute.

vertical merger   A merger in which a company at one level of the manufacturing-distribution system acquires a company at another level of the system.

vertical restraint against trade   An agreement between two parties at different levels in the manufacturing-distribution system to engage in a practice that restrains trade.

vest   To mature, as in the maturing of rights such that a party can legally act on the rights.

vicarious liability   The liability or responsibility imposed on a person, a party, or an organization for damages caused by another; most commonly used in relation to employment, with the employer held vicariously liable for the damages caused by its employees.

virtue ethics   The ethical system which proposes that a decision is ethical when it promotes positive character traits such as honesty, courage, or fairness.

virus   A computer program that rearranges, damages, destroys, or replaces computer data.

void   A term applied to a contract that is not valid because its object is illegal or it has a defect that is so serious that it is not a contract.

void title   Not true title; e.g., the title held by someone who knowingly or unknowingly purchased stolen goods.

voidable   A term applied to a contract that one or both parties have the ability to either withdraw from or enforce.

voidable title   Title that occurs when a contract between the original parties would be void but the goods have already been sold to a third party.

voir dire   The process of questioning potential jurors to ensure that the jury will be made up of nonbiased individuals.

W

Wagner Act   The first major piece of federal legislation adopted explicitly to encourage the formation of labor unions and provide for collective bargaining between employers and unions as a means of obtaining the peaceful settlement of labor disputes.

waiting period   In securities registration, the period between the time an issuer files a registration statement and prospectus with the SEC requesting to offer a security and the time the offer is approved by the SEC, which is a minimum of 20 days.

warehouse receipt   A receipt issued by one who is engaged in the business of storing goods for compensation.

warranty   (1) An assurance, either express or implied, by one party that the other party can rely on its representations of fact. (2) In sales, a binding promise regarding a product in the event that the product does not meet the manufacturer's or seller's promises.

warranty liability   Liability that is attributed when the transfer of an instrument breaches a warranty associated with an instrument.

warranty of title   An assurance, inferred in every UCC sales transaction, that the seller has good and valid title to the goods and has the right to transfer the title free and clear of any liens, judgments, or infringements of intellectual property rights of which the buyer does not have knowledge.

waste   Permanent and substantial injury to a landlord's property.

watered stock   Stock that is issued to individuals below its fair market value.

white-collar crime   A variety of nonviolent illegal acts against society that occur most frequently in the business context.

whole-life insurance   Life insurance that provides protection for the entire life of the insured person.

will   A legal document in which a person outlines how she wants her property to be distributed after her death.

winding up   The process of completing unfinished partnership business.

workers' compensation law   A state law that provides for financial compensation to employees or their dependents when the covered employee is injured on the job.

working papers   The various documents used and developed during an audit, including notes, calculations, copies, memorandums, and other papers constituting the accountant's work product.

World Trade Organization (WTO)   An international organization that facilitates international cooperation in opening markets and provides a forum for future trade negotiations and the settlement of international trade disputes.

WPH process (of ethical decision making)   A set of ethical guidelines that urges us to consider whom an action affects, the purpose of the action, and how we view its morality (whether by utilitarian ethics, deontology, etc.).

writ of certiorari   A Supreme Court order, issued after the Court decides to hear an appeal, mandating that the lower court send to the Supreme Court the record of the appealed case.

writ of execution   A court order that authorizes a local law officer to seize and sell a debtor's real or personal nonexempt property, within the court's geographic jurisdiction, to enforce a judgment awarded by the court.

writing   A type of documentation that shows contractual intent and satisfies the statute of frauds requirement.

wrongful civil proceeding   A tort in which one person wrongfully subjects another to criminal or civil litigation that has no justifiable basis.

wrongful dissolution   A partnership dissolution that violates the partnership agreement.

Z

zoning   The process in which government places restrictions on the use of property to allow for the orderly growth and development of a community and to protect the health, safety, and welfare of its citizens.

Subject Index

Page numbers followed by n refer to material in notes.